A CHART
of the
CARIBE ISLANDS
1707

A Cruising
Guide to
The Lesser
Antilles

[The Islands] are accessible in every part, and covered with a vast variety of lofty trees, which it appears to me, never lose their foliage, as we found them fair and verdant as in May in Spain. Some were covered with blossoms, some with fruit, and others in different stages, according to their nature. The nightingale and a thousand other sorts of birds were singing in the month of November wherever I went. There are palm-trees in these countries, of six or eight sorts, which are surprising to see, on account of their diversity from ours, but indeed, this is the case with respect to the other trees, as well as the fruits and weeds. Beautiful forests of pines are likewise found, and fields of vast extent. Here is also honey, and fruits of a thousand sorts, and birds of every variety. The lands contain mines of metals, and inhabitants without number. . . . [Their] harbours are of such excellence, that their description would not gain belief, and the like may be said of the abundance of large and fine rivers, the most of which abound in gold.

—Christopher Columbus, on his return
to Spain from the Caribbean, 1494

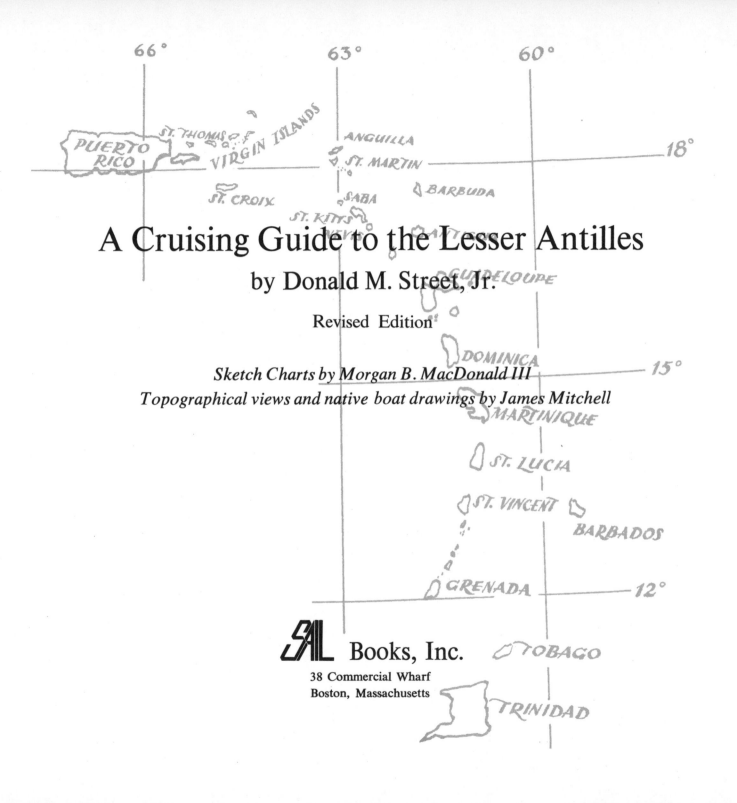

A Cruising Guide to the Lesser Antilles

by Donald M. Street, Jr.

Revised Edition

Sketch Charts by Morgan B. MacDonald III
Topographical views and native boat drawings by James Mitchell

SAL Books, Inc.

38 Commercial Wharf
Boston, Massachusetts

While every effort has been made to insure the precision of courses, ranges, and locations cited in this book, ultimately neither the author nor publisher can fully warrant their accuracy. The charts, headings, and directions herein should be used for navigation only in conjunction with official marine publications.

The symbol ⚓ designates recommended overnight anchorages; the symbol ⚓ designates recommended daytime-only anchorages.

Compass headings are given in magnetic degrees, unless otherwise noted.

Sketch Chart depths are given in feet.

ISBN 0-914814-01-X

Library of Congress Catalog Card 74-81645

Printed in the U.S.A. by Nimrod Press, Boston, Ma.

The cover photograph of *Iolaire* at anchor at The Pitons, St. Lucia, is by the author.

Dedication

The idea for this Cruising Guide was originally conceived in 1963 and it was only through the hard work, perseverance, courage, and self-sacrifice of my late wife, Marilyn, that the original book got off the ground.

Fortunately for myself and my daughter, Dory, I met Patricia Boucher, now my wife, on the beach in Tyrell Bay. She has presented me with two active sons, yet has had time to help in business, in sailing *Iolaire,* exploring, and though she had hardly sailed before our marriage, she has taken to sailing like a duck to water. Her love of sailing was largely instrumental in my decision to keep *Iolaire* when I was thinking of selling her to reduce expenses.

It is only because of Trich's hard work keeping our various business enterprises going in my absence that I have been able to keep the third love of my life, *Iolaire.*

Iolaire has been my mistress for 17 years; at age 68 she is still the type of boat Michel Dufour would appreciate; she is "fast, beautiful and responsive—like a good-looking woman." If she could talk she could tell us stories and, in fact, would probably not need a crew to guide her, having first arrived in the Islands in 1947, remained for a few years, and cruised back to Europe in 1949, from Jamaica to England direct. In 1951, under the ownership of R. H. Somerset, she won her division's R.O.R.C. Season's Points Championship at the age of 45 years, returned to the Islands in 1951, cruised there during the winter of 1951-1952, sailed in the Bermuda Race in 1952, then cruised back to Europe and the Mediterranean. She returned to the Islands in 1954 where she has sailed ever since, except for one trip to the States in 1961. There is little of the Caribbean whose waters have not been furrowed by her hull, and, as some of my good friends will point out, few rocks that have not been dented by her keel!

To my three loves—Marilyn, Trich, and *Iolaire*—I dedicate this book.

—D.M.S.

Preface

When I first arrived in the Islands in 1956 and subsequently purchased *Iolaire,* I found on board her what was then the only cruising guide to the Lesser Antilles in existence—a mimeographed publication produced by the Coast Guard Auxiliary and edited by a Lt. Commander J. M. Buzby. This was followed in 1960 by George Teeple Eggleston's *The Virgin Islands,* the result of a one-month cruise aboard Eunice Boardman's 55-foot ketch *Renegade.*

In 1961, Percy Chubb III, after a cruise through the Lesser Antilles, produced a small, privately printed *Guide to the Windward and Leeward Islands.* In 1964, Linton Rigg authored *The Alluring Antilles,* a combination guide and cruising adventure of a half-year sail from Puerto Rico to Trinidad aboard the 45-foot ketch *Island Belle.*

These seemed to suffice for the small amount of Caribbean cruising done in those days, but starting in the early '60s the charter-boat business suddenly began to expand, and many new boats arrived. It was Frank Burke of Island Yachts who inspired my entry into cruising-guide writing. Figuring that too many of the charter parties were missing the best spots in the Virgins because their skippers had not been in the Islands long enough to get to know them intimately, he asked me to write a cruising guide to the Virgin Islands. This was done and he had it privately printed. I received the magnificent sum of $100—which to me happened to be a veritable fortune in those days.

This small volume later formed the basis of the Virgin Islands section of my *Cruising Guide to the Lesser Antilles,* published in 1966, after I showed it to Phelps Platt of Dodd, Mead, who encouraged me to expand it to cover the whole island chain. This was followed, two years later, by Tom Kelly and Jack van Ost's *Yachtsman's Guide to the Virgin Islands,* and then by Al Forbes' excellent *Cruising Guide to the Virgin Islands,* notable in that, unlike many guide authors, he had sailed the area for many years before he wrote his.

In 1970, following eight years of cruising the Grenadines, I produced the *Yachting Guide to the Grenadines,* after which, in 1973, came Julius M. Wilensky's *Yachtsman's Guide to the Windward Islands,* which covered largely the same territory as mine. Also in 1973, Gordon C. Ayer produced an interesting small guide covering an island group which had never been detailed before—namely, the Passage Islands.

If, in all this, one guide is found to read surprisingly like another, I ask only that you refer back to my original works to see who said what first. If nothing else, it's a matter of pride.

In this present edition of the *Cruising Guide to the Lesser Antilles,* I have tried to include all the information I have gleaned in nearly 20 years of cruising these islands. I have drawn not only from my own experiences but, as you can see from the accompanying acknowledgments, also from the experiences of old friends who are, in addition, good sailors. Thus I feel I have described probably every cove in the Lesser Antilles where one could possibly think of anchoring.

If you find one I may have missed, please let me know. Hopefully, this volume, too, will be updated again in a few years. I boldly asserted in my 1966 guide that the book would never become dated because rocks don't move. Little did I realize how eagerly island governments would actually start moving them, along with creating new islands, making islands into peninsulas, building low bridges, and so forth, as the development of the Lesser Antilles boomed. Further, any guide is destined to go out of date simply because the idyllic uninhabited spot of one year becomes a thriving hotel and cabana settlement the next. Indeed, one of my readers lately took me to task because he was using my original guide and expected to anchor off an island described therein as uninhabited. As he rounded between Pinese and Mopion, he was greeted by a brand new hotel ablaze with celebration, and counted no less than 45 boats moored in the lee of Petit St. Vincent! Please . . . don't blame me.

It is impossible for anyone to say he knows the Lesser Antilles perfectly; after 18 years I was still discovering new little anchorages. But now the time has come to look to new fields. Hence *Iolaire* in the years ahead will, hopefully, spend much of her time in the incomparably beautiful cruising grounds of Venezuela, Haiti, and the Dominican Republic. If she doesn't, it will be more because of the political, rather than the meteorological, climate.

—D.M.S.

Acknowledgments

Since my original *Cruising Guide to the Lesser Antilles* was published in 1966, people have continually asked why a completely revised and updated edition was not formulated. There were all sorts of reasons, but basically it came down to one—no publisher wished to invest the time, money, and energy to produce a book of the size and scope I had in mind. Finally, Bernie Goldhirsh, publisher of *Sail Magazine,* decided to take the bull by the horns. A contract was drawn up, signed by all concerned, and a mad rush ensued to put the whole book together. I was not starting completely from scratch. I had in my office copious notes taken by myself, and others sent to me by various charter skippers and local yachtsmen. Without the help of these people the revised *Guide* not only would never have been completed in such short time, but certainly would not have been anywhere near as complete as it is.

Augie Holland (the only person I know who cruises in a genuine Block Island Cow Horn), Ross Norgrove of *White Squall II,* and Carl Powell of *Terciel* all deserve a special vote of thanks for helping me update the Virgin Islands section. Jon Repke of Power Products, a refrigeration expert, electrician, mechanic, sailor, and pilot, solved many of the mysteries of St. Martin/St. Barts/Anguilla by spending the better part of a day flying me through this area. Carl Kaushold supplied an excellent chart and information on Salt River. Ray Smith of Grenada was most helpful in his suggestions on tides and weather patterns in the Caribbean, and in compiling the list of radio stations and radio beacons. His brother, Ron, solved the mystery of the whereabouts of Tara Island, on the south coast of Grenada, which is improperly marked on the chart. Carl Amour of the Anchorage Hotel solved the great mystery of the rocks off Scott's Head, Dominica. Dr. Jack Sheppard of *Arieto,* Dick Doran of *Laughing Sally,* and Carlos Lavendero of several boats made possible the inclusion of the Puerto Rican and Passage Islands information. Gordon Stout of *Shango* and Peter Lee of *Virginia Reel* made possible the inclusion of Tobago. Jerry Bergoff of *Solar Barque* and Sylver Brin of St. Barts were most helpful in clearing up some of the mysteries on the eastern end of St. Barts. Pieter van Storn of Island Waterworld was most helpful in the St. Martin area. John Clegg of *Flica II,* David Price of *Lincoln,* and Gordon Stout of *Shango* were continually popping up with wonderful odd bits of information which they had gleaned on their cruises from one end of the Lesser Antilles to the other.

Numerous other skippers have, over the years, given me a tremendous amount of help, some of whom are: Joel Byerley of *Ron of Argyle, Lord Jim,* and *Mirage;* Desmond Nicholson of V. E. B. Nicholson & Sons; Morris Nicholson of *Eleuthera;* Simon Bridger of *Circe;* Dave Corrigan of the Mariner's Inn, St. Vincent; Simon Cooper (who unfortunately has now left the Islands); Peter Haycraft of Tortola, a harbor pilot, yachtsman, and food importer; Martin Mathias of the yacht *Bahari,* expert fisherman; Bert Kilbride, diver extraordinary from Saba Rock, Virgin Gorda; Doug and Hugh (Daddy) Myer of *Rosemary V;* Arthur Spence of *Dwyka;* Marcy Crowe of *Xantippe;* Andy Copeland from various boats; Mike Smith of *Phryna.* And old timers Jim Squire of *Te Hongi;* Ron Prentice; Alan Batham, the founder of the Marina Cay operation, now residing in New Zealand; plus many others who, if I have forgotten to mention their names, I hope will forgive me. It is only with the help of experienced yachtsmen like these that a book of this type can be written.

A special vote of thanks must go to Morgan B. MacDonald III, my nephew, who labored hard for three months in Grenada putting together the sketch charts contained in this book. And to Jim Mitchell, who has done a superb job of drawing the native boats and topographical views.

Thanks should also go to Patricia Street, my sister Elizabeth Vanderbilt, her husband Peter, and their son Jay for their help in rechecking many facts.

Finally, thanks should go to my typist, Mrs. Barbara E. Doten, who labored hard and long hours in order to speed up the final stages of the editing.

—D.M.S.

Foreword

The Lesser Antilles stretch southward from St. Thomas to Grenada in a great crescent 500 miles long, offering the yachtsman a cruising ground of unequaled variety. Some of the islands are flat, dry, and windswept, their shores girded by coral reefs, and their land barely arable. Others are reefless, jagged peaks jutting abruptly up from the sea, where they block the ever-present trades and gather rain clouds the year round; water cascades in gullies down their sides and their slopes are well cultivated. The character of their peoples likewise varies—from the charming and unspoiled though desperately poor Dominican, to the comparatively well-to-do and worldly-wise Frenchman of Martinique.

Unless you have a whole season at your disposal, it is foolhardy to attempt all the islands in a single cruise. Not only will you not make it but you will fail to enjoy the slow, natural, and relaxed pace of life in these tropical islands. The first measure of a successful cruise is how soon your carefully worked out timetable gets thrown away. Rule Number One in the Antilles is, don't make any plan more than a day in advance since you will frequently—in fact constantly—alter your intentions to suit the pace and attractions of the locale.

Whether Puerto Rico to the north or Trinidad and Tobago to the south should be considered members of the Lesser Antilles is a question for the gazetteers to squabble over. For the purposes of this book, we welcome all three into the fellowship of proximity. Taken as such, the Antilles conveniently break up into a number of areas suitable for two- or three-week cruises. The start- and endpoints of a cruise will be governed by your own tastes and the availability of air transportation. The air services into San Juan and Trinidad are excellent, for example; but neither of these places is a particularly good spot to begin a cruise. San Juan is dead to leeward of the rest of the chain—and who wants to start out with a hard slog into the wind against a strong current? Trinidad is not much better, the anchorage at the Trinidad Yacht Club being a poor lee. It is probably the only yacht club anchorage in the world where you can get seasick lying to a mooring. The anchorage at the main commercial harbor is a gloomy alternative. Pilferage is so out of control that if you have gold fillings, you are advised to sleep with your mouth closed. Recently, the Trinidad Yachting Association has taken a lease in the old U.S. Navy Chaguaramas Base, just west of the seaplane hangar and ramp. Visiting yachtsmen are welcome and here, at least, the anchorage is excellent.

For the most part, St. Thomas, St. Croix, Antigua, Martinique, and Grenada are the better places to begin or end a cruise. All have airline connections to the States, several good harbors, reliable people with whom boats can be left, and, more important, adequate supplies of fuel and goods to stock a boat for a cruise of any length.

Which of these starting points you choose will say something of your tastes in cruising. If you prefer gunk-holing and short jaunts between many little islands only a few miles apart, if you like snorkeling and little in the way of civilization, then it is the Virgins or the Grenadines for you. But you best hurry down because real estate developers are fast making this a thing of the past. Mustique, for one example, was until recently a private estate in the hands of the Hazel family. But it has been sold to a developer who now is working it over at a pretty fast rate. Well-to-do Europeans are buying up land and building houses, creating many new jobs for local labor but depriving the yachtsman of a wonderful hideaway.

For those of you who want to give boat and crew a good tuning up for offshore racing, set out from St. Thomas up through the Virgins, and then work your way across Anegada Passage to St. Martin or Anguilla and finish with a final leg up to Antigua. In doing so, you will gain a fair sampling of island diversity, and of French, Dutch, and English colonial temperaments. The Anegada Passage is a nice hard drive to windward, which should uncover any weak points in rig or crew.

Those interested exclusively in the pursuits of diving, treasure hunting, or snorkeling should steer for the low-lying islands of Anguilla, Barbuda, and Anegada. The reefs are vast and inexhaustible. Fortune hunters still flock to these islands, where innumerable off-lying wrecks date back hundreds of years, some presumably undiscovered. Consult the source books, but remember—they are low, flat, and encircled by reefs that have been improperly charted; don't let your boat become the next curiosity for inquisitive divers.

Saba and Statia are two attractive islands that are too seldom visited. Their anchorages are exceptionally bad, but when the conditions are right, they certainly are worth a go. Their close neighbors, St. Kitts and Nevis, are of historical interest, figuring as they do in the lives of Alexander Hamilton, Admirals Nelson and Rodney, and Generals Shirley and Frazer.

If you like longer sails, the bright lights of civilization, and a variety of language and customs, the middle islands from Antigua to St. Lucia should keep you happy. The French islands of Guadeloupe and Martinique afford the finest cuisine in the Antilles. The local merchants offer an excellent selection of cheeses and meats from Europe and the best wines available outside of France. The tourist shops are a lady's delight, and the perfumes are at about half the Stateside price. Bikinis, up until a few years ago, were so inexpensive—two for $5.00—that the girls bought them by the dozen. Regrettably, those days are gone—probably forever. There is still a fabulous collection of bikinis in Martinique, but the prices have gone up so much in France that the savings for an American are no longer very substantial. Rough rule of thumb: the smaller the bikini, the more expensive it is.

The universal pastime of girl-watching is alive and well in Martinique, and the visiting seafarer soon gets into the spirit of things. The women there may not be the prettiest in the Caribbean, but they are far and away the most stylish. And the men, sitting at the sidewalk cafes sipping their coffee or punch vieux, cut figures worthy of the gay boulevardiers of Paris. But newcomers, take note: the punch will make a strong man weak-kneed and the coffee tastes not unlike battery acid.

The French and their chicory-laced coffee have distressed visiting foreigners for many decades. A story is told of Count von Bismarck touring France after the Franco-Prussian War. He was ending a fine meal in a country inn and called for the maitre d'hotel and offered to buy all his chicory at ten percent over the market price. The maitre d' agreed and sold him what he claimed to be all he had. Again the Count offered to buy any remaining chicory, this time at 50 percent over the market price; the maitre d' produced a second quantity of the spice. For a third time the Count offered to buy any that remained—at *twice* the market price— and the manager surrendered a small amount, assuring him that this was indeed all that remained. Satisfied at last, the Count concluded, "Very well, now you may prepare me a cup of coffee!"

Dominica is for the adventurous. A ride into the mountains by jeep and horseback will take you to the last settlement of the Carib peoples. Here the natives fashion the distinctive Carib canoes that are also seen in Guadeloupe, Martinique, and St. Lucia. With nothing but a flour sack for a sail and a paddle as a rudder, the islanders set out in these boats against the wind to fish in the open Atlantic. Not an easy way to earn a living.

St. Lucia provides some superb anchorages at Pigeon Island, Marigot, and Vieux Fort, and the truly unbelievable one beneath the Pitons at Sourfriere, shown on the cover. The volcano and sulphur baths are an impressive spectacle, and it is well worth the expense to explore the island by car or jeep, an adventure vividly recounted by George Eggleston in *Orchids in a Calabash Tree.*

St. Vincent, just north of the Grenadines, is a high, lush island richly and diversely cultivated. The island has an intriguing history, highlighted by the almost continual warfare among French, English, and Caribs which lasted from 1762 until 1796 when the Caribs were expelled to Central America. An entertaining taxi driver named McLane will tell you all about the fauna, flora, and local politics of the island. His fares are reasonable and, taking into account his wealth of information, something of a bargain.

Bequia is the home of the fisherman and whalers, an island where any sailor can explore, relax, and "gam" for days on end. The harbor is beautiful, life is relaxed.

Barbados is relatively remote and seldom visited by yachts except those that are coming downwind from Europe. If your plane stops there en route to another island, arrange for a lay-over of a day or two. It is undoubtedly the best-run island in the entire Caribbean. Everything is clean and neat (by West Indian standards); the people are charming and speak in the most wonderful accent. They are solicitous and helpful to visitors. The old carenage in Bridgetown should not be missed, nor should the screw-lift dock.

It is a shame that Tobago is so seldom visited by yachtsmen. It is dead to windward of Trinidad, and from Grenada it is 90 miles hard on the port tack. Even if you manage to lay the rhumb line from Grenada, it will be a long,

heavy slog, and the wind, current, and sea will drive you off to the west. It is fairly inaccessible except from Barbados, from where it is an easy reach southward.

The American and British Virgin Islands have been laboriously described in the various tourist guides, but whatever the evaluation of shoreside life, a sailor can pass a very pleasant month cruising this area.

The character of the various island peoples is apt to vary broadly within a relatively small area. Even among formerly British Islands, each has its own peculiar flavor, its own outlook, and accent. (In fact, natives are known to complain that they can't understand the English spoken on neighboring islands.) For the most part, the people are quiet and law-abiding. Actually, the sort of racially inspired violence that periodically has troubled St. Croix and St. Thomas has been far less a problem in the islands further south.

Hopefully, with the aid of this book you will enjoy the Islands as much as I have for some two decades. Anyone contemplating a cruise aboard a charter boat is well advised to read the supplementary chapters, which will give you much background information. They not only will explain to you why perhaps the charter skipper looks tired (he has spent the last two days fixing his generator under sail while he deadheads to pick you up), but you will have a better idea as to what to expect upon your arrival in the islands. A host of important tips and facts that are not included in the average tourist or charter-boat broker's brochure will, I trust, be found in this book. And needless to say, anyone planning to bring his boat to the Islands should read the whole book carefully with pencil in hand to make notes on what is applicable.

"Sailing Directions" is probably the most important chapter, one that should be read and studied. It should be consulted regularly before finalizing the day's plans. While the navigational features and anchorages of individual islands are described in the chapter concerned with that island, the routes *between* the islands are described in the sailing directions—so be sure to consult them each day.

It must be remembered that the sketch charts are just that—drawings meant only to update and supplement the standard navigational charts; be sure you have an overlapping selection of the latter on board.

Finally, be cautious. Practically every place in the Lesser Antilles where a yacht can anchor has been described or at least mentioned, but not all are easy to enter. Many of these anchorages can only be used in good weather and perfect visibility. Besides, some boats are handier than others, and some sailors are better than others. Thus you must evaluate each anchorage for yourself before entering. The time of day, the weather, your abilities, the weatherliness of your boat—all influence the final decision.

As an addendum to this, some advice to readers who operate bare boat charter fleets: study the book carefully, make your judgments, and mark on the sketch charts of each boat's copy the anchorages you want your charters to avoid.

Fair sailing to all.

—D.M.S.

Contents

Sketch Charts

Illustrations

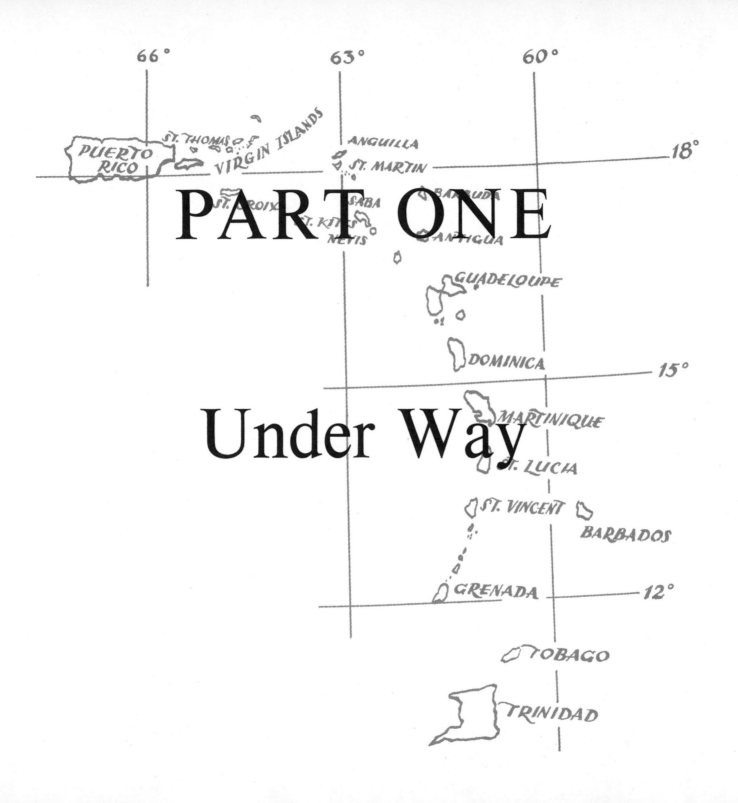

PART ONE

Under Way

CHAPTER 1

Preparations

Cruising through the Lesser Antilles will be more pleasant if some effort is made to equip and/or alter a boat for tropical climes. First and foremost, if you are sending her south on her own bottom, make sure that she is truly rigged for rugged offshore sailing. It can get rough on the trip down and almost every year one or more boats are lost en route. The boat and equipment that stand up fine to Long Island Sound may not be rugged enough to take the gaff in a gale offshore.

Once considerations of physical safety are attended to, the next important factor is physical comfort. Even in steady trade winds, providing for effective ventilation is a must when water and air are both warm. The former holds at about 78 degrees, and the latter frequently hits 85 degrees. But despite what many people may argue to the contrary, air conditioning is totally unnecessary. With adequate awnings, ventilators, and wind scoops, cabins and cockpits never really get uncomfortably hot.

As to hatches, it is important that they be hinged with removable pins and double hinges so that they may be opened to face either fore or aft. If possible, it is advantageous to have them hinged four ways, as sometimes you will be moored to a dock beam to the wind. It is also essential that all hatches be equipped with good watertight dodgers so that when beating to windward, the hatches can be left open facing aft, with the dodger over them to keep out the spray. A buttoned-up boat in the tropics soon becomes nothing but a sweatbox.

A couple of "galley staysails"—i.e., wind scoops—are worth their weight in gold. Keep the air moving and you'll stay cool. Awnings will keep the sun from frying your brain—as long as they are not made of Dacron or nylon. The sun shines right through these materials; you can get sunburned while sitting in their supposed shade, and, perhaps worse, they are noisy. We have all experienced the distraction of a fluttering leech; a nylon or Dacron awning's fluttering will drive you right out of your mind. The best awning material is Vivatex, a mildew-proofed canvas sold by various canvas suppliers in larger cities. It blocks out the sun completely and stands up well to tropical elements. If you have a large awning made up, covering from the mainmast aft, be sure to have its edges roped; it will then last longer and won't tend to stretch. An awning rigged good and tight so that the wind does not blow it around will make life aboard a good deal more enjoyable. Though not essential, if possible carry a second, smaller, awning that can cover the cockpit while sailing. This is all the more a consideration for boats coming from Europe. It's three to four weeks from the Canaries to the Antilles, and a helmsman's brains will be baking from 0900 to 1600 with the sun overhead, the wind dead aft, and little cooling breeze over the boat. All this may seem like the fussbudgeting of a fair-skinned neurotic, but it is well to keep in mind that the Lesser Antilles extend from 19 degrees to 12 degrees north latitude, and the sun is just plain strong—stronger, even, than it is in Florida or the Bahamas. Sunburn can spoil the best-planned cruise.

So can dampness. Going to windward and reaching in a fresh trade wind with a big sea produces large quantities of spray, and the area's rain squalls, while perhaps welcomed at first, can become unpleasant in a hurry. A dodger protecting the whole cockpit will prove to be a real godsend. Similarly, weather cloths rigged on the lifelines on the weather side abreast the cockpit will keep out a lot of spray and solid water. It is well worth the effort to have them made.

The insulation for iceboxes or refrigeration is another area where boats built for the northern climates are frequently deficient. Innumerable times I have been aboard modern yachts, recently built at tremendous expense, and discovered that insulation for the icebox is cork or glass wool. In both cases if the box has been in place for any amount of time, the insulation is soaking wet. The insulating properties of wet cork are about the same as those of old coconut husks. Not only that, but it is a great way to cause rot. The case of my own boat is worthy of note.

When I bought *Iolaire* she had no icebox, so I built one of 200-pound capacity, insulating it with two inches of plank Styrofoam. This setup kept ice for about a week—not particularly efficient. So I put an insulated bulkhead down the center of the box and split the top, getting in effect two totally separate 100-pound boxes. When the ice had melted halfway down in both sides, it was thrown together on one side, so that after no less than five days essentially I started in anew with a full 100-pound box. Then I had a number of extra days in which to take on more ice at my convenience. In addition, since each box was only half the size of the original, when the ice melted down there was not as much area to cool as formerly. The whole of each smaller box stayed cold rather than just the very bottom of the old box. This worked very well, but finally I became concerned about what might be happening behind the icebox, so I tore it out as a precautionary measure. Sure enough, despite the two inches of Styrofoam, condensation was gathering and rot had started eating away at the ceiling of the hull. Luckily, it had not worked its way through to the framing or planking. I rebuilt the whole thing, this time using poured Freon Styrofoam. The result was well worth the trouble.

Freon Styrofoam is expensive, but its insulating properties are superb, as the Styrofoam bubbles are not filled with air but with inert Freon. The expense of rebuilding my icebox was more than justified, due to the saving in time and effort of procuring ice and the further saving of the actual cost of the ice. If the boxes are cold and topped off to their full capacity of 100 pounds each, I can stretch the ice supply to as long as 17 days. Even if you have mechanical or electrical refrigeration, it still pays to reinsulate your box if you plan to visit the tropics. It will keep it from sweating and causing rot, and if the box is really well insulated, it will appreciably reduce the time that you have to run the engine. The great difficulty with mechanical refrigeration is that it is very difficult to get things repaired in the Islands if it breaks down. Some boats have kerosene fridges, others have gas, but all in all, with the time, effort, and expense involved, the simple but well-insulated icebox is difficult to beat. It is bound to work—just buy ice, put it in the box, and everything has to get cold.

Again, what gets you by up north will not necessarily do so in the tropics. To test the ice-holding properties of your system while in northern waters, top off your icebox on a summer Sunday, say, just before leaving the boat. Come back the next Saturday and have a look; if the loss has been more than ten pounds per day, you had better get the box reinsulated before coming down south. For mechanical refrigeration and/or deep freezers, load the box with food and cool it to the desired temperature. If from 10:00 at night to 7:00 in the morning it has lost more than five degrees, it

is time to reinsulate, install new holding plates, or what-have-you. For more chilling details on this subject, I suggest you read the chapter on refrigeration co-authored by Jon Repke in my book, *The Ocean Sailing Yacht* (W. W. Norton & Co.). Repke of St. Thomas is, to the best of my knowledge, the only person in the world who designs refrigeration specifically for the individual yacht. He is himself a yachtsman who has spent more than 15 years in the tropics. His installations are expensive, but they work.

Finding ice is no longer the challenge it used to be. It is usually available on most of the islands—except, of course, when the ice plant breaks down. But for some reason that may be of interest to sociologists, the more civilized the locale, the more difficulty there is in getting ice. In St. Thomas, for example, not only is it expensive and hard to find, but once you have acquired a block the taxi drivers refuse to allow it in their trunks. Bulging burlap bags are red flags to them, so be prepared to walk. I seriously recommend, therefore, that you provide yourself with two smaller bags, so that the load will be balanced and you won't be dragging it on the ground. Better than the standard burlap is a bag made of ten-ounce Dacron, as this will not rot or mildew.

One suggestion to transatlantic voyagers: give the port-side waterline and the area aft under both quarters up near to deck level a coat of cheap, soft bottom paint before your departure. On the way across every boat picks up pin barnacles above the waterline. Remember, the best adhesive known to man, better than epoxy glue, is the glue that a barnacle uses to attach itself to the bottom or sides of a boat. By the time you have removed the pin barnacles, you will have taken a few layers of paint and possibly gel coat with them. The rough spots will have to be reglazed, sanded, and painted. But if you have slapped on a coat of cheap, soft bottom paint (without sand-

ing the boot top and topsides first), a few hours work with wet sandpaper on arrival and you will be down to your original finish. It might need another coat of paint, but it would have needed that anyway.

Another suggestion that will save much work relates to yachts that have varnished rail caps. The day before you leave, slap on a coat of cheap, flat-white house paint *without sanding the varnish*. Again, a sanding on arrival will flake off the white paint, and with a quick coat of varnish your boat will look fresh from the boatyard. Otherwise, you would probably have to rewood the rail cap to make it look decent again. Perform this operation only if your bright work is in really top-notch shape beforehand.

Now we come to the basic ingredients of this venture—the sails. Rule Number One: do not carry too many. You will find yourself loaded down with swim fins, face masks, spear guns, charcoal braziers, etc., etc., and you will not have much space left over for sails. Leave the spinnaker behind; offshore in the Islands it is usually blowing too hard to use it, and even when it isn't, the swell will be rolling the wind out of it. Unless you have a spinnaker net, you will undoubtedly end up with a good wrap. In the lee of some islands where the breeze is light and the sea calm, the wind does continual 90- and 180-degree shifts, so you would really have fun disentangling it. But be sure to bring your light genoa; it will work fine on the end of the spinnaker pole. A small working genoa that just barely overlaps the mast is a useful sail if it is high-cut. But if you have a double headsail rig, that is the greatest asset; being able to douse the jib and leave a staysail up to shorten down for squalls is exceedingly handy.

I remark in the chapter on Weather and Tides that it sometimes blows hard for long periods of time. A small mainsail or a large storm trysail is helpful. *Iolaire* has a large Dacron storm trysail. The same size as the double-reefed main, the trysail is kept stowed in its bag permanently on a switch track for most of the winter. When it pipes up, it is a simple maneuver to drop the main, throw the switch, change the halyard and haul away. At times we have sailed under headsails, trysail, and mizzen, and still averaged seven knots. If you are going to be in the area for any amount of time, bring your sail covers; the sun raises hob with Dacron sails. Apropos of which, have your sails well checked before coming down. Tired sails have a habit of blowing out en route.

But if you limp on to the Islands, you will be pleased to discover that the formerly appalling sail-repair situation no longer pertains. Sails can be repaired in Puerto Rico, St. Thomas, Martinique, Bequia, and Grenada (see Provisions chapter), but, due to the number of yachtsmen who do not bother to check their sails before setting out, there often is a long waiting list.

Needless to say, if you are sailing your boat to the Islands, give the rigging a good going-over. If you have swaged terminals, some preventive maintenance is in order. With few exceptions, there is not a boat in the Islands that has been there any amount of time that does not have cracked swaged terminals on the lower ends of its shrouds. Evidently the salt water that lies in the top of the terminal causes corrosion, which expands and produces hairline cracks in the terminal. Some boats have prevented this condition by cleaning out the top of the terminal with de-rustifier, heating the terminal with a blowtorch, and then sealing the terminal with sealing wax, beeswax, or other preparation. Nothing guaranteed, but it seems to work. Bring enough wire to replace your longest stay, as stocks of stainless wire outside of St. Thomas are none too good. The same holds true for end fittings, turnbuckles, and toggles; bring a few spares as they are very difficult to obtain in the area.

If you don't have a gallows frame, have one installed; trying to hook one of those ridiculous wire pennants from the mizzen mast to the main boom at sea with a big swell rolling is a fine way to have an accident. My own experience with those affairs has been one split-open skull. I am surprised that the ocean racing rules don't require that every boat racing offshore have a substantial gallows frame. Besides the safety factor, it provides a good brace for the navigator and a great place to secure a small awning.

In regard to the engine, check your gasket kit and make sure everything is there that should be. I once opened my gasket kit after I had taken the engine out of the boat only to discover the essential oil seal that costs 15 cents was missing. What with telephone calls, cables, lost mail, the gasket cost me about 20 dollars and two weeks. The same holds true of carburetor parts. It once took me two years to replace standard carburetor parts for an engine that is still being manufactured today.

Diesels are admittedly much more reliable than gasoline engines. However, when things do go wrong, you will discover the diesel-parts situation in the Islands can be excruciatingly poor. Further, when you cable to the manufacturers for the necessary parts, requesting that they be sent air freight or air parcel post, they usually cable back to contact local agents; naturally, one has only contacted the manufacturer because the local agent was without the parts in the first place. For a diesel, I would strongly recommend bringing a complete set of gaskets, a couple of extra valves, some spare injectors, an injector pipe, and—most important—a spare starter motor. Other brands of alternators and generators can usually be adapted, but for a starter motor, only the correct one will fit.

With both gasoline and diesel fuel the greatest problem is dirt and water; be sure you have a large-capacity filter and that you have

plenty of extra filter elements, as they are very scarce in this area. They do have some, but never the type that you need. If your engine needs overhauling, overhaul it. And in any regard, be sure to carry the most complete repair manual that the manufacturer prints—the real mechanic's repair manual, not just the owner's manual.

As to stoves, alcohol stoves leave much to be desired. Drinking alcohol is cheap, but alcohol for stoves is expensive—running $2.50 per gallon and up. (In Bermuda, you may pay as much as $7.00 per gallon.) Primus (kerosene) stoves are the old standby, but there's trouble with them, too. The kerosene (paraffin, to our British cousins) is of poor grade; in fact, much of it is not even kerosene; for some odd reason, I am told, jet fuel is used instead. Great difficulty is experienced with clogged burners; most people use mineral spirits to clean them, but watch out. The mineral spirits burn with a hotter flame than kerosene and sometimes the side of the burner burns out and a most spectacular fire results. Bottled gas is rapidly gaining favor. Bottles can be refilled on all the large islands, but with some difficulty. An adapter filler is needed, which usually turns out to be lost whenever anyone wants to fill an American bottle. For this reason, I urge people to make their own adapter that will accommodate the standard male ending on British and French fillers.

One of the great problems in any tropical area is the cockroach. If your boat remains in the Islands for any amount of time, sooner or later cockroaches will come on board and begin to breed and multiply. Cockroaches on board are not a sign of a filthy boat. The place I am always finding them in *Iolaire*, even after fumigating, is in the winch handle boxes—they love the grease on winch handles. It is possible to have a boat fumigated in the Islands, but it is an expensive and time-consuming procedure. A better way is to buy a bottle of Diazon and an old-fashioned spray gun, follow the directions, mix the Diazon with water, spray all the dark and unventilated corners of the boat, especially the bilge, and you will be guaranteed to be rid of cockroaches. If you have a leaky boat, you can simply pour some undiluted Diazon in the bilge water and let it slosh around. This information was given to me by a former head of the Food and Drug Laboratory in Puerto Rico. He stated that most of the commercially-sold bug sprays in the Islands were more dangerous to the sprayer than to the bug.

As to the bottom of the boat, the specter of the teredo is grossly exaggerated. With good bottom paint and a haul every six or eight months, there is nothing to worry about. However, if your rudder post is not coppered, it is well worth removing the rudder and coppering the post. No matter how hard you try, it is impossible to do a really good job of painting between the rudder stock and the rudder post. If you have a taste for shoal-water exploration, have the deadwood aft of the ballast keel coppered so that if you run aground you will not have the bare wood inviting the worms to dinner.

Another sensible precaution before starting south is to overhaul your pumps. Many a boat heading for the Islands has run into serious difficulty because its pumping system could not cope with more than a small leak. I feel it is essential to have at hand big bilge pumps of the diaphragm type. The old-fashioned Navy pump is next to useless in my opinion, as it is operated with an up-and-down motion; within half an hour your arm is coming out of its socket and no water is coming out of the boat. Plus it is hard to disassemble and is easily damaged. A good big diaphragm pump should be mounted. For ease of pumping, install a handle three times larger than that provided, mount the pump so that it is easily accessible, and make sure the intake and dis-

charge lines have as few bends in them as possible. If your boat has only one pump and discretion dictates that you carry a second, a simple solution is to bolt down a big diaphragm pump on three-quarter-inch plywood and attach two hoses to it long enough to reach from the bilge overside. Then stow it in the lazarette and hope to hell you never have to dig it out except for testing.

Dinghies constitute a definite problem. The average dinghy small enough to be carried aboard a yacht is apt to be inadequate for the constant use to which it will be put in the Islands. There is no such thing as launch service in the Lesser Antilles, and most of the

time you will be unable to lie alongside docks. Also, for diving expeditions, you will frequently have to make passages of a mile or more in moderately rough water loaded down with three or four people, anchor, outboard, diving gear, etc. Often there will be anchorages where a sailing dinghy will provide a pleasant diversion. Thus, you want the largest dinghy that you can possibly carry on board. Weight is not so much a problem as space; even a comparatively heavy dinghy is easily handled if it is hoisted on a sling from the main halyard. But it is necessary to be able to take it on deck. On the passages between the islands, I, for one, do not like to be towing a dinghy. Admittedly,

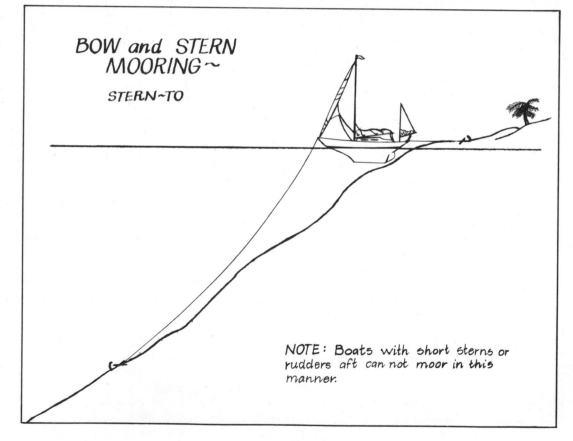

BOW and STERN MOORING~

STERN~TO

NOTE: Boats with short sterns or rudders aft can not moor in this manner.

some of the boats tow their dinghies (in many cases, Boston Whalers with self-bailers) up and down the Islands in all weather. However, my view is that the dinghy is too expensive a piece of gear to be towed behind in rough weather.

Moreover, insurance companies tend to be very feisty when it comes to paying off on lost or damaged dinghies. Lloyd's of London, for instance, does not cover dinghies under tow without a special rider being written, and insists that dinghies be marked with the name of the parent vessel and that outboards be locked in place. This is not so idle a problem, as the theft of dingies and outboards in the Islands has become rampant over the last few years. Not all of it by any means can be blamed on native West Indians; itinerant yachtsmen have also been guilty. If you have an expensive dinghy with a powerful outboard, my advice is to secure it to your boat or to a dock with a good padlock. And even then, make sure your insurance is in force.

Anchors and Anchoring

Anchoring is usually easy, though it has its exasperating and even humiliating aspects, also. If you know what you are about, you will understand that different conditions demand different methods of anchoring, and that there is no one maxim that will let you rest easy every night in every anchorage. Sometimes a Danforth will hold where a CQR plow won't; sometimes vice versa; sometimes neither will do the trick. An old-fashioned Herreshoff will usually work, but it is heavier and harder to handle. I use a 50-pound Herreshoff as my primary anchor. To avoid wrestling with it on the foredeck, I sling it from my bowsprit, where it can be catted without taking it aboard. I do the same with a 35-pound CQR slung from the other side of the bowsprit, and carry a 150-pound three-piece Herreshoff in the bilge as an insurance policy. As to line, for some 15 years I have used five-eighths-inch nylon secured directly to the anchor, its last ten feet protected by canvas chafing gear. This seems to work, though I am careful not to anchor where I can see any coral, as it would cut a nylon rode in minutes. If I can't avoid a coral anchorage, I use chain; it can be backbreaking to lift in the morning but I can sleep soundly all night in preparation for the exercise.

Those of us who prefer rope to chain realize that in Island cruising it is common to anchor two or three times a day. Not being masochists, we choose to play with line rather than struggle with much heavier chain. Besides, line is easier to row out in a dinghy if you are setting a second anchor or carrying one ashore.

Always carry plenty of line. Some anchorages are surprisingly deep and several hundred feet will be required. If you should have to cut away 30 or 40 feet from a fouled anchor, you will not want to interrupt your trip to procure a replacement. Two lengths of at least 200 feet apiece and three anchors are a minimum to carry on board. Also, bring along a float on 20 feet of line to secure to the crown of your anchor. In shallow water this will serve as a handy trip line when an anchor has dug itself in, and if your anchor

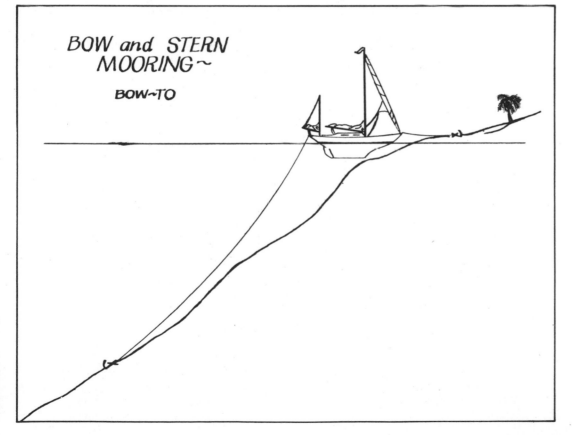

BOW and STERN MOORING ~

BOW~TO

fouls in deep water, you won't have to dive all the way to the bottom to put a line on it. For Island cruising, ten feet of chain per rode will suffice. Anytime a vessel anchors, it is a wise practice to send someone over the side with a face mask to verify that the anchor has properly set.

It is a common occurrence in the Islands to have a strong current running counter to the direction of the wind. Setting the mizzen while at anchor may keep you lying head to wind, but not all the time. The Bahamian sloops have devised a means of coping with this problem which is of special value in crowded anchorages. I call it the Bahamian

Flying Moor. Done right, it can be effective and spectacular; done wrong, a shambles.

Have two anchors made up and ready with plenty of line flaked out on deck ready to run. Slow down and drop your first anchor, then sail on beyond it in the axis of the tide. Pay out the rode fast and coast uptide until you come to a stop, or until you run out of anchor line on your first anchor. Drop the second anchor. Luff up, or drop your sails completely, and let the tide set you back on this second anchor. Set the normal amount of scope, then take up the slack on the first anchor. Secure both rodes at the bow. You should now be lying evenly between each an-

chor and swinging by the bow in a circle whose radius is determined by the length of the boat.

Similarly, it is possible to put out one anchor, get settled, and then row out a second anchor in the direction from which you determine the tide will come when it changes. Since this is usually 180 degrees from your present heading, you can also set the second anchor by letting out double the scope on your first anchor, dropping the second off the stern, leading it to the bow, and paying out line as you pull yourself back up to normal scope on your first anchor. For the old-style boat with the rudder secured to the keel there was no problem with this kind of double rig. However, the advent of short keels and separate rudders has sometimes resulted in a wrap around one or the other, or both. A solution to this problem can be had by securing a small weight to each rode about 15 or 20 feet down from the water level.

What to Bring

No matter how little you bring with you, it will most likely be too much. Yachts are not houses with attics and cellars. Space is at a premium, and for this reason suitcases are a particular nuisance on board. Admittedly, a few of the larger charter boats have stowage areas in the engine room, but these are the exception. No matter how you try to keep them out of the way, suitcases are more trouble than they're worth. Bring your gear in zippered bags. A sailmaker can make them up for you; these are the best variety as they will be thoroughly waterproof. But if you don't have access to a sailmaker, most of the airlines will sell you plastic, zippered, hang-up bags for carrying suits or dresses.

Electric shavers are of uncertain value in the area. In the Grenadines, for example, the 220-volt current which services most of the larger islands will burn out most plug-in shavers

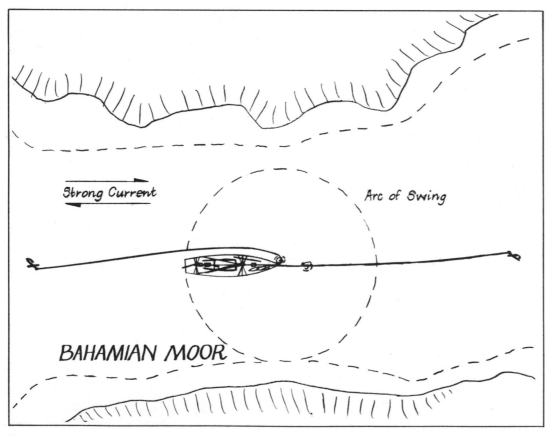

Strong Current

Arc of Swing

BAHAMIAN MOOR

in a second or two. Battery-operated cordless shavers are probably the most convenient on board, until it comes time to recharge them. My own slightly biased advice is—grow a beard!

Most everyone will want to bring a camera. But film can be hard to come by, so it is a good idea to bring with you as much as you plan to use. Keep it dry and, if possible, cold. (At any rate, keep it out of the sun.) An underwater camera will prove to be particularly valuable, and if there is any way short of larceny of laying your hands on one, bring it down. Be sure to use a red filter to counteract the bluish cast that is noticeable in so many underwater photographs. When you are transporting photographic equipment in a dinghy, keep it all in a watertight plastic bag. A waterproof camera should be well secured to your wrist or a thwart. I once capsized a dinghy in breaking seas on the outer reef of Tobago Cays. We lost a fine underwater camera and meter which would be ours today had I tied them down.

Sunglasses are absolutely essential in the area. Bring extras, as they have a way of getting away from you when you need them most. Before you leave the States, drill two small holes in the bows of the glasses. Later a piece of sail thread can be knotted through the holes and passed around the back of the head to keep them from blowing off your nose into the drink. Bring plenty of suntan lotion, since certain brands are not readily available in the Islands. What you want in a lotion is one that will block most of the rays, inasmuch as in the tropics you'll get all the tan you need and then some. If you are in doubt about the most appropriate type, check with a pharmacist. The sun is the real bugaboo of Caribbean cruises. Long trousers and shirts are recommended during the sun-strong hours of the first week, and bring along a pair or two of long-sleeved cotton pajamas and a straw hat with a moderate-sized

brim to wear over your bathing suit. They won't win you a beauty contest, but they'll save you an awful lot of trouble and pain. Two particularly sun-sensitive friends of mine who charter with me regularly even wear the pajamas in swimming. You may not choose to go to these lengths, but certainly if you are in the water for a long while, you should at least wear a cotton T-shirt. After an hour or two of snorkeling, even the most tanned back will take on the look of a well-boiled lobster.

Large broad-brimmed hats are wonderful for strolling around town, but they won't stay on one's head long at sea. Wear the small-brimmed variety and run a piece of sail twine from the hat to a button hole in your shirt. If the hat blows off, all you have to do is lay a hand on the line and clap it back on your head.

Insecticide is not usually needed on the way down. Insects are a major problem only in the Bahamas, but it is good to have one bottle on board just in case. The appropriate tropical insecticide can be bought in the Islands. Look for the ones made in Guyana, as they seem to be the only people who really understand bug repellants.

In general, bring a minimal amount of clothing. Men should take along a jacket and tie for the one or two places they may need to get dressed up. The ladies should bring a couple of fancy dresses which they may not use but which they will be relieved to have on hand should the occasion present itself. They should also bring blouses, bathing suits, and slacks. Bell-bottom-type slacks are the most convenient as they can be rolled up and do not get wet stepping out of a dinghy into ankle deep water. Simple, cool dresses should be carried along, since on many of the islands, shorts and bikinis are not considered proper shore attire.

For the men, shorts and T-shirts are the staple items. Better still are any old, slightly threadbare, long-sleeve cotton shirts. They are cool and provide the best protection from the

sun. It's a good idea to pack a pair of worn-out sneakers to wear in the shallows so that you don't have to worry about sea urchins. Light foul weather gear and a sweater for the evening will come in handy, as will an old pair of socks to protect the tops of your feet and of your tiller hand from sunburn. Sea boots and all that sort of heavy foul weather gear are not needed. Finally, if you are going by air, pack everything you plan to bring in sea bags and hang-up bags except for a pair or two of shorts, shirts, and a dress for the lady. These should be carried in a small, separate bag, so that in case your luggage is lost in transit, you won't spend your days wandering about the tropics in a tweed suit.

Some people, of course, never accede to the local customs of dress. The owner of a small hotel reacted with surprise a few years ago when a Britisher came to supper in a dinner jacket. The owner politely suggested that he might be more comfortable in a shirt and slacks, to which the Englishman replied, "My good fellow, this is not a question of comfort but of how one has been brought up." I told this story to a group of British charter skippers some time later who looked at me rather blankly and said, "Oh, quite."

Water Safety

Much has been written in travel brochures and adventure stories of the dangers of swimming in tropical waters. Perhaps because the sharks, barracudas, and eels have not read the same literature, they are not aware of how dangerous they are. By observing a few simple procedures, you are probably safer swimming the Lesser Antilles than you are crossing 42nd Street in New York City. Here are the fundamentals:

(1) Do not swim at night—the highest rate of shark attacks takes place after sundown.
(2) Do not swim from the boat way off-

shore. Sharks near inshore reefs are well fed and not particularly hungry. But the ones a few miles off are hungry and dangerous.

(3) Do not swim with bright objects of apparel. Leave necklaces, rings, watches, and bracelets on board the boat.

(4) When spearfishing, keep a dinghy nearby. As soon as you spear a fish, put it in the dinghy. A bleeding or fluttering fish will attract a shark in a hurry. Should this happen, leave the fish to the shark as an appetizer. He will eat it up and usually go away. The same applies to barracuda.

Most of the firsthand accounts of shark attacks are told by experienced spear fishermen. If you question them closely, nine times out of ten they will admit to having taken chances in an area they knew to be dangerous, by, say, continuing to swim long after injured fish left in the water began making their distinctive distress cry (a sort of clicking noise).

Besides the shark and the barracuda, there is a third character who must be treated with caution—the moray eel. He is a nasty, mean-spirited customer who hides out in coral caves and holes. Unless sharply provoked, he will seldom attack. Don't go sticking a hand or foot into dark holes in a reef without taking a damn good look first. If you see a lobster and an eel in the same opening, you are advised to leave the lobster alone, for the eel may take offense at the intrusion.

There are four other swimming dangers that present a more common threat than shark, barracuda, or eel. These are: severe sunburn on the shoulders, backs, or legs; sea urchins (they will go right through the sole of a swim fin); being swept away by a current; and getting run down by an outboard. The last is becoming a greater problem every year as more and more yachts come into the area tendered by absurdly high-speed launches. There must be something of the fly-boy mentality in these launch operators who, even when their yachts are moored as little as a few hundred yards off, feel impelled to go ashore at nothing less than full speed, and woe betide the poor swimmer in between. I know of one person who has been killed this way, and I'm sure there have been others. Don't add to the statistics. If there are people joy riding with high-speed outboards, stay close to your own boat or row ashore and swim off the beach. Don't be idly swimming near moored boats, as this is as good a way as any to have your head lopped off.

No matter where you are, check the tide before diving over the side. There are times when there is no way to swim against it. If you are going off on a snorkeling expedition, determine the set of the tide. Don't go when it is running to leeward, and in a strong tide don't swim downstream of the dinghy. In the Grenadines especially, the tides can run very swiftly, and even a strong swimmer with flippers will not be able to make way against it.

And lastly, as tempting as they may look, do not eat the crab apples on the beach. They are manchineel and deadly poisonous.

Insurance

In preparing your own boat for a trip to the Lesser Antilles, it is easy to forget to check your insurance coverage. But don't. Most policies, even on boats hailing from the east coast of the United States, do not cover sailing in the Lesser Antilles. Underwriters usually require an additional premium for the trip down and back, as well they should in light of the number of boats that have been lost and the damage that has been sustained in making this passage. Presently rates are 0.5 to 0.75 percent for a one-way trip, and 1.0 to 1.50 percent for a round trip, with numerous stipulations as to exactly when the trip can be made.

If you are sailing from Europe, you will also be asked to pay an additional premium to cover your passage. Many sailors don't bother. If you do run into trouble on a transatlantic passage, it usually occurs between Northern Europe and the Canary Islands, with the majority of accidents taking place off the Bay of Biscay or off the coast of Spain. Most boats that sail out of European ports are already covered for these areas, and so those bound for the Lesser Antilles merely cross the Atlantic at their own risk, reinsuring once they arrive in the Islands.

It is generally more difficult to obtain coverage if you are heading south with plans to hire out for charter than if you are intending to cruise for pleasure on your own. The usual policy for a charter boat requires an extra fee for every week of chartering. This procedure is acceptable to those who do little business, for their extra premium is small. But for the successful charter skipper, the cost becomes considerable.

Let me cite Lloyd's as a typical example of insurance stipulations. Not too many years ago, Lloyd's was prepared to wash its hands of all Lesser Antilles yacht insurance for the simple reason that they were losing too many boats that were overvalued, overaged, and exhibited a great desire to go to the bottom, usually in water several miles deep. The underwriters became suspicious, but could prove nothing, as there was no *corpus delicti* on which to perform an autopsy. Conditions in the Caribbean are such that even the best-maintained boats tend to deteriorate faster than at the estimated rate, which put Lloyd's in the position of insuring boats for more than their actual value. Rigging deteriorates particularly fast; in one recent year no less than 17 masts were lost within a span of 11 months. At the same time, dinghies were disappearing at an alarming rate, to the point where Lloyd's had just about had enough. Only a last-ditch effort backed by numerous promises to tighten up procedures has saved the yacht insurance business in the

Islands. Today, a competent owner who has his boat surveyed by a reputable surveyor (and the underwriters know just which surveyors can be trusted) and has complied with all his recommendations can obtain insurance in the Lesser Antilles.

Lloyd's prefers to deal with large deductibles (excesses), as the paperwork on small claims is expensive in proportion to the income derived. They are prepared to cover your dinghy under a separate deductible, providing the name of the vessel is on the dinghy, in the hopes that it would be recognized and repossessed if the name were permanently on it. Outboards must be secured with an "anti-theft device" of some kind, and unless an extra premium is paid, dinghies are not covered while being towed in open passages. Similarly, Lloyd's has been deluged with paperwork on small claims of several hundred dollars caused by boats that have moored improperly and have dragged or swung into surrounding boats, causing damage. Consequently, they have now placed a deductible on the third-party "Protection and Indemnity" section of their policies.

The geographic area that insurance companies will be willing to cover varies drastically with the individual underwriters and also with the brokers placing the insurance. However, coverage can be obtained specifically covering the entire Lesser Antilles from Puerto Rico to Trinidad, including the coast of Venezuela. If one broker won't give you the coverage you need, move on to another one.

Rates, of course, also vary considerably, and are the cause of much argument. Frequently the question is asked as to why a beautifully constructed old boat, still in perfect condition and which would still pass a rigid survey, carries such a high hull rate in comparison to a new boat of the same size. The underwriters point out, justifiably, that a 70-foot boat built in 1938 will be valued at probably $70,000 to $80,000, while its modern sister will be valued at $300,000; charging two percent on the modern boat yields a premium of $6,000, while charging seven percent on the old boat realizes a premium of only $4,200. It is not so much the total loss that causes underwriters to lose money, but rather the partial loss: a bashed bulwark, a lost rig, or what-have-you. Replacing the rig in the old boat will be just as expensive as replacing the rig in the new boat; a bashed-in bulwark on the old boat will be, if anything, more expensive to repair than a new boat, yet they are receiving less premium to cover this type of loss—hence the higher rate.

Another problem is that Lloyd's insists on insuring by the ton—the Thames ton—a reckoning which often bears little relationship to the actual size of a vessel. Thames tonnage is calculated by length and beam, which tends to give long, narrow boats a relatively low reading, while fat, beamy boats are given a disproportionately high Thames tonnage. For example, *Flica II*, a converted 12-Meter that is 67 feet long but with a narrow beam, has a lower Thames tonnage than the Alden-designed *Renegade*, 51 feet long with normal beam. Lloyd's wanted more total premium on the 51-footer than on the 67-footer! The only moral I can see is that if you have to insure through Lloyd's, buy a narrow boat.

And now for a personal plug. Insurance coverage can be obtained covering the entire Lesser Antilles from Puerto Rico to Trinidad, including the Venezuelan coast. There are several Lloyd's brokers in the Islands, but Colonel John Jouett on St. Thomas and myself on Grenada handle the majority of the business. Need I say more?

Many yacht owners have little idea of what should be done after a serious accident that will result in an insurance claim. First and foremost, there is the unwritten insurance law backed up by history and innumerable court cases: in case of an accident act as if you were uninsured—protect your own and the underwriter's interests to the best of your ability in the light of circumstances. Second, you should immediately contact by phone or cable both the underwriter and the broker concerned. Third, find a reputable and competent marine surveyor to ascertain the damage. He will then make recommendations on repair or salvage. The nearest Lloyd's agent, who is presumably an expert on insurance matters, is supposed to put you in contact with or appoint a surveyor. Unfortunately, this is not always the best procedure, as the Lloyd's agents here seem to be experts in nothing. Better to contact the surveyor on your own, then ask the broker and underwriter to approve the surveyor's handling everything, thereby bypassing the Lloyd's agent altogether.

In the opinion of myself and John Jouett, the leading yacht surveyors (and the ones we use to settle all our claims) are as follows:

Dave Dana, Jeff Lane—As of this writing Dave has gone north, but the betting is the climate will bring him back again. Jeff Lane has taken over much of his business meanwhile. Contact in St. Thomas over WAH.

Dick Doran—Handles most of the Puerto Rican business. Works extensively in fiberglass. P.O. Box 185, Puerto Real Fajardo, Puerto Rico 00740. Telephone 863-0493.

David Simmonds—General Manager of Antigua Slipway. Does most of the work in the middle islands. Antigua Slipway, Ltd., Box 576, St. John's, Antigua. Telephone 31056.

Mike Forshaw—Formerly yard manager of Grenada Yacht Services. P.O. Box 121, St. George's, Grenada. Cable "Forshaw." Telephone: home 2882, business 3082.

Medical Emergencies Procedures

If off in an out-of-the-way anchorage, get on the radio and start calling. Usually among

PREPARATIONS

the charter-boat parties doctors will be found who will be able to give you advice in person or over the radio. All the major islands have adequate medical facilities in fully equipped hospitals. The quality of care in the hospitals varies from superb to poor. As in the States, emergency wards are a place to try to stay away from. It is best to take the patient to a private doctor if at all possible; if not, contact a doctor and impress upon him the fact that the patient cannot possibly be moved. Doctors do not like to make calls.

Most of the doctors in the Islands are very well trained, but some admittedly have forgotten much of what they learned in medical school. The best method of finding a good doctor is to call one of the hotels, talk to the manager, explain the situation, and ask him to recommend or contact a doctor for you.

In the absence of a doctor, one can fall back on all sorts of West Indian native medicinal herbs and remedies—a book in itself too lengthy to present here. However, one such which might seriously be kept in mind is aloe, a sap squeezed from the flat cactus plant locally called "pingwing." It is without doubt one of the finest burn remedies in the world. Liberal application of aloe saved my wife from being badly scarred as a result of an oven explosion (ashore, not on the boat). This same balm works wonders in taking the burn out of sunburn. Aloe is a cactus-like plant that grows wild all over the Islands. Simply ask a native to get some for you. Slice off the outside; the jelly that pours out should be directly applied to the skin.

CHAPTER 2

From Europe

Getting There

What began years ago as a small trickle of yachts crossing the Atlantic from Europe to the Lesser Antilles reached a torrent in 1970, when as many as four transatlantic yachts could be seen entering St. George's Harbor in a single day. The torrent has now tapered off into a moderate stream, but there are still a substantial number. The actual transatlantic part of the crossing—the long part from Madeira, the Canary Islands, or Cape Verde to the Islands—is in actuality the easiest portion of the trip.

Proper timing is the key to any passage. It is best to leave Northern Europe in August or early September. Then you can traverse the Bay of Biscay and sail on past Spain and Gibraltar without the continual threat of heavy weather later in the fall. But once in the Canaries or wherever you make landfall, it is best to wait until February, March, or April for the second half of the voyage to the Islands. The reason is simple. The hurricane season in the West Indies extends into late October, and who would want to risk the Atlantic during this tenuous period? Besides, as a careful examination of the Pilot Charts reveals, the trades do not really settle down to their full, steady force until February. From late October to December they tend to be light, with intermittent two- or three-day spates of northwest winds which could not do much to help your daily average. Not surprisingly, late October or early November departures seldom, if ever, produce fast passages.

Slow passages are also recorded for the simple reason that all too many people have read inflated stories about "consistent 25- and 30-knot" trade winds and rig accordingly. For many years, most transatlantic passages were made under twin headsails or twin jibs rigged to the helm for self-steering, but these never give enough sail area for the 12- to 15-knot blows which are the more common. Now, with the advent of really efficient self-steering gear, boats are posting better times under mainsail and genoa, with the genoa sheeted to a spinnaker pole. Some even have set spinnakers under self-steering. But there are still those who come across under the traditional high-cut twins, whatever the strength of the seasonal winds, and who inevitably complain of rolling both rails under all the way and making poor time to boot.

My own preference going downwind, which I have used on *Iolaire* and other yachts, improves upon the traditional pairing. It provides the sail area necessary for speed, and it keeps the center of effort low. I have dubbed it the "poor man's twins" and it is rigged as follows: replace the spinnaker halyard block at the top of your mast with a block with a becket on it; shackle a light jackstay wire (the size depending on the size of the boat) to the becket and secure the lower end of the wire somewhere on the bow—to a mooring cleat, a bulwark chock, or what have you; then hoist the Number 2 genoa on the jackstay and wing it out to windward on the spinnaker pole, and set the large genoa on the headstay with a sheet led out to the end of the main boom. With the wind on the quarter both headsails and mainsail will draw. With the wind dead aft and the main doused, the big genoa pulls quite nicely. No extra gear need be carried other than one block and a length of wire. The center of effort of these sails is both forward and low, so that steering is easy and rolling minimized.

Whatever your rig, the speed of your passage is largely a function of the weather, and the most advantageous weather—that is to say strong, consistent northeast trade winds—occurs during the winter and early spring; and this is when most of the record passages have been made.

It is possible for a yacht beginning a cruise in Europe to cross the Atlantic, cruise the Islands, and sail home again, all in about 18 weeks. This is best accomplished by leaving in early April, putting the average 40-footer in Barbados by the end of the first week in May. If seven weeks were spent cruising north through the Islands, the first of July would find one in St. Thomas. From St. Thomas to Bermuda is a five- to six-day trip, from Bermuda back to the Azores is another ten to 15 days, and from the Azores to Europe takes about a week. All of which places one home in mid-August, having enjoyed a glorious summer holiday.

The cruising grounds of Western Europe as far south as Spain are well covered by various European cruising guides. I would suggest that people unfamiliar with the area contact The Royal Cruising Club, the Ocean Cruising Club, the Royal Ocean Racing Club or Little Ship Club for relevant books.

However, Spain, I am told, is not particularly well covered by guides. This country is in the midst of a great yachting expansion; new harbors and yacht clubs are burgeoning everywhere, while old commercial harbors have become increasingly overcrowded, dirty, and generally more unpleasant than ever for visiting yachtsmen.

The 1972 Transatlantic Race finished in

GETTING THERE

Bayonne, Spain. All the yachtsmen gave high marks to this quiet fishing village that has built a modern yacht club facility. The anchorage is good, as a breakwater has been constructed to protect the harbor. The yacht club offers excellent facilities, and customs officials are available right there. The town is old, clean, and the townspeople hospitable.

Funchal, Madeira (southwest of Gibraltar by about 600 miles) has long been a favorite stopping place for yachtsmen—who frequently remain there for months and sometimes years. Food is cheap, the locals are hospitable, and there is the added advantage of a boatyard with hauling facilities and even a side track where boats can be stored for a length of time. These facilities are especially helpful to those who wish to cruise to Madeira in the summer and leave their boat there for a few months until the trade winds have resumed, before setting out for the Caribbean in early spring. At the yacht club there is good drinking water, fuel, and showers available. Reliable mechanics can also be found. The anchorage is normally good in the northeast corner of the harbor, east of the yacht club (Sketch Chart 1), but there are two minor problems. The first is caused by debris on the bottom. To be safe, one ought to set three anchors, two off the bow and one off the stern, particularly if the wind swings to the southwest when a swell can build up in the harbor. But more dangerous are the rain squalls in the hills that produce flash floods. The flood waters roar down the mountain gullies and into the bay through huge storm sewers. They spew out all sorts of debris, including boulders large enough to damage seriously or, in at least one case, sink a yacht. Best to give these storm sewers a wide berth.

Further south, in the Canary Islands, Santa Cruz (Sketch Chart 2) on Tenerife is to be avoided at all costs. The harbor is filthy, open to an ocean swell, and definitely too commercial to be a good yacht anchorage. Luckily, a small fishing harbor has been built one mile east of the main harbor (Sketch Chart 3). But it is hard to find, and many yachts have looked for it and sailed right by. Sailing from the east, if you spot five large oil tanks, you have gone too far.

Once there, anchor on the south side of the fishing harbor, away from the big fishing vessels for which the harbor was especially created. Fuel is cheap, but permission must be obtained before taking it on. The water is good, and there are buses and taxis to the city. Food and marine supplies, I am told, are excellent. By last report, customs clearance was only available in town, but I would advise checking immediately on arrival with yachts already there as to the correct procedure.

Las Palmas, Gran Canaria (Sketch Chart 4) has been unpopular among yachtsmen in the past, but it is now in the process of being rebuilt. The new breakwaters have helped greatly, but you still should anchor bow-and-stern near the yacht club, keeping well clear of the steamers using the steamer quay. Again, the yacht club is hospitable, fuel and water are available, and the food is excellent and cheap. Las Palmas is presently an attractive harbor. I hope it remains so.

Whatever the traditional popularity of the Azores, the latest reports I have heard are un-

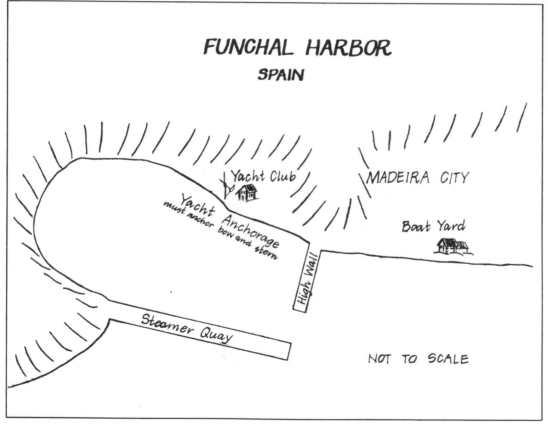

FUNCHAL HARBOR

SPAIN

Yacht Club

Yacht Anchorage
must anchor bow and stern

High Wall

Steamer Quay

MADEIRA CITY

Boat Yard

NOT TO SCALE

SKETCH CHART 1

favorable. The islands were suffering from a persistent drought. No fresh food was available, all of it being shipped in from the outside. For the time being, at least, these islands are best skipped.

Should a transatlantic voyager call at Barbados he will discover that it is a wonderfully well-run island—undoubtedly the best-run in the Caribbean—with a plentiful supply of fresh fruits, milk, vegetables, et al. However, the anchorage is open, exposed, and rolling, with no place to tie up alongside or to land a dinghy. For this reason, the normal routine is to head directly to Grenada. But for my money the thing to do is to head south to Tobago.

Although most attractive, Tobago is seldom visited by yachts from the Islands. It lies 90 miles southeastward of Grenada, 60 miles eastward of the Bocas of Trinidad Harbor, and is to windward against the current. Yachtsmen from both these islands feel the best way to visit Tobago is via LIAT or Arawak, whose planes go to windward very nicely and are unaffected by the current. If you do sail to Barbados first, I would recommend that you still follow the wind to Tobago for a visit, and thence on to Grenada.

Coming Northwest

Sailing through the Lesser Antilles one wonders why there are so many South African yachts and yachtsmen. Due to the lack of harbors and the presence of bad storms on the South African coast, yachting is far from that country's most popular sport. But on reflection it is hardly surprising that so many South African yachtsmen crop up here; Cape Town to the Caribbean is one of the easiest offshore cruises imaginable. Out of Cape Town the next port is St. Helena, 1,700 miles downwind all the way. From there it is 700 miles to Ascension, a good part of it downwind although the doldrums must be traversed as well. From As-

cension to Grenada is 3,300 miles with the trades and a good strong current behind you. The anchorages in Ascension and St. Helena are bad in the extreme, though it is reported that the hospitality ashore more than makes up for the bad anchorage.

Trinidad is not a good landfall when coming from southern waters. Offshore oil rigs are being installed off the east coast, and unbuoyed Darien Rock lingers 22 miles offshore under one-and-a-quarter fathoms. Fifteen miles north of this rock, Emerald Shoal (three fathoms) breaks in heavy weather and is also unmarked. The east coast is low, poorly lit, and generally hard to spot. Boats coming from the south should favor a landfall on the high, well-lit island of Tobago, entering at Scarborough. As I've said, Tobago is a beautiful, unspoiled island, but it is often just too hard to reach from the rest of the Lesser Antilles.

Going South

In the days of the coasting trade between New England, Nova Scotia, and the Caribbean, the old sailing directions to the Islands were rather simple: "You head east so'east until the butter melts, then head south, and when you spot an island, find yourself a fisherman and ask him which island you are looking at." It

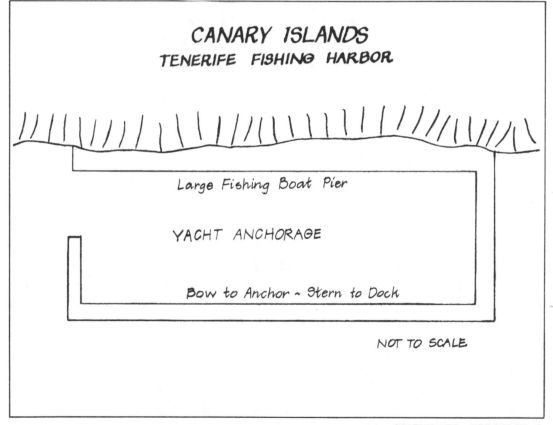

SKETCH CHART 2

worked well enough as long as you spotted one of the high islands before barreling into low-lying Anegada, Anguilla, or Barbuda. In the 19th century, high loss of life at sea was a New England method of population control.

Now every fall more and more American yachts head south to the Lesser Antilles. Most of them aim for St. Thomas, which is probably the most advantageous landfall for a yacht intending to continue on into the Islands. San Juan, though a commodious harbor, is simply too far to leeward. After a long ocean passage, who would relish the tough beat from San Juan to Charlotte Amalie, St. Thomas? And a landfall any farther east than St. Thomas is risky

indeed; just check the number of wrecks on Anegada, Anguilla, and Barbuda. Besides, on St. Thomas you will find every sort of repair facility: electricians, engineers, sailmakers, shipwrights, refrigeration experts, fiberglass experts, hauling facilities for boats up to 50 feet, marine supplies, and food. As a free port, luxury items are relatively cheap; it is a great place to buy yourself a new camera, watch, or spot of Scotch whiskey.

Since summer cruising is good in the eastern part of the United States, most people plan their Antilles cruise for the winter. Coming down in the fall poses a problem. If you leave in September, when the weather is good up

north, you may run into a West Indian hurricane. Wait too long, and you get caught in the winter storms or get iced in before you leave. A check of the dates of hurricanes over the past years and a check of the Pilot Charts will show that November is about the best month to come down. In December north of the 30th parallel you are bound to have a lot of cold weather, and the frequency of gales will have increased greatly. Off Hatteras the percentage of December gales is 22. South of Hatteras the percentage is 13, and toward St. Thomas the percentage is still 12. In three sectors northwest of Bermuda the December percentage runs 7, 10, 15. However, during the month of November, the percentages are between 5 and 7 for the Hatteras area south, while northwest of Bermuda they run 6, 9, 12. Despite the outside possibility of a late-season hurricane, I prefer early November or the last week in October because, with a good long-range weather forecast, your chances of making the trip without getting caught in a gale are good. I will not risk an encounter with a December gale. A yacht in warm weather may weather a 45- to 50-knot gale with no particular difficulty, but when a frigid northeaster comes through and the temperature drops to freezing or below, crew efficiency does not merely deteriorate, it may disappear entirely. Survival becomes more a factor of pure luck than good seamanship. Trying to reef sails or repair rigging from a sleet-covered deck in three layers of clothing, your mittens crusted with rime, is a difficult operation indeed.

There are three distinct types of storms that one can encounter on the way south to the Islands. Foremost is the true tropical hurricane, though these seldom occur after October 25 or early November. If one should happen to develop, the wise mariner will have ample warning of its origin, growth, and progress. Such depressions are now well tracked by satellite; radio WWV announces (at 13 minutes past the

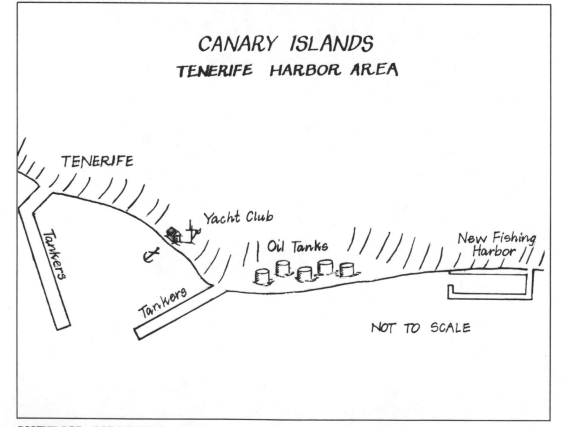

CANARY ISLANDS
TENERIFE HARBOR AREA

TENERIFE

Tankers

Tankers

Yacht Club

Oil Tanks

New Fishing Harbor

NOT TO SCALE

SKETCH CHART 3

hour) all major storms in the North Atlantic, updating its report every four hours. Monitoring this channel will give a few days' warning, time enough to project a storm's course and get out of the way.

A second type of storm that occurs regularly from September to June is the familiar northeaster. These low-pressure fronts sweep across the North American continent, become unstable as they pass over the warmer ocean surface, and roll up on themselves to form intense low-pressure centers. Their arrival is announced by a cold northwest wind blowing anywhere from 15 to 40 knots, and occasional squalls. After the front passes through, the wind will make a switch from northwest to northeast with rain squalls, snow, or sleet. Sometimes the wind shift is gradual, taking as long as a day to swing from northwest to northeast; at other times the shift will take place in a matter of five or ten minutes. The winds may be nothing more than a good solid one-reef sailing breeze or they may pipe up to 50 knots and above.

There is a third type of storm, referred to as a late-season hurricane. It is not a true tropical hurricane as it usually springs up unexpectedly somewhere between 30 to 35 N, 70 to 80 W. These storms are small in diameter, and not particularly long-lived, but they can blow anywhere from 50 to 90 knots. They often give no warning, and the chances of their being picked up on a long-range weather forecast are slight indeed. They have done in a tremendous number of yachts over the years; when the wind blows 60 to 70 knots from east or northeast, Hatteras becomes a deadly lee shore. The Gulf Stream with the wind against the stream becomes a seething mass of breaking seas, where boats lying ahull can be rolled over in no time.

Obviously, the most important thing in going the ocean route to the Islands is to get well south of 30 N without getting involved in any bad storms. The alternative to the offshore route is, of course, the Inland Waterway. You can take it down to Florida in the fall and then work your way east through the Bahamas to St. Thomas. This is good in that you have only one long offshore hop—from Turks Island to St. Thomas. But there are enough disadvantages in this route to discourage most people. For one thing, a yacht drawing more than seven-and-a-half feet cannot negotiate Inland Waterway depths; even a six-foot keel will get stuck now and again. (Consult U.S. Corps of Engineers for latest controlling-depth information.)

Also, there are the distances involved and an easterly wind. From New York to Miami is 1,200 miles, while St. Thomas is another 1,000 miles ESE from Miami. Shortly after leaving Miami, you will reach the trade wind belt, with its constant easterly wind and westerly current. This means sailing hard on the wind all the way, with plenty of extra distance thrown in from tacking, from Bahama-island dodging, and from the leeward set of the current. The Bahamas in general are poorly charted and poorly lit. Many an intended cruise to the Lesser Antilles has been abruptly cancelled on unbuoyed Muchoir and Silver Banks. Other boats have made it half way through the Bahamas before deciding that all this windward work was just

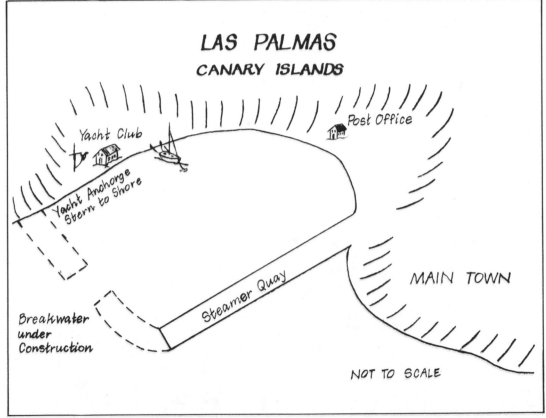

SKETCH CHART 4

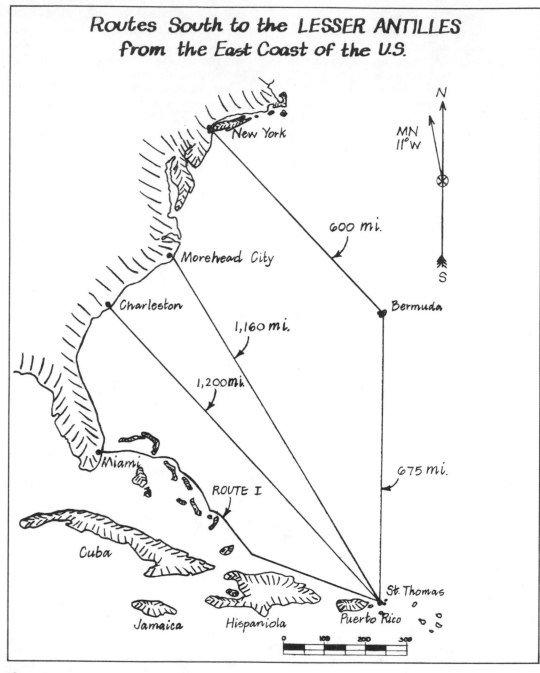

Routes South to the LESSER ANTILLES
from the East Coast of the U.S.

New York

MN
11°W

600 mi.

Morehead City

Charleston

1,160 mi.

1,200 mi.

Bermuda

Miami

ROUTE I

675 mi.

Cuba

St. Thomas

Puerto Rico

Jamaica   Hispaniola

not worth it. It is a very time-consuming process that may take six or seven weeks. Once in awhile you may pick up a chance norther and reach all the way to the western tip of Puerto Rico in 6 days, but such passages are few and far between, requiring a rare combination of luck and skill.

If you set out from New York directly for St. Thomas or Bermuda, you have about 180 miles before reaching the northern edge of the Gulf Stream and warm water; it is also about 700 miles to 30 N, the approximate northern limit of the doldrums and southern limit of the North Atlantic gales. (Roughly the same distances apply from points east of New York. It is interesting to note that the New England coast tends so far east and so little north that Halifax, Nova Scotia, is only 60 miles further from St. Thomas than New York.) As noted, during the month of November the chart covering the area for the first part of the trip shows only 6 to 12 percent gales, but around Bermuda, the percentage runs to 17, reaching 19 in December and 28 in January. (Bermuda attracts gales like a magnet.)

By going first to Bermuda and then heading south, the course is only 150 miles longer to St. Thomas from New York and places you far enough east so that there will probably be no windward work from Bermuda on. The wind roses show relatively little southeast wind in the month of November, so, if you do end up hard on the wind, it probably won't last long. With about a five-day trip to Bermuda and about six or seven to St. Thomas from Bermuda, it is possible to do the trip with two different crews, each using only a week of their vacation.

If the trip is made in two jumps—the first to Bermuda in September and a second to St. Thomas in November—both the winter gales and the hurricanes can be avoided. Hurricanes start about 58 to 59 W, 11 to 18 N. At their formation, they are a minimum of 800 miles in a straight line from Bermuda. They travel in a curve, usually WNW, gradually turning farther north and finally east, thereby traveling some 1,100 miles before they finally reach Bermuda. From the time a hurricane is first spotted to the time when it could possibly be dangerous to a boat en route to Bermuda is about five days. If you check the weather just before you leave in September and no hurricane is reported, you will have clear sailing for at least four to five days. Keep careful track of the weather via WWV radio, and, if no hurricane is reported in the first 48 hours, you should reach Bermuda without difficulty. If one is reported, a check of your position and some time/distance calculations will tell you whether you are close enough to continue, or whether you should turn back to the States. Once you have reached Bermuda, the boat can be left off for the final leg of the trip in November.

During late October or early November, keep a check on your weather and when the report looks good, hop a plane for Hamilton. With the aid of a good forecast and a little luck, you should be able to push south to the doldrums before any gales arrive. Don't be afraid to use the fuel in the beginning of the trip; it is more important to get out of the region of the gales than to worry about getting becalmed in the doldrums. Your course is due south. Once you hit the trades, it will be fast sailing into St. Thomas.

If you sail to Bermuda in September and feel tempted to continue on to St. Thomas—don't. Toward the end of the trip you would not be able to avoid a hurricane, as there would be no more than one or two days' warning. One year a hurricane formed due east of Anguilla and flattened that island before *any* warning was sent out. There was so little advance notice that the boats in St. Thomas Harbor did not even have time to get to Hurricane Hole, St. John, only 20 miles away. A boat ending the final leg from Bermuda would have

been in serious trouble. Again, the Islands should not be approached until after November first.

But for two large, powerful lights on its mainland, Bermuda is not particularly well lit, and a yacht could conceivably pile up on its northwestern reefs in a storm without having seen the lights. Further, the bottom comes up so steeply that unless the channel entrances are pinpointed, a yacht approaching in heavy weather could find itself in real difficulty before realizing how close inshore she had come (witness the bad scare yachtsmen received at the end of the '72 Bermuda race). Finally, the channels into Hamilton and St. George's are very poorly lit.

When a gale is building up, the temptation to fight one's way into the safety of Bermuda may be too great to resist. Such attempts have led to disastrous results: to wit, the sinking of *Romano* in the late 1960's with the loss of five lives. In my own boat, *Iolaire*, I scared the living daylights out of myself and crew in just this way. We made landfall on Bermuda just before a gale; standing off till the gale had passed, we felt, would alarm those waiting for us ashore. So we entered at night with hearts in throats; I assure you this is not something I am likely to try again.

If approaching Bermuda in November when one can continue south without worrying about tropical hurricanes, I would strongly recommend that crews be prepared to make the jump to the Islands without stopping, so that, in the event of a gale, one can stand off and alter course for St. Thomas. From my own experience, I consider the Bermuda route a risky proposition, and I am always very reluctant to recommend it.

Another possible route is to put to sea from Norfolk, at the mouth of the Chesapeake, and head direct for St. Thomas. This way, you will be departing the seaboard in weather relatively warmer than what prevails further

north. The distance is 1,260 miles; for the first 150 miles you will have the Outer Banks and Hatteras on the starboard bow, and in a northeast gale Hatteras is a fearsome lee shore. Its shoals extend 20 miles to sea, and Cape Lookout shoals 20 miles also. The currents and tides are very strong, and the only harbor of refuge is Morehead City, whose channel, with its strong tide, is not the easiest to navigate even under good conditions and one that I would hate to enter on a dark and stormy night.

In a northeaster the wind against the Stream produces continually breaking seas that will cause trouble. Sometimes the gale moves slowly out to the northeast at roughly the same rate as the Stream will carry a boat hove-to. This is what happened to Hardy Wright aboard *Onward III*—he spent three arduous days hove-to in the Stream.

Morehead City is three days south of Norfolk on the Inland Waterway and, for my money, this is by far the best place to set out for St. Thomas, 1,160 miles away. It will gain you very little to go any further along the Waterway, as after Morehead it begins to tend much more west than south. Charleston is 30 miles further from St. Thomas than Morehead and, more important, 180 miles further west. These are hard miles of easting to make up when you set out offshore. Bridge clearance should be no problem. The highway bridge south of Norfolk has an overhead clearance of 65 feet, mean high water. Arrangements can be made to open the bridge by contacting the Virginia Highway Department 24 hours in advance (weekdays 804-545-4685; weekends 804-487-5766 or 420-1938). If you cannot clear the 67-foot fixed bridge at Morehead, an exit to sea can be made at Beaufort where the railway and highway bridges open.

By taking your boat south through the Waterway in easy stages (during weekends in the early fall, say), you can be ready to leave Morehead City without having used any precious vacation time. Morehead City is an ideal take-off point; it has numerous places where you can leave your boat in the fall; there are excellent food stores, and plenty of good mechanics to tune up your engine, check your batteries, or what-have-you. But since Morehead City is a fishing port only, there is very little available in the way of sailboat fittings. One word of caution: they don't know what good hard blue coal is in the South, so bring a supply along with you, if you use a coal stove. Also, scout around town for some five-gallon oil tins; they make excellent disposable fuel drums that can be carried on deck. If you are in a hurry, carry as much fuel as you possibly can, because in November the trades may be light or nonexistent and the doldrums usually extend about 300 miles. One year we burned up 84 hours of fuel and could still have used more.

An accurate long-range weather forecast can be obtained from the FAA at Norfolk Airport. Do not call during the day, as they won't have the time to tell you all you need. Call after midnight when there is little going on. Even in November, the weather is unpredictable, so make sure that you are truly rigged for heavy weather. Depart Morehead City at slack high water. You will catch the first of the ebb in the channel which will really boot you along. With luck it will carry you clear of Cape Lookout. The inner edge of the Gulf Stream is only 60 miles offshore, and this current will set you favorably northeastward. This is the time to pick up your easting, weather permitting. Try to hold ESE until St. Thomas bears SSE, pick up the rhumb line, and you should have a nice close reach.

According to the charts, for the first part of the trip the wind will be in the northerly quadrants, northwest to northeast at about force four. If the wind stays in the northwest, you'll have a nice downhill slide a good part of the way. Around latitude 30 to 31, the wind will fall off to light and variable, so don't forget that big genoa. The final 300 miles should be a fast reach with the wind high on the beam.

The landfall on St. Thomas presents no difficulty. St. Thomas has tower lights on Signal Hill and Crown Mountain at about 1,600 feet altitude, and Culebra to the west has a very bright light also. Charlotte Amalie has grown so much over the years that its loom is now visible 20 or 30 miles off.

As you near the islands, turn on your radio at noon for "The Children's Hour"—the daily boatmen's gabfest on 2638. Some of the boats have quite powerful radios and the skippers are perfectly happy to transmit messages ahead in order to notify your friends of your arrival.

Whichever route you take south, the most important thing is to *get southeast out of the gale area as fast as possible.* If the wind goes light, turn on the mill, use up the fuel; it may save your life by avoiding a gale. If you become becalmed at the end of the trip with no fuel, it may be hot and uncomfortable, but not dangerous.

Practically every winter a boat bound from the States to the Lesser Antilles has been lost. It is not a trip to be lightly undertaken. Some cases can obviously be attributed to bad seamanship or ill-found boats. However, many good boats and good men are no longer with us because they failed to realize the power of a winter gale in the North Atlantic. Complete idiots and superior seamen have gone through the same gale, and many times the good seaman is lost and the idiot survives. On the other hand, some people have made this trip dozens of times with little or no serious trouble. Viv Snow, skipper of Percy Chubb's *Antilles,* has made over two dozen trips on this run; I have made roughly three dozen. The only times I have had bad scares have been when I broke my own ground rules by leaving late and paid the penalty.

It is of interest to note that many marine underwriters insist that boats be south of Hatteras before November 15, that boats of 40 feet or over have at least four crew aboard, and, draft permitting, the Morehead City route be used. Given a good boat, an able crew, and a decent break in the weather, a November trip from Morehead City to St. Thomas can be a wonderful offshore passage, one to be looked forward to and not to be feared.

Coming from the U.S. West Coast

When I first arrived in the Lesser Antilles I was amazed to discover that most of the yachtsmen were either from Europe or the west coast of the United States. The Europeans I could understand, but when you consider that it is roughly 3,000 miles from San Diego to Panama, and another 1,000 miles against both wind and current to the eastern Caribbean, the number of West Coast sailors in the Islands is hard to account for. Perhaps this long trek is an indication of the scarcity of cruising opportunities out West. As my grandfather, who spent all his adult life in Chicago, used to say, "There are a few brilliant people from Mississippi, but they are always *from* Mississippi." There are many sailors from the West Coast, but the good ones always seem to be *from* the West Coast.

Discussing the trip down the west coast of South America is beyond the scope of this book. Similarly, much has been written elsewhere on cruising the west coast of Central America. However, little has been written on coming east from Panama to the Islands, and I shall try to do so here.

The best time to depart Panama is subject to debate. It is more a question of what time is least bad. The first jump is deceptively easy. Between Colon and Cartagena one can usually find good weather and fair winds. En route, you should not miss the San Blas Islands. Regular charts for these islands are poorly detailed, but Kit Kapp, owner of *Fairwinds,* has explored this area for many years and his sketch charts are excellent. They are available at the yacht club at Colon. From the San Blas Islands the next big jump is usually to Cartagena, Colombia, where one can lie at the Club de Pesce. At the Club one will find a small marina, showers, and excellent restaurant, repair facilities, and boat boys who are willing to work hard for low wages. But do not hire anyone without first checking with the dockmaster.

One should stop at Cartagena if for no other reason than to see what is the best-preserved Spanish colonial city in all of South America. There are many other such old settlements but they have been so compromised by the 20th century that it is difficult to separate the old from the new. This is not true in the case of Cartagena. The old city walls are still standing. The inner city and its buildings are unbelievably beautiful, and one should not miss exploring them.

When stopping at Cartagena one should proceed directly to the Club de Pesce. Yachts not taking this precaution have been boarded by local watermen, fights have ensued, sometimes people have been shot, and it is not always the local waterman who has come out on the short end of the stick. If arriving at night, stand off shore, enter in daylight, and go to the club.

From Cartagena eastward it's a long haul. It is best to hug the coast in order to take advantage of a slight easterly back eddy that runs inshore of the predominant westerly current. Furthermore, inshore the high mountains protect you from the onslaught of the trades, and during the early morning or evening it is sometimes possible to pick up a fair breeze.

However, several notes of warning: under no circumstances should one try to stop behind Punta de Bellilo. The chart of this area is completely wrong. Shoal water extends much further offshore than is shown, and there is no hope of finding any shelter here. Secondly, at Cabo Augusta one should stand offshore as the Magdalena River discharges huge quantities of water out to sea. Not only does the discharge disturb the natural wave motion, making it rough off the mouth of the river, but also it inundates the area with large quantities of grass, timber, and other debris. Thirdly, once past the Magdalena River it is safe to stand back inshore, but it should be noted that this shore is low and completely unlighted. Proceed carefully. Finally, resist the temptation to stop at Santa Marta. Every yacht that I have spoken to that has stopped there has been pillaged by thieves. In some cases things have been stolen off boats even while a watch was on deck. In another case, a boat left unattended for just a few hours was completely cleaned out. To make matters worse, the local police are less than cooperative.

East of Santa Marta between Cabo de la Aguja and Cabo San Juan de Guia is a spectacular area referred to as the Colombian Fjords. It is not shown in any detail in any chart, but once again, Kit Kapp's privately printed charts cover the area well. From Cabo San Juan de Guia once more hug the shore, and once more proceed carefully as the coast is low, mostly uninhabited, and therefore mostly unlighted. If the wind swings to the north, it becomes a dead lee shore.

As one approaches Cabo de la Vela (which is regarded locally as the equivalent to Cape Horn), the wind will increase, and right on the nose. The land on both the Peninsula de la Guajira and Peninsula de Paraguana is low. As it heats up from the sun, it sucks the wind in off the ocean. This sea breeze blows across the peninsulas at great velocity. That it blows hard is proven by the fact that the very active racing fleets in Maracaibo stop racing in December and do not commence again until May. It's just too hard on their gear during the winter, though Lord knows, it blows hard in the summertime too. If a ground swell is not running, a good anchorage can be had tucked up tight under the lighthouse at Cabo de la Vela. I would advise any boat proceeding eastwards to go in here and rest for a full 24 hours, because the next 120 miles to Aruba are pure hell with the wind and current hard against you. This is just a case of putting your head down and fighting your way to windward. Some boats have tried ducking into the Golfo de Venezuela, but although one gets out of the current, the Gulf is so shallow that the seas build up and little is gained.

My only unsuccessful delivery has been trying to deliver a boat from Cartagena to Grenada. I can deliver anything that will sail or power, but this particular boat wouldn't sail, wouldn't power, and exhibited a pressing desire to sink. We pumped for four hours with a Whale Gusher 25, by no means a small pump, and were losing ground when we decided to ease sheets, head for Maracaibo, and put the boat on a freighter. At this point we had spent 40 hours making a total distance to windward of 80 miles.

Putting into Maracaibo proved a double error. To begin with, Maracaibo had never seen a foreign yacht in God knows how many years. We innocently sailed up into the harbor with no pilot, anchored, and tried to clear customs. Evidently we broke every rule in the book. They were ready to fine us, put us in jail, and throw away the key. Dr. Daniel Camejo, a prominent Venezuelan yachtsman, heard of our problem and he managed to set it straight with the local officials. But insult was added to injury when, after we had dismantled the boat, packed it up for shipment, and left, the owner decided not to pay the balance of money owed us. Rather, he sent another crew down to bring the boat to Grenada. It took the relief crew 60 days to sail the remaining 600 miles to Grenada. Two years later I was still awaiting the balance of payment pending a court decision in Grenada. No wonder delivery crews are requesting payment in advance.

Don't despair, however. Once you reach Aruba, it is only 60 miles to Curaçao; from there, with a good engine, you're halfway home. From Curaçao one should stand in toward the Venezuelan shore, as once the coast is reached the wind usually dies out in the late afternoon and some respite from the westerly trades can be found during the hours of darkness if you stay within three miles of shore.

Entering Venezuela is difficult. The best place to enter is Pompitar on the Isla de Margarita, 300 miles east of Curaçao. This is, of course, of no use to boats that are coming from the west. At La Guaira (200 miles southeast of Curaçao on the mainland) yachts have reported difficulties with bureaucratic port captains treating them with the same amount of red tape as a 10,000-ton freighter. If you must put into the Venezuelan mainland, you might try Puerto Cabello, 75 miles west of La Guaira, for clearing customs. If you begin here, you can satisfy all customs requirements as you head east by acquiring the standard Venezuelan cruising permit which is good for the entire coast for six months. From Puerto Cabello the next harbors of refuge are three man-made ones that do not show on the chart. The first, Playa Grande, lies just west of Maiquetia Airport, approximately 60 miles east of Puerto Cabello. Ten miles east of Playa Grande is the commercial marina at the Macuto Sheraton Hotel and a private marina in a small basin behind the hotel. About five miles east of the Macuto Sheraton complex is the impressive Club of Puerto Azul, easily identified by the five large apartment buildings which form the Puerto Azul Club complex. The harbor here is large and is protected by a massive breakwater. From La Guaira east, the Venezuelan coast is excellently covered by NO charts which are based on surveys completed in 1940. In general, they are dependable except in the area of Margarita where the currents have moved the sand bottom around a good deal. Caution is a must in this area as the currents and sand bottom produce cloudy water. You cannot eyeball-navigate.

The conditions one meets on the Venezuelan coast are regular and therefore predictable. Wherever there are high mountains close to the coast, it is usually calm during the hours of darkness. Close along the shore in many areas one can find a back eddy that runs in an easterly direction at as much as one-and-a-half knots. This boost is lost as soon as you get too far offshore. Finally, from the Barcelona area eastwards almost to Carupano the normal trade wind pattern disappears. Usually a morning calm is broken before midday by a light westerly that swings to the northwest and increases as the day wears on, only to die out at sunset.

Note: Navigators have complained that radio time signals in this part of the world are impossible to receive, but this is not wholly true. The WWV signals are rebroadcast from the Canal Zone in four five-minute intervals each day. (See entry in "Communications.")

The list of boats that have left Panama heading eastwards and have given up and gone back to Cartagena is considerable. Innumerable other boats have arrived in Grenada having spent half a year making the trip for the simple reason that they had lost their rigs en route and had to wait for new ones either to be built locally or to be shipped in.

Finally, there are those people who have made the trip both ways and who insist that it is easier to get to Grenada from San Diego via the Galapagos, Tahiti, Australia, and the Cape of Good Hope, than to fight your way up from Panama. So be forewarned.

CHAPTER 3

Weather & Tides

The Lesser Antilles are renowned for their consistently fine weather the year round. The daytime temperature ranges from high 80s in the summertime to a mean 84 degrees in the winter. In the evening it falls to about 75 degrees on the water and on a "cold" winter night it might drop to 65. As long as a breeze is blowing, the sun is never oppressive. Out of the wind in the towns it always seems a lot warmer. During the winter months, the humidity is relatively low, and on a well-ventilated boat there should be no problem with mildew. In the late summer and fall when the trades ease up, it heats up and the threat of hurricanes can make things uneasy. This is the time when Island people take their vacations or move from the large towns to a windward shore or to the hills. The temperature drops one degree with every 150 feet of elevation, so that at 2,000 feet it is always cool, particularly during winter evenings.

From Antigua north very little rain falls, a condition hard on farmers but favorable to tourists, sailors, and paint contractors. Here there is no regular rainy season. Precipitation is sporadic and will never last for more than two hours, with spates of bright sunshine in between. South of Antigua the islands' high elevations allow moisture to be gathered from the trades. Here heavy rain squalls occur the year round, but in the dry months of January through June, they never last long. Mid-August to early December is the season of squalls in this area. Life is not as pleasant as during the dry season, except at the southern end of the Antilles from Ile de Ronde to Bequia in the Grenadines, where the sailing is good 12 months of the year.

Since 1970, the weather in the Lesser Antilles for some reason has become very peculiar. In that year, right in the middle of the dry season, Grenada experienced three weeks of very heavy rain. In 1972 the wet season was the driest on record, to the point that the farmers were not planting until November. The rains never really arrived until December, when it rained off and on for a month or so and then died out. In June, 1973, the southern reaches of the Islands down to South America suffered a severe drought. The cause is unknown; it has been allegedly related to cloud-seeding off the coast of Africa, where the U.S. government has been making an effort to cut down on easterly waves and hurricanes. If they are out to stop hurricanes, they certainly were successful. In 1972 there were no hurricanes in the Lesser Antilles. But if to get rid of hurricanes means getting rid of rain, it may be somewhat a mixed blessing.

Though fog is virtually unknown in the Antilles, make sure you are carrying a foghorn and a fog bell on board, as it is required by the Coast Guard and enforced by a $15 fine. At times a haze will form on the horizon, reducing visibility to as little as three miles. When the sun is high overhead, these hazes may be difficult to detect so don't be duped by an apparently clear horizon. I have sailed right by Martinique, within five miles of the coastline, and have never seen a thing. At other times, the visibility will be excellent and the high islands can be seen from distances ranging from 40 to a really extraordinary 70 miles. I was once becalmed at a position in Anegada Passage from which I could see St. Croix, Saba, St. Martin, Virgin Gorda, Tortola, and St. Thomas all at once. Great spectacle though it was, keep in mind that a sudden rain squall can reduce visibility to 50 yards in a matter of minutes.

The weather departments throughout the Islands are famously inaccurate in their reporting of wind velocities. They must keep their anemometers under bushel baskets. Velocity averages over a long period of time paint a false picture, so be prepared for a few surprises. During the winter months it usually blows 12 to 15 knots, a good working-sail breeze. At times it will blow 15 to 20, and it may stay that way for a couple of weeks or may pipe up to a solid 25 or 30. I have kept the lee rail down for a week on end under staysail, storm trysail, and mizzen, but such conditions are more the exception than the rule. Squalls seldom bring more than 30 knots of wind, but on occasion they may mount up to 50. Sometimes they have no wind at all, just plenty of rain.

Even after a couple of decades in the Lesser Antilles, I still cannot reliably predict how much wind a squall will contain. It is wise to prepare for the worst. Squalls are easily spotted and there is no excuse for being caught unaware. They generally move with the trade winds. Sometimes in the hurricane season, when the wind is light, they will come in from the west, but this is highly unusual, and when it does happen, be on your guard: there will be wind aplenty.

The trades are often referred to as northeastern, but this is generally inaccurate. They are more ENE to straight east. During the winter months, the wind will rarely go south of east, but as summer approaches, it will tend to east and ESE, with periods of south and SE. Come midsummer and fall, it will usually be SE to south with variations west of south. The further south you travel, the more north the trade wind is apt to have in it.

Anytime the wind shifts to the north, you can expect a good stiff blow. Except for the hurricanes, there is never so much wind that a 40-foot boat, well handled and well rigged with adequate reefing gear, cannot stand up to it.

The one real variation in the winter trades is what is known as an "easterly wave," which is characterized by high winds, heavy rain, and generally uncomfortable conditions. There is a good description of the easterly wave in Bill Robinson's book, *Where the Trade Winds Blow*: The wave "takes place in a broad stream of air, in this case one that blows initially from east-southeast. . . . The wind gradually becomes northeast, then goes back to southeast and finally settles again in the east-southeast. The wave, with an axis that runs roughly north-northeast/south-southwest moves to the westward at about 15 miles an hour, and the cycle usually takes a day or two to move by. As the wave approaches, the wind decreases as it goes into the southeast, with fine weather and few clouds. After the crest of the wave passes, some medium and high cumulus clouds develop, with a chance of showers, while the wind remains light. In the final part of the cycle, the wind swings back to the east-southeast and strengthens, with heavy showers and sometimes even thunderstorms. It holds fairly strong until the clouds move by and then it settles back to normal seasonal strength."

The barometer gives very little warning of this easterly wave, and it is seldom identified by the San Juan weather bureau until it has passed the Virgins. I have watched barometers for many years in the Lesser Antilles and have come to the conclusion that, except during the hurricane season, you might as well throw them overboard.

Between December and mid-July, you can practically forget about being becalmed. In

20 weeks of cruising within this period, I would never run my engine in gear for more than 20 hours. I finally decided to do away with all the fuss, furor, expense, and frustration of maintaining an engine and yanked it entirely. I have built a comfortable chart table where the engine was and cruised happily ever since. Admittedly I do get becalmed from time to time for an occasional stretch of eight or nine hours, but these are exceptional occurrences spread over a long period of time. Actually, the best months for sailing in the Islands are May, June, and July. The boisterous winter trades have died out, the calms have not yet arrived, and a nice eight- to ten-knot breeze blows day after day.

It is from August to December that *Iolaire* is most likely to miss her engine, but somehow we have managed. Before, when maneuvering in a harbor in light air we had to keep the mainsail up until the last minute. Now with the prop removed we can sail around to our heart's content under staysail and mizzen; she handles perfectly. At a couple of knots the drag of the propellor shaft and strut alone probably amounted to 20 percent of the boat's total drag.

The only thing that foxes me is that with no engine, we have no generator. Kerosene lights are just too hot for the tropics and so we must use electricity. We have installed fluorescent lights which burn cool and bright and use little juice.

At my home on Point Egmont, Grenada, I use a 12-volt wind generator that supplies more electricity than I can possibly use. I would like to mount one on my mizzen mast too, but so far all the ones I have seen are either too large (150 pounds at over 20 amps capacity) or too small (putting out .5 amps maximum). If anyone can recommend a wind generator that will put out two amps at 12 volts in five or more knots of apparent wind with a governor to prevent it from over-juicing

in a gale, I would be greatly indebted.

Whatever may have been said to the contrary, it is possible to make way under sail in the lee of the high islands. Most sailors assume there will be a total lull close inshore, so they pass three or four miles off and find absolutely nothing. But there is a way of skirting close along the lee shore of the high islands, which I discovered in a set of 18th century sailing directions. These recommended two ways of passing the islands either at seven leagues—21 miles—offshore or else close inshore within two "pistol shots." The historian Dudley Pope has explained to me that the "pistol shot" was a recognized measurement in those days and appears frequently in accounts of naval battles. It is the equivalent of 25 yards. Stay within two pistol shots or 50 yards of shore and you stand a good chance of enjoying a smooth, scenic sail the length of a high island. The best time to try it is between 1000 and 1600 hours. After 1600 the breeze falls off rapidly. A big genoa and a mizzen staysail will help you along. Be prepared for the wind to shift radically and to die out completely at times, but it's sure to be a more pleasant way to travel than with the engine droning the whole time.

During the day, as the land heats up there is a good chance of picking up a westerly, onshore breeze counter to the trades which continue to blow higher up. At night the cool air falling down off the hills often will provide a beautiful moonlight sail along the beach. Dawn and dusk are the only times when there is absolutely no wind in the lee of these high islands. I would say that except at these times, you will be successful sailing the lee shore about 75 percent of the time. In the winter of 1965, before I removed the engine from *Iolaire*, during 3000 miles of sailing I used only 35 gallons of gas.

Hurricanes in the Antilles are less a danger than supposed. They have been reported every month of the year, but they are certainly most frequent in August, September, and early October. Not every hurricane that comes whistling out of the south is a threat to the Lesser Antilles. When they make their way through the southern islands they are young ones; their diameter is still small with gale force winds spanning out 60 miles from the center to the northwest quadrant, and 100 to 200 miles in the southeast. A number of them, in the late season especially, churn up to the leeward of the Antilles in the Caribbean or the Gulf of Mexico. The vast majority begin near the latitude of Guadeloupe, pass through the islands in the Guadeloupe-Antigua area, and then curve northward to give a good whack to Hispaniola and the western end of Puerto Rico. There are exceptions, of course. Grenada and Martinique have both been hit hard. Generally the warning system (all local radio stations) is excellent and improving all the time.

The cold print of damage estimates does not give a true picture of the severity of a hurricane. Before the winds even reach hurricane force, the native corrugated iron and tar paper shacks begin to break up and the banana and sugar crops are severely damaged. Imagine the destruction when the winds do reach hurricane force. It is not a pleasant sight— nor is it one to stand around and gape at. Take to a hurricane hole! Everyone down here has his favorite one, best suited to his boat and temperament. The Virgins get the worst hurricane scares and they fortunately have the greatest number of holes. If you plan to spend the late summer and early fall in the Virgins, check with the locals and find one that best suits your needs; when the warning goes out, run for it. Never let yourself go too far from a good hole.

Between Virgin Gorda and Antigua there was, until recently, no harbor of refuge in a hurricane. Now Simson Lagoon in St. Martin

should fit the bill. Admittedly the wind can sweep across the low land but the land is high enough to break all the swell and no sea should be able to build up inside the lagoon. A properly moored boat should have little or no trouble. St. Martin also has the Oyster Pond, which looks fine on the chart, but the entrance is on a dead lee shore. With a heavy swell running in, it would take more guts than I have to enter.

As long as the hurricane does not pass north of the island, which would funnel the wind and sea into the mouth of this northwest-facing harbor, you should be perfectly safe in Gustavia, St. Barts. I would advise against laying alongside the stone bulkhead, as a storm surge could build up and lift you right over it.

English Harbour and Falmouth are both excellent holes and now in Guadeloupe with the dredging of new harbors and the establishment of the marina on the old molasses pier, several holes are available. Similarly, the dredging in Fort de France, Martinique, east of the steamer dock in the Carenage, has created an excellent hurricane hole for yachts. In St. Lucia, if you draw less than eight feet, the new lagoon offers perfect shelter. Also Marigot Harbor is an incomparable hole.

In Carriacou, you can work your way into the inner part of the Carenage; there would be little possibility of damage to a boat moored there.

Grenada has numerous hurricane holes on the south coast, some better than others, but I do not see how anyone can find a better one in the Lesser Antilles than the inner harbor at Egmont. No matter where the wind came from, no matter where the swell came from, it would be impossible to build up a sea or a surge inside Egmont Harbor. Surrounded by high hills on all sides, it receives a tremendous amount of shelter from the wind.

One thing about which people in the Islands tend to be very lackadaisical is the

preparation of their boats for a hurricane once a hurricane has become imminent. They should take a lesson from our northern cousins who have gone through so many. First and foremost, if you fully expect a hurricane to pass nearby, all halyards except the main should be taken down. The main halyard should be well guyed out so it won't pound the mast; all sails should be taken off the spars and the boom well secured into the gallows or, if hanging from the topping lift, guyed off in two directions; ventilators should be removed; in short, everything possible should be done to reduce windage. Similarly, the boat should be well anchored to the heaviest anchors available. Lines that pass through the bow chocks should be heavily protected with chafing gear. Extra chafing gear should be on hand to replace old gear wearing through during the storm. Don't underestimate the possibility of chafe.

If the dinghy is left in the water, make sure the outboard is removed. Either the rain will fill the dinghy or the wind will capsize it. The engine in either case would be under water, and engines don't run very well once submerged. Further, even a boat like a Whaler, which cannot flood because of its double bottom, should have its outboard removed. In hurricanes the wind can get underneath even a good-sized Whaler and flip it upside-down.

When preparing a boat for a hurricane, it should not be secured bow-and-stern but on a Bahamian moor. If a boat is secured bow-and-stern, you are bound to drag when the wind comes on the beam. However, on a Bahamian moor, no matter which way the wind blows, the boat can freely pivot. For such use there is a variation on the Bahamian moor known as a modified Bahamian hurricane moor—three anchors out, two set in a "Y" in the direction that the heaviest wind and sea are expected, and a third in the direction that

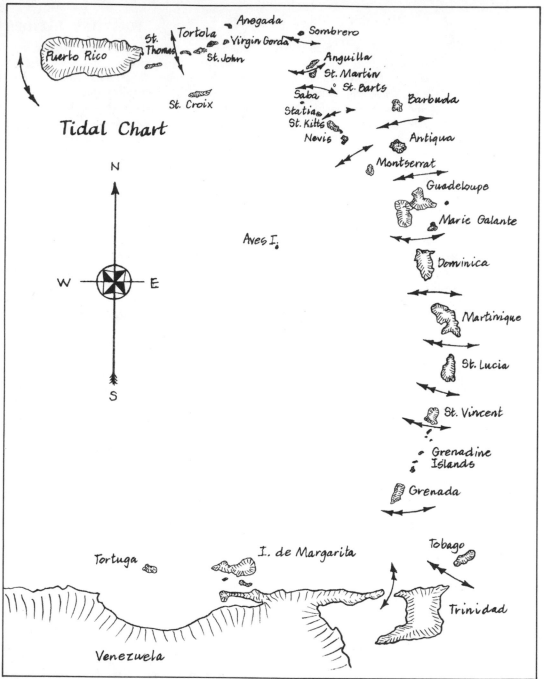

Tidal Chart

Doubled arrows indicate an ebbing tide as re-enforced by westerly current.

TIDAL CHART, LESSER ANTILLES

the wind will commence. Usually as a hurricane passes nearby, there will be a 180 degree wind shift and you must be prepared for it.

Besides the normal anchoring gear, a boat that plans to spend the hurricane season in the Lesser Antilles should have a really large hurricane anchor. I carry a 150-pound, three-piece Herreshoff stowed in the bilge during the hurricane season as insurance.

North Atlantic storms do not make their way as far down as the Islands, but the swells they generate do. They come out of the northwest, seldom appearing higher than six feet. In deep water there may be as much as a mile between crests. In shoaling water they hump up and hit with unbelievable force. I once watched them crashing onto the lee shore of Saba. They passed solid water over Diamond Rocks, some 80 feet high. The spray was driving twice that height, and a fine mist shrouded the entire shore. The swells come in without warning and can build up to dangerous proportions in an hour's time. Offshore they present no threat, but they can make it pretty rough on anchorages with a western exposure. The northernmost islands bear the brunt of the Atlantic swell. None of the harbors exposed to the northwest on the islands of St. Thomas, Tortola, or Virgin Gorda should be used overnight between November and April. As you move south, the swell tapers off. By the time it reaches the Grenadines, it is pretty well under control, although at times it can be very dangerous.

Tides and Current

Anything I say on the topic of tides and currents will be contradicted by someone somewhere. That is a certainty. The movement of water in the Lesser Antilles is not certain, and opinion varies as to its exact nature. Here follow several distinctions which are *almost* universally accepted in the islands.

The terms "tide" and "current" must not be confused. "Tide" refers to water that runs in and out of the Caribbean pulled by the gravitational force of the moon. It results in an 18- to 24-inch difference in water level on the island shores between high and low water. (Use of the term in this section, however, refers to the movement of the water, rather than to its rise and fall on shore.)

"Current" alone refers to water that continually runs in a westerly direction. Its direction is more or less constant—only its strength varies as it is influenced by the wind or tide. An easterly wind increases the strength of the current, a westerly wind (a rarity) decreases the strength of the current. When the tidal water is moving east, it reduces the rate of the current; when the tidal water is moving west, it increases current.

But, of course, there are subtleties to both the tide and the current. The hardest thing to remember about Island tides is that when the tide is rising, or flooding, the movement of the water is west to east—opposite to what one might expect. Similarly, during the ebb tide, the water is moving east to west (see illustration). Thus, a flooding tide slows the current, and an ebb tide increases it.

The current itself is caused by the westerly trade winds that blow unobstructed across open ocean. Several days of heavy westerly winds induce a strong current. The range is from one-third to one-and-a-half knots. The direction of the current also varies. It does not simply run east to west. There are actually two currents, one on either side of the equator. The northern equatorial current runs directly to the Islands, while the southern equatorial current runs up the coast of South America to reach the Islands. (There is besides a back eddy close to the Venezuelan shore that sometimes runs eastward as strong as one knot.) Where the northern and southern currents meet near Ile de Ronde there is a particularly

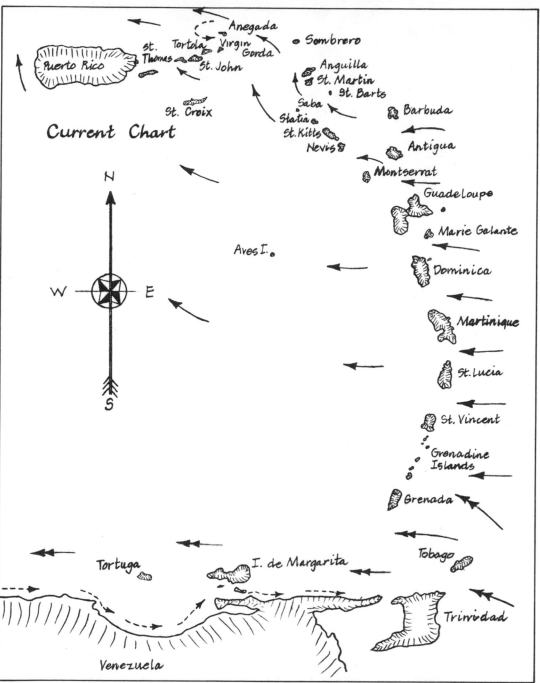

Doubled arrows in the south indicate boost from the Southern Equatorial Current.

CURRENT CHART, LESSER ANTILLES

rough section of ocean. The direction of the current is mostly due west through the islands north of Ile de Ronde, but at Antigua it starts to shift to a more northerly direction (see illustration). In fact, on the back (west) side of St. Martin the current runs almost directly north, only swinging back to northwest north of Dog Island. There is a second major back eddy just west of Anegada where the current passing north of the island loops in over the top of Virgin Bank and frequently runs east onto the reefs of that wreck-strewn island. Finally, it must be reckoned that every island affects the current in its own peculiar fashion, so that close to the shores you may find a variety of different speeds and directions.

Similarly, the tidal flow varies close to shore. I have mentioned that in the channels between the islands the water moves west during the ebb and east during the flood. But during a flood tide, the eastward-flowing water must slide north and south to slip past the obstruction presented by the western shore of an island. Similarly, during an ebb tide, the westward-flowing water must divide and push north and south to pass by the tips of the islands into the Caribbean. In both cases, there is a neutral point near the middle of an island where the tide splits. Thus, if you time a passage up the coast of an island so that you reach the neutral point just when the tide changes, you can carry a fair tide all the way up or down the shoreline. With the aid of a few calculations, some boat speed, and accurate estimates of high (or low) water, it is possible to carry a fair current along the whole lee coast of the large islands.

But to calculate the times of high and low water is not easy. The tide tables are totally inaccurate. Numerous methods of figuring the tide have been advanced, but no two seem to agree. A rule of thumb is that the tidal flow starts to run eastward about two hours after the moon has risen. But you must remember

that this flooding tide is working against the equatorial current, and when the flood is weakest in its first and last stages, the equatorial current negates it. Thus, it is only the middle four hours (approximately) of flood that have a noticeable effect on the current.

To calculate exactly just what this effect is, is considered black magic by yachtsmen in the Islands. Although the rise and fall of the tide is minimal, the amount of water moved by the tide is considerable and there is a large variation between spring and neap tides. Spring tides do not coincide with the full and new moons but usually come three to four and sometimes as much as five days after full and new moons. Neap tides, of course, occur two weeks after spring tides, and run at about half the strength of spring tides.

In order to determine in which direction the water underneath you is moving and how fast, you must consider all the above factors—and one more. In narrow passages and at the north and south ends of islands the tide runs considerably faster—as much as twice as fast.

Let me make a hypothetical case. We are at the northern tip of Grenada, the wind is blowing hard from the east and the moon rose 4 hours ago. The factors are as follows:

EQUATORIAL CURRENT .... ½ knot west (this is constant)	
WIND-BLOWN CURRENT .... ½ knot west (because the wind is from the east)	
TIDE .... 1 knot east	
EFFECT OF LOCATION .... 1 knot east (tide is doubled at tip of island)	
COMBINED INFLUENCE .... 1 knot east	

If the tide were ebbing west at 1 knot, this would be increased to 2 knots because of our location, and the total influence would add up to 3 knots west.

This method suffers from the many approximations it requires, but it does have the

advantage that by observing the time of moon rise (or zenith angle), one can calculate the overall influence of tide and current with surprising accuracy. In any event, you must pay strict attention to the movement of the water beneath you, particularly when you are following a range into an anchorage. The Sketch Charts in this book give the magnetic compass bearings of all ranges. But, as we know, the compass bearing of a range is not necessarily the compass course that must be steered to stay on that range. The current may be pushing you one way or another and the compass course that must be steered is whatever course keeps the range on a steady bearing. Oftentimes in a strong current you will appear to follow a bearing in a crabbing manner, but as long as your bearing stays steady, regardless of the compass course you are actually steering you will be okay.

A second practical consideration has to do with the natural axis of the islands. In the Virgin Islands you do most of your sailing on an east-west axis; in the other islands to the south, you usually sail on a north-south axis. Because the tide and current run mostly east and west throughout the Islands, you have to be careful farther south not to be pushed sideways off course, while in the Virgins you need only worry about the total time consumed sailing in one direction.

A third practical consideration is that the Virgin Islands are diabolically tricky. Since Gorda Sound, Sir Francis Drake Channel, and Pillsbury Sound are basically enclosed bodies of water, the standard rule of the Lesser Antilles of tidal current flowing eastward on the flood and westwards on the ebb does not hold. Rather, it is a case of ebbing and flooding through the various entrances. Depending on which entrance you take, the flood tide entering Sir Francis Drake Channel can be running north, south, east, or west! (See illustration.) It should be remembered that in Sir Francis

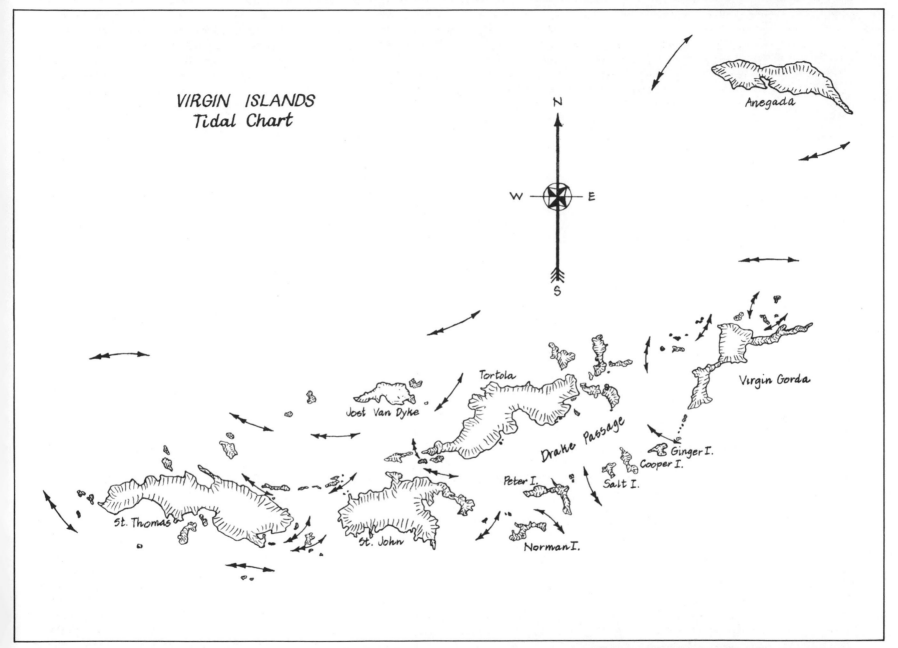

VIRGIN ISLANDS
Tidal Chart

Anegada

Tortola

Jost Van Dyke

Virgin Gorda

Drake Passage

Ginger I.

Cooper I.

Salt I.

Peter I.

St. Thomas

St. John

Norman I.

Doubled arrows indicate an ebbing tide as re-enforced by westerly current.

TIDAL CHART, VIRGIN ISLANDS

WEATHER & TIDES

Drake Channel the tide turns along the St. John and Tortola shores about one hour before it turns in mid-channel.

The game of predicting the tides is ultimately nothing more than educated guesswork, and even the most confident of local "experts" can be humbled by a wrong forecast. As in anchoring, it is best to keep your sense of humor at all times. During the 1973 Antigua Race we were making a final approach on a windward mark when my foredeck captain warned me to stay high of the mark so as to be sure we wouldn't have to tack again. I was not particularly worried as the moon was visible at an altitude of 45 degrees to the east. Thus, the tide should have been lifting me to the east and to windward of the mark. It was not so. The tide was sweeping us to leeward as if there were a vacuum cleaner on my lee bow. We missed the mark by a boat length, had to take two quick tacks, and dropped four boats. Needless to say, I was upset with myself and upon asking several friends what the tide had been doing out there, I was put in my place. "What the hell, Don, the moon doesn't mean anything anymore—the tides haven't been the same since your damned U.S. astronauts took the best rocks away."

CHAPTER 4

Charts

The charts covering the Lesser Antilles are notoriously inaccurate. For the most part they are based on surveys performed during the mid-19th century, and do not take into account more recent changes in the bottom due to coral growth, hurricanes, and dredging. I will attempt to point out discrepancies as I have found them, but the only way to be completely safe is not to poke your nose into unfamiliar coves except when the sun is high and the light is good.

There is a variety of charts covering the Islands, published by American, British, and French authorities. If you are planning a cruise of the entire region, the American charts provide adequate information, but in many areas the British and French charts offer a valuable supplement. In the Virgin Islands, for example, both the American and the British charts should be consulted, especially in the case of St. Croix. The same holds true of St. Martin, St. Kitts, and Antigua. For Barbuda, Montserrat, and St. Lucia the British and American charts are virtually the same, so either one will do. But from St. Vincent down to Grenada the British and American charts show different groupings of islands and each has various detailed inserts. In this case it would be a good idea to have both sets on board. The French charts of Martinique and Guadeloupe are vastly superior to the American and British and one shouldn't consider cruising these grounds without them. I also consider the French 1032 chart, showing the entire length of the Lesser Antilles, the most valuable one for planning or selecting a cruise of any length.

There are several things to bear in mind as you shuffle from one chart to the next. The international buoyage system is the exact opposite of the American, that is, Red *Left* Returning (not too handy to memorize); once you leave the American Virgins it is the international system that is used throughout the Islands. Further, the soundings on British charts appear in fathoms and fractions of fathoms, while French soundings are in meters and tenths of meters. No matter which charts are used, be wary of the markings of channel lights. Although the charts are supposed to be updated regularly, relocated lights are frequently overlooked in the revisions. In 1964 I purchased charts in Washington from the office of the Coast and Geodetic Survey which were marked "corrected through Notice to Mariners" and dated a few days previously. They certainly looked reliable, yet I discovered on closer scrutiny that lights which the Coast Guard had changed eight months before were incorrectly listed. And there is yet another pitfall to reading your charts. The U.S. Hydrographic Office has changed the designation and the numbers on their charts from H.O. and 4 digits to N.O. (standing for "National Ocean Survey") and 5 digits. The Coast and Geodetic Survey—C&GS—charts are still the same.

There are many hang-ups in trying to obtain charts in the Lesser Antilles. French charts are only available on Guadeloupe and Martinique, British charts are only available on the British islands, and American charts are usually only available on the American islands, with the exception that sometimes American charts can be bought at Grenada Yacht Services on Grenada. Wherever you are, you must remember that the tourists all like to buy charts—they call them "maps"—of the particular island that they are on, so that often it is next to impossible to obtain a chart of that island. In the long run, the most reliable method of obtaining charts is to order them before you come down. In the United States, I have had good success over the years with New York Nautical Instruments (address below). Do not order charts from the National Ocean Survey as, being an agency of the Federal Government, red tape delays your order by several months; even then, they will only send charts overseas by sea mail, so that a European's cruise will probably be over before he ever receives them.

In England, I have used Kelvin Hughes (address below), again with good success. They are reasonably quick and their staff corrects all charts up to the date of the last Notice to Mariners prior to shipment. The British charts are more expensive than the American charts, but their paper is superior and thus lasts longer. They are all of regulation size—either 21″ x 42″ or 42″ x 42″—so that they all fit neatly on the standard chart table.

French charts are also expensive, but nevertheless I recommend purchasing the detailed charts of the harbors on Guadeloupe and Martinique, since the American and British charts deal only on a small scale. On the chart list at the very end of this chapter I have starred (*) those French and British charts that I regard as essential. It may seem overly cautious to use the most detailed chart available, but the record shows that there are more accidents in the Virgin Islands than in the Grenadines, and it is no small coincidence that the Grenadines' charts are drawn on a larger scale than those for the Virgins.

In this quest for accuracy and detail I have included the many sketch charts in this book. They have been compiled mostly from my own sailing experience, but also from numerous flights over the islands, from government charts, from sketches loaned me by other charter skippers, and from topographical maps. They have been checked against all available printed material on the islands, double-checked by charter skippers, and triple-checked by anyone who has used my earlier books from cruising the area. The last is perhaps the best check of all, and therefore I ask anyone who finds even the slightest discrepancy to please contact me as soon as he is able.

The sketch charts are not infallible—but it is not always my fault. I know of one party, for example, that left St. Thomas heading for Grenada using only my original cruising guide. The course was set at 163 magnetic and off they went. On the second day out, the on-deck watch reported an island ahead. The skipper refused to believe them, citing my small-scale sketch chart which, omitting tiny Aves Island, showed clear sailing all the way to Grenada. Thoroughly surprised, and without a government chart to consult, they proceeded to pore through the text of my book, where they found that I mention very clearly that Aves Island lies directly on the track. There is a lesson to be learned here somewhere.

It might be noted that Major Mike Hartland of St. George's, Grenada, can heat-seal inside plastic the charts that you most frequently use on deck. This makes them virtually indestructible and plotting can be done on them with a grease pencil, then wiped off clean.

Piloting

It is probably possible (though I wouldn't recommend it) to sail in safety through the length of the Lesser Antilles with nothing more than a gas-station road map and a Boy Scout compass, due to the clarity of the water which reveals the nature of the bottom merely by its color. It takes a practiced eye to sound the

color of the water with any accuracy, but once you get the hang of it, if you sail between 0900 and 1500 when the sun is high, the human eye is an almost infallible pilot. Earlier or later than this, the sun is too low in the horizon to give a really good differentiation of color. Similarly, if you are heading east or west during the earlier or later parts of a day you will run into glare and reflection.

Polaroid sunglasses are well worth the investment, as they accentuate the difference in colors and make reefs and shoals stand out in bold relief.

In general, dark blue water is deep and as the bottom shoals, the water becomes a lighter blue, turning greenish as the two fathoms line is being approached. Once you are in the area of green water, you must exercise caution; depending on the shade of green you will have from two fathoms down to one fathom. At about one fathom and shallower, the water becomes almost white and crystal clear. Coral always shows up as brown, and if you must enter an area that has coral, use extreme care to pilot yourself between the coral heads. Coral literally grows, and in any area that shows scattered coral on the chart, it is recommended that you subtract roughly three to six feet from the given chart depth. Areas of grass show up as a dark patch. Avoid anchoring in these patches as it is difficult to get the anchor to hold.

Underwater visibility varies considerably from day to day, so when piloting shoal water, it is best to heave a lead line a few times to verify that your judgment is correct for that particular day. This is the one time a depth sounder might be useful in the Islands. At all other times it is made useless by the simple fact that as often as not, the bottom rises so fast that a depth sounder would warn you of the impending danger only after you had solidly crashed into a reef.

The most important thing that must be re-

membered about pilotage in the Lesser Antilles is that you must not try it at night. If you are making a long passage, it will of course be necessary to sail at night, but landfalls should be in daylight unless you are entering one of the main ports that are well lit. Even then you must remember that the buoyage and light systems in the Islands are not reliable. For several years now I have pointed out that according to the charts you should be able to see five lights at night from the porch of the Grenada Yacht Club. I have a standing bet: if two or more lights are out, you buy the drinks; if only one is out, we buy each other a drink; if none are out, I will buy. I haven't bought yet, and if I ever do, it will be in celebration of a miracle.

I have noticed in cross-checking the Light List against my own experience that there are numerous changes and omissions that are *not* recorded in the Notices to Mariners. As a general rule, major lighthouses with a visibility of 12 miles or more usually do operate and can be relied on. However, harbor and buoy lights should be viewed with great caution and cannot be relied on. Anyone trying to make landfalls at night is just asking for trouble. As a final word before listing the charts and their suppliers, let me mention two useful publications that you might want to carry with you— *Reed's Nautical Almanac,* East Coast Edition, and the *West Indies Pilot,* Vol. II (H.O. Pub. 22).

International Chart Suppliers

New York Nautical Instruments
and Services Co.
140 West Broadway
New York, N.Y. 10013 ((212) 944-9191)

Kelvin Hughes
St. Claire House
Minories, London EC 3N, IDQ, England

Charts

Coast and Geodetic Survey—Puerto Rico and Virgin Islands

920	Puerto Rico and the Virgin Islands
901	West Coast of Puerto Rico
902	South Coast of Puerto Rico, Guanica Light to Point Tuna Light
903	North Coast of Puerto Rico, Punta Penon to Punta Vacia Talega
	Puerto Arecibo, Puerto Palmas Altas
904	Virgin Passage and Sonda de Vieques
905	Virgin Islands, Virgin Gorda to St. Thomas and St. Croix
908	Bahia de San Juan
909	Jobos Harbor and Rincon Bay
913	Ensenada Honda
914	Culebra and approaches
915	Ensenada Honda to Canal de Louis Pena
917	Pasaje San Juan to Puerto Humacao and western part of Isla de Vieques
918	Port Yabucoa
921	Bahia de Fajardo
922	Ensenada Honda
923	Punta Lima to Cape Batata
924	Port Maunabo
925	Port Arroyo
926	Point Petrona to Muertos Island
927	Bahia de Ponce and approaches
928	Bahia de Guayanilla
929	Bahia de Guanica
931	Bahia de Mayaguez and approaches
932	Bahia de Boqueron
933	Harbor of St. Thomas
935	Christiansted Harbor
937	Frederiksted Road
938	Pillsbury Sound
940	Pasaje de Vieques and Radas Roosevelt

National Ocean Survey Charts

New NO	Old HO	
25008	2318	Hispaniola to St. Lucia

New NO	Old HO	
24032	2319	Martinique to South America
25024	1002	Virgin Islands to Antigua
25243	3904	Tortola to Anegada
25245	0137	Road Harbor
25244	0569	Gorda Sound
25241	1834	Saba, Sombrero, Anguilla, St. Martin, St. Barts, Statia
25242	0371	Detail chart showing harbors on Anguilla, St. Martin, St. Barts
25161	1011	Statia to Montserrat, with inserts showing the harbors in detail
25204	1484	Barbuda
25201	1004	Antigua (should have British chart 2064 also)
25202	0366	St. John's Harbour and Deep Bay, and English Harbour
25203	5725	Parham Sound
25123	0363	Guadeloupe and surrounding islands
25127	1065	Port Louis, Basse-Terre, Fort de Moule
25124	0362	The Saints
25126	0363	Pointe-a-Pitre
25125	0532	Lee coast of Marie Galante
25121	1318	Dominica
25122	0513	Harbors of Portsmouth, Roseau Roads, and Woodbridge Bay
25084	1009	Martinique
25086	1020	St. Pierre Road
25087	1022	Fort de France Bay
25085	1064	La Trinite
25081	1261	St. Lucia, with insert of Gros Ilet anchorage (preferred to British chart, which does not show Gros Ilet anchorage on main chart)
25083	1154	Vieux Fort
25082	1165	Port of Castries
25044	1279	St. Vincent (British chart 791 the better, as it does not cut Bequia in half)
25043	1161	Bays on south coast of St. Vincent and Admiralty Bay
25042	1640	Grenadines (superior to British chart in that it has a detailed insert for the Tobago Cays, but inferior in that it does not have tidal information shown in the British chart)
25041	1316	Grenada (superior to British chart 2921 in that it has a detailed insert for St. George's Harbor, but inferior in that it does not have the detail insert for Grenville Harbor)

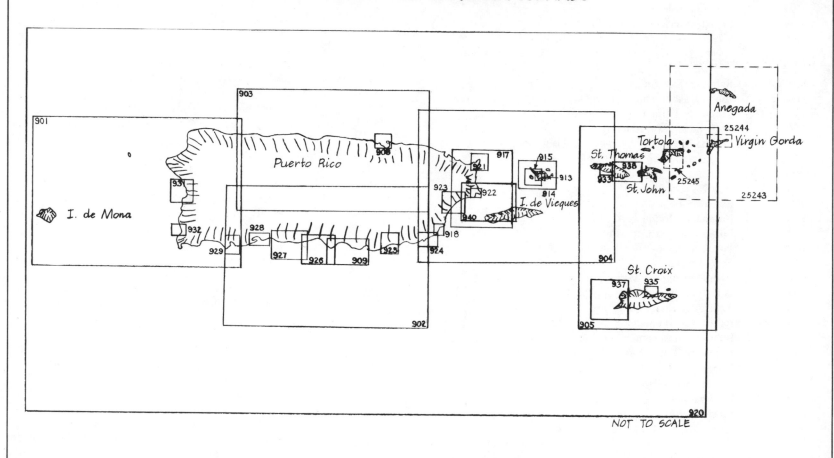

AMERICAN CHART OUTLINES
PUERTO RICO and the VIRGIN ISLANDS

U.S. Charts: Puerto Rico and the Virgin Islands

New NO	Old HO	
25045	1010	Barbados
25046	5253	Bridgetown
24401	5586	Trinidad and Gulf of Paria
		Peninsula de Paria to Dragons Mouth, Trinidad
24406	2115	Chaguaramas Bay, Trinidad, to Port of Spain
24408	135	San Fernando and Point-a-Pierre
24403	355	Ports in Tobago
24402	1618	Tobago
24409	1963	Serpents Mouth, Trinidad

British Admiralty Charts

The (*) following indicates my recommendation for British and French charts as back-ups to or instead of the corresponding American charts.

3408	Mona Passage to St. Thomas
478	Harbors of Guanica, Guayanilla, Ponce, Jobos, Arecibo, and San Juan
* 130	East Coast of Puerto Rico to St. Martin (excellent chart for planning cruise of northern islands)
2183	St. Thomas Harbor
*2452	American Virgin Islands (best chart for eastern end of St. John)
*2019	Tortola, Virgin Gorda, and surrounding islands
*2008	Anegada
2020	Road Harbor
2016	Gorda Sound and approaches
* 485	St. Croix (by far the best chart of St. Croix)
2038	Anguilla, St. Martin, and St. Barts
2079	Crocus Bay, Oyster Pond, Gustavia, Marigot Bay, Groot Bay
* 487	Statia, St. Kitts, Nevis, with inserts showing the anchorages (much better chart than the American chart; much more detailed)
1997	Barbuda
*2064	Antigua, Falmouth and English Harbour (in some ways superior to the American chart, other ways not; both should be carried)
2065	North coast of Antigua and St. John's Harbor
955	Guadeloupe to Sombrero
2600	Mona Passage to Guadeloupe
254	Montserrat

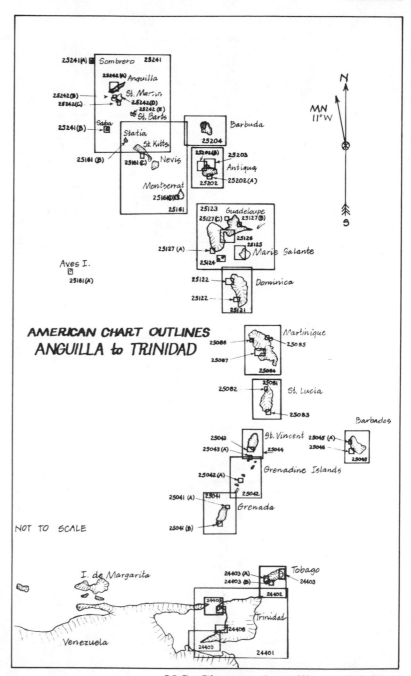

U.S. Charts: Anguilla to Trinidad

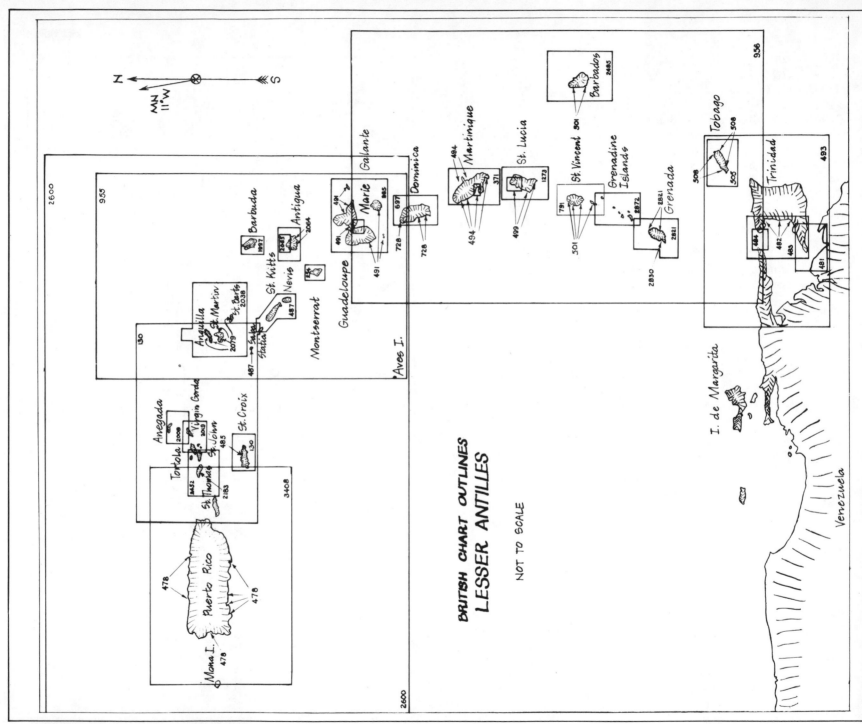

British Charts: Lesser Antilles

885	Guadeloupe and surrounding islands
491	Basse-Terre, Saints, Port Louis, Port du Noule, St. Ann and St. Francois Galet, Grand Bourg
804	Petit Havre, Pointe-a-Pitre, St. Marie
697	Dominica
728	Prince Rupert Bay, Roseau Roads, and Woodbridge Bay
371	Martinique
494	Fort de France, Cul de Sac Marin, La Trinite, Robert, St. Pierre
1273	St. Lucia
197	Northwest coast of St. Lucia, Castries, and Gros Ilet anchorage
499	Castries, Grand Cul de Sac, Marigot, and Vieux Fort
* 791	St. Vincent and Bequia on one chart
501	South coast of St. Vincent and Admiralty Bay
2485	Barbados
502	Bridgetown Harbor
*2872	The Grenadines (superior to the American chart, as it has tidal information not shown on the American chart, but also inferior, as it does not have the detail insert for the Tobago Cays; carry both)
*2821	Grenada, with inserts for south coast and Grenville (superior to the American chart, as the American chart does not have inserts for Grenville)
493	Trinidad and Tobago
481	Serpents Mouth
483	West coast of Trinidad
484	Dragons Mouth
482	Port of Spain, Point-a-Pierre, San Fernando
505	Tobago
508	Ports of Tobago

French Charts

*1032	The Antilles, San Juan to Trinidad (only chart showing the entire Antilles in a single plan)
3423	Guadeloupe
*3125	From Pointe de la Grand Vigie to la Pointe des Chateaux
*3419	From Pointe-a-Pitre to Marie Galante
*4519	Ports of Guadeloupe
*2872	Entrance to anchorages of Pointe-a-Pitre
*3375	From Basse-Terre to Pointe-a-Pitre

FRENCH CHART OUTLINES MARTINIQUE — NOT TO SCALE

French Charts: Martinique

CHARTS

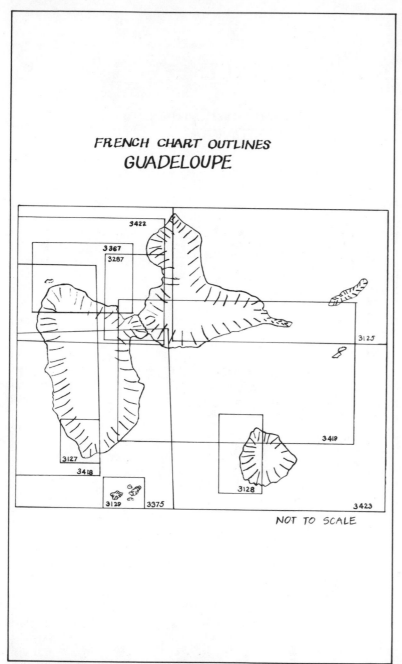

FRENCH CHART OUTLINES
GUADELOUPE

3422
3367
3287
3125
3127
3418
3129   3375
3128
3419
3423

NOT TO SCALE

French Charts: Guadeloupe

*3129	Iles des Saintes
*3172	Anchorage of Basse-Terre to Riviere des Peres at Pointe de Vieux Fort
*3418	From Pointe du Vieux Fort to Pointe Allegre
*3422	From Pointe Ferry to Pointe de la Grande Vige
*3367	Grand Cul de Sac Marin, east part
*3287	Grand Cul de Sac Marin, west part
*3128	Marie Galante
383	Martinique
* 386	Northern Martinique
*5930	St. Pierre
* 384	Eastern Martinique
* 389	Trinite Harbor
* 390	Robert and Francois Harbors
* 385	Southern Martinique
* 391	La Cul de Sac Marin
*5916	Fort de France
5906	Fort de France Road

CHAPTER 5

Sailing Directions

The Lesser Antilles stretch east and south from Puerto Rico and St. Thomas in a great crescent. The entire sweep is best shown on the French Admiralty Chart 1032, the only published chart that shows the Lesser Antilles in a scale suitable for planning a cruise. Spread this chart before you and remember that the northeast trades are a misnomer; they vary from ENE to ESE, sometimes crawling all the way around to the north and more often, especially in the late spring and summer, favoring the SE to S quadrants.

Proceeding South

Most skippers bound for the Lesser Antilles from the north favor a landfall in St. Thomas. Invariably, a few every year are driven farther to the west by southeast winds and must settle for San Juan and for the long haul eastward from there. Leaving San Juan harbor, there is no other way than to sheet her flat and to bull your way east against wind and current for the 60 miles or so to St. Thomas. Arrange your departure from San Juan to pass the northeast corner of Puerto Rico, where it is important that the sun be high, by 1100 hours. Work your way to the east, taking careful bearings. Put a man in the rigging to guide you into Vieques Sound through one of the breaks in the reefs that extend eastward from northeast Puerto Rico. The reefs will afford a moderate degree of shelter. If you like, sheets can be eased and a stop made at Isleta Marina. Or else one can continue on to Culebra or southeastward to Vieques, on both of which islands there are good anchorages and beaches, before the sobering beat east to St. Thomas.

Boats headed for the Virgins from the Bahamas often make their landfall on the west coast of Puerto Rico, where there are good harbors at Aguadilla and Mayaguez. From here the best route east, in my estimation, is along the south coast of Puerto Rico. This coast is somewhat sheltered from the full force of the trades (especially when blowing north of east); the swell is usually less and there are plenty of good anchorages all along. As you work your way east, stay inshore on the Puerto Rican shelf and play the wind shifts for all they are worth. The shelf will act to reduce the westerly set of the current. At night, if they don't die out completely, the trades may frequently shift to north, giving you a reach along the coast into early morning. As the land heats up after sunrise, the wind veers to the east. In the summer months when the wind is east or southeast, the wind will usually die out at night and spring up from the east in the early morning, shifting gradually to the south as the day progresses. Keeping these variations in mind can save you a lot of windward work.

Generally speaking, there are five islands that offer good jumping-off spots for further cruising: St. Thomas, Antigua, Martinique, St. Lucia, and Grenada. They all provide air communication to the States, harbors, shipyards where your boat can be minded in your absence, and stores and markets where you can resupply to continue your trip. St. Thomas is the port from which most cruises of the Lesser Antilles begin, but, being so far to leeward, it makes for a difficult trip to the other islands.

Let us consider a few of the possible routes south:

• St. Thomas through the Virgin Islands, island-hopping to Antigua, 210 miles to windward with possibilities of stopping and resting at various islands.

• St. Thomas to Martinique direct, 337 miles, course 143 magnetic; there is some possibility of laying the course.

• St. Thomas to Martinique via Necker Island Passage; course 152 magnetic.

• St. Thomas to St. Lucia direct or from Virgin Gorda via Necker Island Passage; the same course as that to Martinique except that the distance will be somewhat greater.

• St. Thomas to Grenada direct, 423 miles, course 163 magnetic. The course can be laid once clear of St. Croix.

• St. Thomas to Grenada via Necker Island Passage, 170 magnetic; about 475 miles. An easy reach from Necker down.

The Virgins stretch out to the eastward from St. Thomas, making a cruise through them a dead beat to windward, but this is not a difficult beat, as the islands are close together and, although the wind may blow hard, there will be nothing more than a large chop to contend with. A week to ten days can be pleasantly spent cruising the Virgins.

When departing St. Thomas and proceeding eastward, you may leave Prince Rupert Rocks on either hand. There is plenty of water for normal-sized yachts, but don't go between the buoy and the rocks. You can, however, cut between the rocks and the dock. While sailing along the shore toward Muhlenfels Point, you will have a good chance to tie in a reef. The high hills block the wind and, once clear of the point, the full force of the trades and their attendant swell will be felt. If you have a handy vessel drawing less than 7' 6" and don't mind tacking, or are proceeding under power, you may pass inside the Tri-

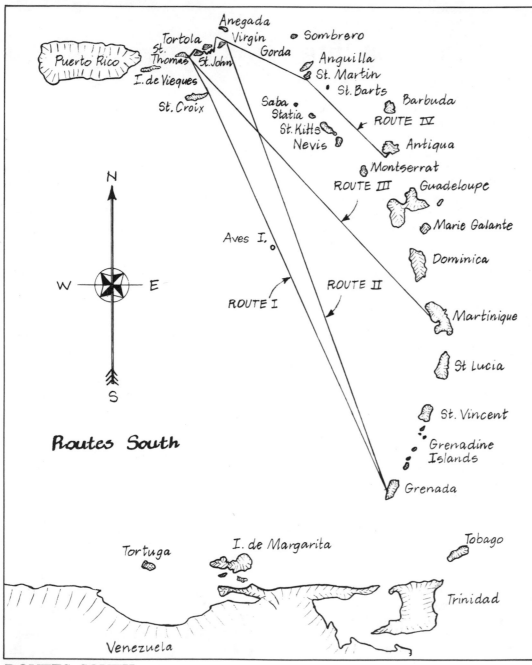

Routes South

angle. Beat to windward along Morningstar Beach, past the low house with a large white roof built on the edge of a low cliff, and stay close aboard the western shore of Green Cay. This will not necessarily save you time, but will keep you out of the sea for the first few miles of beating to windward. Once you have tacked far enough offshore to clear Green Cay, it is usually best to tack back into shore. Work your way along the shore in short tacks and you will avoid most of the ocean swell, but be careful of two dangers. There is an eight-foot spot 800 yards east of Green Cay that is on the direct line drawn from the south end of Green Cay to Long Point. The other hazard is Packet Rock, which is very dangerous, as it has only a fathom of water over it. Despite the fact that there is a nun to mark the rock, it is difficult to spot because the buoy is usually about 40 yards southeast of it.

Stand inshore on starboard tack toward the western shore of Long Point. Tack offshore and continue offshore until you are sure you can lay Cas Cay and Jersey Bay. Do not cut it close, because if you have to tack, there is always a bad sea off this area. This is no place to be caught in stays with a dead lee shore. Directly east of Cas Cay is a 12-foot spot which will bother only the larger boats. Once clear of Cas Cay, stand into Jersey Bay until you can stick your bowsprit ashore. On the next tack you may be able to weather Cow

Route I: St. Thomas to Grenada direct, 423 miles, course 163 magnetic. The course can usually be laid once clear of St. Croix.

Route II: St. Thomas to Grenada via Necker Island Passage, 170 magnetic, a distance of 420 miles.

Route III: St. Thomas to Martinique direct, 337 miles, course 143 magnetic.

Route IV: St. Thomas through the Virgin Islands, island-hopping to Antigua, 210 miles upwind.

and Calf Rocks. If so, continue on until you can lay Current Hole, then tack. If you can't weather Cow and Calf, tack back inshore rather than continuing to seaward, as you will find calm water in behind Great St. James.

When passing through Current Hole, you may pass either eastward or westward of Current Rock. The eastern passage is the widest and deepest, deep enough for any yacht. The high hill to the east of the passage blocks the wind, so it is quite possible that you will have to turn on your engine if you have a foul tide. The western passage is shoal. Evidently the controlling depth is eight feet. I have sailed *Iolaire* (7′ 6″) through this pass for years and have never touched. On the western side of Current Rock you do not lose your wind, but you must be careful, as there is barely room to tack. When using the western pass, remember that the axis of tide through this pass is northeast-southwest. If you have a foul tide and the wind is well north of east, do not attempt this passage, because there will be a strong weather bow tide which will sweep you toward the rocks on the lee side. However, if you are able to head northeast or east of northeast, you have nothing to fear even with a foul tide, as you will be able to lee-bow the tide. Under these conditions, even if you are not quite laying the passage, a quick luff will present your lee bow to the tide and it will push you to the weather side of the channel. A fair tide makes this passage simple. The tide is so strong that, once in the pass, it will carry you through, no matter what the wind.

Once through Current Hole, continue on starboard tack across Pillsbury Sound, but be sure to clear Cabrita Point with room to spare. Off Cabrita Point is a rock referred to as Jumping Rock. It is very difficult to see. A number of boats have come to grief on it. The high hills of St. John produce radical wind shifts, especially when the wind is south of east. Always stand across Pillsbury Sound on

starboard tack until you are east of Steven Cay, for between Steven Cay and Great St. James the tide creates a swell from the south. If you tack to the south you will have this sea dead on your nose. It is so short and so steep that you will make no progress. As you cross between Steven Cay and St. James, check your tide; in this area it runs northwest-southeast, which is at right angles to your course. By adjusting your course to compensate for this tide, you will save considerably in distance sailed. Lay your course for the northern end of Steven Cay. When you pass the end of the Cay, either harden up for Cruz Bay or continue eastward *without easing sheets,* because in the neighborhood of Lind Pt. you will probably be headed. As you reach Caneel Bay, the wind usually swings more northerly, heading you. The passes between Lovango Cay and Hawksnest Pt. have strong tides and you must be careful. I prefer to use the pass between Hawksnest Pt. and Durloe Cays. By hugging the shore, a back eddy may be found which will give you a fair current despite the fact that the tide is against you. The water appears to be smoother on the St. John side of the channel. The only danger in this area is Johnson Reef, easily spotted, as it is usually breaking and there is a buoy off its north end. There is plenty of room to tack between Johnson and Trunk Bay if normal care is exerted.

When proceeding eastward to Drake Channel, the most logical route appears to be through the Narrows. However, I would recommend passing to the north of Thatch. My old *Sailing Directions to the Caribbean,* printed in 1867 when wind and tide were important to a mariner, describes a much better method of getting into Drake Channel. When clearing Windward Passage, stand north and pass to north of Thatch Island. Then stand out into the Sound between Jost Van Dyke and Thatch Island or Tortola. Tack to fetch the western end of Tortola. Pass the rocks on the western

end of Tortola close aboard, then stand over to the Little Thatch Island shore. Do not tack until the very last minute. With luck, if you get one good lift, you will weather Little Thatch and pass on to Drake Channel. At worst, you will need only two quick tacks to clear the eastern end of Little Thatch. This will save you making ten or 15 tacks in the Narrows and, if the tide is foul, will save hours.

Once you are clear of Little Thatch, stand over to the St. John shore and tack only at the last minute. Your next tack should allow you to weather Frenchman's Cay and now, if you work your way along the Tortola shore, you will be out of the worst of the tide. The remainder of Drake Channel is straightforward, except that the southeastern tip of Beef Island should be avoided. There is a tide rip and the high cliffs create a back eddy and disturb the flow of wind.

Anegada Passage

Once you leave the Virgins through Necker or Round Rock Passages, there is little between you and Africa. The seas sweep across 3,000 miles of open ocean and, as they enter Anegada Passage, they are influenced by the tide ebbing and flowing into the Caribbean. The islands on both sides of the Passage disturb the natural flow of the waves, making an area that is always rough and uncomfortable. When the trades really begin to pipe up, the passage is difficult for large boats and well-nigh impossible for smaller ones.

In Anegada Passage the wind is generally east, the current west to northwest at one to one-and-a-half knots—in other words, a dead slog to windward with a foul current all the way. There is some room for play in this passage, however, which I will try to explain with close reference to the chart. The north equatorial current which runs northwestward as it passes Nevis, St. Kitts, Stacia, and Saba, swings toward the west between St. Croix and the Virgin Islands. A strong eddy holds almost due north around the west end of St. Martin and Anguilla, then northwest along Horseshoe Reef and the eastern shore of Anegada. Once it reaches the northern end of Anegada, it goes westward, with a strong back eddy looping eastward below the island on Virgin Bank. This eddy has been attested to by fishermen and pilots who have spotted large accumulations of Sargasso weed between the westerly current and the easterly eddy, and by the surprising number of wrecks on the western reefs of Anegada.

A boat crossing Anegada Passage will be favored by the northerly current on its lee bow. Since this northerly tendency becomes less pronounced the farther off to the south you fall, one should stay well to the north. If you allow your course to sag off toward Saba, you will find the current right on your nose the rest of the way east to St. Martin. (As a general rule, if you can't see Sombrero Light, you are too far off to the south.) For example, if the wind is well in the north, work your way eastward within the shelter of the Virgins, before heading out through Necker Island Passage and standing across to St. Martin; however, if the wind is east or east-southeast, I would advise working your way much farther north before venturing out into the Passage. Take advantage of the easterly eddy hooking around Anegada and lay a northern course such that you pass close aboard the west end of Anegada. Stand far enough north to clear Anegada and Horseshoe Reef in one tack. As you proceed southeastward on port tack, you should have an increasingly strong lee bow current, lifting you favorably. In short, my advice is to stay to the north, granting that there are exceptions to every rule. In the 1973 St. Thomas-St. Martin Race, one boat took a flyer from the rest of the fleet. He stood SE to Saba Bank, then tacked,

beating all his competitors by a country mile and confounding the local sailing authorities.

To Antigua

From Anguilla or St. Martin, St. Barts is only a day's sail, albeit upwind. A decision is required here. One can either make the hard slog 90 miles to Antigua or else ease the sheets for a pleasant reach down to the Statia-St. Kitts-Nevis area. The latter route would require no more than a day. From Nevis to Antigua is an arduous 50 miles dead on the wind. Here the easy alternate is to stand southeast on port tack and sail 70 miles to Guadeloupe. This way one can spend a few days cruising Guadeloupe and the Saints before heading north to Antigua by any of three ways: (1) close-hauled from Deshayes, (2) from Pointe-a-Pitre via River Salee (should it ever re-open), or (3) to English Harbour on a glorious beam reach from the eastern tip of the island, having worked your way to there in easy stages.

If it is decided to sail from St. Barts direct to Antigua, stand southeastward on port tack hard on the wind. Stay north of the rhumb line between St. Barts to St. Johns, Antigua, as the current should be less and the water smoother within the partial lee created by Antigua and Barbuda.

South from Antigua

With the wind well to the north, it is possible to pass to windward of Guadeloupe, avoiding the slow sail in light airs on the back side. Otherwise, reach down to Deshayes. Dominica also can be passed to windward, if you so choose. On the other hand, it is not worthwhile to try to beat to windward of Martinique, since the only available port of entry would be La Trinite, which is not a good anchorage at all. From La Trinite it is a hard

---

Range A: Taffia Hill in line with Channel Rock leads east of Breaking Rock, 030-210 magnetic.

Range B: Northwest side of Channel Rock open slightly from the southeast side of Friendship Hill, 050-230 magnetic.

Range C: Petit Tabac in line with Jamesby leads into Worlds End Reef anchorage, 305-125 magnetic.

Range D: Hill on Frigate Island in line with the 290-foot hill on Union (the hill is west of Pinnacle Hill, which is the highest on Union, 750 feet) leads clear inside Jack a Dan, 023-203.

Range E: Middle Hill on Prune under High North (Mount St. Louis), Carriacou, leads through south entrance to Tobago Cays, 040-220 magnetic.

Range F: The cliff on the northwest end of Saline Bay, Mayero, in line with midpoint of dock. To locate wreck of the *Paruna,* proceed along this range until intersection with Range G.

Range G: Peak on Petit Martinique between easternmost two hills of Palm.

Range H: Sail Rock three fingers open from northwest corner of Petit St. Vincent, 068-248 magnetic. To enter "Windward Side," Carriacou, follow down this range until intersection with Range I.

Range I: Fota closing with southwest corner of Petit Martinique. From where Ranges H and I meet the channel through the reef may be eyeballed.

Range J: Westernmost hill on Mayero over low land of Palm clears the one-and-a-half-fathom spot off Little Tobago to the west.

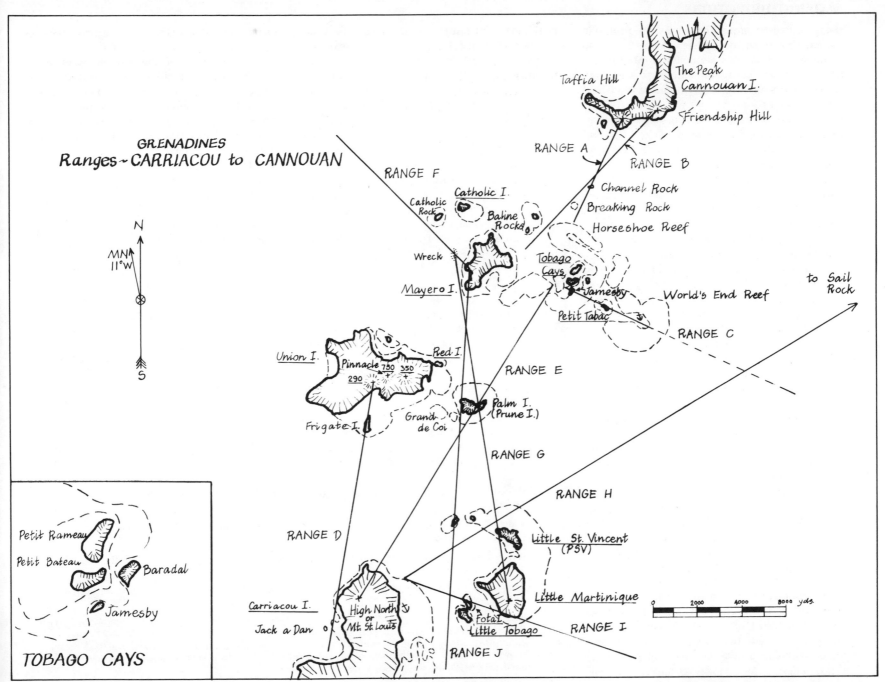

GRENADINES
Ranges~CARRIACOU to CANNOUAN

RANGE F

The Peak
Cannouan I.

Taffia Hill

Friendship Hill

RANGE A

RANGE B

Channel Rock

Breaking Rock

Horseshoe Reef

Catholic I.

Catholic Rock

Baline Rocks

Wreck

Tobago Cays

Mayero I.

Jamesby

World's End Reef

to Sail Rock

Petit Tabac

RANGE C

N
MN 11°W

S

Union I.

Red I.

Pinnacle 750 350
290

RANGE E

Palm I.
(Prune I.)

Frigate I.

Grand de Coi

RANGE G

RANGE H

RANGE D

Little St. Vincent
(PSV)

Little Martinique

Carriacou I.

Jack a Dan

High North or
Mt. St. Louis

Fota Little Tobago

RANGE I

RANGE J

2000 4000 8000 yds.

Petit Rameau

Petit Bateau

Baradal

Jamesby

TOBAGO CAYS

SKETCH CHART 5

beat eastwards along the Caravelle Peninsula which should be avoided at all costs. If you want to take in the east coast of Martinique, enter at Fort de France, and work your way around the south and east corners of the island in easy stages.

From the east coast of Martinique, one can pass to windward or leeward of St. Lucia, an easy reach either way. From Fort de France on the west coast, it is still not too rough a sail to Castries. Do not be discouraged if, when you clear Cape Salmon, you are almost hard on the wind. Usually the wind hooks around the south end of the island, coming in south of east, backing to the east as one sails offshore and to the northeast as Castries is approached.

It is usually possible to sail along the west coast of St. Lucia after 10:00 AM, if you hug the coast. From St. Lucia to St. Vincent, I tend to prefer passing to windward of St. Vincent when the wind is in the northeast. The scenery is extraordinary and there is plenty of wind. If it really pipes up, stay well offshore, as a heavy Atlantic swell will crest in 18 feet and break in 12. From St. Lucia down to St. Vincent is an easy reach.

Departing St. Vincent from Kingstown Harbor, Young Island anchorage, or the Lagoon presents no difficulties. It is almost always a reach to Admiralty Bay. On the other hand, if you want to go to windward eastward of Bequia—"over the top," as the locals say—you must hold high in the event of a lee-going (ebb) tide. Once around, you can stand southeast to Baliceau or south to Mustique. The only danger here is Montezuma Shoal.

Leaving Admiralty Bay under sail is a good test of helmsmanship, since you will be running dead before the wind. Once past West Cay, stand south leaving Cannouan to either side. Windward of Cannouan, beware of the reefs that extend well offshore. These carry seven-tenths of a mile windward of Friendship Hill. There is one danger to look out for between the southeast corner of the reefs off Cannouan and Baline Rock. The course leads directly across the breaking rock southwest of Channel Rock. The best route is to pass Channel Rock close aboard to the southeast and run to the west until Channel Rock opens slightly from Friendship Hill, Cannouan (Sketch Chart 5, Range B). Turn to the southwest and maintain this range, 230 magnetic, until close by Baline Rock.

Passing to leeward of Cannouan, there are no dangers between it and Tobago Cays. Steer course 204 magnetic, making allowance for the current and passing between Baline Rock and the windward reef of Tobago Cays. The sailing directions within the Tobago Cays are given in another chapter, and I will not repeat them here. Basically, eyeball navigation will be required to get you clear of the inner reef; then sail southeastward until the middle hill of Palm Island lines up with High North, Carriacou (Sketch Chart 5, Range E). This range will guide you south between the windward and leeward reefs of Tobago Cays. If your plan is to pass to windward of Palm Island, go east until you come on the range which aligns Friendship Hill between Petit Bateau and Baradal (Sketch Chart 6, Range B). If you maintain this range, you will come right between the two sand islands off Petit St. Vincent. But remember to follow the range rather than the compass course since the currents will be tending to throw you off one way or the other.

If proceeding from the south entrance of the Tobago Cays to the west of Palm Island, a course of 239 magnetic—and an allowance for current—will take you between the reefs of Union and Palm Islands. There are no reliable ranges and a good deal of precautionary eyeballing will be necessary. Also, keep a sharp look out for Grand de Coi, which must be avoided. It can be sailed to the westward by staying west until Catholic Island aligns itself between Union and Red Islands (Sketch Chart 6, Range D) and following this range on south. To pass eastward of Grand de Coi: once the reefs of Palm Island are cleared to port, head up until Glass Hill joins the eastern end of Mayero Island (Sketch Chart 6, Range C). This range should be maintained, keeping clear of the shoal at the southeast corner of Palm. And if your destination is Petit St. Vincent, hold this range until the peak of Little Martinique bears 160 magnetic. Follow 160 midway between Pinese and Mopion. Once you have passed beyond the reefs, you may alter course to Petit St. Vincent.

South and West from Petit St. Vincent

From Petit St. Vincent to the windward

Range A: Peak of Petit Martinique bearing 160-340 magnetic leads between Pinese and Mopion.

Range B: Friendship Hill between Petit Bateau and Baradal leads to windward of reefs off Palm and between Pinese and Mopion, 215-035.

Range C: Glass Hill in line with eastern tip of Mayero passes Grand de Coi to the east, 213-033 magnetic.

Range D: Catholic Island between Red Island and Union leads west of Grand de Coi, 198-018 magnetic.

Range E: Little Tobago one finger open from Fota leads between Pinese and Mopion, between Palm and the detached reef west of Palm, and to the west of the reef at the north end of Saline Bay, Mayero, 010-190 magnetic. If more than half a finger's width of Petit St. Vincent shows to the east of Palm, bear off or else you will come to a sudden stop on the reef at the north end of Saline Bay. (See insert for profile.)

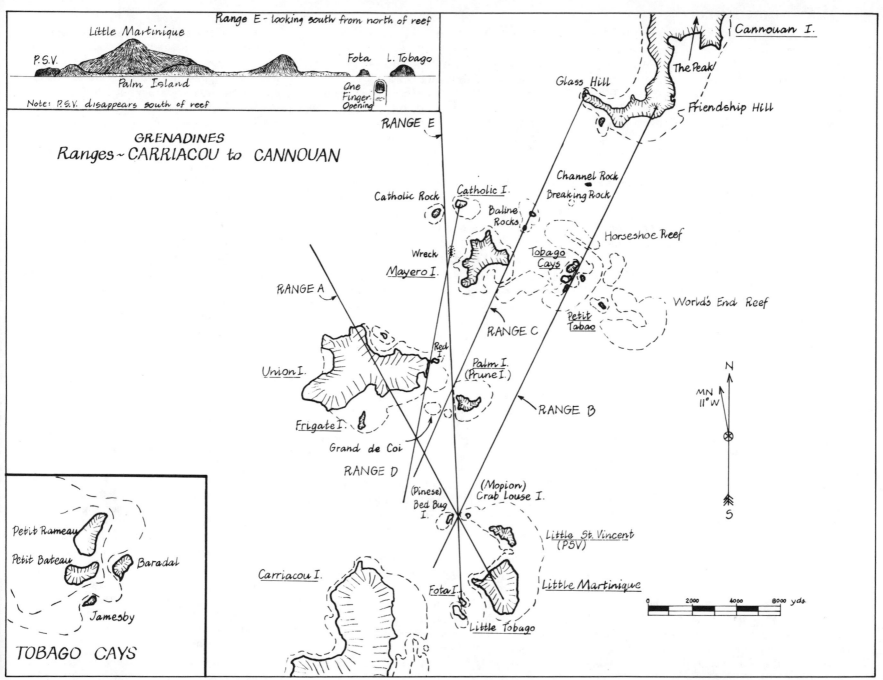

Range E – looking south from north of reef

Little Martinique

P.S.V.

Palm Island

Fota   L. Tobago

One Finger Opening

Note: P.S.V. disappears south of reef

GRENADINES
Ranges ~ CARRIACOU to CANNOUAN

RANGE E

Cannouan I.

The Peak

Glass Hill

Friendship Hill

Channel Rock

Breaking Rock

Catholic Rock   Catholic I.

Baline Rocks

Horseshoe Reef

Wreck

Mayero I.

Tobago Cays

RANGE A

RANGE C

World's End Reef

Petit Tabao

Red I.

Palm I. (Prune I.)

Union I.

N

MN 11° W

RANGE B

Frigate I.

Grand de Coi

RANGE D

(Pinese) Bed Bug I.

(Mopion) Crab Louse I.

S

Little St. Vincent (PSV)

Carriacou I.

Fota I.

Little Martinique

0   2000   4000   8000 yds.

Little Tobago

Petit Rameau

Petit Bateau   Baradal

Jamesby

TOBAGO CAYS

SKETCH CHART 6

side of Carriacou, head west until Sail Rock is three fingers off the northern end of Petit St. Vincent. Carry on this, heading 248 magnetic (Sketch Chart 5, Range H) until Fota is overlapped by the southwestern corner of Little Martinique (Sketch Chart 5, Range I). At this point you will be inside the reef. From here on south along the coast, use eyeball navigation. A skillful reef pilot in a boat drawing no more than seven feet with a man aloft could continue south all the way through Watering Bay into Grand Bay.

A less taxing course from Petit St. Vincent is to sail southwest until the westernmost hill of Mayero lines up with the western side of Palm Island (Sketch Chart 5, Range J). Turn south along this range which will carry you safely to the west of the one-and-a-half-fathom spot southwest of Little Tobago. Once past this danger point, the course should be altered to clear the reef off the eastern point of Carriacou, after which a course approximately southwest may be steered, passing to either side of Ile de Ronde and Grenada.

The west coast of Carriacou is far less formidable. From Petit St. Vincent to Rapid Point is a straight-line course with no hazards. Around Rapid Point it is an easy reach down the coast of Carriacou with no dangers until Jack a Dan, at which time you should hook up with range D (Sketch 5), defined by the peak on Frigate Island placed under the first peak west of the easternmost peak of Union Island. This will carry you clear inside the shoal spot between Jack a Dan and the mainland of Carriacou.

Carriacou to Grenada

From Hermitage Point at the southwest corner of Tyrell Bay to Diamond Island and David Point, Grenada, it is 228 magnetic without taking account of current. This is normally a very broad reach or a dead run. If the wind is in the north, it may be a good idea before

you leave the lee of Carriacou to rig your main boom foreguy to starboard and set your jib on the pole to windward. This will save you a lot of rolling and slatting on the way down.

Once round David Point, the wind tends to hook around the island, often putting you dead before the wind most of the way to Black Bay, Grenada, where it will tend to come more abeam. If your destination is St. George's, the course from Boismorice Point is 178 magnetic, hugging the shore. If you are bypassing St. George's directly to the south coast of Grenada, a course of 214 magnetic from Boismorice Point will clear Long Point Shoal.

Grenada to Trinidad

The sail from Grenada to Trinidad is usually an easy beam reach. The only difficulty is an occasionally strong current along with some tide rips that will set up between the two islands. The normal procedure for most yachts making the passage is to leave Grenada at about 1800 hours, steer 170 magnetic (or 165 if your boat makes a lot of leeway) until you spot the Chocachocare light, and alter your course accordingly. This is a very powerful light which can be seen as far as 25 miles away on a clear night. Do not head right for it as it marks the westernmost Boca and the current will be pulling you in that direction anyway. Most boats favor entering the Gulf of Paria through the eastern Boca in order to save a lot of windward effort. This should put you in Port of Spain early in the morning.

Although the distance from St. Thomas to, say, Antigua is only about 200 miles, the course is practically dead against the wind all the way. There are plenty of islands in between that afford the opportunity to lay over, rest, and sightsee, but the windward legs will be pure hell nonetheless. In a small boat of 30 or 35 feet, your progress against heavy trades may be reduced to nothing.

Bear in mind that there are other ways to reach the middle or southern islands. Depending on the time at your disposal, you can sail from the Virgins direct to Grenada, St. Lucia, or Martinique, and from any one of these islands you can work your way north in easy stages off the wind to Antigua. The strategy is to define the southern reach of your cruise and to proceed north from there. If you are chartering a bare boat and are willing to pay the deadhead fee, you should consider picking up the boat on one of these southern islands. Otherwise, sail the passage yourself. With a break in the weather, you can lay a straight course from St. Thomas Harbor to Martinique (143 magnetic), making it in two-and-a-half or three days. This is not a great deal of time to give up if you are planning a cruise of two or three weeks. The disadvantages are that you will be close-hauled the entire way, and if you have just arrived by air from the States, setting out on a long sail direct from St. Thomas allows no time for the crew to get its sea legs or to build up a tan against the sun. Therefore, a preferable course would be to work your way east from St. Thomas through the Virgins for a few days. This will give you the time to shake down the crew, pick up some precious easting and a tan in sheltered waters, and then to take off through Necker Island Passage for Grenada. The course is 170 magnetic, the distance 420 miles—an easy reach. Even if the wind veers to ESE, you will still be under slightly eased sheets and going like mad. If it is E to ENE, as is usual, you can make the trip in three days. Let me repeat that if you have the time to invest in this passage, I can recommend no better way of positioning yourself for a cruise of the southern islands. You will have reached the southernmost of the Antilles without having strained to windward and with no serious windward work before you.

The course from St. Thomas Harbor to Grenada direct is 163 magnetic, 423 miles.

You will have to hold one point high on the course for the first 50 miles in order to clear the eastern end of St. Croix, but once clear, the sheets can be eased for a nice easy reach to Grenada. The chances of the wind swinging so far south as to put you hard on the wind are relatively slim. If the wind should really pipe up, its direction will back and give you a real sleigh ride. A heavy blow won't faze a small boat, as it will be aft of abeam. For the remainder of the passage there are two things to watch out for: first of all, don't run up on Aves Island, which will be right on your track. The latest surveys place it three miles northwest of its charted position. It is low, uninhabited, and impossible to spot at night. Secondly, take sights to assure that you are not falling off to leeward. It would be an awful waste of time to beat the last 50 miles or so to Grenada. The current runs to the west through here as fast as three knots. Against a three-knot current in the same direction as the wind, it would require six knots through the water to hold your own tacking in 120 degrees.

Proceeding North

Trinidad to Grenada

It is best to depart Trinidad in time to arrive at Point Saline, Grenada, by dawn. More than one boat has grounded on Long Point Shoal tacking up from Point Saline to St. George's. Most yachts can hold a course of 015 from the easternmost Boca to Grenada. Soon after the lights on the hills of Grenada are picked up, Point Saline Light will appear. If entering at L'Anse aux Epines, keep these high lights on the starboard bow but don't approach the coast till dawn or you may come to a sudden stop on the Porpoises. A better course is to head for Point Saline and round close aboard. Hug the coast and short-tack up the beach, passing close to Quarantine Point. This way you will avoid Long Point Shoal,

which is most difficult to spot at night. There is no difficulty entering Grenada harbor at night: anchor in the northeast corner, and proceed at dawn to GYS to clear.

Grenada South Coast to St. George's Harbor

Do not leave harbors like Bacaye or Caliveny until the sun is high, because in the early morning the path of the sunlight is directly in line with the exit course. Once clear of the harbors on the south coast of Grenada, it is best to head directly for Glover Island, keeping an eye open for Porpoise Rocks (Grampuses); pass close north or south of Porpoise Rocks and then head for Point Saline. If you head directly for Point Saline, you will discover that the wind shifts to the south at Hardy Bay and you end up dead downwind, whereas if you stay offshore, as the wind shifts you may head northwest for Point Saline and still be on a reach. Once Point Saline has been rounded, favor the shore. Stay close in to avoid the sea and to take advantage of better wind shifts than could be found offshore. When approaching Long Point, be sure to favor Morne Rouge Beach area, and stay inshore to avoid Long Point Shoal. If under power proceed directly from Point Saline to Long Point, leaving Long Point 100 yards off the starboard side, and proceed directly to St. George's Harbor or Grand Anse Bay clear of all dangers.

Grenada to Carriacou

When proceeding north from St. George's, plans must be made to arrive at Carriacou early in the day and in no event later than 5:00 in the afternoon. This necessitates a very early departure from St. George's. Many boats motorsail all the way up the coast to David's Point and then set sail for Carriacou. If you choose to sail the coast, it is best done close inshore. Every time you get a mile offshore on starboard tack, you should tack back in.

There is little or no wind on the lee coast of Grenada until after 0800 and it dies drastically after 1700. Grenada's highest point is almost 2,800 feet, and the main line of mountains approximately 2,000 feet. Do not make the mistake of standing offshore to find more wind—nine times out of ten you won't find any. Stay in close.

It is most important when proceeding north from Grenada to stay right close to the beach and continue tacking inshore at every opportunity. When David Point (locally known as Tangle Angle, because of the way the current sweeps around it and causes tide rips) is reached, it is again important to tack to the eastward.

In fact, before striking out for Carriacou, you should tack to the east as far as Sauteurs and frequently to Levera. The current runs as much as two-and-a-half knots (normally one to one-and-a-half) to westward through this passage. Although you may think you are laying the course to Carriacou, a strong west-running tide could throw you off 30 degrees if you were doing five knots. Occasionally, with the wind in the southeast, it is possible to lay the course from David Point to Carriacou, but this is very much the exception. Most Grenada-Carriacou races have proved that it is worth tacking to Sauteurs, even with a windward-going tide. In any event, be careful of the shoal spots between Levera Island and the town of Levera, as they can break in heavy weather. Proceed east until you can lay Ile de Ronde, and then set out. Pass between the Sisters and Ile de Ronde and stand north on starboard tack until smooth water is reached in the lee of Carriacou.

The best time to arrive at David Point is when the tides have just begun to run to windward. This will give you four hours of either slack water or a weather-going tide, enough to reach Tyrell Bay before the tide changes.

As you approach Carriacou's southwest point, you should note the tide. If you wish to go to Saline Island or One Tree Rock on the south coast of Carriacou, do so only if the tide is running to windward; otherwise it is almost impossible to get up to Saline Island unless you have a very powerful engine. It should also be noted that it is best not to tack east after Diamond Island (Kick 'em Jenny), as this will put you into the worst of the current. Instead, stand north into the lee of Carriacou; good progress can then be made on port tack in smooth water.

St. George's to Carriacou via the South and East Coasts of Grenada

When proceeding from St. George's to the south coast of Grenada, be careful of the shoals extending from the Islander Hotel over to the Silver Sands Hotel (Range C, Sketch Chart 79, p. 238.

Long Point Shoal off Long Point (locally referred to as Quarantine Point) is most dangerous. The northeast corner of the dock transit shed in line with Government House will clear Long Point Shoal to the northwest (Range B, Sketch Chart 81). Government House may be easily identified as it is a large, dark-colored house, with large verandas on both first and second stories, situated on the ridge northeast of town. It is the only house on the ridge with two flag poles, one east and one west of the house.

The other method commonly used by yachts is to head from St. George's Harbor to Long Point, leaving Long Point to port 100 yards off. When Long Point Shoal comes abeam, head for Point Saline Lighthouse, which course will clear Long Point Shoal to the southeastward; or use Range A, Sketch Chart 81, course 062-242 magnetic. There is deep water along this entire shore and you may sail 200 yards off with no danger and in smooth water. If it is blowing more than ten knots, tie in a reef before rounding Point Saline.

Upon reaching Point Saline, it is best to round the point close aboard; there is deep water 50 yards offshore and very deep water at 100 yards. Upon rounding, unless you draw more than ten feet, the best procedure is to stay close inshore. This will keep you out of the swell and current. Each time a long tack is made offshore, the current and sea will set you to leeward.

Between Point Saline and Prickly Point, there are few difficulties as long as a lookout is kept during starboard tacks inshore. If beating to windward under sail, short-tack along the shore as close as possible, as it will keep you out of the swell and foul current, and will usually give you port-tack lifts; watch for shoals on starboard tack. From Prickly Point eastward, this coast has numerous reefs and sandbanks. All are clearly visible as long as the sun is fairly high.

When proceeding eastward along the south coast of Grenada under power, stay close to shore and keep an eye out for the various shoals. Remember, of course, that you should subtract at least three feet from any depths quoted on the charts, and frequently as much as a fathom. Eastward beyond Fort Jeudy Point, there are a number of shoal spots well offshore: off Westerhall Point, Marquis Point, and Menere Point.

During the winter, if the wind is out of the east or northeast, it is unwise to beat up the east coast of Grenada. It can get very rough with seas breaking fairly far offshore. On the southeast coast there is also roughly a one- to two-knot current dead on the nose. More than one vessel has come to grief in these waters. Not too many years ago a 35-foot cutter, *Tawana*, was boarded by a breaking sea that swept everything before it and sank the boat in a matter of seconds. The crew was fortunate to survive. After the vessel sank, the lashing on the dinghy broke, and the dinghy floated to the surface; the crew bailed her out and rowed ashore.

However, if you elect to proceed up the east coast, note how far offshore the shoals extend north of Bacolet Point. Bear in mind that the current will be setting you onshore. Once Telescope Point is reached, a course should be set for Anthony Rock, which will take you clear of the shoals. The current between Telescope Point and Green Island sets very strongly to the south, so strong that the old Sailing Directions warn vessels about passing and getting south of the entrance of Grenville. The old square riggers were not too good to windward. Thus, if by mistake they sailed past Grenville, they were advised to continue south, around Point Saline, up the west coast of Grenada, and try again. It seems a long distance to go a few miles but in years gone by the sailors had plenty of patience, especially in adverse conditions.

Be very careful not to get involved with the three-fathom spot between Anthony Rock and Sandy Island, as in heavy winter weather the ground swell breaks continually on this spot. The eastern side of Sandy Island kept directly in line with the west peak of Caille Island (Range A, Sketch Chart 89, page 251) will pass clear to windward of this breaking shoal spot.

There is deep water between Sandy Island and Green Island, between Green Island and Levera Island, and between Levera Island and Bedford Point, but the Levera Island side of the channel should be favored for the deepest water. From the northeast corner of Grenada, it is usually an easy sail to Carriacou.

Carriacou Northward

The usual course is to pass along the west side of Carriacou, stopping at Tyrell Bay. When leaving this harbor, pass north of the middle ground, hug the coast, and make allowance for the rocks which extend about 200 yards offshore from Lookout Point (the point south of Cistern Point). Under power or sail, the best course from Cistern Point to Hillsborough Bay is between Mabouya Island and Sandy Island, being careful to avoid the reef on the southwestern tip of Sandy Island. Other than that, there are no dangers in this area unless you have a vessel drawing 12 feet. Beating to windward through this gap is good fun, as there is no sea and usually plenty of wind.

Between Cistern Point and Hillsborough, deep-draft boats can easily run aground. The old schooner range is still a safe one. Put Cistern under the stern and the Hospital Building at the top of the mountain on the bow and proceed straight to the anchorage. Once past Sandy Island, the course can be shifted slightly toward the Hillsborough jetty. North of Hillsborough there is one danger, between Jack a Dan and the mainland. This is a three-quarter-fathom spot with quite a few dents in it. It can be passed inside by placing the hill on Frigate Island directly in line with the 290-foot hill on Union Island, which is the hill just west of the highest and easternmost peak on Union (Range D, Sketch Chart 5, course 023 magnetic). Be sure to stay on this range as this shoal is particularly hard to spot.

Under power, you may steer direct from Rapid Point to the dock of Petit St. Vincent and clear all dangers. Under sail, it will be a dead beat to windward. On port tack, beware of the shoal off Little Carenage Bay and the shoal on the north end of Watering Bay. On the starboard tack, watch out for Pinese and Mopion, the two sand islands northwest of Petit St. Vincent. There is ample water between these two islands, but eyeballing is called for, as the two of them are continually growing and shifting.

To head northward from Petit St. Vincent, pass midway between the two cays and continue on course until Fota and the east side of Little Tobago are one finger open (Range E, Sketch Chart 6, course 010 magnetic). This

will take you east of Grand de Coi and the detached reef off Palm Island. Care must be exerted here, as the current will be at a right angle to your course and will tend to sweep you to leeward. Thus a continual check must be made that you are still on range. This range will carry you inside the outer reefs on Palm Island. A good lookout must be kept, or you may come to a sudden stop before you realize you're too close.

An alternate route clear of Grand de Coi is provided by Range C on Sketch Chart 6, course 033 magnetic. This is Glass Hill on the western point of Cannouan in line with the eastern end of Mayero Island. Glass Hill will appear as a detached island west of Taffia Hill, as it is connected to Cannouan by only a low sand split.

Beating to windward from Rapid Point to the region of Union Island, you will want to avoid Grand de Coi. Catholic Island placed between Union Island and Red Island passes clear to west of Grand de Coi (Range D, Sketch Chart 6, course 018-198 magnetic). North of Grand de Coi, you will have to tack to the east to clear the reefs windward of Union Island.

North beyond Palm and Union Islands is about the most dangerous area of the Grenadines. A reef at the north end of Saline Bay has damaged many yachts proceeding north along the lee coast of Mayero. To clear the end of this reef, put Fota one finger open from the east side of Little Tobago (Range E, Sketch Chart 6, course 010-190). As you approach Grand Coi Point at the north end of Saline Bay, Mayero, check to see if any of Petit St. Vincent is showing east of Palm. If Petit St. Vincent is at all visible, bear off to westward or you will come to a sudden stop on the reef off Grand Coi Point (profile insert, Sketch Chart 6). With this reef behind you, there are no other dangers standing north from Mayero to Cannouan.

Approaches to the Tobago Cays

If proceeding under power, once the northern end of Mayero is cleared, a course may be set straight to Petit Rameau, the northernmost of the Tobago Cays (Range A, Sketch Chart 78, page 233. If you are sailing it, beware of the one-fathom spot southwest of Baline Rocks. Here there are actually three shoal patches, all of them easy to spot.

If coming from Petit St. Vincent, sail west until Friendship Hill, Cannouan, is between Petit Bateau and Baradal (Range B, Sketch Chart 6, course 035 magnetic). This will take you between Pinese and Mopion clear of the reef to the east of Palm Island. Until you are clear to the north of Palm, do not sag below this line. Once near the Cays, bear off until the middle hill on Palm Island lines up with High North of Carriacou (Range E, Sketch Chart 5, course 040 magnetic). Stay hard on this range until you have passed between the eastern and western reefs. The eastern one may be spotted by a small sand island. However, these sand islands are prone to disappearing at irregular intervals.

If you are coming from between Palm and Union and heading for the southern entrance of the Tobago Cays, you must fight your way up to windward, until once again the middle hill on Palm lines up with High North Carriacou (Range E, Sketch Chart 5). Follow this bearing into the Cays.

Tobago Cays to Cannouan

From the north end of the Tobago Cays to the western end of Cannouan, there are no dangers at all. Glass Hill is easily laid from Baline Rocks. If you are bound for the windward side of Cannouan and tacking below Channel Rocks, I urge setting out in slack water or a fair tide. Great care must be taken to avoid the submerged rock one-half mile southwest of Channel Rock. This rock is covered and breaks in a swell. Breaking seas will demolish a small boat in short order. Friendship Hill touching the northwest side of Channel Rock passes clear to the west of the breaking rock (Range B, Sketch Chart 5, course 050 magnetic). Channel Rock in line with Taffia Hill passes the breaking rock clear to windward (Range A, Sketch Chart 5, course 030).

Cannouan to Bequia

This trip should be made at slack water or when the tide is running to windward. The distance is 15 miles, and should the tide be running its full limit of two knots to the west, a vessel making five knots through the water would have to steer 045 magnetic, as opposed to the 028 rhumb line. Unless the wind were southeast, this would put you very close on the wind. During the winter, with the wind toward the north and a leeward running tide, you stand very little chance of laying West Cay, leaving you a tough beat into Admiralty Bay. Against a foul tide be sure to hold high on the course, passing close aboard to leeward of Pigeon Island. There are no dangers on the course to Bequia. If you depart during a weather tide, the only difficulty will be a strong tide rip off the north end of Cannouan. Once Pigeon Island is reached, Quatre and Petit Nevis serve to break the swell, giving a glorious sail the rest of the way in with plenty of wind and smooth water.

Here is a reason to have both a British and American chart, as the latter ends without showing Admiralty Bay, whereas the British shows all of Bequia. Once you have rounded West Cay, you may turn on the iron genoa and head for the anchorage at Elizabeth Town with no dangers in the way, or you can put the sport back into sailing and beat up into the harbor, but be very careful of the shoals on its south side.

Bequia to St. Vincent

Bequia Channel has the well-deserved reputation of being exceedingly rough at times. This brief eight-mile passage has done in any number of small boats and dinghies over the years. The water is smoothest during a leeward tide. A windward tide will offset your leeway, though it will also manage to churn up a nasty, steep sea. I have seen the waves making up into almost box-like shapes—six feet high and six feet between each crest—a great place to lose a dinghy under tow.

From Admiralty Bay round up close aboard Fort Point, watching out for Wash Rock 100 yards off Devils Table. Play the wind shifts close to the Bequia shore and keep inshore until you feel you can comfortably lay Young Island. If this does not seem logical, I must confess that the 45-foot gaff-rigged schooner *Stella Maris* twice beat *Iolaire*—a 45-foot Marconi-rigged yawl—between Bequia and Young Island in just this way, tacking northeast along the Bequia shore before setting out.

Young Island is easily identified by a high peak just south of it on Duvernette Island, which looks like a loaf of French bread put on end. Kingstown will also be readily visible to leeward.

St. Vincent to St. Lucia

There are two routes to St. Lucia from the south coast of St. Vincent. The more usual is to proceed up the west coast in easy stages, stopping off at Wallilabu or Cumberland Bays. The lee of St. Vincent is frequently becalmed, so you may be forced to stoke up the engine. Hold high the course across St. Vincent Passage, as the current sets strongly northwest; at the southwestern corner of St. Lucia it becomes even more severe. If you fall four or five miles offshore when Beaumont Point comes abeam, you're going to have a rough beat inshore.

The other way to St. Lucia is to take off southeastward from Young Island or Blue Lagoon until you are off soundings. When the swell eases up, tack and head directly for Vieux Fort, a distance of about 45 miles. This is a course for able boats to windward and should be undertaken when the tide is running eastward. This is an excellent sail when the wind is in the east or south of east, and less than excellent if it veers northeast.

St. Vincent to Martinique

Castries to Fort de France is one of the finest sails in the Caribbean. The first five miles are sheltered by Pigeon Island on the northeast corner of St. Lucia—smooth water and plenty of wind. On leaving Castries, it is best to come hard on the wind till north of Pigeon Island, and then to bear off direct for Diamond Rock (Rocher de Diamant). The course is 005 magnetic, usually a splendid close reach across 18 miles of open water. The wind swings further aft under the southeast corner of Martinique. Quite likely you will become briefly becalmed under Cape Salmon, a good breeze resuming once you enter the bay of Fort de France. If you are making this trip at night, watch out for the unlit Fond Blanc buoy on the northeast corner of Banc du Gros Ilet; it is dead on a line between Cape Salmon and Fort de France.

Martinique to Dominica or Guadeloupe

I prefer to head south, gunkholing around to the east coast, before taking off from Tartane, clearing Caravelle Peninsula, and laying a course for Scott's Head, Dominica, 45 miles away on a broad reach. If you wish to bypass Dominica, steer 010 magnetic for the light on Petite Terre southeast of Guadeloupe, a magnificent reach all the way.

If you decide to sail up the west coast of Martinique, don't set out before 10:00 AM, as there is no wind before this time. With any luck you will pick up a light breeze along the coast before clearing the lee of the island and setting out for Scott's Head. From Scott's Head to Roseau it is usually flat calm. Not always—I once bore into Roseau with rail down under headsails and storm trysail.

Dominica to Guadeloupe

From Roseau to Prince Rupert Bay is a picturesque day-sail, leaving Roseau late in the morning. There should be enough wind after 10:00 for a high-performance boat. A motor-sailer would probably have to motor. It is a short distance from Portsmouth to the Saints, one that can be made easily in an afternoon. The entrance to the Saints from the south is fairly straightforward.

North from the Saints, your choice of route will be influenced by the amount of time on your hands and whether or not the French Government has succeeded in opening the drawbridge across the river Salee. If it is open, the best thing for my money is to leave the Saints, beat up to Saint Marie—a fine, picturesque harbor—or on to Gros Ilet. Anchor for the night and the next morning proceed up the River Salee and on to Antigua. If the river is closed and you have a boat that sails well to windward, you can work your way along the south coast to Petit Havre or to Francois.

Otherwise, you can sail or motor-sail up the lee coast of Guadeloupe to Barque Cove or Deshayes Bay, before continuing north to Antigua. On the way to Antigua, be sure to take repeated stern bearings, as the current is variable. While south in the Islands the current was on the weather quarter, now it will be on the weather bow as you head north. You will also be harder on the wind. In short, you must make a greater allowance for current than you did farther south. Be sure to leave Deshayes in time to make English Harbour by 4:00 PM at the latest. Should flukey winds put you outside English Harbour at dusk, you will have great difficulty making your way into the anchorage.

From Petite Terre it is a beautiful, long, easy reach to English Harbour, distance 62 miles. But again you must leave early enough to arrive at English Harbour in daylight, which may be almost impossible to do in a small boat unless you are flying a spinnaker.

Antigua to Barbuda

If you want to visit this island from English Harbour, the best plan is to beat around to Green Island, pass the night there or at Nonsuch Bay (an excellent spot when Green Island is glutted with charter boats). Leave early the next morning, timing your arrival in Barbuda, 30 miles away, for no later than 2:00 PM. You will be required to do a tremendous amount of eyeball navigation while you are still well offshore from Barbuda, and this is best done when the sun is overhead.

Antigua Westward

From Antigua, you are in a position to lay just about any island passage. A course can be set southward to Montserrat or slightly north of west to Nevis and on to St. Kitts, Stacia, St. Barts, or St. Martin, all of them easy jumps from one island to the next. One word of warning must be levelled at night passages between the St. Barts-St. Martin-Anguilla area and Virgin Gorda. The current sets strongly to the northwest through here, at times as high as two knots. A number of yachts and commercial vessels bound for Virgin Gorda or Round Rock Passage from this area have received the surprise of their lives on Horseshoe Reef. The current changes erratically from day to day, and there is no telling how it will be running until you get out there. I therefore prefer to leave Anguilla or St. Martin in the evening after a good dinner and lay a course midway between St. Croix and St. Thomas. Both these islands will be visible by dawn, at which time I can alter course accordingly. Fifteen years ago, there were no lights in the British Virgin Islands that were visible from the east. The light on Ginger Island never worked; there was no electricity on Virgin Gorda and very little on Tortola. Now the loom from Road Town can be seen for miles, and on Virgin Gorda, the lights from the houses on the road from Gorda Sound to Little Dix Bay are bright and high enough to be seen on clear nights from 30 to 40 miles to the east.

Virgin Islands Westward

No real problem. To Puerto Rico and the Bahamas you will be dead before the wind. But I have seen boats rolling and slatting before the wind, their jibs alternately filling and collapsing, their mains threatening to jibe, the sun directly overhead frying the crews' brains out. Don't do it this way. Instead, wing the jib on a whisker or spinnaker pole, guy the main boom forward, come down hard on the boom vang, and rig a cockpit awning that can be left up under sail. Then open a beer. Life will be a dream.

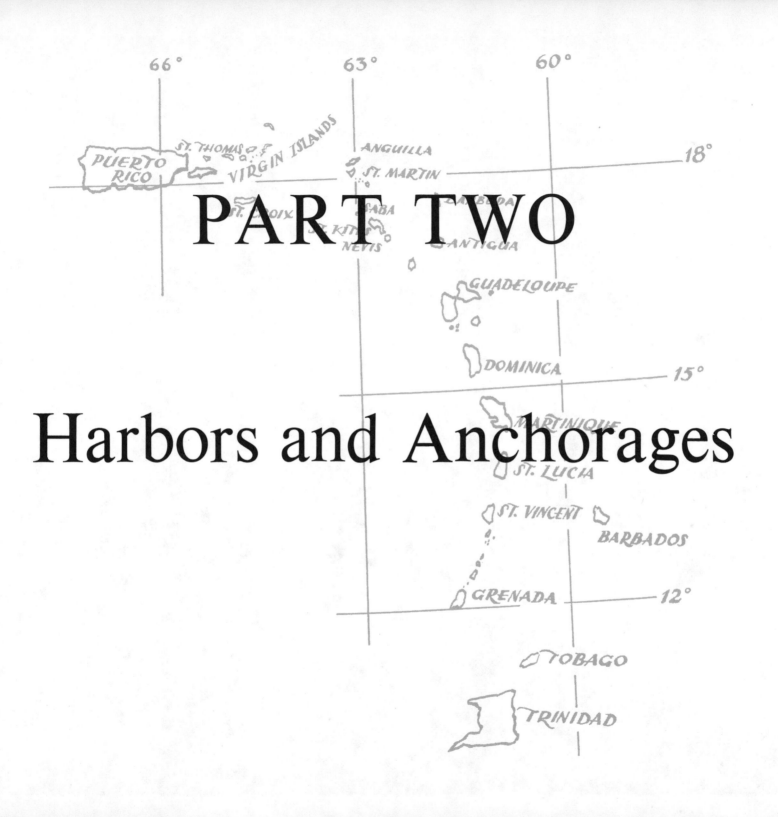

PART TWO

Harbors and Anchorages

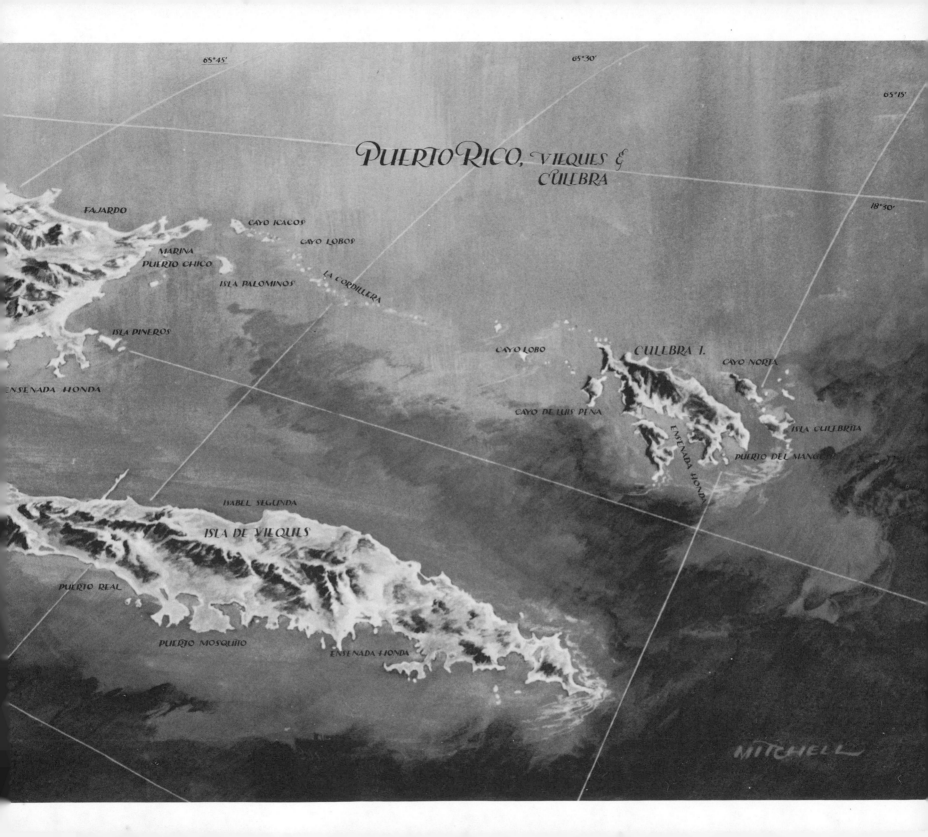

CHAPTER 6

Puerto Rico

C&GS 901, 902, 903, 904, 908, 909, 917, 918, 920, 921, 922, 923, 924, 926, 927, 929, 931, 932

To speak very briefly of a large island, Puerto Rico offers rich opportunities to the cruising yachtsman. The south coast abounds with small coves and deserted anchorages, sandstone caves and white-sand beaches. The waters are well marked and charted. The sight-seeing on the island is varied, rewarding, and, with over 3,000 miles of paved roads, convenient. The nightlife in the major cities is vast even by American standards. Its people have certainly learned how to entertain. Over a million visitors enjoy the island every year, some 200,000 of these by cruise ships. Happily, most of these folks do not venture out of the big cities—some never leave their hotel poolside—so that the countryside and most of the coastline has remained unspoiled.

For some nearsighted reason, Puerto Rico is often derided by Statesiders, and its capital, San Juan, has been referred to as a "Miami with a Spanish accent." This view fails to take into account that Puerto Rico is fundamentally Spanish in its social organization and its outlook on life, while the hotels and nightclubs that cater to American mass culture remain a phenomenon apart. The island can be enjoyed for either separately, but not both together.

The climate of Puerto Rico varies from areas that are arid and desert-like to lush mountains and rain forests. In the principal cities English is the second language, while in the country mostly Spanish is spoken.

For many years Puerto Rican yachting was limited for the most part to power-boating —and some pretty reckless power-boating at that. Woe betide the hapless dinghy that got in the way. True yachting was something of a late-comer, largely due to the fact that along the north coast of Puerto Rico, other than San Juan, there are no sizable harbors. Nevertheless, in the last ten years sailing has gained a definite foothold in Puerto Rico, so much so that in the eastern end of the island there is scarcely the harbor space to accommodate all the new boats. A number of first-class small-boat skippers have emerged, and cruiser-racing has become thoroughly established as well. Some of the most competitive offshore racing in the Caribbean is conducted under the auspices of Club Nautico in San Juan.

Marine supplies and services can be obtained on Puerto Rico without too much difficulty. When dealing with Puerto Rican commercial yacht yards, make sure they will be prepared to do the careful work that yachts require. Many yards catering to larger commercial vessels tend to be rather heavy-handed when it comes to yacht repair.

The Puerto Rican mainland can be spotted from great distances over the water, making landfalls a relatively simple matter. A high mountain range runs the length of the island, and well-lit cities and towns give ample warning to the approaching mariner. The coastal waters have been buoyed and charted by the U.S. Government, and detail charts are available for practically all the harbors. The only interesting area not covered by detail charts is on the southwest coast between Cabo Rajo and Punta Brea, where, until the gap has been filled, I would recommend daytime exploration only. Since an out-of-the-way spot has a way of becoming a little overcrowded with day-trippers during the weekend, I would advise exploring Puerto Rico's smaller anchorages and coves during the weekdays only. Best to pass your weekends in the major harbors, laying in provisions and savoring the delights of civilization, such as they are.

The ports of entry for yachts are San Juan, Fajardo, Ponce, Guanica, Mayaguez, and Aguadilla. Boats approaching Puerto Rico from the east often enter at Fajardo; those coming up from the southern Caribbean enter at Ponce or Guanica; and from the west, at Mayaguez or Aguadilla.

Aguadilla
(C&GS 920, 901)

In normal weather the anchorage is fairly calm. Should the wind come hard out of the north or northeast, a ground swell will prove uncomfortable. Power boats on their way down from the Bahamas and the Dominican Republic will put in to Aguadilla to fuel up alongside the steamer dock. If the anchorage is found to be choppy, proceed southwest around Punta Higuero to Rincon.

Rincon
(C&GS 920, 901)

Here there is a beautiful white-sand beach, many attractive vacation cottages, and some small restaurants and bars—a wonderful place to stop for a hearty meal. Bear in mind that the beach traces its origin to centuries of ground swell—so anchor accordingly. Make sure you anchor on the shelf, as the bottom drops off abruptly from one or two fathoms to 36. The holding on the shelf is excellent. Surfing is a major pastime of Rincon in the winter months. Even in calm weather the waves break on shore, so that care must be taken when landing in a dinghy.

Mayaguez
(C&GS 920, 901, 931)

Mayaguez is the next point of interest

proceeding south along the west coast of Puerto Rico. The harbor is well lit and well buoyed, and the approach is simple and straightforward. On the eastern end of the main dock is a lower section where a yacht can be tied up for short periods. The longshoremen are friendly and will assist you in obtaining water, fuel, and ice. Once you have cleared, it is best to move south to the small private dock just north of the radio towers. There is ten feet of water at the anchorage buoy and six feet along the dock. Ice, fuel, and water may be had at the dock. Minor work can be done at the small yard and hauling facility. Taxi service is available to town and to the countryside. The supermarkets in Mayaguez are, by Caribbean terms, incomparable.

A word about the weather in Mayaguez: the land thereabout is flat with high mountains further to the east. Cumulus clouds build up over these mountains and, blown west, drop their rains on Mayaguez. These rain storms seem ominous as they approach but contain very little wind. No cause for alarm.

Puerto Real
(C&GS 920, 901)

Heading south from Mayaguez, it is possible to hug the shore, using the normal procedures of cautious eyeball navigation. Long open beaches line the shore all the way to Punta Ostiones, where there is a small, protected anchorage near the underwater laboratory run by the University of Puerto Rico. Though it is not shown on the chart, a channel has been dredged privately to accommodate the 72-foot ketch *Isoletta*, drawing nine feet. Since entering here would be difficult without the help of a local pilot, a more practical anchorage is offered by Puerto Real just south of Punta Ostiones. This is an excellent harbor. The only hazard that must be avoided in entering is the shoal southwestward from Punta

Carenero, extending further than the chart shows. Inside is a small pier that is used by the local fishermen and where gasoline, diesel, water, and ice can be taken on board in short order. Feel your way in to the dock; it will carry five or six feet right alongside. Once you have fueled up or what have you, move on; local fishermen are frequently given to moonlighting as thieves.

Boqueron
(C&GS 920, 901, 932)

The next bay to the south, the conditions here are generally good—and I am speaking of the people as well. The reef at the mouth of the harbor breaks the swell in all weathers. Jack Shepard, veteran skipper of Puerto Rican waters, reports that a boat can be left here at anchor for days on end without fear of pilferage or vandalism. Boqueron may be entered with equal facility either to the north or south of Bajo Enmedio reef. The southern entrance is buoyed and the wider and deeper of the two. The northern entrance is sufficiently deep and can be eyeballed in good light. If tacking inside, favor the middle of the channel as the bottom shoals along the north and south sides of the bay. On the northeast corner of the bay is a small-boat dock. Yachts will be seen alongside Boqueron Yacht Club. Fuel, ice, and water may be obtained by shoal-draft boats drawing less than four feet. Anchor in front of town between the small dock and the cottages on the beach south of the dock. Do not go inboard of the line of mooring buoys. There is no water there.

The lagoon behind the beach can be explored in a dinghy. Here, as in so many of the more secluded anchorages on Puerto Rico, clamming, fishing, and birding among the mangroves are rewarding pursuits. The lagoon is a perfect hurricane hole. Its entrance is not properly shown on the chart as it has recently been dredged to ten feet and the channel

marked. Kept here are several power boats from the University of Puerto Rico. Their captain, Mr. German Acusta, is a valuable person to acquaint yourself with; he knows every inch of the west coast of the island, in addition to being an avid fisherman and skin diver. Boqueron is a resort area with restaurants and air-conditioned cottages at reasonable rates. The specialty of the area is the "ostione," a small, sweet-tasting oyster that is beyond compare. The town is rightly considered the most convenient spot from which to hire a car for visits to the towns of Mayaguez, Cabo Rojo, San German, Maricao, and Sabana Grande. With the aid of a road map and a full tank of gas, a rewarding day's outing can be had, sampling Puerto Rican town life and countryside.

South of Boqueron there are no all-weather anchorages, but in settled weather one can enjoyably daysail down the coast and find some good beaches. There is a particularly good one at El Combate south of Punta Moja Casabe where chart 901 shows a road to the shore. Bahia Salinas is not a good anchorage, although the large salt factory there makes for a convenient landmark. On the south side of the bay is a restaurant which many claim to be in itself worth the sail down from Boqueron. The name of the restaurant is Agua Al Cuello, meaning "water up to the neck," which gives some idea of the shoal situation. Anchor off and row ashore. The restaurant is in a small house off by itself at the southern end of the bight. It serves the crispest, tastiest "tostones" to be found in the Caribbean. This is a green plantain smashed into thin cakes and fried till crisp. They are absolutely delicious and understandably renowned.

Reference to the chart of the west coast of Puerto Rico will show the shoaling tendency of this entire shore. The combination of the currents running north to south and the periodic activity of the ground swell tends to move the sand around a good deal. Sand bars and shoals are likely to extend much farther to the west from the points of land than the chart indicates. Don't be put off by this, but be cautious, keep the leadline or depth sounder working, and post a sharp lookout. Only the careless will run aground.

Islands off the West Coast of Puerto Rico

Between the Dominican Republic and the west coast of Puerto Rico are two islands owned by Puerto Rico that should be mentioned, one very briefly:

Isla Desecheo
(C&GS 920, 901)

A pinnacle rock rising 700 feet out of the sea. There is no anchorage off the island and no dinghy landing; in other words, there is no possibility of getting ashore.

Mona Island
(C&GS 920, 901)

An oval island roughly six miles in diameter and flat, Mona is composed largely of limestone, with countless caves. The north and east coasts are lined with high, white cliffs over 150 feet high, making landings from the sea quite impractical. The best anchorages are found off the low land on the south and west coasts. Playa Pajaros is the best anchorage during the winter and during settled summer weather. In a stiff blow the entrance can become very difficult, if not downright dangerous. This spot is adequate for use by yachts of no more than 40 feet with a maximum draft of 6 feet. To make entrance to Playa de Pajaros when coming from the east, head for the lighthouse at Cabo Este, running southwest along the coast off the barrier reef until you spot a large white streak on the cliff resembling an exclamation mark without the period. The

marking has been made by the Coast Guard to designate the entrance and it is the only such mark on the cliff. Bring your vessel abeam of it, make about a 90° turn, and sail roughly 315 magnetic directly toward the mark. As soon as you spot a diamond-shaped wooden post on the beach, align yourself with the range made by it and the mark on the cliff. Abide the range closely as there are coral heads on both sides of this channel. Having established the range, do not sail a compass course as the current and sea will be setting you to the southwest at an appreciable rate. The channel is narrow, one that should be attempted only when the sun is high and never in rough seas. Keep a lookout. Once across the main body of reef, turn sharply toward the small pier on shore. Watch the rock off the starboard corner of the reef, round up, and anchor according to your draft. If no boats have arrived before you, you can tie up to the mooring. This is securely attached to some 40 feet of heavy chain, and the chain to a large engine block. You can also tie up to the four-foot square concrete slab with a heavy, metal ring in its center. This has been put there by the Coast Guard for the work boats that used to make runs between Mona and Puerto Rico. When you want to leave, it is simply a matter of slipping the line from the ring and off you go. This is an extraordinarily beautiful spot and highly praised as an overnight anchorage by yachtsmen bound east from the Bahamas to Puerto Rico.

The water here is crystal clear over white sand. A narrow beach runs along the shore. Nearby there are a few wooden buildings belonging to the Coast Guard.

Behind the dock is a road leading to the lighthouse two miles away. If you want to make the trip to the lighthouse, leave early in the morning, as by mid-morning the sun can become oppressively hot. The view from the lighthouse over Mona Passage and the rest

of the island is splendid. Mona Island is nothing short of a spelunker's paradise. There are said to be so many caves that you can work your way underground from one side of the island to the other. The island supports a varied wild life including iguanas up to five feet long, hundreds of wild goats, and wild boars with huge, white tusks. And at certain times of the year the island supports large populations of doves that have flown over from Hispaniola.

When leaving Playa de Pajaros, stay on the range. Put a lookout forward to watch for coral heads and another on the cabin top facing aft and giving hand signals to the helmsman to hold him on the range. If the sea begins to build up and to break across the entrance, do not attempt to leave under any circumstances. Rather, double up your line and wait for the weather to moderate. It may get uncomfortable inside the reef but it won't be dangerous.

On the south coast of Mona a good anchorage can be had for boats drawing no more than three feet at Playa del Uvero. The approach through the reef must be eyeballed. The south coast is quite beautiful with woodlands stretching all the way down to the beaches.

On the west coast, Sardinera is primarily a summer anchorage. It is frequently untenable during northerly winter weather. The range to guide you into the anchorage will not be apparent until you near the reef. From there you will be able to spot some concrete houses, a partially destroyed pier, and the entrance through the reef which is marked by two rocks, one on each side. The entrance is deep, but the anchorage itself will carry no more than six feet. The bottom is hard sand over a rock slab. If the sea begins to make up, get out right away since an anchor will not hold against the surge. Ashore are four small concrete houses and a partially destroyed dock.

No services are available. A picturesque, lonely spot.

In departing Mona Island for the Puerto Rican mainland, your objective should be to avoid the heavy going in Mona Passage. The wind usually begins to blow by nine or ten in the morning, picking up as the day progresses and reaching its peak about 1700. The best time to depart is late in the afternoon as the wind is abating, motoring or sailing across in less trying conditions. Mona Channel has a deservedly bad reputation. Boats bound east for Puerto Rico will be dead against the wind. The current flows northwest through this passage at a rate alternately reenforced and diminished by the tide. Puerto Rican yachtsmen recommend holding south of the rhumb line since the current will usually cast you northward at a rate greater than the half knot listed on the chart. Puerto Rico may be approached across this Passage at night, as the west coast is well lit. As long as the ground swell is not running, it is feasible to anchor anywhere along the southwest corner and to wait until dawn before making a final approach.

South Coast of Puerto Rico

As you work east along the south coast of Puerto Rico, the winds can be played to considerable advantage. In periods of moderate or light trade wind—at night especially—the wind close inshore is just about due north. As morning approaches, it begins to swing toward the east and into southeast in the afternoon. A boat beating eastward should favor the coast line and exploit these wind shifts for all they are worth. A short tack offshore should be followed by a longer one inshore. Once you are headed by easterly winds offshore, tack in. The same holds true of the north shore: long offshore tacks do not pay. The offshore waters are beset by the westerly current and building seas, and these should be avoided.

Cabo Rojo
(C&GS 920, 901)

At the southwest corner of the island. Judging from the chart, the cove east of the light appears to be excellent. However, I have been told that it is not at all good and should be avoided. The same holds true of Bahia Sucia. Proceeding eastward from Cabo Rojo, care must be taken. The yellow bluffs east of Punta Molina should be read as a danger signal. Just before the place where they end and the mangrove begins is a group of houses known as La Pitahaya. These are almost due north of the western end of Arrecife Margarita. ("Arrecife" is "reef" in Spanish.) Here you must decide on which side you will leave the reef. The outside route is the safer but rougher. Inside, though the water will be calm, you must proceed with the greatest caution. I advise motor-sailing with just the main up, following the blue, deep water. If you are looking for a challenge, it is possible to beat to windward in short tacks between the inner and outer reefs, but make sure the sun is high. Anywhere along the way you can anchor behind the reef and enjoy diving and snorkeling.

East of Arrecife Margarita is one of the most intriguing areas of exploration along the coast of Puerto Rico. A glance at the chart of this entire area will give some idea of its delights. This is the area that is not covered by detail charts. C&GS 901 is the only available chart, and its scale of 1:100,000 is too small to permit close coastwise navigation. Until new charts are forthcoming, put a lookout aloft and proceed cautiously in a favorable light. The regions around Parguera are well worth a look around, and west of Isla Magueyes is a new oceanographic station. The reef can be entered through any number of passages. The westernmost of these is Pasaje de Margarita—perfectly acceptable for an experienced reef pilot. Once inside the reef, stay in the deep, blue water, working your way to the east behind Cayo Enrique where complete shelter can be found. You will be about one mile offshore. From here you can do your own exploring by dinghy or else you can go ashore and hire a local pilot.

An easier entrance to this area is through Pasa del Medio, standing northeastward and entering the inner region between Cayos Enrique and Caracoles. Anchor behind either cay. To gain entrance from the east, enter between Turrumote Island and Arrecife Enmedio. Care must be taken through here as there are various shoal patches to look out for. Once clear of Turrumote, stand in between Cayo Enrique and Cayo Caracoles. It is certainly possible to work one's way the ten miles or so eastward beyond the bay between Punta Montalva and Cayo Don Luis and then to penetrate the reef to seaward, having gained several miles of easting in dead calm waters.

Phosphorescent Bay
(C&GS 920, 901)

This is the bay northeast of Isla Matei—seven feet of water over a mud bottom. It is considered one of the most brilliant phosphorescent bays in this hemisphere, second only to the Gulf of Santa Fe on the coast of Venezuela.

Bahia de Guanica
(C&GS 920, 929)

Easily entered through the buoyed channel. The lighthouse on the cliff on the eastern side of the entrance is visible eight miles. The wreck shown on the chart has been removed. There is no need to worry about the cable across the entrance. Though no clearances are marked on the chart, there is a full 150 feet underneath. Stand due north beyond the commercial pier, keeping your leadline or depth sounder working all the while as the bottom is muddy and not clear enough to eyeball. As soon as the bottom starts shoaling, anchor in nine or ten feet. On a mud bottom it is best to use a heavy plow on chain—certainly more effective than a light Danforth. The shoal water extends well offshore of Playa de Guanica. Do not venture into the northwest arm of the bay as this is the commercial sector.

A dinghy can be taken ashore to the north end of the harbor and from there a taxi will take you up into town where supplies may be bought. If you walk the half mile to the hill east of the harbor, you will find an abandoned fort in excellent repair. It commands an impressive view of the area. Bring your camera. Guanica holds a place in American history as the location of the first landing of American troops in the Spanish-American War.

As you are coming into Guanica Harbor, you'll see a reef on your starboard side. Coarse, gold sand has accumulated to form a small islet. It is safe to pass between this reef and the shore, favoring the reef side. Work your way in until you see Punta San Jacinto. The point divides the area in two. On the western bight is a lovely beach and the Copa Marina Hotel, and to the east are some weekend cottages and several mangrove islands. This is an excellent spot to anchor while exploring the offshore reef in the dinghy. If you really want to go it alone, proceed east from Punta San Jacinto inside Cayos de Cana Gorda. Some skill will be required here, but if you work your way east of Cayos de Cana Gorda, you can anchor bow and stern in a narrow deep-water channel off the beach northwest of Punta Criollo. Slip on a pair of sneakers and comb the reef or dive for shells.

From Guanica to Ponce there is very little to interest the visiting yachtsmen. Guayanilla insults the day with an oil refinery, spewing petrochemical wastes into the sea and larding the air with a godawful stench. At night, the burn-off illuminates a wide area which, viewed from the south on a clear night, appears as a beautiful—if somewhat ghastly—landmark 30 or 40 miles away. The harbor is well charted by C&GS 928 and its channel clearly buoyed. If an emergency so required, it could be safely entered by day or night.

Ponce
(C&GS 920, 902, 927)

The entrance is uncomplicated. Avoid the commercial harbor; instead, move to the Yacht Club in the basin east of Cayo Gato. Anchor off in 30 feet of water, using plenty of line. The bottom is soft mud. If entering, hoist your "Q" flag and row ashore. The club will be happy to notify Customs for you. Space permitting, they will arrange a berth for you alongside. More often than not it will be too crowded, and you will do best to anchor off and conduct your affairs by dinghy. The Yacht Club has a slipway, fuel, ice, water, and taxis into town.

Isla Caja de Muertos
(C&GS 920, 902, 927)

Seven miles southeast of Ponce, this is a popular weekend spot for members of the Ponce Yacht Club. It was formerly owned by the Wirshing family; the late Tito Wirshing was the generous host of some of the most spectacular yachting parties ever to shake the Islands. He claimed never to understand how those giant Americans could collapse into such wet rags after a few hours of rum punch. The ability of Puerto Ricans to consume the island rums in unlimited quantities with no apparent effect is a wonder to behold. I can only prescribe a hearty meal of milk and cream cheese to anyone on his way to a Puerto Rican outing. Isla Caja de Muertos (Coffin Island) has been presented to the Ponce Yacht Club as a tribute to the irrepressible Tito Wirshing, prominent yachtsman and bon vivant.

On the lee side of the island near the smaller of the two promontories is an old pier where one can tie a stern line, anchoring the bow in deep water. Others prefer to anchor northeast of the other hill, which is calm so long as the wind is not piping out of the northeast. A path leads up to the lighthouse and to a commanding view of the south coast.

Cayo Berberia
(C&GS 920, 902, 926)

In settled conditions a good anchorage can be found west of the cay off the mangrove-lined beach. The reef on the eastern shore is prime for shelling and diving.

Playa Santa Isabel
(C&GS 920, 902, 926)

A new dock and restaurant, The Aquarium, has been established here. Except in settled conditions this is not a particularly good anchorage, but some of the shoal-draft boats that really know the area squeeze in behind the mangroves east of the jetty, anchoring in four or five feet of water for a perfect shelter in all weathers.

If conditions are right, one can pass between Punta Petrona and Cayos Cabezazos, staying slightly north of midway between the two. There is a straight stretch of channel— about seven feet deep—with shoal on either side. Inside Cayos Cabezazos is a narrow, deep-water channel; since there are no ranges, strict eyeball procedures must be followed here. The channel is roughly U-shaped, running southeast, east, and then northeast.

Bahia de Rincon
(C&GS 920, 902, 909)

There are several reefs through here. This is a good place for a daytime anchorage and for swimming and snorkeling in good weather.

Do not spend the night. The best anchorage is northwest of Arrecife Media Luna (Half Moon Reef). The island has an excellent beach with lots of shells.

Salinas
(C&GS 920, 902, 909)

A first-rate anchorage—one of the best on the coast. It is only a short hop by taxi to the supermarket. The entrance to Salinas is between Cayo Mata and Punta Arenas; stay midway between the point and the island. Eyeball your way all the way up to the head of the harbor, anchoring in nine feet of water with Punta Salinas bearing about southwest. The bottom is soft mud. There are two restaurants ashore. Alongside the dock you can obtain fuel, ice, and fresh water. Ease on in; it doesn't matter if you touch bottom, as it is soft mud and will do no harm. Boats of seven-foot draft or more should come stern to. Lesser drafts can lie alongside.

Salinas is a convenient spot to rest up before the beat eastward. Proceeding east from here in the morning in good light, one can either stay inside the reef, tacking through calm water and departing through Boca del Inferno, which, though not buoyed, is easily spotted when the sun is high. Or else one can head further east to an anchorage behind Punta Pozuelo and be completely alone, before heading out through Boca del Inferno.

Central Aguirre
(C&GS 920, 902, 909)

No particular reason to put into this harbor. It is the home of one of the principal sugar factories and singularly unattractive.

Las Mareas
(C&GS 920, 902)

This, too, should be avoided, as it is exclusively an oil port and of no use to the yachtsman except in an emergency.

Puerto Patillas
(C&GS 920, 902)

A good spot for shallow drafts. The shoal extends west from Punta Viento further than it appears on the chart. Also, there is a little more water behind the reef than the chart shows. Feel your way in and anchor in six feet of water off the red clay wall. There is six feet close to shore in front of and east of the red clay wall. A good restaurant may be found on the dock. Gas and water can be had alongside.

Punta Tuna
(C&GS 904, 924)

Despite its receptive appearance, there is no anchorage behind this point. In fact, there are no good anchorages for yachts along the entire southeast coast of Puerto Rico. The current sets very strongly to the southwest, and you will simply have to slug it out. Do not try to pass between Arrecife Sargent and the coast; it's too risky.

Puerto Yabucoa
(C&GS 904, 918)

A commercial port only. Pass it by. Further north at Punta Guayanes, the Sea Pines Resort group is planning a big hotel and marina complex. The marina should be open for business by November 1974. This is the same group that built the Sea Pines Resort in Georgia with great success some years ago.

Cayo Santiago
(C&GS 904, 917, 923)

Not particularly good except in settled weather. Half a mile off Humacao, it does offer some respite as you work east.

Puerto de Naguabo
(C&GS 904, 917, 923)

Best in the northeast corner, though not a particularly good anchorage, the swell usually coming in from the southeast. Good local restaurants. East of Puerto de Naguabo a small yacht harbor is in the process of construction.

Bahia Lima
(C&GS 904, 917, 923)

West of Point Lima, it is a fair anchorage sheltered from northeast winds. The land to the east is low, guaranteeing cool breezes.

Ensenada Honda
(C&GS 904, 917, 922)

Northeast of Point Lima and locally called "Rosie Roads"—actually Roosevelt Roads—this is the location of a U.S. Navy Base. As such, it is well charted and buoyed, except that buoy "C" has been moved from the northeast corner of the harbor, where it appears on the chart, to a location further northeast very close to shore. It should be left to starboard when entering. Once passed, alter course to north magnetic and feel your way in carefully as the water is not clear. The day beacons to starboard mark the shoal spots. Head north-northeast to the Navy yacht club in the northernmost corner of the harbor. Although a U.S. Navy Base is officially not open to yachts, the government is usually hospitable and has been very helpful to yachts in distress.

The east coast of Puerto Rico and Vieques Sound is not quite as bad as it may appear from the chart. It is well buoyed, and with the aid of chart C&GS 917 and some careful piloting, the area should present no undue difficulties. Standing north toward Isla Pineros, the local shoal-draft yachts use Passage Medio Mundo. Lead line and eyeball all the way. Off the northwest corner of Isla Pineros, east of the northwest point and between the point and the reef, is a good anchorage when the wind is east or south of east. Pineros will be to the south of you and the reef to the east. There is a good beach ashore. The passage between

PUERTO RICO

Cabeza de Pero and Pineros may be used by boats of up to seven-foot draft. North of Puerto Medio Mundo, the bays are to be avoided. Also, Isla de Ramos is a private island, and visitors are not particularly welcome.

Isla Marina
(C&GS 904, 917, 921)

Playa de Fajardo is a port of entry for the east coast of Puerto Rico and best avoided. Instead, anchor at Isla Marina. If you want to get over to Fajardo for shopping or a meal, take the launch from the dock. Ed Tuma, the manager of the commercial operation, has spent most of his life in the Caribbean and knows the area intimately. He runs an efficient yard and is always most helpful to visiting yachtsmen. It is not difficult to approach the island from the south, as long as the sun is high. The water is usually quite calm.

Marina Puerto Chico
(C&GS 904, 917, 921)

North of Playa Sardinera. Fuel, water, and electricity are available. Incidentally, in navigating the northeast coast of Puerto Rico, the hotel marked on the chart west of Punta Gorda is a landmark that can be seen practically anywhere in Vieques Sound.

Las Croabas
(C&GS 904, 917, 921)

A well known Puerto Rican fishing village. In past years the harbor was filled with small fishing sloops, like those found formerly in Tortola. They are a disappearing breed, pretty to look at, so enjoy them while you can.

The north coast of Puerto Rico offers but one practicable harbor to the cruising yachtsman—San Juan. Otherwise the north coast is to be avoided. The Atlantic swell often comes rolling in out of deep waters and runs up on the steep incline of the Puerto Rican shelf, making the offshore region rough and unpredictable. The only possible stop west of San Juan is Arecibo—feasible only when the ground swell is down and the wind not too far around to the north. I can't imagine planning a visit to Arecibo—it is not very attractive—but it is a spot to keep in mind for an emergency. Feel your way in, and tuck into the northeast corner where you should be able to find at least a moderate degree of shelter.

San Juan
(C&GS 920, 903, 908)

This major port presents no difficulties for the average yacht. Rather, it is the large steamers that have trouble when the ground swell is up. These ships, of course, have the right of way in the channel entrance, so give them room to maneuver. As one enters, the old forts on Punta Del Morro will be clearly visible. Stand on southeastwards to La Puntilla, turning to the east to follow San Antonio Channel. You will find Club Nautico at the east end of San Antonio Channel, and this is an excellent place to stop. Customs can be contacted through the Club; fuel, electricity, and fresh water are available alongside. There are a number of major shipyards in the harbor where repairs can be made, if you don't mind keeping company with large commercial vessels.

CHAPTER 7

Passage Islands

C&GS 904, 913, 914, 915, 917, 921, 940

The numerous islands and cays between Puerto Rico and St. Thomas are collectively known as the Passage Islands. The two largest of these are Vieques and Culebra. Unfortunately, the U.S. government has set aside a considerable part of both for naval exercises. As marked on the charts, areas of water are also restricted during these exercises. The Puerto Ricans have been pressing hard to repossess the land from Uncle Sam, and I wish them luck. Until they succeed, the entire southeast coast of Vieques and the north coast of Culebra are closed to visiting yachtsmen. The times when the various ranges are in use are regularly listed on the Notice to Mariners, or else you can check a day or so in advance by calling Navy Control on the radio.

I stumbled across one of these ranges a few years back when I was navigating a 45-foot ketch, *Antilles,* north from St. Thomas. We had set out from Charlotte Amalie in the early morning with a booming trade that crawled around to NNE. We were soaring along, doing 35 miles per four-hour watch. By afternoon we were running along the north coast of Puerto Rico, when the helmsman reported that we were being chased by a Coast Guard cutter. I refused to believe him and didn't even bother to look up from my book. He swore it was true, and added that this figment of his imagination was now pointing a gun at us. I turned around and, sure enough, there was a cutter chasing us about a quarter-mile off. I had seen her before in Puerto Rico. She was built in the '20s and was now based in San Juan. Though 140 feet long, even with a clean bottom and a following wind she couldn't do better than 12 knots. Since we were doing close to nine, she was having a rough time catching us. Finally, after a long stern chase, she pulled alongside. We received the curt instruction over the bullhorn that we contact her over R/T. The following dialogue ensued:

Coast Guard: This is the Captain speaking. Do you realize you are in the middle of a firing range, that you are interfering with the operations of the United States Coast Guard?

Antilles: No.

Coast Guard: Please clear the area immediately.

Antilles: Certainly. What course would you have us steer?

Coast Guard: 000.

Antilles: Begging your pardon, Captain, but this vessel is a sailing ship. With the wind as it is, we can't steer 000.

Coast Guard: (pause) Well, then steer . . . (various courses mentioned, all in the direction we were coming from).

Antilles: Captain, if, as you say, we are right in the middle of the range, no matter which direction we steer, we will be clearing the area, and since the course we are now on will give us the most speed, let us continue as we are.

Coast Guard: (grudging tones) All right, but make it snappy.

Isabel Segunda
(C&GS 904, 940, 917)

When approaching Vieques from the east, it will be necessary to gain entrance to Puerto Rican waters at Isabel Segunda. The town harbor is a good anchorage when the wind is in the southeast. The combination of a northerly wind and ground swell will make it uncomfortable, however. The anchorage is off the small pier between Punta Mulas and the commercial pier. Isabel Segunda is a typical Puerto Rican town with a few small hotels, innumerable bars catering to U.S. servicemen, and an old fort on the hill. This fort was one of the last built by the Spanish in the New World. Not unlike hardware in the modern arms race, the fort, once completed, was declared obsolete and was soon abandoned. Fuel and water are obtainable, there is a good supermarket ashore, the ferry to Fajardo arrives twice a day, and there is a post office and telephones. A word of warning—don't leave the boat unattended; teen-agers will swarm aboard the minute you leave.

If proceeding westward from Isabel Segunda, you should either follow the buoyed channel or wait until the sun is directly overhead and proceed with careful eyeball monitoring. There are numerous shoals and coral heads just under the surface. Also the shoals extending northward from Punta Arenas are more shallow than the chart shows. Do not try to make it across the bar. Go outside the buoy marking the northern end of the shoal.

South of Punta Arenas is a beautiful white sand beach. The anchorage there is good in most weathers, the main exception being when a north swell hooks around the point. If the anchorage gets rolly, I would advise moving south of Punta Boca Quebrada. Feel your way in, as the bottom shoals very rapidly. A Puerto Rican yachtsman told me of an anchorage for a six-foot draft southeast of Mount Pirata inside the reef. Real skill will be called for here.

Puerto Real
(C&GS 917, 940)

Ten feet can be carried into this anchorage, although the chart incorrectly shows a one-fathom bar north of Cayo Real. Again, this is a case of carefully wending your way inside. This is an all-weather anchorage, sheltered from all but a stiff westerly blow. There is a small dock on the north side of the harbor. A local landmark, called the Frenchman's House, may be visited by taxi, hired car, or on foot.

Ensenada Sun Bay
(C&GS 917, 940)

This is an excellent anchorage with a long, white-sand beach. But deserted it is not; despite the fact that it is extremely popular I am told by the Puerto Rican yachtsmen that it never gets overcrowded. The Puerto Rican government maintains clean showers and changing rooms right on the beach—a consideration one would like to see more of.

Puerto Mosquito
(C&GS 917, 940)

I would be wary of spending the night here without a full arsenal of mosquito nets, sprays, and bombs. Besides its acknowledged insect population, there are other noteworthy features to this spot. At night it is brilliantly phosphorescent. Furthermore, if you have a taste for tree oysters, the area abounds with them. Eastward of Puerto Mosquito is U.S. Navy domain and closed to visiting yachts. As a general rule, when exploring the waters around Vieques, it is best to proceed during the day only. The area is laced with shoals, reefs, coral heads, and all those things which can do in any unwary yacht.

La Cordillera and East

Cayo Icacos
(C&GS 917, 921)

This island and the reefs to the east offer fascinating exploring, diving, and fishing, given the right conditions. In the winter with the ground swell up, the area can be a little treacherous, but it is ideal during the summer. Cayo Icacos is a large enough island to provide adequate shelter. When the wind is southeast, anchor in the island's western bay and when it is northeast, anchor hard by the ruined pier on the south side. The island is brush-covered and uninhabited for the most part.

Cayo Lobos
(C&GS 917, 921)

Here a good anchorage can be had in all weather. Tuck in tight behind the island northeast of the ruined pier south of the reef. The approach to this anchorage will be a matter of cautious eyeball navigation. A Bahamian moor will be required, as there is no swinging room at all. At one time a good deal of money was spent in the construction of a hotel here. For some reason the project was abandoned a little short of completion, leaving a virtual ghost town. But it is privately owned, with a caretaker there at all times.

Isla Palominos
(C&GS 917, 921)

Frequented by weekending Puerto Rican yachtsmen, this anchorage must be approached during the daytime only, as due west of the island's highest land are two coral peaks surrounded by deep water. They rise to within three to five feet of the surface. The best way in is at the northwestern end of the island at Punta Aguila. Eyeball your way southeastward staying close to the shoal water. You will be safe, as the water drops off quite steeply

through here. Continue south until the dock bears roughly east. Anchor to a Bahamian moor between the dock and the shoal to the west. The island will most likely be deserted during the week. The island is privately owned by the Bachman family; the caretaker will be happy to show you around if asked. Little Palominitos is a few hundred yards south of Palominos and has a good sheltered anchorage on its west side. Again, there is no swinging room and a Bahamian moor will be required. This is a fine spot to get away from it all during the week and a good shelter during normal trade-wind weather.

Cayo de Luis Pena
(C&GS 904, 914, 915)

Easily spotted at night by a white-over-red light which is at the top of the island and which is not shown on the chart. An anchorage can be had due west of the peak, the bottom dropping off very steeply. Anchor bow and stern or on Bahamian moor. Good shelter in all normal weather. On the north side of this island there is another anchorage which is strictly an eyeball proposition. This is a cove inside the reefs on the northwest side of the small island east of Punta Rociada. The axis of the channel entrance is roughly southeast in ten feet of water shoaling to six inside. Feel your way in and anchor Bahamian-style or bow-and-stern with the stern anchor in deep water and the bow anchor on the beach. There is a third anchorage in this area which should only be used in the summer when the wind is light. This is on the southeast of Cayo de Luis Pena. The deep water may be seen between the reefs, shoaling inside. Bahamian moor.

Culebra

Isla de Culebra
(C&GS 904, 913, 914, 915)

The major island midway between Puerto

65

PASSAGE ISLANDS

Rico and St. Thomas offers the cruising yachtsmen a wealth of anchorages, exploring grounds, and a few of the best hurricane holes in the northern islands. The area is well covered by the charts, and with their help you should have little trouble negotiating this area. Unlike Vieques, where the Navy has roosted on the best parts of the island, the superior south coast of Culebra is open to all. If you are leaving your boat on the mainland, you can reach Culebra by air or ferryboat from Puerto Rico. The round-trip air fare from San Juan is $16. The ferry makes one round-trip daily between Fajardo and Culebra. The fare is $2.25; a one-way trip, which includes a stop at Vieques, takes about two hours.

Ensenada Honda
(C&GS 913)

Culebra's main harbor, well lit and well buoyed. Use the charts and follow the buoys. The town of Dewey, noted on the chart as Culebra, is in the northwest corner of the harbor. This is no more than a peaceful Puerto Rican village with a few small guest cottages, a gas station, and general store. Fuel and, with some difficulty, water are available. Cars are available for rent. There is a dinghy passage in the cut between Ensenada Honda and Bahia de Sardinas. The cut provides easy access to the reef on the southwestern side of Culebra. The island is dry, even in the wet season. When the wind is down, the anchorages behind the reefs on the eastern side will be cool and bugless, since what little wind there may be will come in off the ocean.

From the main channel into Ensenada Honda swing to the west behind the reef to port. Head for Point Colorado (NO 914, 915)

until you are well inside the reef; then head southwards and anchor Bahamian moor or bow-and-stern with one anchor on the reef and the other on Culebra. From here a dinghy can be taken to Dakity. This is probably the safest way to enter Dakity, though it can be done directly from seaward when the wind is light. From seaward, if it is blowing hard, you will be running dead before it, and with the seas building up between the reefs, this roller coaster ride might be a little more than you bargained for.

From Ensenada Honda take the marked channel toward Cayo Norte. Not too far along the channel you'll spot a reef on your port side and apparently deep water behind the reef. This is Las Pelas, a very good anchorage and very popular with local yachtsmen. Eyeball the entrance. Leave the small island with a house to port and pass behind it. Sandy bottom, good holding ground, and absolute dead calm. No rocks or reefs once you negotiate the entrance, but strictly a noontime operation for the uninitiated.

Puerto de Manglar
(C&GS 913, 914)

In the southeast corner of this harbor is an excellent all-weather anchorage. The entrance to Puerto Manglar is straightforward. Simply sail downwind midway between the two reefs where there is plenty of water. Once inside, turn west around the port hand reef. Hug the edge of the reef until you spot the gap between the exposed coral bank and the offshore reef. Come sharply to port, steering approximately 190 magnetic across the shoal. Stand southward into Bahia de Almodovar and anchor in 20 feet of water with a breaking reef

to windward. What could be better? Even in the heaviest weather, this anchorage will be smooth, and you will be completely off by yourself. Excellent snorkeling, fishing, and shelling.

The bays on the northern side of Isla de Culebra are exposed to the northern swell. The Navy controls most of this area, though from the look of things they may be clearing out soon.

Culebrita
(C&GS 914)

A protected anchorage may be found in the cove on its northwestern side. Because it is somewhat exposed to the north wind and swell, the best anchorage is off the ruined docks due west of the lighthouse. The bottom comes up very steeply here, requiring a double-anchor arrangement. This area is certainly best when the wind is east to southeast. To the west of Culebrita is a shoal called Tierra Media, which is great fishing. Row the dinghy out and anchor. Dinner will be forthcoming.

Proceeding eastward of Culebrita into Virgin Passage, be prepared for some steep, high seas, especially during a flood tide when the current opposes the tide. This is one of those times that comes to all sailors when one must pull his head in and slog it out. However difficult the return, I consider a jaunt through the Passage Islands time well spent, especially for one who has become familiar with the Virgins and is casting about for new cruising grounds. The people are friendly, the food inexpensive, the anchorages quiet and secluded. Give my regards to the U.S. Navy.

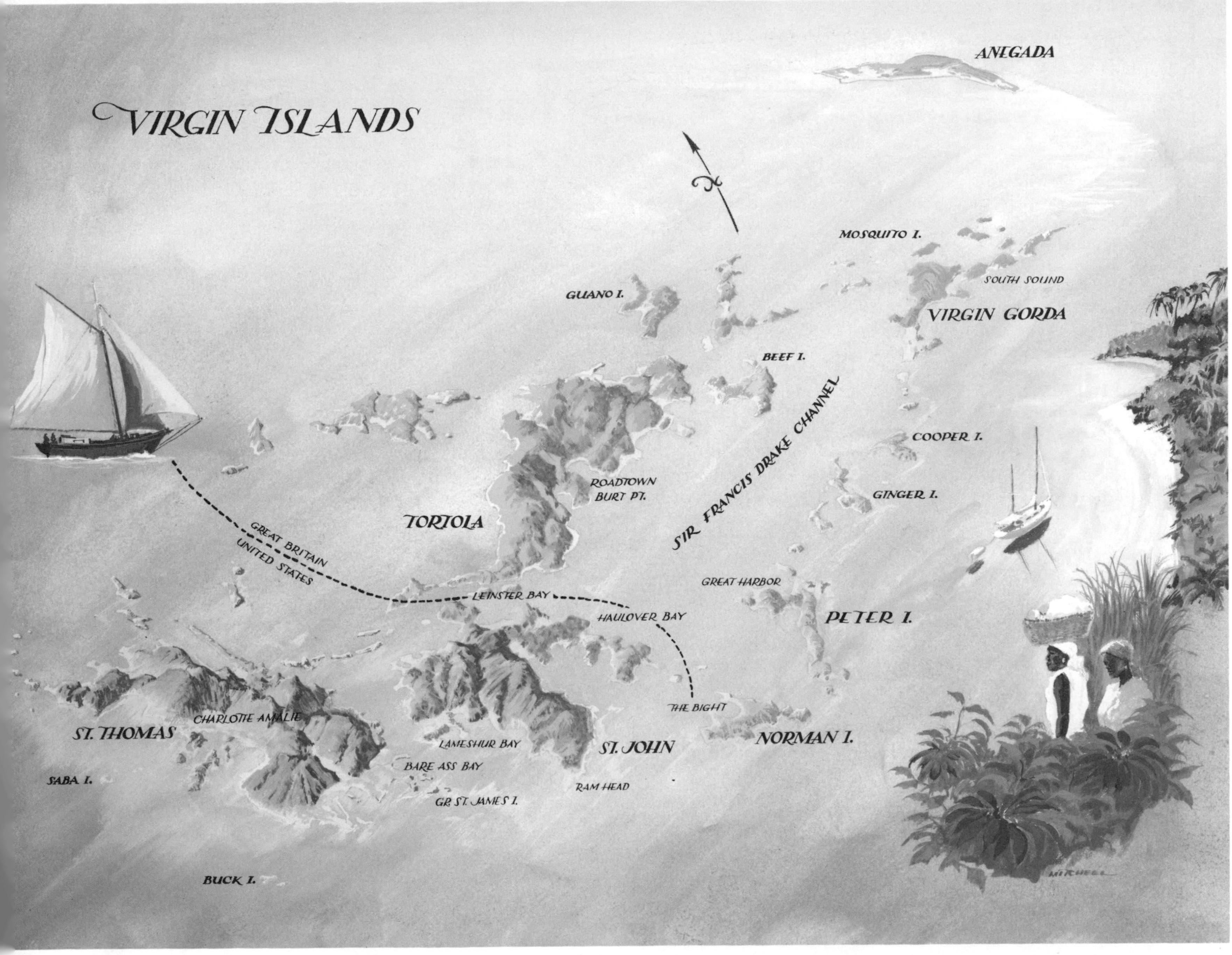

VIRGIN ISLANDS

ANEGADA

MOSQUITO I.

SOUTH SOUND

GUANO I.

VIRGIN GORDA

BEEF I.

COOPER I.

SIR FRANCIS DRAKE CHANNEL

ROADTOWN
BURT PT.

GINGER I.

TORTOLA

GREAT BRITAIN

UNITED STATES

LEINSTER BAY

HAULOVER BAY

GREAT HARBOR

PETER I.

ST. THOMAS

CHARLOTTE AMALIE

LAMESHUR BAY

ST. JOHN

THE BIGHT

NORMAN I.

SABA I.

BARE ASS BAY

RAM HEAD

GR. ST. JAMES I.

BUCK I.

CHAPTER 8

U.S. Virgin Islands

C&GS 905, 933, 935, 937, 938; BA 2183, 2452, 485

Thirty-five miles due east of Puerto Rico lies the group of islands commonly referred to as "The Virgins." They stretch from St. Thomas in the west to Virgin Gorda in the east, and include St. Croix, which, though 35 miles to the south, is nevertheless considered part of the chain. Except for St. Croix, all the islands are close to one another, offering excellent shelter from the ocean swell. But owing to the fact that the islands lie on the same axis as the trades, these waters are not so protected that they break the force of the ever-present easterlies. While you may have to do a little more windward work than you might like—and you should keep this in mind when selecting a boat to cruise on in the Virgins— the islands are so close together as to afford numerous anchorages, all within easy sailing distance of one another. With many calm, comfortable anchorages and a steady, cooling breeze, it is hard to find better cruising grounds than the U.S. and British Virgin Islands.

The three major U.S. Virgins—St. Thomas, St. Croix, and St. John—are each discussed separately herein. These are one of the few remaining U.S. possessions. They are part of the U.S. and pay whopping federal taxes. The total revenue, matched by subsidies from Washington, should produce an island paradise but it doesn't; why it doesn't is a book in itself.

There happens to be such a book. For those who want the background of how the Virgin Islands changed from sleepy, pleasant little islands where everyone knew each other to the present strife-torn state they are today, I highly recommend Edward A. O'Neill's *Rape of the Virgin Islands*. Unless something happens to make the American Virgins change radically for the better, my advice to yachtsmen is to arrive, take care of your business, repairs, stores, and depart for a secluded anchorage where no one will disturb you. Don't go wandering around town unless you are in a fair-sized group or are a karate specialist who wishes to test his skill in combat conditions. This is unfortunate; only a decade or so ago, my late wife and I thought nothing of wandering around town at night or having a drink at a West Indian pub. Six tough men would be necessary to do the same thing today.

The American Virgins are generally more "developed" than the British. By contrast, the latter have retained some of their backwoods, barefoot charm, although they are not so undeveloped that there isn't a television in most houses and Kodak film in every drugstore.

The trades in the Virgins blow an average of 12 to 15 knots out of the east, but you must be prepared and rigged for a good deal more as often they will pipe up to 20 or 25 and howl for a few weeks. At other times, a front will blow through, attended by heavy squalls and plenty of wind and rain. The only thing to do then is to ride it out in a secure harbor for a day or two with a good book and a deck of cards. During the winter months of December to April the wind will occasionally sneak around to northwest. This is a slow process and easily detected. If it does occur, many of the customarily calm anchorages become lumpy, uncomfortable, and even dangerous. Be forewarned. Toward the end of April, the winds lighten and crawl southward, bringing on what many consider the best cruising weather of the year. A comfortable, full-sail breeze usually remains steady through July. August through October, of course, is the hurricane season with light and variable winds and a good deal of rain and humidity. The best way to proceed at this time is with plenty of stout ground tackle aboard, one ear tuned to the radio, the other ear tuned to local talk and consensus, and both eyes on the weather map.

The temperature varies only slightly. In the summer and fall the high is 90 degrees; in winter, it is 86. But so long as there is a breeze it should never get really hot on board a boat.

The tidal rise and fall in the Virgin Islands is only about 18 inches, but this is not to be scoffed at. In some places—in narrow cuts or around the tips of islands—it can run very fast and significantly affect your course and sailing time. Generally, the tide floods in an easterly direction and ebbs in a westerly direction, so that if you are careful to watch the rise and fall on the shoreline, you can keep on top of the situation. But it is not always so simple. During periods of heavy weather with high winds from the east, the tide has been known to ebb (westerly flow) for as long as 24 hours; and when the weather turns calm again the flow can be eastward for as long as 24 hours. In addition, the many juts and curves of the islands tend to alter the direction of the flow significantly so that careful analysis must be made to predict the strength and direction of the tide at any one given place and point in time.

Buy charts ahead of time; they are difficult to obtain locally. The American charts cover the area barely adequately and it is my recommendation that you purchase several British charts, too. Some guides to the Virgins, and many bare boat charter operators, continually maintain that the only chart one needs to cruise the Virgin Islands is C&GS 905.

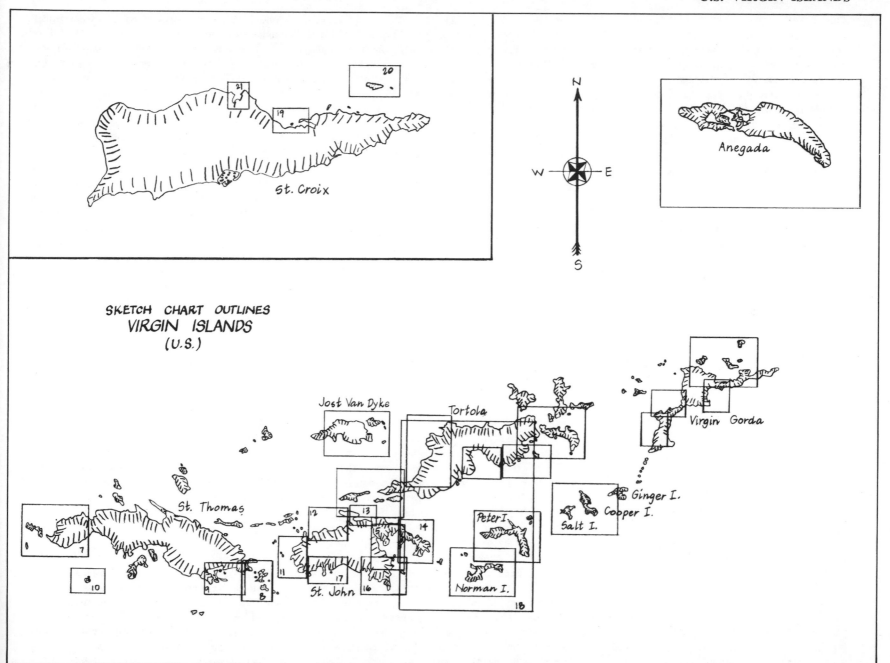

SKETCH CHART OUTLINES
VIRGIN ISLANDS
(U.S.)

St. Croix

Anegada

N
W E
S

Jost Van Dyke

Tortola

Virgin Gorda

St. Thomas

Ginger I.
Cooper I.
Salt I.

Peter I.

St. John

Norman I.

This, I feel, is the height of foolishness, as the scale is such that no details are shown for many of the favorite anchorages. Buy all the available charts of the Virgin Islands (see Charts chapter for detailed list).

The United States purchased the Virgin Islands from the Danes in 1917, mainly as a defense measure; the Navy needed another coaling port, and, more important, the Navy was afraid that the Germans might buy them. The islands continued for many years strictly as a naval base, with the commanding officer of the base in charge of the whole operation.

Eventually they came under civil government, first with an appointed governor, and, just lately, with an elected governor. Now the U.S. Virgin Islands are frequently cited in the UN as an example of United States' colonialism. Although it is not officially stated, I am sure that the Interior Department would just as soon give the islands back to the Danes or grant them their independence. This would certainly save the U.S. government a tremendous amount of time, money, and embarrassment.

When all is said and done, the Virgin Islands nonetheless provide some of the world's best sailing—if you store ship and clear out to a secluded anchorage. Then you should have no trouble. As Lord Nelson said, "Ships and men rot in port."

St. Thomas

The harbor at Charlotte Amalie, St. Thomas, has been popular with sailors for hundreds of years. Originally pirates of various nationalities used it as an R-and-R port. Finally the Danes came in and established a modicum of control. I say "modicum" as they did not chase the pirates out, just asked that they behave a little better and leave Danish ships alone. The Danes made St. Thomas a free port. This meant that privateers (and the fine line between privateers and pirates is a fine

one indeed) and warships of all nations could come into the well-guarded harbor and sell off their legally and often illegally acquired goods and ships.

St. Thomas reached its heyday in the years between 1790 and 1815. In these years there was almost continual warfare in both the Old and the New World, much of it at sea; prizes and booty needed to be disposed of, and St. Thomas soon became a key market in this operation. Comparing old accounts of the port in those years, it is interesting to follow the growth of business and the development of the population. The total population of St. Thomas was barely 15,000 in 1780, while by 1815 it was pushing 45,000, a startling fact when it is noted that its entire population in 1955 was again at 15,000. With trade the basis of its economy, the percentage of whites, free coloreds, and slaves was strikingly different from the other islands of the Lesser Antilles, which were strictly agricultural. It is true that sugar was grown on the steep hillsides of St. Thomas—witness the old ruins and windmill on Fortuna Hill—but the number of windmills does not begin to compare with the number of windmills on St. Croix where the slave population was considerable.

During the long peace after the Napoleonic Wars, St. Thomas languished, and the Danes grew eager to sell the island to the U.S. In 1867, a number of powerful senators were well bribed to assure passage through Congress of a bill purchasing the island. However, the newspapers got wind of it, and the situation soon became so hot that many senators felt that voting for the purchase would be to admit having taken a bribe, and the bill failed to pass.

During the next 50 years the island became a major coaling and repair port but the income so earned was not enough to support the island. Life was grim. Coal was loaded by women carrying hundred-pound basket-loads on their heads; the wage was a penny per bag.

Conditions have improved to an extent under American dominance.

The town of Charlotte Amalie—almost universally called St. Thomas—is really quite fantastic. It is a free port frequented by as many as five cruise ships in a single day. The shops are dazzling; don't let your wife get near them or she will spend in a few hours more than you could spend on a two weeks' charter. There are some beautiful old Danish mansions on the hillsides and some picturesque old churches, including one of the oldest Jewish synagogues in the Western Hemisphere; quaint little West Indian houses are flanked by gardens reached by a narrow alley or by a long, steep flight of steps. Regrettably, Charlotte Amalie must also claim some of the worst slums in the Caribbean.

Anything can be purchased in Charlotte Amalie; as a rule luxuries are cheap and essentials expensive. A few odd things may confuse the visitor. Though a U.S. island, cars drive on the left. After the U.S. purchased the island, right-hand drive was instituted for a time. It was not entirely successful. Frequently, a farmer, returning home in his cart in the wee small hours of the morning, would fall asleep, his donkey would cross over to the habitual left-hand side. When a car came along at full tilt, the collision would usually kill the donkey, wreck the car, and disturb the sleep of the farmer. It was decided that it would be easier to instruct motorists to drive on the left than to retrain donkeys to walk on the right.

St. Thomas Harbor
(C&GS 933)

St. Thomas Harbor is one of the safest harbors in the entire Lesser Antilles. In all weathers it is completely sheltered. For many years it remained remarkably free of commercial shipping. What few ships there were, moored along the West Indian dock, leaving the rest of the harbor clear for yachts. More recently the harbor has been dredged to accommodate the influx of tourist ships, which anchor in the middle, restricting yacht anchorage to only a few areas. These yacht sectors are labelled on the chart as "C" and "E" and located on Long Bay, northeast of the buoys that mark the ships' turning basin and north of a line drawn due west from Fredericksburg Point.

The harbor is one of the few that is safe to enter at night. If you are unfamiliar with the area, use the main entrance only. A night approach through Gregerie Channel can lead to difficulties on Porpoise Rocks or, west of Lindberg Bay, on the rocks off Red Point. Through the main entrance, it is simply a matter of following the range lights on Berg Hill until the Rupert Rocks Buoy lies abeam. Anchor off town and wait till morning to clear Customs. Incorrectly described on the 1972 chart, the range lights are green rather than red, the usual color for a range light. I suppose too many sailors climbed the hillside looking for the red-light district! If you are coming from the States or Puerto Rico and have no need to clear Customs, head for the anchorage in Long Bay. But be careful; this has become a very crowded anchorage.

There is another good anchorage close under Bluebeard's Hill Hotel, with the hill bearing roughly due east magnetic.

When entering through the main channel during the day, you can see all the dangers clearly. To save yourself the beat to windward, you can pass inside Rupert Rocks and round up around the west side of West Indian Dock and stand on into the bay.

Similarly, if you are entering on the west side, all the hazards can be seen by day, including an unlit buoy on the western end of Lindbergh Bay which marks the shoal area north of Red Point. Once in West Gregerie Channel, be sure to pass *north* of the red flasher at Sandy Point. There is a very exten-

sive shoal area between it and Water Island, and passing to the wrong side of this buoy has brought more than a few boats to grief.

Haulover Cut has no more than nine feet of water and even that may be pushing it. Any boat with more than an eight-foot draft should steer clear. Close-winded boats can sail through this passage, but they should enter on the eastern side practically kissing the reef. Just when you feel that you have completely lost the wind, it will hook around the point of Hassel Island and you'll be home free.

Pacquereau Bay
(C&GS 933)

On the eastern side of the main entrance to the harbor, this is excellent in all weathers. It has two beautiful white-sand beaches, a sand bottom, and it is seldom used by yachts. Although you are a longish dinghy ride from town, the total peacefulness of the area more than makes up for your effort.

Long Bay
(C&GS 933)

The traditional anchorage for cruising yachts since well before World War II, when the present Yacht Haven Dock was no more than a sunken barge. For some time to come the dockage situation at Yacht Haven will be somewhat unpredictable with many of the docks under repair.

Let's hope that the new management of Yacht Haven will have brought some order out of the present chaos. Prior to May, 1973, the toilet and shower facilities, the electricity, and the water supply ranked with the worst in the world. Much of the potentially good dock space is taken up by old hulks that are barely afloat and which should have been sunk long ago. It does, however, deserve one true word of praise. Right on the dock is the only coin-operated laundromat in the Lesser Antilles. Here you can do your own laundry cheaply,

while everywhere else in the Islands your laundry bills may well become your largest single expense.

Freddie's Bar at Yacht Haven is an institution. Opening at 8:00 AM, filled by 10:00, and closing in the early evening, it is certainly the cheapest drinking in the entire Lesser Antilles. There you meet them all: the proper yachtsman, the rugged salt, the blowhard, the local businessmen, and natives—an assortment of every island type.

Unless yours is a large yacht with chain rodes, I would not recommend lying stern-to anywhere on the waterfront, except to clear Customs; the Customs House is located at the western end of the wharf east of the Antilles Air Boats Ramp. Put in with plenty of fenders, clear, and get out! Don't wait around for your rode to be cut by some hot-shot launch jockey.

Fredericksberg
(C&GS 933)

Between Fredericksberg Point and King's Wharf, this area is being used more as the years go by. It is not a good spot when the wind goes around to the south, but during the winter when the wind is in the north, it is excellent. Feel your way in carefully and do not lie too close to shore in case the wind shifts.

Cay Bay
(C&GS 933)

Also called Mud Hole. Incidentally, the British chart (BA 2183) incorrectly lists Ballast Island as visible; it has been safely underwater for more than 20 years. The real advantage of Cay Bay is that it has everything you need right there—a restaurant (The Quarterdeck), ice, water, electricity, a market nearby, a bar, and taxi service to town. Watching the sailboats dodge the aircraft landing in the Bay is good for a few laughs. Dick Avery's marina and boatyard, called The Boathouse, boasts what is probably the only monorail hauling system in the world. Dick Avery established his charter boat and marina business in the late '50s. He occupied a small boathouse in a tiny wooden shack at the edge of Haulover Cut. As he puts it, the operation "just done and growed" but it has remained "The Boathouse" ever since. It is not the best place to lie overnight. The wind blows across a mile of open harbor and builds up quite a chop, which is increased by the wakes of the many launches on Haulover Cut.

West Gregerie Channel
(C&GS 933)

Crown Bay anchorage is not particularly good due to the wash from launches. Some boats like to anchor behind Sandy Point. It is not particularly accessible to town facilities, but you are off by yourself in peace and quiet and it is well protected in all conditions. Shoal draft boats can anchor behind some abandoned freighters which provide good breakwaters.

Krum Bay
(C&GS 933)

An overhead power cable crossing obstructs Krum Bay. The clearance is less than that marked on the chart, and this has been the cause of more than a few accidents. Best to avoid the Bay entirely; it is noisy and foul. Leave the power company to its own devices.

Lindbergh Bay
(C&GS 933)

A good anchorage in normal weather, it should be avoided if the wind is in the south or if there is a heavy ground swell from the north which somehow manages to hook around the west end of St. Thomas and sweep into the area. Also heavy weather from the east-southeast can work up a terrific swell that has accounted for the loss of many boats, including my own *Iolaire*. In 1958 she was declared a total loss on the beach in front of the Carib-

bean Beach Hotel. I salvaged the wreckage, went on to rebuild her, and she is still going strong at age 68.

Druif Bay
(C&GS 933)

Locally known as Honeymoon Bay. On Water Island, it is an excellent anchorage in normal weather. Do not anchor in the deep water in the mouth of the bay, as you may find your anchor wrapped in the remains of a World War II torpedo net. Work your way well inside where you will find good holding on a sand bottom. It is likely to be crowded on the weekend, but during the week there is seldom more than a boat or two. There is a discouraging $5.00 landing charge. Per person! How long this bilking operation will remain in effect is uncertain. A short walk along the road brings one to the ferry at Providence Point which runs over to the sub-base on the mainland, where one can find a taxi to town.

Flamingo Bay
(C&GS 933)

On Water Island, this anchorage is rarely used by yachts, although a dredging job has opened up the inner lagoon, which would seem to forecast a new marina for the area.

Brewers Bay
(C&GS 905)

Good in normal weather. The white-sand beach is deserted during the week and inundated on weekends. Few yachts anchor here. Perhaps they shy away from the aircraft homing in on Harry S. Truman Airport.

Mermaids Chair
(C&GS 905, Sketch Chart 7)

An excellent spot for one boat at a time —and only one—so long as the wind is well to the north, or in calm weather. Anchor in the cove west of Mermaids Chair; there's deep

water close to shore, but no swinging room, so anchor bow and stern. One finds a beautiful sand beach, separated from the ocean by a spit of sand. Cross over and enjoy the surf on Sandy Bay.

West Cay
(C&GS 905, Sketch Chart 7)

There is a fine anchorage in the small bay on the southwestern side of West Cay. Here again, this is only to be undertaken in settled weather or when the wind is well to the north and during the day.

Although the chart does not show water in Big Current Hole, there is at least eight feet, and one can sail or motor through here. From the north, it can be done on a beam reach. Otherwise you will just have to crank up the iron genoa and chug your way through until Little St. Thomas comes abeam.

North Coast of St. Thomas

Sandy Bay
(C&GS 905, Sketch Chart 7)

Totally useless during the winter trades, as the swell hooks around Botany Point. The beach is exposed to northern ground swells. But during the summer in a southeast wind, Sandy Bay provides a good anchorage.

Botany Bay and Stumpy Bay
(C&GS 905, Sketch Chart 7)

The same holds true for these bays, the latter being an especially good spot away from the usual traffic of summer charters.

Santa Maria Bay
(C&GS 905)

Another instance of a summer retreat where one can get away from it all. Few yachts have ever poked their noses in this area. It is not covered by any chart, and good exploring can be had here.

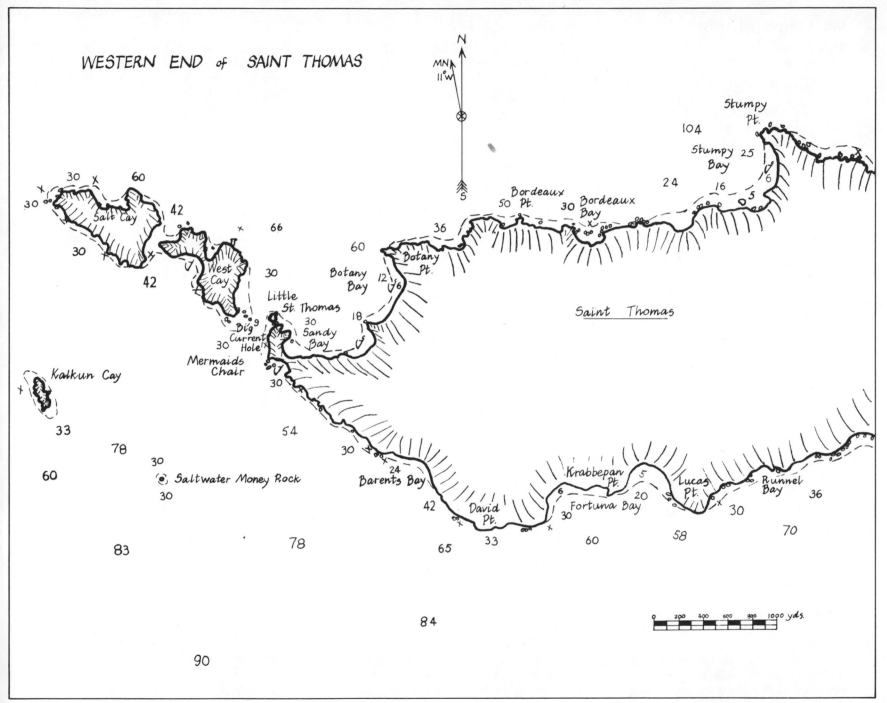

WESTERN END of SAINT THOMAS

N
MN
11°W
S

Stumpy Pt.
104
Stumpy Bay
25
24
16
6
5

Bordeaux Pt.
50
30
Bordeaux Bay

36

60
Botany Pt.

Botany Bay
12
6
18

Saint Thomas

30
60
42

Salt Cay
30
X
60
42
30
66
X
30

West Cay
30

Little St. Thomas
Big Current Hole
Sandy Bay
30

Mermaids Chair

Kalkun Cay
33
78
30
60
30
Saltwater Money Rock

30
54

Barents Bay
24
42
30

David Pt.
33
65

Krabbepan Pt.
5
6
20
Fortuna Bay
30
60

Lucas Pt.
58
30

Runnel Bay
36
70

78
83
84
90

0 200 400 600 800 1000 yds.

SKETCH CHART 7

U.S. VIRGIN ISLANDS

Magens Bay
(C&GS 905)

If you are interested in seeing the north side of St. Thomas, Magens Bay makes for a good stop to break a trip, provided there is no ground swell from the north. It is sheltered from all normal weather but completely open to the northwest, so keep an eye out for a changing sea. The best anchorage is at the head of the bay in the easternmost corner in six fathoms of water. Be careful of the shoal at the head. It is easily seen if the sun is high. Ornen Rock at the mouth is extremely difficult to spot. To be sure of clearing it, favor Picara Point when making your approach.

From Picara Point to Red Hook Bay there is not much in the way of secure anchorages. The whole stretch is open to the prevailing winds, and little protection is afforded by St. John, which is three to five miles across open water.

Red Hook Bay
(C&GS 938)

Lying north of Cabrita Point, this has become virtually the second port of St. Thomas. Years ago it was a sleepy little bay with no more than a small dock and do-it-yourself boatyard. The rest was all mangroves, mosquitos, peace, and solitude. Now it is a bustling harbor replete with expanding dock and marina facilities, ferry boats shuttling to St. John and back, fishing boats making early morning departures to the banks further north, and the familiar panoply of visiting charter yachts. Fuel, ice, and electricity are available here, as is taxi service to the Fort Milner Shopping Center. Harms Lagoon Marina is located on the north side of the bay. However, it is not the most attractive or comfortable anchorage in the Antilles. Its bottom is muddy, the water unclear, and it is open to the continual chop from the east. I suppose its popularity should be ascribed to its convenient location on the passage between St. Thomas and St. John.

Great Bay
(C&GS 938, Sketch Chart 8)

When passing from Red Hook to Great Bay, give a wide berth to Cabrita Point. Jumping Rock is well offshore and difficult to spot. It has been struck by many yachts over the years. Great Bay itself is no more than a large exposed anchorage off Bluebeard Beach Hotel. I would put no faith in it at all.

Cowpet Bay
(C&GS 938, Sketch Chart 8)

Beyond Current Cut and also known as Secret Harbor, this is the home of the Virgin Island Yacht Club and a fine spot it is for small-boat racing. But as a permanent anchorage it is not all that good. It is on a lee shore that is only partially protected by Great St. James. The bottom is sand and good holding, but if a rode chafes through, you will be on the beach in no time at all. Maybe this is why the Yacht Club discourages yachts from anchoring overnight. Just the same, the club welcomes yachtsmen from other clubs during the day.

Nazareth Bay
(C&GS 938, Sketch Chart 9)

If you wish to spend the night in the area and have found that Christmas Cove at Great St. James is too crowded, sail around the corner to Nazareth Bay where there is a beach north of Beverhout Point that is excellent in normal weathers, as long as the wind is not south of east-southeast.

Brenner Bay
(C&GS 938, Sketch Chart 9)

East of Long Point lies the Jersey Bay area with a low mangrove-covered lagoon to the west and Brenner Bay to the north. The entrance is east of Cas Cay. The only danger in Jersey Bay is a 12-foot spot, but there is no reason for a boat large enough to strike this shoal to be in the bay in the first place. West of Rotto Cay is a marked channel leading off to the northwest and turning east-northeast as it nears Bovoni Cay. This channel leads into Brenner Bay, the home of a number of small powerboat yards and of the Antilles Yacht Corporation with its Travel Lift and large storage area. The channel is supposedly four-and-a-half feet deep, but boats drawing only four feet keep running aground. Just the same, I have also seen boats that draw six feet at the Yacht Corp. dock; how they got there I don't know. Since Tom Kelly of the Yacht Corp. swears he can get six feet into Brenner Bay, my advice is to anchor behind Coculus Rock, go ashore in the dinghy, find Kelly and bet him a case of beer that he can't get your boat into Brenner Bay.

The lagoon to the west of Brenner Bay used to be full of fish, birds, and oysters. But as each year goes by more and more of the mangrove is bulldozed away, leaving nothing but raw, scarred earth in preparation for yet another real estate development.

Small Islands near St. Thomas

Little Saba
(BA 2452, C&GS 905, Sketch Chart 10)

Provides an excellent anchorage in all normal conditions. It is seldom used by other yachts and is a great place to start up or wind down a cruise out of St. Thomas Harbor. Anchor off the low land at the north end of the island. Make your approach when the sun is high so that the detached rocks at the west end of Turtledove Cay can be seen.

Buck and Capella Islands
(C&GS 938)

An excellent anchorage is the westernmost

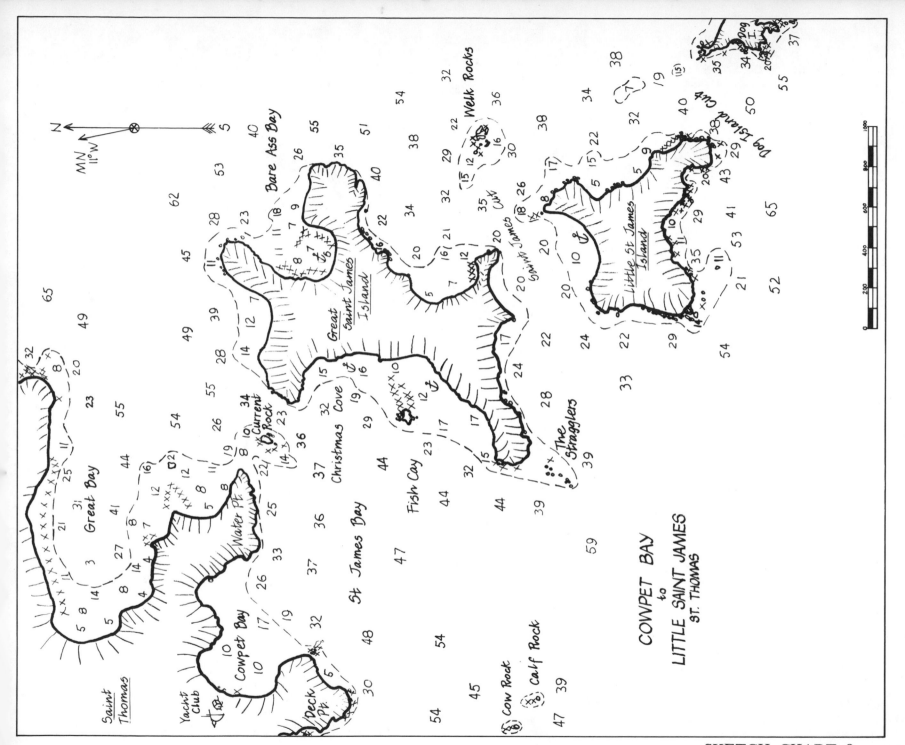

COWPET BAY
to
LITTLE SAINT JAMES
ST. THOMAS

SKETCH CHART 8

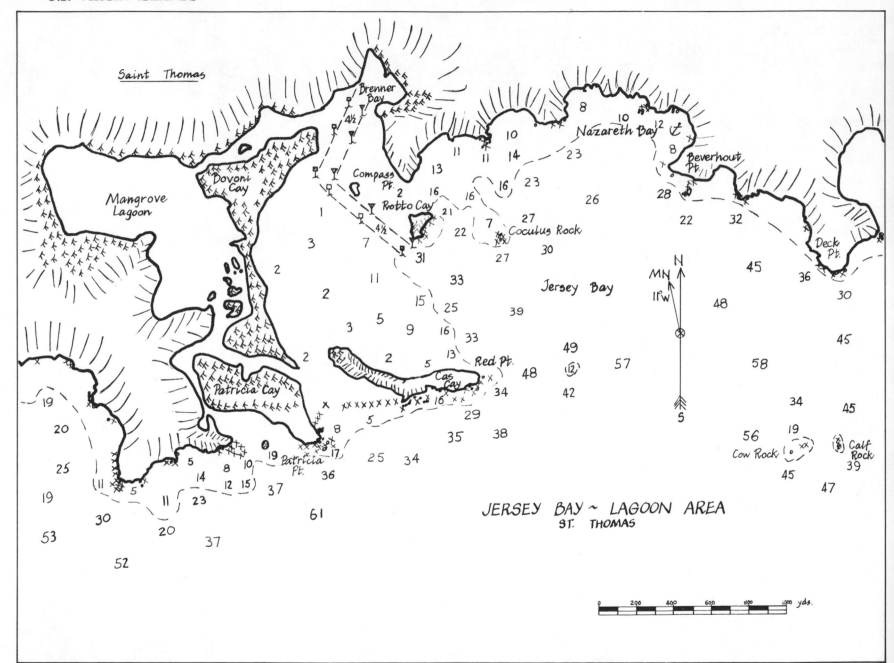

Saint Thomas

Brenner Bay

Mangrove Lagoon

Dovoni Cay

Compass Pt.

Rotto Cay

Coculus Rock

Nazareth Bay

Beverhout Pt.

Deck Pt.

Jersey Bay

Patricia Cay

Cas Cay

Red Pt.

Patricia Pt.

Cow Rock

Calf Rock

JERSEY BAY ~ LAGOON AREA
ST. THOMAS

0   200   400   600   800   1000 yds.

SKETCH CHART 9

cove of the western island. The cove is steep-to and there is a full eight feet at the end of the ruined jetty. It has a rocky bottom, so don't anchor too far out, as you may have to dive your anchor out. If you must anchor off, rig a tripping line to the anchor crown. This is an excellent spot in all normal trade-wind weather. In late summer and fall it is not recommended as it is wide open to the west. Another anchorage on the northwestern side of Buck is good for daytime use only. In the winter the swells sweep around the point. But in the summer, when the wind starts swinging south, this is a pleasant spot. Use the southeast corner of the cove for anchoring.

Great St. James
(C&GS 938, Sketch Chart 8)

Of the two anchorages here, the best-known and most popular is Christmas Cove. There is no problem whatever in entering as long as you take care to avoid the reef extending northeastward from Fish Cay. There is ten feet of water between the reef and the shore towards Great St. James. Elsewhere the cove is plenty deep north or south of Fish Cay. North of the Cay a Bahamian moor is best as you are likely to catch some of the current from the cut. This is an all-weather anchorage. Swimming and snorkeling are always good. On weekends it is likely to be crowded, since it is the first and last stop for large numbers of bare boat charters from St. Thomas Harbor.

Bare Ass Bay
(C&GS 938, Sketch Chart 8)

An excellent anchorage for shallow drafts of five feet or less. The name does justice to its seclusion. If someone is there before you, stay clear, as there is not enough room inside for two boats. Except when the wind is hard from the northeast, it is an excellent anchorage, but it should not be entered unless you are familiar with eyeball reef navigation. Enter from the northeast, favoring the western side of the bay; round up behind the reef and anchor to a Bahamian moor. It is a constricted bay with no more than six feet of water, but well worth seeking out if you can be the first one there.

Little St. James
(C&GS 938, Sketch Chart 8)

The chart does not post soundings in the passage between the two St. Jameses. There is, in fact, ample water (over 15 feet) and excellent snorkeling and diving, but beware of the strong current. The bottom used to be chocked with lobsters, which have been pretty well fished out of late. There is a beautiful white-sand beach on the north side of St. James. Anchor in close but be sure to use a Bahamian moor since there is a strong reversing current that could very well cause you to drag or swing ashore.

Grass, Mingo, Congo, and Lovango Cays
(BA 2452, C&GS 938)

These afford really no overnight anchorages at all. Grass has some little coves on the north side of the island, but these are only

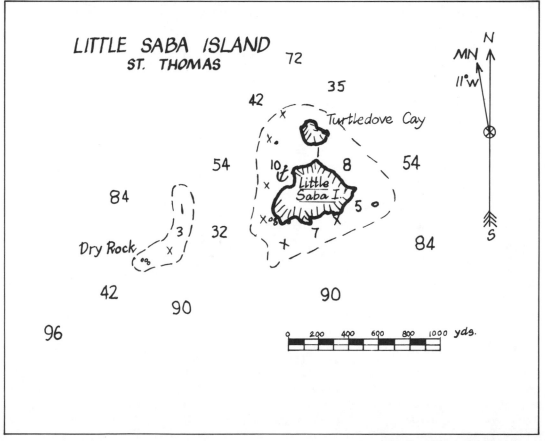

visitable by outboard in the summer months. The coves have tiny secluded beaches flanked by 100-foot rock cliffs.

Boats bound for St. Thomas Harbor from the north are likely to use Middle Passage. What is shown as an awash rock on the British chart and as a submerged rock on the American chart is in fact a submerged rock under five feet of water which extends well to the west of the position marked on the chart—beware! The passage between Mingo and Grass Cay cannot be used; you can use the passage between Mingo and Lovango, but there is a very strong tide, much stronger than one finds in Current Hole.

The anchorage between Lovango and Congo Cays off the small sand beach on Lovango is good in settled conditions with the wind in the southeast. Anchor by chain as the bottom is stone and loose coral.

Little Hans Lollik and Great Hans Lollik
(BA 2452, C&GS 905)

For the past 15 years a great deal of ink has been spilled on the subject of a big real estate development on these two islands. I tend to discount this sort of Caribbean rumor until the first hotel graces the skyline. Friends have told me of an anchorage on the west side of the reef that links the two islands. I have never anchored there but I would suspect that it would have a considerable reversing current and require bow and stern anchors. I can't recommend it outside of the summer months when the wind is in the southeast and not heavy. It would be practically useless in the winter.

There is an anchorage on the southeastern side of Great Hans Lollik behind the reef. This is viable only in moderate winds as the reef does not provide adequate protection in heavy weather. Six feet is the most that can be taken inside this reef. Enter from the south favoring the shore, and anchor anywhere inside away

from coral heads. Six feet will clear the sand bottom but the scattered coral heads stick up a couple of feet. The British chart is the better one for this area.

Inner Brass Island
(BA 2452, C&GS 905)

"Real estate development" has been in the works for many years. It's that same old tired song, and I'll believe it when I see it. I advise not going to this island in the winter months because of the surge. At best, it may be worth a lunch stop in the quieter waters west of the island.

There are abandoned pens on Lovango Cay where in days gone by lobsters and turtles were stored. When the pens were filled to capacity, the load was dumped on a boat and sailed full tilt over to St. Thomas before it spoiled.

St. John

The island of St. John lies two miles east of St. Thomas, and is connected by ferry from Red Hook. Pillsbury Sound, between St. Thomas and St. John, can get very rough. With the strong north-running tide, the sea gets up against the wind, producing boxy, nerve-wracking, six-foot seas with six feet between crests.

The island is unlike St. Thomas and St. Croix, as it is almost unpopulated and has remained so for hundreds of years. When the Danes first settled on St. Thomas, many families set up second plantations on St. John to provide employment for younger sons. When it was discovered that St. John was more fertile and wetter than St. Thomas, the island soon prospered. The main town was in Coral Bay, which was fortified by numerous batteries, some of which can be seen today. A second port and small fort were later established in Cruz Bay.

In the middle of the 18th century the

slaves revolted and managed to kill everyone on the island except the few who tried to find refuge at the Durloe Estate at what is now Caneel Bay. Durloe had built his estate house in the form of a miniature fort and mounted a number of cannon right inside the house. With these the slaves were held off. Finally, troops were brought in from St. Thomas and Martinique, and the rebellion was put down. A large number of slaves chose to leap to their death in the sea off Mary Point north of Francis Bay. The locals say that the moaning noise sometimes heard north of Whistling Cay is the spirit of the dead slaves.

Although the slaves were defeated, the island never recovered. Estates were allowed to go to seed, the Danes left, the squatters moved in, and peace and poverty reigned until the early '50s when the Park Department took over. Now the Park Department is busy preserving the island for the North American tourist but this has certainly been hard on the people who have lived there for many years. In many instances families have been dispossessed of their lands; others have been allowed to remain on their land until they died, though their children are forbidden to inherit it.

Besides its rich collection of harbors, St. John provides excellent grounds for exploration on foot or by rented car. The roads being as rough as they are, I would advise hiring a car and driver.

Years ago, you were awakened early in the morning by the crying of peacocks—how anyone came to keep peacocks in Cruz Bay is beyond me. The only night life in those days was a small bar at Galge Point (called Gallows Point by locals). The bar was always a lot of fun, run by Duke Ellington—not the musician, but the one who wrote the Fat Man radio series back in the '40s.

The most interesting attraction on St. John to my mind is the old fort marked "Government House" on the chart. Looking through the fort you can see why the old pirate ships were able to seize the forts in the West Indies, inasmuch as the walls were simply not built high enough.

Cruz Bay
(C&GS 938, Sketch Chart 11)

Cruz Bay is St. John's main port. Some basic supplies—frozen meat, canned goods, bread, etc.—can be picked up here, but it definitely can't be regarded as a place for stocking up a boat. Better to hop a ferry to St. Thomas if you're really in need of provisions. If approaching Cruz Bay from the south, it is possible to sail between Steven Cay and St. John (Range A). However, this passage has numerous rocks in it, and care must be taken. Line up Carval Rock (the rock east of Congo Cay) with the west hill of Jost Van Dyke at 023 or 203 magnetic. Follow the range carefully—more so than your compass, as all too many yacht compasses are inaccurate.

When entering Cruz Bay favor the north shore, which is steep-to; the south shore light on pilings marks the end of the reef. However, bear in mind that the southwestern side of the bay is shoal; keep on favoring the northern half. Do not go alongside the dock, as it is used by ferries; they get precedence, and you get banged up. Moor in the northern half of the bay clear of ferry traffic. I would strongly advise not spending the night here, because the ferries to Red Hook incessantly charge back and forth far into the evening and start right in again early in the morning. Their wakes not only disturb one's sleep, but constitute a threat to your anchor set.

Frank Bay
(C&GS 938, Sketch Chart 11)

In fair weather, a good refuge from the ferry wash in Cruz Bay. But it's choppy in bad weather, and in the winter admits a swell.

Turners Bay
(C&GS 938, Sketch Chart 11)

A good harbor only if the wind is north of east. Sand has been dredged from the bay for fill used elsewhere so there's water, but it's strictly eyeball navigation. If the wind comes south of east, best to move on.

Great Cruz Bay
(C&GS 938, Sketch Chart 11)

This seldom-used spot is actually an excellent anchorage. Dredging has made the bay considerably deeper than the chart shows. Eyeball in, and anchor as close to the head of the bay as your draft permits.

Chocolate Hole
(C&GS 938, Sketch Chart 11)

An excellent anchorage, but not overly attractive. It tends to be hot and airless, and its name is derived from the water's Hershey-brown color. A worse name could have been thought of. But it's one of the better places around for clamming. The bottom is mud, not sand.

Caneel Bay
(C&GS 938, Sketch Chart 11)

North of Cruz Bay, this is another excellent anchorage in normal weather, so long as the ground swell is not rolling in. This factor is not to be taken lightly; at times the swell builds up to the extent that it washes over the beach and literally laps at the ankles of guests in the hotel dining room. The whole area from Caneel Bay north to Hawksnest (sometimes Hogs Nest) is part of the Rockefeller Caneel Bay Plantation. This elegant resort is described as an ideal place for "newlyweds and nearly deads." Night life ashore is virtually nonexistent; the doors are locked and bolted come 10:00.

The Rockefellerian attitude toward yachts is difficult to ascertain. Sometimes they have been known to be very friendly, and at other times have turned an icy shoulder. Perhaps it has to do with the price of Standard Oil on the Exchange.

The hotel here is like any number of other swank establishments in the Islands, and for that reason leaves me cold. However, I am somewhat of a traditionalist and many people may like the well-groomed landscape and sophisticated atmosphere. In the back of the hotel are the partially restored ruins of the old Caneel Estate, once a sugar plantation. Like most ruins, they are well worth exploring. (The plantation used to be armed with guns, and was the one spot in St. John that held out against the slave revolution in 1733.) But a feel for the history of the sugar mill has been partially dampened by the recent addition of a snack bar at the top terrace, which nevertheless provides a striking view of the sweep of the bay and the yachts lying in the area to the northwest.

You can anchor anywhere in the bay but there are several large cruisers which use the dock, so I would advise giving them plenty of room to maneuver. There is a space at the dock where you can tie up your dinghy and the club asks that you use that space rather than pulling up on the beach in the designated swimming area which is marked by buoys (an orange cross in an orange diamond).

Henley Cay
(C&GS 938)

An anchorage can be had off the beach on the south side, but currents sweep around both sides of the cay, making it not too secure. It's mainly academic anyway, since the cay is privately owned and was obviously purchased to get away from people. I have not tested the patience of the owner, as I believe in respecting the rights of privacy. A property owner's frame of mind is tough to predict. I can only suggest that you make inquiries on the mainland.

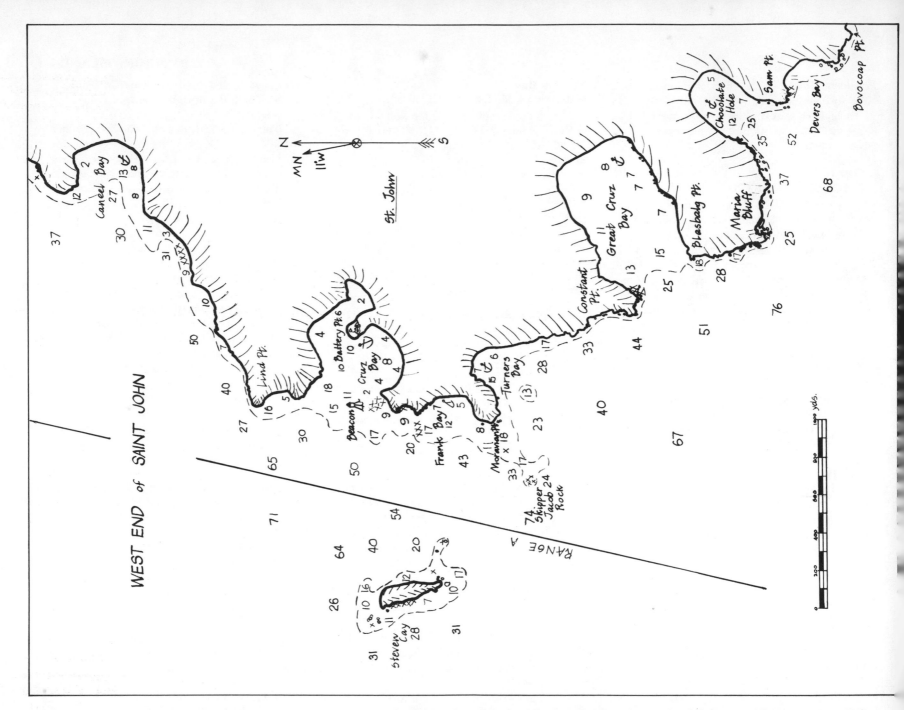

Range A: Carval Rock, east of Congo Cay, in transit with the west hill on Jost Van Dyke clears all dangers between Steven Cay and St. John, 023-203 magnetic.

SKETCH CHART 11

Hawksnest Bay
(C&GS 938, Sketch Chart 12)

Excellent anchorages are to be had off the beach in the southeast corner—when the ground swells are not running. A good place to get away from the crowd at Trunk Bay.

North Coast of St. John

Trunk Bay
(C&GS 938, Sketch Chart 12)

The only hazard in this area is Johnson Reef. The number of boats that have hit it is astounding, but how they manage to do so is mystifying. It is easily seen, is almost always breaking, and is marked by buoys. You can sail either north or south of it. The bay is an excellent daytime anchorage in the lee of Trunk Cay—provided, once again, that the northerly swell is not running. Because of the possibility of this swell making up, do not spend the night there. The beach is quite steep, so you can anchor close inshore. Try to arrive in the morning so you can have your swim and depart before the various tours from St. Thomas arrive and inundate the place. The beach is exceptional and there is good snorkeling. In particular, there is an underwater trail for beginners, complete with signs identifying the coral and fish. Spearfishing is prohibited. On the hill to the east of the beach is a modest lunch counter and a fantastic view.

I for one no longer visit this bay. There are many other less crowded bays around that have not lost their natural charm under the good intentions of the Park Department. But it didn't always used to be cluttered with picnic tables and aluminum outhouses. When the Bulon family owned it, there was only a vast stretch of natural beauty, and the charter skippers who anchored there took pains to keep it that way. Along came the P.D., and one of the first things they did was to buoy the anchorage area such that it was impossible for more than two moderate-sized yachts to fit. The charter skippers promptly declared war on the Park Department and its set of new regulations. One of the most amusing battles (won by the skippers) took place at the anchorage buoys. The skippers discovered that the buoys were held in place with nice new anchors and chains. Within a few days each rig had been replaced with rusty chain and old flywheels. The skippers also took to harassing the officials by facing the underwater signs the wrong way, causing all sorts of confusion. But, of course, the Park Department was there to stay, and so it remains to this day. At least the developers have been kept away.

Cinnamon Bay
(C&GS 938, Sketch Chart 12)

Cinnamon Bay is not as nice as Trunk Bay, which is probably why the Park Department is not so officious here. There are no anchorage buoys, but there are camping facilities ashore. This is a good anchorage in reasonable weather, except with a ground swell coming in from the north. If spending the night you should be on a Bahamian moor to keep from being swung around, should the wind die out and a ground swell come in.

Maho Bay
(C&GS 938, Sketch Chart 12)

A good anchorage in the summer, but uncomfortable in the winter with the swell. There's a nice long sandy beach that can be used by yachtsmen, but the area is private, so stay on the beach and don't go wandering around. The entrance is easy, but the bay is only six or seven feet deep. Boats drawing more can find water in the deep finger of the bay between American Point and Maho Point; watch the color of the water carefully and set bow and stern anchors, as there is no room for deep-draft boats to swing. The holding is good on hard sand.

Francis Bay
(C&GS 938, Sketch Chart 12)

An excellent anchorage in all weathers—the best in northeast St. John. Whistling Cay evidently breaks the ground swell. But be absolutely sure your anchor is well set before going ashore. The bottom drops sharply from seven or eight feet to 50; if your anchor drags off the edge, it won't hold on the backside of the shelf, no matter how much scope you have. Also, since the sand overlays rock and coral, it is essential to doublecheck your anchor; in some places it will bury in a few inches, hit rock, and fail to set. The extra precaution is well worth the effort. There is a good white-sand beach and the swimming is delightful. Snorkeling, however, is rather fruitless, as there is nothing to see on the bottom but more white sand. On the southwest corner of Whistling Cay is an old customs guardhouse from Danish days, placed there to prevent smuggling between the Danish and British islands.

The house overlooking Francis Bay was built many years ago by Mrs. Ethel McCully. As the story goes, she was on her way to Tortola aboard a local sloop which tacked into Francis Bay to avoid the current in the Narrows. Mrs. McCully decided on the spot that this was where she wished to live. The skipper refused to put her ashore, so she dove overside, swam ashore, found the owner of the land, and promptly bought it. She built her house in the early '50s when there was practically no ground transportation on the island. All the materials were sailed to Francis Bay, piled onto the backs of waiting donkeys, and toted up the hill. A book on the subject, *Grandma Raises the Roof* (also called *She Did It With Donkeys*), is of interest.

Whistling Cay
(C&GS 938)

The "whistling" comes from the fact that

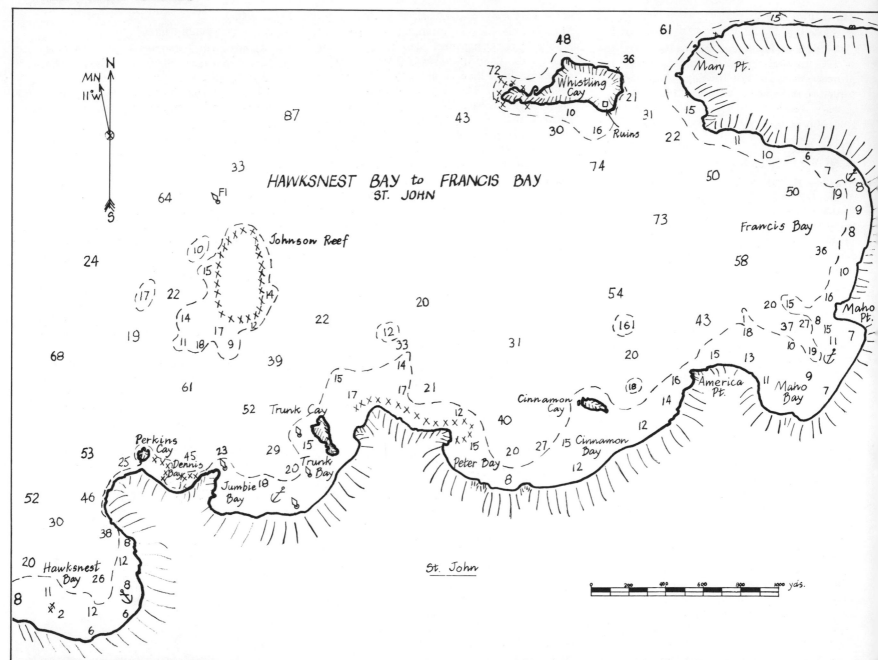

HAWKSNEST BAY to FRANCIS BAY
ST. JOHN

SKETCH CHART 12

if you are sailing downwind close aboard, you can actually hear the wind screeching through the high cliffs on the north side. The locals claim that this is the moaning of rebel slaves drowned below Mary Point. Rather than surrender, the slaves jumped to their death off Mary Point Cliff, sometimes called Bloody Point.

The shore between Francis Bay and Leinster Bay to the east is steep-to all the way. One can short-tack through the Narrows against the foul current, but I strongly advise against it. I prefer going north of Great Thatch Island and back down through Thatch Island Cut when coming from the west (see Sailing Directions, chapter 5).

Leinster Bay
(BA 2452, C&GS 905, Sketch Chart 13)

With its four separate anchoring spots, Leinster Bay is one of the favorites of this coast. The most commonly used anchorage is at the east end of the bay in what is commonly called Watermelon Bay; here there are no dangers whatsoever. Sail right in, anchor close to shore in deep water. The sand bottom is good holding but be careful to avoid the several patches of grass. Trying to get your anchor to hold on grass is well nigh impossible. From this anchorage, a row ashore brings you to the ruins of an old lime tree plantation. On the hill north of the bay is another old ruin, which was at one time used as a school. The view from here is superb.

On the southeast corner of Watermelon Cay there is a fine anchorage. You can practically sail up to the beach, throw an anchor on the sand, and drop a stern anchor to hold you off. The island is completely deserted with a good sand beach, shelling, and snorkeling. It is not too heavily frequented by boat traffic, and you may well have the island all to yourself.

Directly north of the sugar mill in the

middle of the bay, it shoals to six to seven feet. Shoal draft boats can sail in and anchor right on the shoal. The point to the east gives ample shelter from the swell. Great Thatch Island to the north cuts the worst of the ground swell, and the wind sweeping across the water keeps the bugs away. A short dinghy ride will take you to a landing which is below the sugar mill.

At the westernmost edge of Leinster Bay, Mary Creek affords an excellent anchorage, but one that is generally thought too shoal for the average boat. However, a reliable reporter insists that six feet of water can be carried over the middle of the bar at low water. You must

feel your way in. On the other side it deepens to eight or nine feet. The sand is good holding. In the early morning the mangrove to the west is a bird watcher's delight. Clams can be found in the shoals by the mangrove. In the Virgin Islands wherever mangroves are found in mixed mud and sand, clams usually abound. Prior to World War I, clamming was a regular employment in the Virgins. Presently it seems to be monopolized by a few cagey charter skippers.

The wind sweeping Leinster Bay guarantees to make it bug free, but there is not enough fetch to build up a chop; an excellent anchorage in all weathers.

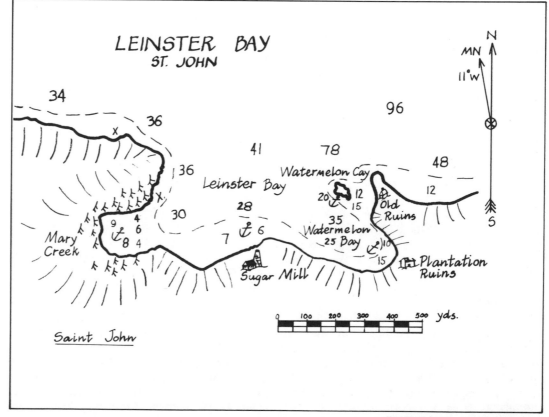

SKETCH CHART 13

U.S. VIRGIN ISLANDS

Haulover Bay
(BA 2452, C&GS 905, Sketch Chart 14)

Three-and-a-half miles east of Francis Bay, it affords an excellent anchorage in the southeast corner off a white-sand beach. Enter midway through the reef; there will be a submerged rock on the port hand as you come in. Anchor as close to shore as your draft will permit, using bow and stern anchors or a Bahamian moor. Some people prefer to drop a stern anchor out and to row a bow anchor ashore and bury it in the sand. In all but a northeast wind the shelter in the corner is superb.

Haulover Bay takes its name from a practice of years gone by when in rough weather the local sloops, not wanting to round the eastern end of St. John, would sail to this bay, anchor, offload the cargo destined for Coral and Round Bays, and haul it across the low land to dinghies waiting in Round Bay. The cargo sloop then continued on to Tortola, Virgin Gorda, or Anegada. There is room for two or three boats in this cove but absolutely no more.

Haulover Bay charts are puzzling in that both the British and the American ones show a rock in the southeast corner of the bay, while Al Forbe's *Cruising Guide to the Virgin Islands* speaks of a tree in 40 feet of water. According to recent reports, the tree is no longer there and an unpublished C&GS survey shows no rock in the southeast corner of the bay. I can only advise that you keep your eyes peeled as you enter.

New Found Bay
(BA 2452, C&GS 905, Sketch Chart 14)

The charts notwithstanding, there are nine feet at the head of the bay. The bay may be identified by an eight-foot-tall pinnacle rock on its south side. The rock is covered with guano and appears white at a distance. The entrance is from the northeast midway be-

tween the reefs. Stand on in and round up, using a Bahamian moor as there is very little swinging room. If a boat is already inside, do not enter, since there is simply not room enough for two. This is no anchorage for a novice—experienced reef-pilots only.

Privateer Bay
(BA 2452, C&GS 905, Sketch Chart 14)

West of Privateer Point is a satisfactory daytime anchorage when the wind is well in the north. There is deep water right up to shore, a mixed sand-and-rock bottom, and a shingle beach. Not the best anchorage in the world but a good spot to get away from it all.

Round Bay
(BA 2452, C&GS 905, Sketch Chart 14)

The 19th century *Sailing Directions to the Caribbean* point up some interesting changes in the Coral and Round Bays area. The leading mark for entering Coral Bay was described as a white-walled fortress on the hill above Moor Point. The town and Governor's House were described as a half-mile inside Moor Point, which would put them up in the northeast corner of Round Bay. This area is now totally overgrown, and I would not be surprised if ruins could be uncovered with a little machete work. Further exploration may be had on the wreck of the *Santa Monica* which is marked by four buoys or right at the two-and-a-half fathom mark on BA 2452.

In the past, the most common anchorage was just west of the southern tip of Moor Point. Here there were a few permanent moorings that could be used; otherwise it was a case of anchoring in 35 feet of water over a sand and grass bottom. A better anchorage is found if you continue north from Moor Point until you come to the Old Cameron, an easily spotted house with a striped roof. Off the house south of the rock there is 15 feet of water over a sand bottom. From this sheltered an-

chorage a dinghy can be taken to the *Santa Monica*.

Haulover Bay South
(BA 2452, C&GS 905, Sketch Chart 14)

The next anchorage west of the Cameron house can be dubbed Haulover Bay South as it has no official name on the chart. It is surrounded by high hills; use a Bahamian moor to keep yourself from swinging every which way in the current. From here it is a short walk to Haulover Bay on the north side of St. John.

Hurricane Hole
(BA 2452, C&GS 905, Sketch Chart 15)

North and west of Turner's Point is Hurricane Hole and the small bays of Bork's Creek, Princess Bay, Otter Creek, and Water Creek. The anchorage in these inlets is apt to be hot, airless, and, during the wet season, quite buggy, but during the hurricane season they do afford a perfect shelter. Where the chart marks White Sand Bay, there is good swimming and snorkeling, although it requires anchoring in about 70 feet of water.

Coral Harbor
(BA 2452, C&GS 905, Sketch Chart 15)

An excellent anchorage. There is a dock and six feet of water at the head of the bay. Oddly enough, the tiny town of Coral Harbor is an official port of entry for the U.S. Virgin Islands. There are a few good sights in the area. The old Moravian Mission is fun to poke around in, and on the eastern side of Battery Point are the remains of the original Danish fort. Some of the old cannons lie below the fort at the water's edge. There is plenty of water in the outer reaches of the harbor. If you anchor with the stone house—on the low spit of land on the north side of the harbor—bearing northeast, you will be in two-and-a-half fathoms of water. Further in to-

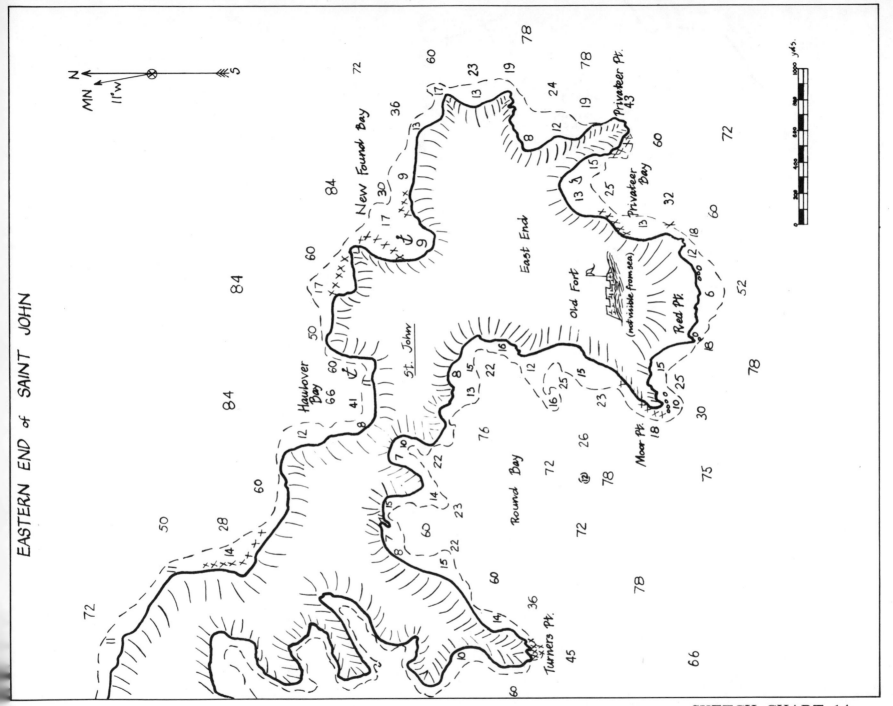

EASTERN END of SAINT JOHN

SKETCH CHART 14

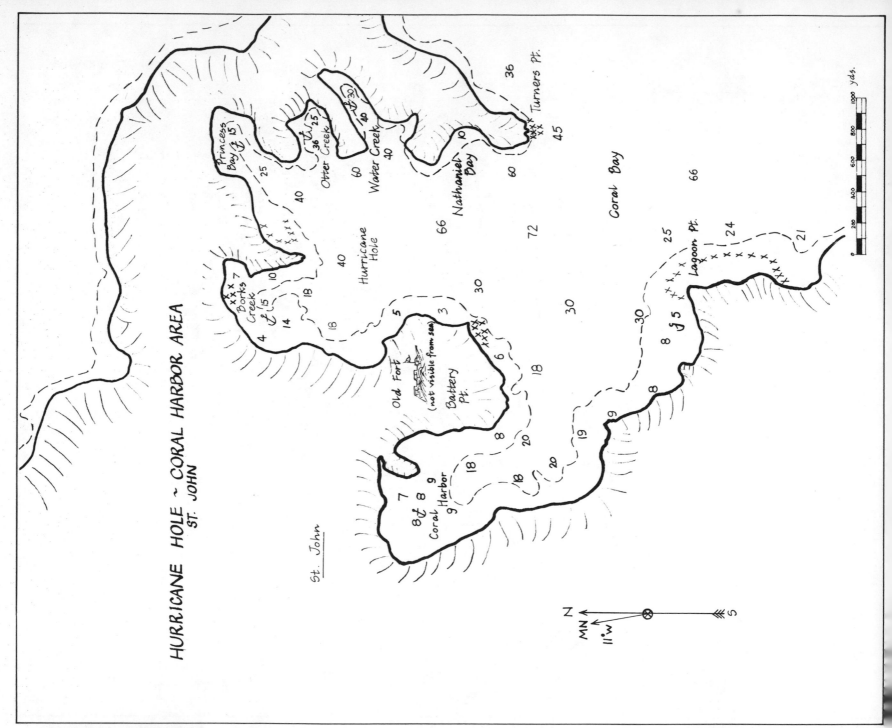

HURRICANE HOLE ~ CORAL HARBOR AREA
ST. JOHN

St. John

Coral Harbor

Old Fort (not visible from sea)
Battery Pt.

Borks Creek

Princess Bay

Otter Creek

Water Creek

Nathaniel Bay

Turners Pt.

Hurricane Hole

Coral Bay

Lagoon Pt.

N
MN
11°W
S

0 200 400 600 800 1000 yds.

SKETCH CHART 15

ward the head, the water shoals rapidly, although with care six feet can be taken right in to the small dock.

Lagoon Anchorage
(BA 2452, C&GS 905, Sketch Chart 15)

Below Coral Harbor just at the mouth of Coral Bay is Lagoon Point. Here the reef projects well out to sea so as to form a small protected basin just behind the point. There is six feet of water over a grass bottom, which is poor holding. The reason I mention this marginal anchorage is that from here it is only a short ride by dinghy to the reef on the windward side of the point where exceptionally good diving and spearfishing can be enjoyed by an experienced diver. Beyond the reef the bottom drops precipitously to 14 fathoms.

Between Lagoon Point and Ram Head to the south there are no other anchorages. When passing south between Leduck Island and the St. John shore, favor the western shore giving a wide berth to Eagle Shoal. The shoal itself is not correctly shown on the government charts. It actually consists of three very narrow pinnacle rocks that are within about four feet of the surface. They are widely separated, two of them some 50 yards apart and the third about 200 yards to the northwest. Spread out like this, they cause no break in the swell and have created havoc for a number of boats heading from Sir Francis Drake Channel to Ram Head. This shoal can be avoided easily if the southeastern end of Flannegan Island is kept in transit to the extreme western end of Peter Island (Range D, Sketch Chart 19). This is an easy range to spot and will safely clear Eagle Shoal.

South Coast of St. John

Beyond Ram Head lies the beautiful but seldom-visited south coast of St. John. There

are nine or ten good anchorages between Ram Head and Bovocoap Point alone—a sum that offers a week's good cruising.

Ram Head Anchorage
(BA 2452, C&GS 905, Sketch Chart 16)

With the wind well in the north, an anchorage can be had anywhere behind Ram Head; anchor very close to shore using a Bahamian moor or bow-and-stern. The bottom is loose rock and drops off very steeply. The beach is shingle and not much for those wanting to bask on white sand.

Salt Pond Bay
(BA 2452, C&GS 905, Sketch Chart 16)

Northwest of Ram Head is the superb anchorage of Salt Pond Bay. It is easily entered and deep enough for all but the largest boat, though somewhat restricted in space. Booby Rock is easily recognized and avoided, since it is 35 feet high and covered with guano. There is a reef at the entrance, with ample water to pass on either side of it. I think it best to leave the reef to starboard and round on up into the bay, carrying a full two fathoms of water to within 100 yards of shore. Deep-draft boats can anchor on a Bahamian moor; shoal-draft on a bow anchor up on the sand, and another from the stern in deep water. Wind sweeps across the low land between Coral Bay and Salt Pond, making the anchorage cool at all times. A short walk ashore will bring you to Salt Pond. During the dry season large salt crystals frequently form around the pond's edge —free rock-salt for the taking. Within the bay the snorkeling is good fun, and more experienced divers will enjoy the deeper water around Booby Rock.

Unnamed Bays
(BA 2452, C&GS 905, Sketch Chart 16)

West of Kittle Point and Salt Pond Bay lie two other excellent harbors, each with deep

water right up to the shore. Again, either a Bahamian moor or bow-and-stern with one anchor ashore will do the trick.

Great Lameshur Bay
(BA 2452, C&GS 905, Sketch Chart 16)

Once the site of the Tektite Project, the government's experiment in long-term undersea existence, all that remains now is a stone dock. The government's loss is the yachtsman's gain: sail in, put a bow line to the dock and a stern anchor to hold you off. This is a reliable anchorage in any but the worst weather.

Little Lameshur Bay
(BA 2452, C&GS 905, Sketch Chart 16)

Yet another good anchorage with deep water right up to the shore. On the starboard hand there are shoals to the head of the bay. The best anchorage is halfway up the bay. Bow anchor ashore; stern anchor out—unless a swell is hooking around the point, in which case it is better to anchor in the axis of the swell. Swimming and snorkeling are delightful in the clear water.

Reef Bay
(BA 2452; C&GS 905, 938;
Sketch Chart 17)

The problem here is that the bay is wide open to the south. The point east of the bay does not hook far enough south, and the southerly swell washes in directly. However, a decent enough anchorage can be had at the head of the bay (referred to on #938 as Genti Bay). Approach with care, as the gap between the reefs is scarcely 150 yards wide. Always anchor to the swell's axis, or your appetite will be rolled out in no time. A beach landing may seem impossible by dinghy due to the breaking of the swell; the Sketch Chart shows a recommended landing area where calm water can be found no matter how rough it gets on the north beach.

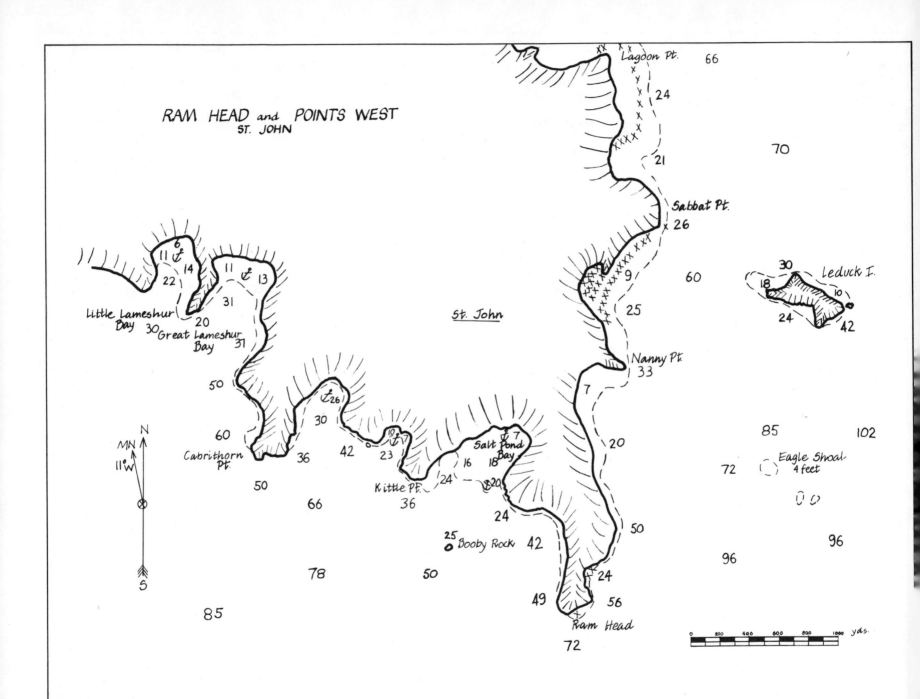

RAM HEAD and POINTS WEST
ST. JOHN

Lagoon Pt.   66

24

70

21

Sabbat Pt.
26

30   Leduck I.
18   10
24   42

9   60

St. John

25

Little Lameshur
Bay   20
30 Great Lameshur
Bay   31

Nanny Pt.
33

7

85   102

50

26

20

30   Eagle Shoal
60   4 feet
Cabrithorn   42   10   72
Pt.   36   23   72

Salt Pond
Bay
16   18

50   24   20

Kittle Pt.   24   96
36   24

25   96
Booby Rock 42

78   50   24

49   56
85

Ram Head

72

N
MN
11 W
S

SKETCH CHART 16

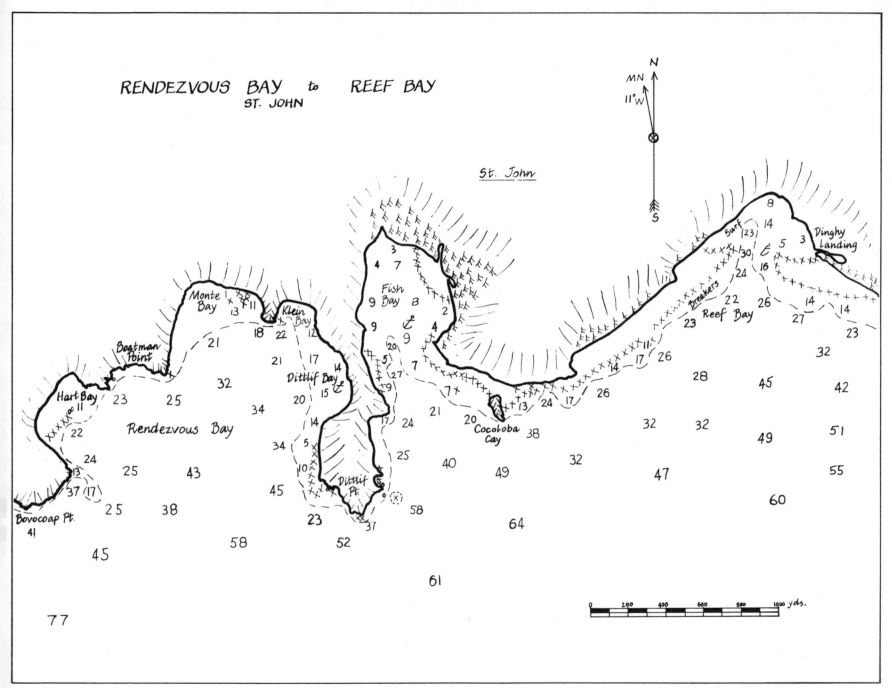

RENDEZVOUS BAY to REEF BAY
ST. JOHN

St. John

N
MN
11°W
S

Dinghy
Landing

SKETCH CHART 17

A worthwhile trip is to follow the path up to the old rum factory, which as of this writing is not yet in such a state of disarray that it could not be got running again with a few weeks' work. Follow this path further up the hill and some rare Carib carvings can be found. There are relatively few of these anywhere in the Virgins. Shortly before the arrival of Columbus, the Caribs came and conquered the Arawaks, tossing most of them into the pot, and continuing on their rapacious way westward to Puerto Rico and the Bahamas. Unfortunately for this tribe, their rapaciousness was soon outdone by the Spaniards, who rapidly killed off everyone, leaving little remains of native civilization.

Fish Bay
(BA 2452, C&GS 938, Sketch Chart 17)

Since the names given to West Indian shores often explicitly hark back to some rudimentary condition (viz., Chocolate Hole), it's a good bet that anything called Fish Bay is loaded with fish and oysters. But unless you're an avid fisherman, the bay with its low land to the east impresses me as a poor stopover for the night. Fish Bay is shoal, but six feet can be taken well up into it, provided you feel your way carefully. In such marginal situations, remember that the Carribean is lower in the spring and early summer than in the winter—sometimes substantially lower.

Rendezvous Bay
(BA 2452; C&GS 905, 398;
Sketch Chart 17)

There are practically no dangers in entering this seldom-used but nonetheless excellent anchorage. Stand to the south rounding Dittlif Point and, keeping discretely west of the reef alongside this point, round up into the bay. Once more you can sail practically up to the shore before dropping your anchor. I'm told there is good fishing and clamming here.

A word of warning about the entire south coast of St. John from Ram Head westward to Rendezvous Bay: none of the anchorages are safe if the wind swings to the south. It is more apt to do this from early August until the trades arrive in December, but there are exceptions. For example, in January, 1973, it blew steadily south and southeast for weeks on end.

Basically it should be kept in mind that the south coast is best in the winter, while New Found Bay, Haulover Bay, and Trunk Bay on the north coast are favored in the summer when the wind is likely to be south of east.

St. Croix

The largest of the Virgin Islands lies approximately 35 miles due south of the other Virgins, separated from them by extremely deep water. Many people cruising the Virgins tend to skip St. Croix because of its relative remoteness, but it is an island well worth visiting. The main harbor at Christiansted is excellent; Buck Island, a morning's sail from Christiansted, offers superb snorkeling and diving; the yacht club in Tague Bay hosts weekend racing; the entire area inside the reef on the northeastern side of the island is a perfect place for small-boat sailing; and to the east of Tague Bay the waters are completely sheltered and virtually always calm, providing unparalleled snorkeling among coral heads.

St. Croix's topography and climate are different from the other Virgins. The northern and eastern parts are hilly, while the northwestern end is mountainous. The eastern climate is practically like a desert, but west of Mt. Eagle one finds lush tropical forests where huge mahogany trees reign. The southwestern portion used to nurture mile after mile of sugar cane, stretching as far as the eye could see from the mountains to the ocean. This, of course, was before development struck.

Despite some touristy pretenses, the island ought to be explored ashore, preferably by car. If you happen to be there when the Landmarks League is conducting tours of houses, be sure to join up. Many of Christiansted's imposing old houses have been restored (one is on permanent exhibit), as have a number of the town's historic buildings. A sugar mill (on the Whim Estate along Center Line Road on the southwest side of the island) was in the process of restoration as this is being written, and probably is open to the public by now. In fact, the whole lower part of Christiansted is a National Trust area in which the facade of buildings cannot be altered without official sanction. In my opinion, parts of this section constitute the most attractive area in the whole Lesser Antilles chain. The old Danes were practical architects. The ground floors of their buildings were warehouses, while the second and third floors, housing countingrooms and living accommodations, were built out over the sidewalks, supported by tidy stone arches. As a result, in the lower part of town the sidewalks are shaded, making the walking cool on sunny days and dry on rainy ones.

Whereas trading was once prime on St. Thomas, agriculture was St. Croix's industry. Some of the Danish planters became so wealthy through sugar and cattle that when they visited the mother country they made a bigger splash in Copenhagen than did the King. (As a result, the King of Denmark was embarrassed into passing a law that restricted the number of liveried servants and outriders who could accompany a coach through the streets.) Until the mid-'50s, St. Croix remained an agricultural economy; cattle was first, sugar second, and tourism a weak third. Sugar is now completely gone, cattle are disappearing, and tourism and industry (i.e., the oil refinery and aluminum plant on the south coast) have taken over.

In the two decades or so I have been frequenting the area, many, if not most, things have changed in the Virgins. But thankfully one old reliable has held out staunchly: Ted Dale's Comanche Club. The Comanche in question may have changed from a 72-foot yawl to a schooner with two small mizzens, but Christiansted Harbor's colorful watering spot has stayed the same. The dock looks like it's about to give up the ghost, but I wouldn't bet any money on it. It has been there since about 1955, looking exactly the same. The imposing Mr. Dale and his henchman Duke (who's even bigger than Ted) banged the facility together in two weeks with 55-gallon drums, railroad iron scrounged from God knows where, a couple of sledge hammers, and a box of cigars for Duke. Everyone predicted that it wouldn't last the season. The Club also boasts a tower fashioned by Ted and advertised as a honeymoon cottage. It's often available as a cheap room if you don't happen to be traveling with a bona fide bride. Sitting on top of the tower with a cool drink in your hand as the moon comes up over the yacht harbor spread out at your feet is one of the Virgin's not-to-be-forgotten experiences.

Ted and Duke are both quite some sailors. They used to sail the old 72-footer off the dock, around the harbor, and back and forth from Puerto Rico without engine or winch. I found the story hard to swallow until one day I asked Duke to haul me to the top of *Iolaire*'s mast, and showed him to a winch. He just laughed. He hauled me up hand-over-hand so fast that when the halyard two-blocked I almost kept going into space like a moon rocket! Ted also has a predilection for outlandish small craft. At one point he kept a genuine Venetian gondola in which he rowed around the harbor, and when last checked in on he was sailing a Carib war canoe whose rig consisted of five Sunfish lateen masts—the only five-masted lateen schooner in existence.

St. Croix is covered by C&GS 905, Chris-

tiansted Harbor by C&GS 935, and Frederiksted Harbor by C&GS 937. I feel it is essential to carry BA 485 also, since its 1:58,400 scale shows much more detail than 905's 1:100,000, and it also gives numerous profiles, ranges, and so forth, making navigation in and around St. Croix infinitely easier.

One can sail directly from St. Thomas to St. Croix (course 170 magnetic; distance 36 miles, sea buoy to sea buoy), but you will be making leeway and facing a weather bow current of one-half to one-and-a-quarter knots, which would necessitate steering a course between 160 and 163 depending on the leeway made by the individual boat. (It should be remembered that many of the bare boats make a tremendous amount of leeway and if you're sailing a real sand barge you would do well to steer closer to 150 magnetic.) If the wind is at all southerly it will mean that you will be hard on it, making for a rough all-day sail. Chances are you wouldn't get there until twilight, and Christiansted should not be entered at dark under any circumstance.

From St. Thomas, it is better to leave from Buck Island, as that will shorten the distance by a good four miles. Head for the well-defined notch east of Christiansted. As you approach the island and pick up the town of Christiansted, do not head directly for it, as the town is well westward of the harbor entrance. Continue heading for this notch until you pick up the radio tower on Fort Louise Augusta (WIVI, 970 kHz), and bring that to bear on magnetic 170, which will lead you through the channel. There is a range into the channel, but it is difficult to pick up; the radio tower is easier.

Better still, depart from Norman Island or the eastern end of St. John. The advantage of the latter is that you will not have to go through Customs and Immigration upon arrival, which you will have to do if you come from Norman Island. The course from Salt Pond Bay is 180 magnetic, from the western

end of Norman Island 196 magnetic (distance: 32 miles). Both courses should result in a beam or broad reach with little leeway being made, and only the set of the current to reckon with. In leaving Norman Island, be careful to avoid Santa Monica Rock by holding to 180 magnetic until the south tip of Peter Island appears from behind Norman; then you will be safely south of the rock (Sketch Chart 18 gives ranges for this area). Santa Monica Rock is marked one-and-a-quarter fathoms on the chart, but it can still be hit by the average draft, as a yacht can drop on it in a swell, and frequently the rock causes waves to crest.

When approaching St. Croix from Norman or St. John, again head for the saddle between the two hills east of Christiansted until the city itself comes into view. Immediately upon discerning the city, head for its eastern edge to pick up the radio tower; if you continue too far southerly, the range from the saddle will lead over the western edge of Scotch Bank. This bank breaks in heavy seas and has shoals with as little as a quarter of a fathom of water over them. Continue heading for the eastern part of Christiansted until the foot of the radio tower at Fort Louise Augusta bears 170 magnetic, and follow 170 degrees into the channel.

Christiansted Harbor
(BA 485, C&GS 935, Sketch Chart 19)

It should be noted that the British chart does not show the dredged channel westward of Protestant Cay to the western end of the harbor.

When entering Christiansted Harbor, stay absolutely in the channel with the radio tower placed squarely between the buoys at 170 magnetic—red to starboard entering. (At night, the range lights on 174 magnetic can be used.) Scotch Bank shoal will be to the east, Barracuda ground and shoals (also called Long Reef) to the west. Rather than sail the turns inside, stand on in directly to Fort Louise Augusta

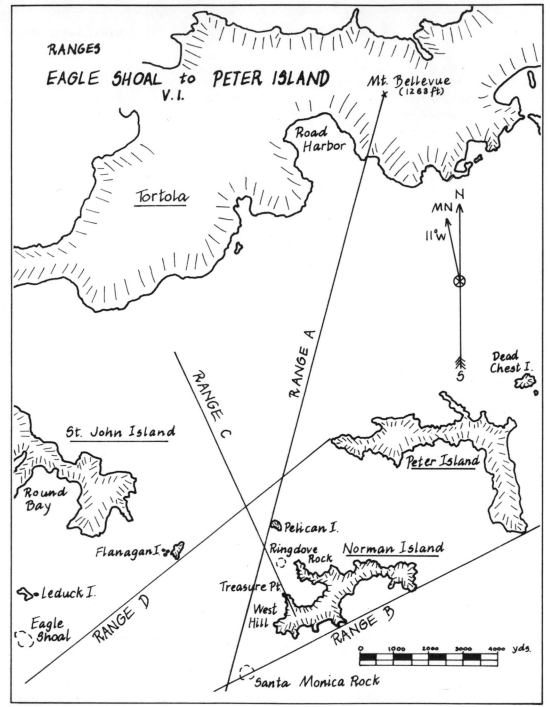

RANGES

EAGLE SHOAL to PETER ISLAND
V.I.

SKETCH CHART 18

until Flashing Green "7" is brought abeam, then bear off to a course of 205 magnetic, leaving the red-and-black buoy to starboard. Gradually bear off to the west, passing east of Round Reef, thus following the old schooner channel. When Protestant Cay is slightly forward of abeam, you may either round up and anchor among the yachts off St. Croix Marine and Development, or bear off running down between Protestant Cay and town, rounding up and anchoring behind the Cay. Do not anchor any distance to leeward of the yachts moored west of Protestant Cay, as not only does the water shoal, but also the area is used as a seaplane landing. A sailboat may have the right of way, but . . . .

If by any chance an attempt is made to enter this harbor at night (which I strongly discourage), you must be absolutely certain of your ranges and buoys before proceeding. Innumerable yachts have come to grief on either Barracuda Ground or Round Reef—most on the former, having mistaken the flashing green two-and-a-half-second "9" marking the northwest corner of Round Reef for "7," a green four-second flasher. If this is done, you are bound to pile up.

Secondly, you can come a cropper by bearing off before the red and black can marking the division of the channel at Round Reef is

Range A: Pelican Island slightly open to east of Mt. Bellevue passes safely to the west of Santa Monica Rock.

Range B: The two southeastern points of Norman Island in line with the southeasternmost point of Peter Island leads over Santa Monica Rock.

Range C: West Hill in line with Treasure Point clears Ringdove Rock to the westward.

Range D: Western end of Peter Island in transit with southeastern tip of Flanagan Island clears Eagle Shoal to the south.

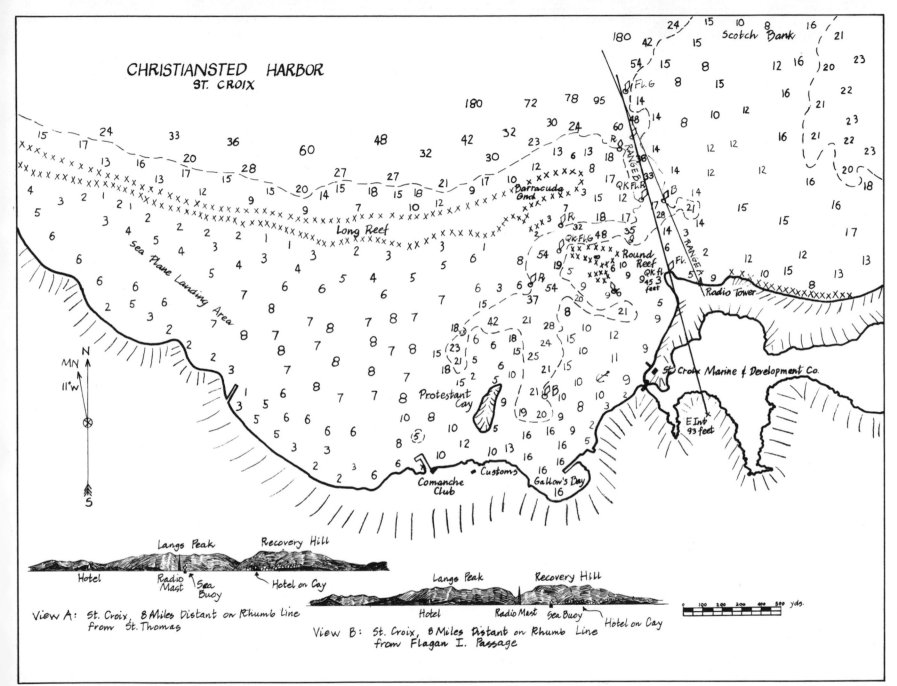

Range A: Radio mast lined up between sea buoys, 170 magnetic.
Range B: Ft. Augusta Light in line with 93-foot E Int range light, 174 magnetic.

SKETCH CHART 19

abeam. This is a difficult mark to spot, as it is not lit. Do not begin to bear off until quick flashing green "11" is abeam, then head 200 magnetic, following the shore, until the anchorage off St. Croix Marine and Development is reached. One can then head westward, passing between Protestant Cay and the mainland, and anchor in the lee of the Cay. (Use C&GS 935

for approach, rather than the BA chart.)

Another error can be made even after the outer channel is safely negotiated. Inside, sailboats at night try to follow the main deepwater channel (the steamer channel) but are a little slow in gybing and end up hard aground on Round Reef, which is exposed to the swell.

One more word of caution. When anchor-

ing west of Protestant Cay, a strong easterly current will be experienced, especially in heavy weather. Surf comes in over the reef, runs eastward continually, and then pours out the mouth of the harbor. Thus a Bahamian moor is essential. Otherwise you may find yourself stern to the wind with a slack anchor line, swinging around in huge circles.

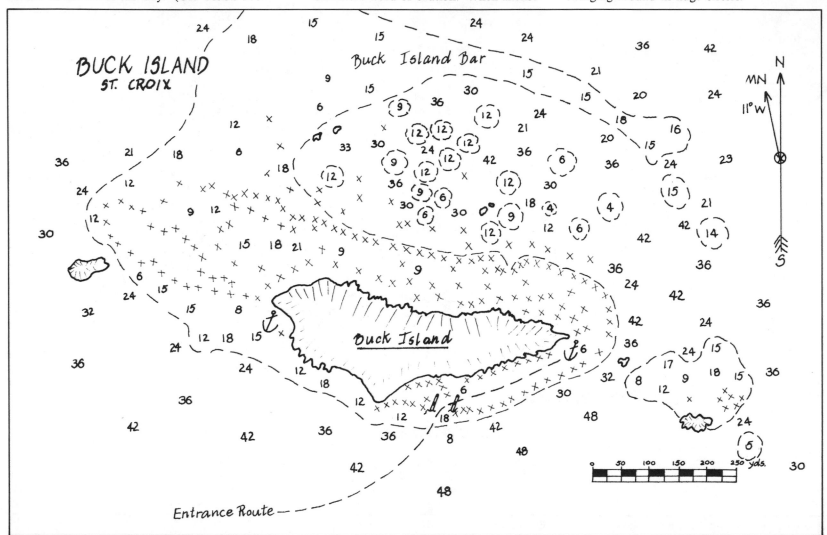

SKETCH CHART 20

Buck Island
(BA 485, C&GS 905, Sketch Chart 20)

Four-and-a-half miles northeast of Christiansted, Buck Island provides an excellent day's sail. Take off in the morning and beat to windward in calm seas. Spend a few hours exploring the island and its magnificent reefs, and then enjoy a nice easy run home before dark.

Many years ago Buck Island (not to be confused with St. Thomas's Buck Island) was given to the government on the stipulation that it never be developed, thus making a wonderfully wild park for local Cruzans and tourists. Charter skippers were diligent in cleaning the area before they left, and every so often the Yacht Club would come over to tidy up the beach, plant trees, and maintain its unspoiled beauty. But somewhere along the line the Park Department decided it could improve on nature by erecting picnic tables and outhouses, and labeling all the coral for the benefit of literate scuba divers. Well, better so than a 40-floor hotel and a lot of "Keep Off" signs.

When sailing to Buck Island from Christiansted, do not tack inshore inside buoy "7" off Fort Louise Augusta, as there are two shoal patches here which have already nabbed plenty of boats. Once clear of these shoals, it is best to hug the shore as closely as possible to gain the shelter of Shoy Point and Green Cay. The U.S. chart is wrong in that it shows ten feet of water between Green Cay and the mainland. This is not so. With care and a local pilot, a maximum of seven feet can be carried, but five feet is more like it for the inexperienced visitor. When you are clear of Green Cay, hug the shore until the west end of Buck Island can be laid, then stand out toward Buck. The white-sand beach on the western end offers the best anchorage. Sail right in toward the shore. Shoal draft boats can actually come close enough to have someone jump ashore with the bow anchor; but be sure to have a stern anchor out to hold the boat off.

For those who are veteran rock-dodgers, it is possible to sail eastward along the island to a gap in the reef marked by two stakes. Power inside the reef and anchor in an area clear of coral heads. Then you can hop in your dinghy (take an anchor) and motor around to the northeast corner of the island where a marked trail begins. Keep in mind that this is a protected area subject to regulations.

If you don't feel like taking your own boat, charter one of the catamarans or trimarans for an exhilarating sail to the island. And to meet one of the local characters—a true oldtime Cruzan and a gentleman of the highest order—find out which of the charter boats is being skippered by Bomba, an institution of a man with the sunniest smile and the biggest feet in the entire Antilles.

Tague Bay
(BA 485, C&GS 905)

Tague Bay at the northeast end of St. Croix is the base of the St. Croix Yacht Club and is a superb place for small-boat racing, being completely sheltered by a barrier reef. It's also a glorious spot to sail cruising boats in; there's not terribly much room, but the water is smooth and there's always plenty of wind whistling in across the reef. To enter Tague Bay, make your way east past Green Cay and Pull Point. The entrance to Tague Bay is easily spotted by the dry sand bar north-north-east of Green Cay Estate. Once past this bar stand eastward until the mill at Coakley bears south, then tack southward. Enter midway between the reef to the east and the dry sand bar to the west. Once inside the reef, start tacking eastward again. There is plenty of water, but watch out for isolated coral heads. This should not be attempted except when the sun is high. Good anchorage can be had anywhere off the Yacht Club, but do not try to get too close to shore, as the water shoals to five feet fairly far out.

Be careful when anchoring. Make sure your anchor is well buried, because there are occasional patches of grass, and holding well in them is doubtful.

Yachts can continue eastward of the Yacht Club, as proved by John Burr, who used to anchor his seven-foot-draft *Iolanthe* off his home at the eastern end of the island. But extreme care must be taken. Perhaps easier is to get into your dinghy and take it east to a secluded spot for some isolated snorkeling and bathing.

The Yacht Club is open every afternoon for light lunches and snacks and conducts small-boat racing on Sundays and sometimes on Saturdays.

Salt River
(BA 485, C&GS 905, Sketch Chart 21)

This is the only other harbor on the north coast of St. Croix. When proceeding westward be sure to stay outside White Horse Reef, which will break even in normal weather. Before setting out, it is advisable to check with local yachtsmen on what the conditions are at Salt River. Sometimes there is extensive shoaling of the sandbanks just inside the entrance due to the ground swell from the north.

To enter Salt River pick out the break in the reef and head in midway between the breakers steering a course of about 190 magnetic; immediately upon passing between the reefs come abruptly around to 100 and continue east until you spot a day marker to starboard; alter course to 190 and feel your way in. In the spring of 1973 it was reported that six feet could be safely brought into the inner harbor.

Exactly what will become of Salt River is anyone's guess. A fancy private marina was started with much ado at Judith's Fancy on the eastern side of the river—great activity, dredging, docks, breakwater—then all died. Another marina is now under way, and an eight-foot marked channel leads off to the

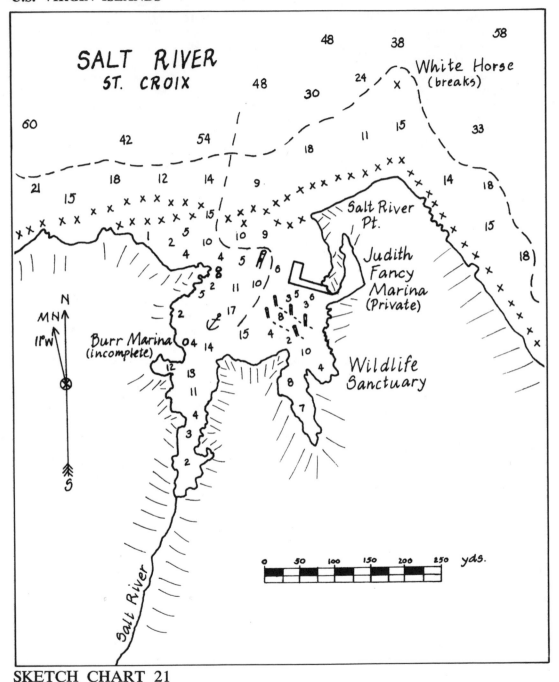

SKETCH CHART 21

southeast to the wildlife sanctuary.

Don't attempt to enter without checking with local yachtsmen first, but once you have directions, as long as the ground swell is not coming in from the north it does make an interesting, if somewhat hot, anchorage.

South Coast of St. Croix
(BA 485, C&GS 905)

The British chart is not quite right in that it only shows the one harbor at Kraus Lagoon; now there is a second one at Limetree Bay. Though both may be used in an emergency, they are strictly commercial harbors with no facilities for yachts, and I would try to avoid them.

Eastwards of Limetree Bay are some anchorages which look promising when the wind is well into the north. Kit Kapp on *Fairwinds* did some fairly extensive exploration on the south coast of St. Croix with seven feet of draft and reported that every time the tide went out, he found himself aground. One must conclude that the south coast is open to exploration only by boats drawing five feet or less.

West Coast of St. Croix
(C&GS 937)

This area is seldom visited as it is dead to leeward of all other anchorages in the island and completely open to the ground swell. Besides, the bottom drops off so steeply that it is difficult to find an anchorage.

The town of Frederiksted lies on the west coast. It was formerly a listless sort of place with few signs of commercial activity. Now with the infusion of industry on the south coast and the influx of tourist ships, the town has taken a new lease on life. It certainly is not as good-looking a town as Christiansted, but there are a number of old buildings that have a great deal of charm. The fort is worth exploring and a car can be rented to tour the rest of the island.

Anchorage may be had anywhere along the west coast; it is just a case of finding the bottom. Don't try to anchor by the southwest tip of the island, however, as the swell sweeps around the point and the current is very strong.

The 14,000-acre Virgin Islands National Park, preserved by the U.S. National Park Service and Caneel Bay Tourist Development, was established in 1956 and has been attracting an increasing number of tourists ever since. Campsites and beach privileges are available to yachtsmen. The public areas are shown here inside the dotted lines. The remainder of the island of St. John (striped) is privately owned.

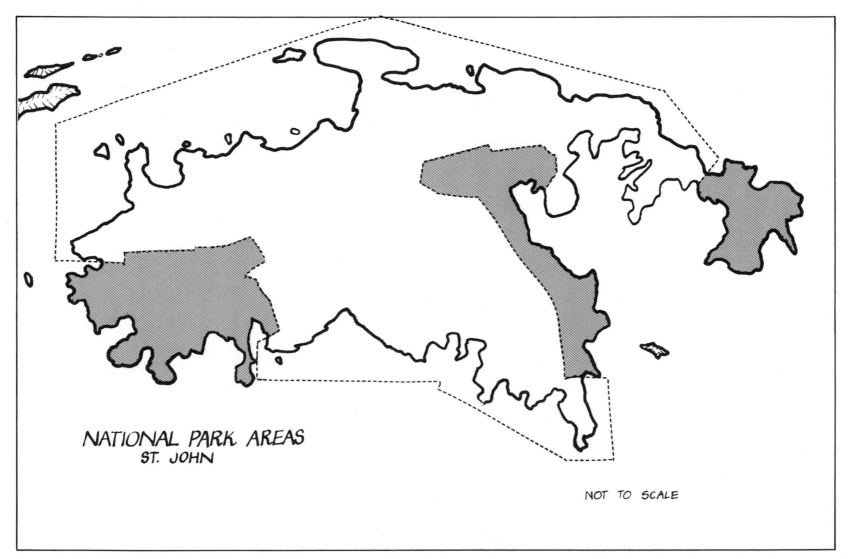

NATIONAL PARK AREAS
ST. JOHN

NOT TO SCALE

CHAPTER 9

British Virgin Islands

C&GS 905; NO 25241, 25243, 25244, 25245; BA 2008, 2016, 2019, 2020, 2038, 2452

The British Virgins are comprised of the two major islands of Tortola and Virgin Gorda; the six minor islands of Norman, Cooper, Peter, Ginger, Jost Van Dyke, and Anegada; and cays, islets, and rocks too numerous to mention. This small gathering east of the U.S. Virgins is, alas, one of the last few remaining outposts of the British Empire. Perhaps it is thanks to this fact that the crime rate here is comparatively low, since, although the islands have a local legislature, the British government is responsible for internal law and order as well as for their external defense. In any event, murder is rare and robberies few.

The law is enforced zealously, even by Tortola's police launch. Visiting yachtsmen should take pains to keep everything aboveboard, since the police enjoy their launch so much that they would love to acquire a few more. According to the islanders, the constabulary is just itching to catch a visiting yacht with a store of illegal drugs on board. If they do, they certainly will impound the boat, put the crew in the cooler, and sell the yacht at auction. A few such seizures and they should easily be able to afford all the police launches they desire.

The smaller islands are still sparsely populated, but development is beginning. One hopes the powers that be have taken note of what happened to St. Thomas and St. Croix and will learn from their mistakes. Luckily, the British Virgins have traditionally maintained what might be called a one-class economy, in that there has been no landed plutocracy controlling everything for itself. Some people own more than others, to be sure, but there is no

particular ruling class as happens in many other small islands of the Lesser Antilles.

When I first came to the British Virgins in 1955, electricity was available only in Road Town, the capital. A small generator serviced the government house, the hospital, and a few houses along the waterfront. Fort Burt on Road Town Harbor, then the only hotel, existed on kerosene lanterns and kerosene refrigeration; the lantern they used to hang out on the patio was more visible at sea than the rudimentary battery-powered light marking Fort Burt Point. Telephones were nonexistent. Radiotelephones occasionally worked, but more often did not. Virtually all intra-island commutation was by boat, since the longest paved road was then one mile. Anyone who wished to visit the incomparable beaches on the north side of the island was obliged to hire a horse in Road Town and follow a path over the mountaintop. So few did this, however, that the mountain long remained a favorite place to grow sugar and brew illegal rum. This local practice, unfortunately, is one of the casualties of progress on Tortola.

The island is now crisscrossed with paved roads connecting the two villages of West End and East End with Road Town. Judging from the capital's name, thoroughfares have been on the minds of the islanders for some time, but it was not until around 1960 that there was a road between West End and Road Town. Public Works built one, declared it open, and invited the Administrator to drive his Land Rover over it. The road was so bad that he left the vehicle in West End, returned to Road Town by boat, and ordered Public Works to

improve the road and retrieve his Rover. Thanks to the sensitive seat of this gentleman's pants, you can now drive over the mountaintop in relative comfort.

There is now considerably more electric power, a few telephones, and finally television, the hallmark of an emerging economy. Outboard motors have also arrived, scuttling in their wake the some hundred Tortola sloops that were actively used in the '50s, but which now have entirely disappeared. I look upon this loss to the sailing world with mixed emotions. It was most embarrassing to beat to windward in a modern cruising yacht and discover that a tired old Tortola sloop with a baggy sail could keep right up with you. I always wondered that they could be so fast and finally discovered that their rapid progress was not due to inherent boat speed, but to the skipper's absolute knowledge of local wind shifts and currents.

Road Town is the only bona fide town in the British Virgins. In the past, acquiring supplies in Tortola was a project. Now it is easier, and although the grocery shelves are not so extensively stocked as in St. Thomas or St. Croix, they are certainly adequate, and the prices are not that much higher. A small point of interest to stamp collectors is that Tortola is the only place in the world where British stamps, printed in England with the Queen's imprint on them, are sold with U.S. currency designations.

Tortola

West End
(BA 2452, C&GS 905)

West End is shown on the charts as Sopers Hole. It is practically impossible to run aground without first putting your bow up on the beach. The harbor is so deep that the only good place to anchor is in the northeast corner where there is a small shelf. Make sure you are well onto

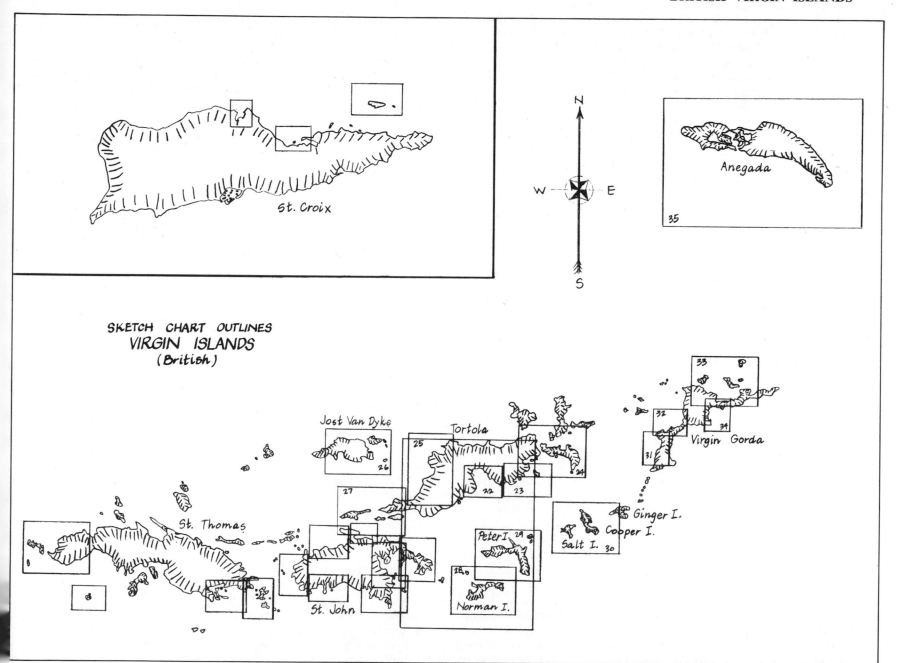

St. Croix

Anegada

35

N

W · E

S

SKETCH CHART OUTLINES
VIRGIN ISLANDS
(British)

Jost Van Dyke

Tortola

33

32

31

Virgin Gorda

34

25

26

24

8

27

22

23

Ginger I.

Cooper I.

St. Thomas

Peter I.

29

Salt I.

30

28

St. John

Norman I.

the shelf or you will suddenly find your anchor hanging 50 feet straight down. There is a small marina at West End run by Paul Gouin. Available are fuel, water (sometimes), showers, and ice (again, sometimes). Everything depends on the island water supply, which can run quite short. West End is also a port of entry and the ferries from St. Thomas and Road Town stop briefly at the dock. I use "briefly" as an understatement here. It can be great fun to watch the goings-on when the ferry arrives. Everything happens so fast that it looks like a Charlie Chaplin movie run at double speed. Chickens squawking, children crying, motorcycles roaring, fish dripping fresh blood—man and beast trundled aboard posthaste. A few basic supplies can be purchased in West End, but for anything outside of the basics, you must taxi to Road Town via Drake's Highway.

There is a dinghy passage between Frenchman's Cay and the mainland. I am told that late in the evening and early in the morning there is good fishing in the flats at either end of the passage. However, pelicans are often interested in fishing lures, so be careful. A pelican puts up a good fight at the end of a light tackle and furthermore, trying to remove a hook from his mouth is a good way to lose a finger.

East of Sopers Hole the charts show a shoal, one-half mile off the ruin, midway between Fort Recovery and Nanny Cay. In truth, the shoal is only about 200 yards offshore, but there is little reason for a boat to come upon it anyway, as the best place to get out of the adverse current when working eastward is on the St. John shore.

Nanny Cay
(BA 2019, C&GS 905, NO 25245)

The charts of Nanny Cay are outdated. For one thing, they are presently dredging out the basin behind Nanny Cay in order to build a marina and condominium complex. The sit-

uation changes constantly, so request up-to-date information at West End.

Sea Cow Bay
(BA 2019, C&GS 905, NO 25245)

Again, dredging has outdated any charts. Check at West End.

Road Town
(BA 2019, C&GS 905, NO 25245,
Sketch Chart 22)·

Both American and British charts of Road Town, though recently corrected, are completely wrong. The accompanying Sketch Chart is more accurate.

When entering Road Town at night (a practice I advise against), there are red range lights that line up on a bearing of 300 magnetic. Follow these in. In daylight, run in on a bearing of 300 magnetic on the commercial dock. Once Fort Burt bears 180 magnetic, turn to port and head for the Tortola Yacht Services. The anchorage off the main dock tends to be rough, and the bottom is loose sand and weeds. Do not, under any circumstances, go alongside the commercial dock. You are bound to suffer damage from the surge or from the commercial freighters. Further, it is inadvisable to bring a dinghy alongside the dock, as the swell will bang it to pieces. And too, anything left in the dinghy will undoubtedly be stolen.

Most suppliers in Road Town are convenient to the Tortola Yacht Services dock. If it is your first stop in the British Virgin Islands and you plan to take a taxi into town to clear Customs and Immigration, bring along several canvas bags and visit the new ice plant. The years of the old slush ice are finally over, and not a day too soon.

At the landing on the south side will be found an English pub transplanted to the Caribbean: good drink, fellowship, and food. On the north side of the landing is a small grocery store owned by Peter Haycraft, one of the

larger importers on the island. What they don't have in the way of provisions they will try to find for you.

When sailing out of Road Town Harbor be very careful of the shoals east of Wickam Cay. Do not go north of the line between the Harbor Spit Buoy and the main dock. This is all foul ground and to be avoided.

Treasure Island Marina
(BA 2019, C&GS 905, NO 25245,
Sketch Chart 22)

Where the chart shows Wickam Cay, there is now a yacht harbor. The harbor entrance is marked by two rows of stakes. Entrance is simple. Merely line up the stakes and enter. The passage is ten feet deep but only 80 feet wide, and should not be attempted at night. The channel markings follow the international buoying system. Inside, you will find a brand new facility with water, ice, showers, fuel, electrical outlets, and even a sewage disposal unit. In a southeasterly wind a chop can roll in the harbor and make it uncomfortable at the dock.

Port Purcell
(BA 2019, C&GS 905, NO 25245,
Sketch Chart 22)

The main steamer dock; not to be used by yachts unless they are in the 100-foot-and-over category. In case you've got such a yacht, there is plenty of water at the dock even at low tide.

Bauger Bay
(BA 2020, C&GS 905, NO 25245,
Sketch Chart 22)

On the eastern side of Road Town Harbor there is the excellent anchorage of Bauger Bay, protected in all but a southerly wind. Quiet and peaceful, it is far removed from everything—either a blessing or a headache, depending on your point of view.

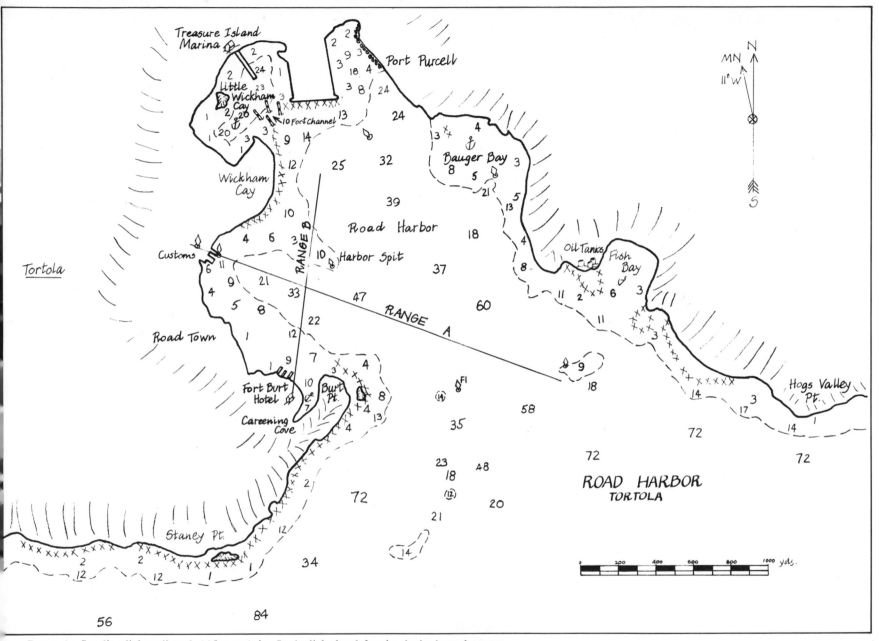

Treasure Island Marina
Port Purcell
Little Wickham Cay
Fort Channel
Wickham Cay
Bauger Bay
Road Harbor
Oil Tanks
Fish Bay
Customs
Harbor Spit
RANGE B
RANGE A
Tortola
Road Town
Fort Burt Hotel
Burt Pt.
Careening Cove
Hogs Valley Pt.
Staney Pt.

ROAD HARBOR
TORTOLA

N
MN
11° W
S

0 200 400 600 800 1000 yds.

Range A: Leading lights aligned, 300 magnetic. In daylight head for the dock along the same bearing.

Range B: Fort Burk Hotel bearing 180 magnetic leads into Tortola Yacht Services dock and anchorage area.

SKETCH CHART 22

BRITISH VIRGIN ISLANDS

Fish Bay
(BA 2020, C&GS 905, NO 25245,
Sketch Chart 22)

Fish Bay is too shallow for most boats except shoal draft catamarans and trimarans. For those that can fit in, it can be private and beautiful, as long as you keep your eyes on the bottom and avoid the oil tanks on shore.

Brandywine Bay
(BA 2020, C&GS 905, NO 25245,
Sketch Chart 23)

The British and American charts of Brandywine Bay differ so much as to suggest that the surveyors took the name of the bay to heart when going about their appointed task. I regard the U.S. as the more accurate of the two. Good anchorage with wind north of east.

Half Moon Bay
(BA 2020, C&GS 905, NO 25245,
Sketch Chart 23)

This anchorage is limited, but beautiful. It is shallow with only three or four feet and it is sheltered only as long as the wind is north of east. But it may be dredged in the near future, so check in Road Town before dismissing it.

Paraquita Bay and Paraquita Lagoon
(BA 2020, C&GS 905, NO 25245,
Sketch Chart 23)

Private property surrounds Paraquita Bay and Paraquita Lagoon. There is obviously an entrance to the lagoon, but whoever knows about it has kept silent. Looking in from Sir Francis Drake Channel, you will probably see the mast of a sailboat rising above the low shoreline. Do not be deceived. It is indeed a sailboat—a shoal draft centerboarder. The lagoon is shallow. I have been told that the Royal Navy blasted a four-foot channel into the lagoon several years ago, but I have never seen the results of their work. Nevertheless, the lagoon is navigable by dinghy; one can fish among the mangroves, or birdwatch, or dig clams in the shoal mud.

Maya Cove
(BA 2019, C&GS 905, NO 25243,
Sketch Chart 23)

Maya Cove is shown on the charts as Hodges Creek. Caribbean Sailing Yachts are presently using the cove for their fleet of charter boats, but I am told that they will be moving to Baughers Bay, Road Harbor, in September 1974. Exactly who will crop up next in the cove is uncertain.

The channel to Maya Cove is not shown on the charts. To enter is easy enough, though sailing out to windward through the narrow entrance can be more than exciting. From Drake Channel, Maya Cove can be seen at quite a distance. West of Buck Island, on a promontory about 100 feet high, there is a conspicuous white house with a windmill to the east of it and a white pillared house to the northwest of the windmill. The cove is beneath this little complex. To enter, run down the range formed by the windmill and the passage between Ginger and Cooper Islands. The range is 308 magnetic from the windmill. Given the usual easterly trades, you will probably find yourself running broad off. As you approach Maya Cove, you will notice an old oil drum with a stick in it, marking the port side of the entrance. This concrete-filled drum stands on the eastern extremity of the western reef. Favor the port side of the channel, giving the oil drum a berth of 15 yards. There is another reef on the eastern side. Turn slowly to port (this usually requires a gybe) as the oil drum comes abeam and head west, running along the inside of the reef. A large basin will open up to starboard. To anchor, merely bear off to starboard to give yourself plenty of room inside the reef, and then round up and drop the hook. Sheltered no matter what the wind and sea conditions are, you are nevertheless cooled by a gentle breeze that sweeps across the low reef and drives off any mosquitoes. There is at least ten feet of water throughout the basin, and the channel is reported to have a depth of eight feet.

Maya Cove is an excellent place in which to sail a small boat. You can sail inside the reef over to Paraquita Bay or eastward inside Buck Island to East End (marked Fat Hog Bay on the charts), and then on through the passage between Tortola and Beef Island to the small bays and coves on the western end of Beef. All told, there is a six-mile strip of coast which can be traversed in complete safety in a small dinghy.

Fat Hog Bay
(BA 2019, C&GS 905, NO 25243,
Sketch Chart 24)

Fat Hog Bay was the home of many native Tortola sloops and cargo schooners. Alas, about the last time a sloop or schooner was built in Fat Hog Bay was the early '60s. A walk along the shore today reveals nothing but skeletons of sailing days past.

The beach shelves gradually, so keep your lead line going, and when you reach a depth of two fathoms, let go your anchor. It is a long dinghy ride ashore and not the world's best anchorage, as it is open to the east. But it is interesting—old wrecks and derelicts, fishermen, small boats, etc.

Along the north coast of Tortola there are miles and miles of isolated beaches. Long stretches of beautiful, soft, white sand have been piled up by the relentless ocean swell. The coast is exposed to the full force of these swells and there are no harbors that offer real protection or safety. It becomes impossible except by land to visit the beaches in the winter when the swell has built up. In the summer and occasionally in the early fall, when the wind tends to come more out of the south, one can anchor off these beaches, but at no time would I regard these as overnight anchorages.

Belmont Bay
(BA 2019, C&GS 905, NO 25243)

Belmont Bay is on the extreme west of the north shore of Tortola, and I have been told that there is a good anchorage in behind the eastern arm of the reef. Although I have not checked them myself, depths are reported to be ten feet.

Cane Garden Bay
(BA 2019, C&GS 905, NO 25243, Sketch Chart 25)

There are some people who regard Cane Garden Bay as the most beautiful bay in the entire Virgin Islands. The ruins of some old buildings and a rum distillery can be seen. In the past, the bay was completely isolated. There were no roads and natives were warm and hospitable. This is no longer the case. Now a road has brought with it all the disadvantages of tourism.

When entering Cane Garden Bay, favor the north side of the bay and then swing in behind the reef and anchor. In the winter, this is a lunch stop only. A swell can build up to unmanageable proportions in no time and with little warning. More than one Tortola cargo schooner has ended up high and dry on the beach as a result of an unexpected swell.

Brewers Bay
(BA 2019, C&GS 905, Sketch Chart 25)

Brewers Bay is my candidate for the most

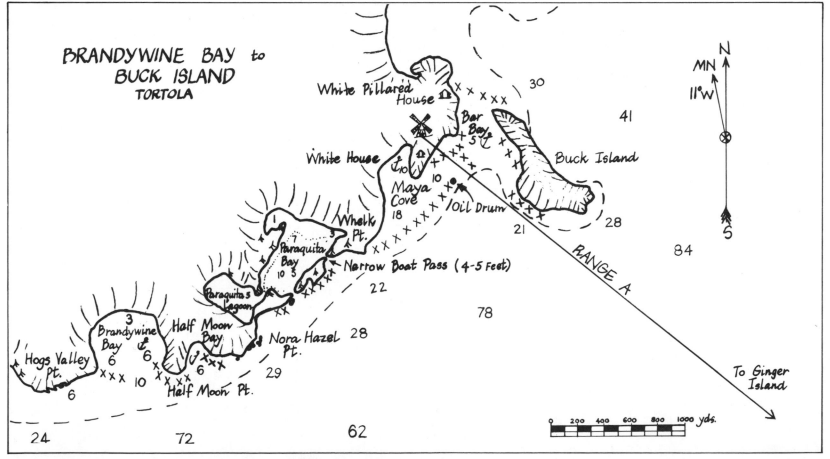

Range A: Windmill bearing midway between Ginger and Cooper Islands, 308 magnetic.

SKETCH CHART 23

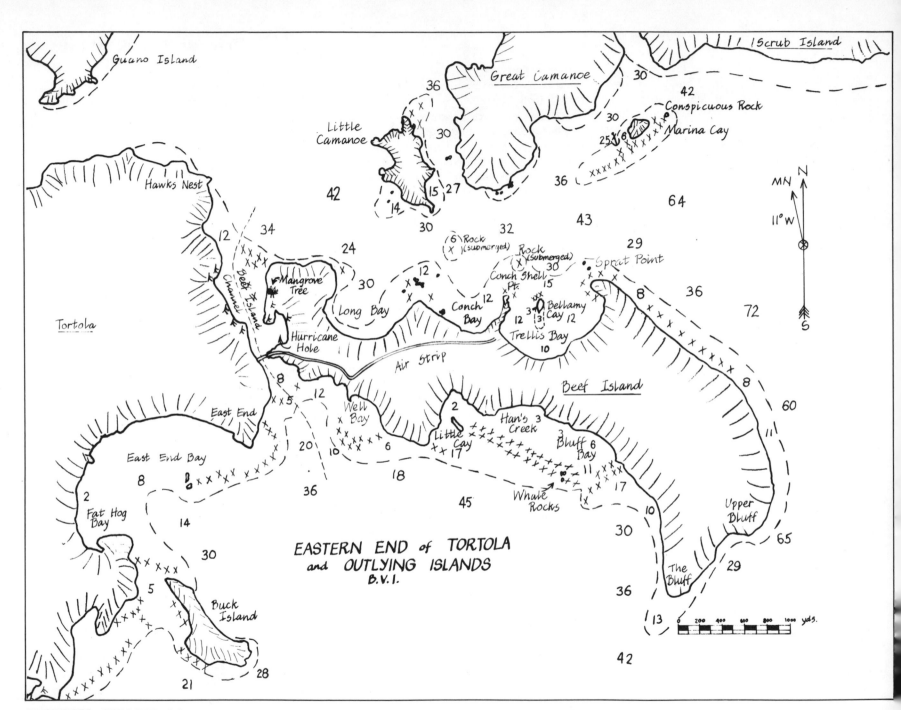

EASTERN END of TORTOLA and OUTLYING ISLANDS B.V.I.

SKETCH CHART 24

beautiful bay in the British Virgin Islands. Unfortunately, most of the time all you can do is sail in, look around, and sail out again. It is completely exposed to the ground swell. In summertime, it can occasionally provide a good anchorage, but one must be careful, as the bottom shelves up very steeply, and there are extensive shoals lying well offshore. If you plan to stay, throw one anchor in deep water to hold you off, and then sneak in and pitch another anchor into the shoal water. The beach is soft white sand and deserted; the snorkeling is excellent.

Buck Island

Buck Island
(BA 2020, C&GS 905, NO 25243, Sketch Chart 23)

Exactly why no one ever anchors behind Buck Island is beyond me. It is completely sheltered unless the wind swings to the southeast, which happens so infrequently that it is not to be considered a real danger. A cool breeze usually blows over the low land. Beaches and bottom are sand. The area offers good shelling and the romance of a deserted island. Buck Island was the original site of the airport serving Tortola back in the late '40s. It had a direct crosswind runway and a rough grass strip. The pilots must have been superb.

Buck Island was also the home of Buck Island Bucks. Years ago, the owner of the island minted coins that were similar in size to the U.S. silver dollar. Everyone thought it very humorous—except the U.S. government. They nearly threw him in jail for counterfeiting, though he rightly pointed out that he was merely creating his own currency and that if someone was fool enough to accept his currency, more power to him. The Federal government still did not see the humor of the whole situation, and Buck Island Bucks soon passed out of circulation.

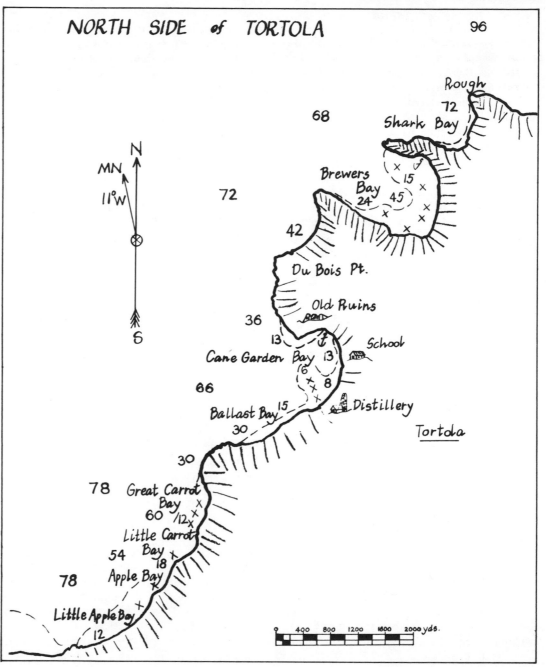

BRITISH VIRGIN ISLANDS

Beef Island

Beef Island is due east of Tortola, to which it is connected by a bridge. There was formerly an arduous though navigable channel between the two, but the bridge, which once opened, is now permanently closed. The clearance is ten feet, which effectively closes it off to masted vessels. The last time I recall its being opened was during a Round-Tortola Race several years ago. One of the starters made arrangements with the operator to have the bridge opened at an appointed time. He breezed through the channel, the bridge was cranked up, and our friend shortened his Round-Tortola distance by many miles. An uproar ensued, not so much because he had taken the bridge, but that once opened, it couldn't be closed for several hours, and the traffic to the Beef Island Airport was backed up most of the way to Road Town.

Allan Batham, the original owner of Marina Cay, has kindly helped with the sketch of this channel. His directions, which are primarily of interest to launches and powerboats, are as follows: At the southern end of the cut there is about five feet at high tide. The clearance beneath the roadway is ten feet. The channel at the north end, approaching from the north, is complicated by a reef, with the entrance at the west side, close to the Tortola shore. The channel runs from this entrance southeast behind the reef toward a single mangrove tree at the water's edge. It has been blasted cross-current through sand, and it may well silt up again. Before blasting, the depth was three feet. Close to the mangrove tree the channel goes toward the bridge and deepens.

Coming from the opposite direction, with the mangrove tree astern and traversing the main channel in a northwest direction, there are three peaks visible in the skyline. Steer on the right-hand one and, when this sinks behind the others, the turn to starboard can be made. Don't try it at night!

If a heavy swell is coming in from the north, and particularly when the tide is setting against it, do not approach the Tortola shore on the north entrance. Come in squarely to the reef from well to seaward and keep the reef as close on your port hand as possible, the face of it being quite sheer and some 12 feet at this point. The same applies going out in the reverse direction. There are reefs off the Tortola shore which are dangerous in a heavy sea.

Traveling south from the bridge, the channel heads southwest of the big rocks at the mouth, there being the shallowest water—five feet—just inside off the end of the reef, which stretches out on the starboard hand. Once clear of the gap, there are no further hazards to the south.

Bluff Bay
(BA 2019, C&GS 905, NO 25243, Sketch Chart 24)

Located on the southeast of Beef Island, Bluff Bay was for long a seldom-used anchorage. Until recently everyone was convinced that only six to eight feet could be carried inside the bay until veteran charter skipper Ross Norgrove, in *White Squall,* drawing nine feet, made it one of his favored anchorages. Sail toward Beef Island, working your way cautiously into the shelter behind the high hill at the southeastern end of the island. A reef will be found extending along the south shore of Beef; look for a low white rock, which on closer inspection you will see to be guano-covered. Work your way east. About 300 yards before Whale Rock a gap will be found in the reef. The axis of the channel leading inside is approximately northeast magnetic; sail in on starboard tack; once past the western reef, ease sheets and head due north. Anchorage can be made in 12 feet.

One afternoon Norgrove, lying at anchor, watched a bare boat sailing up Bluff Bay toward him. It was late afternoon and the sun was low in the sky, but despite the poor visibility the boat confidently zigzagged its way in and anchored beside *White Squall.* Amazed to find a bare boat charter with the ability to make such a tricky anchorage in poor light, Ross invited the newcomers over for a drink. Several rums later it came out that these fellows had seen Norgrove's boat anchored comfortably in the bay, and they had just sailed right in, never suspecting that there was a reef between them and the anchorage.

Trellis Bay
(BA 2019, C&GS 905, NO 25243, Sketch Chart 24)

Trellis Bay on the north side of Beef Island was formerly the main anchorage for Beef Island. There was a marine railway, a hotel, and a powerboat dock. Exactly why Vladic Wagner built a slipway in this most inaccessible spot beggars the imagination, but he did. For many years it was the major shipyard of the British and American Virgins. Now the railway and the hotel have been abandoned. The dock is still used for launch service to Marina Cay. To enter Trellis Bay, sail in west of Bellamy Cay. At night, do not rely on the light shown on Bellamy Cay in the charts. It hasn't been lit for years. You can anchor under the lee of the Cay in about three fathoms of water. If it is crowded, move on and anchor south behind the sandspit which extends south from the Cay. This is a good anchorage in all weather. No sea ever reaches into this bay and the holding ground is good.

Marina Cay, the Camanoes, and Guano

Marina Cay
(BA 2452, C&GS 905, NO 25243, Sketch Chart 24)

Marina Cay lies one mile north of Trellis

Bay and offers one of the most comfortable anchorages in the entire Virgin Islands, with no wind, no sea, no current; just a continual cooling breeze. There is room for 20 boats, and it is so sheltered that not the slightest chop will build up, no matter where the wind is from.

In the early '60s, Allan and Jean Batham developed a resort hotel on Marina Cay. They built several cottages and a main house with a dining room and an open-air bar. They built their island paradise into a thriving business. Attempts to expand to Beef Island proved unsuccessful, but their son, Michael, with his wife, Terry, brought the family business successfully to Great Camanoe Island. Allan and Jean ended up buying Ross Norgrove's *White Squall I* and then set out for New Zealand, where they live now.

Marina Cay Harbor is easy to enter. From the west, you can sail right in. Coming from the southwest (Drake Channel), begin by staying well off Beef Island. The tide makes it sloppy near shore and you will lose your wind under the cliffs even on the windward side of the island. There are no hazards to speak of. Coming from the east or northeast, it is easiest to pass north of Marina Cay. There is good water to the north, right up to the conspicuous long rock (six feet high) on the northeast tip of Marina Cay Reef. To enter the anchorage, run down between Marina Cay and Scrub Island; then round up, douse sail, and pick up a mooring. This will save about ten minutes over beating up from the lee end (southwest corner) of the reef. It is also the best way to leave Marina Cay if you are heading east, because it keeps you out of the channel between Beef Island and Marina Cay with its strong tide and steep chop.

Another entrance to the Marina Cay anchorage is from the north between Great Camanoe and Scrub Islands. There is ample water but the channel is quite restricted and should not be attempted unless you know what you are about. Reefs on both sides of the channel are visible when the sun is high.

Once arrived in Marina Cay, there are moorings available for visiting yachtsmen. The eastern buoys have seven feet of water under them, and the western buoys have 12 feet.

There are two dangers in this area. There is a middle ground with three feet of water over it two-thirds of the distance between the southwest tip of Great Camanoe and the rock pile which is visible on the shore at the eastern end of Long Bay. Since this middle ground is hard to spot, hug the northern side of the channel and you will clear it. The second danger is a rock 100 yards northeast of the westernmost arm of Trellis Bay. Again, use the north side of the channel and you will be safe. In years gone by this rock was a great help in supporting the shipyard at Beef Island. Boats would haul, go back into the water, start to run down the channel, and hit the rock. They would then turn around, go back to the yard, and haul again.

Great Camanoe and Little Camanoe
(BA 2019, C&GS 905)

Although it is possible to land a dinghy on Great Camanoe and Little Camanoe, neither island offers any anchorages of worth to the average cruising boat.

Guano Island
(BA 2019, C&GS 905)

Guano Island is owned by the Bigelows and the Guano Island Club. They have their houses high up on the hill and have no facilities for visiting yachtsmen. However, they seem perfectly happy to have yachts stop at White Bay and use their beach. There is no way to get up to the club other than by foot, and it is a long way, all uphill. Although the beach is attractive, White Bay is not a good anchorage. It is difficult to find water that is shallow enough to anchor in and still far enough offshore that it prevents your swinging into coral heads when the breeze dies down at night. For this reason, I advise mooring bow and stern. Usually the swell hooks around the point and it is most comfortable lying east-and-west, so that the boat rides meeting the swell with its bow or stern.

Jost Van Dyke

"JVD" is a small, relatively unspoiled island, still a quiet backwater off the mainstream of Island progress. Until recently, there were no cars and no roads—only tracks suitable for horses—and the only settlement was the port of entry at Great Harbor. But who can be so innocent as to think this idyll will last?

Great Harbor
(BA 2452, C&GS 905, Sketch Chart 26)

For years the only place offering meals and entertainment was the Tamarind Restaurant at the south end of the beach in Great Harbor. Run by Feliciano Callwood (also known as "Foxy"), it started out as a lean-to affair, a few palm branches thrown over a couple of packing cases in which were stored the ingredients for a really fabulous rum punch. The Tamarind has grown to become one of the most famous entertainment spots in the entire Lesser Antilles.

JVD's main harbor is normally sheltered, except when the wind veers well to the south. The northern end of the bay is reef-encumbered. East of the reefs on the northwest side of the bay, there is an anchorage in 12 feet of water about 300 yards offshore. To reach Settlement Dock, row your dinghy east until the dock bears 010 magnetic. A gap through the reef will lead you ashore. The town is very small, with no supplies available except some good "informally distilled" white rum. There's a way of spotting the really good home-distilled white rum. Drop an ice cube into a glass of it.

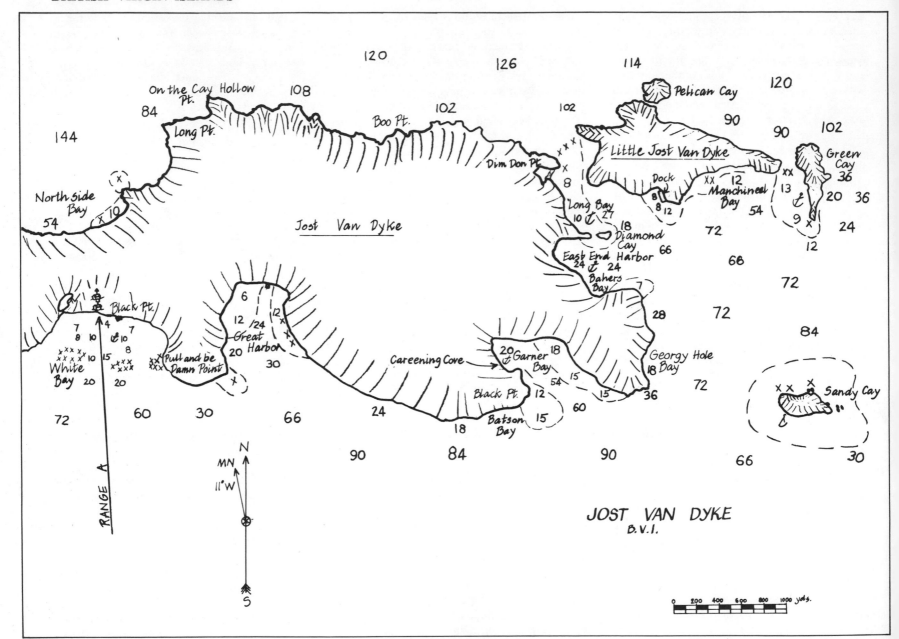

120   126   114   120

On the Cay Hollow Pt.   108   Pelican Cay   90   90   102

84   84   Boo Pt.   102   102   Little Jost Van Dyke   Green Cay   36

144   Long Pt.   Dim Don Pt.   Dock   12   Manchineel Bay   13   20   36

North side Bay   54   x 10   8   Jost Van Dyke   Long Bay   10   27   18   Diamond Cay   8   12   54   9   24

East End Harbor   66   72   12

Black Pt.   6   24   24   Bahers Bay   68

7   10   4   7   12   /24   12   Great Harbor   28   72

10   8   Pull and be Damn Point   20   30   Careening Cove   20   Garner Bay   18   Georgy Hole Bay   72   84

White Bay   20   20   Black Pt.   12   54   15   18   36

72   60   30   66   24   Batson Bay   15   60   72   Sandy Cay

18   90   84   90   66   30

RANGE A

N
MN
11°W
S

JOST VAN DYKE
B.V.I.

0   200   400   600   800   1000 yds.

Range A: Two rooftop stakes, one triangular, the other square, in line lead through the break in the reef.

SKETCH CHART 26

If the cube sinks to the bottom, you'll know you're dealing with some potent brew.

White Bay
(BA 2452, C&GS 905, Sketch Chart 26)

West of Great Harbor lies what was until recently a beautiful, deserted white-sand beach. It is not so deserted any more. Entrance can be gained around the western end of the reef or through a break in its center. This break used to be difficult to spot, but the Myricks, who operate a small guest house and restaurant ashore, have helpfully placed a range off their beach bar which leads through the break (see Sketch Chart). There is disagreement as to the exact depth of water inside; personally, I wouldn't take more than seven feet. A good anchorage can be had outside the reef in the northeast corner of the bay, northwest of Lower Flat Rock, where there is ten to 15 feet of water over sand bottom. However, the surge sometimes makes White Bay uncomfortable, and the place has become popular with the bare boats.

Garner Bay
(BA 2452, C&GS 905, Sketch Chart 26)

Also known as Little Harbor, it lies east of Great Harbor, and although it is open to the southeast and very deep, it is more sheltered than one would expect. It is a picturesque spot with hills on three sides rising abruptly from the water. Unless you anchor close by, you will find yourself in 15 fathoms of water. One popular anchorage is in the southwestern corner in Careening Hole. Bury a bow anchor in the sand ashore and drop a second anchor astern. The swimming is magnificent.

East End Harbor
(BA 2452, C&GS 905, Sketch Chart 26)

East End Harbor is wide open to the east. By all counts it should be a hopeless anchorage, but for some reason its northwest corner is usually good—cool and breezy with only a slight swell. As it is on a dead lee shore, I would advise using a two-anchor rig, making sure that each is firmly set. Lay them down ahead of you in a "Y" configuration, and swim down with the face mask and check them out.

Along the north coast of Jost Van Dyke the cliffs drop vertically into the sea. There are one or two shelves along this coast, making the depths a lot less than the chart shows. No one has closely investigated the area, but it is believed that Saddle Bay, North Side Bay, and Cherry Cut Bay (south of Long Point) may have possibilities as daytime summer anchorages.

Under no circumstances should the north shore be approached in the wintertime. The Atlantic swell rolls and crashes against the cliffs, sending waves of solid water a hundred feet high. In the old days when the people of Jost Van Dyke fished for a living, each winter two or three people were lost fishing from the cliffs on the north side. Occasionally a fisherman was knocked from his perch on the cliff by an extra large wave, and that was the end of him.

Little Jost, Green and Sandy Cays, and Tobago Island

Little Jost Van Dyke
(BA 2452, C&GS 905, Sketch Chart 26)

On the south side of Little Jost Van Dyke there used to be a small hotel-restaurant where honky-tonk music could be heard till the wee small hours of the morning. But it is no more —a fire—and no one is sure when it will be rebuilt. The dock is still there, nonetheless, with eight feet of water alongside. Rumor has it that all of Little Jost Van Dyke will be developed by a Canadian consortium that will run roads over both islands and build an expansion bridge in between—maybe.

Green Cay
(BA 2452, C&GS 905, Sketch Chart 26)

Due west of Green Cay's sand bar is an exceptional anchorage that is very well protected from the sea. The wind sweeps across the bar to make it cool and comfortable. No need for a Bahamian moor here as the wind will keep you off. It is best to come up close and anchor on the bar; the water increases sharply to ten fathoms as you move away, and should your anchor drag any distance, it might fall right off the ledge. During the winter the ground swell manages to wend its way between the Cay and Little Jost Van Dyke, making the spot untenable overnight on occasion.

Sandy Cay
(BA 2452, C&GS 905, Sketch Chart 26)

East of Jost Van Dyke, it offers a fine beach and good snorkeling. If the wind is in the southeast, anchor off the northwest corner of the island. If in the northeast, anchor off the southwest corner. This is strictly a daytime lunch spot; the beach should not be missed. Eyeball your way in and anchor in a suitable depth.

Tobago Island
(BA 2452, C&GS 905)

Tobago Island is seldom visited, but does provide an anchorage for one yacht at a time as long as the ground swell is not running. It is a small cove close under the cliffs off the sand beach on the western side of the island. There are three hazards in the vicinity of Tobago Island. One is Mercurius Rock, east of the island; with approximately six feet of water over it, it crests and breaks in heavy weather. Another is King Rock, south of Tobago, which, though just under the surface, seldom breaks. Watson Rock, west of Tobago Island, rises steeply from seven fathoms with a shelf dropping to 20-25 fathoms on its western side. It has excellent diving and can be easily gained from the Tobago anchorage.

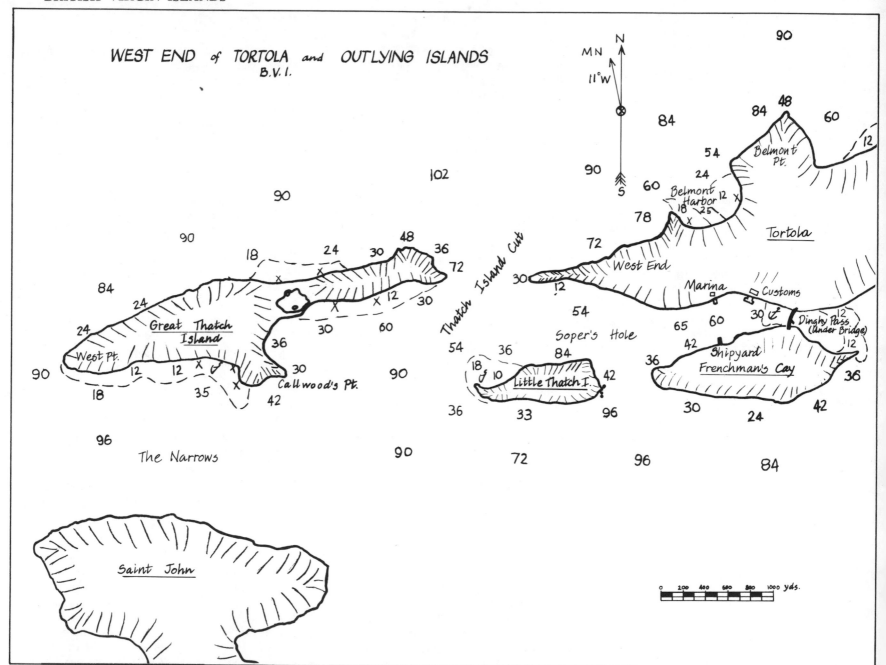

WEST END of TORTOLA and OUTLYING ISLANDS
B.V.I.

90

MN N
11°W
S

84
84 48
60
Belmont Pt.
12
54
24
90
102
90
60 Belmont Harbor 12 X
18 25
90
78 X
Tortola
90
18 24 30 48 36
72
West End
84 24 30 X 12 30
Marina Customs
Great Thatch Island
24 36 60
30 ⌁ Dinghy Pass (Under Bridge)
West Pt.
30 Thatch Island Cut
65 60 42 12
54 Soper's Hole
12 12 X 30
36 Callwood's Pt.
54 36 84 Shipyard
18 42 Frenchman's Cay 36
90 90 8 10 Little Thatch I. 42
18 35 42 33 96 30 24 42
96
36 72 96 84
The Narrows
90

Saint John

0 200 400 600 800 1000 yds.

SKETCH CHART 27

Great and Little Thatch Islands

Great Thatch Island
(BA 2452, C&GS 905, Sketch Chart 27)

Completely uninhabited, and while I have never known anyone who has been ashore, I know several who have anchored comfortably just west of Callwood Point. Here you can lie parallel to the beach, sheltered from the ground swell. A second anchor should be set in the southeast to prevent a south shift in the wind from swinging you ashore. The snorkeling is excellent, and if you're lucky, you may pull in a lobster or two.

Little Thatch Island
(BA 2452, C&GS 905, Sketch Chart 27)

The home of what I call the "on again, off again Finigon Hotel." The Finigon was the first small hotel on the western end of Little Thatch. Since 1954, the hotel's owners and managers have come and gone with great frequency. The only stable residents of the place seem to be the mountain goats. The island is without a good anchorage, and clearly this has detracted from its commercial success. There is one anchorage off the northwest corner which is good for the summer months only. During the winter the ground swell rolls in through Rock Island Cut, producing a turbulence that can be dangerous at times. Before making the trip to the Finigon, check at West End to find out if it is open.

Norman Island

Norman Island is reputed to be the island that Robert Louis Stevenson had in mind when he wrote *Treasure Island*. It is entirely possible, as there are several anchorages that seem to fit into the scheme of that classic adventure. A total of seven anchorages are scattered around the island: The Bight, Miner/Carstarphen Cove, Benures Bay, Money Bay, Windward Sound, Treasury Point Caves, and Privateer Bay. Treasure-hunting is still much bruited about. As recently as 1972 a gold doubloon was supposedly found in one of the caves.

The Bight
(BA 2019, C&GS 905, Sketch Chart 28)

The Bight is the largest and best anchorage on Norman, and the best place in The Bight is in the extreme northeast corner. Feel your way in with a lead line because if you miss the shelf in the northeast corner, you will be anchoring in seven or more fathoms of water. The bottom is sand and the holding good. Gusts of wind may blow down off the hills, but there will be no sea. The beach ashore is fair, but watch out for sea urchins. There are also ruins ashore which may be explored. Coins, pottery, and tile fragments abound. Finally, be careful of the livestock. They don't often see human beings and are anything but friendly. If you ever run across a French sloop moored there, stay and watch the fun. The Frenchmen run the cattle down to the water, herd them out to their boat, and hoist them aboard by their horns. Needless to say, the cattle object to this treatment and sometimes run the Frenchmen into the water instead.

Miner/Carstarphen Cove
(BA 2019, C&GS 905, Sketch Chart 28)

So named for the yachtsmen who popularized this anchorage, it lies southwest of the northwestern arm of The Bight. In Miner/Carstarphen Cove the wind loops over the hill, so you will lie with your stern toward the shore the entire time. The bottom is mixed sand and rock in about five fathoms. If you have a yawl or a ketch, it is best to leave your mizzen up to prevent you from waltzing around and fouling your anchor or your rode on the rocks on the bottom. There is good snorkeling right under the point at the south end of Privateer Bay.

Treasure Point Caves
(BA 2019, C&GS 905, Sketch Chart 28)

The third commonly used anchorage on Norman Island is off the caves, which are about 300 yards south of Treasure Point. Many different stories are told about the treasure found in the southernmost cave. I don't know which is the true one and I don't think anyone knows the whole truth, but you can hear some interesting tales from the older natives. At this anchorage the bottom is deep. Again, the wind loops over the hill and you will lie stern to the shore, but you are more exposed, and I would advise against spending the night here. All three caves may be explored by dinghy. Snorkeling is good all along the shore. For the strong swimmers and experienced spearfishermen, there is some good fishing, albeit in rough water, south of the southwesternmost point on Norman Island.

Privateer Bay
(BA 2019, C&GS 905, Sketch Chart 28)

Augie Holland reports that with the wind in the southeast in the summer months, the anchorage in the southern end of Privateer Bay is excellent. It is a short swim to Caravel Rock, where there is good snorkeling, spearfishing, and underwater spelunking. You can watch the pelicans soar above the cliff, fold their wings, and plunge into the water with the force of a cannon ball. The beach is rock. A Bahamian moor is called for to keep from swinging ashore, as the wind will continually box the compass.

Benures Bay
(BA 2019, C&GS 905, Sketch Chart 28)

On the north side of Norman Island there is an anchorage in Benures Bay that offers protection when the wind is in the south. Anchor as close to the white-sand beach as you dare; the bottom is sand and provides good holding. Above, the wind whistles between two 250-foot-

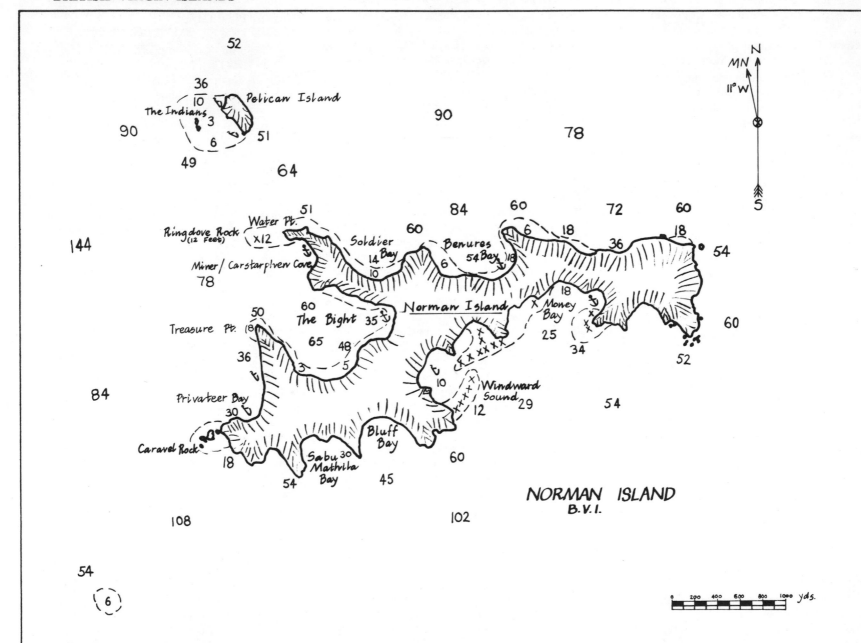

52

36

10

Pelican Island

The Indians

3

90

6

51

49

64

90

78

N

MN

11°W

5

144

Ringdove Rock (12 Feet)

Water Pt.

51

×12

Soldier Bay

60

84

60

72

60

6

18

36

18

54

Miner/Carstarphen Cove

14

Benures 54 Bay

18

78

10

6

Norman Island

18

Money Bay

60

50

60

The Bight

35

×

25

34

60

Treasure Pt. 18

65

48

×

×

52

36

3

5

10

×

Windward Sound

12

29

54

84

Privateer Bay

30

Bluff Bay

Caravel Rock

18

Sabu 30 Mathilda Bay

45

54

60

NORMAN ISLAND
B.V.I.

108

102

54

6

0 200 400 600 800 1000 yds.

high hills, guaranteeing a cool and bug-free anchorage the year round. I am told that on the ridge to the west are the ruins of an old estate.

Money Bay
(BA 2019, C&GS 905, Sketch Chart 28)

With the wind well into the north, Money Bay provides a calm anchorage and still another beautiful, white-sand beach. The chances of finding another boat there are slight, and there is room for only two or three boats anyway. To conserve swinging room, I would strongly recommend a Bahamian moor or bow and stern anchor. It is a deep harbor and, with proper scope out, the swinging radius on just one anchor will be considerable. Tuck yourself up in the northeast corner if possible, as it is quietest here. From Money Bay you can take your dinghy the three-quarters of a mile to Windward Sound.

Windward Sound
(BA 2019, C&GS 905, Sketch Chart 28)

Windward Sound is a reef-sheltered anchorage—for the courageous only. To enter, it is best to put a man in the rigging. There is ample water once inside, but the channel itself is only six to seven feet deep, narrow and zig-zag. It leads diagonally from the northeast to the southwest and there are breaking reefs on both sides. The harbor will take only one boat at a time. Don't bother to launch your dinghy. The harbor is small enough to explore by swimming off your boat. This is only a place for the competent seaman.

Peter Island

Little Harbor
(BA 2019, C&GS 905, Sketch Chart 29)

The entrance to Little Harbor presents no problems. Sail in, drop your hook, and you are set in normal trade wind weather. Tortola

blocks any ground swell that might upset the harbor, so the only risk would be from a northwester, which comes on in the winter with a slow, gradual shift. A more real threat is overcrowding. Little Harbor is extremely popular due to its accessibility to Road Town and its picturesque setting. To control swinging, I advise everyone to use a Bahamian moor.

Of the numerous anchorages on Peter Island, Little Harbor is the one most often visited by yachtsman. It is easily identified from a distance by the white roof of Sir Brundel Bruce's house. Sir Brundel Bruce was well known for an effective method of curing litterbugs of their bad habits. If anyone threw garbage overboard in the harbor, they would receive several bullet holes in their mainsail—a rather drastic but effective remedy to a mounting problem. Perhaps this old-fashioned solution should be revived.

The area ashore is owned by Percy Chubb III, who bought the land to "get away from it all." His privacy should be respected. Try to keep your anchoring blunders to a minimum as Mr. Chubb is the head of Chubb & Son, one of the largest yacht underwriters in North America. Sitting on his porch, he has watched the antics of the bare boat charterers sailing through the Virgin Islands and his observations have had much to do with his reluctance to insure bare boats or charter boats in the Antilles. If fewer people complained about the difficulty of obtaining insurance and more people improved their anchoring techniques, we might straighten out the current insurance situation in the Islands.

Great Harbor
(BA 2019, C&GS 905, Sketch Chart 29)

The next bay east of Little Harbor is Great Harbor, which is also sheltered in all normal weather. It is deep—so deep, in fact, that unless you have a tremendous quantity of line, it is difficult to find a suitable anchorage.

On the south side midway between the mouth and the head of the harbor, there is a three-fathom shelf. Don't anchor here. Rather, drop your hook on the north side, one-third of the way up the harbor where there is another three-fathom shelf. To use the southern anchorage is to make enemies of the local fishermen. Every afternoon the fish come in along this side of the harbor and any boat lying there, even just a dinghy running around, has been known to spook the entire school and send it back out to sea, leaving a group of rather indignant fishermen. Similarly, they pass the word not to use outboards anywhere in Great Harbor. These people have been making a living for the past 150 years or so by net-fishing in this harbor and it would be regrettable to spoil their livelihood.

If you look up on the eastern hillside in the afternoon you will spot a watchman looking out to sea for the arrival of the fish. When he signals that the fish are in, a net is run out from shore, around the school, and back to shore. The net is slowly drawn tighter and the fish are driven into a large penned area, where they are kept alive until they are taken to market. If the catch is a good one, you can buy fresh fish at a reasonable price. Once they have finished their work, you can sail right up to the beach, drop a stern anchor, throw a line ashore, and the fishermen will tie it to a sea-grape tree. Make sure your stern anchor is well set, and you will be moored for the night. No dinghy is needed. You can jump ashore dry-shod from the bowsprit.

Sprat Bay
(BA 2019, C&GS 905, Sketch Chart 29)

Sprat Bay is to the east of Great Harbor on Peter Island. The name is not shown on either chart. The U.S. chart does show seven feet of water inside the harbor, while the British shows nothing. Formerly this was a quiet little bay known to very few. Now Peter Island

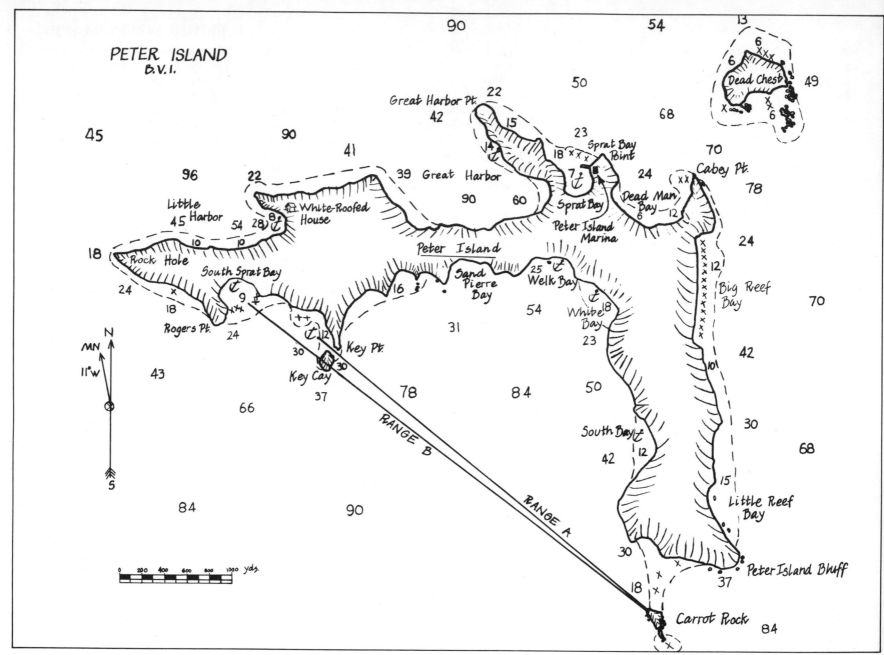

PETER ISLAND
B.V.I.

Dead Chest

90   54   13
                              6
                         6
            50
                    68   49
                                   70
Great Harbor Pt.   22   Cabey Pt.
42   15   78
                    23   Sprat Bay
45   90   41   14   Point
96   18
            22   39 Great Harbor   24
                                        Dead Man
Little   54 28   White-Roofed   7   Bay
45 Harbor   House   90   60   Sprat Bay   6   12   24
18   10   10   Peter Island
Rock Hole   Marina   12
24   Big Reef
            South Sprat Bay   25   Bay
18   16   Sand   Welk Bay   70
Rogers Pt.   9   Peter Island   Pierre
            24   Bay   54   White   18
                12   31   23   Bay
MN N   Key Pt.
11°W   30   101   42
43   Key Cay   78   84   50
66   37   South Bay   30
                                               42   12   68
84   90   15
                                                              Little Reef
                                                              Bay
                                        30
                                   18   Peter Island Bluff
0 200 400 600 800 1000 yds.   37
                                        Carrot Rock   84

SKETCH CHART 29

Range A: When Carrot Rock appears between Key Point and Key Cay, 139-319 magnetic, round up and anchor.

Range B: Carrot Rock in line with Key Cay leads into South Sprat Bay, 136-316 magnetic.

Yacht Club has opened a marina at the mouth of the harbor. Docking space and electricity are available and, sometimes, fuel and water. The Yacht Club is run by a Norwegian and is rapidly building up a reputation as the best marina in the Lesser Antilles. Coats, ties, and dresses are required for dinner.

The entrance to Sprat Bay is amply deep, having a good three fathoms. Hug the reef on the east side of the channel, douse sail as you pass the new concrete dock (there is seven feet of water off the end), and anchor in the middle of the bay. This harbor is always windswept and cool. Swimming is good and the snorkeling on the reef is fascinating. A short walk to the east along the new road which crosses the saddle of the two hills will bring you to the shore of Deadman Bay. This is a captivating, uninhabited, white-sand, palm-fringed beach. A short walk to the west will bring you to the shore of Great Harbor and to a view of the fishing operation.

Deadman Bay
(BA 2019, C&GS 905, Sketch Chart 29)

Deadman Bay is a wonderful daytime anchorage, but it is not comfortable at night. The swell usually sweeps around the eastern point and hooks into the harbor. The seas are rarely large enough to be dangerous, but even the small swell hitting you on the beam tends to make you roll. The best anchorage is in the extreme southeastern corner. The beach is superb and the snorkeling excellent. For those who like to go for big fish, swim around the northeastern point of the bay and you will find plenty, including a couple of large tarpon.

South Bay
(BA 2019, C&GS 905, Sketch Chart 29)

South Bay is not the best anchorage on Peter Island, but it is a place to stop. There is no beach, but plenty of shells, and probably plenty of whelks. Moor close to shore with bow and stern anchors, as the wind coming over the 450-foot cliffs will haul in from the west to blow you onshore.

White Bay
(BA 2019, C&GS 905, Sketch Chart 29)

White Bay is so-named for its gorgeous white-sand beach and its combing surf. Though the ground swell from the north is mostly broken up by Tortola and the other islands, some of the surge still sneaks into White Bay, building up the white-sand beach. Again, there is deep water suitable for anchoring close to shore, but rig bow and stern anchors, or a Bahamian moor, as there are high hills that tend to suck the wind into the beach.

Whelk Bay
(BA 2019, C&GS 905, Sketch Chart 29)

The beach is shingle and loaded with whelks. Ross Norgrove advises that in hunting for whelks, "Always remember that they can hear you. When you make a noise, you can see the whelk move a few inches, but those few inches will be just enough to put him under a rock and out of view. So you do not use a motor to go ashore, do not beach the dinghy roughly, do not run on the shingle beach, and do not talk—in no time you will have a bucket of whelks. Whelks are delicious when properly cooked. Take the pressure cooker, put an inch of half saltwater and half fresh in the bottom, throw in the whelks, and put it on the fire. Bring the pot to full pressure and only then start timing. Cook for 45 minutes at full pressure. At the same time, make up a sauce of melted butter, lime, and your favorite spices. Whelks can provide a fabulous free meal, and when correctly prepared, they can hold their own with escargot."

Key Point
(BA 2019, C&GS 905, Sketch Chart 29)

There is an excellent anchorage west of Key Point. To enter, stand in from the south, keeping the high point bearing approximately 045 magnetic and favoring the Key Cay side to avoid the reef on the west side of the entrance. By the time Carrot Rock disappears behind Key Cay, you should be fully prepared to drop your hook. Immediately upon resighting Carrot Rock, round up, douse sail, and anchor. Here you are protected in all weather, and a gentle breeze blows in from between the Cay and Key Point, keeping the anchorage cool at all times. There will be good snorkeling within swimming distance of the boat.

South Sprat Bay
(BA 2019, C&GS 905, Sketch Chart 29)

Another cozy anchorage on the south coast of Peter Island. Inside there is ten to 12 feet of water and room for only one boat. The entrance is narrow; the entrance bearing brings you onto a broad reach or a run, so watch out not to get going too fast. Enter on a northeast heading (about 045 magnetic) pointing for the western peak of Peter Island. Once Carrot Rock begins to close in behind Key Cay, turn to 315 magnetic and run down this line of bearing with a lookout forward or in the rigging. As soon as the reefs are spotted, alter your course to pass midway through the gap in the reef, round up, and anchor on a Bahamian moor, which will be good insurance against swinging onto the reef at night. This is a small bay, so be careful.

Dead Chest Island
(BA 2019, C&GS 905, Sketch Chart 29)

Northeast of Peter Island lies the island where William Teach is supposed to have stranded a group of recalcitrant crew members. He left them with a cutlass, a bottle of rum, and certainly no hope of getting ashore since they didn't know how to swim.

There are no good anchorages on Dead Chest Island. Blonde Rock, between Peter and

115

Salt Islands, will scare the living daylights out of you if you pass over it. There is roughly eight feet of water over it, so stand clear unless you have a shoal draft boat or you wish to join the ranks of William Teach's crew. You might try snorkeling near it; rising sharply out of 70 feet of water, it should be alive with fish.

Salt Island

Salt Pond Bay
(BA 2019, C&GS 905, Sketch Chart 30)

Salt Island is a good place for a lunch stop, but don't spend the night there. The anchorage is off the settlement in three fathoms, but it is exposed and the water is rough. Ashore, the natives make their living by gathering salt from the pond behind their village. The pond is community operated, but technically owned by the Queen. Each year the Commissioner of the British Virgin Islands comes to the island and accepts an annual rent of one sack of salt. Most of the residents have now moved to Road Town so that their children may benefit from the school system there. However, several older locals still live on, staving off boredom by showing visitors around and consuming quantities of "the big drink," which amounts to any alcoholic beverage that they can beg off a sympathetic visitor.

On the southwest extremity of the island you can dive on the wreck of the *Roan*, a steamer sunk by a hurricane in 1869 with great loss of life. It makes interesting diving, but you really need an aqualung to see anything. Sailing close to the northwest end of the island, you will see a perfect silhouette of the British Lion gazing northward. It makes a nice photograph in the late afternoon sun.

The Sound
(BA 2019, C&GS 905, Sketch Chart 30)

On the east coast of Salt Island, between Groupers Nest and Salt Island Bluff, the Sound seems to be completely obstructed by a shallow reef. I have never explored it via boat, but from the air it appeared to have only two or three feet of water over the reef with plenty of water inside. I thought at the time that someone should blast a channel through the reef, as the harbor would make a perfect anchorage with the wind sweeping in over the reef, a deep sandy bottom, and a white-sand beach. From the air it seemed that only a dinghy could get inside, but later one of the charter skippers reported seeing a 35-foot boat —undoubtedly a centerboarder—at anchor there. So apparently it can be done.

Lee Bay
(BA 2019, C&GS 905, Sketch Chart 30)

In periods of light weather, I see no reason why one could not anchor in this bay. The bottom drops off steeply so you would have to anchor bow-and-stern; otherwise it looks like a delightful spot. Similarly, with the wind in the northeast, I would think South Bay (same Sketch Chart) would be a good anchorage. Again, a double moor would be called for.

Cooper Island

Manchioneel Bay
(BA 2019, C&GS 905, Sketch Chart 30)

This is Cooper Island's northwesternmost bay. It has a sand bottom, a good beach, and a grove of palm trees. The only drawback is the wind looping over the hill and causing you to tail off stern to the beach, so don't anchor too close to shore. There are a few small cottages built by some sun-worshipping Continentals. The southernmost of these is interesting, as it is built on the ruins of a colonial estate. From a distance it looks to be a hot and airless spot, but a closer look reveals that the planters were no fools: the wind eddies around the two hills, and there is always a breeze from across the point.

The southern half of the island is rocky and exposed. There are no anchorages, but if you visit the area in a dinghy, you will discover good fishing.

Carval Bay
(BA 2019, C&GS 905, Sketch Chart 30)

Makes an excellent anchorage when the wind is in the north. The water is deep right up to shore. Its possibilities as an anchorage were first recognized by my old friend, Ross Norgrove, who put in during a very heavy blow out of the northeast, expecting to spend no more than a couple of hours. It was such a nice spot and so well sheltered that he passed the night there and has used the anchorage regularly ever since. As a general rule of thumb, when the wind is south of east, anchor north of the point in Manchineel Bay; if north of east, anchor south in Carval Bay.

East of Cooper Island, Ginger Island is uninhabited and without beaches or harbors. There is a blinking light on top of it which is supposed to be visible for five miles. I sometimes think that this light is nothing more than a candle held high by a little native boy and made to flash by cupping a hand over it.

Northeast of it is Round Rock, the highest and southernmost of the rocks south of Virgin Gorda. It has no habitation or landing. North of it is a series of rocks awash, called The Blinders. And north of these is Fallen Jerusalem, so-called as it was thought to resemble ruins of Jerusalem after the Roman Conquest. A pro tem, calm-weather anchorage can be found off the beach on the north end of the island. It may be a little rough, but you will have complete privacy, since few boats stop there. The snorkeling is excellent, and the spearfishing is reputed to be good.

This entire area between the south end of Virgin Gorda and Round Rock is very poorly charted and dangerous in the extreme. I'm sur-

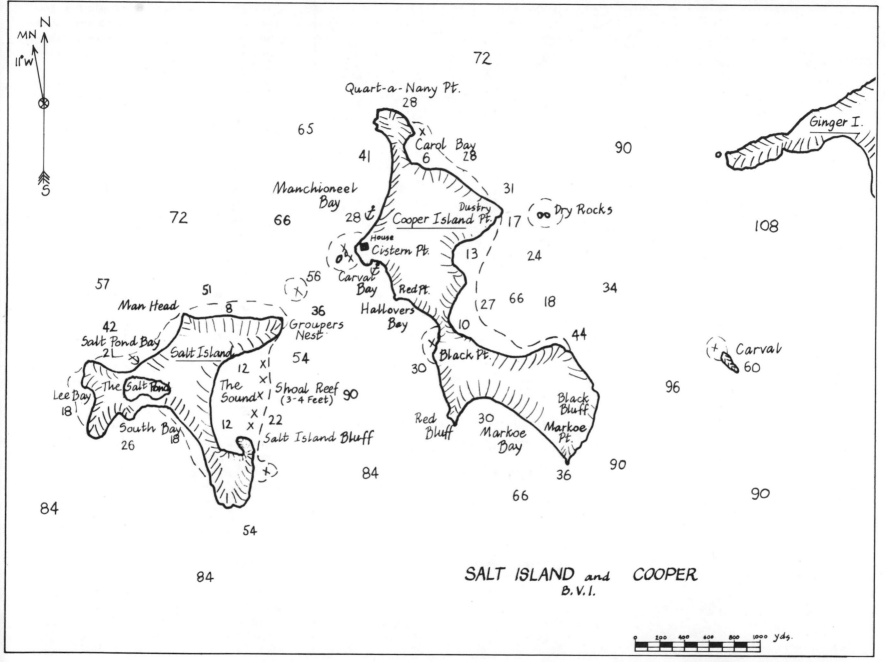

N
MN
11°W
S

72

Quart-a-Nany Pt.
28

65

Carol Bay
41   6   28

90

Manchioneel
Bay   31

72   66   28   Cooper Island Pt.   Dustry   17   Dry Rocks

House

108

Cistern Pt.

56   Carval   Red Pt.   13   24

57   51   Bay

Man Head   8   Hallovers   27   66   18   34

42   36   Groupers   Bay   10   44

Salt Pond Bay   Nest

21   Salt Island   54   30   Black Pt.

12   The   Shoal Reef   90

Lee Bay   The Salt Pond   Sound   (3-4 Feet)   Black

18   12   22   Bluff

South Bay   18   Salt Island Bluff   Markoe   Markoe

26   Red   30   Pt.

Bluff   Bay   90

84   84   54   84   66   36   90

Ginger I.

96   Carval   60

SALT ISLAND and COOPER
B.V.I.

0   200   400   600   800   1000 yds.

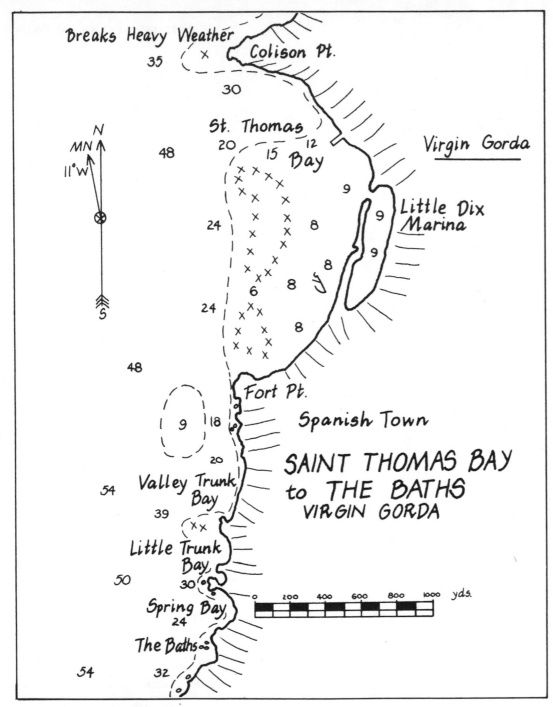

Breaks Heavy Weather

Colison Pt.

35

30

St. Thomas

48   20   15   Bay   12

Virgin Gorda

N
MN
11°W
S

9

Little Dix
Marina

24   8   9

9

8

24   8

6   8

8

48

Fort Pt.

9   18

Spanish Town

20

54   Valley Trunk
Bay

SAINT THOMAS BAY
to THE BATHS
VIRGIN GORDA

39

Little Trunk
Bay

50   30

Spring Bay

24

0   200 400 600 800 1000 yds.

The Baths

54   32

prised more boats have not been lost here. There are numerous discrepancies among the various charts. NO 25243, for example, shows a rock with six feet of water over it between Round Rock and the southernmost Blinder, while no such rock appears on the British chart. Flying over the area, I have spotted a few other uncharted rocks sticking out of deep water. In short, the passage between Virgin Gorda and Round Rock should not be tried except in good daylight and in calm weather with a man in the rigging. The current runs strongly here; the sea is choppy, and it is almost impossible to make this passage against the current if the wind is blowing hard against you.

Virgin Gorda

Virgin Gorda is the second largest of the British Virgin Islands. It used to be refreshingly backward. There were only a few people living there on the barest necessities but who were nevertheless healthy, happy, and extremely hospitable. Time has brought progress, and with progress, development; but the unique charm of Virgin Gorda is still very much to be found just a short walk inland, away from the marinas and other marks of the modern world.

Electricity has arrived in Virgin Gorda, which is a boon to the mariner, as on a clear night the lights from Virgin Gorda can be seen 40 to 50 miles to the east. This should reduce the number of vessels lost on Anegada Reef, but it will not eliminate all losses; if the visibility is not absolutely perfect, a ship can hit Horseshoe Reef before it sees the lights—witness the freighter that hit and was a total loss in the spring of 1973.

An airport has also been built. It has a crosswind runway that is a good test of a pilot. Some don't pass the test. On the day of the airport's inauguration ceremony, the first plane to land on the new strip crashed, killing the pilot and four passengers. It was reported that the plane had hit the wire holding up the WELCOME sign, and had spun out of control. To date, the case has not been settled in court due to the novel circumstances at the time of the crash. The Rockefeller Organization, which had built the airport, was in the process of signing it over to the Virgin Islands government. Needless to say, when the case was brought to a preliminary hearing, each side insisted that at the time of the crash, the airport was the property of the other.

The western shore of Virgin Gorda is well known for its beautiful beaches. But if one is willing to do a little exploring, there is some wonderful scenery on the east side of the island, too. Equip yourself with shoes, long trousers, shirt, and hat, and walk east over the hills in the general direction of Africa. There is no land between that continent and Virgin Gorda, and, if the trades are blowing, the seas that have built up over the vast expanse of ocean crash spectacularly against the rocks. A walk further along the shore toward the north will bring you to Cooper Mine Point and the old copper mine which reaches far out under the floor of the ocean. Every time the price of copper goes up, there is talk of reopening the mine, but at yet nothing has come of it. The bays and reefs north of Copper Mine Point provide excellent snorkeling and spearfishing for those who are accustomed to rough water. However, these bays are only accessible by land. Being on the windward side of the island, they are too exposed to risk bringing a boat into them. Of course, there is always the exception. One yacht sailed across the Atlantic, became lost, bounced over the reefs outside of Tady Bay, and came to rest in one piece within the bay. Later, she was towed out in calm weather before continuing on her way.

The Baths
(BA 2019, C&GS 950, Sketch Chart 31)

This is the most popular part of Virgin Gorda, a beach along the southwestern tip of the island known as "The Baths." It is so-called because of the huge boulders, larger than most houses, that time has thrown together helter-skelter one on top of another. Waves wash in among them and create a series of pools of crystal-clear water, made even more beautiful by the sun filtering through openings in the rocks. Warmer than the ocean water outside, the pools are more enticing than a suburban bathtub.

To reach The Baths, anchor off the second beach up from the southern tip of Virgin Gorda. Once ashore, work your way south. You can't miss the passageway. Try to get there early in the morning, or the lunchtime spread put on by the Little Dix Hotel, complete with tables, white tablecloths, and jacketed stewards, tends to destroy the illusion of the beautiful, unspoiled Virgins.

If anchoring directly off The Baths, you must be careful. The bottom drops off steeply and there are submerged rocks directly off the beach that have only six feet of water over them. This group of rocks is on a line drawn between the westernmost rocks of Virgin Gorda and the high point of Fallen Jerusalem. Do not spend the night anchored off The Baths. Even in daytime it is best to leave someone on board because the ground swell can build up quickly and pivot you around stern to the beach in a short time. There is always a swell, so it is advisable to leave your mizzen up so that the prevailing easterlies will blow you directly offshore and keep you there. Ordinarily, with care, a dinghy can be taken through the surf, but sometimes it is not possible to land at all. The snorkeling around the rocks is excellent. There are many small colored fish—pretty but too small to spear.

Spanish Town
(BA 2019, C&GS 950, Sketch Chart 31)

This is the old settlement of Virgin Gorda

on the south end of St. Thomas Bay. Enter from the north end of the reef behind Colison Point, turn southwards from the Little Dix dock, the large dock at the north end of St. Thomas Bay; pick up channel buoys (international buoyage system), stay directly in the ten-foot (reported) dredged channel, and swing on into the basin. Shoal draft boats drawing six feet or less can anchor in the basin outside, behind the reef, if they wish. Dockage, ice, water and electricity are available, but the price of ice is dear. Best to stock up in Road Town.

Little Dix Bay and Savanna Bay
(BA 2019, C&GS 905, Sketch Chart 32)

These harbors are beginning to become popular as anchorages. However, it must be noted that both bays are completely open to the northwest ground swell. Although the charts show off-lying barrier reefs, these are not high enough to effectively block the swell, which will sometimes break all across the entrances.

The best way to get to Little Dix Bay is to anchor in St. Thomas Bay and take a taxi over the hill. There are two fathoms of water inside the reef, but only two feet over the reef itself. The entrance is unmarked and requires eyeball navigation. If you do go in, don't stay the night. There is little shelter from the northerly swell. Rather, enjoy your stay there but allow plenty of time in the afternoon to sail out to a secure anchorage.

Savanna Bay is strictly a summer or calm-weather anchorage. The winter swell rolls right over the reef and can break across the entire entrance channel; again, clear out before evening. In the summer months, however, Savanna Bay can be a secure anchorage. Enter 30 yards north of Blowing Point and continue eastward, following the reef around to port. Favor the reef side of the bay, as the beach side is littered with obscured coral heads. Anchor with the low land between the hills bearing southeast. The wind usually sweeps in through this gap, keeping you cool and bug free. Once anchored, hop in the dinghy, explore north to Pound Bay, Maho Bay, and Tetor Bay. They all provide excellent snorkeling and spearfishing.

The remainder of the western coast of Virgin Gorda is beautiful but is without good anchorages. It is continually exposed to the rollers from the northwest and there are no barrier reefs north of Tetor Bay where one might find shelter.

Gorda Sound
(BA 2016, NO 25244, Sketch Chart 33)

Gorda Sound on the northern end of Virgin Gorda provides the yachtsman with numerous good anchorages that are protected in any weather. The main entrance to the Sound is between Colquhoun Reef off Mosquito Island and the reefs off Cactus Point on Prickly Pear Island. Both reefs are visible at all states of the tide. Tack well to the north of Mosquito Island on your approach to be sure that you can make the entrance with ease. The entrance itself is closer to Cactus Point than to Mosquito Island, and the course through the hole in the reefs is southeast, 135 magnetic. Some eye-balling is called for. You are by no means home free once you are through this initial opening. In fact, Bert Kilbride on Mosquito

Island counted 50 groundings in one year in this tricky channel. So bear with me through the following directions. They are complicated, but hopefully foolproof.

The course through the entrance is south-east, 135 degrees magnetic; maintain this course until Necker Island (off to port) disappears behind Cactus Point (Range A, point A); alter course to due south, 180 magnetic. (Do *not* turn west of south, and do *not* turn and head for the dock on Mosquito Island.) Continue south, looking off to starboard; eventually you will be able to see Seal Dog Rocks in the channel between Mosquito Island and Anguilla Point (Range B, point B). When the Seal Dogs disappear behind Anguilla Point, you have the whole of Gorda Sound before you. But to reach Mosquito Island from this imaginary point B, you still can *not* turn directly for the dock. From point B, turn west to a course of 285 magnetic. You should be heading directly for Anguilla Point. If Seal Dog Rocks reappear, you are too far north. Head further south and keep the rocks just hidden behind Anguilla Point. Continue on 285 magnetic until you see Necker Island appearing off your starboard quarter from behind Cactus Point (Range C, point C). When the whole of Necker Island is visible, turn northward and head for the anchorage off the dock at Mosquito Island. You will be well protected there, for though it is possible for a small chop to build up, no sea can find its way through the small entrance to Gorda Sound.

There is a fine view of Gorda Sound from the top of the hill on Mosquito Island. A path on the north side of the island leads you to the top. Wear sneakers, as there are prickly plants. Swimming off the beach, the snorkeling on Colquhoun Reef, and the *pina colatas* at the open-air bar—all are most enjoyable.

The second entrance to Gorda Sound is between Mosquito Island and Anguilla Point. This narrow channel is frequently used by na-

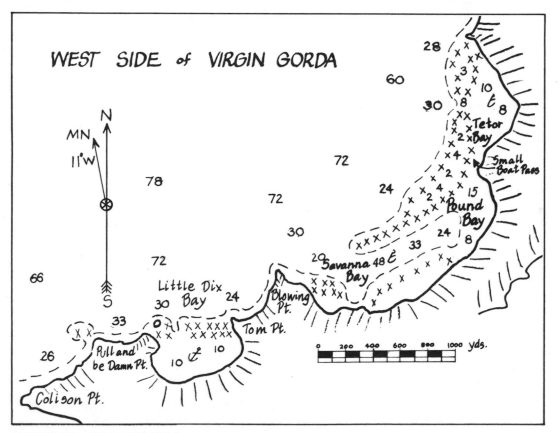

SKETCH CHART 32

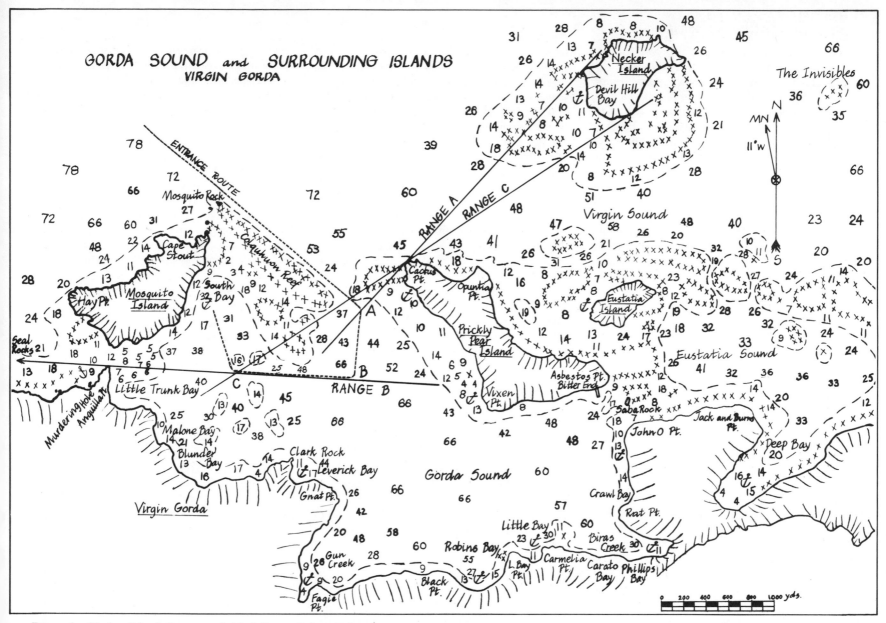

Range A: Necker Island disappears behind Cactus Point—Point A on Entrance Route.

Range B: Seal Rocks (NO 25244) disappear behind Anguilla Point at Point B. Range leads clear of shoals southeast of Colquhoun Reef.

Range C: Necker Island opens to the north of Cactus Point. At Point C course may be altered into South Bay.

SKETCH CHART 33

tives and others sailing in small boats. It saves you considerable distance and keeps you out of rough water when the trades begin to pipe up. Enter in mid-channel, but once east of Anguilla Point, swing to the south and steer about SSE magnetic (157 degrees). More than anything else it is a question of using your eyes and aiming for the narrowest section of the sand bar. You should carry seven feet through the channel safely. Fergus Walker of *Poseidon* assures me of this, and *Te Hongi*, which draws seven-and-a-half feet, has used this passage without any trouble. However, the Anguilla Point entrance to Gorda Sound should not be used if there is a large ground swell running, as the swell will break completely across this area.

Anguilla Point
(BA 2016, NO 25244, Sketch Chart 33)

In the summer when there is no danger of a ground swell, there is an excellent anchorage directly west of Anguilla Point with good snorkeling on the reefs in the southwest corner of Mosquito Island. From here Gorda Sound can be visited by dinghy. It is beautiful and cool with wind sweeping through the gap between Mosquito Island and Anguilla Point.

An one enters Gorda Sound through the northwest entrance, instead of following the preceding complicated directions all the way into the Mosquito Island anchorage, there is a beautiful, small, secluded, white-sand beach that offers an ideal anchorage for one boat. It is along the shore of Prickly Pear Island on the port hand as you come in. Two words of caution: in the afternoon it can be oppressively hot, so bring something for shade. And don't eat the crab apples; they are manchineel and very poisonous.

A diving camp is located at Leverick Bay, run by Bert Kilbride, who probably knows more about scuba diving and wreck sites than any man in the Virgins. If you have an interest

in diving, you might as well hire the best and go with Kilbride. He can be reached on the ship-to-shore during "Children's Hour" at noontime. I am told he is soon moving his operation to Saba Rock at the north entrance to Gorda Sound.

Gun and Biras Creeks
(BA 2016, NO 25244, Sketch Chart 33)

Gun Creek is always a popular anchorage, and I am told that the old village there has changed very little over the years, except that it now has a road running over to the Rockefeller Development in Spanish Town. Another road runs east along the coast to Biras Creek. Biras Creek itself is a superb anchorage, separated from the Atlantic to the east by a short spit of low land over which the wind sweeps, keeping the area cool and bugless. A Norwegian group is fashioning a marina and hotel at Biras Creek at the present time. When making your approach, beware of Oyster Rock which is awash and which is the only hazard in the eastern end of Gorda Sound. A further anchorage is available along the shore west of Biras Hill. A good restaurant, The Bitter End, is within easy reach.

During the winter the anchorage between Biras Creek and Saba Rock may resemble a New York Boat Show. Best to arrive early and stake your claim. Run a bow line to a mangrove tree and a stern anchor to hold you off. Incidentally, this is a favorite area for clammers.

Prickly Pear Island
(BA 2016, NO 25244, Sketch Chart 33)

Uninhabited, for the most part. Anchorages can be made due west of Saba Rock. Use a Bahamian moor, as the reversing current can be tricky. It is a short row to the Bitter End Restaurant on Asbestos Point. Gorda Sound is so well sheltered that you can anchor most anywhere along the coast of Prickly Pear. Just

west of the land marked on the chart as Vixen Point or Observation Point, you can put your bow right onto the beach, anchor bow and stern, and forget about using the dinghy. The south and southwest coasts of Prickly Pear offer swimming, diving, and exploring as good as you can find anywhere.

Eustatia Sound
(BA 2016, NO 25244, Sketch Chart 33)

Great place for diving and exploring. The area is sheltered enough to anchor close aboard any of the reefs, so you swim directly off the boat without launching the dinghy. The channel between Saba Rock and Biras Hill is seven feet and should be negotiated with careful eyeballing. Make sure the sun is high and don't return any later than three in the afternoon. There's no way you can make it back with the sun in your eyes. If you are foolish enough to have stayed late in Eustatia, there is a slightly wider and deeper alternate route between Prickly Pear and Eustatia, but again this is strictly an eyeball proposition.

Before leaving Eustatia Sound, I should mention Deep Bay, a nicely protected, bug-free, and breeze-cooled summer anchorage. I am told that here, too, the clams are plentiful.

Beyond Eustatia Island there is a good anchorage between the island and the reef to the west. It's a fabulous spot for shoal-draft boats, but it should not be used overnight except during the summer. The winter ground swell makes the area quite untenable. It is impossible to leave after 1600; if the swell builds up, you are trapped.

Necker Island
(BA 2016, NO 25244, Sketch Chart 33)

One of the few fairly large islands in the Virgins that is still uninhabited. Bear eastward across Virgin Sound until the hill on the southwest corner of the island is bearing due north magnetic. Stand on in, heading north and favoring the land. When the high peak bears east-southeast, you should be able to find about ten feet of water. Put down a proper moor, and you will be well set for the day. The anchorage should not be used overnight except in the summer, but even then make sure you are moored well before dusk. The approach must be eyeballed in good light.

South Sound
(BA 2019, NO 24243, Sketch Chart 34)

The most secluded anchorage in Virgin Gorda is South Sound on the south coast. Only recently have people started coming here, in complete desperation to get away from other boats. It has proved excellent in any weather for a skillful seaman who has boat enough to beat the six-and-a-half miles from Round Rock to South Sound. Remember when you are attempting this feat that there will be nothing between you and Africa and that the Atlantic swell will have become short and steep. The windward side of Virgin Gorda in normal conditions is rough in the extreme.

South Sound can be entered; head for Lance's Bluff, with a man aloft to guide you. As Lance's Bluff is approached, bear towards Great Hill, bringing that to bear approximately due north magnetic. As the coast is approached, a gap in the reef will open not more than 50 yards wide. In the middle of the gap will be seen a shoal spot; there is plenty of water north and south of the shoal spot. Ross Norgrove advises staying south of the shoal and swinging northwest around the end of the reef before running due south. The reef gives complete protection; 15 feet can be carried as far down as Mattie Point and eight or nine feet can be carried further south than this, all the way down into South Creek. Anchored in South Creek, one has an ideal little hurricane hole—*for one boat only*. The reef provides perfect protection, excellent snorkeling, and does not obstruct the breeze.

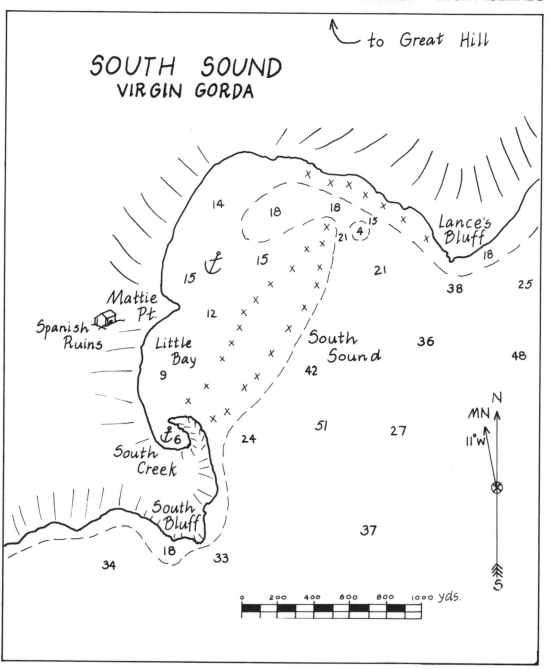

SKETCH CHART 34

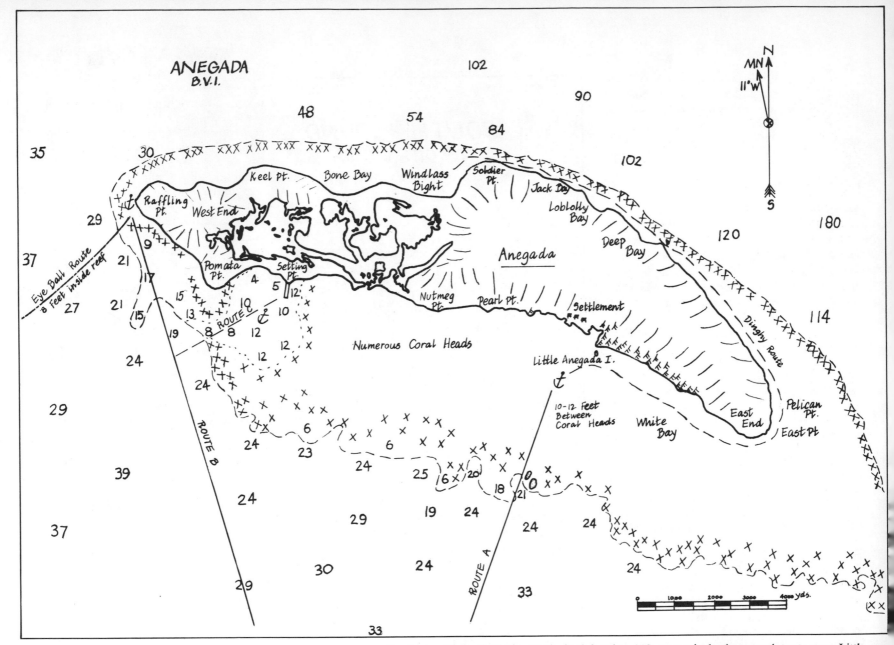

Route A: Peak of Virgin Gorda back-bearing 210 magnetic leads to anchorage near Little Anegada. Numerous coral heads require careful monitoring.

Route B: 355 magnetic from northwestern entrance of Gorda Sound leads to anchorage of West End. (Back bearings must be checked, as current varies east and west.)

Route C: Dock and buildings bearing roughly 060 magnetic will lead to channel through the reef.

SKETCH CHART 35

Anegada

Anegada
(BA 2008, NO 25243, Sketch Chart 35)

Anegada lies 15 miles to the north of Virgin Gorda, a flat island whose reefs are strewn with the wreckage of literally hundreds of ships. It was justly listed on the old charts as Drowned Island. For many years, in fact until quite recently, the main source of revenue on this island has been from the salvage of wrecks. It is very low, the highest point of elevation being only 30 feet, and it is surrounded by reefs. You can run aground on Horse Shoe Reef long before there is any possibility of seeing the island of Anegada.

Scarcely a year goes by that some yacht or native schooner doesn't wreck in this area. Needless to say, the reefs are a diver's delight, and the island itself, being difficult to reach, has remained relatively unspoiled. For a distance of three miles south of the island, the chart shows no soundings, only coral heads. But they are not so numerous that you cannot pick your way between them.

If you have made up your mind to travel to Anegada, it is best to depart Gorda Sound early in the morning, in time to arrive at the outer edge of the coral heads by 11 AM. Be prepared to spend the night, since by the time you have made it into the anchorage off the Settlement and done your diving, the sun will be around to the west and you will be unable to see the way out through the glare. If the weather looks the least bit unsettled, forget about swimming and *get out*.

To reach this anchorage from north of Gorda Sound, stand to the east until Virgin Gorda Peak bears 210 magnetic. Run down this line of bearing (course 030 magnetic, although plus or minus allowances must be made for the current) until you see the Settlement (Range A). You will probably spot the houses before you do the land beneath them. Head for the Settlement, keeping a constant lookout for coral heads, with one man aloft and one on the lead line. There is no marked channel, and you must eyeball it for three or four miles. Moor "when the bottom gets close to the top." How far in you go depends on your draft—and your courage. Don't be fooled by the native sloops; they seldom draw more than four feet. For diving you can anchor a mile off in ten feet over a sand bottom. The reef to the east breaks the sea, but a sizable chop can build up, and it is not a comfortable anchorage. From the anchorage off the Settlement there is a dinghy route inside the reefs clear around East End to Windlass Bight on the north coast.

The better way to Anegada is to start out early in the morning from Gorda Sound, setting a course for West End. The rhumb line is 355 magnetic (Range B), but be sure to continually check your back bearings on Gorda Peak as there is sometimes a strong easterly current on Virgin Bank south of Anegada. An unwary boat could get pushed well to the eastward and end up on the coral heads south of the island. Anegada is so low-lying that it is easy to underestimate one's distance offshore. Off Raffling Point at West End eight feet can be carried inside the reef. It is a tight squeeze and should be attempted by the experienced only and must be avoided in the winter when the ground swell could build and push you ashore or trap you inside the reef. Despite this difficulty, people like the spot for the good beach within easy reach of the dinghy.

About three miles east of West End, near the Setting Point area, a jetty and small hotel have been built. Whether the hotel will ever open is in question, but an eight-foot channel has been blasted southwest from the dock through the reef. Joe Soares, the owner of an excellent restaurant and bar in the area, is intending to buoy the channel. I suggest that you contact Soares on the radio and ask for directions. When the dock and hotel, the only buildings around, bear approximately 060, you should be off the channel entrance.

The first airstrip was built on Anegada in the early '50s, in part to help service a shark fishery that was making a go of it at the time. The fishery fell through and the strip was abandoned. Some years later a doctor from Tortola who flew his own plane tried to make a call to Anegada by air. Having inspected the airfield from above and everything looking okay, he went in for his landing, touched down, and all went well until an 18-inch ditch across the runway sheared off his landing gear. It seems that one of the locals wanting to drain a salt marsh had dug the ditch across the runway. Such is aviation in the West Indies, and so it remained on Anegada until the late '60s when the island was leased whole-hog to a British corporation that intended to put in a monstrous jet strip for SST's and jumbo freight jets. It was at this time that the hotel and jetty were built, but for one reason or another the whole shooting match fell through, and the lands were returned to the government.

Among the numerous wrecks of boats on Anegada is the original *Ondine*, a 53-foot yawl. Many of its fittings, including the mizzen mast and boom, ended up on *Iolaire*.

Sombrero

Sombrero Island
(BA 2038, NO 25241)

Forty-two miles east of Anegada, Sombrero is small, flat, and British-owned. It is mainly remarkable for a bright, flashing white light that is visible for 18 miles and was one of the earliest lights established in the West Indies. If you should be in its vicinity at night, beware of the steamer traffic from Europe. I know of only a handful of yachts that have put in to Sombrero, and they agreed that it was not worth the effort. The anchorage is west of the light on the island's western shore.

CHAPTER 10

Anguilla

NO 25241, 25242; BA 2038, 2079

Anguilla is a wonderful spot for a summer cruise in settled weather. Perhaps because of the inadequacy of the charts, the area is largely unvisited by yachts. The standard BA chart uses a scale of 1:174,000 and the NO 1:145,000, which only a Talmudic scholar could follow in any detail. Besides the smallness of their scales, NO 25241, NO 25242, BA 2038, and BA 2079 are incorrect in many respects.

The island is a British colony 70 miles east of Virgin Gorda. It is low and flat, and thereby totally different from its towering neighbors, St. Martin, St. Barts, and Saba. Long and narrow, the island takes its name from "snake" in Spanish. Its highest elevation is 200 feet, which earns it very little rainfall nor the mosquito- and fly-infested swamps that are found on the high, lush islands to the south.

Many West Indian schooners make their home port in Anguilla. The primary sources of income are shipping and salt. The salt from the salt ponds is shipped to the Grenadines for curing fish. The Anguillans enjoy an excellent reputation as sailors, making this one of the best islands in the Caribbean to find a competent native crew. The Anguillan schooners were the last of the northern island schooners to take down their topmasts and install engines. The Anguillans have always been an independent lot. For decades they chafed under the government of St. Kitts, which they finally chased off the island in 1969. The reverberations of this action spread throughout the world. The insurgents were compared to Castro, the villain of the Caribbean. At tremendous expense the British mounted an invasion of Anguilla, complete with warships, strike force, and parachute drop. Most of the equipment was dropped from aircraft using highly sophisticated electronic gear. But the location of Anguilla had been mischarted by a couple of miles, and the precious expeditionary equipment fell into the sea. The British Foreign Office was not amused, and the affair dragged on far too long. A tremendous amount of money was spent on the assault force, money which could have been put to much better use in the construction of a salt-water distillation plant, extending the airport runway, building more docks, or surveying the harbors.

So much for history. Today Anguilla is not the place to stock up a boat for a major cruise, although most basic supplies can be had here. Anguillan ice is far and away the coldest and hardest in the Islands. No marine supplies are available, but there are a few mechanics and a good machine shop. Anguilla and the islands that surround it are known for their fine harbors and anchorages. A wind in the southeast favors the harbors on the north side of the island, and conversely a north wind favors the south side. If a really big northwest ground swell makes up, many of the harbors will become untenable, even on the south side of the island.

Anguilla and its off-lying islands, being low and relatively unlit, have brought many boats to grief. If you are coming from the north, Anguilla will be backed by the highlands of St. Martin in such a way as to make true distances difficult to judge. When approaching Anguilla from the east or the southeast, it is no problem, as St. Barts and St. Martin will be visible well before Anguilla, permitting the navigator to fix his position correctly. The same holds true out of the south or southwest. Coming directly from the west or northwest, great care must be exerted. Eight miles northwest of Anguilla is low-lying Dog Island, surrounded by many hazardous reefs and shoals. Due east of Dog Island are Prickly Pear, Seal, and the Seal Island reefs, all of which would be impossible to spot at night. You would be aground before you could spot the Anguilla lights. The light at the western tip of Anguilla is supposed to be visible for ten miles, but I have my doubts. Finally, as for making a landfall at night from the north or northeast, I consider it unimaginable. Maybe one fool tries it a year—only Lloyd's would know for sure.

If you are passing from west to east around the end of Anguilla, I would *not* go between Anguillita Island and the mainland. Although there is ample water, the wind and a very stiff current would be dead against you, making it a hard slog through a narrow passage. There is the additional hazard of a rock under three feet of water about 100 yards southwest of the tip of Anguilla. On the other hand, if coming from the east, running downwind, this passage presents no difficulty. Simply favor the Anguillita side of the channel and stand through.

On the south coast there are ports of entry at Blowing Point Harbor and Forest Bay. BA chart 2038 shows a place called Boat Harbor just east of Blowing Point, but I was unable to locate this either by sailing along the coast or from the air. If it is the same harbor as that labeled on the topographical map as Little Harbor, then it is only for the very experienced reef pilot in a boat drawing no more than three or four feet.

Road Harbor
(BA 2038; NO 25241, 25242)

The main town and harbor on the north coast, it is also a port of entry, as is every other harbor on the island. No one seems to be very worried about formalities here; just go report yourselves to the police. Road Harbor is well sheltered in all normal trade wind weather. It is only exposed to the west wind, which is uncommon in the Antilles, and when a west wind does blow, it may be time to scout around for a hurricane hole. Seal Island and its reefs afford the harbor

some protection from the northerly ground swell, but if the swell really begins to roll in, it's best to move on to one of the harbors on the south side of the island. Approaching Road Harbor from the west, favor the Anguilla shore, as north-northwest of Road Harbor are the twin dangers of Dowling Shoal and Sandy Island. Both are unmarked and unlit, though easily seen by day. This is no place for a stranger at night. The entrance to Road Harbor is straightforward. There is ample depth of water in the main harbor, though for most yachts I would recommend

the northeast corner to avoid the swell. Work your way in as close to shore as possible, anchor, and row ashore for a look around. There are only a few small stores. Behind the low spit of land is a salt pond which, as late as 1972, was still in commercial operation, one of the few of its kind. Taxis may be hired for a tour of the island. A good beach and excellent swimming are right off town. As often as not, you will see a schooner under construction or hauled for repairs.

West from Road Bay are a series of beaches backed by steep cliffs. These are

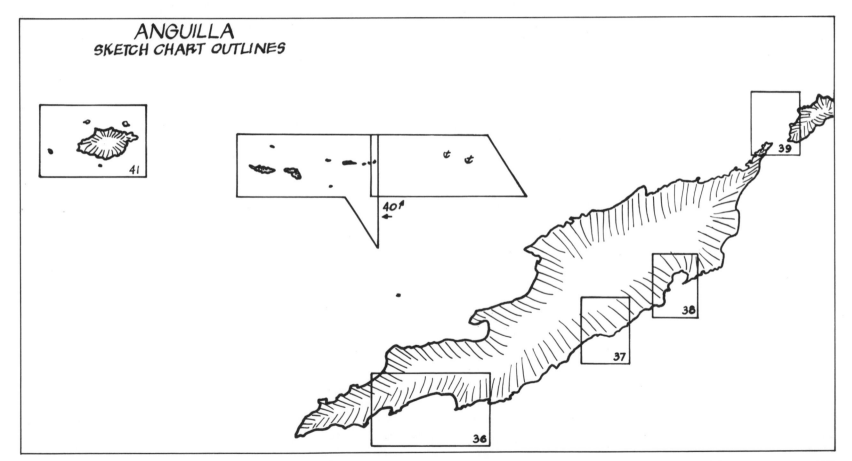

ANGUILLA
SKETCH CHART OUTLINES

41

40

39

38

37

36

ANGUILLA

within dinghy distance of the main harbor and thoroughly secluded. With the wind in the southeast in calm summer weather a pleasant daytime anchorage can be had off this shore. Under no circumstances should this area be so used in the winter.

Cove Bay
(BA 2038, NO 25241, Sketch Chart 36)

Shoal Bay and Maundays Bay, the two southernmost bays on the island, are not particularly good, exposed to the east and shallow. You are better advised to proceed eastward to Cove Bay, where an anchorage can be had in the northeast corner of the bay in one-and-a-half fathoms. Keep your lead line working, since it is hard to judge the gradually shoaling depth of this bay, even though the water is crystal clear. A lovely sand beach stretches for a mile and a half.

Rendezvous Bay
(BA 2038, NO 25241, Sketch Chart 36)

A beautiful, wide expanse, unencumbered by coral heads. The only danger is Shaddick Point, which extends much farther to the southwest than is shown on the chart. My favorite anchorage is in the northeast corner of the bay over a white-sand bottom. The only difficulty is a non-stop generator on shore that tends to interrupt the peace.

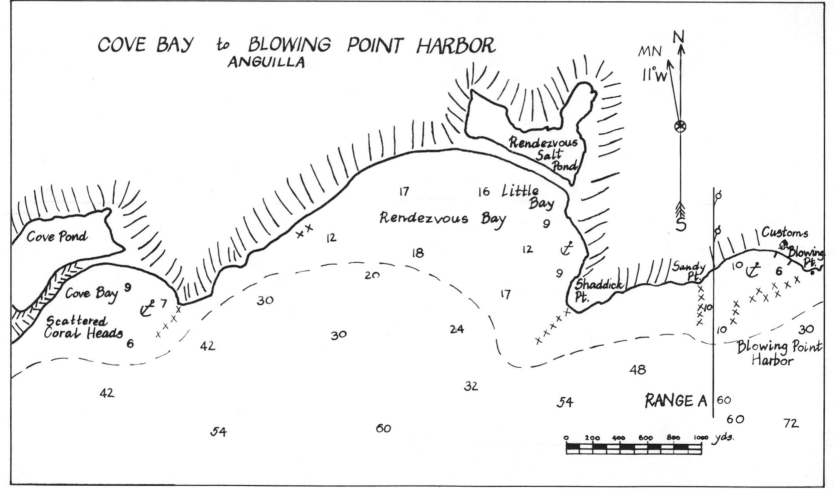

Range A: Two white markers in line, 010 magnetic.

SKETCH CHART 36

Blowing Point Harbor
(BA 2038, NO 25241, Sketch Chart 36)

Just between Sandy Point and Blowing Point, this is the oft-frequented harbor of the small boat traffic between St. Martin and Anguilla. The land behind Blowing Point Harbor is so low and featureless that it is impossible to relate any ranges or bearings. I will say that it is not shaped anything like what the chart shows. The harbor may be spotted from a distance by the many masts of moored boats. Another landmark is the 100-yard spit of coral that has been piled up by the current off Sandy Point. To enter, favor this bank of dead coral and pick up the range marks, two white shapes lined up on a bearing of 010 magnetic. This leads between the bank of dead coral and the reef to windward which is submerged by two or three feet; stand in to the harbor, and round up to the east. Anchor anywhere in the middle where there is roughly ten feet. There is a small jetty where you can row ashore and clear. There are usually a number of schooners and sloops moored in the harbor. One of them, the *Endeavor,* a former smuggler of great repute, is undoubtedly the largest sloop in the Lesser Antilles. She was built many years ago along the lines of a knockabout Gloucester fishing schooner—with overhanging bow, no bowsprit, no forefoot, low freeboard, fine rounded counter, and a carved wooden railing around the stern. She is sloop-rigged, with roughly an 80-foot boom, the largest and longest main boom I have ever seen. Moored in Blowing Point Harbor when I last saw her, she looked to be doing six knots just tied to her mooring buoy. She is said to be capable of 12 knots on a reach. Even allowing for gross exaggeration, she must have been very fast. But not fast enough to outrun the new Customs launches which soon managed to put her out of business.

Boat Harbor/Little Bay
(BA 2038, NO 25241)

Too shoal- and reef-encumbered for the average yacht.

Forest Bay
(BA 2038, NO 25241, Sketch Chart 37)

East of what is marked as Boat Harbor on the chart, it can be identified by its small custom house and jetty. Though this is the deepest harbor on the south coast of Anguilla, it is not very well protected and is difficult to enter. The reefs are not high enough to break the swell, which has tended to limit its use to the larger Anguillan vessels. The channel is ten feet deep on into the center of the harbor, but it is more tricky than it appears. Entrance is made from the southwest; head in for the jetty until inside the reef; lower sail and anchor in the middle of the harbor. The bottom shoals on both sides.

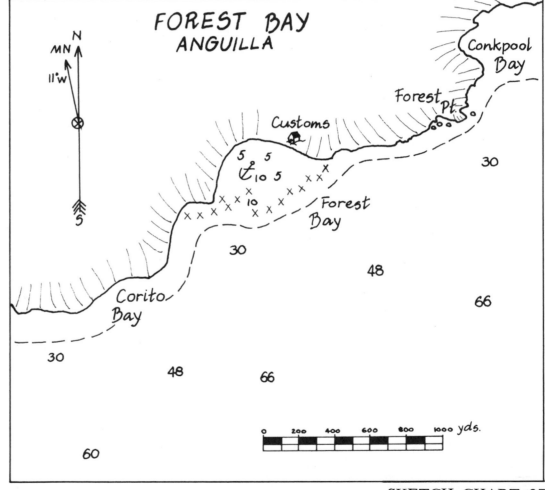

SKETCH CHART 37

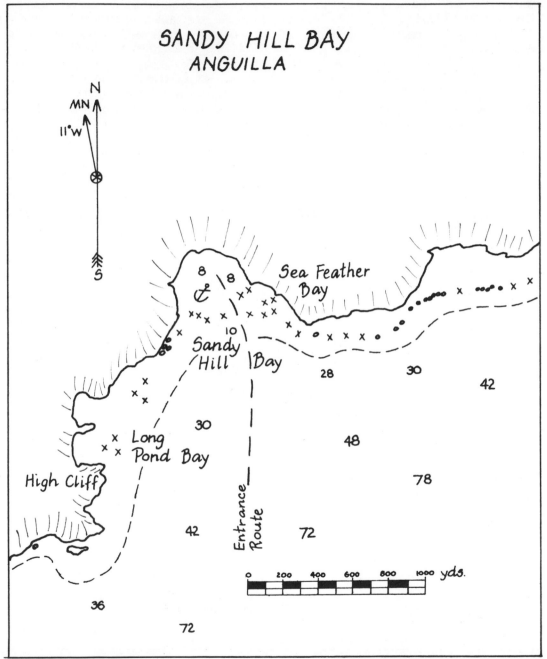

SKETCH CHART 38

Sandy Hill Bay
(BA 2038, NO 25241, Sketch Chart 38)

A first-rate anchorage well up the coast of Anguilla. It can be spotted by the houses around the beach and by the small boats anchored in the western part of the harbor. This is not a port of entry. Approaching Sandy Hill Bay from the south, the appearance may convince you that there is not enough water all the way inside. But as you will see from the Sketch Chart, an anchorage can be reached within. Reefs extend from the eastern side of the harbor. West of these are three coral heads with about three feet of water over them. Pass between the two eastern ones and sail on into the bay, anchoring in about eight feet of water. The bay has a beautiful white-sand beach which makes it a favorite picnic spot of the Anguillans.

East of Sandy Hill Bay, on the south coast of Anguilla, there are no harbors whatsoever—only exposed bays and beaches. The same holds true of Little Island Harbor behind Scilly Cay, which is very tricky and will carry no more than four feet. I would advise against this harbor unless you have a highly skilled local pilot on board, and even he would have to have luck going for him.

Crocus Bay (NO 25242) on the north side of Anguilla was at one time one of the main ports, a fact which I have never understood as the bay is wide open to the ground swell. Thus it is best avoided, even though the chart shows an anchorage behind Flat Cap Point. The only vessels that frequent the area are the tankers off-loading the island's fuel supply.

Islands off the Coast of Anguilla

The islands off the coast of Anguilla provide opportunities for exploring, archaeology, diving for wrecks, beachcombing, or plain old lazing about. These areas are recommended for summer use when the ground swell has subsided.

Scrub Island
(BA 2038, NO 25241, Sketch Chart 39)

East of Anguilla, Scrub Island has a fabulously beautiful beach, which can only be approached during the summer months. The approach to the shore at Scrub Bay on the western side of the island is largely obstructed by coral and grass. However, from the middle of the bay bearing on the middle of the beach is a narrow white-sand channel. Follow this channel along toward the beach and anchor Bahamian style or bow-and-stern. The holding is good—no coral or grass to interefere with the proper set of your anchors. On the eastern end of the island is Dead Man's Bay, which is fully exposed and full of coral heads. I have flown over and seen campers inside, but there is certainly no anchorage here, the only way of approaching it being by outboard-driven dinghy.

Sandy Island
(BA 2038, NO 25242)

Northwest of Road Bay, this is a fine daytime anchorage when it is not blowing too hard. You can put in to anchor along the shoal west of Sandy Island. Dowling Reefs to the northwest are good for swimming and snorkeling. This is the very image of the deserted tropical island—a small sand spit under a few palm trees with white-sand beach and crystal water stretching all around.

From Prickly Pear eastward there are a series of exposed reefs, small unnamed islands, and sand spits over a distance of seven miles. In settled weather, this is an incomparably fine area to anchor and swim.

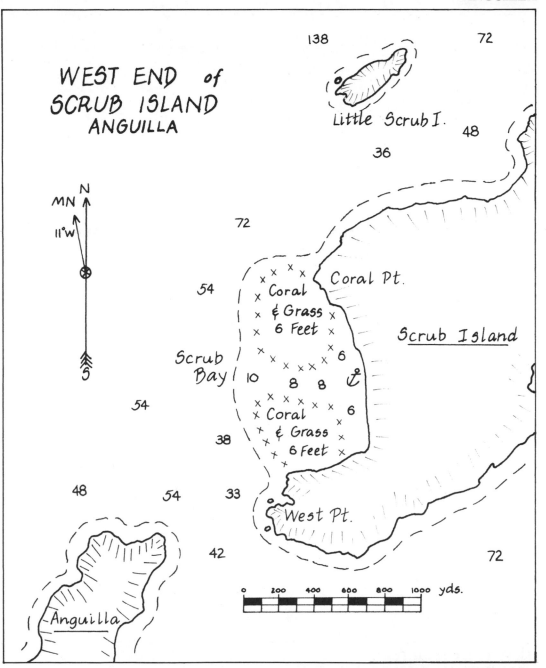

SKETCH CHART 39

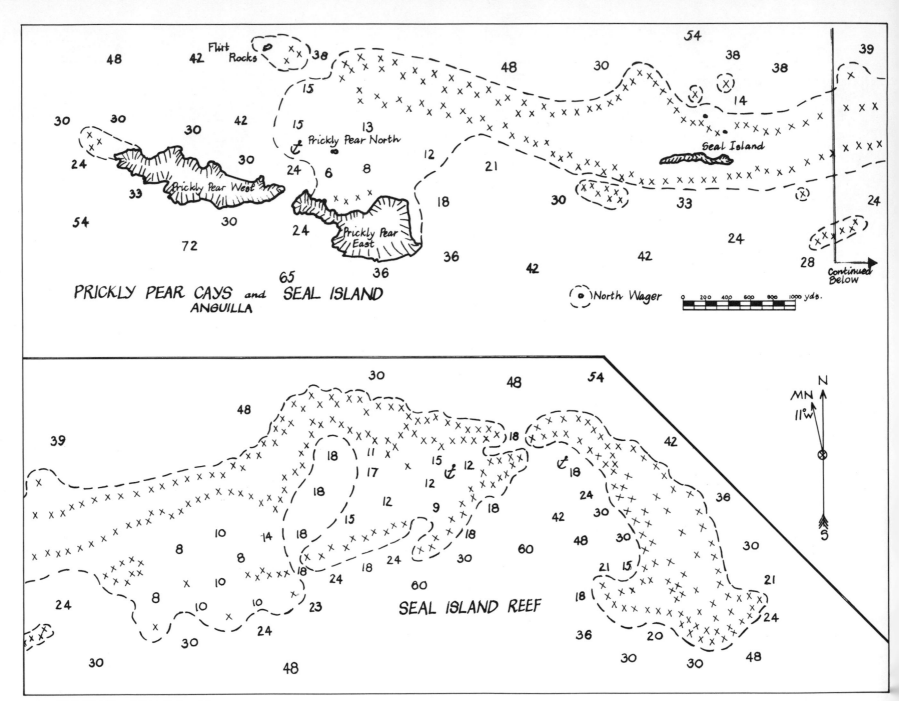

PRICKLY PEAR CAYS and SEAL ISLAND
ANGUILLA

SEAL ISLAND

Flirt Rocks

Prickly Pear North

Prickly Pear West

Prickly Pear East

Seal Island

North Wager

200 400 600 800 1000 yds.

Continued Below

SEAL ISLAND REEF

N
MN
11°W
S

SKETCH CHART 40

Only the Tobago Cays come near to rivaling them. Anchorages can be had almost anywhere behind the reef or in among the coral heads. The area is not charted in sufficient detail, so that careful eyeball navigation will be required. The most sheltered anchorage is on the west side of Prickly Pear North (Sketch Chart 40), which is nothing more than some six-foot-high rocks north of Prickly Pear Cays. For a reason no one can fathom, there is a landing strip on Prickly Pear West, which I have never seen used.

Dog Island
(BA 2038, NO 25241, Sketch Chart 41)

There are three good anchorages along the west coast of Dog Island. There is ample water for yachts of normal draft to sail between Dog Island and West and Mid Cays, although the charts don't show it.

Spring Bay, on the northwest corner of the island, has a sandy beach which is beautiful to look at but not to swim from, since from the water's edge down it is all coral and loose rock. This beach also boasts a prodigious

crop of natural sponges. There is an old landing strip on the island that is no longer used.

South of Spring Bay lies Bailey's Cove—strictly a dinghy landing spot. The dinghy must be anchored bow-and-stern to keep it off the rocks. The snorkeling is superb and I imagine the fishing is quite good.

If you continue sailing southeast you will arrive at what I will categorically declare to be the finest beach in the Lesser Antilles. Great Bay is the home of this paradise, and as long as the ground swell is not running

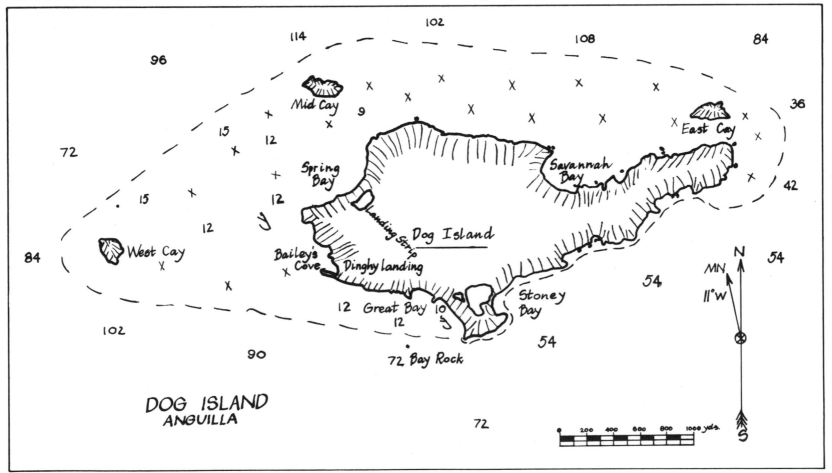

DOG ISLAND
ANGUILLA

and the wind is not in the east, a good anchorage can be had in the southeast corner of the bay. When entering, be careful to avoid Bay Rock which just barely breaks and could easily do in a hapless yacht. The beach is about 500 yards long and divided into halves by a four-foot-high stone wall. (Two particularly short couples can skinny-dip in complete privacy.) At the western end of the beach, the sea has hollowed out a bowl in the rocks into which the sea sluices from time to time, creating a clear, warm, salt water bath. If you are moored in Spring Bay, this beach can be reached by walking over the ridge southeast of the end of the runway and around the salt pond; head south and pass the western edge of the salt pond and "voila!"—the perfect beach.

One of the interesting things on Dog Island, as with many of the other islands in the area, is that stone walls four feet high and two feet thick have been built crossing the island at various points, from the northern shore to the southern shore in a straight line. Like the New Englander, the Anguillan had to remove the rocks from his fields before he could farm, hence the stone walls. I must say that they had excellent stonemasons, as these dry stone walls are about the best I have seen in the Islands.

There are wonderful cruising opportunities throughout this area. In settled weather one could easily spend from ten days to two weeks exploring the coast of Anguilla and its off-lying islands. But the yachtsman is well advised to do so quickly before the hoteliers and tourists move in for keeps.

LESSER ANTILLES—
NORTHERN

DOG I.
SEAL RKS.
SCRUB I.
ANGUILLA
St MARTIN
ORIENT BAY
St MAARTEN
St BARTHÉLEMY
GUSTAVIA
(St BARTS)

SABA

SABA BANK

BARBUDA

COCO PT.
PALASTER REEF

TERRE

THE NARROWS

NEVIS

ANTIGUA
FIVE ISLANDS HBR.
PARHAM SOUND
NONSUCH BAY

63°W
62°W
18°N

CHAPTER 11

St. Martin

NO 25241, 25242; BA 2038, 2079

When, years ago, I first arrived in the Lesser Antilles, the small, high, and sparsely populated island of St. Martin was enjoying the beginnings of a tourist boom. It was rather nice. The positive aspects of civilization (electricity, frozen meat, ice, and a few hotels) had arrived without the curses of neon lights, traffic jams, and insolent taxi drivers. Air communication with St. Thomas, Antigua, and San Juan was meager. Since that first visit, however, the airport has expanded until now direct air service exists from Europe, the United States, and South America. Americans have flocked to the island to escape high taxes and pollution. St. Martin is now booming with hotels from the huge casino type to little guest houses. The influx of tourists and hotels has completely taken over the economy of the island to the point where it is difficult to find any sign of the original small, sleepy villages of Philipsburg on the Dutch side or of Marigot on the French.

The foundation of this curious two-country situation was laid in 1648, when squabbling French and Dutch settlers agreed to divvy up the island between them. The Dutch took 21 square miles in the south and the French 16 square miles in the north. Although now into its fourth century, the treaty is still in force. The island can be discussed as a single entity, however, inasmuch as no one seems to care about the border.

St. Martin (or Maarten) is developing pretty much as one unit even though the Dutch are well ahead of the French in tourist development. The Dutch side is drier than the French; the French northeastern corner is lovely: rolling hills, lush grass with cattle grazing—a genuine farm economy. This is in marked contrast to the dependence on tourism that saturates the southern side of the island.

The French are a competitive people. The airport was in Dutch territory, so the French built a small, cement strip on the northern half of the island. The Dutch dredged a channel into Simson's Lagoon from their side; the French promptly dredged a like channel from French territory. Although the Dutch have had their troubles, they did finally organize the opening of their bridge at Simson's Point. The French, however, in a similar fashion to the trouble-plagued bridge at Point-a-Pitre, Guadeloupe, have as yet been unable to effect the opening of their bridge. As late as mid-1973, a masted vessel had to enter the lagoon from the Dutch side.

St. Martin is developing into a yachting center. On the French side there is a small yacht yard, while the Dutch expect to have a floating drydock in the years to come. In addition to a floating dock, Island Water World on Simson's Lagoon has marina facilities, ice, fuel, and water. At present, boats with drafts up to 54 inches can use this dock. Island Water World hopes to be able to take care of boats that draw up to eight feet in

ST. MARTIN
SKETCH CHART OUTLINES

43

the future. They plan to do more dredging and to expand their marina facilities. Captain Frank Mundus expects to have a travel lift capable of taking boats up to 65 feet and 40 tons. But it may be several more years before all this comes to pass. Also in the same area is Lanseair, specializing in the design and construction of lightweight catamarans similar to the well-known *Blue Crane* which Peter Spronck originally designed and built in Grenada. (Peter has sailed *Blue Crane* up and down the Islands for the last ten years at great speeds and with little difficulty.)

Boats can enter Blue Lagoon through the bridge in Simson's Bay, at the eastern end behind Pelican Point. No charts are available, but *Black Swan* with a draft of 14 feet has entered the lagoon. Once you are inside, you must depend upon local knowledge, since the charts do not show the results of the dredging operations.

All sorts of foods can be purchased at both Philipsburg and Marigot. Imported luxury items—cheeses, wines, liquors—are relatively inexpensive; but the basic necessities—meat, vegetables, and fruit—are quite dear. Ice used to be worth its weight in gold, but now you can take a taxi to the fishing station at Witte Cape in Philipsburg where you can buy block ice.

Both Marigot and Philipsburg are free ports and quite casual in their attitude toward customs and immigration. Fly your "Q" flag when entering either port. If no one has arrived from officialdom by the time you have anchored, furled your sails, and rigged your awning, go ashore and locate the appropriate persons: French side, it's the Gendarmerie; on the Dutch side, the police station.

St. Martin lies 72 miles southeast by east from Virgin Gorda by way of Necker Island Passage, and is the usual landfall for boats proceeding eastward from the Virgin Islands. With two fairly good harbors, it is sufficiently high and well lit that it can be spotted at night from a safe distance. Do not approach St. Martin from the north or northwest at night, since St. Martin rising over the low land of Anguilla is apt to make you misjudge your distance off the latter island. Should this happen, you will be on the reefs before you realize your mistake. In fact, there are four miles between St. Martin and Anguilla, but at night this distance is not apparent.

Boats approaching from the south must watch out for Proselyte Reef (Man-of-War Reef). With only two-and-a-quarter fathoms over it, in rough weather it sometimes breaks and is the single danger on the southerly approach. The ranges to clear this reef are given with Sketch Chart 42.

Boats rounding the western end of St. Martin must take care, as Terre Basse Point is continually extending to the westward. At night give this point a berth of at least one-and-a-half miles; during daylight, do not approach the point closer than one mile without putting a lookout in the rigging. Numerous boats have grounded on this point and many have been lost.

Philipsburg
(BA 2038, 2079; NO 25241, 25242
Plan C)

A good harbor in most weather, but it is open to the south. When the wind is south of east, it is wise to go to Marigot on the French side. Also, a big ground swell from the north is apt to make Philipsburg uncomfortable: sometimes this swell sweeps all the way around the island and enters Philipsburg from the south! Should this happen, set two anchors, so your boat will lie facing south despite the wind. A single anchor could break out and your vessel would be ashore before you could do anything. For the most part, though, the harbor is breezy and cool with only a slight swell in normal trade wind weather.

The outer harbor, on a line between Fort Amsterdam and Witte Kappe, is amply deep. There is a steamer pier on the west side of Witte Kappe. Across the entire harbor stretches a bar with at least seven to eight feet over it. The deepest water is at the eastern end; if you line up the Sea View Hotel (the first large white building on the beach) with the saddle between the two hills behind the town, this range follows a channel of about 10 feet deep. The anchorage for small boats is off the town pier, where you will find from eight to ten feet of water. (The bottom changes so often that positive depths are impossible to predict.) Anchor about 200 yards south of this dock, which is strictly a dinghy landing with a sporadically burning light. Customs will come out to your boat. They are usually fairly prompt.

There is a light on Fort Amsterdam, but it does not seem to have the visibility claimed on the chart (six miles). The lights on the steamer pier, however, are visible eight to ten miles off.

Simson's Bay
(BA 2038, 2079; NO 25241, 25242)

West of Philipsburg Harbor the only other true anchorage is behind Pelican Point in Simson's Bay. This anchorage is satisfactory in normal weather, but when the ground swell is rolling, the surge tends to swing all the way around the point. The swing-bridge and entrance to Simson's Lagoon are here. Arrangements must be made ahead of time to have the bridge opened; to do this, contact Arthur Brown, the bridge operator, at his home at 224 Cole Bay. As I have mentioned in the introductory remarks, be sure to obtain up-to-date local directions before you attempt to enter.

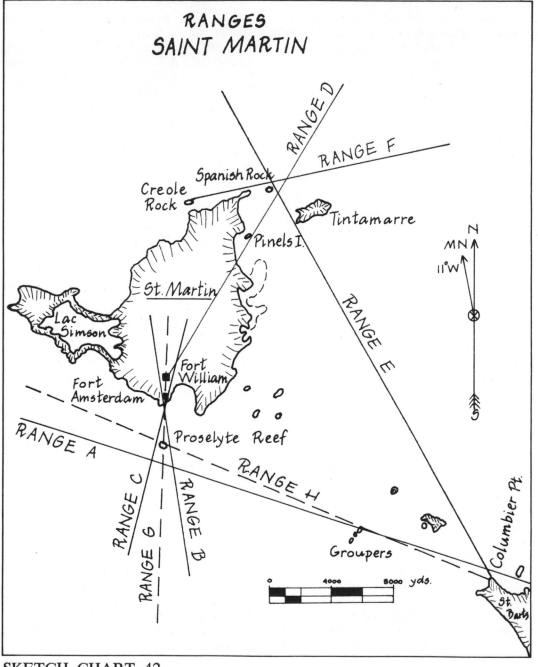

RANGES
SAINT MARTIN

SKETCH CHART 42

Marigot Bay
(BA 2038, 2079; NO 25241, 25242
Plan B)

The French port and town of Marigot Bay is an open roadstead and at one time boats had to anchor quite far offshore. An excursion ashore would uncover a small, sleepy village with one four-room hotel. Marigot has since expanded drastically. The road westward of the beach is now lined with hotel after hotel, nightclubs, and restaurants—including one small floating bar: a catamaran anchored in the harbor. (Although it cost almost nothing to build, the catamaran has become one of the town's most popular water-

Range A: Great Groupers open to the north of Columbier Point, St. Barts, clears Proselyte Reef to the south.

Range B: Fort Amsterdam in line with the west face of steep hill below ruins of Fort William clears Proselyte Reef to the east.

Range C: Fort Amsterdam in line with east face of steep hill below ruins of Fort William clears Proselyte Reef to the west.

Range D: Fort William seen over the eastern high land in line with the highest part of Pinels Island at its east end leads southeast of Spanish Rock.

Range E: West high land of St. Barts in line with southwest point of Tintamarre clears Spanish Rock to the northeast.

Range F: Creole Rock just open of the northeast point of St. Martin leads clear to the north of Spanish Rock.

Range G: Fort William and Fort Amsterdam in line passes over Proselyte Reef.

Range H: Great Groupers in line with the northwestern high land on St. Barts passes over Proselyte Reef.

ing spots and is a prime example of a minimal investment that brings in a large cash return.)

To find the best anchorage, get the Fort bearing due east; then feel your way in with a lead line over the gradually shoaling bottom. The farther in you go, the more comfortable you will be, as seas do tend to swing around the point to the eastward.

Exert special caution when the ground swell is running because the shoal spots towards the western end of the harbor actually crest and break even in less than extreme conditions.

Marigot is bound to become popular with sailors, as it has at this time one of the nicest and best-padded docks in the entire Lesser Antilles. Despite the fact that this is a commercial jetty, all pilings are covered with heavy rubber tires to protect your boat's topsides.

Both the Fort and the Roman Catholic Church are worth visiting. The shops are loaded with luxuries that are fantastically cheap and with essentials that are horrendously expensive.

East of Marigot Bay, all-weather anchorages are almost nonexistent. In calm weather you can find an anchorage in Anse Marcelle but this is strictly a case of eyeball navigation. You can sneak down into the south corner of Marigot Bay in the summer, but only if the wind is in the southeast.

Other anchorages on the coast of St. Martin are the west side of the island of Tintamarre, Oyster Pond, and Orient Bay. When proceeding through Anguilla Channel, the navigator should have no problems, as there is deep water close to shore on both islands. If you are heading south between Tintamarre and St. Martin, however, beware of the dangerous rock, Bse. Espagnole (Spanish Rock), which breaks in heavy weather only and under normal conditions is difficult

to spot. See Sketch Chart 42 for ranges to spot this rock.

Passing through Anguilla Channel in the region of Tintamarre, do not close Creole Rock with St. Martin. If you intend to beat south through the passage between Tintamarre and St. Martin, stand well to the eastward in Anguilla Channel and tack when you are far enough to windward to lay the line of bearing between Tintamarre and the high land of St. Barts.

A pleasant daytime anchorage may be found under the lee of Tintamarre. Off the white-sand beach on the western shore you can anchor on a clear bottom in four fathoms of water. Exciting snorkeling can be found off the north and south coasts; the island is uninhabited, and exploring on shore is interesting. During and for the first years after World War II, Tintamarre was used as an airfield, so you might find old bits and pieces of aircraft lying around. Since no one seems to know what was going on at the airport at that time, the speculation potential is unlimited.

Possibly my first *Cruising Guide* discouraged the exploring of the east coast of St. Martin, since I pointed out that it is a deadly lee shore open to the Atlantic. Thus for many years most everyone assumed that the east coast offered no anchorages. When I became tired of the same anchorages and of being surrounded by charter yachts, I tried some exploring in *Iolaire*. Adding the knowledge gained from my own forays to that gleaned from other adventurous yachtsmen, I have concluded that the east coast of St. Martin has at least four perfectly acceptable anchorages.

Ilet Pinels
(BA 2038, NO 25241, Sketch Chart 43)

This little island provides two anchor-

ages. The easier and more protected of the two is west of the southern point of Ilet Pinels. The entrance is dead simple if you are careful. Spot the rock southwest of Pinels Island; sail in with the rock bearing approximately northwest; watch out for the rocks that extend from the southern point of Pinels. When these rocks are abeam, harden up and head almost due north. As you round into the bay, keep an eye out for a submerged rock that has four feet over it to the west of the point. Round up between this rock and the point; work your way as close inshore of the sandy beach as you can. Using the lead line, feel your way in where you will find good holding ground on a gently shoaling sand bottom.

Although there is a channel between Pinels and the mainland, this is accessible only to powerboats or dinghies. To enter the north anchorage, you must eyeball your way in heading approximately southwest. As soon as you find yourself in some shelter from Pinels Island, round up and anchor. I doubt that boats drawing more than seven feet will be able to work their way into the sheltered water in this northern anchorage.

I expect that some sort of marina or harbor will someday come into existence at the head of Orient Bay in its northwestern corner, since the dredge was hard at work there in 1973.

Cay Verte (Green Island)
(BA 2038, NO 25241, Sketch Chart 43)

An excellent shelter and a superb anchorage with a simple entrance. Sail into the middle of Orient Bay where you will find the water amply deep. Stand south towards Cay Verte, favoring the shore of the cay rather than the mainland. Using eyeball and lead line, work your way as far to the south as your draft will allow; anchor with a Bahamian moor, as the swinging room is limited.

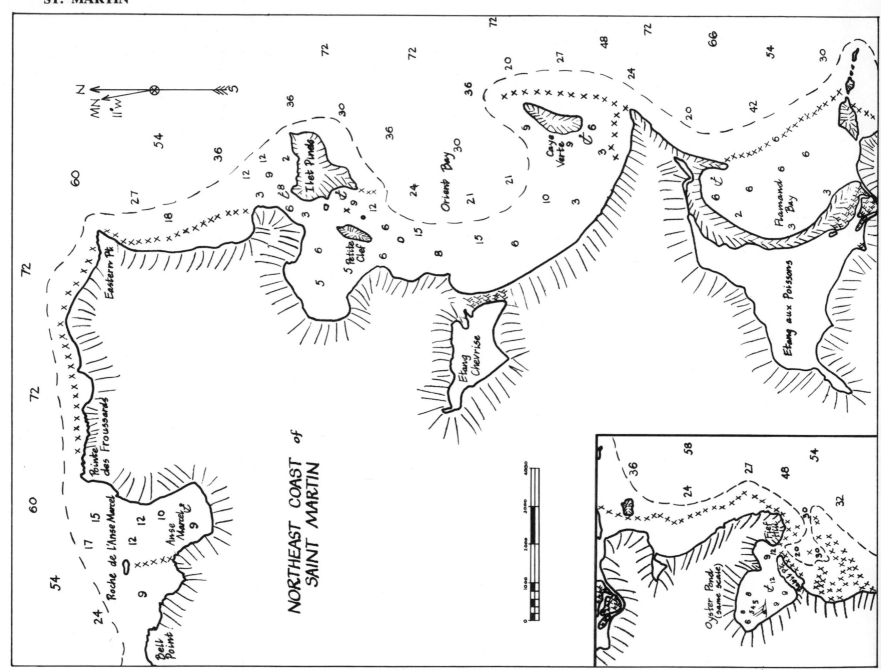

NORTHEAST COAST of SAINT MARTIN

SKETCH CHART 43

Here you will enjoy an absolutely peaceful stay with nothing to disturb you. There are no roads going to the beach at Cay Verte and the only way a determined individual can reach you is by wandering through about a mile and a half of cow pasture and by climbing over barbed-wire fences. And if someone needs to get to you that badly, you probably don't want to know about it.

Flamand Bay
(BA 2038, NO 25241, Sketch Chart 43)

On the roadmap of St. Martin, Flamand Bay is called Bay de l'Enbouchure. It provides splendid shelter to anyone brave enough to enter. Even if I were on familiar terms with this area, I would be leery of the on-shore breakers at the entrance to this harbor. There is no possible range, since the land behind the harbor is low and flat. Behind Lime Reef at the head of the bay you will find excellent protection provided you have a shoal-draft auxiliary (drawing four to five feet) that can slip through the narrow break

in the reefs. Once in, you can run down behind the reef and anchor at the north end of the bay. It can be done. We did spot a 35-foot sailboat, undoubtedly a centerboarder, inside the harbor at the north end of the bay, but figured she must have been a local boat and familiar with the area.

Oyster Pond
(BA 2038, NO 25242 Plan D,
Sketch Chart 43)

According to Morris Nicholson of *Eleuthera*, this harbor is not as scary as it looks on the chart. Although many sailboats have entered it, do not try it without a pilot unless you are very experienced at reef sailing. If it is blowing hard, I would call an engine an absolute necessity to aid in navigating through these reefs, although buoys have been established which mark the northern reef and the obvious breaker on the southern reef. It used to be difficult to spot Oyster Pond, but the establishment of the large Oyster Pond Hotel complex on Babil Point has made the harbor

easy to recognize. Line up the breakers with the cliffs bearing 270 magnetic; run in until you pick up the reef on the starboard hand; follow this around to starboard, favoring the weather side of the channel. Once you pass between Babil Point and Fief Hill, you will find yourself in deep water close to shore on both sides. Inside is complete calm, delightful hospitality at the Oyster Pond Yacht Club and Hotel, and the wreck of the *Norlandia*. This wonder of maritime history sank a few years ago and it is a shame that such a fate should have befallen her. She was a three-masted schooner that carried cargo from Norway to Iceland, Greenland, Newfoundland, Nova Scotia, and back again, frequently crossing the Atlantic with a crew of no more than a skipper, mate, cook, and cabin boy. She sailed through World War II without an engine. After the War, she made a few transatlantic passages carrying commercial cargo—still without an engine—between Europe and Newfoundland.

CHAPTER 12

St. Barthelemy

NO 25241, 25242; BA 2038, 2079

Universally known as St. Barts, the island is one of the most popular in the entire Caribbean, as it is the "free-est" free port in the whole area. This has been the case since 1784, when France ceded the port to Sweden in exchange for trading rights in Stockholm. At that time an agreement was made to the effect that St. Barts would forever remain a free port, thus guaranteeing the French a harbor in which they could unload the loot from their privateers. Later, St. Barts developed into a port for smuggling goods into the British islands, which in fact it still is today.

The Swedish colony proved so unsuccessful that by the middle of the 19th century most of the Swedes had left, and in 1877 Sweden gave the island back to the French. The only Swedish name left on the island seems to be Marius Stacklebough. While a large portion of the island's population have blue eyes and fair hair, this coloring probably stems from the Norman French who came in the 1880's.

The economy of St. Barts is based largely on trade, both legal and illegal. In 1960 Hurricane Donna destroyed most of the working sloops and schooners that were owned and sailed by locals. Although most of these boats were uninsured, that storm did not financially devastate their owners, nor did it put an end to the St. Barts' trading fleet. In traditional thrifty French fashion, the skippers slit open the mattresses where they had been stowing their profits over the years and went to Guadeloupe and with the help of the French Government bought motor vessels. Just the same, it amounted to yet another body-blow to working sailboats.

In years gone by, local schooners had an ingenious law-beating gimmick. Although it was illegal to import cattle into French islands from non-French islands, St. Barts, being a free port, did not have to abide by such regulations. The St. Barts schooners would sail to Tortola or St. Croix and buy several head of cattle, sail to St. Barts, sell them to a "brother," buy back, reload, and sail off to Martinique or Guadeloupe with papers that proved the cattle had been bought in a free port acceptable to the French. Later, these entrepreneurs did not even unload the cattle; they simply bought and sold them while the vessel remained at anchor.

Today, liquor and cigarettes are the main items of sale. The French don't waste their own energy smuggling; instead, they sell to others who want to smuggle. In 1973, Mount Gay Eclipse Barbados rum sold for $1.50 a bottle in Barbados and in most other British islands. In the free port of Gustavia, St. Barts, the same rum sold for $6 a *case*—and sometimes less. Small island sloops sail 400 miles from Grenada to St. Barts, pick up a cargo of Barbados rum, and sail 400 miles back to smuggle the rum into Grenada. Thus the rum travels 800 miles to be smuggled into an island that is only 90 miles from where it was made!

Dick Ames, owner of *Andiamo*, always maintained that he could buy rum for the best price in the entire West Indies. He would visit a dealer and the two of them would sit down over brandy and cigars and start haggling over the price of 20 cases of rum. Dick

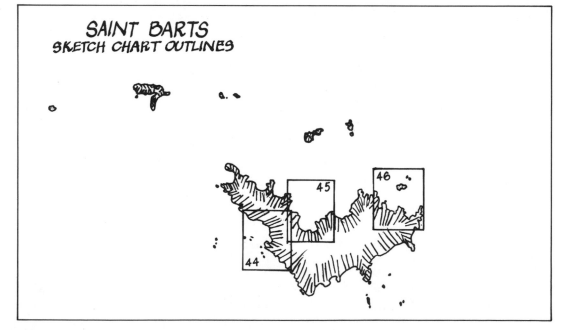

SAINT BARTS
SKETCH CHART OUTLINES

45

46

44

would finally scrape the price down to $5 a case. Then, he said, he always felt so guilty that he would take the dealer out for a good lunch. At the end of the lunch and the wine and cigars and drinks, Dick figured that it would have been cheaper for him to have bought the rum at $7 a case. But he had so much fun haggling and feasting that he felt the experience was well worth the difference.

In addition to liquor, cigarettes, and perfume, many other good buys can be unearthed in St. Barts. You might find wonderful old copper kerosene anchor lights and running lights which have internal chimneys and which don't blow out. Tremendous quantities of marine supplies are available at the Alma store. You would have trouble locating these anywhere in the world, least of all expect to find them on the little island of St. Barts.

The owners of Alma, the Magras family, run a vast business enterprise. Monsieur Magras wanders between the three stores run by his sons while managing to keep a watchful eye on his myriad other enterprises, prominent among which is the St. Barts Yacht Club, the old house on the western side of the harbor where you can always buy an excellent dinner. Years ago, when there were no banking facilities on the island, money was kept in an old shoebox in the Magras office. If you went in to cash some checks, Magras would open a drawer and there would be lying tens of thousands of dollars in various currencies. When too much money was on hand, which happened occasionally, it was stuffed into a brown paper shopping bag, handed to the mate of one of the schooners heading for St. Thomas for deposit in the bank there. Now St. Barts has a bank, and the procedures are predictably stuffy.

Do not plan on picking up either fuel or water in St. Barts. Gasoline and diesel fuel are available alongside the dock, sold strictly by appointment in five-gallon tins. Water is very hard to come by; and ice, although you can purchase it, will cost you an arm and a leg. Stock up on all three of these before reaching St. Barts. Little fresh food is available on the island. Frozen food is flown in from San Juan and is very expensive. Do not attempt to stock up on anything other than liquor and luxury items.

Gustavia itself is well worth some exploration. Many of its buildings date back to the days of the Swedish occupation, and the massive stone architecture is quite different from the typical West Indian houses. The town is essentially French. The houses belonging to the wealthy people present a stern and forbidding exterior; but in back you will usually find a beautiful, cool, walled-in garden where the family entertains.

You can walk to Ft. Coral, to the east of town, take in an exquisite view, and then go down to the lovely white-sand beach that was created when the harbor was dredged. (Although the natives claim no success spearfishing there, the last time we fished the beach, one of our party caught a 40-pound grouper.) If all this walking has made you thirsty, stop by Marius Stacklebough's bar, La Select, at the head of the dock, both to pick up news and for a spot of booze. You will meet all the locals there. Marius, St. Bart's last Swede, can recommend a restaurant and arrange for a taxi. He is certainly one of the more informed of the local inhabitants in island lore.

Visit the fishing village in the Baie de Curazo by taxi or dinghy; it is totally isolated from the rest of St. Barts. Until recently, the village had no road; and now that it does, most of the villagers still travel to and fro by small boat.

The completion of a wharf in 1960 removed one of the most interesting spectacles in St. Barts. Formerly, ships had to anchor off the outer harbor and lighter their cargo ashore. The lighters were propelled by two oars, one rowed in the usual way on the side, the other over the stern as a sculling oar. Why they didn't go around in a circle beats me. The loading and unloading of cattle was a particularly good show—as long as you were not a member of the ASPCA.

Although the landing strip has been given a coat of tarmac, it can still give a strong man a weak heart. It is rightly regarded as the most dangerous airstrip in the Islands, with a record of many crashes to assure this status.

Now there are several hotels on St. Barts. Which is currently the best I would not venture to say. My advice would be to check out details of hotels and restaurants with the locals at La Select.

In the early 1950s, St. Bartians were considered the best of the West Indians for yacht crews. Their English was abominable, but they were skilled divers and good small-boat sailors, quick to learn, honest, hardworking, and fearless. There was the added bonus of their cooking prowess. After a few days out, a St. Bartian crew would be heard to mutter, "Yes, I am not a cook but I make something in the kitchen for you." In no time at all, marvelous smells would emanate from the galley, and from then on the smart charter skipper would surrender the galley to the man who insisted he was not a cook.

Many such islanders crewed on charter yachts, then moved on to high-paid jobs aboard large, lush, U.S. yachts, and with the true frugality of French West Indians, they spent virtually nothing. After 15 or 20 years, they took their substantial nest eggs back to St. Barts where they invested in small guest houses, restaurants, and stores.

Despite the expansion of small enterprises on the island, St. Barts itself has not changed at all; no development money for St. Barts has come from outside the island, which is the way the islanders want to keep it. The honesty of these islanders is legend: if you load a car with groceries, liquor, a camera, or hang a gold watch from the dashboard, it could safely be left unlocked in the middle of town.

St. Barts is a part of the "department" of Guadeloupe. A department is a sort of state, the same as a province in France, which means St. Barts has its representative in the French legislature in Paris. This can be a mixed blessing, since it brings with it the inevitable gendarme. Clearing-in at St. Barts is usually a matter of going ashore and, in your own sweet time, wandering up to the Gendarmerie, turning in a crew list, and meandering out the door. But it doesn't always happen that way. Last time I was on the island, the sergeant jumped on me with both feet, gave me a 15-minute lecture in French (which I pretended not to understand), made me go back to the boat and bring him everyone's passports and hoist my "Q" flag. When I arrived back at the Gendarmerie, the sergeant had left and the corporal who was there couldn't figure out what all the papers were for. He made me fill out the crew list and wished me bon voyage.

If you are approaching St. Barts from the south, leave Pte. Negre and Les Saintes to port. There are no dangers along this part of the coast and there is ample water between Les Saintes and the mainland. You can tell the maximum depth by the color of the water. When Ft. Octave is abeam, start rounding up and flattening sheets, stand into the harbor on starboard tack, make one or two tacks, and you will be in the anchorage. It is steep-to close to shore. If you make passage outside the Saintes, watch out for the shoals that extend north of them.

Coming from the west and the northwest in daylight, there are no dangers for a yacht.

Everything is visible above water and steep-to. At night north of the island, Roche Table is dangerous; it is low and hard to spot. The details of the light at Ft. Gustavia are shown on BA 2079. This light is group occulting, three colors: red, white and green. It is confusing in that, at the extreme of visibility when you cross from one sector to another, the light disappears. The white sector of the light is visible 14 miles, the green 10 miles, and the red 9 miles. It is red from northwest to north, and from south-by-west to west-southwest. The light is white and green for the rest of the west half of the compass. The green sector covers the area that is encompassed by Ile Syndare and Le Pain de Sucre (NO 25242). This means if you are in the white sectors of this light, you are in good water and not in danger. Remember, this light is obscured by high hills northwest-by-north clockwise around to south-southwest. Do not approach St. Barts from directions where the light is obscured. Since there are few recognizable lights on shore on a dark night, you could be on the beach before you realized it was there.

During the day, pass close aboard the rocks off the western end of Baie Colombier; hug the coast, staying 100 yards off, as it is steep-to all the way. The old *Sailing Directions* warn that "the vessel must be at all times kept under command as the flaws coming from the highland may catch the vessel aback." Being caught aback was a great danger for an old square-rigged ship which had great difficulty maneuvering in restricted waters. These same "flaws" are of great advantage to the modern yacht: tack on every header, take advantage of the lifts, and you will really make good to windward with considerable time saved.

If you should be forced offshore, beware of La Baleine, an awash rock 250 yards east of Ile Syndare.

Gustavia
(BA 2038, 2079; NO 25241, 25242; Sketch Chart 44)

The town and port is not as it is shown on the chart. In 1960 the northern half of the harbor was dredged to a depth of 12 feet and a dock was constructed on the eastern end of the harbor. Gustavia is now a first-rate, if somewhat dirty, port that is sheltered in all winds. Even the ubiquitous ground swell is not too bothersome.

Before the latest dredging, the harbor was restricted to medium-draft yachts. The wind would waltz around the compass; boats would swing at their moorings; pushpits would end up in pulpits and pulpits in pushpits. Dredging has opened up a depth of 12 feet right up to the harbor head, with a slight shoaling around the edges. Now the average-sized boat can lie stern-to anywhere in the entire basin. Although this has not turned the harbor into a perfect hurricane hole, it certainly provides more than adequate shelter in all but an absolute hurricane.

Anse a Corossol
(BA 2079, NO 25242, Sketch Chart 44)

This is an attractive anchorage and an alternative to the dirty harbor of Gustavia. The bay has a white-sand beach, a small fishing village, and a single restaurant right on the beach that is owned by an ex-yachting crew. The only disadvantage to this idyllic spot is the racket from a power plant that runs all night.

Anse du Public
(BA 2079, NO 25242, Sketch Chart 44)

Listed on the British chart as Publiken Bay, this is another excellent anchorage and also much cleaner than the town anchorage. It is isolated enough to allow an early-morning skinny dip, yet is only a short dinghy ride from town.

Baie de Colombier
(BA 2038, NO 25241)

The north shore of St. Barts provides two good anchorages. Bay Colombier on the northwest tip of the island is satisfactory as far as the shelter is concerned, but the holding ground is poor (mixed sand and grass), so be sure that your anchor is well set. This anchorage is only practical in normal trade wind weather; if the ground sea makes up from the north, move around to Gustavia. The cove is easily recognized by the large house built by one of the Rockefellers above the beach. Everything is steep-to and you should find no problems in approaching. It is legal to land there and you will find an appealing sand beach. Under French law, everything from 14 feet back of the high-water mark to the shore is public property. To remind Mr. Rockefeller of this fact, the local French have picnics on his beach on the big French holidays. This being the game, I doubt that Rockefeller could object if visiting yachtsmen did the same.

Baie de St. Jean
(BA 2038, NO 25241, Sketch Chart 45)

Easy to spot because of the Eden Rock Hotel, owned by Rene de Haenen who settled on St. Barts during World War II and has been there almost ever since. For many years Rene had the only hotel on the island, the only aircraft, served as mayor and at other times as the elected representative to the French Legislature. You will not find this harbor on the standard chart. The Sketch Chart will give you an idea of the approach. Put your stern on Isle Bonhomme (I. Chevreau [Goat Island] on the chart), steer a course of 165, aiming for a conspicuous group of four coconut trees on the beach, one of which is painted with white stripes. Keep your bow on the striped tree and run on in. Do not be confused by the buoy which marks

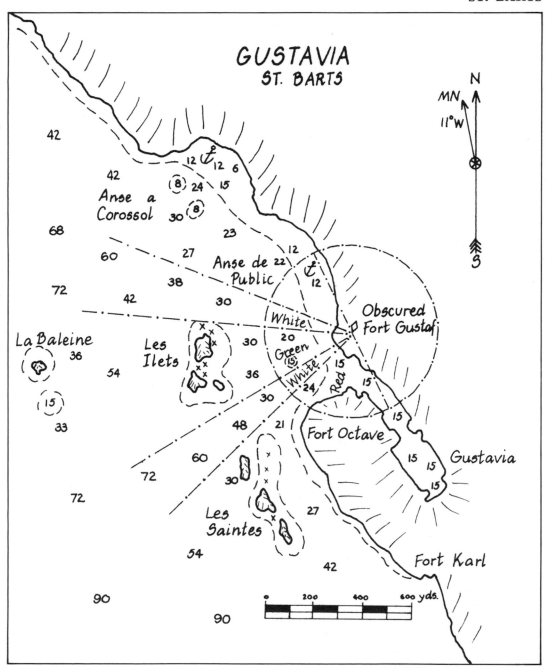

SKETCH CHART 44

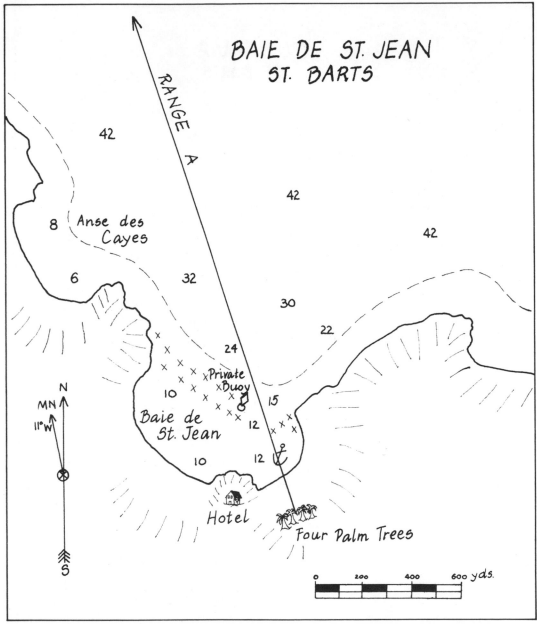

BAIE DE ST. JEAN
ST. BARTS

RANGE A

42

42

42

42

Anse des
Cayes

8

6

32

30

22

24

×
× ×
× × ×
× × ×
Private
× × × Buoy

10

Baie de
St. Jean

10

15

12

12

Hotel

Four Palm Trees

N
MN
11°W
S

0   200   400   600 yds.

Route A: Palm tree painted with white stripes brought to bear 165 magnetic leads between the reefs.

SKETCH CHART 45

the reef on the western side of the harbor, as the buoy may or may not be in the correct position. Do not enter unless the sun is high, since you must use eyeball navigation. As soon as you pass the reef on the port hand, round up and anchor. A boat drawing ten feet can be taken inside the reef. This is only a settled-weather spot. During the winter months, when the ground swell is apt to build up, the reef is not high enough to provide shelter.

Anse de Marigot
(BA 2038, NO 25241, Sketch Chart 46)

Both the U.S. and Admiralty charts are completely incorrect in this area so beware of them. Anse de Grande Cul de Sac and Anse de Petit Cul de Sac are, as the names suggest, entirely obstructed by reefs; only a small dinghy could make it over the reef and into the bay. Similarly, no passage exists between La Tortue and the mainland; it is totally shoal and reef-encumbered. An entrance to Anse de Marigot can be found, however: sail eastwards until you see the beautiful, white-sand beach at the mouth of the harbor on the eastern side of Anse de Marigot. Proceed eastward until you can run downwind with the house on the south of the ridge bearing approximately southwest. The entrance between the two reefs is very narrow so eyeball navigation is a must. In fact, I think a pilot is essential to enter this anchorage. Run in between the reefs, and, as you pass the tip of the eastern reef, start altering your course to the west. You should be heading for the beach at the top of the bay. Once the bay opens up, you can round up and anchor near its head in eight to ten feet of water.

This information was given to me by courtesy of Jerry Burgraff of *Solar Barque,* the only yachtsman I have ever met who has actually entered this harbor. Once inside, he reports, a boat is perfectly sheltered.

Anse de Grande Saline
(BA 2038, NO 25241)

If the wind is in the east and not blowing too hard, Anse de Grande Saline is a lovely daytime anchorage, well tucked-up in the northeast corner. You will find a white-sand beach and no roads; you will probably have the whole place to yourself.

North of St. Barts are numerous islands which are reputed to provide splendid spear-fishing and diving for the adventurous. Most of these islands have no landing, however, so the yacht would have to heave-to off the island while the divers went in by dinghy.

Iles Fourche
(BA 2038, NO 25241)

This island provides one decent anchorage, but only one. Iles Fourche is referred to as though it were five islands because, when seen from a distance, its five peaks appear as separate islands. It is shaped like the thumb and index finger of the right hand: thumb faces south; index finger faces west. In the northeast angle you will find an excellent anchorage in three fathoms of water. Be careful of the exposed rock off the western tip and the submerged reef off the southern tip. This exquisite anchorage has a beach and some lovely views, but there are no bushes, trees, or water on the island. It would be a good place to abandon a mutinous crew.

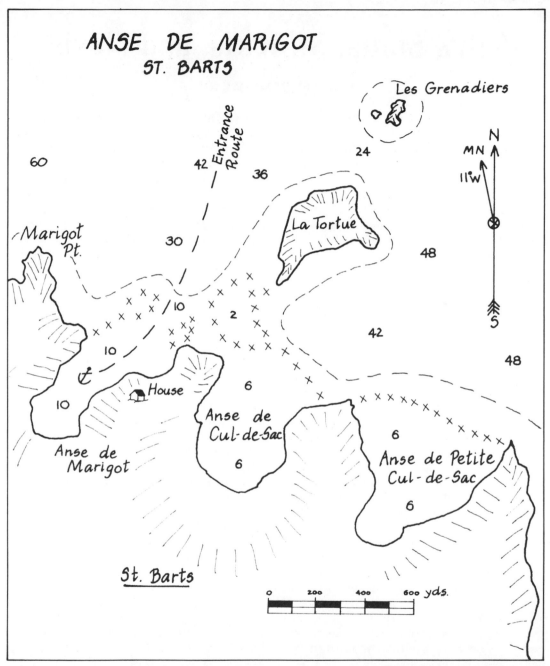

SKETCH CHART 46

CHAPTER 13

Saba, Statia, St. Kitts, and Nevis

NO 25161, 25241; BA 487

Saba

Eighty-four miles southeast of Necker Passage and 23 miles southwest of St. Martin, Saba is a pinnacle of rock rising 3,800 feet out of the sea. It is a most frustrating island to be sailing to, in that it is visible 40 miles off on a clear day; you can spot it by dawn and it can still be tantalizingly out of reach at nightfall. And even on arriving, it is often too rough to land. There is no harbor, nor any hope of building one, and only bare traces of boat landings. Nor is there any arable area to speak of. One wonders why the Dutch chose to settle there at all, with many more attractive islands nearby.

Nonetheless, once you get there, you will find it to be an exceptionally interesting place, totally unlike any other West Indian island. The two towns make one immediately think of Holland. Their houses are neatly painted white, surrounded by gardens that are beautifully tended; the women sit in the doorways making lace, for which they are justly famous. Because there is so little agriculture, Saba's men turned to the sea, being rigorously trained for it in the island's surfboats. For hundreds of years Sabans have held an enviable reputation as the best sailors in the West Indies. Today you will find master mariners in various ports of the world who began their careers in Saba. But now the surfboats are virtually a thing of the past. One wonders what will become of the new generation once the skills of launching, maneuvering, and landing these craft are entirely absorbed by motor. Probably more and more of them will

be going to work in the oil refineries at Aruba and Curacao, and eventually the Saban tradition of consummate seamanship will be lost.

The island is high, steep-to, and, although it has substantial rainfall (its peak is usually hidden in a cloud), the climate is healthful. There are no lowlands to breed mosquitoes and the various fevers and sicknesses found on other islands. For this reason, the Sabans are a hardy sort and seem to live forever. Maybe after all the settlers did know what they were doing.

The main town is inside an extinct volcano and is called Bottom. The other village, on the crater's rim, is called Top; to get to Bottom one must first go to Top. This used to be achieved only by dint of a laborious climb up the mountain over steps cut into the rock, but in the early '50s the Sabans succeeded in building a few roads, so that the climb is no longer necessary. In 1960, they also succeeded in carving out a small airstrip for single-engined planes in the appropriately named location of Hell's Gate. But this didn't open the floodgates to tourists, as the so-called airfield is strictly for the brave. It is cut through a saddle in the hill, and mountain peaks rise sharply on both sides; at both ends of the runway is a sheer drop into the ocean 1,000 feet below. No place for engine failure.

Saba is seldom visited by steamer, and even less frequently by yachts; most of the time it is too rough to land or anchor, although on occasion it can be as smooth as a millpond. Even in the latter instance care must be exerted, as the sea can build up very quickly. There are two anchorages: South

Side Landing on the southeast corner, and Ladder Landing on the southwest. At the former is the Customs House, a road, taxis, and a dock, constructed around 1972. The small freight-carrying steamer that connects Saba to the outside world lays alongside this dock when it calls, and its passengers get ashore over a gangway, rather than, as before, leaping from the deck of a surfboat.

If the weather is calm, it is possible to lay alongside this dock. However, make sure you have plenty of fenders, fenderboards, dock lines, chafing gear, and—most important—a breasting-out anchor to hold yourself off the dock, as even in the calmest weather there will be some surge.

The weather in Saba is unpredictable, so do not chance leaving your boat alongside the dock except with enough crew on board to take the boat to sea if the swell begins to build up. When anchoring off, rig a trip-line: the bottom is mixed sand and rock. Back eddies off the mountain may swing the stern too close onshore for comfort; use two anchors in a "Y," one set off to the south. If the weather is such that you have to anchor off, think twice before attempting to use your dinghy, as no matter what the weather there is always large surf onshore. The beach is loose rock, guaranteed to reduce the average yacht-tender to kindling in short order. Rather, signal for a surfboat to come out and get you. One probably will, since the Sabans welcome tourists. And again, leave adequate crew aboard; if the weather worsens, your boat may be forced to leave in a hurry.

In such an instance, it is advisable to move around to Ladder Landing, which is more likely to be smooth, particularly in the summer when the wind is apt to be in the southeast. The disadvantage here is that you still have to climb the crater on shanks' mare; there is still no road, and hence no taxis. Leave someone aboard here, too; if the ground swell begins to roll in, it has to be seen to be believed. Once when we were *becalmed* off Saba, we estimated that the surf was sending solid water some 150 feet up the cliffs!

Despite all this hair-raising description, if the weather is good Saba is well worth the effort. Some boats have liked it so much that they have remained for days, the crew staying aboard in shifts. My own feeling is that a visit to Saba, even with its built-in difficulties, is an experience one will have only once in a lifetime and is supremely worthwhile.

As an addendum: to the south of Saba lies Saba Bank, an area where it is impossible not to catch a boatload of fish in a few hours. (Don't eat barracuda caught here, however: they are likely to be poisonous.) The area is shoal—bottom can almost always be seen—but it is not so shoal that any but the largest steamers will run aground. *But do not beat to windward across it.* When coming from the Virgin Islands, under no circumstances allow yourself to sag down onto the bank; tack to the northward if necessary. The current runs

strongly to the *west* (despite what various Sailing Directions and Pilots say to the contrary) across Saba Bank. Its shoal water causes the seas to become short and steep, sometimes even square—six feet high and six feet between crests. Even a power boat driving into this head sea can get into difficulty. I know of one that broke every bottle of beer in its lockers; the crew thought it had started to leak until they discovered they had lost 20 cases of beer into the bilge. Despite the extra distance, discretion is the better part of valor;

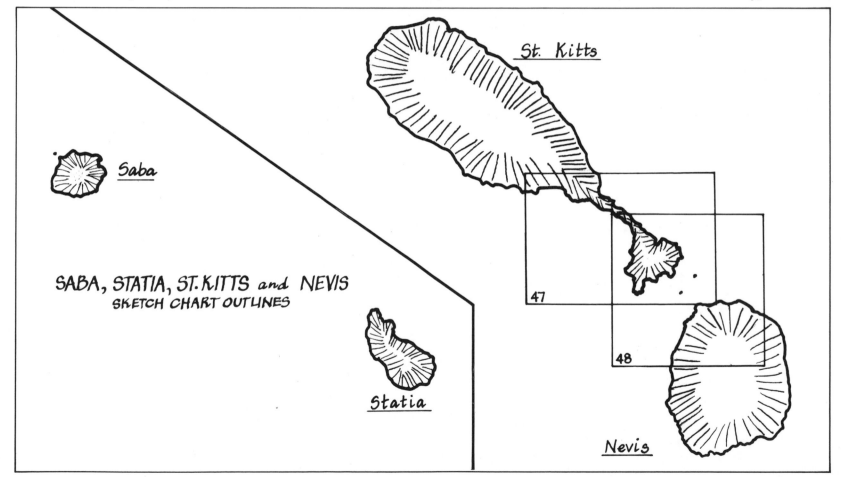

Saba

SABA, STATIA, ST. KITTS and NEVIS
SKETCH CHART OUTLINES

St. Kitts

47

48

Statia

Nevis

when heading east, alter course to travel around Saba Bank.

The islands of St. Eustatius (Statia), St. Christopher (St. Kitts), and Nevis are charted entirely on NO 25161 and BA 487. Although inserts on both charts depict the anchorages, the British is to be preferred over the U.S. chart because it has more detail and shows names of various bays not noted on the American.

These three islands lie on the eastern side of the Anegada passage about 30 miles south of the Anguilla-St. Martin-St. Barts group. They are all essentially mountain peaks with their heads in the clouds and no real harbors on the shores. Statia, a Dutch island, is sparsely settled and has a subsistence enonomy. St. Kitts is a British-associated state, heavily populated, and grows a great deal of sugar. Nevis, politically part of St. Kitts, is a realtively populous island whose people grow a variety of crops on small holdings. Historically, the three have had their day in the sun but are now in eclipse and are trying to find something new to bolster their economies.

None of these islands is large enough to effectively block the trade wind, so the climate is sunny all year round. The rainy season brings showers and squalls, rather than the all-day torrents that deluge the high islands to the south. Tides are only about one foot. No really narrow passages exist to block the flow of water, so the currents are minimal.

Statia has little to offer in the way of food. Unless you wish to lighter ice, fuel, and water out through the surf, do not plan on provisioning from this island. No hauling or repair facilities exist on any of these three islands.

St. Kitts has plenty of frozen meats, canned goods, and ice, but little fresh produce. You can take water and fuel aboard if you are brave enough to go alongside the

eastern commercial pier.

Nevis does have excellent fresh produce at a market right near the head of the dock. This island has little canned or frozen food, but you can buy ice. Tie up at the commercial dock if you need water and fuel.

St. Kitts and Nevis have air service via LIAT; Statia, at last, has an airstrip, so it is possible to fly to Statia from St. Martin via air charter.

Statia

Historically, Statia had the distinction, in 1775, of being the first place that accorded a salute to the American flag in foreign waters. It was a free neutral port where privateers and pirates could unload and auction off their captured goods. Then, in 1781, Rodney captured the island, seized the goods, condemned them, and auctioned off goods, ships, and sundry miscellany as prizes of war. He burned what he could not auction off and spent the rest of his life involved in lawsuits brought by the merchants of St. Kitts.

Since that time, Statia has been practically a ghost island. Nothing but an open beach with a ruined jetty greets the visitor where at one time he would have seen hundreds of sailboats anchored in the roadstead and innumerable warehouses on shore and on docks for unloading. Statia's one anchorage southwest of town is sheltered from the normal trade yinds. An uncomfortable swell almost always makes in, however, so the anchorage is predictably rolly. The swell makes landing on the beach an experience best avoided.

Oranjestad is built on the top of the cliff looking down into the roadstead and is hard to see. The ruins of the warehouses stand at the foot of the cliffs and a road leads up to the town. Northwest of town lies an old battery; a fort (in ruins) southeast of town makes

a good exploring spot; and numerous fine beaches run along the north side of the island.

Statia has begun to be exposed to 20th century tourism. A few hotels have opened, a few more are in the process of construction, and visitors are trickling in. But if you want to explore an island that still reflects a 1950's atmosphere, stop in at Statia and slow down your life.

St. Kitts

While Mt. Misery, the main peak on St. Kitts, is 4,314 feet high and usually hidden in the clouds, the island slopes therefrom gently into the sea. This fertile, well-watered low land is covered with sugar cane, a remnant of what at one time constituted the sole economy of the island. A true one-crop island, St. Kitts estate owners made little attempt to diversify into other crops or to introduce new industry. In recent years this attitude has somewhat changed, and, especially high up in the hills, open tracts of pastureland and plowed fields reflect a new versatility of agriculture.

St. Kitts is the last refuge of the sailing lighters in the Antilles. Since St. Kitts has no steamer dock, all cargo is off-loaded into lighters and brought to the small piers. The lighters are open boats 35- to 45-feet long, with 15 feet of beam and rigged very crudely. Some have a single leg-of-mutton sail with a mast raked well forward and the boom pointed up at a 45-degree angle. The larger lighters carry loads all the way to Nevis and are sloop-rigged with overlapping jib, short mast, a boom longer than the mast and peaked up high to clear the cargo. The mainmast is Dutch style, with a short three-foot gaff which looks more like a giant headboard than a gaff.

St. Kitts is attempting to become more attractive to tourists and is in the midst of a major expansion of its airport. Hotels are being built, but the dry climate at the southern end of the island presents problems. This is where the tourists want to stay, but there are no roads, no power lines, and no water. These basic situations must be dealt with before tourism can become a serious part of the economy.

As is Barbados, St. Kitts is known as Little England. Many of the island's lovely old sugar estates have been in the same family for 300 years. The St. Kitts Club is reputedly the oldest private club in the Americas.

Basseterre is the main town and port of entry of St. Kitts. There is no real harbor; the port consists of an open roadstead which is only semi-sheltered from the normal trades. The trade wind whistles across the low land southeast of the town and during windy spells it feels as though the hinges of the gates of hell are about to be blown off. Sometimes we have not been able to row the dinghy against the wind. If these conditions are prevailing, do your business in town and leave for the anchorages on the southwestern side of St. Kitts or Nevis. The anchorage is acceptable only when the wind is down.

When you go to clear in, anchor due south of the westernmost dock in three to four fathoms. Usually, the Customs Officer will come out; but if he doesn't, you may go ashore to find him. Native boats selling things will probaly come alongside you, so be sure to rig your fenders and boarding nets. Do not leave your oars and oarlocks in your dinghy or your outboard on the dinghy stern when you are alongside the dock, for obvious reasons.

If you are approaching St. Kitts from the west, tack up to the lee of the island as soon as you can. If you are approaching from the north, from St. Barts, St. Martin, or Anguilla, round the northwestern side of

St. Kitts one-half mile off, and then work down the shore. The flaws in the wind will probably drive you offshore so you should make frequent tacks back close in. You will find plenty of water along the whole coast, smooth water close to shore, and spasmodic strong puffs of wind that come off the mountain. These vary as much as four points, so be careful of being caught aback. As for The Narrows between St. Kitts and Nevis, see further.

Frigate Bay
(Sketch Chart 47)

If you decide that the anchorage at Basseterre is too rolly and you wish to move elsewhere, you might try Frigate Bay slightly southeast. But sometimes this is as uncomfortable as the town anchorage, in which case continue farther south along the coast of the larger bay and you will gaze on a splendid selection of white-sand beaches. You can come right up to the steep shore and use either a Bahamian moor or you can set a bow and stern anchor and lie in the axis of the swell. During the winter, Frigate Bay and the anchorages immediately to the south are apt to be rolly, but in the summer they are calm and smooth. The beaches stretch on deserted for miles, inaccessible except by sea; so if solitude is what you want, you should be ecstatic. Also, the small bay with the shingle beach just northeast of Rock Point is often an excellent, calm anchorage. Stand in toward shore and anchor at a reasonable depth.

Shitten Bay
(Sketch Chart 47)

The temptation to make a bad joke is waived in deference to the quality of this anchorage. The small bay with its shingle beach lies just north of Horse Shoe Point. The anchorage is calm and offers good shelling.

Major's Bay
(Sketch Chart 47)

If the ground swell is rolling in along the whole coast as it might be in winter, sail around Horse Shoe Point and up into the northern end of Major's Bay. Unless the wind gets well around to the south, you should be comfortable here. Nevis, only two-and-a-half miles away, shelters this anchorage even in winter, and even with the wind in the south it is not bad. This is an exceptional place to lie because it is completely deserted and has white-sand bottom and beaches. Major's Bay makes a wonderful place to start your exploration of St. Kitts. Old, abandoned ruins of a fort can be found on the ridge, extending northward from Horse Shoe Point. You might also try snorkeling off both points at the end of the bay, since the area abounds in lobsters.

Mosquito Bay
(Sketch Chart 47)

East of Major's Bay is Mosquito Bay, also called Banana Bay. The anchorage is in the northeast corner with Scotch Bonnet bearing southeast. Here, the wind whistles over the hill and you are likely to waltz around your anchor. The holding ground is none too reliable and a Bahamian moor is definitely necessary. You can go by dinghy over to the Cockle Shell and the Banana Beach Hotel on the western side of the harbor, but do not anchor off them since you will find a fair chop in this sector.

Sand Hill Bay
(Sketch Chart 47)

On the east coast of St. Kitts, this can be entered in the summer months if the wind is in the southeast. It is dangerous and shoal, however, and boats drawing more than six feet should not attempt it. It cannot be reached by road, and this of course means

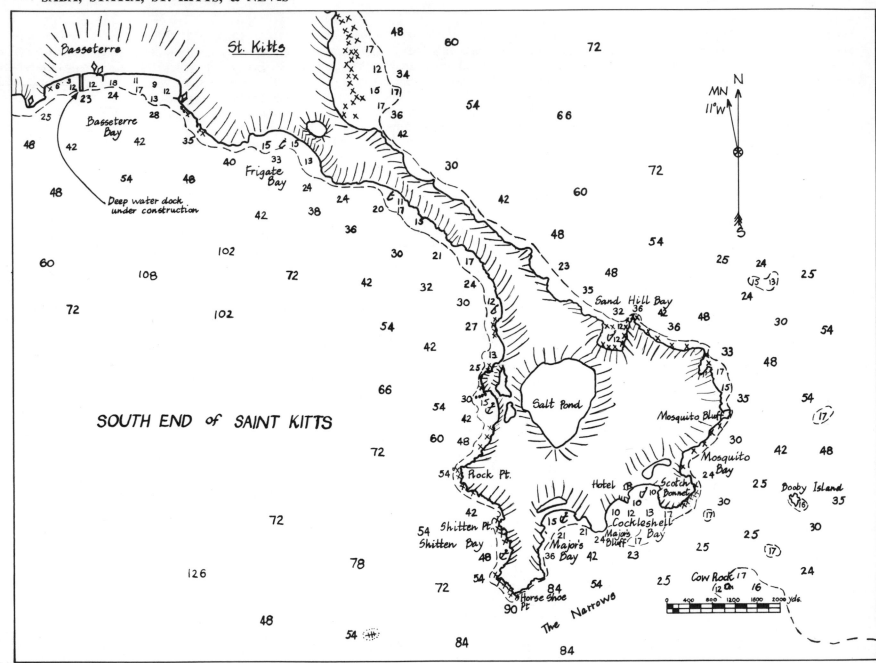

St. Kitts

Basseterre

Basseterre Bay

Deep water dock under construction

Frigate Bay

SOUTH END of SAINT KITTS

Salt Pond

Sand Hill Bay

Mosquito Bluff

Mosquito Bay

Rock Pt.

Hotel

Scotch Bonnet

Cockleshell Bay

Dooby Island

Shitten Pt.

Shitten Bay

Major's Bluff

Major's Bay

Horse Shoe Pt.

Cow Rock

The Narrows

N
MN
11°W
S

0 400 800 1200 1600 2000 yds.

SKETCH CHART 47

that you will be all by yourself there. The diving around the edges of the reef is bounteous.

Deep Bay
(NO 25241)

Also called the Punch Bowl. In the northeast corner of St. Kitts, it was probably used as a loading point for sugar in the past when no adequate roads existed. This is strictly a small-boat harbor for fishing boats that can be hauled out of the water once they are inside the reef. It is not a yacht harbor of any kind.

You cannot leave St. Kitts until you have visited Brimstone Hill, referred to as the Gibraltar of the West Indies. This was the scene of a brilliant and valiant defense by Generals Shirley and Frazer against the French at the time of the American Revolution. (The names Shirley and Frazer keep cropping up in the military history of the West Indies, a subject well covered by Alec Waugh in *A Family of Islands*.) On Brimstone Hill stands a big bronze cannon with the inscription: *Ram me well and load me tight/I'll send a ball to Statia's height.*

If you ride around the island to see the sugar operation and the beautiful old estates,

Range A: Mosquito Bluff at 182 magnetic. When Sandy Hill comes abeam, alter course toward Booby Island.

Range B: East side of Booby Island in line with Lowland Church, 205-025.

Range C: Booby Island in line with Cow Rocks, 229-049 magnetic.

Range D: North end of Booby Island in line with Brisco Old Mill, 296-116 magnetic.

Range E: West side of Booby Island in line with west slope of Hurricane Hill, 182-002 magnetic.

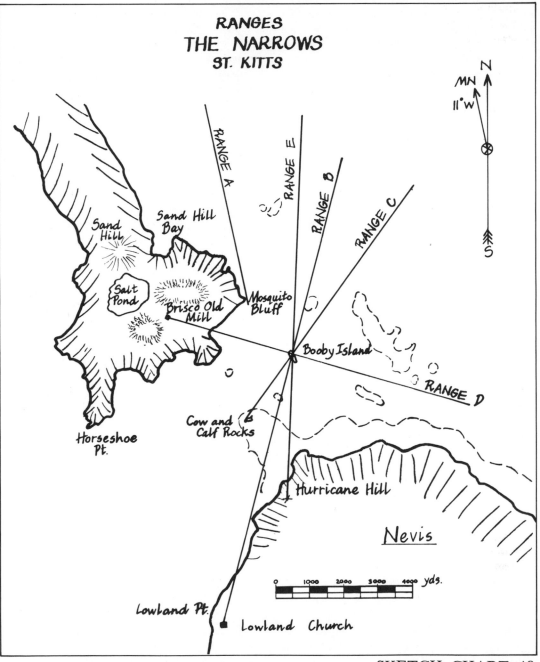

RANGES
THE NARROWS
ST. KITTS

you will be impressed by the drives leading up to many of the estates. These are lined with the most magnificent palms I have ever seen.

And you might explore the beaches on the east side of St. Kitts: soft black sand—and hot.

The Narrows
(Sketch Chart 48)

The passage between St. Kitts and Nevis referred to as The Narrows is filled with reefs and shoals, some of whose depths are less, I'm quite sure, than those shown on the charts. Because the ranges are not easy to identify, this passage should be navigated in mid-day and with extreme care.

If you are approaching The Narrows from the north, it is possible to pass west of all the shoals. Steer for the eastern extremity of Mosquito Bluff, and, while still well off-shore, bring Mosquito Bluff to bear 180 magnetic. Run down this range (Range A) until Sand Hill Bay is abeam; then head for Booby Island until Mosquito Bluff is abeam. Ease sheets and run down the south coast of St. Kitts; or proceed to Nevis, leaving Cow Rocks to port.

If you are approaching The Narrows from the northeast, keep well off the shore of St. Kitts until the west side of Booby Island lines up with the church at Lowland Point (Range B). Or, if you cannot bring Lowland Church into view, get a bearing on the west coast of Booby Island and the farthermost westerly point of Nevis. Go west of this bearing by the width of Booby Island and you will avoid the shoals to the east. Do not head east of this range to be sure that you do avoid the shoal water. Then bear off directly for Horse Shoe Point if going to Basseterre; or, if continuing to Nevis, leave Cow Rocks 200 yards off the port hand and run down the coast.

Should you be coming from the east, stand to the north until Booby Island is in line with Cow Rocks. Then run down this range (Range C), leaving both Booby Island and Cow Rocks to port. Once you have Cow Rocks abeam, dangers are cleared.

The approach from the southeast is the most difficult, as the range is hard to spot. Brisco Old Mill is not shown on the U.S. chart, but you will find it in the valley north-east of Sugarloaf on St. Kitts and it can be seen over the beaches of Mosquito Bay. The range is Brisco Old Mill, St. Kitts, in line with the north end of Booby Island (Range D). Once you have Hurricane Hill (St. Kitts) abeam, you may alter your course to west magnetic until Cow Rocks are in line with the western end of Nevis. At that point, all dangers are passed.

Beating to windward through The Narrows is not easy, particularly during the winter when the trades are boisterous and the shoals breaking. Do not pass between Cow Rocks and Nevis unless your boat is shoal draft. The best passage is north of Cow Rocks, favoring the St. Kitts shore. From Mosquito Bay, tack to the south, if necessary taking a few extra tacks to get to weather of Booby Island, tacking to the north when Booby Island lines up with Lowland Church (Range B).

If you can lay this range, fine. If not, do not sag below the range established by the west side of Booby Island in line with the west slope of Hurricane Hill (Range E). If you cannot lay this last range, either tack back to the eastward, or ease your sheets, run off, and bring Mosquito Bluff to bear 180 magnetic over your stern; then pass inside the shoals.

Nevis

Although Nevis is separated from St.

Kitts only by The Narrows, the two islands are very different. In keeping with this fact is the old rule of thumb concerning St. Kitts-Nevis anchorages: if the anchorage at Basse-terre is bad, it will be good at Charlestown, and vice versa. When heading from Basseterre to Nevis, there are no dangers. Monkey Shoal has four fathoms over it; and if anyone has a yacht that draws four fathoms, please let me know. The anchorage at Nevis is off the town of Charlestown. If you approach it from the north, you will find no dangers; from the south, be sure to give Fort Charles at the south end of town a good berth, as the shoal extends almost one-half mile offshore. The anchorage is due west of the dock; expect three fathoms and a sand bottom that means good holding.

The contrast in the two islands of St. Kitts and Nevis can immediately be seen. St. Kitts is a hustling, bustling, populous island of large sugar holdings. Nevis is the land of the small farmer who grows a bit of everything, really has no money, yet is much more pleasant to deal with than his St. Kitts cousin. Large plantation houses almost totally abandoned stand on the hillsides, their vast palm groves unworked. Squatters have taken over most of the land, and small villages dot the countryside.

The town of Charlestown is architecturally interesting. Most of its buildings are of heavy, cut-coral blocks and date back to the 18th century when Nevis was a great sugar island and health resort. The hot springs were reputed to cure all ailments, so people came from all over the world to bathe in the restorative waters. The bathhouse is standing today. If the caretaker can be located, it is still possible to enjoy a hot sulfur bath.

Right on the waterfront at Charlestown are two of the most magnificent old brass cannons I have ever seen. After bathing in antiquity, if not in hot sulfur, enjoy a beer and fresh lobsters at the Alexander Hamilton Centenary Hotel, right behind the cannons.

Other hotels are beginning to be built. Reputedly, Dulcina Island Club, a large development, is planning to install a marina. If this projected marina has a sufficient depth of water to take a large boat and is out of the ground swell, the island of Nevis will improve immeasurably in the eyes of yachtsmen.

The island is changing and hotels are opening up often enough that it would be well for a visiting yachtsman to contact the tourist board for further information on Nevis.

CHAPTER 14

Antigua and Barbuda

NO 25201, 25202, 25203, 25204; BA 1997, 2064, 2065

Antigua

Antigua lies well to the east of the St. Kitts group and due north of Guadeloupe. It owes its popularity within yachting circles to its most eminent anchorage, English Harbour, and the incomparable shelter which this harbor provides. Antigua itself is relatively low with its highest bench mark at 1,300 feet. Though it suffers from an almost perpetual drought, the dependable trades make it cool and ventilated. The innumerable hotels luxuriate in the cool weather, but are hard pressed to keep themselves supplied with fresh water.

Antigua was first settled for the British by Sir Thomas Warner and, with the exception of a brief French occupation in 1666-67, has remained British ever since. In the early 18th century the British were made aware of Antigua's strategic importance and the superb shelter afforded by English Harbour. They proceeded to fortify the hills above the harbor and built a dockyard for naval supply and repair. With the introduction of large steampowered ships in the 19th century, English Harbour went into a decline from which it did not recover until recent years.

For most yachtsmen English Harbour epitomizes Antigua; it is surprising that so few of them explore the countless coves, reefs, and inlets that are Antigua's best assets. Easily a week could be spent cruising the coast of this British island, entering a different anchorage every noon and night. The eastern side of the island has great Atlantic rollers crashing on shore. Beating to windward is an exhilarating experience and a good test of spirit and rig. The lee side of the island has that ideal combination of steady winds and no sea. One of the thrills of a lifetime is to hold a

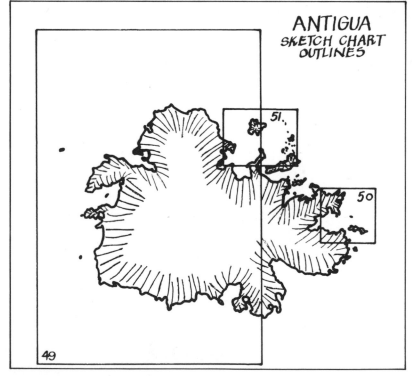

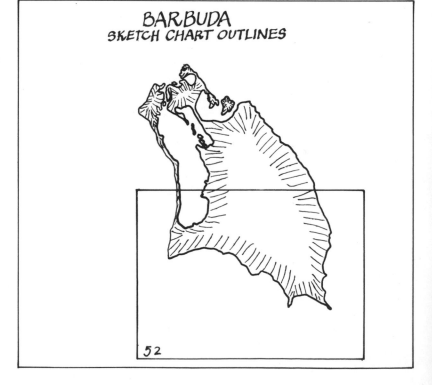

156

booming reach along the lee shore of Antigua, rail down, over smooth, crystal-clear water, the magnified terrain of the bottom slipping by below.

There is regular and frequent air service from Antigua to all parts of the world. While the telephone and telegraph communication from the capital, St. Johns, to the rest of the world is good, calling St. Johns from English Harbour can be like wringing water from a rock. The required charts are NO 25201, 25202, and 25203, and BA 2064 and 2065.

Range A: The Inn over the beach house at Freeman's Point leads into English Harbour.

Range B: Old Road Bluff in line with Dow House Wall ruins leads south of Cade Reef (NO 25201), a distant range difficult to spot.

Range C: Johnson Point in line with Old Road Bluff leads through Goat Head Channel, 121 magnetic.

Range D: Conspicuous white roof of Curtain Bluff Hotel in line with the second valley north of Old Road Bluff leads through western end of Goat Head Channel and clear of the reefs.

Range E: Sandy Island in line with the highest of the Five Islands leads inside shoals off southwest tip of Antigua.

Range F: Hawkes Bill Rock in line with Pelican Point leads through Five Islands Channel, east of largest of Five Islands.

Range G: Ferris Point, the western point of Galley Bay, in line with Fort Barrington (the signal station on Goat Hill) leads over Hurst Shoal.

Range H: Belmont Hill over Maiden Island leads over Pelican Shoal.

Range I: Fort James in line with Belmont Hill clears Warrington Bank to the southwest.

Range J: Fort Barrington, which is the signal station on Goat Hill, in line with Mt. Thomas clears Diamond Bank and Warrington Bank to westward.

Range K: Great Sister in line with whitewashed Old Field Mill leads through Diamond Channel.

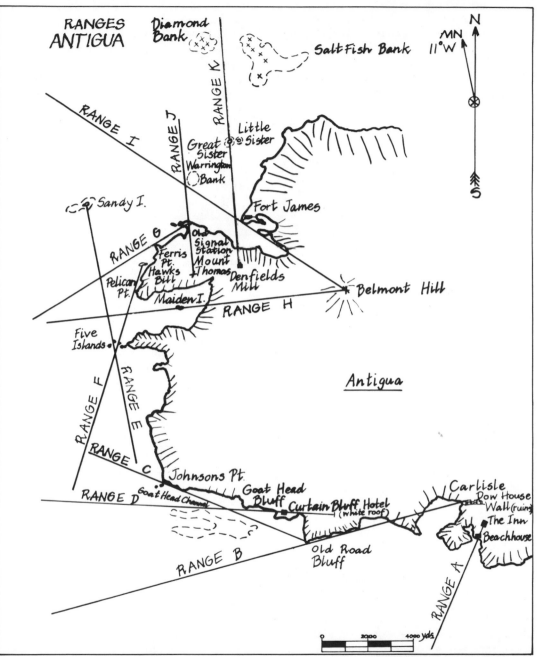

SKETCH CHART 49

ANTIGUA & BARBUDA

The British are more accurate and have a more manageable format than the American charts, while the American provide many valuable ranges not included by the British. Although the U.S. charts base themselves on British surveys, they contain a number of inaccuracies and discrepancies. There are five rather important ones: (1) The wreck of a four-masted square-rigger awash in Deep Bay, south of Shipstern Point, has been omitted. (The wreck dates from 1920!) (2) There is no water inside Hawkes Bill Rock. (3) Between Little and Great Sister there is a scant nine feet of water. (4) In the northern entrance to Nonsuch Bay, the easternmost reef has no more than nine or ten feet over it. (The chart lists two fathoms.) (5) Similarly, the reefs north of the island have in every case less water than is noted on the chart.

Approaching from the south from the lee side of Guadeloupe, lay your course for English Harbour. Once Antigua becomes clearly visible, head for Shirley Heights, a flat-topped hill with ruined fortifications on the eastern side of the harbor. When shore details can be seen, post a lookout for the Pillars of Hercules, a clearly distinguishable rock formation that looks like the entrance to a Greek temple in the cliffs forming the eastern side of the harbor entrance. Do not approach at night, as it is possible to mistake the lights of the Curtain Bluff Hotel on Morris Bay to the west for those of The Inn in Freeman's Bay, English Harbour. The manager of Curtain Bluff, Howard Holford, told me that on the average one boat is lost on the reef off Curtain Bluff every year.

Approaching Antigua from the west and southwest, care must be taken to avoid the shoals along the western side of the island and the exposed reefs south of Johnsons Point. It is best to get inside Cade and Middle Reefs if proceeding east to English Harbour. That way you will be sailing over calm water as far as Curtain Bluff. Once inside the reef, keep in mind that the outer reef, Cade, will be breaking while the inner reef, Middle, will not be and can only be spotted by the color of the water. Do not confuse the two reefs.

If coming from the northwest, to avoid the shoals west of the southwestern part of Antigua pass ouboard of Five Islands; then put Sandy Island on the northeast side of the highest of the Five Islands (Range E, Sketch Chart 49), continuing south until you have cleared the reefs off Johnsons Point.

Making approaches from the north or northwest, put a man aloft on the upper spreaders. The north coast is lined with reefs that are notoriously difficult to spot and I would advise against trying to pick through unless you are familair with the area. The only adaptable range is along Diamond Channel at the western end of this tangled line of reefs. The range is Great Sister in line with Denfields Mill, a whitewashed ruined mill (Range K, Sketch Chart 49). Once through this channel, Warrington Bank is buoyed, and Hurst Bank may be easily avoided by staying close to shore. The north coast is low and featureless, and while there are several radio towers in the vicinity of the airport, they are not marked with sufficient accuracy on the chart to fix a position. As soon as you get into about seven fathoms of water, be very cautious. Long Island is low and hard to spot, and the reefs north of Bird Island Reef can give you an awful scare. From the northeastern corner of Antigua to the southern coast, there are no off-lying dangers, and it is an easy matter to lay a course south along the east coast to English Harbour.

English Harbour
(BA 2064, NO 25202)

This is the principal yacht anchorage of Antigua, and a port of entry. It affords complete shelter in every weather, being virtually landlocked. The wind sweeps across the island through low valleys, making the harbor cool through most of the year. In good British fashion, the entrance is unbuoyed and unlit—not a spot to be entered at night for the first time. (I am firmly convinced that the British government does not establish a good buoyage system because they don't want to put the local pilots and shipwreckers out of business.) There were absolutely no lights on the entire south coast of Antigua until tourism took hold. Now the nights on the south shore are emblazoned with hotel lights, which serve as beacons of a sort. If you reach the south coast at night, stand off until dawn. By day the approach is not difficult. Once the Pillars of Hercules have been spotted, head directly for them until you are close to shore, bearing off to clear the reef off Charlotte Point. The beach house at Freeman Point placed in line with The Inn, the large white hotel higher on the hill, leads clear of all dangers. Barclay Point is steep-to, but be careful of the submerged piles off the dock on the north side of Hart Point. Once inside the harbor, shorten down. You can moor stern-to anywhere along the bulkheaded dockyard or further north at the Admiral's Inn where seven-and-a-half feet can be taken stern-to. Officials will come on board to clear you. Once cleared, you may anchor where you wish. Freeman's Bay is completely sheltered and offers good swimming.

English Harbour was once the main anchorage for the British West Indian Squadron. Abandoned in 1899, the dockyard has recently been restored as a Mariner's Museum by the Friends of English Harbour. Watching the old square-riggers entering English Harbour must have been an awesome sight. A 19th-century *Sailing Directions* gives some idea of the laborious measures involved: "Intending to enter the harbor with the prevailing wind at east, stand boldly in under the heights, a little to windward of Fort Charlotte Bluff. Keep the ship under full plain sail, trimmed by the wind, hug the lee shore, giving the bluff a berth of one cable length, and having rounded the buoy close aboard to starboard, keep the leading mark on until the dockyard staff is on with the end of Fort Barclay, then luff close up, take in the course, and if you have a strong way, you will probably shoot around the point to Fort Barclay, before the wind from the highlands comes off from the northern shore. If the ship loses way and becomes unmanageable before this, you must anchor immediately; if you succeed in shooting in, be prepared to wear short around, and when in the center of the channel, clew up, as you will most probably have sufficient way to carry you to the anchorage off the dockyard."

Great progress has been made to usher English Harbour into the 20th century. Electricity has been installed; fresh water is available; and the two notorious foul-smelling cubicles which were passed off as shower stalls have vanished under the assault of the jackhammer. In their place has appeared a pair of immaculate, white-tiled showers—a major improvement. Commander V. E. B. Nicholson, his two sons, and their wives conduct a many-sided business out of English Harbour: a yacht brokerage office, a radio service (2725 kilocycles at 0900 daily), a mail pick-up, a marine store, hotel, and travel agency. This all dates back to an afternoon 25 years ago when the Commander and his family happened to put into the harbor during a proposed round-the-world cruise.

His office in the old paymaster's house maintains a fascinating scrapbook of photographs and short histories of just about every boat that has come through English Harbour since 1955—a veritable history of transatlantic passages. The Commander is one of the most amusing individuals on the island and entertains frequently. His house is the converted powder magazine on the point between Tank and Ordnance Bays.

The Antigua Slipway, across the harbor from the old dockyard, is ably managed by David Simmonds. The facility is capable of hauling yachts of any size. Gasoline, diesel, oil, and water are available alongside. There is a marine store at the slipway where you can probably scrounge up needed supplies. One corner of the yard gives perfect shelter from the wind, an ideal section of the harbor to leave a boat for a few months under the supervision of the yard. There is good local labor available, but be sure to check out qualifications and the going wage beforehand from the local skippers. Sail repairs can be made at Vanessa Hornidge's shop.

Indian Creek
(BA 2064, NO 25201)

A small, sheltered, and deserted cove one mile east of English Harbour. There is a dangerous rock at the entrance which can be spotted by the breaking sea. Inside is plenty of water, though the space is limited. This is a good hurricane hole—if you can get there first. The snorkeling is excellent on the eastern point of the cove.

Mamora Bay
(BA 2064, NO 25201)

This, too, is a good shelter; it has plenty of water in the middle and shoals along the sides. A hotel, casino, and small Florida-type marina that were built a few years ago are now pretty much defunct. The bay will carry at least nine feet. To enter, hug the reef on the starboard side.

Willoughby Bay
(BA 2064, NO 25201)

A large, sheltered bay, somewhat difficult to enter. Isaac Channel is overgrown with coral, leaving Horse Shoe Channel as the only entrance. This should only be attempted in good light with a lookout aloft.

Green Island
(BA 2064, NO 25201, Sketch Chart 50)

Between Willoughby Bay and Green Island there are no viable bays except for a hell-bent surfboarder. Green Island is very attractive and offers two small anchorages. The larger and better of the two is Rickett Harbor, which has room enough to accommodate three or four yachts. Protected from normal trade wind weather, it is exposed only to a summer southeast wind and swell. If Rickett Harbor is crowded, try the small cove east of it, called Tenpound Bay on the American chart and unnamed on the British. There is only room for one boat here—total seclusion. The entrances to both harbors call for careful eyeball procedures in good light. Feel your way in, being careful to avoid the reef east of Rickett Harbor which extends farther south than the chart indicates. All dangers will be clearly visible in good daylight.

Nonsuch Bay
(BA 2064, NO 25201, Sketch Chart 50)

A large, protected bay with innumerable anchorages. It is an ideal spot for dinghy sailing, swimming, and snorkeling. The northernmost cove, called Ledcoff Cove on the British chart, unnamed on the American, affords an excellent anchorage. If the light is good, you may anchor among the reefs downwind of Rat Island and explore the reefs directly from the boat without having to launch the dinghy. South of Bird Island is another first-rate anchorage over a beautiful white-sand bottom which is good holding and where the reef breaks the swell. It is sure to be breezy and cool, with good diving under the bowsprit. A favorite anchorage of mine is in

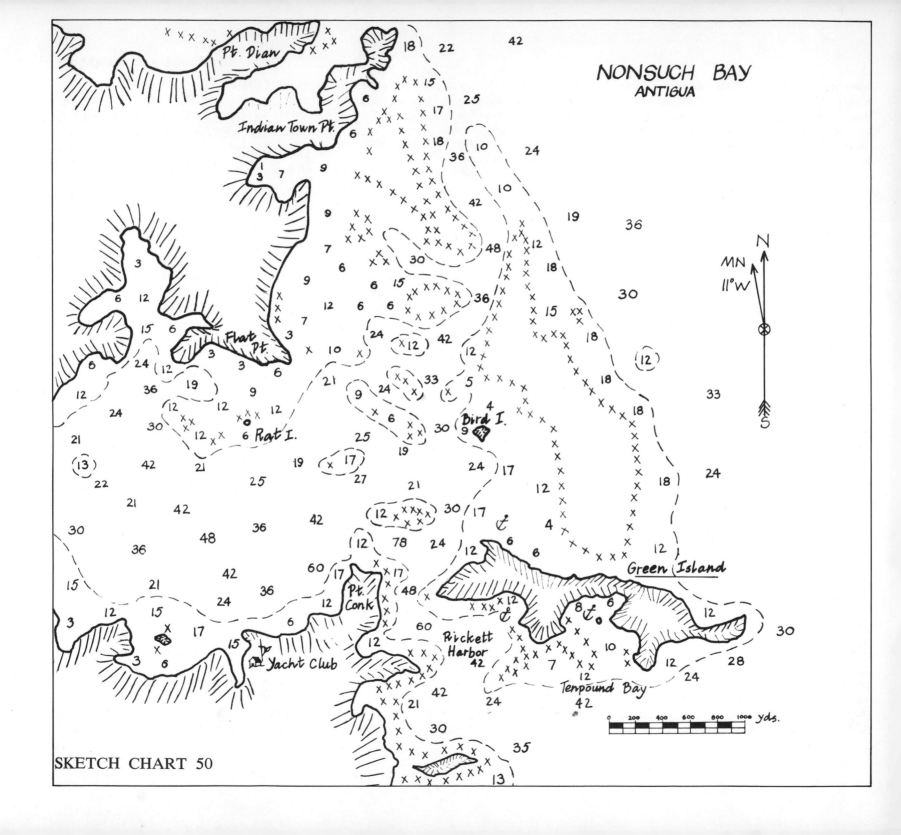

NONSUCH BAY
ANTIGUA

Pt. Dian

Indian Town Pt.

Flat Pt.

Rat I.

Bird I.

Green Island

Pt. Conk

Yacht Club

Rickett Harbor

Tenpound Bay

MN 11°W

N / S

SKETCH CHART 50

0 200 400 600 800 1000 yds.

the minute cove on the northwestern tip of Green Island, which offers complete privacy and a lovely sand beach.

A word of caution in regard to Nonsuch Bay: the entrance and exit should be made to the west of Green Island. The northeastern entrance—called Spithead Channel on the British chart—is incorrectly sounded. The eastern side of the channel will not carry two fathoms; it is scarcely a fathom and in many cases much less. Besides, there is no maneuvering room in the channel. I have twice received bad scares departing Nonsuch through here, which has not left me eager to renew the acquaintance. It can be done, however, but you must have a close-winded boat, and the wind must be out of the east, not the northeast, as you have a dead lee shore. To my mind the channel is nowhere near wide enough for most sailboats to tack in. Thus, without an engine and except in ideal circumstances, it should be avoided.

Belfast Bay and Guana Bay
(BA 2064, NO 25201)

These are completely sheltered—so much so that I would advise against attempting entrance without the aid of a local pilot. Similarly, beating out of them against stiff trades and a hefty Atlantic swell might be more excitement than one has bargained for. In fact, when the trades are at their most boisterous, you would be wise to steer clear of Antigua's east coast entirely. The seas can be immense; as they near the coast, they will become steeper and crest—nothing for a small yacht to tangle with.

Parham Harbor
(BA 2065, NO 25201, 25203;
Sketch Chart 51)

A complete shelter with reefs all around. The channel has recently been buoyed by the U.S. Navy, but I would proceed cautiously

just the same. A number of uninhabited islands on the sound invite leisurely exploration.

Jumby Bay
(BA 2065, NO 25203, Sketch Chart 51)

This is on the western side of Long Island. The anchorage is 100 yards offshore in two fathoms of water. Long Island is a private island, but the owners allow visits by well-behaved tourists. Also, if you are interested in shelling, a visit to Maiden Island is called for. An anchorage can be had in the lee of this island. For those who like to dive, the whole eastern end of North Sound is a fabulous spot. The anchorage here is in the lee of the reef north of Great Bird Island. There is also an anchorage in the lee of Great Bird Island between the two arms of the reef on its western shore. Feel your way in and anchor according to your draft. There are two good beaches, and the island is a well-known nesting place for migratory birds. It is likely to be crowded with visitors on the weekend, so plan your trip accordingly. A channel runs out of North Sound in the northeast corner, called Bird Island Channel. This should only be used by shoal-draft boats in settled weather, and even then only if you have reliable power to fall back on. This entire area is shoal- and coral-infested and should be navigated only when the sun is high.

Leaving this area and proceeding westward, care must be taken to avoid the reefs on the north coast. Put a man in the rigging and eyeball it. Whether to pass inside or outside of Prickly Pear Island is something of a toss-up. Be governed by considerations of wind and sea. West of Parham Harbor, the north coast of Antigua offers no anchorages. Soldier Bay is a nice lunch stop and has a pretty beach, but being exposed to the northwest, it is not a spot to pass the night.

Dickinson Bay
(BA 2065, NO 25202)

A beach runs for a mile along the shore; hotels are scattered throughout. This is a likely spot to visit if you crave a little nightlife. The bay is none too deep; ease your way in with the lead line and anchor in a convenient depth. This bay is also open to the northwest and apt to be rolly in certain weathers.

St. Johns Harbor
(BA 2065, NO 25202)

The capital of Antigua, the largest town, and a port of entry, St. Johns is seldom visited by yachts. The harbor is muddy and unattractive. Recently a channel has been dredged so that there is deep water right up to town. This is a commercial anchorage with no yacht facilities whatsoever. Most yachtsmen inclined to visit St. Johns make the trip by cab from English Harbour.

Deep Bay
(BA 2065, NO 25202)

South of St. Johns, it offers fine anchorages and beaches. Two fathoms will carry quite close to the beach at the head of the bay. It may be rolly when the ground swell is running. In entering, watch for the wreck due south of Shipstern Point. The wreck is awash and is good fun for a snorkeler to poke around in. Lobsters can usually be found in its mast stumps.

Passing south along the west coast of Antigua is superb sailing, provided that you stay right on the ranges. The American chart notwithstanding, there is no water inside Hawkes Bill Rock. Beyond this rock, hug the shore. Ten feet can be taken inside Pelican Rocks and the rocks past Pelican Point. Favor the Pelican side of the channel. Then put Pelican Point in line with Hawkes Bill Rock, a range which will lead you through Five

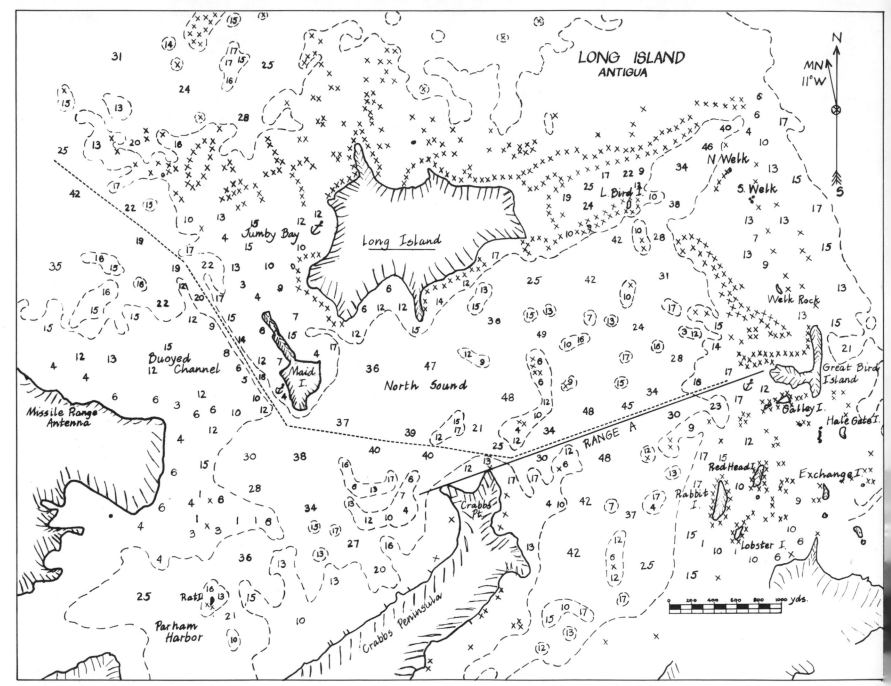

LONG ISLAND
ANTIGUA

N
MN
11°W
S

31

(15) (X)
(14)
(X) 17 17 15 25
16

24

(X) 13
(15)
13 28
13 20 16
25
17
42
22 (15)
19
35 (16)
(15)
16 (16)
22 20 17
(15)
15 15
15

4 12 13
Buoyed
12 Channel

Missile Range
Antenna
6 6 3
6 6
12
4
6
15
30 38
28
4 4 × 6
4 3 3 1 1 6
36
25 Rat I (16)
13 15
21
Parham
Harbor (10)

Jumby Bay
15
19 22 13 10
12 (12)
3
9
12 9
V4
8
5 18
8
12 7
10
12
5
6
10 12

37
30
17 17
16
6
7
8 13 (17) 6
(13)
34 7
12 16
(15) (17)
27 16
(13)
13
20
13

L.Bird I
25
19 24
Long Island
6
6 12 12 14
12
15 (15)
(15) (13)
36
47
North Sound
36
48
45
40 40
39 (15) 21
12 (17)
25 (12)
12 13
17
Crabbs
Pt
Crabbs Peninsula

17 22 9
40 46
N Welk
34 (X) 13
S.Welk
38
13 13
7
13
31
25 42
(10)
X 28
42
X
(10) 24
49
(10) 16
(12) 9
(X) 6
(X) (9)
48
(12)
(15)
(17)
34
48
30
(12)
(17)
(X) 6
30
48
13 7
(17) 4
Rabbit
I.
4 10 42 (7)
37
(12)
6
×
(12)
25
(17)
13 42
(15) 10 17
(15)
(13)

40 4
10
17 22 9
6
6
17
10
13
15
13 13
7
15
Welk Rock
13
(17)
14
17
18
34
23
9
15
1
10
15
×
17
(13)
(17)
37 4
15

Great Bird
Island
21
15
12
12
Galley I.
Hale Gate I.
Red Head I
10
15
Exchange I
9
Lobster I 6
10
6

RANGE A

SKETCH CHART 51

Range A: Two tips of Crabbs Point in line leads into anchorage off Great Bird Island

200 400 600 800 1000 yds.

Islands Channel to the east of the highest of the Five Islands. The depth is ten feet. Or else you may pass inside all of the Five Islands, again in ten feet of water. Once past Five Islands Channel, place the highest of Five Islands in line with Sandy Key; the range will lead clear of all dangers. Once the shoals off Johnson Island have been cleared, a course may be laid inside Middle Reef (Sketch Chart 49). There are numerous anchorages along this western shore; all tend to be shoal, so ease your way in to a suitable depth.

Five Islands Harbor
(BA 2064, NO 25201)

This is one of numerous anchorages along the western shore. Anchor off Maiden Island and avoid the eastern half of the bay, which is shoal and mosquito-infested.

Mosquito Cove
(BA 2064, NO 25201)

Okay, despite the unsavory name. The mosquitoes have cleared out, leaving a good anchorage for moderate-draft boats and some good beaches. To avoid the shoals, anchor midway between Mosquito Hill and Reed Point in one fathom.

Ffryes Bay and Crab Hill Bay
(BA 2064, NO 25201)

These are viable short-term anchorages, with a tendency to shoal. Both are lunch spots off deserted white-sand beaches.

Goat Head Channel offers a smooth passage to the east when the light is favorable. Ranges are of no real use since, tacking upwind, you will be criss-crossing all the way. If the light fails before you have cleared the reef, there is an anchorage of sorts in Cade Bay. The same holds with Morris Bay, though if the wind is south of east, this will tend to be rolly. Don't try to use the Danforth; the bottom is full of weed and poor holding. It

once took me five tries to set a 50-pound fisherman before I finally dived down and shoved the fool thing in! The Curtain Bluff Hotel on Morris Bay is one of the best on the island. The owner, Howard Holford, gives an enormous party every year, which is one of the highpoints of Antigua Week.

Carlisle Bay
(BA 2064, NO 25201)

A beautiful, palm-lined anchorage. The shores are rimmed with coral, but the center of the harbor is clear of hazards and calm as long as the wind is not south of east. But Rendezvous Bay, the next one down, is wide open and frequently untenable.

Falmouth Harbor
(BA 2064; NO 25201, 25202)

The major harbor just west of English Harbour and, like English Harbour, sheltered in all weathers. There is ample water if you proceed carefully. Enter in mid-channel, heading for Blake Island until Bishop Rocks on your starboard hand are well aft of abeam; then turn to the east, favoring the southern side of the bay. Anchor in the southeastern corner of the bay in two to three fathoms over sand bottom.

At the north end of the harbor is the Catamaran Club, a hotel-restaurant run by Hugh Bailey. Hugh got his start crewing on yachts out of English Harbour. He quickly rose to mate and skipper, salting away his savings to invest in the hotel. Now he is a yachtsman in his own right, racing his 45-foot sloop *Invader* with considerable success. Ten feet of water can be carried to the anchorage off the Catamaran Club. The way must be eyeballed in good light. If the light is waning, send the dinghy over to the club and Bailey will arrange for someone to guide you in.

A good anchorage also can be had north of the Antigua Yacht Club dock. The club is

not particularly active during the week, though things tend to pick up around Friday night.

Barbuda

The island of Barbuda (NO 25204, BA 1997), 25 miles north of Antigua, to whom it belongs, is well off the beaten track of customary inter-island cruising. It is low, flat, and featureless, and thus cannot be seen from its sister island. Somewhat inhospitable-looking, it was never heavily colonized. For many years a settlement was maintained on the island for the grim, sole purpose of breeding slaves, a sort of stud farm in human flesh. The Codrington Family owned the island for almost 200 years, and, after the slaves were freed, contined to use the island as a game-hunting ground. The accounts of 19th-century visitors to the island speak in a single voice of its absolute poverty. Its present economy has not much improved.

Barbuda, nonetheless, has some superb beaches and is an attractive, quiet, cruising ground—provided you maintain a healthy respect for the inaccuracy of the charts. Best to arrive there early in the day and rely on your vision and good light. If a squall springs up, it would be well to stand south until the weather clears.

In approaching from the south, your best landmarks will be the Martello Tower on the southwestern part of the island, the hotel a few hundred yards to the east of it, or the hotel on Cocoa Point. From the southwest—that is, from the western side of Antigua—head for the Martello Tower until your bearing to the buildings on Cocoa Point indicates that you are well inside Codrington Shoals and Codrington Bank. From there, work your way eastward.

From the eastern side of Antigua, I advise heading directly for Cocoa Point. keeping the point to bear north by east. Keep a good

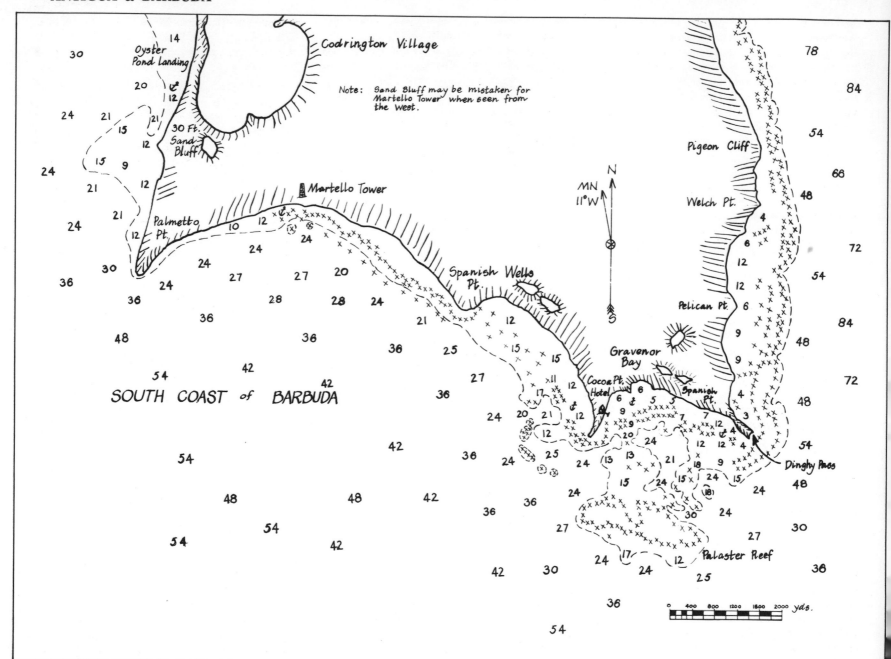

SKETCH CHART 52

lookout as there is a seven-foot shoal spot five miles offshore. On a hazy day you could hit the shoal before even sighting the island.

Actually, there are many off-lying hazards, among them Codrington Shoals to the south and the alleged nine-foot spot on the north corner of Codrington Bank. The charted depths over these shoals are unreliable, as the coral has grown appreciably since the last surveys. Spanish Wells Point and Palmetto Point have extended much farther to the south. In general, the entire south coast is littered with coral heads not shown on the chart. On the west coast, do not try to cross the nine-foot bank; it is considerably less than nine feet, as several yachts have discovered to their chagrin.

You must clear Customs in Antigua before sailing for Barbuda. Antigua will give you coastal clearance to Barbuda. The police in Barbuda told me that it was not necessary to go into Codrington to clear in Barbuda, but that if you happened to go ashore, you should bring the coastal permit with you.

The town of Codrington is a village, not a town; the population is poor but friendly. Its main claim to fame is the fact that its fences are held up by posts which actually are old carved posts of four-poster beds. How an island that has always been dead poor acquired literally hundreds of beautifully carved four-poster beds is beyond me.

Spanish Point
(BA 1997, NO 25204, Sketch Chart 52)

Of the several anchorages on the south coast of Barbuda, the best by far is the one west of Spanish Point. Here again the chart is wrong in that a full two fathoms can be carried right up behind the point. Yachtsmen who use this spot differ on the best way to approach. Andy Copeland of *Flica* favors passing to windward of Palaster Reef, following in toward Spanish Point until the breakers

on the reef south of the point are spotted, then bearing off behind this reef, and rounding up into the anchorage. On the other hand, Dave Price of *Lincoln* suggests an approach from the west, working eastward between Palaster Reef and the mainland until Spanish Point bears roughly southeast, then easing on in through the coral heads and anchoring in a suitable depth with Spanish Point bearing about southeast. Both agree that scrupulous eyeballing is required. No matter how hard the wind is blowing, no matter what the height of the ground swell, this is a calm anchorage. When departing the area, it is possible to sail in a near-straight line between Spanish and Cocoa Points, but post a lookout.

Gravenor Bay
(BA 1997, NO 25204, Sketch Chart 52)

This is an excellent shoal-water anchorage east of Cocoa Point. It is best with the wind in the north. However, with a full mile of fetch to windward, the bay can become choppy when the wind is south of east. The break in the reef is easily spotted. There is ten feet at the entrance and seven or eight feet just inside, shoaling rapidly to five feet. Round up just past the break and anchor. A boat of no greater than five-foot draft can be taken anywhere in Gravenor Bay with care taken to skirt the coral heads.

Cocoa Point
(BA 1997, NO 25204, Sketch Chart 52)

West of this point is a good anchorage when the swell is down. Anchor off Gravenor Bay. There is a hotel ashore that is inhospitable—even hostile—to visiting yachtsmen. On running westward from Cocoa Point toward the Martello Tower, give a wide berth to Spanish Wells Point, where the shoal and coral heads extend well offshore. There is a

tolerable anchorage off the tower. The prime anchorage is southwest of the tower, but if you are feeling enterprising, you can swing in among the coral heads and anchor in relatively calm waters, with the tower bearing northeast. There is a small hotel near the tower where taxis may be hired to take you into Codrington.

Palmetto Point
(BA 1997, NO 25204, Sketch Chart 52)

Again, an undersea area that has grown out considerably, to the southwest perhaps as much as a mile more than shown on the chart. In general, do not try to anchor off the western shore of Barbuda in a ground swell. Otherwise, when the swell is down, a beautiful anchorage can be had off Oyster Pond Landing. En route north, let me repeat the warning not to cross the "nine-foot" bank beyond Palmetto Point. The neck of land at Oyster Pond Landing is narrow enough to permit carrying a dinghy across, from where it is a short row to town. Some frequenters of the area prefer an anchorage between Tuson Rock and the mainland. Head due east from Tuson Rock, which is visible only from the spreaders, and anchor in suitable depth. Here again the dinghy can be dragged overland for the trip to town. An adventurous eyeballer in a shoal draft boat could make it all the way north around the west coast of the island past Cedar Tree and Billy Points, feeling his way back down south through the channel, ending up at Castle Landing.

Palaster Reef
(BA 1997, NO 25204)

Not as it appears on the chart, but rather a series of reefs with breaks that permit entry for a safe anchorage inside. Use a Bahamian moor, and, if the wind picks up, use two anchors off the bow and one astern. This is an ideal spot in settled weather.

CHAPTER 15

Montserrat and Redonda

NO 25161, BA 254

Montserrat has always been the bridesmaid but never the bride. The island lies 35 miles south-southeast of Nevis, 35 miles southwest of English Harbour, and 35 miles northwest of Guadeloupe. Hence, many yachts stop there en route from one place to another, but seldom do they remain long on the island; like Dominica, Montserrat is a farmer's delight and a sailor's nightmare. It is high, beautiful, and lush, but has no harbor; the only port of entry is Plymouth and it is the merest excuse for a harbor.

The island is most famous for its black natives who speak English with an Irish brogue, and for the difficulty of landing on its open beaches. I have read four books written between 1830 and 1900 on traveling in the West Indies. All register the same complaints against Montserrat—a great surge on the beach, the boatmen not experienced seamen, and everybody arriving ashore soaked to the skin. Wandering across the island in wet woolen clothes did not improve the temper of the 19th-century tourist, nor will it improve yours, and you will get wet—so be forewarned.

About 500 yards south of the dock in Plymouth, nestled among the coconut trees, you will find a very nice, small hotel with a most hospitable owner. If you arrive by boat, the first drink is on the house—a wonderful custom all too infrequently found. At the other end of town is a new air-conditioned motel; it looks to be straight out of New Jersey. In other parts of the island, various cottage clubs with hotels attached, a la Miami Beach, are rapidly sprouting up.

Recently there has been an influx of real estate developers. If you pretend that you are interested in buying land, they will show you the whole island. This is cheaper than hiring a taxi! If you should hire a taxi, be sure to visit the forts on the top of St. George's Hill. If you are touring by foot, visit both the Catholic and Anglican churches and their attendant graveyards. It is interesting to note the names and the short life span that prevailed in years gone by.

LIAT has daily scheduled flights out of Montserrat to other islands. I don't know the schedule, but LIAT usually doesn't either, and whatever it is, it is subject to change without notice. Their favorite trick is to book you on a flight that doesn't exist and their favorite pastime is to lose your baggage. Carry all your essentials in your hand.

There are no marine supplies available of any sort on Montserrat, nor is fuel or water available unless you are willing to lighter it out yourself. Wrestling a 55-gallon drum into a boat and launching through the surf is not my idea of yachting. Ice is available, and a moderate selection of food can be found. By all rights, there should be an unlimited selection of fresh fruit and vegetables, but there isn't. I don't know whether it is all bought up by the canneries, or whether each farmer hoards what he raises. There is some produce sold in the market, but nowhere near what you would expect.

Montserrat is covered by NO 25161 and BA 254; there is nothing to prefer between them. When arriving in Montserrat, remember that Customs is strict. Anchor first off the main dock, clear, and then go about one-quarter south to the first cove south of town, home of the hospitable hotel which I mentioned. The bottom is sand and should provide good holding but does not. An unbelievable collection of garbage, large waterlogged timbers, lengths of wire, and whatnot will inevitably foul your anchor. There are other anchorages on the lee side of Montserrat, namely Cars Bay or Old Road Bay, but neither is very good; they are wide open and rolly. The lack of good harbors has played a major role in slowing the development of the island.

Redonda

Midway between Montserrat and Nevis lies the pinnacle rock of Redonda. Redonda is now uninhabited but remains a dependency of Antigua, which is 25 miles to the eastward. This is a place that few yachts visit, as there is no anchorage and no apparent way to get ashore. It does faithful service as a turning mark for the Sir Thomas Lipton Race, but that is usually as close as one now gets to this pile of rock.

This was not always the case. At one time a flourishing mine was operated on the island. Fritz Fenger, who cruised through the islands in a 16-foot batwing canoe before World War I, reported that he landed at a large buoy on the western shore from which they lifted him and his canoe out of the water onto a cable car which carried them both to the manager's house 1000 feet above.

I had always supposed that they mined sulphur on Redonda, simply because that was what they used to mine on Saba. But recently a West Indian history book set me straight. At its height, just after the turn of the century, the mine on Redonda was yielding 7,000 tons of alumina per year. That would be 140 tons a week, which, considering the primitive gear used then, indicates a bustling operation.

Despite its forbidding shore, for the adventurous, the mountain climber, or the historically inclined, Redonda might make an interesting day's diversion in calm weather.

Aves Island
(insert A on NO 25161)

For want of a more logical place, uninhabited Aves (or Bird) Island, 125 miles west of Dominica, is entered on the chart for Statia to Montserrat. Less than half a mile long, some 300 yards wide, standing no more than 12 feet high, and changing size and shape with every storm, it gives me the willies just to think about it. Some say it is the eeriest, most desolate spot in the world; others claim it is the most beautiful. Though it has been nightfall every time I have passed it (lying as it does on the direct route from St. Thomas to Grenada), I tend to agree with the former view. An anchorage of a sort can be made in sand and coral in the island's lee; it will be rough, as the swell hooks around both ends of the reef.

Owned by Venezuela, Aves is now a turtle and bird sanctuary, but it has a long history of tragedy and near-tragedy. Turtles go there in the hurricane season to lay eggs, where they are pursued by hunters and naturalists. Any number of West Indian turtle schooners have been wrecked on its shores. They would anchor in the lee, relying on the trades to keep them off, and when the wind died out, the swell would pitch them high and dry on the beach. In the late '60s, the famous Norwegian lifeboat *Ho Ho*, which had sailed around the world in the '30s, went out to Aves in the hurricane season to gather turtles. Nothing has been heard of boat or crew since. Even more recently, a young French couple anchored and went ashore to study turtle life at night. At dawn they discovered that their boat had drifted out of sight. Two nights later they were able to signal a passing freighter; lo and behold, what was being towed astern but their yacht! Some people are very lucky.

Others, however, are not. Perhaps one reason Aves has such a bad reputation is that the charts have it positioned wrong. Actually, it is roughly three miles to the northwest of where it is shown on the charts. In any event, be sure to give it a wide berth at night, and keep a sharp lookout for it by day.

CHAPTER 16

Guadeloupe

**NO 25123, 25124, 25125, 25126, 25127; BA 491,
804, 885; French 2872, 3125, 3127, 3128, 3129, 3287,
3367, 3375, 3418, 3419, 3422, 3423, 4519**

Aside from some civil instability and occasional riots, Guadeloupe is one of the finest islands in the Caribbean. Perhaps because of the restiveness of its natives, it is overly neglected, but the worst that happens is that foreigners and tourists are ejected before the real fireworks start, and then the French come in, bloody some heads, and restore order. Nonetheless, yachtsmen have been tending to give it a fairly wide berth. Some may take a quick look at the anchorage at Basse-Terre and clear out. Others may try Pointe-a-Pitre, but the noise, heat, and filth of the commercial harbor drive them away immediately.

But possibly the real reason that the island is not a favorite among yachtsmen is that they rely mainly on U.S. and British charts, which is a mistake, as the French charts are considerably better, more numerous, and more detailed. Guadeloupe and its nearby islands of Petite Terre, Desirade, Marie Galante, and Les Saintes are covered by five NO charts, three BA charts, and some 13 French charts.

Large, lush, mountainous, well cultivated, civilized, and heavily populated, the capital of the French West Indies is well worth investigating. Its geography is varied. The western half, called Grande-Terre and actually an island unto its own separated from Basse-Terre by the Salee River, is low and flat. Guadeloupe abounds with history, all of it brutal and bloody; the carnage during the French Revolution and the Napoleonic Wars was unbelievable. The infamous Victor Hugues made his headquarters in Guadeloupe while he "visited" the other French islands in the name of the Revolution. He traveled well equipped, carrying his own portable guillotine which he toted along to do in on the spot those to whom he objected.

There are numerous small hotels on the island which are comfortable, charming, and serve outstanding meals. Since the mid-'60s a number of large, so-called modern hotels have been erected. Personally, I prefer the older type: the food is better, they are usually run more congenially, and the prices are much more reasonable. I am suspicious of any ostensibly French restaurant that prints its menu in English.

Air communications are good—by West Indian standards. Cable and wireless are available only during the day, and mail service is no better or worse than on any of the other islands.

Like Martinique, Guadeloupe is a good spot to load up on food, wine, bread, and cheese, but the one time I stocked up on eggs

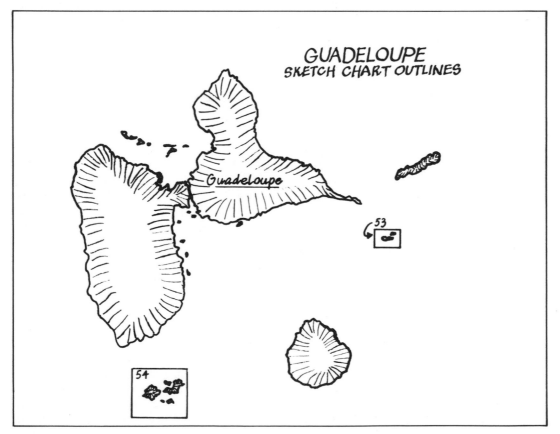

GUADELOUPE
SKETCH CHART OUTLINES

Guadeloupe

53

54

I lived (barely) to regret. They must have been World War II surplus, and were rotten when purchased despite being labeled "fresh." Ice is widely available. In Basse-Terre fuel comes only in drums, and there are few facilities for going alongside unless you have lots of guts and plenty of fenders, as there is always a surge at Basse-Terre. At Point-a-Pitre, the old molasses dock has been rebuilt as a fully equipped marina.

Basse-Terre
(BA 491; NO 25127; French 3127, 3418, 3375)

In the southwest corner of the island, Basse-Terre is a stop frequently used by yachts to pick up supplies or drop off guests. That is all the port is good for. It is open, rolly, steep-to, and the bottom is littered with anchors, cable, and waterlogged timber. Unless you enjoy diving in murk, rig a trip-line on your anchor. None of the charts yet show the new dock that was built in 1963. The best anchorage I have found is north of the new dock inside the innermost buoys. Once your anchor is set, run a stern line out to one of the buoys, as the wind waltzes around, the tide is strong, and there are many eddies. A stern line to a buoy will prevent you from fouling your anchor. Usually it is not necessary to use your own dinghy; a local fisherman will often take you for the fee of a pack or two of American cigarettes, which are harder currency than dollars. Customs will come out. Don't forget to rig your fenders as soon as you arrive.

The town itself is far more stimulating than its harbor. A good restaurant is Robinson's at the top of the hill. One of the Customs officers, Rufus Fab, speaks English and loves to guide visitors. Fort Richepanse is a fascinating old place—from the outside. I would love to explore it, but have never figured out how to get in. The French seem to value their old forts highly, and keep them locked up.

It's also a fine shopping and provisioning center. A few years ago I stopped at a small shop to buy some shorts for my wife, but I didn't know her size in French. I tried to describe her to madam, who suddenly stopped my gestures and called out six girls from the back room who had been busy sewing. I pointed out one that appeared to be about Marilyn's size, and for the next half hour she happily modeled various shorts for me. I bought a few pairs, which turned out to fit perfectly. Only on a French island could you get free modeling service.

From Basse-Terre buses run to all parts of the island, but most leave earlyish in the morning. The ride to Pointe-a-Pitre takes a couple of hours and is good fun if you bring a cushion with you; the wooden benches get rather painful after a while. Taxis also can be hired, but if you wish to visit Pointe-a-Pitre, it is better to set out from Deshayes at the northwest corner, as the ride is shorter. Some people like to get off at Basse-Terre, taxi around the island, and meet up with their boat at Deshayes.

Anse a la Barque
(BA 885; NO 25123; French 3418, 3375)

Six miles north of Basse-Terre lies what used to be a beautiful and quiet cove. Now, however, I have been told that there are so many small yachts moored permanently at its head that it is almost impossible to get in far enough to find bottom for anchoring. Also, apparently the two steamer buoys to which one used to be able to moor are no longer there. All this is academic anyway, since heavy traffic along the coast makes sleep nearly impossible. If you do decide to have a try, the cove is small but easy to spot. Anse a la Barque is supposedly marked by a fixed green and group flashing white. In the day-time you will see a concrete dock with a number of small boats moored nearby. If you can't get in close, remember the cove is very deep, and you will need lots of line out.

Running north from Anse a la Barque, hug the coast within two pistol shots. With luck you will hold a breeze, and if you don't, the water will be calm enough for easy motoring. There are two dangers that must be avoided. North of Islets a Goyaves and Pigeon is Point Malendure, which has a six-foot shoal slightly north of it. A mile north of Goyaves lies Point Mahaut, with a four-foot spot 200 yards offshore. For what it's worth, I have also heard of a few boats that either have had the living daylights scared out of them or actually suffered a bullet hole through a sail. It seems that there is an army firing range along this sector of the coast; it is seldom used, but when it is, the militia is less than careful about where they are aiming. Or are they *very* careful?

Islets a Goyaves
(BA 885; NO 25123; French 3418, 3375)

There is a nice cove here that is well sheltered from the south. I haven't come across anyone who has stopped, but I have been told by locals that it is an interesting island with good swimming. Whether or not anchoring is possible, I don't know. It might be a case of having to stand off the island and of sending a dinghy ashore.

Deshayes
(BA 885, NO 25123, French 3418)

At the northwestern end of Guadeloupe, this is the ideal landfall when coming south from Antigua, and likewise a good departure point when leaving for Antigua. As a port of entry, it is unique. Row your dinghy ashore and walk to the northern end of town. There you will find a small bar, and the barmaid will not only serve you a drink but will give you all the necessary entry forms. You no longer have to trudge up the hill to the Gendarmerie (but the view is still worth it).

The town itself is unusually picturesque, with numerous fishing boats drawn up on shore, nets drying, small boys sailing model boats, and an assortment of workshops making furniture of beautiful wood but in unbelievably bad taste. One such shop is almost completely taken up by the biggest and most complicated woodworking machine I have ever seen. Its operator evidently knows how to run it; Stan Young of *Limley* had him lengthen his cabin top by four feet, and the man did a beautiful job of it in six days. There is not much available in the way of supplies, but a visit to the bakery late in the afternoon will be rewarded with bread hot out of the oven. South of the town is a small stream with a two-track road paralleling it. Follow the road along the stream, and when it ends, start climbing. You will find small waterfalls, exquisite little pools suitable for fresh-water swimming, and some fine bird-watching. Chances are you will be in complete solitude, as there is no habitation along the stream.

The anchorage at Deshayes is straightforward enough. Sail on in to about five fathoms, round up, drop the hook—and watch for fish pots. The holding is in good sand. The ground swell can roll in, but not dangerously. If the swell is running, all anchorages in this area will be uncomfortable. One word of caution, however: if approaching from the south do not round up at the southern end of the bay. Rocks extend from the shore further than might be expected. I found out the hard way.

The northern waters of Guadeloupe— the great reef-encumbered bay between the two halves of the butterfly—is covered in detail by French charts 3287, 3422, and 3367. But for some unknown reason they ignore the details of Port Louis, the only real town in the area. However, Port Louis is covered in detail by charts NO 25127 and BA 491.

From the look of the chart, these reefs have to be some of the best diving and their shores some of the best exploring in the Antilles. A boat drawing six or even eight feet could go most places—with care. Shallower draft boats can navigate Grande Riviere a Goyaves without danger, since it's all soft mud (and great exploring); they used to be able to use Riviere Salee when there was an opening bridge at Pointe-a-Pitre. As of this writing the bridge is stuck, and there is the further problem of high-tension wires. The French pilot office informed me the clearance was 57 feet, which information I dutifully put in my earlier guide. A few years after it was published, I received a letter from someone whose mast was considerably shorter than 57 feet. He had touched the overhead wires and nearly fried himself and crew. Sparks went in all directions, he said, and his rigging was fused. So I cannot recommend a river passage except with reliable local advice. Make inquiries ashore.

On the western shore of Grande-Terre there are numerous waterways leading back into towns, villages, and cane fields. Some day I should like to poke along some of them, as I suspect one could find ruins dating back to the days when sugar was the area's prime asset. As scary as exploring may seem on the chart, there are rudimentary aids to navigation—a local system. When proceeding eastward, leave all red buoys on the starboard hand, and white ones to port. What you do when you are going north and south, I can't say. Personally, I wouldn't trust the system; if the buoys are there at all, I'm sure the white ones will be so rusty that they will appear red. Eyeball navigation is the only safe way to get around; find a reef to anchor behind before the sun gets so low that navigation is difficult.

Le Moule
(BA 491, 885; NO 25127; French 3125)

The northeast coast is bold and steep-to, and only this port is subject to analysis. The British Admiralty's *Sailing Directions,* which, of course, is published for large vessels, warns of difficulty of entry and states that it is unsafe from October to March. It does not say why; I presume it would be on account of the ground swell. The wind also can come directly out of the north during these months. Both of these factors would conspire to make a large power vessel virtually unmanageable in restricted quarters. In view of the BA's concern, I don't think I would try it in a sailboat either, except under ideal conditions. I've attempted a visit some four times now, but was always rebuffed by the weather and the swell. However, Henry Strauss, owner of *Doki,* reports that he was most intrigued by the harbor when he sailed in during the summer of 1972. He cautions, though, that it should be attempted only when the rollers are not running.

Enter on the range given on the chart until breaking water can be seen to port on Mouton Dehaut, then favor the eastern shore marked by a row of huge anchors which make it look like Tarawa after the battle. If you examine the French chart's insert carefully, you will see that these anchors are numbered. Once the light and signal mast bear due west, feel your way in very cautiously, as the bottom shoals gradually. Once in, it definitely calls for a Bahamian moor or a bow line tied to shore with a stern anchor out. Otherwise you will be swung onto the reefs when the current reverses.

Under no circumstances should you attempt to follow one of the small fishing boats in, as they snake their way through chinks in the reefs that will not tolerate a deeper draft. Once anchored, a diverting side-trip by dinghy is to the head of the harbor and on up the river, which extends well into the center of Grande-Terre; along the way the skeletonized remains of a once-flourishing sugar industry can be seen. Additionally, the town itself is not without interest. An old battery, off the beaten track on the west side, is definitely worth exploring.

Ste. Marie
(BA 804; NO 25123; French 3419, 4519, 3125)

From Basse-Terre, one might admire the perfect shelter offered by the two rows of reefs and detached coral heads, but it seems to be a flip of the coin as to whether you can gain it by sea. I know of two yachts that have successfully sailed in, and townspeople talk of three yachts that were lost there within six months. If the sun is high and the water clear, you might feel bold enough to venture the numerous reefs. It is reported that the entrance is buoyed, but also that the water is often murky. The rain squalls which frequently blot out the town flood the rivers, which in turn carry mud into the harbor, with the result that you can't see the reefs. It is a reach in (and a reach out), and there is anchoring anywhere the depth looks good. Le Gros Loup gives excellent shelter from the sea, providing a beautiful and cool anchorage. The Goyave River north of town undoubtedly would be fun in a dinghy.

Pointe-a-Pitre
(BA 804; NO 25123, 25126; French 3419, 2872, 3375)

Guadeloupe's main city and the capital of the French West Indies, the harbor is nonetheless much neglected by yachtsmen. Although it is well buoyed, well lit, and well sheltered, it is no place for yachts. For one thing it is a commercial harbor, and just plain filthy. It is also noisy, beset with pilferage, and the smoke from a nearby sugar factory

adds to the altogether unsavory atmosphere.

The entrance to Pointe-a-Pitre is very deep and buoyed, but it must be remembered that in all waters except the U.S. Virgins, it is the European system: black is left to starboard when entering. The buoys are placed precisely at the end of the shoals they mark, so that it is impossible to cut them even by a few feet, and the channel is so narrow that if there is a ship in it there is no room left for a yacht.

Despite the above-mentioned drawbacks, with the accent on yachting in Guadeloupe there is now a full-fledged marina with all facilities in the harbor. It is located on the old molasses loading pier—the long pier marked on the chart north of Fouillole Point. Diesel, gasoline, electricity (single-phase 220), and water are available; I might mention that this is one of the few marinas I have ever been to where the water at the end of the dock still has tons of pressure. At the head of the dock are showers, the main road into town, and an ice truck every morning.

The marina is run by Pierre Lemarie, a French Canadian from Quebec, with his wife and five sons. No matter what you have on your boat that has broken down, one of the five sons will turn out to be an expert on it, and will repair it. As in Grenada, the nice thing about lying at the marina is that you don't have to keep using taxis. Just hop in your dinghy and make the short run to the Yacht Club de Guadeloupe, an excellent jumping-off spot for Customs, shopping, and what-have-you. The Club is most friendly.

On Rue Gaspail is found Henri Martin's fabulous marine supply establishment—undoubtedly the largest south of St. Thomas. It is convenient in that it is in the cove north of the Dardoucier Sugar Factory and can be visited by dinghy en route to town, or by taxi. You can walk in the back entrance of the establishment and see literally hundreds

of outboards, Del Quay dories, Boston Whalers stacked up by the half dozen, Sailfish by the dozen—you name it, he has it. He carries the complete set of French charts for the area, but remember, if you're in Martinique and going to Guadeloupe, buy your Guadeloupe charts in Martinique as Henri, because of the demand, may be low in stock for Guadeloupe. The gear is mainly for power boats and small sailboats; not many big heavy items but all sorts of bits and pieces that are unobtainable elsewhere in the Caribbean.

In 1940, the two most talked about events in Guadeloupe were the Fall of France and the building of a drawbridge over the Salee River. Neither lasted very long: France recovered in 1945 and the bridge stopped opening around 1968. In 1972, a new opening bridge was constructed; the power line was going to be buried under water, and the river was supposed to be dredged to 12 feet, making it a blessing for yachtsmen sailing to and from Antigua. Unfortunately, someone goofed, and the bridge didn't work. Exactly when it is scheduled to be fixed I don't know, despite several queries to officials. And the high-tension wires are still an overhead threat.

La Grande Baie
(BA 491, NO 25126, French 3375)

Southeast of Pointe-a-Pitre, this is a good sheltered anchorage as long as the wind is in the northeast. With the wind from the southeast, it becomes rough and uncomfortable. It shoals very gradually, so feel your way in. At present there is no nearby habitation, so you can be completely by yourself yet only a mile and a half from town by dinghy. However, this area is also being eyed for development, and by now there may be a marina there.

Le Gozier
(BA 491, NO 25126, French 3419)

Four miles east of Pointe-a-Pitre lies this

excellent anchorage and its surprisingly bustling village. The mainland and Ilet du Gozier give complete shelter to the northwest of the island on a sand bottom. There is plenty of water with gradual shoaling. Feel your way in; the further east you go, the less swell will be encountered. There is good snorkeling and a number of hotels along the beach. It is only a short taxi ride to a number of towns along this part of the coast, and night life is active. This anchorage is also handy to the airport. If you anchor fairly far offshore behind the reef, there should be plenty of breeze and no bugs.

Petit Havre
(BA 885, NO 25123, French 3419)

There are other small harbors along the south coast of Guadeloupe that look enticing and reasonably accessible (at least on the charts), but I have found few sailing people who have visited them. Petit Havre, however, two and a half miles east of Le Gozier, comes well recommended as being an excellent anchorage in the winter months when the wind is north of east and the swell is from a northerly direction. In the spring and summer, though, I would be careful, since if the wind goes into the south, the harbor will not be good.

Ste. Anne
(BA 885; NO 25123; French 3419, 4519)

No matter what quadrant the wind is blowing from, the harbor of this attractive town looks to be perfectly protected by the surrounding reefs. It is not, however, when the wind is south of east. There are two entrances, both of which are buoyed, but it still should not be entered except when the sun is high. The eastern channel affords the best entrance, and the western the best exit. Shoal draft boats can sneak up behind the reef to the east and gain complete shelter, but deeper

boats should regard the harbor strictly as a daytime stopping place. In fact, I would recommend that any boat drawing more than six feet not try it at all, as the harbor is quite shoal.

The picturesque small town is not officially a port of entry, but gendarmes there seem quite content to receive a crew list and wish you a good day. A number of hotels boast good French dining rooms. At the western end high on a promontory is the new Caravelle Hotel, famous for its fabulous food and a frantic floor show. To the west of this point is a reliable anchorage as long as the wind is east or north of east. Ice is available, and a small market is held each day. The beach in front of the town is lined with the typical Saintes boats found in the south of the island.

This gorgeous beach stretches eastward for miles, providing tourists a popular resort spot and yachtsmen an unbeatable stretch for bikini study. The equally extensive reefs outside offer outstanding diving. I have seen power boats anchor off and in a few minutes fill themselves with fish.

St. Francois
(BA 885, 491; NO 25123; French 3419, 4519)

This small village-cum-harbor is mainly frequented by French fishermen from Desirade who come to sell their catch. Like Petit Havre and St. Anne, the harbor is open to the south and therefore should be viewed with a jaundiced eye in spring and summer. In the winter, however, it ought to be comfortable.

The harbor's anchorage is small in the extreme; buoys on the outer reef lead to the inner anchorage. To enter the eastern anchorage, pick up the outer buoy, pass it close aboard to starboard, and steer 338 magnetic. Round up once the eastern reef gives shelter.

If you want to get away from it all, a mile eastward of town is Passe Champagne, which is ideal for shoal draft boats to lie behind the eastern end of the reef.

Islands off the Coast of Guadeloupe

La Desirade
(BA 885, 491; NO 25123; French 3125, 3423, 4519)

The name means "desired one," but why anyone should call it that is beyond me; it has little or no fresh water, no timber, and its permanent population barely ekes out an existence. Maybe it is just as well that none of the charts listed above cover the island in detail. French 4519 is at least helpful to some degree, in that it carries a profile map of the island and of Anse de Galet, though the range marks of a tree in line with a mud-and-wattle thatch hut doubtless disappeared decades ago. The anchorage at Anse de Galet would appear less than inviting. The island is long and narrow, lying in the same direction as the wind and sea. I don't think it would give much protection in normal trade-wind weather. And when the northerly ground swell starts rolling in, I'd forget it.

However, the British Admiralty *Sailing Directions* refer to an anchorage off Grande Anse on the south coast and state that with local knowledge a vessel drawing five feet or less could enter between the reefs. If so (it's hard to tell from any of the charts) the anchorage would probably be quite good if the wind is well around to the north. The *Pilot* mentions a third anchorage at the eastern end —Baie Mahault—but again cautions that it is accessible only with local knowledge.

A lighthouse keeper on Petite Terre has kindly sent me some information on his neighbor to the north. La Desirade has a population of about 1600, all of them fishermen and their families. There is only one road on the island, running along the south coast near the shore. Mahault has a restaurant, but no hotel. In the main town, Grande Anse, on the south coast, is a small inn serving reputedly good French food. He agrees that the harbors should be entered only with local advice and shoal-draft boats. My suggestion is that if you really want to see the island, either fly over to it from the mainland, or charter a launch headed there from Petite Terre. The faster one makes the trip in about 35 minutes. There's been a rumor outstanding for some time now that a marina was about to be built in Mahault. I would inquire in advance if this has yet been done, as rumors in these parts hang on for years without embodiment.

Petite Terre
(BA 885; NO 25123; French 3423, 3419; Sketch Chart 53)

Petite Terre is one of the most attractive

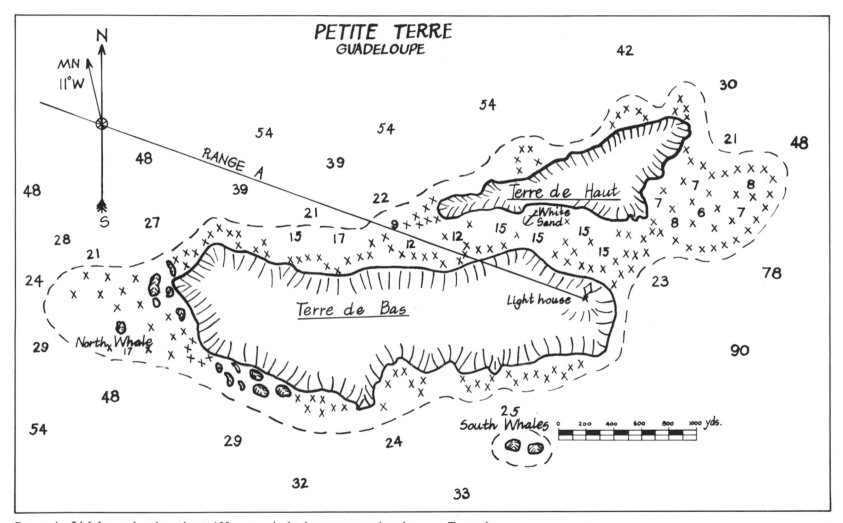

Range A: Lighthouse bearing about 120 magnetic leads over outer bar between Terre de Haut and Terre de Bas. Watch for coral heads.

SKETCH CHART 53

anchorages I know in the Lesser Antilles—if the weather is right. It is well known and appreciated by the French yachtsmen from Guadeloupe who visit on weekends, but during the week apparently no one ever goes there except fishermen. When I visited a short time ago, we were told we were the first foreign vessel ever to have anchored among these islands!

The islets show up quite well on French 3419, and I've supplied a few more details on the Sketch Chart. I do this because after visiting there myself I wondered if the chartmakers had ever done likewise. The western entrance to the channel between the islands is completely swept by breakers in heavy weather and the eastern entrance is blocked by coral reefs. The only entrance to the anchorage is from the northwest, but don't attempt it in a northerly swell. Even in good weather don't attempt it unless the light is perfect. Stand in on port tack with the lighthouse bearing about 120 magnetic. There is nine feet of water between the coral heads, but the coral heads stick up a minimum of three feet from the bottom, so stay to the white sand and work your way eastward. Once the western end of Mouton de Haut comes abeam, favor the north side of the channel, where the coral heads disappear and the depth increases to around 15 feet. Continue eastward until you spot a small white-sand beach on the port hand. The beach is steep-to, practically vertical. Drop a bow anchor, run a stern line ashore, and warp in as close as you dare. If you anchor from the stern and run the bow in, you'll probably be able to jump right onto dry land. Having done this, you can confirm the inaccuracy of the French charts from the top of the lighthouse by observing that there is no passage from the east, but only from the northwest.

Naturally, there is great snorkeling between the two islands, and on the exposed outer shore of Terre de Haut is some fine fishing. A path handily leads from the white-sand beach to the outer shore. There's no dinghy landing out there, though, so it's a case of swimming from shore, catching your fish, and swimming back with it.

For those who like to explore ruins and lighthouses, a stop at Terre de Bas is a must. The view from the lighthouse is incomparable, and for what it's worth, the structure is reputed to be the oldest lighthouse in the Western Hemisphere still in continuous operation, dating back to 1835. (Desirade Light is older, having been built in 1828, but since has been completely rebuilt.) It is interesting to note that in the early 19th century the French erected lighthouses on dangerous landfalls, whereas the British have yet to establish lights on Anegada, Anguilla, or Barbuda, despite their total number of wrecks now pushing on one thousand. Petite Terre's lighthouse keeper—now replaced by automation—insisted that there were *no* wrecks surrounding either Desirade or Petite Terre.

Terre de Bas was originally a privately-owned estate. You can see its extensive remains from the lighthouse. If you go exploring, make sure you come back before dusk. The island is so mosquito-infested that during the wet season the lighthouse keepers lit huge bonfires to keep the mosquitoes at bay.

Iles des Saintes
(BA 491, 885; NO 25124; French 3129, 3375, 3423; Sketch Chart 54)

The popular archipelago of islands ten miles south of the mainland is best served by the French charts, which are the right size to use easily. There are two main islands, Terre d'en Haut and Terre d'en Bas, rising 1,000 feet out of the sea with numerous rugged peaks, plus innumerable little rocks and cays. There is an excellent anchorage off the town of Bourg des Saintes, lots of beaches, and attractive settlements populated by fishermen. These islands are a prime vacation spot for Guadeloupians, as the climate is always wonderful. But the breeze and dryness create the area's one major problem: lack of fresh water.

In each of the coves you will see the distinctive Saintes boats, with their high flaring bow, low heart-shaped stern, long low mainsail, and genoa jib. In the worst weather they will be seen hove-to under oars, one man holding the bow to the sea while the remainder of the crew tend hand lines. They catch beautiful fish, but it is almost impossible to buy fresh fish in the Saintes. At the end of the day they sell all their fish to a "buy boat" that lies in the main harbor. Then they take their money and go ashore to buy hard dry salt cod that has been shipped from Nova Scotia! The reason that they never bring fish ashore is that the boats are worked on shares and each man is afraid if anyone brings home a fish, it might unbalance the shares; hence they sell the catch for cash and split the cash.

The small hotel that overlooks Bourg des Saintes used to be run by one Al Cassino, who left Brooklyn in the early '30s. He ran the hotel and the power plant, went through several wives, and sired countless children. For some reason he and the priest—the island's two most prominent figures—had a running fight going for years. They never spoke to each other, but only through intermediaries. There was always an air of mystery about him, but Al never confided his past to me. I found out after he died that he had been on the losing side of a gang war just at the end of prohibition, and a contract was out to fit him with cement shoes. He decided that the climate in the Antilles was much more salubrious than the States, and took hold in his new land so quickly that no stranger had a chance to approach without his knowing about it. When indeed "friends" arrived, they invariably found Al standing at the dock waiting to "greet" them. Instead of dying with weighted boots on, he expired peacefully in bed. But his sign lives on: BAR RESTAURANT.

At the head of the dock is another small restaurant, the Coq d'Or, with its intimate balcony overlooking the harbor. Any number of houses along the main street have also been converted to bars and restaurants. Frequently what looks like a charming private home can on short notice conjure up a very good meal. I don't know where they get their ingredients, but somehow they do it. The majority of the larger houses are summer homes for the mainlanders, who come here to escape the heat and rain of Guadeloupe.

Except for salt, fish, and rice, the only food that you can purchase is bread, distinctive in that it is excellent the first day, tasty to put in the soup the second day, makes a good wooden mallet the third day, and from the fourth day onward you can drive nails with it. No fuel, water, or ice is available.

The main anchorage is off Bourg des Saintes; its approaches are not difficult when coming from the north. If entering west of Ilet-a-Cabrit, there are no dangers until Passe du Pain de Sucre is reached. There the only danger is Haut Fond, a pinnacle rock south of the eastern end of Ilet-a-Cabrit. This rock is well marked with a buoy. If approaching from the north and passing eastward of Ilet-a-Cabrit, there are the double dangers of Baleine du Large (just breaking) and La Baleine (two feet high). The Sketch Chart provides the ranges.

In Anse du Bourg the best anchorage is to the north of the dock; watch out for the shoal that extends out from the bow of the sunken ship coming out of the cliff. Anchor close to shore in three fathoms with plenty of scope; the bottom shelves off quite steeply. If it is blowing hard, put out two anchors; the

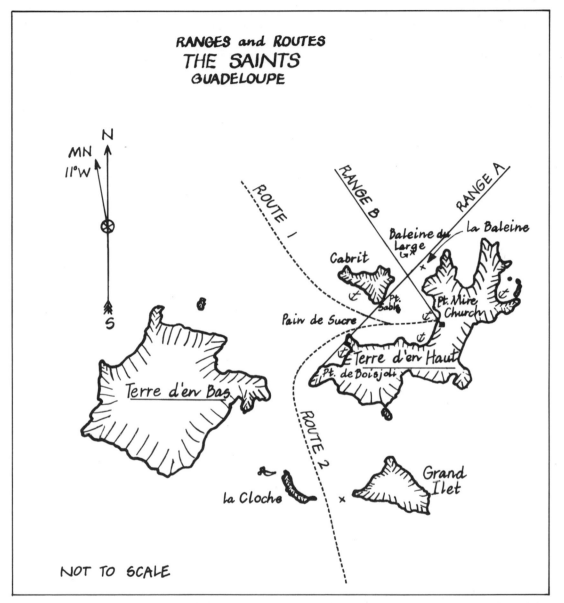

Range A: Point de Boisjoli, Pain de Sucre, and Point Sable in line leads between La Baleine and Baleine du Large, 232-052 magnetic.

Range B: The church open to the west of Point Mire leads to the west of La Baleine and Baleine du Large, 165-345 magnetic.

SKETCH CHART 54

gusts from the hills cause you to sheer around badly. There is also an anchorage south of the dock at Petite Anse.

Take a crew list ashore to the Gendarmerie, but don't tie your dinghy up to the main dock at what appears to be a dinghy landing. It isn't. We found out the hard way. The ferry from Guadeloupe mashed ours up, and when we complained to the captain, he told us (in colorful French) where to put the shattered remains. We answered that if such was his attitude to visitors, we would complain to the owner. The captain said *he* was the owner. We replied all right, then, we would bring the matter to the mayor. He said *he* was the mayor. On applying for aid from the local constabulary, all this proved to be true, and, to add insult to injury, the sergeant threatened to throw us in jail if we continued arguing with this captain-owner-mayor—insulting a French official is a serious offense. About a year after this incident, I anchored there again, this time pulling my dinghy up on the beach and walking to the Gendarmerie. The same little sergeant was there. He took one look at me and immediately started ranting in French. From what I could gather, the point was that I had better behave myself or he would run me off the island. Gendarmes have very long memories and very short patience.

For those who have the courage, there is a small airport with regularly scheduled service to Guadeloupe. It is undoubtedly one of the shortest runways in the world. If you stay, you'll find the swimming in the harbor excellent. A walk up to Fort Napoleon is well worth the effort, but hiking up to the watchtower at the west end of Terre d'en Haut is more of a project. An invigorating all-day outing is to pack a picnic lunch and walk over to Baie de Pontpierre, where there is a deserted beach with fine swimming and snorkeling. From there one can swim across to the island of Roches Percees and climb to the top. Straight down over the undercut cliff to the sea 100 feet below is the most awesome display of surf imaginable.

The Baie de Pontpierre is completely protected, but sailing in and out of it is difficult, in that there is a rock with only four or five feet of water over it smack in the middle of the channel. A wind anywhere near the northeast would make leaving very difficult. This rock, which French chart 3129 shows at a depth of 1.7 meters (5.5 feet), has not recently moved despite the fact that several yachts entering without incident insist it is no longer there. I personally have seen it from the top of Roches Percees, and, just to double check, circled the bay in an airplane; it is definitely there. Therefore, favor the western side of the channel. If you can spot the rock, there is enough room to pass to leeward of it.

There is an excellent anchorage south of Le Pain de Sucre where you can usually find complete isolation, but you must sail in very close, as the beach drops off sharply. Again, excellent swimming, and the breeze blowing over the low land between Le Pain de Sucre and the island makes for a cool and quiet night.

Baie du Marigot is not as attractive as it seems by the charts. The water is quite muddy and the area does not have much of interest, except that you'll be able to see the stern of the sunken ship whose bow projects into the harbor at Anse du Bourg. She was going so fast when she hit the island that she went right through the mountain—or seemingly so.

Terre d'en Bas is notable in that it is mostly agricultural with its main village at the center of the island away from the shore. There are dinghy landings at Grande Anse, Anse de Muriers, and Anse Fideling, plus, on the lee side, Petites Anses.

When coming from or leaving for Dominica through the Passe des Dames, make sure you are exactly in the center, as there is shoal water on both sides. Also keep an eye out for the rock that pops out of 25 feet of water off Les Quilles; even a shoal draft boat could be damaged if it bottomed out in the trough of a wave. Otherwise if approaching the Iles des Saintes from the south, pass to windward of Grand Ilet with sheets eased, running through the Passe du Grande Ilet, then head up into the anchorage.

Marie Galante
(BA 885, 491; NO 25125; French 3128, 3423)

Low, flat, and nearly circular, for some reason this island is disdained by both yachtsmen and tourists, which, perhaps, is all the more reason to seek it out. There are three industries on Marie Galante—sugar, fishing, and cotton. The last-named was dying until recently, when demand for long staple cotton increased drastically. All through the islands where it was formerly grown, in fact, cotton fields are again being tilled. It is somewhat a mixed blessing, however; the field hands regard picking cotton with as little enthusiasm as cutting sugar cane.

There are three anchorages, of which the first is Capesterre on the southwestern end. Caye du Vent, the highest reef, is situated on the eastern side of the channel, so the harbor should be tried only with local knowledge, and even then with lots of guts. Recently I made the happy discovery that Air Guadeloupe will fly you in a morning, and on the cheap, from Pointe-a-Pitre to Basse Terre, the Saintes, Marie Galante, and Desirade. The flight gives a spectacular view of the area, and all the harbors, reefs, and rocks can be spotted without fear of running aground. On the basis of this flight, I will state categorically that Capesterre Harbor is strictly for small fishing boats that can be pulled up on the beach and not recommended for a cruising yacht.

The second anchorage, St. Louis, is probably fine in the summer months, but in the winter, with the wind from the north, I am sure it would not be comfortable.

Grande Bourg, in the southwest corner of the island, is the main town and the best anchorage. If your draft is less than eight feet, it is possible to turn south once you have passed between the two reefs. Although the channel is buoyed, feel your way along with the lead and go as far to the southeast as you dare. But don't go south of the dock unless you draw less than six feet. Moor with two anchors in case the wind dies and the tide swings you around. The southern reef looks like it should give good protection from the swells, but it doesn't. The swell rolls in over the reef, making this a very uncomfortable harbor.

Marie Galante is another base for the innumerable fishing boats of the type referred to as Saintes boats. Their captains must be damn fine sailors to fish in the open channel with its strong current and with nothing between them and Africa. Every time we saw French fishermen ashore they were drunk; my wife said it was because a man would have to get drunk before he would go out and risk his life in one of those little dinghies.

Actually, anywhere along the lee shore of the island would likely provide a decent anchorage. Guadeloupe itself evidently breaks the ground swell from the northwest, and there are endless miles of attractive, deserted sand beaches in the middle of this northwest coast to which the swell doesn't find its way. The one report I have of this shore states that there is an excellent anchorage off Pointe du Cimetiere—when the wind is south of east. There is good holding in sand bottom. But best of all, there are no charter boats, and the beaches are deserted.

CHAPTER 17

Dominica

NO 25121, 25122; BA 728, 697

Dominica lies between Martinique and Guadeloupe. High, lush, and rugged, it is a farmer's delight—and a sailor's nightmare. Its central ridge rises to nearly 5,000 feet with a sheer drop to the sea on both sides. This mountainous ridge wrings the moisture from the trade winds, accounting for the 300 or so rivers and streams that cascade down its slopes. So effectively does the ridge block the trades that there is almost a total calm in the lee of the island.

Dominica was discovered in 1494 by Columbus on his second voyage to the New World. During the next century and a half every attempt to settle the island was successfully resisted by the local Carib tribesmen. The Caribs entrenched themselves in the mountains from which they would periodically make forays against the early settlers, driving them off to neighboring islands. By the Treaty of Aix la Chapelle the colonial powers agreed to declare as neutral the islands of Dominica, St. Vincent, St. Lucia, and Tobago. Peace was not long at hand, however, as the British and French continued to squabble over Dominica until it was recaptured by the French in 1778. During the American Revolution, the British lost control of their Caribbean territories until Admiral Rodney broke the French hold on the Antilles in the Battle of the Saints in 1782. After a few years of peace, hostilities were resumed during the Napoleonic Wars. The British acquired permanent possession of Dominica, St. Lucia, St. Vincent and Grenada by the Peace of Vienna.

Dominica is precariously connected to the outside world by LIAT airways. The airfield is very poor, and it is small wonder that so few flights come in there. A number of good hotels have been built on the island in recent years. Some are right on the beach, some high in the mountains. If you are to dine in a mountain hotel, bring along a heavy sweater. Come sundown, the men will certainly want a jacket, especially if a rain squall comes whistling through.

The shops in the town of Roseau are fairly good, but the harbor is miserable and the taxi service to the interior is irregular and expensive. Cars may be rented. It is only recently that decent roads have appeared in Dominica. If you want to visit the Carib reservations, hire a Land Rover. In the reservations fine straw baskets are made, woven so tightly that they can hold water without losing a drop. The Caribs also build rugged sailing canoes which can be seen in the Antilles as far south as St. Vincent. They may look frail and unseaworthy, but it was in just such boats that the Caribs once traveled throughout the Lesser Antilles. When Columbus arrived, they had conquered all the islands as far north as Puerto Rico, occasionally making raids into Hispaniola and the Bahamas. They were fierce warriors and fabulous seamen. Today they are fishermen. Early each morning they launch their canoes and beat to windward, often against the full force of the winter trades, to fish the bank east of the island, returning home in the afternoon and running their canoes through the surf onto the exposed windward shore. The sight of one of these canoes bursting forth from a squall, the crew flat out on the trapeze, the flour-sack sail

streaming, is indeed impressive and totally deflating to the modern yachtsman with his trendy electronic aids, zipper-footed dacron sails, and roller-reefing gear.

The climate of Dominica can be summed up in a word—wet. The only difference between the so-called dry and wet seasons is that during the wet season it rains all of the time and during the dry season it rains most of the time. Along the lowlands of the shore it is hot, but as the altitude rises, the temperature drops off rapidly. The tide is minimal, with the rise and fall less than one foot. The tidal current generally runs north and south parallel to shore on the east and west coasts, and a strong westerly current is usually found off the north and south points of the island which is seldom overcome by the flood tide.

If you are anchored at Roseau or Woodbridge and notice the tide running north, time your departure correctly and you can carry a fair tide all the way to the north end of the island. (See chapter on tides.)

The coasts of Dominica are steep-to and for the most part free of danger. A sail up the windward coast is an exciting experience, though, since there are no anchorages, few boats do it. The scenery is unbelievable. This is a dead lee shore, and it is apt to be rough, so keep well off. The scenery is good on the west coast, too, but the calm in the lee can be frustrating.

Dominica is charted by NO 25121 and harbor chart NO 25122. The corresponding British charts are BA 697 and BA 726. Both sets conform closely to one another, even in their inaccuracies. For example, the rock off Scott's Head—the only danger along the west coast—is incorrectly marked on each. I have looked for it where they say to many times and have never been able to spot it, even from the rigging. Among charter skippers a reliable consensus of opinion places the rock 300 yards west of Scott's Head, further north than the charts show it, and under six feet of water (while the charts claim it bares). Sometimes the seas break on it; other times it can only be spotted as a discoloration of the water. Sailors have been continually spotting a rock very close on Scott's Head and have mistaken it for the rock shown on the chart. As a result they shortly hit the rock that is supposed to be above water but usually isn't. It has recently been confirmed by Carl Amour of the Anchorage Hotel that there are, in fact, three separate rocks west of Scott's Head with approximately six feet of water over them, 300 yards offshore. He also found that the rocks directly north of Scott's Head extend offshore further than are shown in the chart. The upshot of all this is: when passing Scott's Head, stay well offshore or you are likely to come to a very sudden stop.

Except for this one spot, the best way to sail the western shore of Dominica is in close at a two-pistol-shots distance. At night the cold air falling off the mountain will produce a light breeze sufficient to propel a high-performance boat close inshore. Early morning and dusk are pretty much hopeless sailing times. If you plan to sail within the lee of the island, there is really no point in setting out before 11 or 12 in the morning. During the day as the land heats up, the hot air rising from the island will draw the cool air in from the sea and frequently give you a light onshore breeze from mid-morning to early afternoon. This breeze can only be found very close in and dies out completely a few hundred yards off.

One word of caution about proceeding along shore—have your sheets and halyards ready to run. In the lee of this island very violent squalls occasionally strike. They approach with no warning and last for a short time. They consist of cold blasts of air blown down from the mountain passes with great ferocity. Not only is the velocity of the wind dangerous but its angle is, too. Usually winds are horizontal to the water and will spill out of the sails as a boat is knocked down. But here the wind blows downward and exerts *greater* force as the boat heels. I have yet to experience one of these clear-air squalls, but I've heard enough hair-raising stories not to doubt their existence.

Scott's Head
(BA 697, NO 25121)

If you can manage to skirt the aforementioned rocks, this locale at the south end of Dominica offers a sheltered anchorage for a daytime rest. It is not good at night, as the winds are variable and, since the bottom falls off steeply, you will be anchored close to shore. There is very good view from the top of Scott's Head, and there is excellent skindiving offshore. But watch the current.

Soufriere
(BA 697, NO 25121)

North of Scott's Head is a town which many people like to tour. Soufriere is not a port of entry, but it *is* the home of famed Rose's Lime Juice. Anyway, anchoring is all but impossible. Probably the best way to do it is with your anchor in deep water and some stern lines ashore. But this will serve only as a temporary expedient since at night the area is prone to squalls booming out of the hillsides at every sort of crazy angle.

Roseau
(BA 697, 728; NO 25121, 25122)

The capital and port of entry offers an anchorage below Old Fort Hotel, which is a good spot to lie while clearing Customs. Row to the dock and tie up. The Customs building is a short walk to the south of the dock. If you happen to clear early in the morning and you like a good breakfast, trot over to the Green Parrot on Front Street. Some say it is the best breakfast in the entire Lesser Antilles. Finding even a tolerable breakfast in the Islands is a bit of a feat; finding a good one is a major victory.

A mile south of the dock is the Anchorage Hotel. Its owner, Carl Amour, has installed out front a number of heavy, first-rate moorings suited for yachts up to 65 feet. There is no charge for their use. The hotel is well run and extremely popular with visiting yachtsmen. One room has been set aside for charter boat crews who can come ashore and get a hot shower, again free of charge. Amour is a Dominican and knows the island well. If you notify him beforehand, he can arrange for tours through the island, for the delivery of fresh fruit and vegetables, or for your laundry to be done. And while there are no yacht services on the island, he can probably locate a carpenter, mechanic, or electrician to help out in an emergency.

Woodbridge Bay
(BA 697, 728; NO 25121, 25122)

One mile north of Roseau, it is the only natural anchorage in the southern portion of Dominica, though here again there is the problem of deep water. The best spot is off the fuel docks. Feel your way in and anchor at a depth to suit you. But take care: the bottom is very poor holding. Once you feel secure, there are taxis available to town.

Laylou River
(BA 697, NO 25121)

Five miles north of Woodbridge Bay, the mouth is none too easy to spot, but if you pass close inshore you will see an opening in the trees, a small village, and surf breaking across the mouth of the river. Anchor north of the river; the bottom is sand and good holding at two to three fathoms. There is sometimes a swell and the weather must be watched. Instead of rowing through the breakers, wait awhile—the canoes will probably come out and a ride ashore can be arranged. The beach is black sand. Bring your diving gear; there are large fish in the river and lots of small crawfish. The latter make delicious eating. The crew should bring shampoo and any clothes they want to wash, as the Laylou offers fresh water unlimited. There is a pleasant walk to be enjoyed along the river bank through the Hillsboro valley. A hotel, the Castaways, has been built with restaurant and beach bar.

Prince Rupert Bay
(BA 697, 728; NO 25121, 25122)

At the north end of Dominica, it fronts the town of Portsmouth. The harbor is excellent and there is good anchorage off the town in four fathoms with good holding, sand bottom, and no hazards or difficulties at all. The town itself is nothing more than a little village. There is no restaurant or hotel. It can boast of little more than the world's worst phone connection. Raising even Roseau on the phone has to be considered a miracle of communications.

In 1964 I helped to arrange an evening of dock-side entertainment in Prince Rupert Bay. There used to be no parties in the Islands from the end of Carnival to Easter. This particular evening was during Lent, and a license was required for the band to play. After the most delicate negotiations with the local authorities it was determined that five dollars to the local church would salve consciences, two dollars to the police would secure the special permit, and that for three dollars and a bottle of rum the Department of Public Works would rig up some lights on the dock, which we were assured would continue to run as long as the band would play. The musicians were eager to play for $20, though we ended up giving them $25. All of this was split among three boats for an enjoyable evening.

A decade or so later, I doubt that you will find a steel band in Prince Rupert Bay at these prices. Though that much has changed, the rest has not been altogether for the worse. Ten years ago, the island girls would not think of going to the beach, let alone in a bikini or slacks. Their dress was plain and subdued. Now they read all the American and European fashion magazines and do themselves up in the latest styles.

On East and West Cabrite Hills there are the ruins of an old fort and barracks. You will find cannons strewn far and wide among the bushes and below at the water's edge where they were dumped when the fort was ransacked by French raiders centuries ago. The Indian River flows into Prince Rupert Bay, and a dinghy trip up this river is a delightful way to pass several hours. The way is simple; there are no breakers or bars at the mouth, and inside it is wonderfully cool and peaceful, with large trees overarching the stream and shafts of sunlight filtering down. The current is swift enough to require an outboard during the ascent. Don't be discouraged by the old rusted-out bridge. Continue beyond, feeling your way around the various snags and shoal spots, until you reach the first of the rapid water. Here the dinghy can be dragged over the shoals by hand. Further on, the river will open up into deep pools that are good for swimming or a midday meal. On the way back, keep the outboard off. Paddle or pole down quietly and you will see any number of fabulous birds. It is possible to get close right beneath them in their trees. The river is a great way to spend a morning; start early and take along some supplies.

Douglas Bay
(BA 697, NO 25121)

This is a fair anchorage if there is no swell and the trades are south of east. Anchor close in.

LESSER ANTILLES—
SOUTHERN

GUADELOUPE

62°W

BASSE TERRE

POINTE-
A-PITRE

St. FRANCOIS

DÉSIRADE

61°W

TERRE DE HAUT

PETITE TERRE

TERRE DE BAS

ILES DES SAINTES

MARIE GALANTE

16°N

PLYMOUTH

ROSEAU

DOMINICA

SCOTT'S HEAD

MARTINIQUE

MT. PELÉE

St. PIERRE

FORT DE FRANCE

CUL DE SAC TARTANE

LE FRANCOIS

15°N

ANSE D'ARLET

DIAMOND ROCK

STE. ANNE

CHAPTER 18

Martinique

NO 25084, 25085, 25086, 25087; BA 371, 494;
French 383, 384, 385, 386, 389, 390, 391, 5906,
5916, 5930

MARTINIQUE
SKETCH CHART OUTLINES

This is one of the largest islands (425 square miles) in the Lesser Antilles. The spoken languages are two strains of French, one fairly pure and the other an indecipherable patois. The natives regard themselves as Frenchmen rather than West Indians, and this notion is reflected everywhere. Fort de France is a sort of Paris of the New World. Its women are beautiful and well dressed, and the sidewalk cafes are always filled with an assortment of types sipping their punch vieux and admiring the passing scenery. The restaurants are of a very high quality, and the local boutiques offer many of the latest fashions.

Martinique is high and lush. Mountains tower over vast fields of cane and banana. Country roads vary from beautiful four-lane highways to grotesque contours of rubble and mud. The good beaches are on the east coast for the most part and difficult to reach, except by boat. It is only recently that tourism has arrived in wholesale fashion. As late as 1965, it was considered a noteworthy event to have ten yachts moored off the Savanne. In December, 1973, I counted 86; and cruise ships plow in and out all winter long. I have seen as many as three enter Fort de France on a single day. Hotels and guest houses have sprung up throughout the island. Most of the new ones are expensive, geared to the needs of the modern tourist. Some of the old-fashioned ones are not only less expensive, but are much more fun, and have better food. The Hotel Europe comes to mind in this regard. Also, there are many fine small restaurants on the island which do not appear in the travel brochures. On a French island, one should never worry about the outside appearance of a restaurant. Simply arrive around 12:30 and observe the clientele. If it is predominantly French-speaking Martinicans, sit down and enjoy a meal. Like the Frenchman, the Martinican demands good food and value for money spent.

Martinique is a prime spot to stock up on foods of all kinds. The various self-styled "supermarkets" carry an excellent selection of imported meats, cheese, and poultry. A word of caution about French poultry: it is frequently sold plucked and frozen but not cleaned. Be sure to gut it as soon as it thaws. The quality is excellent. As for wines, the various merchants will more than accommodate your expertise; or, if you happen to be an uninformed wine enthusiast like myself, they will ably guide you in making a selection. The market in Fort de France is really superb and should not be missed. Don't arrive too early, as things don't get fully under way before 0800. All the buying and selling is conducted in French. If you don't speak the language, find an interpreter. He will more than earn his wages. A number of the taxi drivers speak English. One such driver, Joe Ratin, has taken good care of me over the years; he is helpful and informative and can usually be found in the vicinity of the Hotel Europe.

Mail can be addressed in care of American Express, Fort de France. It will end up with Roger Albert, the American Express Agent, or with the American Consul—check both places. Heini Hafliger, M. Albert's assistant manager, speaks English and will be able to answer many of your questions about the island. The overseas telephone and telegraph service is not particularly good, operating during workday hours only, 8 AM to 4:30 PM and closed Saturday afternoon. The shopping hours are slightly different from English islands: 8:00-12:00, 2:30-5:30, with a large number of small shops opening at 3:00 and closing at 6:00. Wherever they go, the French take a two-hour lunch. Air connections to and from Martinique are good by Caribbean standards.

Martinique is one of the best-charted islands in the Caribbean. The French charts are far and away the best and most thorough. The American National Ocean Survey publishes four charts of Martinique (NO 25084, 25085, 25086, 25087). The British have two (BA 371, 494). The French, on the other hand, publish ten, all of which have been kept fairly up-to-date, and since they are far and away best, I will cite only their numbers following. The east coast of Martinique is covered in especially minute detail. One thing to bear in mind—when the French chart notes coral with a series of "x's" and no soundings are shown, it indicates an area of less than five feet where there were too many coral heads for surveying. What these markings do not show is that there are usually breaks in the coral large enough for a power boat or dinghy to pass through. Also, the wooden beacons that are shown on the charts will not always be found where they are supposed to be, or some will have rotted away at the waterline, while others may prove difficult to spot from any distance. Inside the reefs, channels are sometimes marked with wooden stakes—not unlike the oyster stakes in Chesapeake Bay. These are locally maintained, and the system they use is apt to vary from place to place, but they can be very helpful, once you figure out the plan.

Baie de Fort de France

Fort de France Harbor
(French 5906, 5916)

In this one instance you need only carry NO 25087. It is copied from the French, but with soundings in fathoms rather than meters, it is more easy to work with than the French. Fort de France Bay is commodious, containing many anchorages and coves that will provide shelter in all weathers. If one of these becomes rough under certain conditions, you only have to move the short distance to a more favorable spot.

The principal yacht anchorage is off the town at the Anchorage des Flamands. Anchor southwest of the covered pier, due west of the north end of Fort St. Louis. Feel your way in with the lead and anchor at a convenient depth. The bottom shoals very gradually. If you are passing the night, keep an eye on your outboard. Some islanders find them exceedingly adaptable to their fishing canoes. The anchorage is satisfactory in normal weather; when the wind swings around to south or southwest, it is time to move along. When this happens, I would advise crossing the harbor to Anse Mitane.

The advantage of anchoring off the Savanne is that it is only a short dinghy-ride ashore. You can tie up at the Club de Voile on Point Simon or to the fueling pier where, besides fuel, fresh water and ice are available. Take the dinghy up the Riviere Madame to the market. An ice house is right nearby. This way, you can load everything right on the dinghy and avoid the traffic jams at the other supermarkets. The Riviere Madame, like many French rivers, doubles as the town sewer. If you fall in, it would be the end. If there is a fuel shortage in Fort de France, I would contact M. Daniel Valin of Martinique Charter Service. He can be reached by radio on 2527 or frequently at the fuel dock northeast of the yacht club.

Anse Mitane
(French 5906, 5916)

Listed on the chart as Anse de Cocotiers, Anse Mitane is the local name and the more commonly used. This is an indisputably fine anchorage and understandably popular with the French. It has one of the few decent beaches in the area within easy access of the town—a three-mile reach coming and going. A word of warning to those sailing from the anchorage off the Savanne: do not head directly for Anse Mitane or else you will come to a resounding halt against the shoal which extends southwest from Ft. St. Louis. Instead keep west of the line bearing 210 magnetic from the Savanne pier. When the large flashing buoy approaches the port beam, head for the Bakoua Hotel at the northern end of the anse. There are two other hazards to be reckoned with in the approach to this area. Due west 500 yards off the hill on the north end of the beach is an unbuoyed shoal with coral heads. Once you have cleared the shoal off Fort St. Louis, this one may be avoided by laying a course direct to Pointe du Bout and thereafter hugging the shore south to the anchorage. Reverse the procedure on the way out. Many boats have hit this reef because it lies on a line between the anchorage at Anse Mitane and at Fort de France off the Savanne. The final hazard is a big steel ketch which has been lying at the bottom of Anse Mitane for a good 25 years. Seven feet of water cover it. It is located off the beach two-thirds of the way from the Bakoua to Auberge de Anse Mitane. The buoy which used to mark its location has disappeared.

Excellent meals are available at the Bakoua. No supplies can be had at Anse Mitane, although a ferry runs every hour to Fort de France, if you want to do some errands in town. A variety of small and inexpensive restaurant-bars line the beach. A few of these may have rooms to rent, which are probably the cheapest accommodation on the entire island. On the weekend Anse Mitane is inundated by the French from Fort de France. They love to tear around the bay at full-throttle in their little hot-rod outboards. Swimmers take heed: if you want to get ashore, row.

Leaving Anse Mitane for Fort de France, hug the shore until past the Bakoua, and then head for the buoy marking the end of the shoal off Ft. St. Louis. If you are bound for Pointe des Negres, again stay inshore until the Bakoua is abeam, as otherwise you may

clip the five-foot spot that lies on the line between Mitane and Pointe des Negres.

Baie du Carenage
(French 5906)

East of Fort St. Louis, this is the home of the yacht club—a good shelter if you are willing to put up with the heat, the dirt, the odor, and noise. The yacht club is most hospitable, with a well-stocked bar, shower rooms, and fresh water. Boats drawing six-and-a-half feet can moor stern-to for short periods. The smell is so atrocious that I can't imagine anyone staying more than an hour or so. On the east side of the bay are the steamer docks and the main drydock. There are Customs offices near the passenger reception terminal on the docks.

Baie des Tourelles
(French 5906)

East of the steamer dock, Baie des Tourelles has a first-rate yacht yard run by M. Jean Grant. Unless the charts of this area have been updated, they do not show that deep water now carries all the way up the mouth of the river just east of M'sieu Grant's. Favor the eastern shore.

Pointe des Negres
(French 5906)

This is an excellent shelter in normal weather. The only difficulties are posed by deep water and the lack of swinging room. However, arrangements can usually be made to moor stern to the dock, where fuel and water can be found. A rugged old fort can be found nearby. Unlike Baie des Tourelles, the water here is clear and pleasant to swim in.

Ilet a Ramiers
(French 5916)

This is the little island at the southwest corner of Fort de France Harbor. The preferred anchorage is in the channel between

the island and the mainland. Anchor in ten feet of water over a white-sand bottom. Drop the hook when the dock on the island bears due north. This channel shoals to six feet east of Ramiers. Here, too, the swimming is excellent. Visit the fort ashore—that is, if the French will let you land. Periodically, the French, indulging a taste for mystery, close the island to all visitors. What they find to do with an 18th-century fort I can't imagine, though I doubt that it is any cause for world alarm.

Trois Ilets
(French 5916)

In the southwest corner of Fort de France Bay, this is an out-of-the-way spot, difficult to reach by car and seldom visited by yachts. There is an excellent restaurant ashore that serves good meals at a very reasonable price. The anchorage (due north of town) is mud bottom. The harbor is frequently used as a hurricane hole. The holding is not too good, but if you drag, there is only soft bottom to end up on. When going to Trois Ilets, be careful of the numerous shoals that litter the eastern side of Fort de France Bay. They are all buoyed and there is plenty of water between them. If anyone has the exploratory urge, a lot of fun can be had with a dinghy or outboard in the various rivers and canals that radiate from the harbor of Fort de France. Many of them extend quite far inland to towns east of the harbor.

Southwest Coast

Grande Anse d'Arlet
(French 385)

This is the first cove south of Cap Salomon and one of two good anchorages on the southwest coast. The bottom is white sand and good holding with two fathoms in the southeast corner of the harbor. A slight roll is not too bothersome. The swimming is excellent. Make sure you are on the edge of the shelf before you anchor, as the bottom drops off very steeply here. There is no real town at Grande Anse d'Arlet, only a fishing village with a variety of canoes, nets stretched out to dry, dogs, cats, goats, roosters, and small bare-bottomed urchins running to and fro. At the north and south ends of the beach are some beautiful small cottages owned by wealthy citizens of Martinique, who come here in the summer to beat the heat of Fort de France. Feel your way in and anchor in the extreme southeast corner.

Petite Anse d'Arlet
(French 385)

This is the next cove south of Grande Anse and not as sheltered, but it has the advantage of a good restaurant and ferry communication to Fort de France. Anchor off the town, but be careful of the coral bank at the northern end of the harbor; here, too, the bottom drops off steeply. The anchorage in the northeast corner usually avoids the swell. If you want to get away from town, a small beach to the south provides privacy and a satisfactory anchorage in two fathoms. This bay is also a resort for the well-to-do French, who come and go by water, thereby avoiding the long and circuitous drive on kidney-busting roads.

Petite Anse du Diamant
(French 385)

A small white-sand beach but not a very good anchorage. I do not advise stopping here. The most spectacular sight on the south coast of Martinique is the Rocher du Diamant or, as the British prefer, H.M.S. Diamond Rock— so called because the British Admiral Hood somehow managed to establish a warship-like gun battery at the top of the mountain. The guns swept the channel between Diamond Rock and the mainland, closing it to all coastal traffic. Against the best efforts of the French, the British succeeded in holding out for some 18 months. When they finally surrendered, the French arranged for their immediate exchange as prisoners, as it was felt that men so brave and resourceful should not be left to rot away in prison. How wars have changed!

How the French have changed! They have lost their sense of humor. Recently, their Navy was sending a squadron to Martinique to celebrate a national holiday. Two young Englishmen decided to have some fun. The night before the squadron was scheduled to arrive, they scaled the cliffs of Diamond Rock and hung a huge white ensign, the symbol of the British Navy. In the morning as the French squadron sailed past H.M.S. Diamond Rock, the white ensign was clearly visible on the south face. The French admiral was apoplectic; he ordered a helicopter to lower a man on the rock to destroy the flag. The French complained through diplomatic channels, and before the dirt had settled, it had become something of an international incident.

South Coast

This coast offers little in the way of anchorages except for Passe du Marin and St. Anne. Care must be exercised when sailing this shore, as the shoal water extends as much as a mile offshore in some places. There are many exposed coral heads, but by far the greatest danger is Caye d'Olbian, an unbuoyed one-fathom shoal one-quarter mile due south of the eastern end of the beach at Anse du Diamant.

Marigot du Diamant
(French 385)

This is the location of the Diamond Rock Hotel. Be careful of the reefs that extend out from Pointe du Marigot. A small dock under the hotel in the southwest corner offers fuel and water alongside. Do not go north of the buoys in the center of the harbor, since it shoals rapidly here. A good anchorage, in clear water.

The unnamed cove east of Grosse Pte. and Anse du Ceron both appear to have possibilities as anchorages for those who want to get away from it all. I have no first-hand experience with either. Anse des Trois Rivieres appears to be too open for comfortable use unless the wind is all the way round to the north.

Riviere-Pilote
(French 385)

I have not passed a night here, but I have sailed in and there appears to be a comfortable, isolated anchorage behind Pointe Figuier.

Although the distance from Anse d' Arlet on the southwest coast to Ste. Anne in the southeast corner is only 13 miles, it is best to allow the better part of the day for the trip, since there is a strong westerly current along the coast. You should try to stay as close to shore as the shoals will permit. As you tack inshore, the wind will become variable; play the lifts and headers for all they're worth and you will save considerable time. Back bearings taken between Diamond Rock and Ste. Anne and Diamond Rock and the light on Ilet Cabrit will keep you clear of the shoals and out of the worst of the current. Do not try to push on beyond Ste. Anne after 11 AM, for you will be unable to reach the harbors on the east coast before the light fails.

Cul-de-Sac du Marin
(French 391)

If the wind swings to the south, it is only a short sail to this harbor. Though the area is well charted, particular care must be taken to avoid the shoals. Most of these are marked with stakes, but you can still get into trouble. The harbor is sheltered in all winds no matter what their direction. The land is low, the harbor likely to be hot, airless, and bug-ridden. I would advise against anchoring for the night unless the anchorage at Ste. Anne has become uncomfortable. The Club Mediterranee has recently established itself at Point du Marin at the mouth of this harbor. Visitors are not welcome ashore unless they are members of the Club, an attitude that will be made clear to you in no uncertain terms.

Mouillage de Ste. Anne
(French 391)

An excellent shelter in trade wind weather. The entrance is simple and straightforward; anchor due west of town in two fathoms of water, feeling your way in with the leadline. The bottom shoals very gradually. The town has a few small grocery stores, a small market, and a hotel right on the beach. Just south of town, 15 minutes if you walk along the coast road, you will find the restaurant Au Mahogany, delicious and inexpensive. A wide veranda overlooks the harbor of Ste. Anne.

East Coast

This coastline is thoroughly charted by French 384, 385, 389, and 390. The east coast should be explored only by an experienced yachtsman sailing a good, weatherly boat, a cruising guide in one hand, the appropriate French chart spread before him, and a man on the pulpit. Or, better, on the spreaders. It offers wonderful cruising in an area where you are not likely to encounter many yachts. It may be rough or windy at times, but there are any number of harbors and coves that are completely sheltered and calm as a mill pond. At Francois, Robert, and Trinite, food

186

and supplies can be bought. Lobsters are plentiful and inexpensive. Sudon, the Caribbean cherrystone clam, can be found in the shoal water. In planning a trip up the east coast, bear in mind that this is a lee shore with a strong current setting on it. Until Passe de Vauclin is reached, there will be no protection from off-lying reefs. Once the reefs have been reached, they will dampen the swell to give you a great sail. But you must stay on your toes as you thread through the reefs; looking back, it will not seem as bad as you anticipated.

Cul-de-Sac Anglais
(French 385)

The anchorage outside is really excellent. For many years I was eager to visit this area, but the conditions were never right. Each time I was left with a dead downwind entrance, with the prospect of little room to round up in and a tough beat out. I have only managed to penetrate this anchorage once since then aboard another yacht. We were pressed for time and spent only a few hours, but it is certainly an area that warrants the most thorough exploration. The entrance is moderately straightforward; enter from the southeast on a course roughly northwest. Watch out for the rocks on the port side as you come in and round up under Ilet Hardy. Proceed as far north toward shoal water as your draft will permit, and anchor.

It is possible to take seven feet up into Cul-de-Sac Anglais. Its inner harbor is nothing more than soft mud with mangroves around the sides—good fishing, I suspect, but not a very spectacular anchorage. The dinghy can be taken northeast to Ilet Lezards, a mile away across reef-sheltered water and white-sand bottom.

The chart shows an entrance between Pte. Baham and Ilet Toisroux. This may be so, but I would not attempt an entry without

surveying it from a dinghy beforehand. I have studied the channel from aloft, and while I managed to distinguish a narrow channel, there appeared to be a rock in the middle of it. If you are coming up from the south and trying to sight Cul-de-Sac Anglais, look for the black cliffs on Toisroux.

Vauclin
(French 384, 385)

This is the first town of any size that you will encounter going up the east coast. It is easily spotted from seaward by its church, which has a new green roof. A red flare burns nightly from the steeple. The harbor is wide and shoal. The chart shows an anchorage three-quarters of a mile due east of town behind a small unnamed cay south of Baril de Boeuf reef. This puts you a long way by dinghy from town, so I would advise going to Cul-de-Sac Grenade and walking overland.

Cul-de-Sac Grenade
(French 384, 385)

Cul-de-Sac Grenade is not very well spoken of by the French, but I found it a delightful spot, a perfect anchorage, and a wonderful place to try out the sailing dinghy or explore with an outboard. In fact, with a dinghy one can stay inside the inner reefs and visit almost all the remaining east coast of Martinique, all the way to Robert, ten miles to the north. Spotting the break in the reef that leads into Cul-de-Sac Grenade is none too easy unless you have someone high up in the rigging. In the spring of 1973, a Morgan 41 missed the channel entrance, hit a coral head, and sank. (In fact, put a man in the rigging when cruising *anywhere* on the east coast of Martinique.) The outer part of the channel is deep, with seas breaking on the reefs on both sides, giving a definite line of demarcation. Once the break is spotted, the course is about southwest by south magnetic;

minimum depth in the channel is eight feet, sounded with a lead line.

As you pass between Petite Grenade and Pte. de Vauclin, you will notice a low spit of land on your port; round up behind the spit of land and anchor. It is a beautiful cove with no habitation around, but this may not continue, as someone has put through a road. The cove is 20 feet deep and deep right up to shore; you can put out a stern anchor and run your bow line to a tree. There is a beautiful white-sand beach on the point, but it turns out to be a great disillusionment—there are ony six inches of beautiful white sand over soft gooey black mud.

There is a small fishing village at the head of the Cul-de-Sac, where a taxi could probably be obtained or a bus found for a ride to Vauclin. The unnamed bay northwest of Petite Grenade is also a good deserted anchorage. Although there are no soundings shown on the chart, I found fairly regular soundings of eight feet through most of the bay, gradually shoaling when the inner edge of the reef was approached. I had no difficulty in finding a break in the reef for the dinghy, allowing me to enter Passe du San Souci.

Passe du San Souci
(French 384, 385)

This is another good anchorage with plenty of water and no town or village of any sort. Anchor near the mouth of the pass, as the land is low and swampy at the head of the bay, where it would tend to be hot, airless, and bug-infested.

Grande Passe du Simon
(French 384, 385)

This passage is fairly open to the east. It is littered with reefs that are so steep you could round up under just about any one of them and drop your anchor right on it. If no

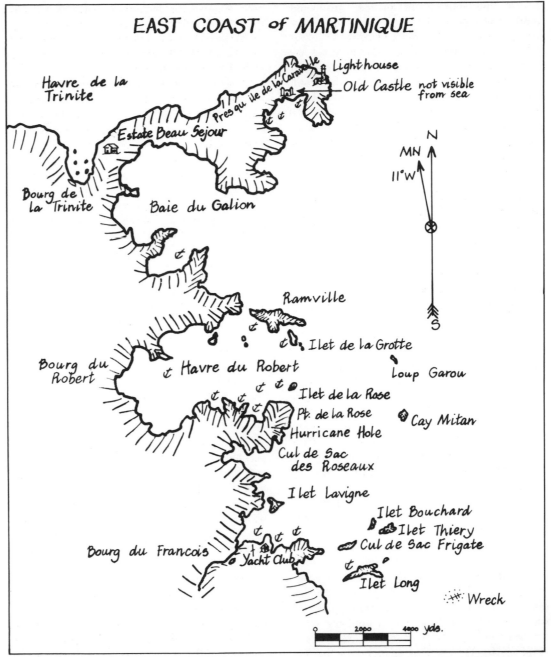

SKETCH CHART 55

MARTINIQUE

contact with shore were desired, you could comfortably spend the night with the likelihood of a nice cool breeze.

On the south side of Grande Passe du Simon is Pointe de la Prairie, with a reef and shoal water extending quite far to seaward. There is little or no water over this shoal, strictly a dinghy area. Slightly south of Pointe de la Prairie is Cap Est Hotel. It is very popular, expensive, and has good meals, a swimming pool, etc. The hotel has a dock, but this again is strictly a dinghy area.

Cul-de-Sac Fregate
(French 384, 385, 390)

Easy to spot and easy to enter. On the north side of the entrance is Ilet Thiery, a good landmark. On the island's northeast point is a large white house with a large veranda around the entire house. Also on the east side of Ilet Thiery is a black cliff with a large cave at the water's edge. When entering, sail between the two easily spotted reefs, which are always breaking. But before you ease sheets, make absolutely sure of your bearings and pass outside—that is, northeast of— the ten-foot shoal. The shoal always breaks in heavy weather. Favor the reefs on the north side of the channel; they are more steep-to and more clearly defined than the reefs on the south side. Once your position is definitely established, run on in and anchor in the lee of one of the many islands.

We found the anchorage off the house of M. Hayot the best. Run along the north shore of Ilet Long past the small cove with the fishing boats, give the point to the west of the cove a berth of 100 yards, jibe over, then harden sheets and round up in the next cove. There is a white house with a small marine railway to the east of it. There is plenty of water close to shore, so run in until the western point of the cove lines up with the western point of Ilet Thiery. This anchorage is perfect

no matter what direction the wind blows, and the holding ground is good. If you would like to be nearer diving water, you may move to the lee of Ilet Thiery; be careful of the detached coral heads.

Although the chart shows coral heads and no soundings, a draft of five feet may be taken between the western end of Ile Aubin and the mainland. Go slow, keep your lead line going, and try to make some sense out of the private stakes placed by the locals to mark the shoals. Pass close to the western shore of the island, hold a course of west-northwest; you should spot two stakes that mark the channel. However, be careful and don't rely too much on local marks. There is also a dinghy pass around the western end of Ile Long into Grande Passe du Simon that can be used to visit Cap Est Hotel.

Francois
(French 384, 390; Sketch Chart 55)

A typical middle-sized French town of Martinique. Full-scale tourism has not yet arrived, though it is nonetheless possible to buy a good meal; sometimes ice is available, and fresh fruit and vegetables, freshly baked French bread, cheese and wine, and lobsters are sold at reasonable prices. A man can survive quite well on this diet. This town is especially attractive; there is a drainage canal that runs up into its heart, enabling one to take the dinghy right into town. The two landings are always a scene of riotous activity: people coming and going and arguing about the price of fish and the price of transportation, the fishermen making passes at the girls, and the girls trying not to be coy but without success.

This whole area near the towns of Francois and Robert is especially interesting, as many people live on the various islands, others in little coves on the mainland that are not connected to the main roads, with the result

that there is a continual flow of canoes to and fro, some rowing, some sailing, and others motoring, almost completely hidden but for their great bow waves.

Mouillage du Francois
(French 384, 390; Sketch Chart 55)

Can be entered by either the Passe du Francois or via the channel north of Ilet Thiery and Ilet Bouchard and south of Fond Blanc. If using the southern entrance, be careful of the six-foot spot north-northeast of Ilet Thiery. The eastern end of Ilet Thiery aligned with the eastern end of Ilet Long leads over this shoal. The northern pass leads between Petits Cays, which are always breaking, and Cay Brigantine, which is supposed to be marked by a day beacon that may or may not be there. I would strongly advise against entering by the Passe du Francois; running dead downwind between the two reefs that frame the eastern entrance leaves no margin for error. I tried it one day before suddenly realizing that I had placed myself in a false lead. We had to round up and beat back through heavy surf. It took several years off my life.

Once inside the harbor, keep your eyes peeled for the various shoal spots. There are three coves on the south side of Mouillage du Francois. The first two east of Pte. Michele have picturesque fishing villages on their shores. However, I would not advise spending the night, as I think that they would tend to be hot, airless, and full of bugs. A better anchorage is in the third cove, where they have a yacht club with showers, a restaurant-bar, fuel, water, and what-have-you. Dockage is available or you can anchor out. On Sundays, Frenchmen from all over the east coast come here for an all-out three-hour banquet. The fact that there are few foreigners means that it must be very good indeed.

Francois may be visited by taxi or by

outboard; going by outboard, take it easy—you may churn up mud at various points in the canal. And don't capsize. I don't know which would be worse—to drown in a Martinique canal or to be rescued from one. The canal is hard to spot; but if you continue southwestward alongshore from the yacht club, you will have no trouble picking it up.

Ilet Lavigne looks most attractive and there appears to be an excellent anchorage behind the island, with plenty of water right up to shore. Here again a shoal water passage connects with the next bay.

Cul-de-Sac des Roseaux
(French 384, 390; Sketch Chart 55)

This is just north of Francois. I have not visited it. However, I did climb to the top of Pointe de la Rose and enjoyed a commanding view of the entire area. The main harbor of Cul-de-Sac des Roseaux is easy of entrance, but of course the shoal water must be reckoned by eyeball. On the north side of the harbor along the south shore of Pte. de la Rose are two coves. The easternmost of these is the more interesting, with 10 to 12 feet of water right up to shore and not too much land growth to gather mosquitoes—a perfect hurricane hole. The entrance is narrow and must be cautiously negotiated; all three of the passes shown on chart 390 off Pointe de la Rose are amply deep and wide. A path leads from a small dock up the hill to the road; the climb is well worth it—follow the road to the westward and you will come to the ruins of an old sugar mill from which you may survey the entire area.

There is another cove to the west of Pte. Chauve Souris, which has plenty of water. It makes a good hurricane hole and a nice spot to visit by dinghy. Don't spend the night. The hills rise vertically on three sides, and no air reaches the cove at all. Looking down on it from the hill above the fishing village, I could not see a ripple in the water, although the trades were blowing so hard they almost blew me off the ridge. The western part of Cul-de-Sac des Roseaux is shoal at its head and you would have to anchor quite far offshore. There is little or nothing to attract one ashore.

Havre du Robert
(French 384, 390; Sketch Chart 55)

The largest harbor on the east coast and a sister town to La Trinite, it is beautifully shown on the detail chart 390. This harbor is wide and easy to enter, with innumerable coves on both sides of the harbor. There is an anchorage at its head near the town of Robert. Robert itself is beautifully perched on the edge of a hill. A delightful open-air restaurant is located right next to the dinghy dock. The one difficulty with the restaurant is that they have no menu and they don't speak a word of English; I can vouch for the sudon and langouste. As usual with French towns, there is plenty of bread, cheese, wine, fresh fruits, vegetables, and seafood.

The east coast of Martinique is so featureless that a stranger may not know exactly where he is. Some of the towns are not visible from the sea. Let me list the key Robert landmarks to look out for: Vauclin—church with a restored roof; Ilet Thiery—a large house on the northeast end with a veranda all around, and the black cliff with caves on its eastern shore; Cay Pinsonnelle—the reef always breaks and a wreck of a sunken steamer is visible at the south end; Loup Garou—a small, bleach-white sand island off the entrance of Robert.

The chart gives ranges for entering Robert, but the ranges are for large vessels standing in from seaward and not for inside the harbor itself. The dangers are easily seen; stay in the center of the harbor until Petit Martinique bears due north, after which great care must be exerted, for the water is not clear, the shoals are very steep, and the beacon stakes are broken off almost flush with the water. I found a good anchorage where Point Cotterel bears northwest magnetic and the clock towers of Robert bear west by north magnetic. Sounding with the lead showed we could have continued much further inshore if we were careful. However, there are so many coves that I think that it would be easiest to moor nearer the mouth of the harbor and visit the town by dinghy. The bottom off town is soft mud, with plenty of grass; all right for an old-fashioned fisherman, but not good for a plow or Danforth.

The first anchorage on the south side of the harbor is to the west of, and in the lee of, Ilet des Chardons. There is deep water right up to the reefs on both sides, dinghy passages among the reefs, excellent diving, and lobsters galore. Very close to this anchorage is another in the lee of Ile Madame. Deep water carries close to shore on the western side, a long arm of the reef extending out to the north and a solid reef across to Pte. de la Rose give complete protection. Both these anchorages are good and there should be plenty of wind to keep you cool and bug-free.

To the west of Pte. de la Rose is Baie de Saintpierre; be careful of Banc de la Rose when entering. Best anchorage is under the lee of the reef with the north end of Pte. de la Rose bearing due east. There is plenty of water all the way to the head of the bay, but the head is all mud flat and mangroves. Take a dinghy, tie to the mangroves, and walk up the hill to the old sugar mill: a wonderful view, a cool breeze, soft grass, and a big spreading shade tree.

The next cove, unnamed, between Pte. de Sable Banc and Pte. Hyacinthe, is completely sheltered and deep. Watch Banc Guillotine when you enter; four feet could easily bring you to grief. The pond at the head of the bay is full of mosquitoes; I would advise mooring near the mouth of the cove where there is a breeze.

East of Pte. Royal is the last noteworthy cove on the south side. Easily spotted by an old sugar mill with a modern house next to it, a number of old cannons pointing seaward, and three or four boats moored in the cove. There is never a problem with bugs and always a breeze in this perfect shelter. The house is mainly used as a summer residence.

(A word about habits of the Martinicans. Like the Frenchman, he takes his vacation in late July and August, deserts the city, and goes to the beach. The west coast of Martinique is hot, muggy, and wet, while the east coast is not only cool and dry but also has the sand beaches. Hence in the summer you will find the east coast heavily populated, but in the winter the various summer residences will be empty. The locals will tell you that it is winter and cold, even though the temperature is in the low 80s all day.)

You really may anchor anywhere in the north side of the harbor of Robert, but there are two anchorages that are better than the others, the first one on the south side of Ilet Ramville well west of Ilet Duchamp (Ilet de la Grotte). An even better anchorage can be had closer west of the buildings on the north end of Ilet Duchamp; deep water goes right up to shore, with sand bottom, good holding, and no swell; it's breezy and bugless besides. The chart is wrong; there is no passage, except for a dinghy, between Ilet Ramville and Ilet Duchamp. But there's good snorkeling, and the area is a good place to teach children to swim—great sand flats with only one foot of warm water over them between the two islands. If you wish to visit Rocher de la Grotte, it is best to leave the dinghy at Ilet Duchamp and wade across from the island. The cove of Ilet Duchamp on the south

side of Ilet Ramville is shoal and reef-encumbered. I would not advise entering it in anything but a dinghy. However, on the western end of Ilet Ramville off the farm buildings is another anchorage, provided the wind is not very much south of east.

The lee of Petit Martinique in the northern part of the harbor is an anchorage, as is the area off the sugar plantation of La Grange. The latter has a dock, but I am not sure of the depth alongside.

Baie du Galion
(French 384, Sketch Chart 55)

A large open bay with several anchorages but not much to warrant more than a lunch stop. A reef runs south from the mainland east of Pte. Brunet, giving good shelter from the sea. Moor close to the reef at its northern end as close to shore as you dare. This puts the boat out of the swell, but there is still plenty of wind sweeping across the reef. Another good anchorage is north of Pte. Brunet, off an old farm that is still in operation. There are numerous reefs in the bay; the water is none too clear, so be careful. I circled Ilet du Galion and found nothing of interest except to a mountaineer eager to practice belaying. I did not visit the village of Galion, but I did find an old jetty near the cane cutters' cottages on the western shore of Baie du Galion. The cottages are below the old sugar plantation. A landing can be made at the jetty; a short walk up the hill brings you to the main road, where there is frequent bus service to La Trinite. A taxi may be hired for the ride back; the driver will take you down the hill to your dinghy. If you speak French, it might be possible to get a tour of the sugar estate.

Cul-de-Sac Tartanne
(French 384, Sketch Chart 55)

Also referred to as Treasure Cove or

Treasure Harbor, reputedly a pirate hideout in days of yore. It is one of the most beautifully sheltered harbors I have even seen. We were there in September, 1964, when a hurricane up north was kicking up a ground swell over six feet high along the east coast of Martinique, large enough for the seas to crest in 15 feet of water. Lying in the northeast corner of Cul-de-Sac Tartanne, we felt not the slightest motion; it was as smooth as a mill pond, with a pleasant breeze hooking around Pte. Caracol, and no bugs. There is no detailed chart available; it is a case of eyeball navigation, but the water is either shoal or very deep and everywhere steep-to. I was able to lay *Iolaire* parallel to the shore so close that you could step from the port side of the boat into one foot of water. We put a tackle on the main halyard and heaved her down far enough to paint the waterline. Even so, there was water enough to dive between the sand bank and the boat's bottom and to come up on the other side.

When entering, it is easy to see the reefs on both sides, as they always break; once in the pass, head for the lighthouse on the hill, skirting the western edge of the reef that will be in your path and rounding up north of the reef. Shoot across on the back side of the reef, drop your hook off the stern, snub up, and drop a bow anchor once you have actually reached the reef. Be sure to lay your anchor on the reef, as on the north side it is a near vertical drop into 50 feet of water. Make sure that your stern anchor is well set; when the wind drops at night, the current running out over the top of the reef will tend to shove you into shoal water.

There are numerous small fishing boats, all chasing squid, and I can vouch for the lobsters in the area—I caught one while checking the anchor. There are other anchorages in the western side of the bay behind the main reef. Though the northwestern corner of the bay is reef-encumbered, it does provide some perfect hurricane moorings. The water is deep between the reefs; it is possible to place the anchors on top of the reefs and run stern lines to trees ashore. With hills on three sides and overlapping reefs at the entrance to the harbor, it would be hard to find a more ideal spot.

For those who like to explore, there are the ruins of the old pirate stronghold. It is high on a ridge but so overgrown that it is impossible to spot from seaward. It must have been quite a place in its day; it included a reservoir (now a mudhole) and a dam some 30 feet high that must have held a good-sized pond 200 years ago. Old bits and pieces of iron abound, some huge molasses pots known as people pots (what they cooked the missionaries in), sugar cane machinery, an old powder magazine—a whole morning could be spent rummaging about. A walk up the hill leads to the main road to Tartanne and La Trinite, with wonderful views along the way. To find the old castle, land the dinghy in the cove to the west of the middle point projecting out into the bay where a group of fishermen are always making fish pots or working on their canoes. From there a path leads up the hill to the ruins. Above the ruins you will find a road eastward to the lighthouse of Tartanne. The lighthouse keepers are most happy to give you a tour.

North Coast

There is only one port, La Trinite, worth mentioning on the north coast of Martinique. La Trinite is an excellent harbor in the summer months when the trades are south of east, but in the winter I think the swell from the north would make the anchorage too rocky. The harbor is well buoyed and easy to enter. La Trinite is shown on French charts 384 and 389. When leaving, if you are planning to pass eastward around Pte. du Diable, do not go south of the line between Loup Ministre and Pte. Diable when it is blowing hard or when the ground swell is running.

The town of La Trinite is much the same as the other towns on the east coast of Martinique, only larger, with facilities and good road communication to Fort de France. La Trinite is a port of entry for Martinique and a port of clearance. The Customs and Immigration building is, for some reason, all the way south at the head of the harbor, one-half mile from town. The anchorage at La Trinite is poor even in the best of circumstances, and in a northeast wind unimaginable. Also, there is absolutely no place to tie up a dinghy. All in all, I would not recommend La Trinite except to clear Customs, if so required.

In my original book I mentioned that there was reputed to be a harbor south of Ilet Tartanne. Since that time I have studied the location by car; there's no harbor that can really be described as such, just a cove from which fishing boats sail daily and pull up on shore. It may be worthwhile visiting overland, but I could not recommend it by boat.

West Coast

St. Pierre
(French 386, 5930)

The town was totally destroyed by the eruption of Mt. Pelée early this century. A museum commemorating the catastrophe is a spectacular tourist attraction. The anchorage is not good; for the the most part it is an open roadstead; the swell usually runs in, and the bottom drops off very steeply. Make sure that you are on the shelf before you let go the hook. Many a boat almost lost its anchor when its fathometer registered bottom—on the second time around.

CHAPTER 19

St. Lucia

NO 25081, 25082, 25083; BA 197, 499, 1273

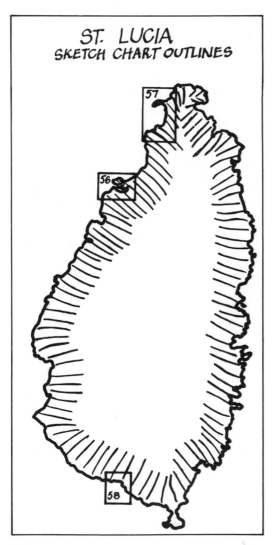

St. LUCIA
SKETCH CHART OUTLINES

St. Lucia, a semi-independent British affiliate, lies between Martinique to the north and St. Vincent to the south, and on most days it is visible from both these islands. There are two good harbors and sundry anchorages on its western side. The harbors were the cause of violent clashes between colonial powers in the 18th and early 19th centuries. Castries, the capital of St. Lucia, was important to the British as a fleet harbor in the 18th century and as a coaling station in the 19th. It was continually built up and fortified until the early years of the 20th century. During the 1920s, its importance declined with the passing of coal-burning ships, and the island fell into an economic depression. The activities of World War II and the establishment of a large American base at Vieux Fort revived the economy for a brief period, but soon after the war the air base was closed, and the island returned to third-world oblivion. In the very earliest colonial days the island had grown rich off its sugar; now a second economy based on sugar, bananas, and tourism is being set in motion, and St. Lucia is stirring again.

Because of its many hills and mountains, St. Lucia is naturally one of the wet islands. During the wet season, it seems to rain almost continually, tapering off in the dry season to a couple of short squalls per day. Although the island is high, it is not the solid block of Dominica. It is more like a series of ventilated hills, and a breeze is usually to be found along the western coast close inshore.

The tides are minimal, so much so that they are not listed on the tide tables. I found an old British chart that listed the HWF&C as 1 h 36m. (High water full and changed: the average interval between the transit—upper or lower—of the full or new moon and the next high water.) The current north and south of the island sets into the Caribbean at a knot or more.

St. Lucia is covered by the following American charts: NO 25081, the island plus Gros Islet Anchorage; NO 25082, Castries Harbor, Grand Cul de Sac, and Marigot; NO 25083, Vieux Fort Bay. The British charts BA 1273, 499, and 197 cover the same area in the same detail (and level of accuracy). The British chart does not show a causeway to Pigeon Island; neither the British nor American charts show the dredging in Castries; these are shown on my Sketch Charts.

St. Lucia has a number of good hotels and restaurants, most of which are new and outside Castries. There is one in town—Antoine's—which overlooks the harbor and has an excellent reputation. The island has very good air transportation to all the other islands, and, unlike flying from St. Vincent or Grenada, it is not necessary to spend a night's layover in Barbados.

There is a good open-air market in the town of Castries, as well as three or four stores where frozen foods, canned goods, and so forth are available. The yachtsman will have no problem securing all the normal food supplies.

When approaching St. Lucia from the north, there are no dangers lying off the coast. Castries is easily identified during the day by the forts on Vigie Point, and at night by the lights on either side of the harbor entrance. Do not stop at Pigeon Island before entering Castries; wine smuggling is a great occupation here, and the authorities take a dim view of stops being made before clearing. When coming from the south, unless you are heading for Vieux Fort (a port of entry), head directly for the Pitons, which are very easy to spot at a great distance, appearing like two loaves of French bread standing upright. There is only one hazard. On the lee side of St. Lucia, off Grand Caille Point, the rocks extend 200 to 250 yards offshore. They have only a few feet of water and a tide rip over them most of the time. Give them a wide berth.

Castries
(BA 1273, 197; NO 25081, 25082; Sketch Chart 56)

Neither British nor American chart correctly shows the dredging in Castries harbor. The Sketch Chart, however, gives a more accurate view. The harbor is deep, well sheltered, well illuminated, and easy to enter. So easy is the entrance that during World War II a German submarine entered after dark, sank a freighter along the dock, and departed, allegedly leaving an unexploded torpedo imbedded in the soft mud under the town. There is deep water up to fairly close inshore. Watch the rocks just off St. Victor Point. Once the old fueling dock has been reached (south side of the harbor—flashing green light) be careful to avoid Vielle Ville Shoal, marked by a flashing red beacon and a day marker. Don't be confused by boats in the cove, as they are moored north of this shoal.

At night, follow the range—two fixed red lights—right into the harbor. The range may seem to cast you very close to the south shore of the harbor, but this is correct and there is nothing to worry about except that the dredge companies are notoriously lax about lighting their equipment. In a contest of yacht vs. dredge, the latter will win. Keep an eye out.

All the area by the Harbormaster's office has now been filled in; no longer can you moor your dinghy safely there while you do your shopping or watch a schooner hauled by a steam-powered winch.

To clear Customs, sail alongside the north side of the main dock and hoist your "Q" flag. If no one comes, the skipper can go ashore and clear on the dock.

After clearing, best to go to Vigie Cove and anchor off, or go astern to the Privateer Marine Services dock, better known as Ganter's. Eight feet can be squeezed in. The marina is reputedly in the process of expansion, and a good stock of marine supplies was to be available shortly. Even if it is not, it is a worthwhile stop to meet Gracie Ganter, who has been taking care of itinerant yachtsmen and charter skippers for more years than she would like to admit. Unfortunately, Russ

Johnson's coin-operated laundromat is no more. Instead, Gracie has a number of two-legged laundry machines operating, picturesque but not as efficient as the coin-operated ones. Also, there is no dryer. If you hit a patch of rainy weather, you will never get your laundry dry. Beverly Pringle of Carib Cruises has her office in Ganter's; she is most helpful, but raising her on the radio leaves much to be desired. Either Beverly or Gracie will be able to advise you on any help or service you may need. Ice may be easily obtained by sending a taxi for it. You can row a dinghy to town and leave it, but I would be wary of the pilferage. For this reason and because

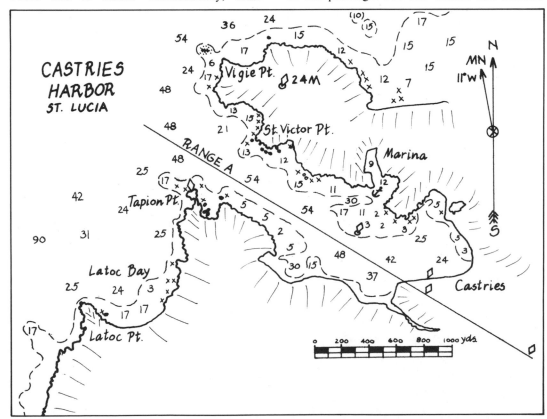

Range A: Castries Harbor leading lights in line, 135-315 magnetic.

SKETCH CHART 56

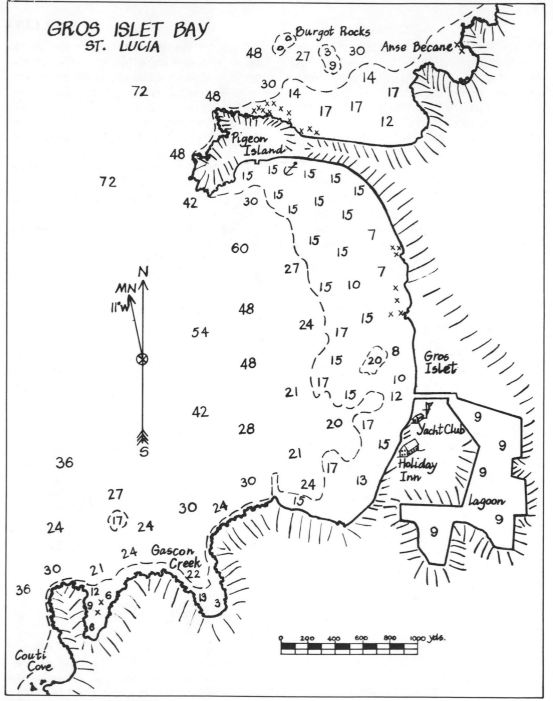

GROS ISLET BAY
ST. LUCIA

Burgot Rocks

Anse Becane

Pigeon Island

Gros Islet

Yacht Club

Holiday Inn

Lagoon

Gascon Creek

Couti Cove

N
MN
11°W
S

200 400 600 800 1000 yds.

SKETCH CHART 57

of the noise and the dirt in the main harbor, I would advise moving on to Vigie Cove, once you have cleared.

Vigie Cove is perfectly sheltered, with a soft mud bottom. Don't try to cut the beacon, as it is shoaled immediately inside it. Right at the water's edge in Vigie Cove is the Coal Pit Restaurant, where you can find excellent food, good drinks, a superb wine cellar, and first-class service at first-class rates. Best to reserve ahead. The advantage of this restaurant over others is that you can come and go by dinghy.

Pigeon Island
(BA 197; NO 25081 as Gros Ilet
Anchorage; Sketch Chart 57)

An excellent anchorage for yachts. It is illegal to put in to Pigeon Island if you are coming from Martinique. You must clear through Castries beforehand. Pigeon is an island in name only, as it has been connected to the mainland by a causeway. This gives full shelter from the sea hooking around the northern corner of the island, and the causeway is low enough that it doesn't block the wind, allowing for a cool and bug-free anchorage in 18 feet of water. The causeway has created a wonderful harbor, though it has spoiled the seclusion of Pigeon Island. The island was formerly a bird sanctuary, but I suspect the influx of cars and day-trippers has driven the birds away.

If you are approaching Pigeon Island from Castries, hug the coast. There are no hazards and you should be able to make it in one tack. Head for the thatch huts on the south side of the island, round up behind the causeway, anchoring about 200 feet offshore. Don't get to close to Pigeon Island, as this is a lee shore. The wind will blow hard here, but the causeway gives shelter, and the island of St. Lucia is a close enough fetch that only a small chop can build up.

The island was formerly owned by Mrs. Josette Leigh, better known among the yachting circles as Madame Snowball. Her thatch-cottage hotel on the beach vied with Mary Pomeroy's Beachlands on Nevis as the most famous and hospitable hotel in the Lesser Antilles. Mrs. Leigh sold out a few years ago, and the hotel is no more. The thatch cottages still stand. Visitors are welcome to tromp about or visit the old ruins. A climb to the top of the watchtower at Fort Rodney is well worthwhile.

These waters may be the only place in the world where fish are still caught with rocks. Two or three mornings a week, about 25 dugout canoes assemble off the beach. Nets are strung out at right angles to the shore and the canoes are laden gunwale-deep with rocks gathered from shore. The canoes arrange themselves in a line some few hundred yards off, where the fishermen wait for a school of fish to come along. When the fish are sighted, the natives throw the rocks to drive the fish into the nets, which are then looped together and dragged ashore. This is a wonderful opportunity to take some good photographs, as well as to obtain fresh fish at reasonable prices. The fishermen are friendly and enjoy having strangers help them haul the nets.

Gros Islet
(BA 197, NO 25081, Sketch Chart 57)

South of the town of Gros Islet is a newly dredged channel into the lagoon behind the hotels that line the beach. Channel and lagoon have been dredged to a depth of eight feet. I don't know who planned the lagoon, but he certainly did not do his homework. A large number of the plush charter and private yachts that visit the area draw well more than eight feet. If they had dredged the channel and part of the basin to 12 feet, the big boats (the ones with money to pay their bills) would be encouraged to enter and stay. On the south side of the entrance channel to the lagoon is the St. Lucia Yacht Club, active over the weekend, but not so much during the week. Don't be scared off by the "members only" sign; someone forgot to add "and visiting yachtsmen."

Grand Cul de Sac Bay
(BA 499, NO 25081).

Two miles south of Castries, this bay is not too attractive. Shoal water extends quite far offshore and the bay is exposed to the swell. The only feature of interest is the sugar factory. Behind the factory the landscape is low and unattractive. A harbor best skipped.

Marigot Harbor
(BA 499, NO 25081)

Four miles south of Castries, this is a narrow, deep harbor. In years gone by, before the construction of the hotel and guest houses, yachts usually sailed right by without taking notice. Now it has become a popular anchorage. You will notice small cottages along the water's edge on the north side of the harbor, and four or five new houses on the steep hillside forming the south side. Entering is easy; favor the south side of the outer harbor; shoal water extends 200 yards west by north from the southern tip of the palm-covered spit on the north side of the entrance. Shoal water can easily be spotted in this outer section of the harbor. Tacking through the narrow neck to the inner harbor, there is deep water close to shore. In fact, it is perfectly possible to lay a large vessel alongside the end of the palm-covered spit on the north shore and moor to the trees with plenty of water. If you do this, set an anchor out to the southeast to hold her off. The one disadvantage of palm-tree anchorages is the mosquito. For this reason, I prefer the middle of the inner basin off the new hotel and dock.

In all weather Marigot Harbor is perfectly sheltered, even in a hurricane. It is always calm and peaceful. Its quiet is only ruffled by the hum of the hotel generator, which definitely needs a new silencer. The hotel service is excellent, nonetheless. Water and fuel are available alongside the dock. Univest, a northern investment group, has bought up the hotel and dock and plans to have a fleet of Morgan 41's on bare-boat charter operating from Marigot in the near future. The diving is good off the mouth of the harbor, and it is a wonderful place to sail dinghies or sailfish.

Soufriere
(BA 1273, NO 25081)

South of Rachette Point, north of Petit Piton, Soufriere is the second largest town in St. Lucia, though it is not a port of entry. You must stop first at Vieux Fort or Castries to enter. Anchoring at Soufriere is difficult as there is deep water right up to shore. The best policy is to moor stern to the jetty, with a light anchor and plenty of line from the bow.

The major attractions of Soufriere are the sulphur baths and volcano. A taxi may be hired to take you to both spots. The baths are reported to be refreshing and invigorating, something just short of a fountain of youth. The volcano is one of few in the world whose crater can be explored without a lot of mountain climbing. It is immensely popular, though some people may say that it is nothing more than a blowhole on a hillside.

Anse des Pitons
(BA 1273, NO 25081)

A short way south of Soufriere is by far the most spectacular anchorage in the Lesser Antilles. On either side are the Pitons, towering 2000 feet in the air. At the head of the bay in the northeast corner is an excellent anchorage, off the Jalousie boathouse, so long

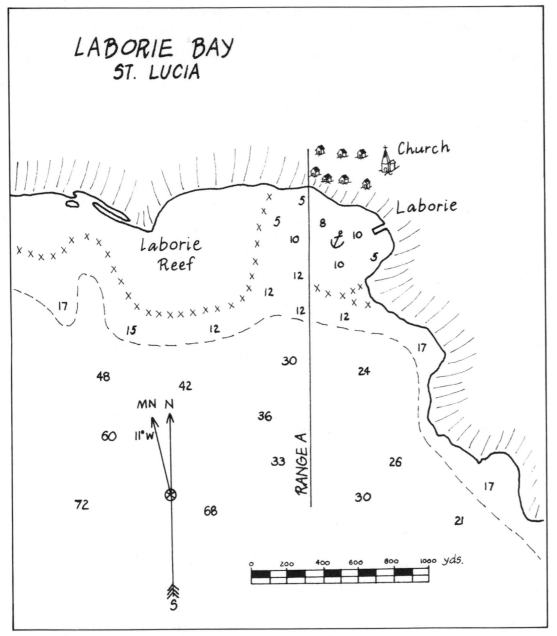

LABORIE BAY
ST. LUCIA

Laborie Reef

Church

Laborie

Range A: The western end of the village brought to bear roughly north magnetic. When reef is abeam to starboard, head up into anchorage.

SKETCH CHART 58

as you are able to find bottom. The only way to moor is to sail in close, drop a stern anchor about 50 yards offshore, luff up, and have someone jump off the bow with line to tie to a coconut tree. I have lain within half a boat length of shore and had plenty of water under the keel. The cover photograph will give an idea of how close you can get. Be sure that your stern anchor is well set as hard gusts (back eddies off North Piton) can blow you down on the rocks to the south of the boathouse. Further, though it seldom happens, the ground swell can sometimes find its way into this northeast corner; if it does, you will have to get out fast before the stern anchor drags and you are high and dry on the beach.

Ashore you will find a most interesting set of ruins, along with an operating coconut plantation. The workers are friendly and will very happily give you a tour of the place. Watching men scramble up the 80-foot-high coconut trees is a sight to behold.

If you enjoy exploring the countryside, my friend John Clegg says to take a cab down the Choiseil Road from Soufriere. Go about four miles and take the road to the right. It's not much of a road and the driver will probably protest, but take it just the same. Bounce along for another mile until you reach a group of houses. Though the inhabitants speak no English, for five or ten dollars one or two of them will guide you to Gros Piton. If the weather has been dry, it will be about a two-and-a-half-hour scramble. The route swings around the south of Gros Piton at roughly 600 feet and climbs the west ridge from there. At the top you will find yourself in the thick of a mahogany forest. Climb a tree and take a gander. The view will prove well worth the struggle.

The hike to Petit Piton is another worthy struggle. Again you will need a guide. The route goes up the col from the anchorage toward Soufriere to about 800 feet, then down again to about 200 feet before winding its way up the northwest ridge. For the most part, the trip is a pretty standard scramble through thorn scrub, with the exception of a 30-foot patch of rock where some basic climbing technique may be required. The top of the piton is open and breezy. If you clamber down about 150 feet and climb a tree, you can get a good shot of your boat anchored at Jalousie. Allow about six hours for the entire trip up and back. Be damn sure to bring some liquid refreshment.

Laborie
(BA 1273, NO 25081, Sketch Chart 58)

One harbor that is on the chart but seldom visited is Laborie, a most intriguing anchorage. This harbor should only be entered under ideal conditions with the sun high. The man who made the Admiralty chart appears never to have seen the harbor. The reef on the eastern side of the entrance to Laborie Harbour is not as indicated on the chart but extends at least 150 yards westward from the eastern point.

To enter, bring the houses on the western side of town to bear about north magnetic and keep a good lookout to starboard. Once the reef is abeam to starboard head northeast toward the church, round up and anchor wherever it is convenient. There is about nine feet of water in the harbor.

Mike Smith of *Phryna* has warned to keep an eye on the rain clouds before entering Laborie. In heavy rainfalls the stream that empties into the harbor spews out so much mud that it is impossible to find one's way in or out. Thus it might be wise to avoid this anchorage during the summer rainy season.

Vieux Fort Bay
(BA 499, NO 25083)

On the south end of St. Lucia, this is a large banana-loading port as well as a port of entry. Well to the eastward on the way north, it is difficult to lay from St. Vincent and is seldom visited by yachts. However, if you are disposed to visit Soufriere or Marigot without going to Castries first, you would do well to clear through Vieux Fort. In normal trade-wind weather this is a good anchorage. Use the area to the southwest of the large pier. When coming from the south, approach with Gros Hill (the hill northward of Battery Point) in line with Morne Bellevue. The one danger in this bay is the ruined beacon marked on BA 499, NO 25081, and NO 25083. I have looked and never been able to find it.

The locals inform me that the structure has collapsed, and the remains can only be seen at dead low tide, when some of the iron work is just flush with the water. I don't mind a one-fathom sand shoal, but the thought of an iron pipe skewering my garboards is most disconcerting. Check your bearings carefully when entering. Hoist your "Q" flag, go ashore, and find Customs.

There is not too much else ashore at Vieux Fort, but there is excellent reef diving and lobstering thereabouts. If you are the lazy sort, lobster are for sale cheap.

The eastern shore of St. Lucia has some small coves that are used by the natives for launching canoes, but there is nothing that can be really called a harbor. I know of no yacht that has visited this area.

One last word of warning: *under no circumstances should one swim in St. Lucia's streams.* There is a parasite in the water that can enter the blood stream and cause all kinds of trouble. This is the same parasite that plagues the upper reaches of the Nile in the area of the Aswan Dam.

CHAPTER 20

St. Vincent

NO 25043, 25044; BA 501

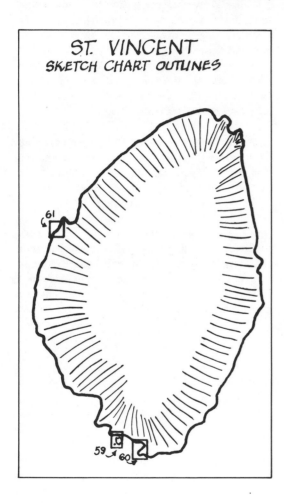

St. Vincent is somewhat smaller than St. Lucia, its neighbor to the north. It is a lush, wet island with peaks rising to well over 3,000 feet. Sections of it have been lavishly cultivated, the crops laid in neat green tiers reminiscent of the English countryside. From the sea, the town of Kingstown presents a pleasing view, nestled in a hollow with mountains rising around. The island was discovered by Columbus on his third voyage to the New World. Like Dominica, it had been populated by Carib Indians who resisted every attempt to colonize the island. Only when the Caribs became embroiled in their own civil war were the Europeans able to establish a presence on the island. In 1675 a slave ship bound from Africa went down off St. Vincent. Many of the slaves swam ashore and settled, producing through intermarriage the Black Carib of today.

The story of St. Vincent is one of continuous warfare. The Caribs entrenched themselves in the north end of the island while the British settled and fortified the towns of Kingstown and Calliqua. The Caribs were supported against the British by the French who imported other Caribs as mercenaries from neighboring islands, primarily St. Lucia. These hired Caribs always landed on the northeast and northwest of the island, grouped, and proceeded south overland against the British. It is for this reason that many of the old fortifications on the island, such as those at Duvernette, Dorsetshire Hill, Richmond and Sion Hills, and the earliest ruins at Fort Charlotte, all have their cannon aimed inland.

When the Caribs were finally conquered, around 5,000 of them were placed on the island of Baliceaux and later shipped to British Honduras. How they managed to cram 5,000 onto an island the size of Baliceaux beggers the imagination, and I suspect the loss of life was heavy.

There are a number of good hotels on St. Vincent. Kingstown has two supermarkets, Corea's and Hazel's, either of which can be reached by radio-telephone. The open-air market is excellent and operates every day from 0800; but if you want to get the best, you should arrive early in the morning. Ice is available at the ice plant or the ice cream factory, and it is seldom that both operations are broken down at the same time. Fuel is obtainable by appointment with the Shell agent at Hazel's Store, and arrangements can be made for it to be delivered at the steamer dock. The dock was clearly not designed with yachts in mind. It is a miserable place to lay, especially when the ground swell is running. Unfortunately, this is the only place in Kingstown harbor where fresh water can be had.

There is deep water all along the jetty. The best place to anchor at Kingstown, a port of entry, is around the northeast corner. Get your bow close to shore, drop anchor and ease your stern into the dock right next to the steps where the small bum boats off-load. Once you have cleared, I would advise moving out to another anchorage as soon as possible.

But if you are coming from the north, I hardly think it worthwhile to clear through Kingstown. From Johnson's Point it is a hard beat to the jetty in the northeast corner of the bay. Much time is lost in maneuvering your way safely to the jetty, and thence through Customs. Once cleared, you are required to leave, and from the jetty it is two and a half miles against wind and current to the nearest amenable anchorage at Young Island. The better way by far is to take a beam reach from Johnson's Point to Bequia and then a short sheltered beat up to Admiralty Bay. This is a fine anchorage where you may clear at your leisure and pass the night. If you then wish to visit St. Vincent, you can sail directly to the anchorage at Young Island or Blue Lagoon, thereby postponing indefinitely the suspect pleasures of the Kingstown jetty.

Dave Corrigan of Mariner's Inn is planning to install some permanent moorings at Young Island. Corrigan was one of the kingpins in the development of Petit St. Vincent and the organizer of the PSV "jumpup" parties. He is a former Canadian schoolteacher who decided that catering to tourists could not be much worse than riding herd over kids in a schoolhouse. Corrigan probably knows as much of the services available on St. Vincent as anyone in the area and he can fill you in on mechanics, electricians, or refrigerationists. If you're in desperate straits, he might be convinced to do most of the repairs himself. Also, his wife Jo can arrange to have your laundry done in one day's service.

There are very limited facilities for yachts in St. Vincent other than the Caribbean Sailing Yachts operation in Blue Lagoon. But the Vincentians are patient and ingenious; I have seen a 55-foot deep-draft ketch hauled out with nothing more than some big wooden rollers, a makeshift cradle, and a bulldozer. I've been told that the Adams brothers are building a heavy-duty drydock of 200-ton capacity in Wallilabu Bay. Exactly how this will function in a big ground swell I do not know, but I'm sure they will find some way.

St. Vincent is not without its oddities. A favorite of mine was a sign, which has since disappeared, in the middle of town which read, "WINDWARD TRAFFIC KEEP RIGHT— LEEWARD TRAFFIC KEEP LEFT." The Catholic and Anglican Churches in Kingstown

are across the street from one another from where they conduct a certain liturgical rivalry. They are both so high-Church that it is hard to tell which service you have wandered into. The first time I went to mass in St. Vincent, I was on the communion rail before I realized I was in the wrong church. Now, since the changes in the Catholic Mass, it is perfectly easy to tell the difference: if you walk in and hear what sounds to be a good old Catholic Mass of years ago, you'll know you are in the Anglican Church.

Among the charter skippers that sail the Islands there is a great debate as to whether a boat can be better stocked in St. Vincent or Grenada. Without joining either cause, I can only judge that since there is this dispute in the first place, you can stock a boat for a long cruise in either place, and which you choose is only a matter of personal preference.

Tourism is making its mark on the island. The hotels, restaurants, shopping centers, and cruise ships have arrived in the customary profusion. The expansion, however, has been hampered by the lack of a good airport. For years it was assumed to be impossible to build any airstrip on St. Vincent, until a young Grenadian engineer designed and executed a small one for DC-3's. To get around the space shortage, he built the strip uphill. The planes landed uphill and took off down, with gravity doing the extra work in both cases. Flying out in one of those old DC-3's fully loaded was the experience of a lifetime, and if it was blowing really hard in the wrong direction, you just didn't take off, occasionally for two or three days. Sometimes the stewardess would take the passengers from the last four rows and cram them up against the door of the cockpit so that, with the weight of the plane forward, the pilot could get the tail off a little faster. Works fine in the Islands, but I wonder how an FAA inspector would have reacted to the procedure. Now with the new

LIAT Avro's there is no problem landing or taking off; it is more a question of when LIAT is motivated to dispatch a flight to St. Vincent.

A taxi ride around the island is diverting. Mr. Elford McLean (telephone 2831) has been conducting tours for many years. He is a council member for the city of Kingstown, and knows every inch of the island. If he can't make it, he will send one of his friends, and any friend of Elford's will be completely reliable.

Kingstown Harbor
(BA 501, NO 25043)

If possible, avoid, for the reasons described above.

Young Island
(BA 501, NO 25043, Sketch Chart 59)

For many years this has been the most popular anchorage in St. Vincent. The Young Island Hotel is usually quite crowded during the winter, and it is best to make reservations.

Anchoring off Young Island should be done with great care. It is frequently crowded, and when the tide starts running to windward, the boats have a tendency to roam about a little erratically. Many a bow pulpit has been bent out of shape at the change of tide. The Bahamian moor is strongly recommended. To my mind the best spot to anchor is in the shoal water off the northeast tip of the island. This will put you out of the worst of the tide and close enough to the beach for easy swimming. Best to arrive early, as space is on a first-come basis. Keep an eye out for the underwater cable that runs from the northeast tip of the island over to the mainland. If you hooked into this one, you'd put the hotel right out of business.

A few of the savvy yachtsmen prefer to anchor in the shoal water well east of the former Aquatic Club. They drop a main anchor close to the shoal, and back off a ways

199

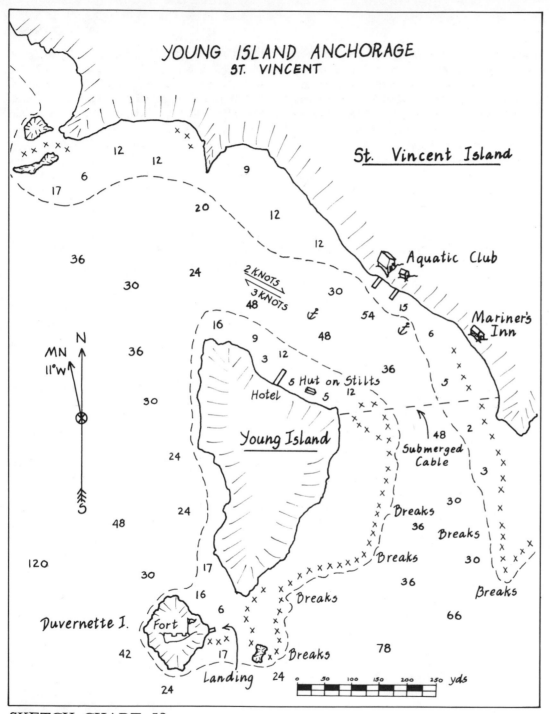

YOUG ISLAND ANCHORAGE
ST. VINCENT

St. Vincent Island

2 KNOTS

3 KNOTS

Aquatic Club

Mariner's Inn

MN
11°W

N

Hut on Stilts

Hotel

Young Island

Submerged Cable

Breaks

Breaks

Breaks

Breaks

Breaks

Breaks

Duvernette I.

Fort

Landing

0   50   100   150   200   250 yds

SKETCH CHART 59

and run a light Danforth ashore off the port bow to prevent the reversing current from swinging them out into the main stream. The tide eddy is such that there is no worry of the stern swinging northward onshore.

The anchorage at Young Island may be entered through either the southeast entrance or the west entrance. Normally the latter is used. There is deep water close inshore on both sides. It is a somewhat tricky anchorage to sail into when the tide is running to leeward. A two-knot current will tend to set you back on any moored boat you try to pass to windward. I recommend it only to the most experienced sailors. If you are using the southeast entrance, be sure to post a lookout in the rigging. The reefs are steep-to. Steer midway between the breaking water and follow the deepest water by eye. However, do not leave via the southeast entrance unless the tide is running to windward. Otherwise the foul tide in this very narrow area would make even powering out a difficult proposition. A departure through this opening is justified only when you are headed across to the top of Bequia, as this will set you favorably to windward.

There is excellent swimming and snorkeling around Young Island. If you would like a dinghy expedition, row around to the west side between Young and Duvernette Islands. On the northeast corner of Duvernette you will find a landing stage. Be sure to moor a dinghy bow-and-stern, or else it will thrash itself to splinters on the rocks. Climbing to the fort at the top of Duvernette is a close second to a walk up the Washington Monument. That they managed to trundle cannon and materiel up to the top of this rock is quite unbelievable.

Calliqua Bay
(BA 501, NO 25043)

An open, turbulent, and generally unattractive anchorage, unless you have it in mind to stop in for a short while, row ashore, and watch the fishing boats being hauled up on the beach in the afternoon. These are interesting native boats, though not so well finished or maintained as the boats of Bequia.

Blue Lagoon
(BA 501, NO 25043, Sketch Chart 60)

An excellent spot which in days to come may well become the major yacht harbor of St. Vincent. At this writing Caribbean Sailing Yachts, which is the big bare boat agency, has the only facility in the area. It is a small yard providing fuel, electricity, and water—for its own boats only. The main entrance is through the channel in the break of the reef on the southwest side. The axis of the channel is 067 magnetic and is sometimes marked; one must proceed with alert eyeballs. Put a man in the 'rigging to spot the breakers on both sides, align and follow a course of 067 midway through the break. The channel is narrow and should not be attempted in a heavy swell.

There is another entrance to the Blue Lagoon on its northwestern side. The channel is usually marked by four stakes. It is reputed to be six feet deep and a bare five feet at extreme low water. Proceed very slowly and ease your way in. Once inside the lagoon, you can anchor anywhere, but bear in mind that the water is 50 to 80 feet deep throughout, requiring a tremendous amount of scope. In the northeast corner of the harbor you can

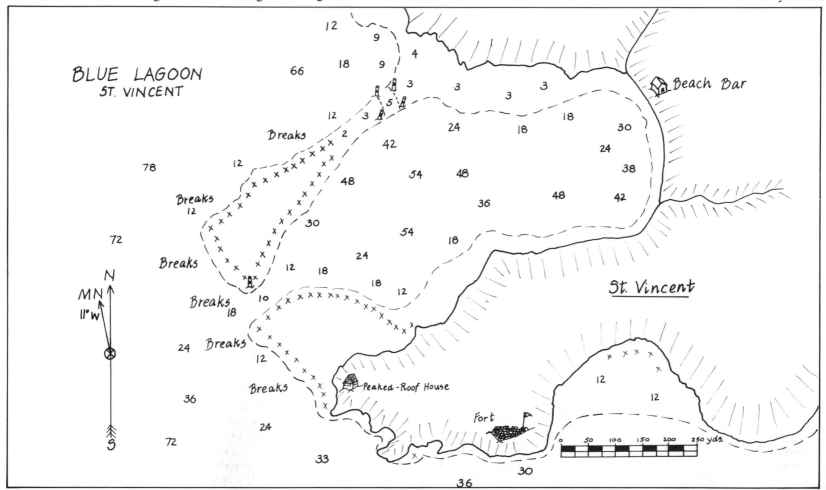

SKETCH CHART 60

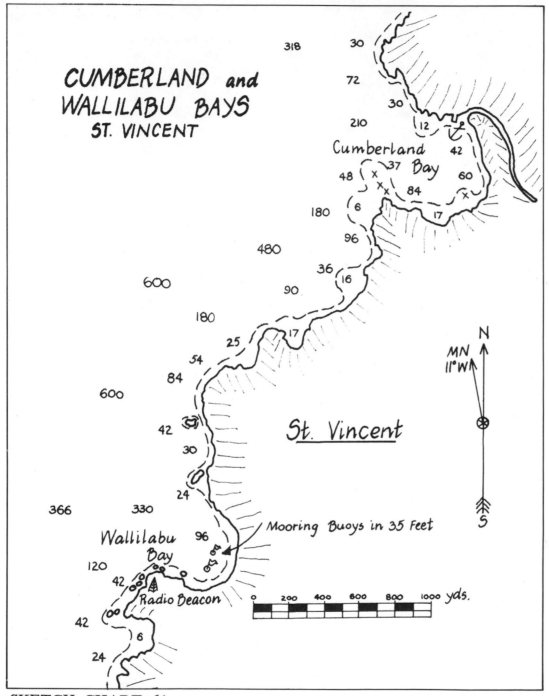

CUMBERLAND and WALLILABU BAYS
ST. VINCENT

Cumberland Bay

St. Vincent

Wallilabu Bay

Radio Beacon

Mooring Buoys in 35 Feet

MN 11°W

0 200 400 600 800 1000 yds.

SKETCH CHART 61

sail in close and pitch the bow anchor up onto the beach and run a light stern anchor to hold you off, without leaving your boat. In the northern corner there is a beach facility run by the Sugar Mill Hotel, and near to it the home of Caribbean Sailing Yachts. Through the hotel you can arrange for rooms and meals ashore. On the south side is the Blue Lagoon Hotel which can outfit you with the same sort of accommodations.

At all times of the year the Blue Lagoon ranks as a prime anchorage. It is well sheltered from the east, and the ground swell that hooks around the south end of the island is effectively abated by the reefs on the south and west sides of the lagoon. It should not, however, be regarded as a hurricane hole. If the eye of a storm passes to the south of St. Vincent, the lagoon would be protected from the heavy sea to the east. But if it passes north anywhere near St. Vincent, the wind and sea would then be booming in out of the southwest, and the prognosis would be bleak for any vessel tendered in the Blue Lagoon.

Cumberland Bay
(BA 501, NO 25044, Sketch Chart 61)

One of the few anchorages on the west coast of St. Vincent, this spot is safe enough for the most part. It usually does not get much of the ground swell, though at times it can be inhospitable. This has been a popular anchorage for boats bound from St. Vincent to St. Lucia. From Young Island to Castries, at the northern end of St. Lucia, it is an 80-mile sail, which is longer than most charter parties care to make. Cumberland Bay hence became the natural overnight layover. The bottom here drops abruptly from the shore. The best method is to ease in slowly, checking for bottom. As soon as you see it, drop a stern anchor and continue on ahead toward shore. Then you can either row the bow anchor into the shoal water or nudge your bow against the shoal, drop from there, and haul back on your stern line. Make sure your bow anchor is well set or you may find yourself out to sea during the night. If you are entering the bay from the south, give the southwesternmost point a wide berth. There is a rock with six feet of water over it. A number of yachts have failed to do so and have left behind large portions of their keels to commemorate the oversight.

Fresh water flowing into Cumberland Bay gives the opportunity for bathing and laundering. But don't roam too far—I have heard reports of stolen dinghies and pilferage in the bay. There now seems to be a certain amount of ill will between the natives and visiting yachtsmen, which leads me to suggest that you avoid this bay unless you are prepared to post watch.

Wallilabu Bay
(BA 501, NO 25044, Sketch Chart 61)

Because of the local problems in Cumberland Bay, nearby Wallilabu Bay has become the preferred anchorage within this area. Ashore, the Andersons have a craft shop and small beach bar; they report that the anchorage is a good one and at its best in the southeast corner of the bay. Anchor 30 yards from shore and run a stern line to a palm tree. There is a dry dock under construction in the northeast corner, though when it will be finished is anyone's guess. The radio tower is incorrectly listed on the British and American charts. As you see on the Sketch Chart, it is on the hill forming the south corner of Wallilabu Bay.

Chateau Belair
(BA 501, NO 25044)

The most northern town on the island of St. Vincent. Here again, although the charts do not properly show it, the bottom drops off very abruptly to 30 or 40 fathoms within a hundred yards of shore. The only way to anchor is with one ashore and a second one to seaward. The best anchorage is on the small shoal north of the Fitzhughes Estate as marked on NO 25044. This is only good in calm weather when the swell is down, but it's the best spot from which to set forth on an expedition of north St. Vincent.

There are the ruins of an old estate at the village of Wallibu. This is reputed to be one of the most primitive areas of the Lesser Antilles, by romantic accounts not unlike regions of darkest Africa. From here or Morne Ronde Village (which can only be reached by dinghy) a guide can be hired to take you to the crater lake, where, when the weather is right, some fabulous vistas can be enjoyed. The crater lake can just as well be approached by taxi from the east. The nearness of your approach to the base of the crater will depend on the willingness of your driver. From there it is a good hike to a view of the lake. Anytime you are climbing in wooded areas higher than a thousand feet in the Lesser Antilles it is a good idea to wear heavy shoes and to bring along some foul weather gear. Carrying a little liquid refreshment is also advisable, as one can work up a pretty good thirst in these rocky climes.

To reach Soufriere, the more or less extinct volcano of northern St. Vincent, take a cab to Orange Hill. From there the path is well trodden. John Clegg reports that his pride of physical achievement was somewhat diminished by encountering a party of nonchalant picnickers making their way down from the summit, followed shortly after by a nun in full habit. The view from the east rim at the top is liable to be clouded. If it is, follow the path around to the south and down to the southeast edge of the crater, where the view should be quite clear. Instead of doubling back from here for the trip down, at the east-southeast corner of the rim you can scramble down another 400 feet—it is fairly steep going—to rejoin the trail.

There used to be some pretty good fishing in the crater lake until quite recently when there was a quickening of subterranean activity. So active, in fact, that the entire northern end of St. Vincent was evacuated for a time, the temperature in the lake rising to 170 degrees. The water level fell drastically, and now an island 60 feet high has emerged from its depths.

The explosion of Mt. Pelee, Martinique, is the one that always captured the imagination, but when Soufriere in St. Vincent blew up the day before Pelee, 2,000 people were killed. Amazingly, some were killed all the way down in Kingstown, by small pieces of flying rocks. People in Kingstown heard the explosion, rushed outside to see what had happened, and many were struck down.

A final place of interest to yachtsmen on St. Vincent is the waterfall at Grand Baleine at the north end of the island. The falls are quite spectacular and make for a good daytrip from Chateau Belair. One can proceed from Chateau Belair the six miles to Grand Baleine either by dinghy or under sail. If you sail, you must leave some of the crew on board the boat to stand off under shortened sail while the rest visit the falls. There is no hope of anchoring at Grand Baleine, as the cliffs are vertical to a great depth. In a way, this is typical of the problem faced by the yachtsman in St. Vincent. There is much to be seen ashore but a definite shortage of dependable anchorages from which to set out.

CHAPTER 21

Barbados

NO 25045, 25046; BA 502, 2485

Barbados lies 80 miles due east of St. Vincent. It is one hard windward slog to reach it, and very few of the boats that cruise the Lesser Antilles ever attempt it. As good as *Iolaire* is to windward, I've found that nothing goes into the wind quite as well as a LIAT plane, and to my mind this is the best way to get there. In most cases the yachts you will see in Barbados have arrived there en route from Europe.

Too bad that Barbados is so far upwind (and has so poor an anchorage once you get there), because it is a very attractive island. Despite its being one of the most heavily populated areas in the world with 1400 people per square mile, it is neat, clean, and orderly. Certainly it is the best run of the Lesser Antilles. The people are polite, friendly, and helpful. They speak in the soft, musical tones of the Bajan accent and regard themselves rather as Englishmen than West Indians. For centuries Barbados has been referred to as "Little England," and justly so. The beautifully tended landscape little suggests a tropical island. There are neatly clipped lawns, a racing turf, cricket field, and a proper little bandstand. The police are impeccably dressed, and the harbor police in their straw hats and white jumpers look like something out of another era. The spoken language is English; there is no patois or corruption with a foreign language. In short, the island shows clear signs of being the only one in the entire West Indies that has remained under a single flag.

The northeast trades have been its life-blood, making travel from England a simple matter. By the same token the trades were its protection from rival colonial powers to the west. In those days of wooden ships and iron men, the windward ability of a warship was roughly that of a bathtub toy. It was impossible for the French to keep a fleet assembled through a long beat out to Barbados. They tried once or twice and became hopelessly scattered and had to give it up.

From the Antilles the island is best approached from a point north or south of Barbados, depending on the season, In the spring and summer when the wind is in the southeast, the best place to start is from the south end of Grenada. Put to sea on the starboard tack, and check your progress by RDF (Barbados Radio at Black Point: 705 mHz; Sewell Airport Beacon: 345 kHz) or celestial sights. The current runs to the northwest, so watch that it doesn't set you north of the island. Barbados is low-lying and it is possible to miss it. Native schooner captains have a way of returning to their home ports in the Islands with the explanation that "Barbados done sunk. We was where she is, but she ain't dere no more."

In the winter months with the wind in the northeast it is best to set out from Martinique or St. Lucia. Here is the method used by the schooners from St. Lucia: stand north from Castries until the light of Ile Cabrit—the southeastern corner of Martinique —is abeam; go about on port tack, and stay as close to the wind as you can; if you don't see Barbados in 24 hours, turn around and try again. These are not the most explicit sailing directions in the world, but they seem to work one way or the other.

Despite the generally low aspect of Barbados, its highest peak, Mount Misery, is 1069 feet. This is altitude enough to produce clouds that will often serve as a landmark well before the island itself comes into view.

Barbados is well lighted and well charted; making a landfall at night presents no real difficulties. All corners of the island are marked with lights visible at great distances. While there are no off-lying hazards, bear in mind that there are a number of reefs on the coasts of the island, so do not hug the shore too closely. On the southeastern coast especially, the reefs extend offshore in places one-and-a-half miles, and the current sets on shore. The current can mount to two knots at times, so again do not approach too closely. There are a number of small-boat passages through this reef, but a good deal of local knowledge is required.

Carlisle Bay
(BA 502, NO 25046)

The major anchorage in Barbados is off Bridgetown in Carlisle Bay, due north of the fort on Needham's Point. It is a relatively poor anchorage because it is open to the rollers from the northwest, and the normal trade wind sea hooks around Needham's Point. When the northwest swell is severe, it is well nigh impossible to land ashore in a dinghy. The Aquatic Club and its pier, which for so many years was a haven to transatlantic yachtsmen, has regrettably been absorbed by a Holiday Inn. Yachtsmen and their dinghies are most definitely not welcome.

Once you have rounded Needham's Point, proceed north and anchor right off the Carenage, which is due south of Customs and marked on the chart. The customs official will usually come out to clear you. Once cleared, it is best to relocate to the Holiday Inn vicinity and anchor. Dinghies can be landed on the beaches at either of the two below-mentioned yacht clubs.

No sailor should miss the Carenage. It is chocked with vessels of every shape and size. There are always a couple of schooners being loaded at the pier, water taxis shuttling about in every direction, and the harbor police maneuvering to keep the mayhem under control. During rush hour one of them stands in a dinghy ceremoniously directing traffic. Colorful though it is, I wouldn't recommend leaving a yacht for any time in the Carenage. It gets to be a little noisy; the water is, of course, foul, and I suspect the pilferage is beyond belief.

In years gone by, everything was lightered out to the ships anchored offshore, and passengers were brought in by rowing wherries. It was a picturesque sight, and the arrangement provided needed employment for the locals who built and ran the little boats. Now, as in all the islands, a large deep-water dock has been built. The boatmen are unemployed, the wherries are rotting away in the Carenage, and the people who were dependent on them for their livelihood are looking for work.

Bridgetown is a major transfer point for pasengers and cargo. Many freighters stop here, as do most of the cruise ships and airlines. Whatever you may have heard of cargo lost in Trinidad holds true of Barbados as well.

There are a number of good hotels within walking distance of the anchorage and regular bus service to the heart of town. If you are an early riser, for a change of pace try watching the trainers give their horses a workout every morning at dawn at the race track.

Many small-boat fittings can be obtained on the island, but it is practically impossible to locate fittings for larger boats. Basic marine supplies such as paint are much cheaper here than in the rest of the Islands, since no duty is paid on any marine supplies at all. For the most part you will find supplies that you were unable to find anywhere else. The major distributors of engines, mechanical equipment, paints, tools, and what-have-you are based on the island, usually in Bridgetown. It is indeed a pleasure to deal directly with the supplier.

The machine shops and hauling facilities are really excellent. Their mechanics are used to working on boats. The screw-lift dock can lift any size of yacht. In fact, this screw-lift is well worth a look around, even if you don't need to use it. It was installed by a Scotch designer sometime in the 1880s. The original steam engine has been replaced by diesel. Each section of the dock assembly disengages and lowers away to allow access for bottom and keel repairs.

There are two yacht clubs—the Barbados Yacht Club north of the Holiday Inn Pier (marked Aquatic Club on chart) and the Barbados Cruising Club south of that pier. The Barbados Yacht Club looks like something right out of an Edwardian novel—with large, cool reading rooms, tennis courts, a monumental bar, and just the sort of quiet atmosphere one expects of a well-heeled British club. It was formerly the *Royal* Barbados Yacht Club and it is still listed as such on the charts. The reason for the change, I am told, dates back some years to a time when Prince Philip was paying a visit to the government of Barbados. He had immensely enjoyed the company of Barbados' premier and, discovering that he, too, was a yachtsman, invited him to the Royal Barbados for a drink. The premier replied that he was not a member of the club and furthermore was not permitted to become one. A day or two later the Royal Barbados became just plain Barbados Yacht Club. Maybe they have loosened up. In the past, they used to feed visiting sailing teams on the beach out front instead of in the clubhouse proper. But this attitude has now changed entirely, and visiting yachtsmen from other clubs are now welcome.

CHAPTER 22

Northern Grenadines

NO 25042, 25044; BA 501, 791, 2872

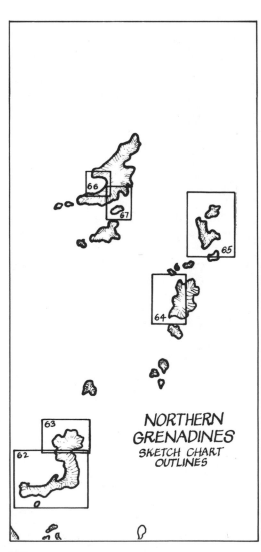

NORTHERN
GRENADINES
SKETCH CHART
OUTLINES

The Grenadines comprise a string of small islands stretching 45 miles northeastward from Ile de Ronde to Bequia. They are a varied lot, ranging unpredictably in size and topography. While the Tobago Cays are low and flat, neighboring Union Island soars high into the air. During the popular charter season in the winter, most of the islands are dry and windswept, but in the rainy season their colors change abruptly from dull brown to a bright, lush green. In sailing the Grenadines, the runs are very short; most passages can be made in two hours and the longest ones never last more than five. There are anchorages virtually everywhere, but these must be carefully negotiated. What distinguishes this area from the rest of the Antilles—and the Virgin Islands in particular—are the vast reaches of shoal water. There is an indescribable thrill in sailing across these banks with only two or three feet of water below the keel, and to watch the bottom slipping by from your place on the spreaders.

Most of the islands lie along a northeast-southwest axis, allowing you to lay a course close-hauled when coming from the south. This contrasts with the Virgins, where you are either dead before or dead against the wind. There is very little chance of getting becalmed in the low-lying Grenadines. Soon the days of the unspoiled tropical cay will have passed. Many of the islands are undergoing the throes of long-term development ventures.

Both Chapter 22 and Chapter 23 are organized from south to north, as if cruising from Grenada.

Cannouan Island
(BA 2872, NO 25042, Sketch Chart 62, 63)

The British island of Cannouan is one of the largest in the Grenadines and remains one of the least known and least populated. In the last century, Cannouan was a major outpost of the whaling ships. During winters in the 1890s as many as 20 New Bedford schooner-whalers could be seen anchored in its lee. Although whaling finally died out in the '20s, one still encounters scattered remains of whale boats in the area.

The island offers a variety of good anchorages to visiting yachtsmen. If you are approaching from the south, the westernmost peak of the island, Glass Hill, will appear as detached from the rest. The narrow, low-lying, sand spit which separates it from Taffia Hill is hard to spot from any distance. Approaching from the north, Cannouan is the first sizable island after Mustique or Bequia. Its main anchorage is Charlestown Bay. The south side of this bay is far shallower than indicated on the chart. One popular spot is in the south-eastern corner of the bay off the dock, as there is a good sand beach and it is not far from town. There are two posts about ten feet high, striped yellow and gray, which define a range for entering this part of the bay. They are lit by a couple of kerosene lanterns whose function, as far as I can tell, is purely ornamental. At least I have never been able to spot them at night. Although lots of people use it, I hesitate to recommend the anchorage, however, because the holding is poor (sand and grass) and it is exposed to the swell.

The best anchorage to my mind is in the northeast corner of the bay, just off the fish house, which is a relatively new, white building with a small dock in front. There are two fathoms of water off the dock. The north and south sides of the channel are shoal. The axis of this 20-foot channel is 100-280 magnetic. With the lead line feel your way in to the

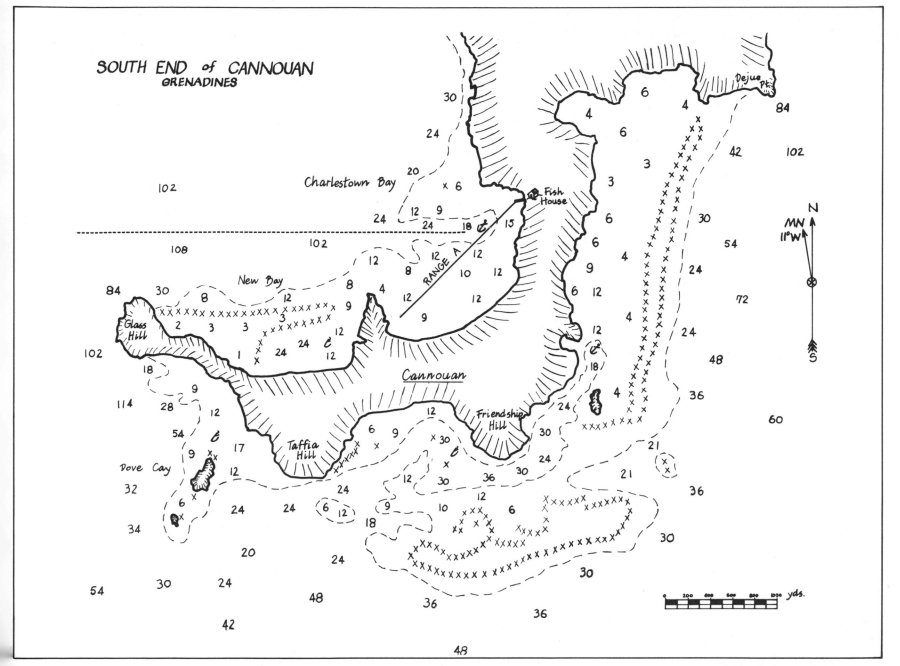

SOUTH END of CANNOUAN
GRENADINES

Charlestown Bay

New Bay

Glass
Hill

Cannouan

Taffia
Hill

Friendship
Hill

Dove Cay

Fish
House

RANGE A

Dejue Pt.

N
MN
11°W
S

yds.

Range A: Fish house brought to bear roughly 045 magnetic.

SKETCH CHART 62

mouth of the channel and follow the southern edge in toward shore. When the fish house bears northeast, turn to port and head for it. Off the fish house there will be no ground swell. The wind will appear to be from the west. These are the trades hooking over the hills to the east and forming a back eddy. The eddy will cause no great difficulty, although putting out two anchors will make for a more relaxed night's sleep.

According to the chart, there is a seemingly good anchorage in the bay due north of Taffia Hill in New Bay. From an airplane it also looks to be an ideal anchorage. I have only visited this spot once, and I was rocked all night long. The reef on the north side of the bay affords less protection than the chart indicates. There are three or four feet of water over the reef, enough to let the ground swell from the north come rolling in. For the winter

months, therefore, I would have to rule out this spot. Only in the summer when there is no ground swell and the wind is in the southeast is this adequate for anything more than daytime stops. The bottom is grass, and the holding wretched. The night I spent there, I had to dive to the bottom, dig a hole, and bury my anchors before they would hold. The reef appears excellent for snorkeling, and in the cove on the eastern side of the bay there is an

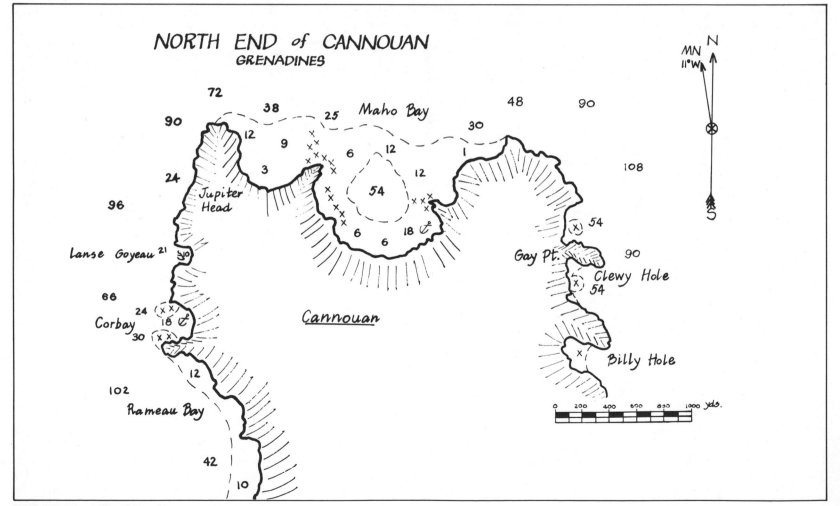

SKETCH CHART 63

attractive small beach. Over the bar at the entrance it is eight feet. You must stay within 50 yards of the eastern point as you enter. When the sand beach falls abeam to port, bear off toward the middle of the harbor. There is plenty of water inside the reef—anchor anywhere, but don't plan to spend the night.

Again if the ground swell is not running or it is not blowing too hard, there is another lunch-time anchorage between Dove Cay and the mainland. Due north of Dove Cay is excellent. Sail in and check it out. If it looks calm, drop the hook and enjoy yourself. Further east, between Taffia and Friendship Hills, another anchorage is to be found. The approach requires careful eyeballing. Post a man in the rigging and stand in cautiously under power or on starboard tack. There is good holding here on a white-sand bottom, excellent swimming, and not too much of a swell unless the wind is from the southeast.

For the seasoned sailor, deep water can be carried to windward around Friendship Hill and a good ways north inside the reefs (Sketch Chart 62). Boats drawing eight feet have gone up through here. Within the reefs the current is always running south and at times too strongly for a man to swim against. You will find complete privacy here, good swimming and snorkeling, and great shelter. A boat drawing five feet or less can easily make its way north all the way to the head of the bay—carefully. Marcy Cromwell took his *Xantippe,* drawing six feet three inches, all the way to the village at the very end of the basin. A good deal of skill is required. The deepest water is fairly close to shore off the beaches and at the points of land no more than 30 yards offshore. It is a matter of feeling the way with a boathook or with someone leading the way in a dinghy. When you reach the head of the basin, there is an old church ashore which is worth a look around.

It has been claimed possible to enter this basin from the north through a break in the reef, but I tend to discount this as a local boast of derring-do. I have observed the area from the air, and the approach looked quite impossible, though I suppose one or two boats may have done it. I am pretty certain that where the charts say three fathoms there are no more than two.

The other bays on the northeast corner of Cannouan are not feasible as they face out into the eastern wind and swell. The only exception is Maho Bay (Sketch Chart 63) on the north end of the island, where there is a beautiful summer anchorage and no ground swell when the wind is in the south. If it is used in the winter, one should rig two anchors and be prepared to move out if the swell makes up. There is a beautiful white-sand beach here. The best spot to anchor is in the extreme southeast corner very close inshore. The cove is seldom visited; it is a good place to get away from the herd.

On the western coast of Cannouan I recently found two beautiful coves which I determined to be excellent anchorages, although I had never heard them mentioned as such. The two are L'Anse Goyeau and Corbay, as marked on the Sketch Chart. Corbay is the nicer and has room for two boats. Rocks extend from the north and south points, and these must be avoided, but once you are inside, the water is completely smooth and clear. There is a white-sand and shingle beach that is very steep-to at the water's edge. In the winter this spot will do as a fine daytime anchorage when the swell is down and in the summer it can be used overnight. L'Anse Goyeau, the more northern of the two, is quite a bit smaller and recommended for day use only.

Petit Cannouan
(BA 2872, NO 25042)

Four miles northeast of Cannouan, this is steep-to and offers no anchorage possibilities.

Savan Island
(BA 2872, NO 25042)

Well to windward of Petit Cannouan. If heading south from Mustique, this is a possible place to anchor for a night in settled conditions. One can anchor in the lee of this island, or between the islands with one anchor on the windward of the two and a second anchor on the reef to leeward. The current runs strongly there, which no doubt accounts for the excellent fishing. Without the fishing, I suspect that this little pile of rocks known as Savan Island would be totally uninhabited. The people charge visitors for the right to camp or fish. If it is blowing hard, passing from north to south makes a rather spectacular sail between the islands. Be sure to have your camera ready on the starboard side as you emerge from the channel. You will see a massive stone arch which the tides have formed.

Petit Mustique
(BA 2872, NO 25042)

A small, steep island south of Mustique with no anchorages and of little interest. It is not visited by yachtsmen so far as I know.

Mustique
(BA 2872, NO 25042, Sketch Chart 64)

This has always been a favorite of mine, but the times they are a-changing. Out to windward of the rest of the islands, it was seldom visited by the charter yachts. For many years the island was owned by the Hazel family of St. Vincent. The first time I visited the island there was a small fishermen's camp on the northwest beach and a small community of farmers barely scratching out an existence. The island is now in the hands of new owners who have imported farming equipment, increased the tillable acreage, and built new houses and roads; in short, they have done much to raise the standard of living. The island is now being developed as a resort for

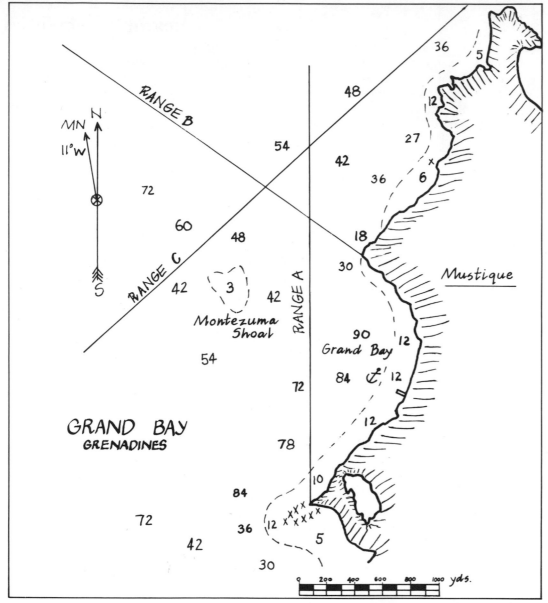

Range A: Southwestern point of Mustique in line with the southeastern corner of Petit Mustique clears Montezuma Shoal to the eastward, 010-190 magnetic.

Range B: Rocks at north end of Grand Bay bearing 135-315 magnetic passes clear to the northeast of Montezuma Shoal.

Range C: Westernmost of the Pillories in line with the northern mountain on Baliceau passes clear to west of Montezuma Shoal, 230-050 magnetic.

SKETCH CHART 64

the very wealthy from Europe. **Princess Margaret** and **Lord Snowdon** are among those building houses here. The old cotton warehouse has been converted to a hotel which I consider one of the most attractive buildings in the Lesser Antilles. The hotel is a good one, though quite expensive. Generators, when they are working, supply electricity to the whole island. A landing strip has been built to accommodate the vagaries of LIAT and the assorted charter and private flights. There is an active nightlife in the club that has been built near the dock. There are two sets of ruins on Mustique, one at the north end and one on top of the hill in the middle. From the top of this hill there is a beautiful view from where an old plantation house stood. Basic supplies can be had from the grocery store. Ice is available, but fuel and water are not, at the present time. "Mustique" takes its name from the French mosquito. Although a valiant effort has been made to eliminate this pest, my advice is to get off the beach before sundown.

Mustique should be cautiously approached. The off-lying Montezuma Shoal has done in any number of ships, more recently the *Lord Jim,* which might easily have become a total loss had a tug not hauled her off. The shoal bears 309 magnetic from the dock at Grand Bay. If you are beating up from Bequia against the easterly trade, under no circumstances should you fall eastward of range C on Sketch Chart 64 until you have passed clearly north of range B, which bears 135 magnetic on the rocks at the north end of Grand Bay. Staying northeast of range B, stand in toward shore until east of range A, before working down into Grand Bay.

The best anchorage in Grand Bay is off the new dock. Feel your way in and anchor where the depth suits you. The current here is not particularly strong. It comes and goes at intervals, and frequently during the night you will find yourself rolling for a few hours as the current swings your beam onto the wind, but I have never found it too uncomfortable. The bay is normally deserted here except when there is a British holiday or on Sundays when small boats come over from Bequia loaded with day-trippers. Often in the evening the fishermen come down from Cheltenham to set their nets in the northeast corner of the harbor, so don't anchor there, as they dislike having their fishing disturbed by yachts at anchor. Since they are making a living from the sea, and we are just playing, give them a break. It is magnificent to watch a pair of these big double-enders coming around the point, bending their oars in perfect unison and staging a brief racing sprint for the benefit of the visitors from up north.

If fishing interests you, it will be worth a trip up to Cheltenham. The fishermen store their gear in a few crude sheds that line the shore. In the afternoon they can be found sitting on their sea lockers in the shade of a sail rigged as a tent, playing cards, repairing gear and corning (salting) fish. They are quiet and shy, but if you talk to them for a while, they will loosen up a bit and soon be telling you stories of chasing whales or pilot fish or of the one that got away. Cheltenham itself is not a good anchorage as it is small and exposed to the swell.

Besides Montezuma Shoal which I have mentioned and which is difficult to spot even on a clear day, there is a second hazard at Mustique which must be reckoned with. This is the shoal at the south end of Grand Bay, which extends much farther to the southwest than the chart shows. This shoal is growing continually and must be given a wide berth.

Baliceaux
(BA 2872, NO 25042, Sketch Chart 65)

A small island one-and-a-half miles long and a quarter-mile wide, north-northeast from Mustique. This high, rugged, seldom-visited island is inhabited by transients. No one lives here permanently, but there is a continual influx of fishermen who camp on the beach for weeks or months at a time. There is an anchorage in the cove on the southwestern corner of the island. With the ground swell running this is a totally impossible anchorage; the surf breaks so heavily onshore that even the fishermen cannot launch their boats. But during the spring and summer, this can be a great spot.

As you approach from the south, feel your way up favoring the eastern shore. The reef on the western side is extremely difficult to spot. There is only room enough for one or two boats, so if it is crowded here when you arrive, other anchorages can be had anywhere along the western side of the island, once you have skirted the reef. Once anchored, go ashore and enjoy the view from the top of the hill. The fishermen here are a hardy lot. Many come down from Bequia for the day only. They leave Paget on the southwestern coast of Bequia early in the morning in their 20-foot boats, beat eight miles out to Baliceaux, arriving before dawn, fish through the early morning and then reach over to St. Vincent to sell their catch. Late in the day they beat around the eastern end of Bequia and finish up with a final run down to Paget. This amounts to an 18- or 20-hour day; sailing, fishing, and rowing. It's small wonder that the Bequians are such a lean breed. I have the greatest respect for them.

Battowia
(BA 2872, NO 25042, Sketch Chart 65)

So far as I know, this, too, is seldom visited by yachtsmen. There is no harbor whatsoever. If the trades are not blowing too hard, an anchorage can be had west of the reefs extending to the west of Church Cay. A Bahamian moor will be required here, since the current runs strongly through the break between Battowia and Baliceaux. I am told by the fishermen that a landing by dinghy can be made in the cove on the southeast corner of the island. Here, in the past, small boats would land to drop off and pick up supplies. The island was a sugar island, the only reminder of which is a ruined smokestack at the head of the cove. This is the island where the British detained several thousand Carib tribesmen captured on St. Vincent in the 18th century. How they managed to cram so many on such a small island, let alone feed them, is beyond me. In any event they were ultimately shipped out to Honduras, where their descendants may be found today. Now Battowia is uninhabited, but it remains a delightful place to visit when the weather permits.

Pigeon Island
(BA 2872, NO 25042)

Southwest of Bequia, little more than a rock sticking out of the water with no harbor, no beach—and no reason to stop.

Isle Quatre
(BA 2872, NO 25042)

Pretty to look at, but one must be something of a mountain goat to appreciate it. The only anchorage is below the house on the northwestern shore in three fathoms of water. The house is perched on a ridge 400 feet above the sea and facing directly into the trades. It must have one of the best views in the entire Caribbean. There is no chance whatever of anchoring in any of the coves on the windward side, although there looks to be great snorkeling there.

Petit Nevis
(BA 2872, NO 25042)

The island where the whales caught by the Bequians are brought to be butchered. Whale bones are strewn along the shore. Most of the

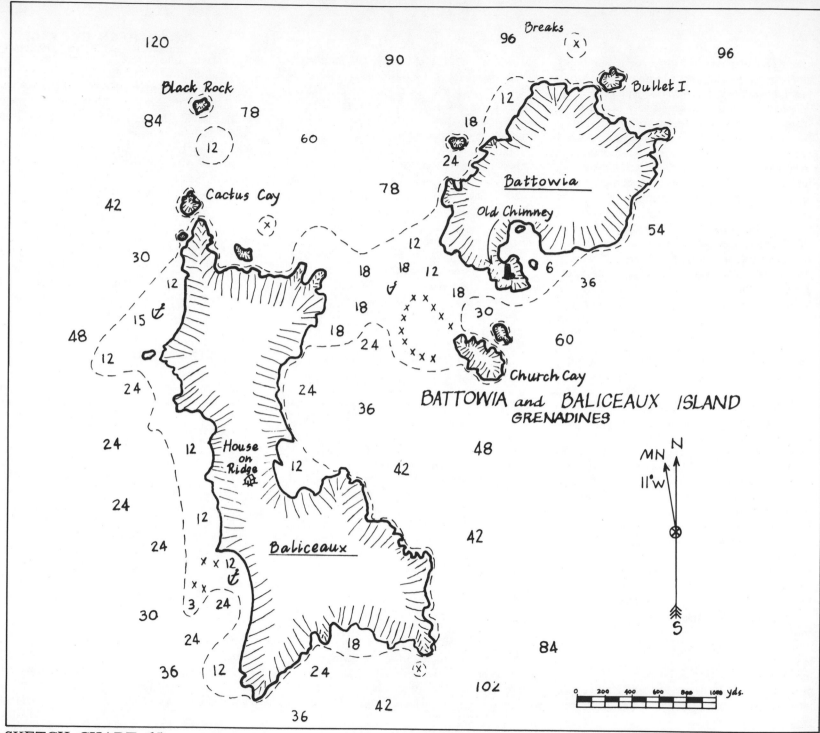

120

Breaks

96

90

96

Black Rock

84   78

Bullet I.

12

Battowia

18

24

60

78

54

Old Chimney

42

Cactus Cay

30

12

12

6

36

18   18   12

12

18

18

30

15

60

48

18

24

12

24

Church Cay

24

24

36

BATTOWIA and BALICEAUX ISLAND
GRENADINES

24

House
on
Ridge

12

12

48

42

24

42

24

12

N

MN

42

11°W

Baliceaux

x x 12

x x

30   3   24

24

84

36   12

18

102

24

42

84

36   42

SKETCH CHART 65

time you will find the island deserted, unless there is a butchering operation going on or during weekends and holidays when the people of Bequia come across to let the good times roll. There is a good anchorage off the western shore of Petit Nevis, but the bottom falls off so steeply here that you must nearly set your bow ashore before dropping anchor. When the anchor's down, feed out plenty of scope. It is always calm here when it's windy. You can walk over to the windward side where the beach varies from white sand to loose gravel, depending on the storms that year. This is an excellent picnic spot and no matter the condition of the beach, it is always cool with the trades blowing through the palm trees. Nevis, unfortunately, is now in the midst of real estate development; exactly what will happen in the next few years, my crystal ball doesn't show.

Bequia

The island of Bequia has been celebrated by sailors for hundreds of years. I have read glowing first-person accounts of Admiralty Bay by officers of the Royal Navy during the Napoleonic Wars. Esteemed by legend and heralded by song, it has always been a fine place to careen a ship, muster a crew, or replenish stores. There is a good deal of Yankee blood in the people of Bequia, harking back to the New Bedford whalers who took wives and settled here. In Paget on the western tip of the island are the descendants of the early French settlers, a group that has remained remarkably separate from the rest of the island.

Bequia is the last refuge of the sailing-fisherman. Even now, the sail-fishermen outnumber the motor-fishermen by a large number. An attitude still prevails there that a motor is an auxiliary to the sail. When the fishermen gather for the sailing races on the major holidays, the level of the competition is as high as you will find anywhere. These people think nothing of sailing down to Grenada in a 17-foot open boat.

Admiralty Bay
(BA 501; NO 25042, 25044;
Sketch Chart 66)

A beautiful anchorage and excellent in all weathers. It is the major anchorage and the port of entry for Bequia, and is easily entered in daylight, although one should be wary of Wash Rock off Devil's Table. Give Devil's Table a good 150-yard berth. Once around Fort Point, a course can be laid for the church in Elizabeth Town (106 magnetic), providing you draw less than nine feet. If you are tacking in, care must be taken to avoid Belmont Shoals, which is foul ground and full of coral heads. If you are approaching from the west, a clear course can be set from West End directly to the town dock.

The best anchorage can be had due west of the church. There is deep water quite close to shore so allow plenty of scope. The hard, sand bottom is excellent holding. It may take a moment or two to set, but once it has, you won't budge. Do not anchor south of the line of boats extending southwest from the church, as these are moored right on the edge of the shoal. Admiralty Bay is a popular spot, and there may be as many as 30 boats anchored within. As always, space is on a first-come basis, which may require anchoring well offshore, leaving you a long row into town. A way of avoiding this problem is to sail right up to shore just north of the church. The bottom drops off so steeply here that it is possible to lie close in, with a stern anchor holding you off and the bow anchor run up and buried on the beach. This arrangement, however, has at least one liability. There is a large, bronze bell in front of the church. Now, I don't mind a bell for calling the faithful, but when every village drunk takes to clanging it at all odd hours of the morning, this is too much. On one Whitsunday Weekend, I counted 103 rings over one night and early morning. The next time I hit Admiralty Bay, I'll be packing a hacksaw!

Anchored in Admiralty Bay, you may notice many boys chasing model yachts through the water to and fro across the harbor. Model boat racing has been a pastime here since time immemorial. The kids used to make models of the local schooners; now they make them of the charter boats that frequent the area. A feature of the big holiday weekends is the racing of these models. Each model is attended by its young owner swimming furiously to keep up with it, as the rules provide for one person to adjust sails, rigging, or direction. If some are not strong enough to keep up with the boat, they follow in a dinghy, diving in to make adjustments whenever necessary. Without the aid of self-steering gear, these model yachts manage to hold a true course and stand up well to the breeze.

These models are to my mind the best souvenirs that can be brought back from the Caribbean. And it is interesting to note that only in Bequia do the children have the skill and interest to build model yachts that can really perform. No wonder they grow up such fine seamen.

A good time will be had by all in Admiralty Bay. Visit the Sunny Caribee, whose broad terraces and shaded bar are just a short walk down the beach. The Frangipani Hotel is also on the beach. It is run by Son Mitchell, who is presently the Premier of St. Vincent. The Crab Hole Boutique is something of an institution on the island and is worth a good browsing. The Whalebone Bar and Restaurant is a favorite of many. In the winter of 1973 the island's first nightclub opened. I'm sure others will have followed.

Beyond the southernmost of the great shade trees along the beach you will find the

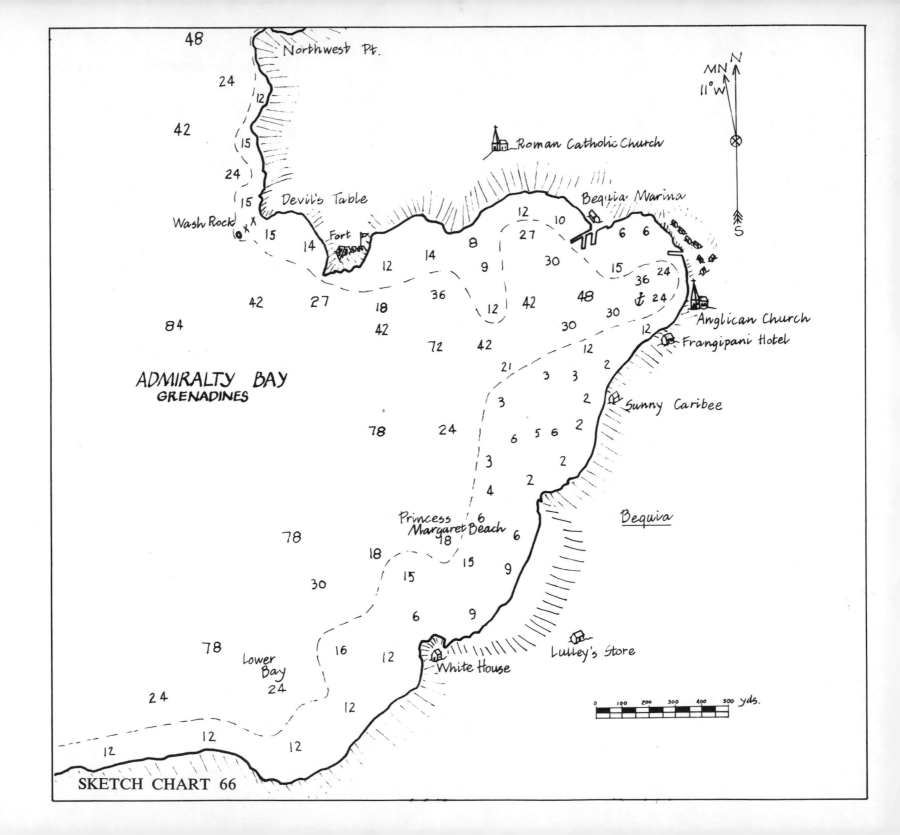

SKETCH CHART 66

Estella Frederick Bakery. Her ovens consist of nothing more than a couple of 55-gallon drums stoked with firewood and coconut shells, but they manage to turn out the most delicious bread. Each loaf has a strand of palm leaf down its center. Maybe this is their secret. I like to drop by in the late morning and persuade Estella to sell me a loaf of hot bread despite her protestations that too much is "bad for de tommy." Combined with a little cheese, bread, and honey, and a bottle of white wine, it can be mighty "good for de spirit." Right next door to Estella is the Lincoln Simmonds Sail Loft. Simmonds has been repairing sails and awnings, splicing rigging, and generally bailing visiting yachtsmen out of trouble for as long as anyone can remember. What he can't do himself, he can tell you who can. Just below his loft is a small machine shop run by Ken Walker. On the north side of the harbor and labeled "Marina" on the Sketch Chart is the Bequia Slipway—a misnomer as after six years in business there was still no slipway. Ice, water, and fuel can be purchased here at expensive prices.

There are three good beaches here, the one in front of town and two on the south side of the harbor. The easternmost is now called Princess Margaret (formerly Tony Gibbon Beach), the western one is called Lower Bay. Both beaches are beautiful and frequently deserted. At the western end of Princess Margaret Beach is a cave through the rock which leads to another small beach about 20 feet wide with overhanging cliffs on all sides. Presumably this too was a favorite of Princess Margaret.

A path leads up the hill from the western end of Princess Margaret to a road above from where it is only a short walk to Ross Lulley's Store, where you will find the world's best bargains in spearfishing equipment, fishing gear, shackles, knives, and other oddments. There is a beautiful view here and the coldest beer in

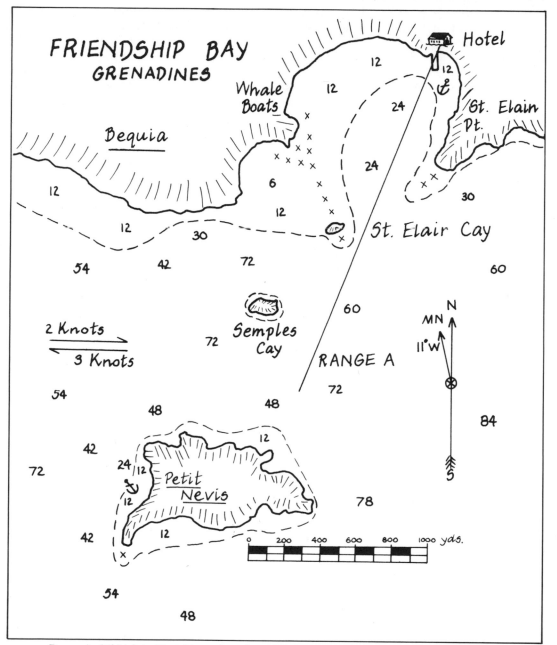

Range A: Midpoint of hotel brought to bear 030-210 magnetic leads into Friendship Bay.

SKETCH CHART 67

the island, kept in his kerosene deep-freeze. Unfortunately, I can't speak as highly of Ross's homemade wine.

For fresh food, seek out Sydney McIntosh, who runs a farm on the south side of the island. He can supply you with vegetables, eggs, chicken, fresh fruit, and other produce. He will also arrange barbecued dinners. Make your reservations in advance, as he has only the facilities to handle one or two boats at a time. His chicken farm is nearly the most efficient operation on the island, second only to a visiting dentist I once found pulling teeth, forceps in hand, under the large shade tree south of the church. His dental chair was an empty whiskey case; the anesthesia was a shot of rum. He pulled 55 teeth in one day.

Near the western tip of Bequia on the north side is Moon Hole. This is a cave which passes directly through the island, in which one Tom Johnson has built a house. There is an anchorage off Moon Hole in very deep water that is good for calm weather only. Johnson moved up there to get away from it all, but since an article in *National Geographic*, I believe he will have to unearth some other place to find his peace and solitude.

On the south side of the western end, there is an anchorage off Paget Farm. It is

usually calm here and undisturbed by the ground swell, but there is always a wind which tends to put you onshore. Care should be taken when anchoring in this bay.

On the west side of the northeastern point of Bequia is a cove seldom visited by yachtsmen, L'Anse Chemin. With the wind east of southeast this anchorage is a calm one. It is three fathoms close to shore. There is good snorkeling and ashore are the ruins of an old sugar plantation.

Friendship Bay
(BA 791, NO 25042, Sketch Chart 67)

Well worth a visit by boat or taxi from Elizabeth Town. It is easy to enter: merely stay in the middle of the entrance to the harbor, steering 015 magnetic for Friendship Bay Hotel flag pole. Anchor in the eastern corner of the harbor where there is the best protection from the ground swell. This is a smooth anchorage for the most part, though it is prone to some turbulent periods. The dock at the Friendship Bay Hotel is for dinghies only. The beach bar is to the west of it. There is good snorkeling on the reef out front. The hotel discourages spearfishing. A long, white-sand beach extends from the hotel west to the settlement at Friendship. The beach is lined with the pretty man-

chineel trees whose apple-looking fruit is deadly poisonous.

At the western end of the beach are the whale boats. These are big, heavy boats, weighing as much as a ton each, but to watch the Bequians in the early morning before dawn launch them swiftly from the shore and bring them back up in the evening is a sight to behold. It's a rough way to earn a living. They go out after the humpback whale, a variety which usually travels in pairs, so that when one is caught, the second can be caught also. Oftentimes, the charter boats will come racing down to watch the whaling boats after the first whale has been taken, making it very difficult to capture the second. The humpback is very fast and sharp of hearing. It is easily scared off, so it is best to stand off while the whalers conduct their business. Whaling in Bequia is the livelihood of an impoverished people and should be distinguished from the reckless plunder carried out every year by large nations. Only about half a dozen whales are caught out of Bequia in a good year for all their effort. The entire animal is used. The oil is sold to the States, the meat is eaten by the poor, and the bones are sold to the tourist as scrimshaw. What could be neater?

CHAPTER 23

Southern Grenadines

NO 25041, 25042; BA 2821, 2872

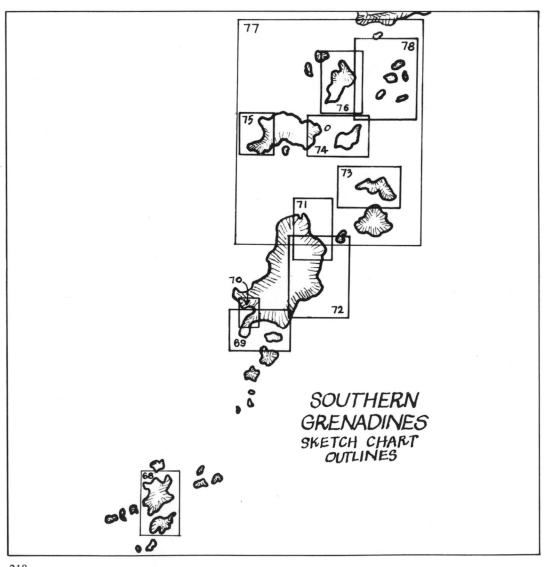

SOUTHERN
GRENADINES
SKETCH CHART
OUTLINES

Ile de Ronde
(BA 2821, NO 25041, Sketch Chart 68)

From Grenada north to Carriacou is 38 miles; if the current is running to leeward and the wind is in the north, this can be one of the longest beats you will encounter coming from the south. Many break the trip by stopping off at Ile de Ronde. The island is particularly vulnerable to a northwest ground swell, but in settled weather you couldn't find a better lunch spot. The fishermen keep their boats on the beach on the southwest shore. Here, if you sail in close and anchor on the edge of the shelf, you will find a passable anchorage. The tide runs swiftly and it is likely to be a bit rough, but the great attraction is a really beautiful beach. A path, marked on the Sketch Chart, leads past the lake (which is a pond in the dry season) to the beach and reef on the windward side. From this anchorage you can also visit Ile de Caille, the tiny island south of Ile de Ronde made famous by Fritz Fenger's *Alone in the Caribbean*. Whale Bay on Ile de Caille is only recommended for dinghy trips in calm weather.

Corn Store Bay is the westernmost bay of Ile de Ronde and perfectly adequate in settled weather. However, a ground swell can be enough to force your stern ashore. Two boats have been lost here in this way. If you elect to pass the night here, be certain to use a Bahamian moor. Feel your way in with the lead line and anchor off the little beach in three fathoms with the hut bearing northeast. The snorkeling is fairly good, and with any luck you should be able to spear a few pan fish for lunch. The cove on the north face of the island may be visited by dinghy. The swimming and snorkeling are good here, but I would not recommend taking the boat inside unless you were very adept at reef navigation and your boat drew no more than three feet. As it stands now, the reef does not afford enough protection from the sea; no doubt some enterprising developer will soon arrive on the scene to remedy this.

London Bridge
(BA 2821, NO 25041)

This small island is about one mile north of Green Island and noteworthy only for the hole that the sea has washed through it. It is a fascinating and picturesque rock formation, a good view to bolster your photo album.

Diamond Island (Kick 'Em Jenny)
(BA 2821, NO 25041)

The etymology of the variant is a mystery; it is probably some untraceable corruption of a French place name. There is no landing here at all. A strong current north of the island frequently sets up in a direction against the wind and kicks up quite a chop. It should also be noted that the shelf drops off steeply from 25 to well over 100 fathoms.

Les Tantes
(BA 2821, NO 25041)

To windward of Diamond Island and Ile de Ronde, Les Tantes are a series of uninhabited islands. A rough anchorage can be had off their western shore but I recommend it for the adventurous only. The swell and a stiff current are invariably a problem. Transient fishermen camp on these islands from time to time; otherwise they are deserted.

In sailing between Diamond Island and Carriacou, always hold well high of the course. Though it is only a six-mile run, it can get very rough at times. Flying over this area is a real eye-opener. Tide rips can be seen cropping up in every sort of unpredictable place. If it is possible, you should carry the dinghy on deck to avoid a swamping. If the current is setting you to windward, you will have no trouble laying the course, but it will be rough going. A set to leeward will give smoother water though some tacking will be required.

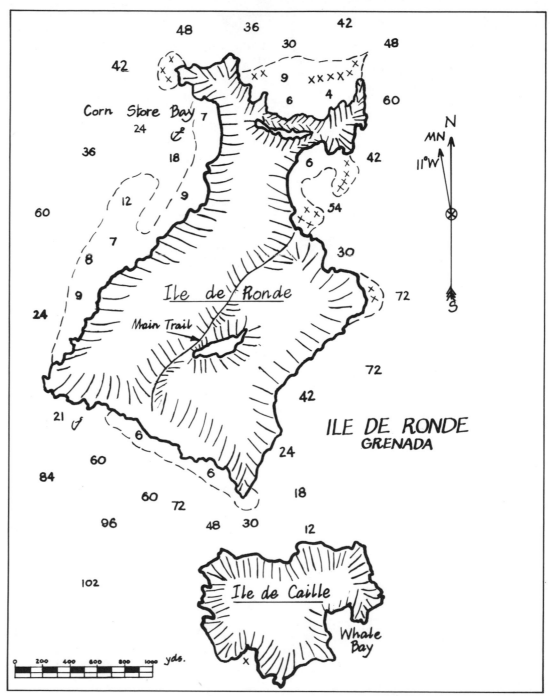

SKETCH CHART 68

SOUTHERN GRENADINES

The best time to set out from Ile de Ronde is at slack water before the tidal disadvantages make themselves felt.

Bonaparte Rocks
(BA 2872, NO 25042)

This is the small pile of rocks south of Large Island. I have never heard of anyone making a landing here, and I can't imagine anyone wanting to. The tide rips by them at four knots at times. They are best avoided.

Large Island
(BA 2872, NO 25042)

The chart shows an anchorage in the northwest corner of this island but the beach facing it is not particularly good. There is an abandoned estate ashore, but a strong current makes the approach difficult.

Frigate Island
(BA 2872, NO 25042)

One of two islands so named in the Grenadines, the other being south of Union Island. Here again, strong currents and narrow beaches make the island less inviting. Some have found it convenient to anchor off the western shore of Frigate. From here the dinghy can be taken around the northwestern tip and into the bay on the north. The bay is extremely shoal and should not be entered except by dinghy, the chart notwithstanding. There is good shelter on the southeast corner of the bay, but I cannot recommend this.

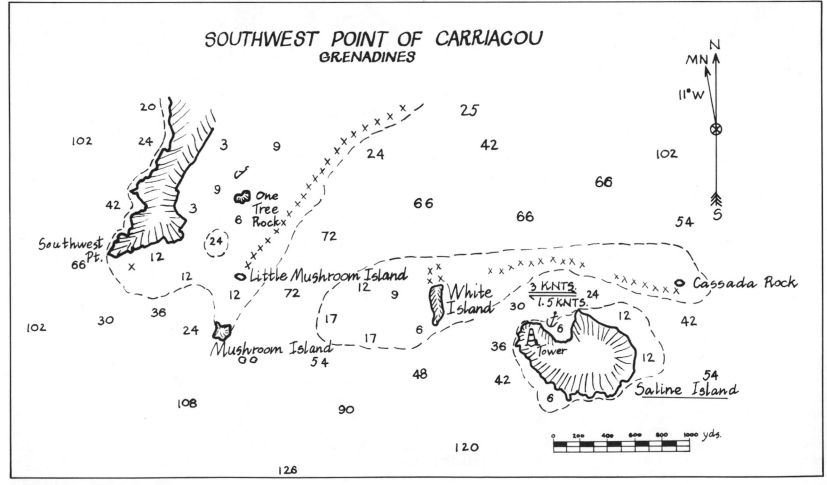

SKETCH CHART 69

Even a very shallow-draft boat (three feet maximum) would have a rough time of it.

Saline Island
(BA 2872, NO 25042, Sketch Chart 69)

Just south of Carriacou lies Saline Island, seldom visited by yachts and one of my favorite islands in the Caribbean. It is possible to anchor between Saline and the reef to the north, but the tide runs a solid three knots down this channel, requiring a heavy anchor and Bahamian moor. However, inside the cove on the north side of the island is a superb anchorage for shoal-draft boats. The southeastern portion of the bay is completely out of the tide. The shelf is one fathom, dropping off steeply at the northwest corner of the harbor near the old lime kiln. Deep water can be found by nosing right up to the shoal, dropping a bow anchor onto it and setting a stern anchor from the stern to hold you off. With the kiln bearing southwest, you will find yourself out of the tide in three fathoms of water. Exercise caution in making your approach, as the bottom shoals from two to one fathom within 30 feet. The western tip of the island drops off so steeply that you can dive from the beach straight down into the sea. The snorkeling on the southwest corner is as fine as anywhere in the Caribbean. Stay close to shore and make allowance for the tides; once caught by the current off Saline Island there is no swimming back to shore.

Carriacou

This is the most populated of the Grenadines. As one becomes acquainted with the island, one wonders how the inhabitants support themselves, much less maintain so many respectable homes. As it turns out, for many generations the sons of Carriacou have made their living by going to sea or to the oil fields of Venezuela and Aruba. They stay away for many years, sending home money to their families and eventually coming home themselves to marry in middle age and raise a family. An alternate source of income for many years used to be the smuggling trade, which was carried out with surprisingly little government interference. It was argued that as long as the government did not intervene, a sizable part of the population was kept off the public dole. Now the governments of Grenada and St. Vincent have their own patrol boats and the trade is rapidly dying out. In Tyrell Bay it used not to be a rare occurrence at night to hear a sloop working its way into the harbor with no running lights. It anchors silently close to shore; the headsails come down, and the main is left sheeted flat—the marine equivalent of the idling engine of a getaway car. You can hear the motors of unlit cars and the slapping of dinghies shuttling back and forth to shore. After 15 minutes or so, she brings in the anchor and off she sails around Cistern point to Hillsborough, there to be found the next morning, anchored docilely off town, legally entering a regular cargo.

One Tree Rock
(BA 2872, NO 25042, Sketch Chart 69)

If you are beating up to the windward side of Carriacou from the south, a good anchorage may be had inside the reef extending northeast from Mushroom Island. Enter to the west of Mushroom and anchor behind One Tree Rock. This is a wonderful spot. Approach Mushroom Island from the south, keeping Little Mushroom and One Tree Rock on the starboard hand; round up north of One Tree and anchor in one-and-a-half fathoms over white sand. The many coral heads to windward break the worst of the swell and are a good area for spearfishing. In one hour we took ten fish and three lobsters. The times I have stopped there have been during the summer in calm weather, but the Bequia fishermen tell me that even in winter it never gets too rough through here. The only problem they speak of is the winter swell which pours over the reef and pours out again through the south entrance, setting up a stiff current that could give a swimmer quite a scare. Incidentally, a boat drawing four or five feet of water can sail up inside the reef to Manchioneal Bay and get away from the heavy traffic.

Tyrell Bay (Harvey Vale)
(BA 2872, NO 25042, Sketch Chart 70)

This is the customary anchorage for boats coming to Carriacou from the south, and it is excellent in all weathers. Plenty of breeze and good holding over a white-sand bottom. The U.S. chart is incorrect: the shoal in the middle of the harbor marked one-and-a-half fathoms is actually shallower. *Iolaire* brushed it at seven-and-a-half feet, as have others with even less. The spot is easily seen in good light, and it is safe and advisable to steer north or south of it. The north side is probably the best route, but as you tack in along the north shore, watch out for the shoal in the corner of the harbor near the entrance to the Carenage. Similarly, if you tack in along the south shore, you must watch out for rocks 200 yards offshore below the cliff. If the rum shop at the head of the dock is brought to bear 075 magnetic, you will safely pass south of the middle shoal and north of the rocks. If you must enter at night, which I don't advise, the rum shop is usually lit by a kerosene lamp until late. Most nights the open-air theatre south of the rum shop is easily spotted. If this is brought to bear 065 magnetic, you will also pass clear. The best anchorage is off the dock or south of it. Do not go further inshore than the end of the dock or you will run aground.

An interesting diversion is to sail a dinghy into the Carenage, where the old, wrecked

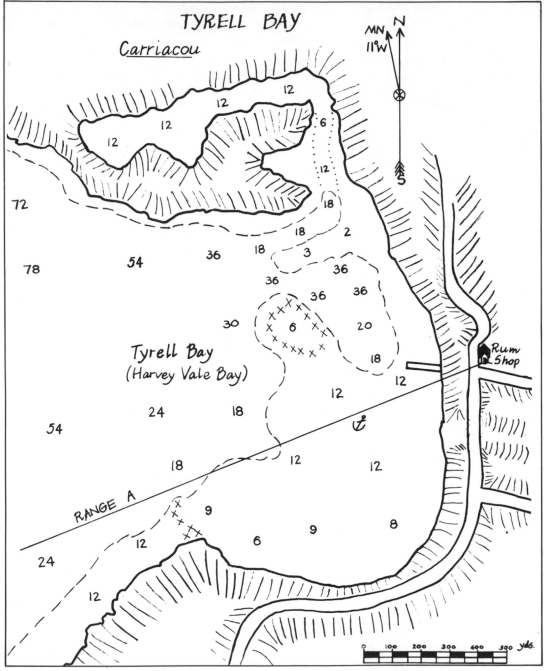

TYRELL BAY
Carriacou

MN
11°W
N

12
12
12
12
12
6
12
72
18
18
2
18
18
3
54
36
36
78
36
36
36
36
20
30
6

Tyrell Bay
(Harvey Vale Bay)

18
12
12
24
18
12
12
12
8
54
18
9
9
RANGE A
9
12
24
6
12

Rum Shop

0 100 200 300 400 500 yds.

Range A: Rum Shop at head of dock brought to bear 075-255 magnetic leads into Tyrell Bay south of the middle ground and north of the rocks below the cliff.

SKETCH CHART 70

schooners lie. You can tie up among the mangroves and fish in total quiet and solitude. The mangroves are alive with birds who will flit close around you. As this is written it is possible to carry seven feet into the Carenage, but I would make a point of checking with local yachtsmen before you enter.

L'Esterre Bay
(BA 2872, NO 25042)

Lies south of Sandy Island, southwest of Hillsborough. It is shallow and the wind tends to sweep in from the north. All but the shallowest draft boats must anchor far from shore. I can recommend it for daytime use only.

Sandy Island
(BA 2872, NO 25042)

The island is owned and protected from development by the government of Carriacou. The people of Hillsborough frequent the island on weekends and holidays. Charter boats often anchor off its southwestern corner, their parties going ashore for lunch and snorkeling. Spearfishing is prohibited. This is a good and justifiably popular daytime anchorage.

Hillsborough
(BA 2872, NO 25042)

The principal town on Carriacou. The inter-island schooners can be seen off-loading cargo from a dock at the eastern end of town. Customs and Immigration and the Post Office are at the head of the dock and, after hours, at the police station. Basic supplies can be purchased in Hillsborough, but this is not the best place to provision a boat for an entire cruise. The Mermaid Tavern is owned by a friendly American couple, Tom and Betsy Vickery. Tom is most helpful to visiting yachtsmen. He will relay messages over his radio between 0800-0900 and 1500-1600. During the winter the hotel is fairly full and dinner reservations should be made ahead of time. Over the radio is the easiest way.

The first weekend in August, known as August Monday, is one of the big weekends of the year in Carriacou. The workboat race in Hillsborough and a yacht feeder-race from Grenada flood the island with people. A good chartering idea is to take a boat in late July through the Grenadines, timing your arrival in Hillsborough for August Monday. The spectacle of some 40 Grenadine workboats vying for cash prizes is really stunning.

The anchorage in Hillsborough tends to be rolly; in the winter it can get all but impossible. The usual anchorage west of the dock is not the best. Northeast of the dock is far better. Work your way as far northeast as your draft will permit and anchor tucked in behind the east point. Boats drawing seven feet will have to anchor outside the shoal off the small hotel. Those drawing six feet or less can sneak in behind the shoal and anchor close to shore. The channel leading into the basin east of the shoal is best approached from the north—an eyeball proposition. The sand bottom is good holding in front of the hotel.

Wherever you anchor, care must be taken in the event of the wind swinging around from the north. At such times the south shore of the harbor becomes a dead lee. I came damn close to losing my boat along this shore when my anchor engaged in a ham tin on the bottom and dragged. Somehow it was fouled in such a way that I couldn't haul it back aboard. I had to cut the rode and sail out after banging once on the shoal. I recovered the anchor later with the fluke stuck through the ham tin, which kept it from burying to its normal depth.

A taxi can be hired in Hillsborough for a drive around the island. The view from the windward side is quite impressive. The roads are really first rate and well above the norm

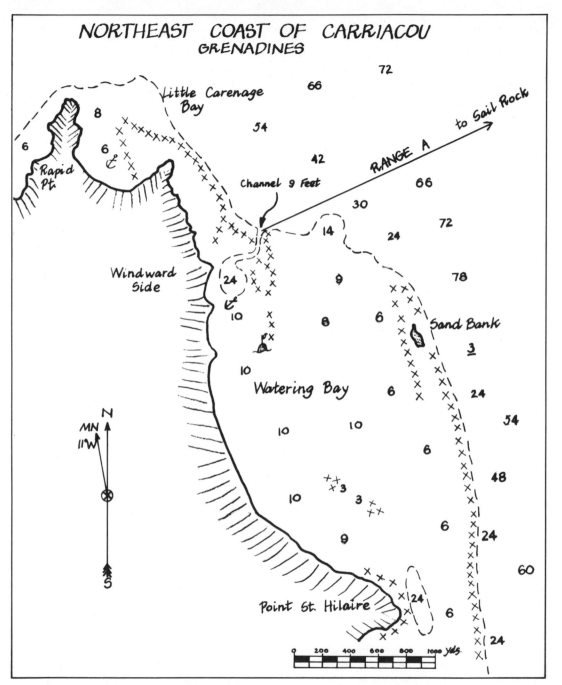

Range A: Sail Rock three fingers open to the northwest of Petit St. Vincent leads to channel into "Windward Side," Carriacou.

SKETCH CHART 71

for this part of the world. They date back to the days when the British and the French were squaring off for control of the Islands. The British controlled the seas around Carriacou and the French the land. The French built roads to give their ground forces mobility against the British fleet wherever it tried to land. If the British fleet, thwarted at one landing, decided to haul up and sail down to the next inlet, the French would simply hitch up their cannon and follow them overland. So it went for many years, while an elaborate set of roadways sprang up crisscrossing the island.

The coast of Carriacou north of Hillsborough provides no overnight anchorages. There are only one or two places where you might put in for lunch and a swim. There are some spectacular beaches along this shore. Standing north from Hillsborough, hug the shore until past the three-quarter-fathom spot between Craigston Point and Jack a Dan. Placing the hill on Frigate Island in line with the 290-foot hill beyond it on Union—the first hill west of Pinnacle hill—will carry you safe inside Jack a Dan (Range D, Sketch Chart 5, page 43).

Little Carenage Bay
(BA 2872, NO 25042, Sketch Chart 71)

Due east of Rapid Point is a cove called Little Carenage Bay where there is an anchorage for shoal-draft boats behind the reef, and a good beach. It is best suited for multihulls, centerboarders, or shoal-draft motorsailers.

Watering and Grand Bays
(BA 2872, NO 25042, Sketch Chart 71, 72)

On the east coast of Carriacou, locally called Windward Side, is Watering Bay. The entrance to the bay is slightly intricate and should be made when the sun is right overhead. If you are lucky, you can follow one of

the local sloops which frequent the area. When coming from the north, proceed until Sail Rock is three fingers open on the northwest corner of Petit St. Vincent. (West Indians say two fingers but their hands are bigger.) Then turn west on this range, 248 magnetic, until Fota joins Little Martinique. When these two join, the man in the rigging will have to con you into the channel, which first heads south, then west, into the basin—generally nine feet of water. You can, if you choose, head south, leaving the stone daymarker to port, and sail through Watering and Grand Bays, making an exit through the pass at Kendeace Point (Sketch Chart 72). The best water is near shore, but you will have to eyeball it for yourself. On the chart there appears to be a break in the reef off Jew Bay, but I have tried twice to enter through here with no success. If entering at Kendeace Point, proceed carefully with a man aloft, and you should have no problem. The channel is narrow, deep, and easily spotted by the breakers on the reef to windward. Because the wind and current will be setting you to leeward, hold high and stay as close to the weather side of the channel as the color of the water will permit. Inside it is calm and secluded. You can sail in a rail-down breeze against no more than a light chop. Anchor close to the reef and stay there for days undisturbed by traffic of any sort.

Island Dependencies of Carriacou

Little Tobago and Fota
(BA 2872, NO 25042)

No anchorage and little of interest except to the geologist. The same holds true of Fota, another hunk of uninhabited rock, except that in calm weather there is a tolerable anchorage off its lee shore. They do provide a number of helpful ranges, which are drawn on Sketch Charts 5 and 6 in Chapter 5.

Little Martinique
(BA 2872, NO 25042)

If you visit this dry, windswept island, you will notice rows of houses like the wooden salt-box houses of Nantucket. Back in the old days the locals must have learned house building from the New England whaler crews. High in the hills on the northern tip of the island is the Catholic Church, where the view is stupendous.

The islanders make a living by going to sea for legitimate trade or illicit smuggling. At times, the Customs inspector comes over from Carriacou but his visits are always well-advertised and the people have time to put their island in order. I suspect that if the government chose seriously to crack down, Little Martinique would soon be uninhabited. Basically the people of Little Martinique are hardworking, honest men.

A good daytime anchorage can be had, so long as the swell is down, due west of a small jetty at the northwest corner of the island. From here to Petit St. Vincent is a short hop, but watch out for the shoal marked one-and-a-half fathoms between the two islands. I sailed across it in *Iolaire* some years ago heeled over and drawing no more than six feet, and I touched repeatedly. I advise sailing around this spot altogether.

Island Dependencies of Union

Petit St. Vincent
(BA 2872, NO 25042, Sketch Chart 73)

The island is commonly referred to as "PSV." It was formerly a beautiful deserted island, but I am not particularly surprised that it has been built up. It is an attractive land with good anchorages and beaches. The hotel on PSV is spectacular in every respect, right down to the bill that will be tendered you at the end of your stay. Lunch or dinner reservations can be made by radio over 2527.

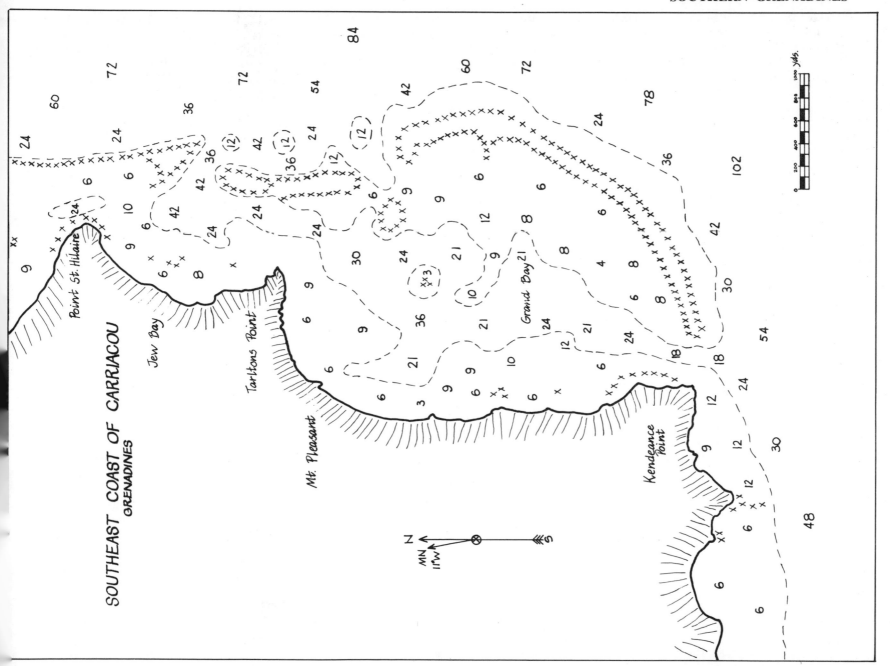

SOUTHEAST COAST OF CARRIACOU
GRENADINES

Point St. Hilaire

Jew Bay

Tarltons Point

Mt. Pleasant

Grand Bay

Kendeance Point

SKETCH CHART 72

SOUTHERN GRENADINES

Ice and fuel are available on the island; water is hard to come by, though you could probably get some in a real emergency. PSV is part of St. Vincent. If you are going there from Little Martinique or Carriacou, you must first clear through Clifton Harbor, Union. Considering the growing number of yachts visiting the area, I would not be surprised if PSV were some day made a port of entry. In the meantime, the customs regulations are strictly enforced: do not stop at Palm (Prune) or PSV before entering Union, no matter what the time of day. A number of boats have been arrested at dusk in PSV and made to return to Union to clear and to pay a fine.

The shoreline is a string of beaches, separated one from another by intermittent outcroppings of rock. It is possible to walk around the island by wading through the shallows around the rocky points, but I would suggest wearing a pair of sneakers unless your feet are more leathery than most. The shelling on the rocks is unusually abundant; diving expeditions can be made to the reefs windward of the island; small boats can be rented from the hotel.

The normal anchorage is off the south coast. The larger boats favor a location due south or slightly east of due south of the highest peak on the western end of the island. Smaller boats can tack farther east between the reef and the island, ending up at anchor south of the saddle formed by the two hills. The bottom is hard sand and good holding. The current reverses along here so I would recommend a Bahamian moor, especially when the anchorage becomes crowded. Since the completion of the new dock, the shoals along the shore have been growing and shifting—proceed with caution. When leaving the anchorage, boats drawing eight feet or less can pass to windward of the shoal, before turning to the south and west. This is sometimes an easier way out than threading downwind

through a crowded anchorage. The chart shows a ragged sort of channel through the reef between PSV and Little Martinique. Some of the work sloops sail this channel going downwind. Upwind it is just too narrow. And either way, you would have to be one hell of a seaman to make it through. I would strongly urge newcomers not to use this channel. An error could prove fatal. The first time I saw a boat in this channel with seas breaking all around, I thought I was watching the preliminary maneuvers of an elaborate suicide.

Some boats in search of privacy anchor north of the island or else work their way along the south coast through the reef to an anchorage east of the island. Both possibilities are indicated on the Sketch Chart.

Pinese
(BA 2872, NO 25042, Sketch Chart 73)

This is the westernmost of two sand cays off Little St. Vincent. The other one is Mopion, meaning Crab Louse. The translation of Pinese is Bed Bug, and perhaps both are distant relatives of Las Cucarachas (the cockroaches) off the northeast tip of Puerto Rico. When passing to leeward of Mopion, be careful of the shoal, since the island is continually extending to the south and southwest farther than is shown on the chart. Many yachts have struck this shoal, as many a Lloyd's underwriter will attest. There is a channel east of Mopion, known among experienced Island yachtsmen as Crazy Corrigan's Crooked Channel, named after Dave Corrigan of Mariner's Inn, St. Vincent. It is perfectly safe for the experienced reef pilot, but there are no ranges whatsoever. I will give the general gist of the directions heading southeast, but you will have to eyeball it for yourself. Head a little bit to windward of Mopion until you spot the break in the reef. Enter and head roughly southeast following the color of the deep water. As Mopion comes abeam, the channel

curves to the south, and, as you pass Mopion, it curves again to the southwest. Follow the channel around, and once clear in deep water, head for PSV. In the annual race between Tobago Cays and PSV, this channel saves about half a mile of windward work.

Union Island
(BA 2872, NO 25042, Sketch Chart 74, 77)

As the Grenadines go, Union is fairly large. Its population is sparse, with only two small villages at Clifton and Ashton. It is easily spotted from a distance by rock pinnacles that bristle the sky like large spikes. The island is three miles long and two miles across at its broadest. A less than super "supermarket" has been built in recent years, and a beautful hotel has sprung up on the northeast corner of Clifton Harbor. A large dock at Clifton serves the boats that come over from Martinique to pick up lobsters from the pens ashore. (The pens, teeming with lobsters and turtles, are an interesting attraction.) East of the hotel is a large slipway, which is bound to draw more and more yachtsmen to the island as years go by. I suspect that like the Beef Island Slipway in Tortola, this one will be hamstrung by the dearth of materials and supplies on the island.

The entrance to Clifton Harbor will be confusing to the newcomer. The chart is inaccurate in several respects. The best approach by day is to head in until you spot the outer reef. If you wish to moor near town, leave to starboard the big concrete pillar with a light on it. Sail on in and anchor anywhere in the middle of the harbor. The holding is good but the water is very deep, 35 to 40 feet, as opposed to the four fathoms marked on the chart. The American chart shows a solid reef extending from the stone pillar all the way to the shoreline. In fact, this is a middle ground, and it is feasible to sail to windward between this ground and the point forming the northeast corner of the harbor, so as to anchor directly behind the outer reef. My favorite anchorage is directly downwind of the little reef island known as Green Island. I normally sail in behind the outer reef, douse sail, and round up, backing the mizzen to keep me off the ground. (Keep the engine running so that you can back down.) Drop the anchor in shallow water close aboard the reef. The holding ground is excellent and you can swim directly from the boat without having to break out the dinghy to shuttle swimmers back and forth.

At night the channel into Clifton is marked by a white flasher, but this is not always operational. Two kerosene lamps—the red light on the Customs Dock placed under a white range light on the hill—define a range of 159-339 magnetic (Range A, Sketch Chart 74). Whether these lights will be lit is another story altogether.

Ashton, west of Clifton and the main town, has no harbor for boats carrying more than three feet. A path leads up from Ashton or Clifton to The Pinnacle, the highest peak on Union. Coming from Clifton, according to John Clegg, the best approach to the peak is from the east, heading for the smaller pinnacle

northeast of the main one. From the small one to the summit of the large there are two or three routes and which one is more convenient depends upon where the century plants have been growing that year. None should present any problem, but beware the Jack Spaniard wasp. He won't kill you, but he gives one hell of a nasty sting. He looks like the North American wasp, only a mite larger.

Frigate Island
(BA 2872, NO 25042)

This is the small island just off Union,

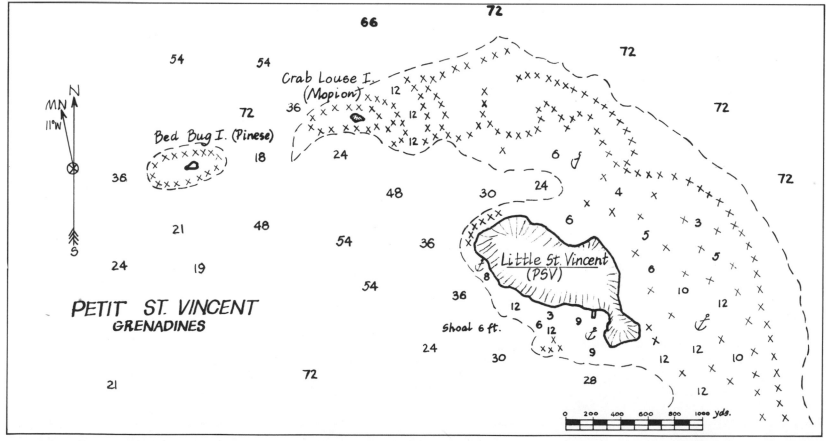

SKETCH CHART 73

and behind it there is a good anchorage, indeed. Deep water extends much farther north than the chart indicates. I normally anchor with the high hill on Frigate bearing approximately southeast. It is always sheltered and cool here. There may be some chop, but this is more than made up for by the total seclusion. It is pleasant in the evening to lie back and watch the frigate birds circling lazily around the peak towering above you. The harbor behind the reef is a perfect place for dinghy sailing. The water is shallow and the wind is always good. If the kids capsize they can stand in the shallows and right the boat.

Chatham Bay
(BA 2872, NO 25042, Sketch Chart 75)

The other good anchorage of Union Island, Chatham was uninhabited until some years ago an individual in search of privacy built a small cottage. He is seldom visited by anyone except a few of the local fishermen. Inside Chatham Bay, hard gusts have a tendency to blow out of the hills with surprising force. They are not dangerous in themselves, but they may lead you to believe that it is howling outside. Boats have hung back timor-

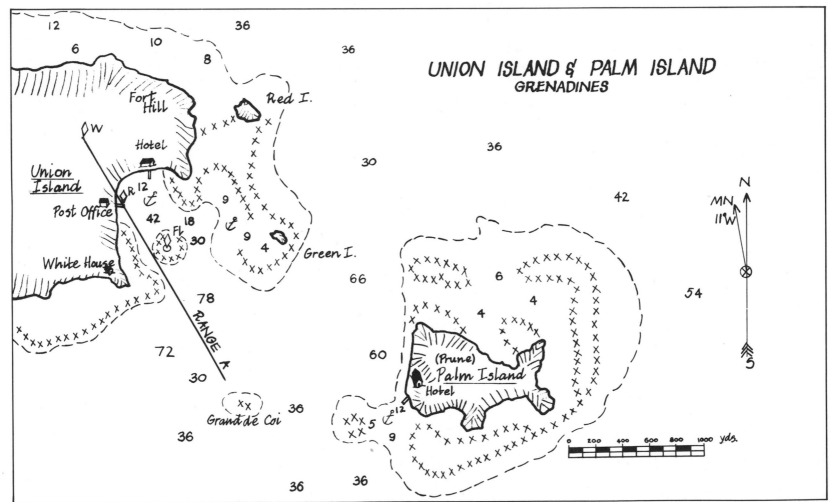

Range A: Leading lights, if working, in line lead into Clifton Harbor, 159-339 magnetic.

SKETCH CHART 74

ously in the harbor for days on end expecting raging gales outside. Finally venturing out, they have found it blowing no more than ten or 15 knots. Don't be deceived. From here you can travel to the northeast tip of the island, where the reef diving and spearfishing is of the very best. Yachts seldom anchor in the area, but it is good nonetheless. The best place is in the northeast corner in two fathoms. The southeast corner is shoal and exposed to the wind.

Palm Island
(BA 2872, NO 25042, Sketch Chart 74)

Formerly called Prune Island, Palm Island is under a long-term lease to John Caldwell. In American folklore, Johnny Appleseed planted apple trees from coast to coast. Here in the islands it is Coconut John who has planted palm trees throughout the Caribbean. For this reason Prune Island was renamed when John took over. Caldwell has had an interesting career. He was married in Australia during World War II. When the war ended, he found himself in Panama with no means of returning to his wife in Australia. Though he was not a sailor, he bought a small sail boat and, with more guts than brains, set out for Australia. He got as far as Fiji before wrecking and damn near losing his life. The fiasco resulted in Caldwell's first literary effort, *Desperate Voyage*. He and his wife moved to San Francisco where he received a graduate degree in sociology, thereafter setting out in a gaff-rigged Tahiti ketch for Australia. The passage was successful and resulted in a second book, *Family at Sea*. He worked in Australia for several years before building his present boat, *Outward Bound*. With his family on board he sailed westward halfway around the world to the Caribbean. That was some 15 years ago, and he has been in the Islands ever since. He considers the lower Caribbean the best sailing in the world.

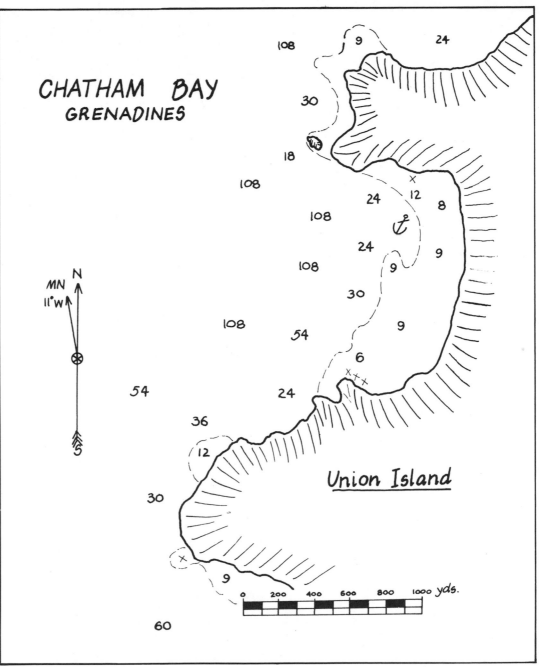

CHATHAM BAY
GRENADINES

Union Island

SKETCH CHART 75

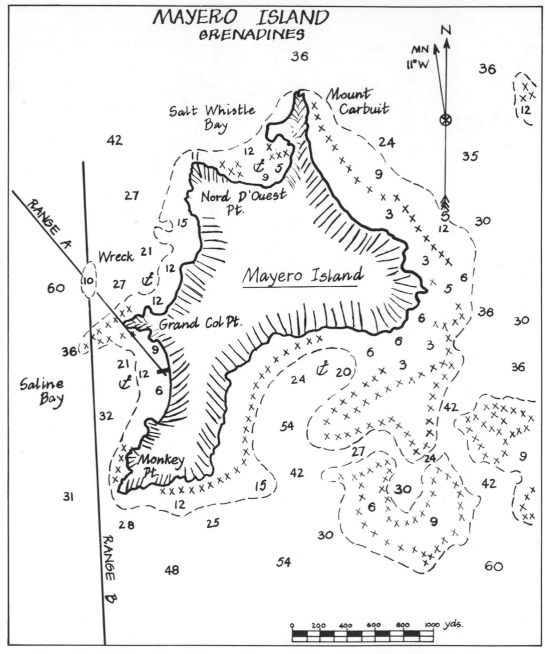

MAYERO ISLAND
GRENADINES

Mount Carbuit

Salt Whistle Bay

Nord D'Ouest Pt.

Mayero Island

Wreck

RANGE A

Saline Bay

Grand Col Pt.

Monkey Pt.

RANGE B

MN 11°W

N

Range A: Cliff of Grand Col Point in line with midpoint of Saline Bay Dock leads over wreck.
Range B: Peak of Petit Martinique over western low land of Palm leads over wreck.
Note: use ranges cautiously and only for finding wreck; otherwise you may become one yourself.

SKETCH CHART 76

The north shore of Palm is completely surrounded by reef. There is much less water inside the northeasternmost reef than is shown on the chart. You would need a shoal boat drawing less than four feet to penetrate safely inside. (Such a boat, in fact, could circumnavigate the island *inside* the reef.) The best anchorage is off the dock on the southwest corner of Palm. Watch out for the detached coral head 300 yards southwest of the southwest corner of the island. You can carry a full nine feet between the coral head and the main reef, but keep a sharp eye for the former. A Bahamian moor is usually recommended, since the current tends to swing around the corner and in the winter the boisterous trades will kick up a considerable chop. But the bottom is excellent holding; John Caldwell reports that the only boats to have dragged here were run by idiots who did not know enough to test the set of their anchors and had not allowed enough scope.

Caldwell has made a full-scale development of Palm, and it compares with the best. His radio standby is on 2527. LIAT flights land on the grass strip that he built himself. His two sons run a scuba operation; they can fill your tanks, rent you equipment, take you diving, or tell you where the best diving can be found. They may even be able to help you with minor engine repairs. Ice and some basic groceries are available. Lunch and dinners are served at the hotel.

Mayero Island
(BA 2872, NO 25042, Sketch Chart 76)

Three miles north of Union, Mayero's peaks should not be confused with those of Union, being only half as high. A few years ago the people of Mayero were living at a bare subsistence level. Today, the island appears much more prosperous; the old houses are being fixed up and painted, and some new ones built. (Tourism has certainly brought

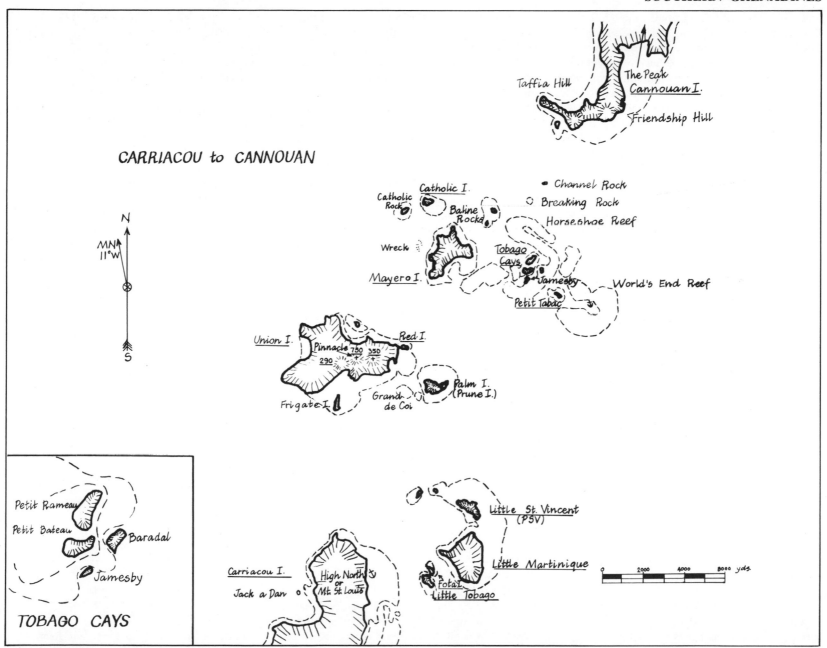

CARRIACOU to CANNOUAN

Taffia Hill
The Peak
Cannouan I.
Friendship Hill

N
MN
11°W
S

Catholic I.
Catholic Rock
Baline Rocks
• Channel Rock
○ Breaking Rock
Horse-shoe Reef
Wreck
Tobago Cays
Mayero I.
Jamesby
World's End Reef
Petit Tabac

Union I.
Pinnacle 750 350
290
Red I.
Palm I.
(Prune I.)
Frigate I.
Grand de Coi

Petit Rameau
Petit Bateau
Baradal
Jamesby
TOBAGO CAYS

Carriacou I.
Jack a Dan
High North or Mt. St. Louis

Little St. Vincent (PSV)
Little Martinique
Fota I.
Little Tobago

0 2000 4000 8000 yds.

See Sketch Charts 5 and 6 (pp. 43, 45) for ranges.

SKETCH CHART 77

some advantages to these small islands.) Saline Bay is a large open bay on the southwest side of the island, with a dock on its northeast corner. The water extends much closer to shore than the chart would have you believe. This is a beautiful spot with a half-mile-long white-sand beach that is usually deserted. Best to spend your time on the beach, as the ground swell hooking around the point makes laying-to a rolly affair. When leaving for the north, give a wide berth to the shoal extending from Grand Col Point. It has a longer reach than the chart will give it credit for, one that has dented a surprising number of boats in recent years. A safe range is discussed in Chapter 5. North of this reef you will find the submerged wreck of a World War I gunboat, *Paruna*. It must have struck the reef off Grand Col going full tilt, bounced over, and hobbled along for a few feet before sinking. The Sketch Chart provides ranges for locating the wreck. The current is very strong, so plan your diving expeditions for slack water. The bay directly east of the wreck is a nice lunchtime spot when the swell is down. The beach is beautiful here, but this is definitely not recommended for overnight stops.

At the north end of Mayero is one of the most attractive anchorages in the Grenadines —locally called Salt Whistle Bay. As the Sketch Chart shows, the shoal extends south and east from the northwestern point of the harbor; however, there is a full five feet south of the reef, and this depth can be carried inside the reef well up into the northeast corner. Proceed slowly, as the bottom comes up gradually. Use a Bahamian moor or anchor bow-and-stern. Note the condition of the tide: if you sneak too far in and the tide goes out from under you, it may be a few hours of rough bumping before you get out. Beware that the ground swell does not make up while you are inside, as this would make getting out a hazardous proposition. This is a good anchorage

in settled weather only. Ashore is a beautiful, long, deserted beach. If there happen to be other visitors in the area, walk around to the windward side of the island. You will find another vast beach that is excellent for shelling. There are a few sheltered pools inside the reef that offer warm-water bathing. These are only two or three feet deep, and by late in the afternoon the sun will have warmed them to bath-like temperature. A great spot to float and relax. An especially attractive pool may be found all the way down in the southeast corner near the cliff.

There is one good anchorage off Mayero Island. On the southeast coast there is deep water inside the reefs. Sail up inside, round up, and anchor close behind the reef where the Sketch Chart indicates. Use two anchors to keep you off in case the wind dies. A final note on the chart: a one-fathom passage is shown around the eastern point of Mayero. Looking at it from the hill, it does not seem to exist, but *Brabantine* with a six-foot draft succeeded in getting through at high tide.

Catholic Island
(BA 2872, NO 25042)

There is nothing to attract yachts to this small island northwest of Mayero. It is noteworthy only as a hazard for boats working north from Mayero. The bank extending well to the east of Catholic threatens boats beating north against a leeward-setting tide. Low-lying Catholic Rocks to the west are unlit—no place to investigate after dark.

Tobago Cays
(BA 2872, NO 25042, Sketch Chart 77, 78)

The approach ranges to Tobago Cays are discussed in Sailing Directions; once you have latched onto one of these ranges, it is strictly a case of eyeball navigation. When you have entered the channel between the two sand cays—which may be under water in years to

come—you have a choice of three routes. Vessels drawing seven feet or less may hold a course northeast (Route 1, Sketch Chart 78) leading between the two coral shoals to the west of the Cays. The minimum depth between the two is nine feet. Once through these shoals, you may stand to the north and tack into the slot between Petit Rameau and Petit Bateau, or else power through.

Deeper boats should favor Route 2, which follows deep water all the way. As soon as you pass the two disappearing sand cays, sail east until the channel between Petit Bateau and the reef off its leeward shore become visible. Pass north through this channel, turning east again gradually following the line of deep water, and anchoring wherever you like.

Boats bound directly north beyond Baline Rocks should favor Route 3. This is an eyeball proposition, the course bearing roughly 350 magnetic. Once clear of the reef, set your course for Baline and stand on north from there. This route is sometimes used by sailboats bound for the Cays that cannot— with the wind in the north—lay a course between the reefs. They then hook around toward Petit Rameau, as shown on the Sketch Chart. It goes without saying that navigating the Cays requires skill and a good boat and crew.

The approach from the north is simple. Pass to windward of Baline along Route 4.

Range A: North end of Petit Rameau in line with north end of Mayero clears shoal south of Baline Rocks, 120-300 magnetic.

Range B: Baline Rocks in line with east end of Mayero leads over shoals south of Baline Rocks, 215-035 magnetic.

Range C: Southeast end of Petit Rameau in line with the cut in the hill north of the low area of Mayero Island (see profile).

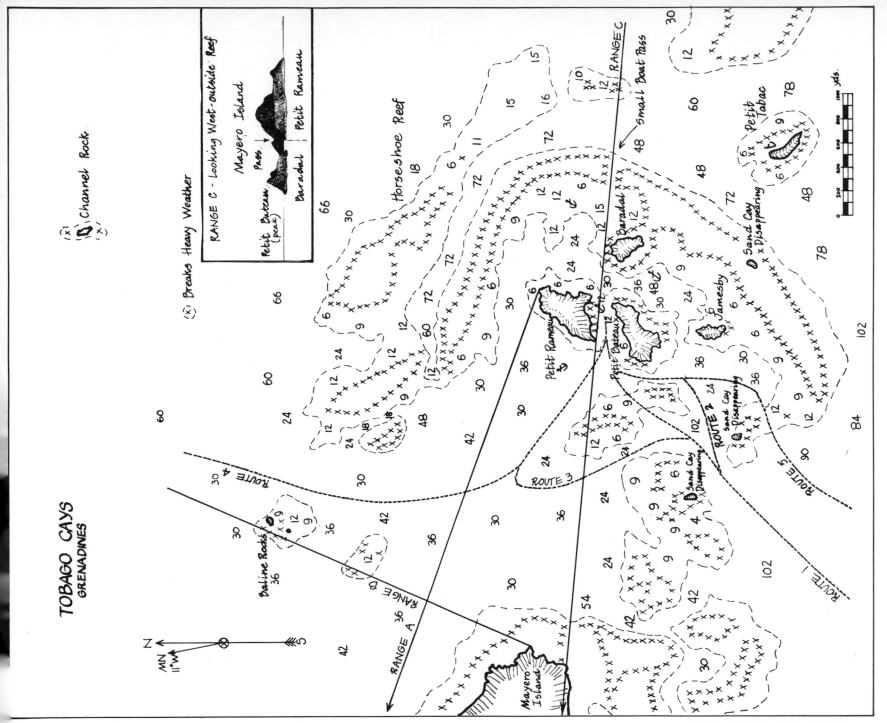

TOBAGO CAYS
GRENADINES

SKETCH CHART 78

Post a lookout for the shoal and you should have no problem. Coming from the west, follow Range A—course 300 magnetic—which will carry you clear of the reef south of Baline Rock. This reef is in fact three separate shoal spots and not the single reef as the chart would have you believe. These triple shoals are about 600 yards off Baline on the straight line drawn between Baline to the eastern tip of Mayero. This range bears 215-035 magnetic, and is marked as Range B on Sketch Chart 78.

These are without a doubt the most popular, most photographed, and most publicized anchorages in the entire Caribbean. A Tobago Cays anchorage is the *piece de resistance* of an Island charter. Many years ago the Cays were deserted and unvisited. Now you can expect to see other boats in the area, but so far there are plenty of anchorages to go around, and with any luck you should be able to anchor in relative privacy. Of course, there is no preventing the next boat from anchoring on top of you once you are secured. The Cays are low, dry, and uninhabited, surrounded by mile after mile of fabulous reef. The Bequia fishermen will be seen camping on the beach. They are skilled swimmers who can dive to 60 feet with no more than a face mask. With sufficient inducement they may allow you to accompany them on an afternoon's dive; they can show you stretches of reef like nothing

you have ever seen. This should only be undertaken by expert swimmers, as you will be in deep, rough waters. For the less ambitious the shelling on the shoals surrounding the Cays is sure to be profitable. Put on a pair of sneakers to protect your feet as you wade about. And finally, for the complacent, a fine time may be had just lazing about under a deck awning, listening to the water slapping against the hull, or ashore under the shade of a palm tree. In the evening some visitors like to have a barbecue on the beaches. There is usually enough driftwood for fuel. Be sure to clean up afterward. Don't join the ranks of the crass polluters.

The tides run swiftly through the Cays, and your movements and activities—especially diving—should be planned accordingly. A swift tide can take you by surprise; and every season at least one insurance claim is made for yachts colliding in these narrow straits. If you are approaching a crowded anchorage, you may be wise to drop sail and motor in.

Once into the Cays, you may anchor anywhere along the slot between Petit Rameau and Petit Bateau in a full two fathoms. I prefer to moor on the south side of the slot near the shoal forming the western end of the beach on Petit Bateau. Best to use a Bahamian moor; otherwise when the tide runs to windward, it will swing your stern into the wind, even when blowing 20 knots through the slot. The effect

will be to waltz a boat in a 300-foot circle. This could present a problem when there are other boats in the area. Large boats usually anchor leeward of the Cays. If the anchorage within the slot is too crowded, a good anchorage can be had close to shore southwest of Baradal. There is plenty of room here and no need for a two-anchor rig.

For those who value privacy and wish to be close to a reef, an anchorage can be had close behind Horseshoe Reef. It is cool, breezy, calm, and bugless. If you are planning to stay more than a few hours, two anchors are recommended: a Bahamian moor during full or new moon if the wind is light; or during a small moon—neap tides—and heavy weather, use two anchors ahead in a "Y."

The true adventurer in a centerboarder or a bilge-keel boat can anchor behind the reef east of Petit Tabac. A boat drawing three-and-a-half feet can enter the break in the reef at the northwest corner of the island. There are about five feet in behind the reef.

It is not surprising that the Tobago Cays are so highly esteemed by generations of cruising yachtsmen. Their beauty is very much their own, no matter how it has been brandished in the pages of island guides or as an advertiser's honeymoon tableau. One hopes that when the other islands have been surrendered to the developers, the Cays will remain as they are today.

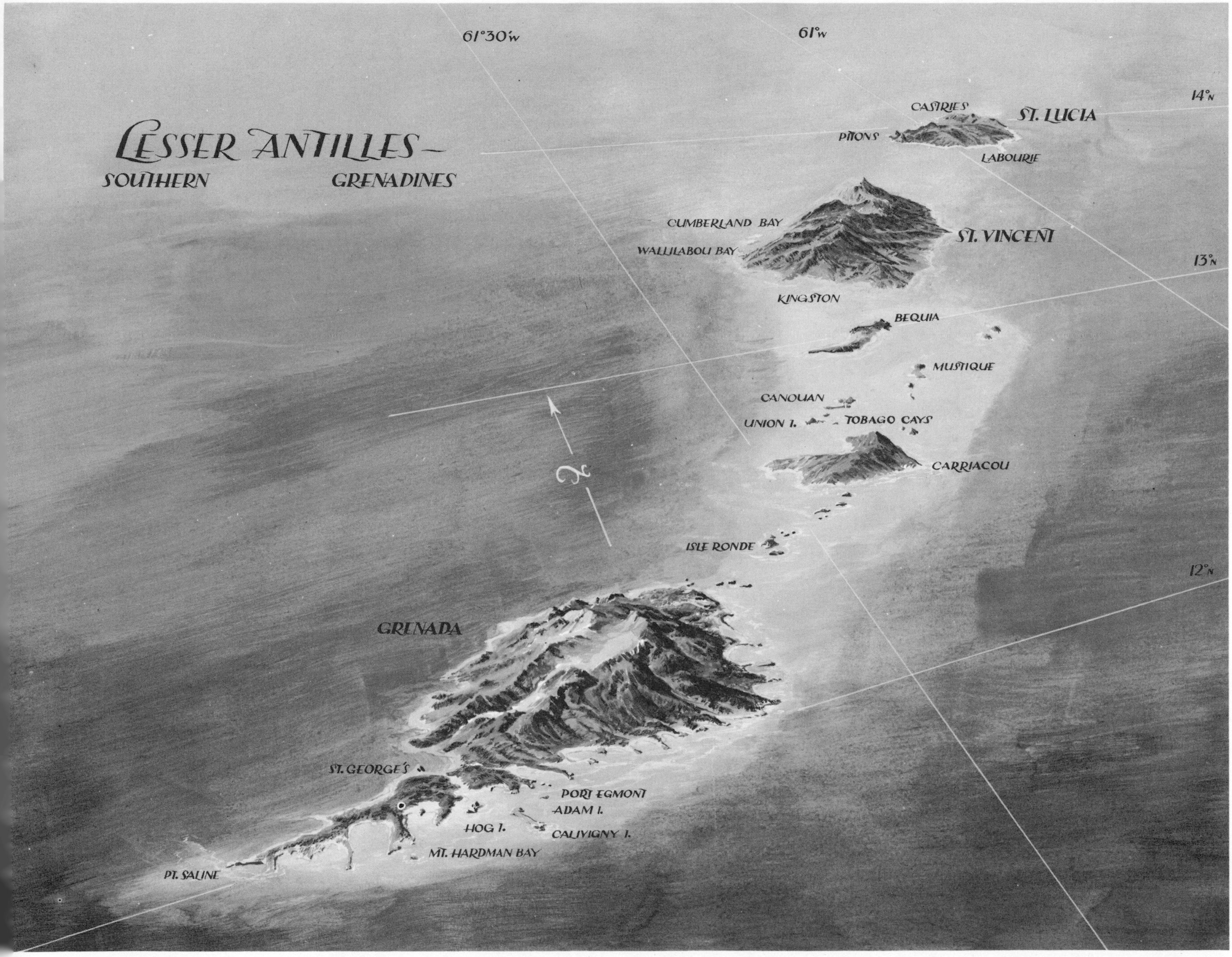

LESSER ANTILLES —
SOUTHERN GRENADINES

ST. LUCIA
CASTRIES
PITONS
LABOURIE

CUMBERLAND BAY
WALLILABOU BAY
ST. VINCENT

KINGSTON

BEQUIA

MUSTIQUE

CANOUAN
UNION I.
TOBAGO CAYS

CARRIACOU

ISLE RONDE

GRENADA

ST. GEORGE'S

PORT EGMONT
ADAM I.
HOG I.
CALIVIGNY I.
MT. HARDMAN BAY

PT. SALINE

61°30'W

61°W

14°N

13°N

12°N

CHAPTER 24

Grenada

NO 25041; BA 2821, 2830

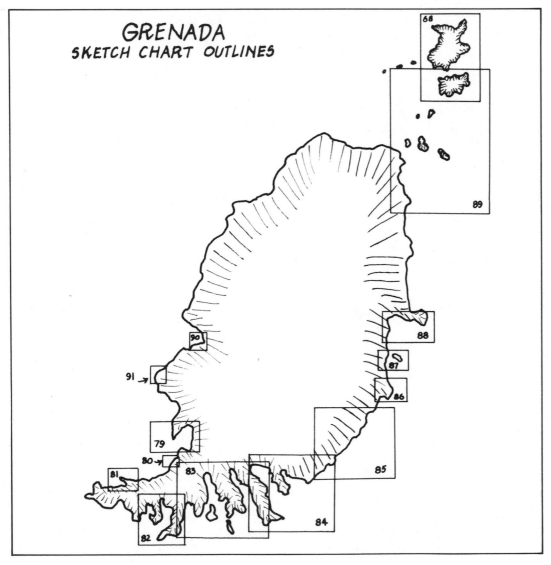

GRENADA
SKETCH CHART OUTLINES

Grenada is a large, lush, and populous island, roughly 460 miles east-southeast of San Juan. A mountain range extends practically the length of the island and catches enough rain to make Grenada verdant throughout the year. It has been traditionally called "The Spice Island," although after the great hurricane of 1955 severely damaged the nutmeg, cocoa, and major spice crops, the industry has never been the same. Since then tourism and banana exports to Great Britain have saved the island from economic devastation. Grenada is a place of small landowners, who are far easier to get along with than the people of other islands, where most of the land is owned by a few wealthy families.

A French colonial influence persists in the commercial habits of the island. The two major towns are St. George's and Grenville. Everything revolves around the capital, St. George's. Produce grown throughout the island is shipped to the market at St. George's where it is sold, loaded into carts, and trundled back out to the countryside. The market itself is a spectacle to behold. It is open six days a week, the best days being Wednesdays and Saturdays. Any Saturday of the year, a profusion of cargo schooners and bright red sloops can be seen lying peacefully at the waterfront, set off against the bright green hillsides whose slopes are zig-zagged by the narrow tracings of roadways. The market itself is piled high with wonderful collections of fresh fruits and vegetables, trussed-up chickens and hens, squealing pigs and goats, and cluttered with hordes of small children underfoot. Brightly uniformed policemen gesticulate smartly to unsnarl the traffic through town. Colorful busses from the countryside line the streets. The names emblazoned on their sides are eye-catchers: "Trust No Friend," "Fool's Paradise," "Happy Home."

A tour of the island may be had by rented car or taxi. The taxi drivers are courteous and honest, but on longer trips it is best to check out the fare beforehand. There are four taxi drivers who are favorites with yachtsmen: George Leid (telephone 2819), Wesley Matthews (4209), William Francis (2508) and Wilfred Lewis (2743). If you are interested in the flora and fauna, call Wilfred Lewis, who has a thorough knowledge of all the best places to visit in the botanical gardens, spice estates, and rain forests.

Grenada was originally settled by the French and taken over by the British during the 18th century colonial wars, when spices had become as valuable as gold. The value the British assigned to this trade can be judged by the number of old forts now to be seen on the island. Fort George still stands today as it did in the early 18th century. A small fort on the top of the hill to the north of town was once connected to Fort George by an underground tunnel. On the hills east of town are Fort Frederick, Fort Lucas, and Fort Dalfas with their large parade grounds out front. Dalfas is presently a jail. Fort Jeudy, on the south coast, was built to protect the entrance to Egmont Harbor.

This island was long considered the yachting capital of the lower Caribbean, but now it is feeling some competition from Antigua, Martinique, and Union Island. St. George's is an outstanding harbor that offers easy access to hauling facilities and boatyards, marine stocks, and provisions of every sort. Emile Erbin (call 2981), formerly of NASA, and undoubtedly the finest machinist in the Lesser Antilles, keeps a shop next to Lincoln Ross's Combined Workshop at the southwest corner of the Lagoon. The Combined Workshop (call 3018) does iron work and welding. It may not be of the high quality of the best yacht yard, but it is strong, rugged, and the price is right. Claude Paterson's Chandlery and the Custom Clearance Office is in the south wing of the Combined Workshop (call 3269). Yacht Main-

tenance, run by Mike Tate in St. George's (call 2895), keeps a staff of sail-repairers, electricians, mechanics, and refrigerationists. Spice Island Boat Yard in Prickly Bay on the south coast has first-rate facilities for boats of 55 feet on down. It also has a good marine chandlery and excellent sail-repair facility.

The Grenada Yacht Club in St. George's is an old and hospitable organization that has entertained yachtsmen from all over the world. The frequency with which it is visited by overseas yachtsmen in proportion to its size would place it alongside the Island Sailing Club at Cowes. Since the closing of the Suez Canal, interoceanic voyages take the Cape route, and more often than not the Grenada Yacht Club is an inevitable lay-over. Its bar enjoys a commanding view of the harbor and is certainly one of the most pleasant places in the world to enjoy an afternoon sundowner. The club manager, Ray Delzin, is most courteous and has been very helpful to many yachtsmen in forwarding messages, mail, and cables. He can be found at the club in the morning from eight to noon and from four to six in the afternoon (call 2022).

St. George's
(BA 2830, NO 25041, Sketch Chart 79)

There is no problem in entering. The ranges in the outer harbor are for large ships and may be disregarded. There is plenty of water all the way in. If arriving at night, it is best to anchor in the northeast corner of the Carenage. The range lights shown on the chart may not be working, but there are no hazards, and you should have no trouble entering if you mind the charts. The "official" yacht anchorage is in the northeast corner beyond a line drawn between the fire house and the Texaco agency (dotted line, Sketch Chart). Stay well up in the northeast corner to be clear of the maneuvering big ships. It is best to drop anchor in the shallows and then pay out into

deeper water. The center of the harbor is 60 feet deep over a poor-holding, mud bottom. Yachts are not permitted to go alongside the main wharf unless they have made previous arrangements with the harbormaster. It is reserved for large vessels. (Many of these tie up stern-to with the wind holding them off.) It goes without saying that you should anchor clear of the fairway, but more than once I have seen yachts anchored at the mouth of the harbor right smack in the middle of the commercial channel.

There is always a great deal of activity in the Carenage, with water taxis and fishing boats shuttling back and forth all day long. These water-taxis (bum boats) are the most economical way of getting from one side of the harbor to the other; the fare is ten cents. The fare from the Carenage to the yacht club or to Grenada Yacht Services is 50 cents, and this is faster and less expensive than by land. They will also row you to the Food Fair where you can load all your groceries from right alongside.

The recess south of the Carenage is known as the Lagoon. A narrow channel leads inside. No more than 12 feet can be carried through here at high water. The entrance to the Lagoon is easily spotted by day as there are posts on both sides of the channel. It is possible, though not recommended, to sail through this channel; the axis is 150 magnetic. If your engine is not working, arrange for a tow from the Grenada Yacht Services inside the Lagoon or from the yacht club. (The name of the handyman at the yacht club is Oliver.) Grenada Yacht Services can arrange for Customs. If you decide to anchor off the dock at GYS, as it is called, bear in mind that the bottom is the softest mud and poor holding. This is the place to use your heaviest anchor and plenty of chain. The advantage of lying in the Lagoon is the easy access to town and the fact that you are out of the way of the heavy commercial traffic.

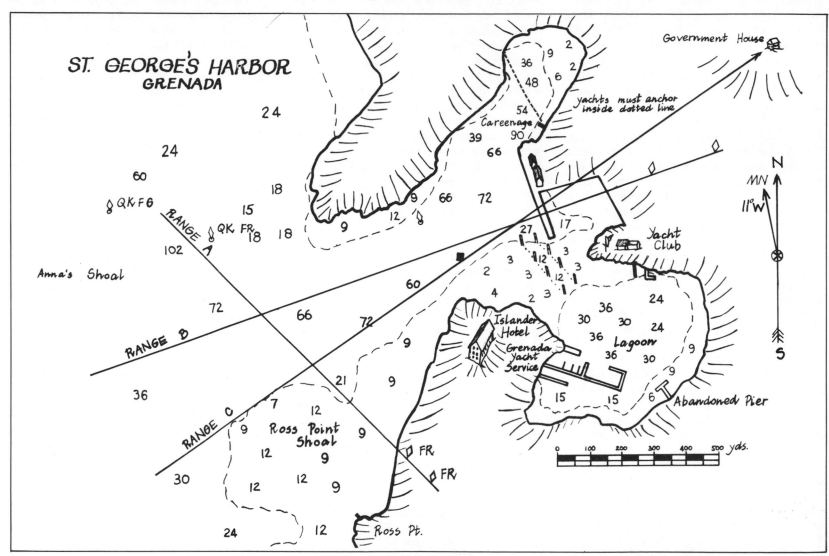

ST. GEORGE'S HARBOR
GRENADA

Government House

yachts must anchor inside dotted line

Careenage

Anna's Shoal

QK F6

QK FR.

RANGE A

RANGE B

RANGE C

Ross Point Shoal

Ross Pt.

FR

FR

Islander Hotel

Grenada Yacht Service

Yacht Club

Lagoon

Abandoned Pier

MN

N

11°W

S

0 100 200 300 400 500 yds.

Range A: Two red lights ashore in line leads east of Anna's Shoal, 142-322 magnetic.

Range B: Two red-orange lights in line lead along Harbor Channel, 079-259 magnetic.

Range C: Harbor reef buoy (oil drum) under Government House leads clear of Ross Point Shoal, 060-240 magnetic.

SKETCH CHART 79

However, it does tend to be muggy at night and the water is too foul to swim in. The best dinghy landings in town are off the Food Fair, the Nutmeg Restaurant, and Portofino Restaurant. The last is probably the best for long stops, as it is the only one with a fender.

Grand Anse
(BA 2830, NO 25041, Sketch Chart 80)

If you tire of the Lagoon, it is possible to find a good anchorage fairly near town at Grand Anse. This is very good in the summer and somewhat variable in the winter when the ground swell is up. At such times the best thing is to anchor bow-and-stern in the axis of the swell. If you are approaching from St. George's, steer a course of about 250 magnetic from the harbor reef, which is marked by a buoy (an old oil drum) at the southeast corner of the harbor. This course will clear the shoal off Ross Point, after which a course may be steered further inshore, although you must be very careful of Dathan Shoal north of the Silver Sands Hotel, a white three-story building with porches on all floors. The shoal is about 350 yards offshore along the range drawn between the thatched shack at the end of the hotel dock and the round, white, dance pavilion (Range A). Anchor 150 yards offshore; there is a nice beach all along Grand Anse Bay. The most popular anchorage seems to be between the Silver Sands and the Grenada Beach Hotel. (Be careful of the shoals to the west of the Aquatic Club.) You would do well to dive over to inspect the set of your anchor, as it is all too easy to wrap a rode on a coral head here. During the winter there is always a good deal of activity on the beach. Small boats may be rented from Grenada Water Sports near the Grenada Beach Hotel.

Morne Rouge Bay
(BA 2830, NO 25041, Sketch Chart 81)

This is west of Grand Anse and south of

Long (or Quarantine) Point. Draft permitting, a far superior anchorage to Grand Anse. Feel your way in carefully and anchor in the mouth of the bay. Well offshore the bottom rises abruptly from five fathoms to a fathom-and-a-half and to one fathom. The bottom is hard sand with patches of grass. Shoal-draft boats can work their way in farther using the lead line or sounding pole. Long Point Shoal offers a good deal of protection from the ground swell hooking in from the west around Long Point. Normally a yawl with its mizzen up will lie to the axis of the swell; she will hobby-horse gently rather than pitch wildly.

The bays between here and Saline Point can only be regarded as lunch stops. There are several beaches along this stretch, but all of them are exposed to the northerly swell—good in calm weather only. When heading westward from Grand Anse to Point Saline, avoid the shoal extending northwest of Long Point. You may pass inside the shoal by placing the southwest corner of the warehouse on the dock at St. George's Harbor under Government House (Range A, course 062 magnetic). Or you may pass outside by placing the northwest corner of the same warehouse under Government House (Range B, course 069 mag-

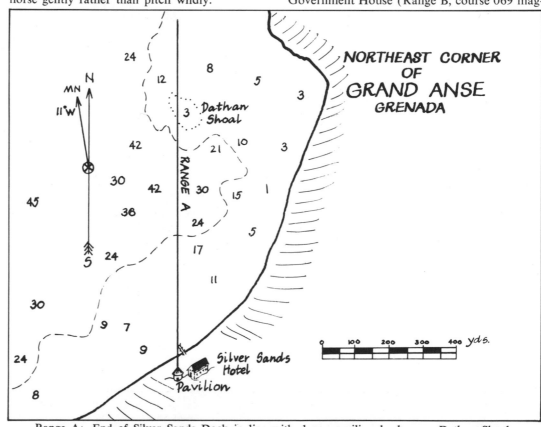

Range A: End of Silver Sands Dock in line with dance pavilion leads over Dathan Shoal, 008-188 magnetic.

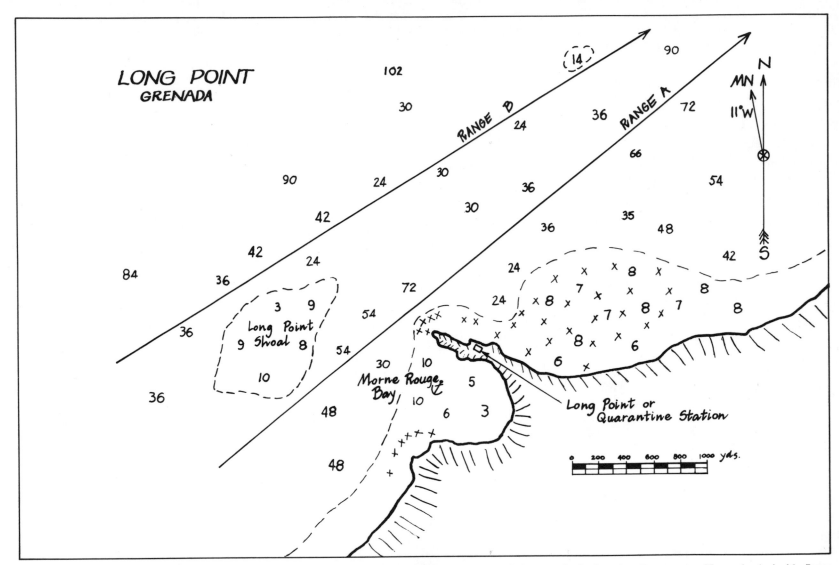

LONG POINT
GRENADA

Range A: Southeast corner of the transit shed under Government House leads inside Long Point Shoal, 062-242 magnetic.

Range B: Northeast corner of transit shed under Government House leads northwest of Long Point Shoal, 069-249 magnetic.

SKETCH CHART 81

netic). When passing around Point Saline, you can expect the wind to step up suddenly. If there is more than a ten-knot breeze before rounding, you should put in a reef. About 150 yards southeast of Point Saline and unmarked by the chart is a rock with six feet over it. I discovered this one the hard way during the Easter Sunday Race in 1973. *Iolaire* received a good thwack, though *Rosemary V* following directly behind passed safely by. It could be that we knocked the top of it off, but I mention it just the same.

Glovers Island south of Point Saline is seldom visited, except as a lunch stop in its lee. From here you can row ashore and explore the ruins of a Norwegian whaling station.

Hardy Bay
(BA 2830, NO 25041)

This is seldom visited, though quite attractive. The bay is wide open to the southeast and should be used overnight only when the wind is well to the north. The Bay is deep in the center all the way up toward its head and shoals along both sides as you enter.

True Blue Bay
(BA 2830, NO 25041, Sketch Chart 82)

The water is not very clear, and it shoals at the head. A protected anchorage can be had northwest of the point on the eastern side of the bay. The bay is easily spotted from seaward by a flagpole on the point and by several buildings that were built for an exposition in 1969. When entering, be careful of the reef off the west corner of the bay.

Prickly Bay
(BA 2830, NO 25041, Sketch Chart 82)

East of True Blue, Prickly Bay (or L'Anse aux Epines, in the French), is the most popular anchorage on the south coast of the island. This is the home of the Calabash Hotel and the Spice Island Boat Yard. At the head of

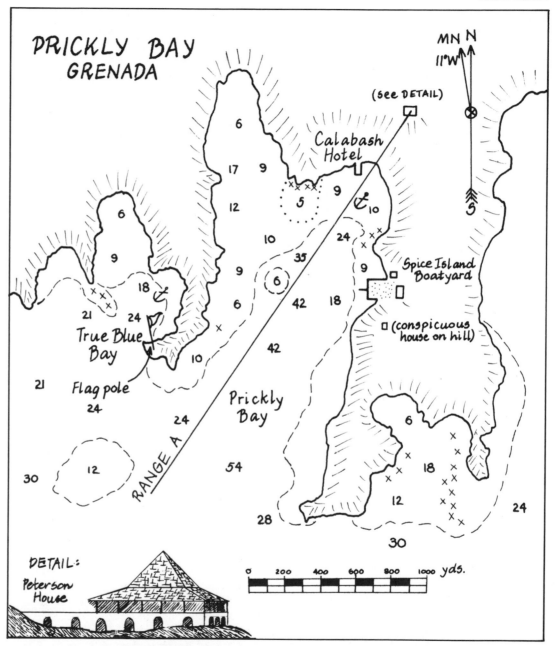

Range A: Peterson House bearing northeast (045 magnetic) leads east of six-foot shoal.

SKETCH CHART 82

the bay is a beautiful white-sand beach. Nearby is the Red Crab, an English Pub where you can get draft beer on tap. The best anchorage is in the northeast corner of the bay. The bay may be rolly during the winter with the swell hooking around the point and piling up into the harbor. This is not a dangerous situation, only an inconvenience. Once you have cleared to windward of the shoals east of True Blue Point, bring Bob Peterson's house (detail, Sketch Chart 82) to bear at 045, which will take you clear to windward of the reefs west of Spice Island Boat Yard.

The harbor is a four-mile taxi ride from St. George's. Taxis may be called at the Calabash or at the boat yard. Dinner reservations at the Calabash should be made ahead of time. Hauling facilities and dock space are available at Spice Island Boat Yard. The yard is one of the few that will allow you to do your own bottom work. Be careful of the shoal west of Spice Island Boat Yard. (Range A will keep you clear.) The Horseshoe Hotel and Restaurant, run by Aggie and John Yarwood, is out near the tip of Prickly Point. It can be reached by dinghy, and the food is excellent. Here, as at the Calabash, a necktie and, for the ladies, a dress are expected.

The Porpoises are a group of awash rocks three-quarters of a mile east-southeast of Prickly Point. There is deep water all around them, except that 40 yards north of the easternmost Porpoise is a rock under six feet. Although the chart doesn't mark it, Bill Stevens, local yachtsman and hotel owner, discovered this one by bouncing hard off it in a Hughes 38.

Mt. Hardman Bay
(BA 2830, NO 25041, Sketch Chart 83)

This is the next anchorage east of Prickly Bay. (The harbor on the point between it and Prickly Bay is shoal and for dinghy use only, despite what the chart shows.) Making entry to Hardman Bay will require a certain amount of reef-dodging. There are a number of ways to enter; the one I prefer is to hug the reef along the western shore. Pass through the break and continue on until Secret Harbor Hotel comes into view; head directly for it and stand on into the harbor. An alternate approach is to stand east from Prickly Point until Mt. Hardman Peak bears 022 magnetic; stand in along this line of bearing, bearing off when the hotel bears 330 (Route I). What the chart shows as an exposed sand bar is now a foot under water, and the reef to the south of it has built up to an island six feet high. Called Tara Island by the locals, it is no more than a heap of slab coral that was thrown up by the heavy seas of Hurricane Flora in 1963, and yet it abounds with sea life and appears to be growing in size all the time. The water is shallow and a strong current sweeps by it in such a way that there is no convenient lee in which to make a dinghy approach. If you go ashore, wear a pair of sneakers and bring two light dinghy anchors along, one to hold the stern off and one to bury ashore.

The anchorage is good anywhere in Mt. Hardman Bay; one that is guaranteed to be cool and bug-free is behind the low saddle at the south base of Mt. Hardman. The east breeze sweeping through this notch in the land is most refreshing. Nearby, the Secret Harbor Hotel high on a hill on the western side of the harbor offers excellent food and service. It is run by Barbara Stevens and is certainly one of the most beautiful hotel projects in the Islands.

Hog Island
(BA 2830, NO 25041, Sketch Chart 83)

East of Mt. Hardman Bay is an unnamed anchorage behind Hog Island, which is one of the finest spots on the south coast. To get there from Hardman Bay, you have only to swing around the reef off-lying Hardman Point along a wide semi-circle. The shoals extending west of Hog Island must be eyeballed. You can anchor anywhere in the basin between the island and the mainland. I prefer a spot due west of the north hill on Hog. There is a dinghy passage into Clarke's Court Bay between the island and mainland. It is possible to take a boat through here, but I hesitate to recommend it. For shoal-draft boats, I provide the following directions: coming from the west, approach the gap favoring the starboard side of the channel; as the point on Hog Island is approached, veer to the left on 010 magnetic for a distance of 40 yards; then veer right and you are through. The controlling depth is five feet and the channel is 30 feet wide at its narrowest.

If you are approaching the anchorage behind Hog Island from seaward, you must eyeball it. The shoal due south of Hardman Point is more shoal than the charts let on; consequently you should continue east until the hill on Hardman Point bears north magnetic; run in on this bearing, keeping your eyes peeled for reefs on either side. Slowly head up, working your way eastward behind Hog Island and into the anchorage.

Clarke's Court Bay
(BA 2830, NO 25041, Sketch Chart 83)

This large harbor contains many coves.

Range A: Conspicuous white house on Pt. Egmont bearing 225-045 leads through coral heads along eight-foot channel southeast of Hog Island.

Range B: Middle of palm grove east of Rocky Pt. at 005-185 leads into Clarkes Court Bay.

Range C: White house on Pt. Egmont at 335-155 leads between reefs off Caliveny and Adam Islands, and near anchorage behind Adam.

Range D: Eastern shore of Pt. Egmont and eastern point of Gary Island in line leads into outer Egmont Harbor, 170-350. When south end of Caliveny comes abeam, start to favor the Fort Jeudy side of channel.

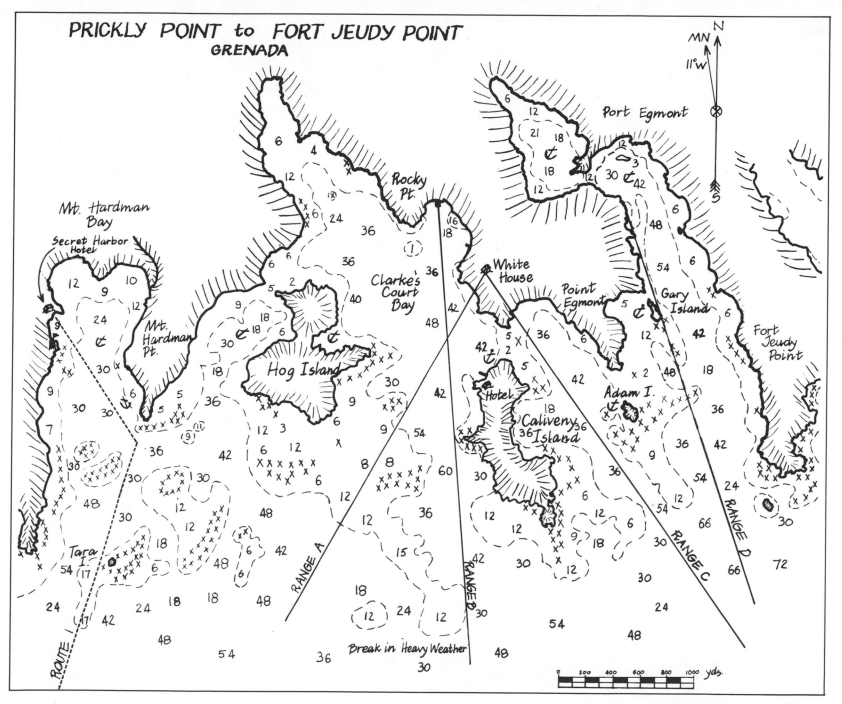

PRICKLY POINT to FORT JEUDY POINT
GRENADA

SKETCH CHART 83

GRENADA

Caliveny Island forms the eastern side of the harbor, and one of the best anchorages in the area is between it and the mainland. You may sail right up to the shoal, throw your anchor on top and back off. A stern anchor should be used overnight when the wind has died down and when the current has a tendency to swing you around. Best to use a heavy anchor as the bottom is grass. Caliveny Island was developed in recent years but is now abandoned.

If you continue into the bay until you spot the first cleared land on Point Egmont, you will find an anchorage near a groin below the modest hilltop house I call home. The bottom is very steep-to so that it is possible to jump ashore and carry the bow line to a palm tree. In the center of the harbor, directly south of Rocky Point, is a large shoal spot with about one foot over it. Because this is extremely difficult to make out I would strongly advise against going to the head of the bay unless the light is perfect.

There is another good anchorage in what I have come to call Saga Cove on the eastern shore of Hog Island. *Saga*, owned by Harry Disharoon, frequently anchored here and he considered it one of the best anchorages on Grenada. Good swimming and snorkeling, and as this is on the lee side of the harbor, there is always a good breeze over calm water.

When entering this bay, care must be taken of the shoals whose depths are significantly less than shown on the charts. The way must be eyeballed in good light. It is possible to sail upwind across the shoals southeast of Hog. Range A on Sketch Chart 83, course 045 magnetic, will carry seven feet—and no more—safely over the shoals. Certainly the safest way to enter is to stand eastward, taking care to avoid the two-fathom shoal south by east of the hill on Hog. This frequently breaks in heavy weather. Continue east until Stevens Beach dock bears 005 mag-

netic (Range B). The beach may be identified by a line of palm trees, a cliff on either end, and a small stone dock in the center.

Five feet can be carried between Point Egmont and Caliveny Island. One must stay 50 feet off the Point Egmont shore and feel the way along with a sounding pole. The channel may be spotted by heading about 50 yards north of the point south of the conspicuous white house. As you approach shore, start curving south, following the shoreline around the point. Once round, head north, east, and then south to the Adam Island anchorage. It is advisable to test this route beforehand from a dinghy. Even so, you will save time over the long beat around to Adam Island.

Adam Island
(BA 2830, NO 25041, Sketch Chart 83)

The anchorage behind this island is a good deal better than the chart indicates. The chart does not reflect the extent to which the small reef south of the island hooks to the west. If you tuck behind—northwest—of this reef, you will be sheltered at all times. From my house on Point Egmont I have never seen it rough behind the reef. To enter from seaward, place the white house marked on the Sketch Chart on a bearing of 335 magnetic (Range C). Put a man aloft and watch your course carefully, as there is very little room for error through here. Follow this bearing and round up immediately after passing the west reef; head in and anchor when the house on Adam Island bears southeast and the west reef closes with the south end of Caliveny Island. Between Adam Island and the mainland there is a dinghy passage with 18 inches of water.

Gary Island
(BA 2830, NO 25041, Sketch Chart 83)

There is a good shoal-draft anchorage behind this island which will carry no more than four feet. A deeper daytime anchorage

(two fathoms) can be found immediately south of Gary Island. It is well sheltered from normal trade-wind weather, but open to winds from the south.

Point Egmont
(BA 2830, NO 25041, Sketch Chart 83)

The inner harbor here is the most protected harbor on the south coast of Grenada. Almost completely landlocked, it is surrounded by high hills on all sides. Even in the most violent hurricane, I cannot imagine a boat incurring damage in Egmont. The entrance is simple as long as you proceed when the sun is high. Steer east offshore until the eastern end of Gary Island is in line with the eastern side of Point Egmont (Range D, 351 magnetic). There is ample water until Fort Jeudy Point comes abeam, when you can safely swing eastward to the center of the channel and continue on north into the harbor. The wind hooking around Fort Jeudy Point is likely to put you dead before it. As you approach the head of the harbor, watch out for the shoal along the western side and for an unmarked shoal north of the anchor-mark on the Sketch Chart. Both can be hazardous.

The inner recess is steep-to on both sides of the gap. On one occasion, tacking out through the narrows, I actually put the bowsprit onto the mangroves without running aground. You may anchor anywhere in the inner harbor. It is so sheltered that there will be very little strain on the rode. The swimming and fishing are excellent and the seclusion perfect.

In leaving, the wind will be dead against you, so that it is probably advisable to motor out and set sail under the lee of Fort Jeudy Point. As you leave, stay east of Range D until Prickly Point separates from the south tip of Caliveny Island. This will keep you from bearing off onto the shoals south of Adam Island.

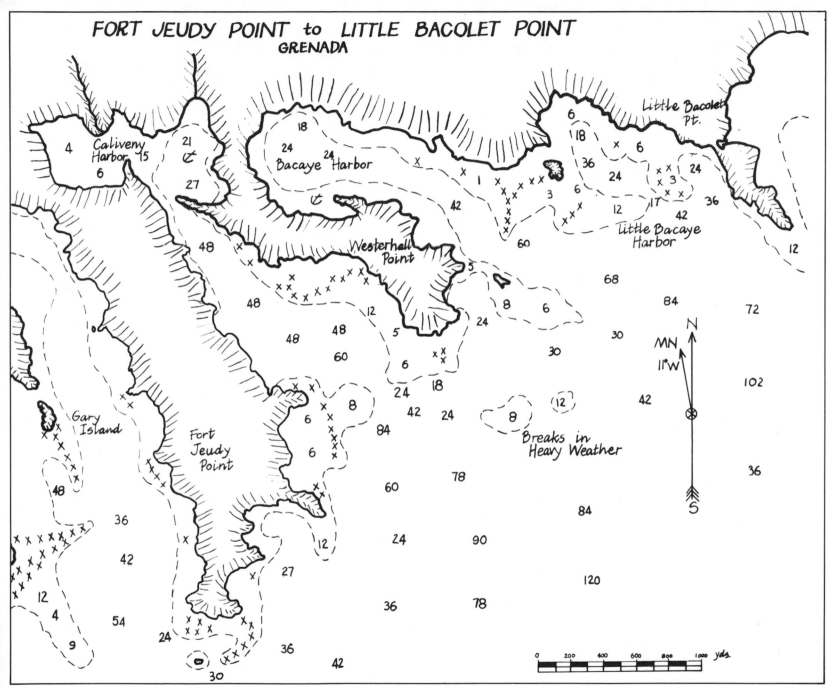

FORT JEUDY POINT to LITTLE BACOLET POINT
GRENADA

Little Bacolet Pt.

Caliveny Harbor

Bacaye Harbor

Little Bacaye Harbor

Westerhall Point

Breaks in Heavy Weather

Gary Island

Fort Jeudy Point

MN 11°W

N
S

0 200 400 600 800 1000 yds.

SKETCH CHART 84

GRENADA

Caliveny Harbor
(BA 2830, NO 25041, Sketch Chart 84)

The next harbor east of Point Egmont, this is not to be confused with Caliveny Island. The old sailing directions speak highly of this harbor, inasmuch as the square riggers could sail in without having to anchor first and warp their way up to the anchorage at its head. The outer entrance is very narrow. The shoals extending southwest of Westerhall Point are shallower than the chart indicates. On the western side of the channel the one-and-a-quarter-fathom spot extends quite far to the east and connects with the reef off Fort Jeudy Point. This is a case for eyeball navigation in good light. The shoals on the starboard hand are more easily discernable than those to port. Favor the Westerhall Point side as you enter. Stand right on up the harbor, keeping to the middle. You may anchor anywhere within the inner harbor. Some boats prefer to drop a stern anchor and sail right up to the sand spit, which is very steep-to. You can jump ashore and tie a line to a bush or bury a hook in the sand. There is abundant fishing to be had among the mangroves on the western side. You will find a good dock on the Westerhall side of the harbor. Westerhall Point is a large, private development put together by Beres Wilcox. The houses are expensive and beautifully landscaped in this rather nice preplanned community, which is on the main road from St. George's, 20 minutes away by car. The guard at the entrance will probably allow you to use the phone to call a cab.

Bacaye Harbor
(BA 2830, NO 25041, Sketch Chart 84)

North of Westerhall Point, Bacaye is an excellent anchorage, though seldom used on account of the gross inaccuracy of the charts. The deep-water passage shown between the point and the small island east of it has shoaled. The two- and three-fathom spots noted further southeast have become more shallow. The three-fathom spot breaks in heavy weather, and the two fathomer has no more than eight or nine feet and breaks continually in heavy weather. Give both spots a very wide berth.

Access to the harbor is along an east-west axis; it should not be entered after 1300 or the sun will be in your eyes. The depth sounder will not substitute for careful eyeballing, since the reefs are steep-to and would not show up on the dial before you were hard on them. The best anchorage is in the cove on the south side of the harbor. The chart notwithstanding, there is no more than nine to ten feet of water in here. The bottom is soft mud, so be sure to use a good heavy anchor.

The best time to leave is after noon and under power. At 0900 the sun will be directly on your line of bearing, making an exit difficult, if not impossible. Many years ago, I ran aground in four feet of water trying to tack out in the early morning, having misjudged the end of the reef on the north side of the harbor. No damage was done thanks to a full-length lead keel, and with the aid of a strong anchor windlass I managed to kedge off.

St. David's Harbor
(BA 2830, NO 25041, Sketch Chart 85)

Few yachts venture to anchorages east of Westerhall Point, though there are a number to choose from. St. David's Harbor is very good, as long as the wind is not in the south. One must follow all the way up to the head of the bay and anchor on the eastern side close ashore. I would suggest a bow-and-stern mooring along a north-south axis in anticipation of the swell which tends to hook around St. David's Point. Stand eastward as you enter until St. David's Point bears 010 magnetic; then bear off and run in on a course due north, watching for the detached rock on the western side of St. David's Point and for the one-fathom spot on the western side of the harbor.

La Sagesse Bay
(BA 2830, NO 25041, Sketch Chart 85)

The only anchorage is on the eastern half of the bay, west of Marquis Point. A beautiful white beach always has some surf on it. The bay is easily identified by an old estate house on the northeast corner of the beach. This is a popular spot with the Grenadians on weekends and it is a good lunch stop for the visiting yachtsman, but it's not for overnight use.

Lascar Cove
(BA 2830, NO 25041, Sketch Chart 85)

This heretofore unnamed cove was sounded by Bill Gould and myself aboard his *Lascar,* hence the name. It is a beautiful spot, located between Marquis Point and Petit Trou Point, with a small, first-rate anchorage in its northeast corner. There is a slight roll in the northwestern corner where a small stream enters. The cove is difficult to spot from seaward. A small white building that looks like a church and is marked on the chart as a courthouse will come into view as you work eastward. Bring this to bear at 355 magnetic and it will lead you directly to Lascar Cove. Entrance should be made in good light as the reefs impinge closely from either side. The opening is no more than 100 yards. Once inside, head for the beach in the northeast arm of the bay and anchor off in two fathoms. Stay to the west of the reef on the starboard side. Another reef projecting south breaks the harbor into eastern and western halves. There is enough room to round up and anchor, but I would advise using a Bahamian moor, especially if there is more than one boat inside. The diving and fishing are very good in here.

Petit Trou
(BA 2830, NO 25041, Sketch Chart 85)

There is a pretty, deserted beach here but the shelter is not good, so that I can only recommend it for daytime use in settled weather.

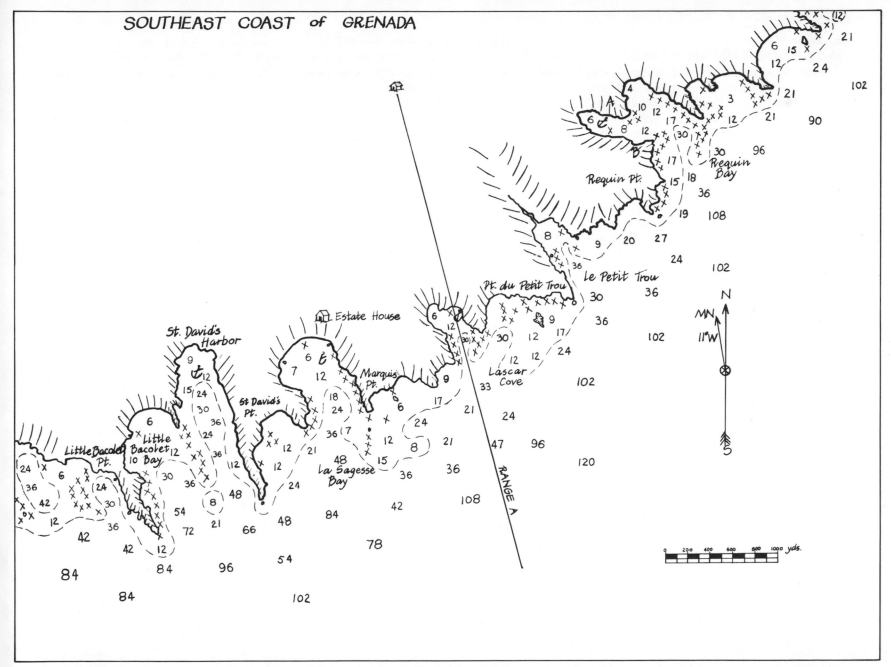

SOUTHEAST COAST of GRENADA

Range A: The church, labeled "Court House" on the chart, brought to bear 335 magnetic leads to entrance of Lascar Cove.

SKETCH CHART 85

GRENADA

Requin Bay
(BA 2830, NO 25041, Sketch Chart 85)

This bay may be hard to make out; a pair of rock arches marks the next bay east of it, from which you should count back one bay to Requin. Once Requin has been identified, stand to the northeast until point A appears from behind point B (Sketch Chart). Bear off to a course of roughly 335 magnetic, which leads up to the white-sand beach on the northeast arm of the bay. This is a dogleg channel requiring eyeball navigation. The reef extends from the eastern point of the bay farther than the chart shows. Once you have cleared the eastern reef on starboard tack, head up until you are past the other reef on your port side. Then bear off and run down into the western arm of the bay. The best anchorage is due south of point A, since farther west the bottom becomes grassy and poor holding. Eight feet may be carried all the way to the dock on this western arm. The eastern arm has a slight roll most of the time. There is a fine beach ashore where Little Requin River empties; but it's the old story of the good beach that seldom gives a good anchorage. Beware of the turtle nets as you enter. They are used all along the southeast corner of Grenada. Their buoys are almost flush with the water, set wide apart, and difficult to spot.

Between Fort Jeudy and Marquis Island there are a number of bays that I have not investigated but which seem to have possibilities. La Tante Bay has a good beach but poor shelter. The bays to either side of Menere Point look promising. Behind Crochu Point looks very good indeed. Great Bacolet Bay (Sketch Chart 86) is probably not a good anchorage but it has a beautiful beach.

Marquis Island
(BA 2830, NO 25041, Sketch Chart 87)

Anchorages may be had behind the island or between the western tip of the island and the mainland. The former is the more protected, though a double moor is required as the wind looping over the top of Marquis will waltz you in every direction. It is not a particularly good shelter.

Grenville Harbor
(BA 2821, NO 25041, Sketch Chart 88)

The only port of entry on the east coast, Grenville is the second largest town on Grenada. Food supplies are available but in nowhere near the quantity as St. George's. The windward reef affords total shelter while the wind blows in to make the place cool. There are two beautiful old churches, many buildings, and an altogether pleasant atmosphere ashore.

The town is best visited on Fridays or Saturdays. The small sloops from Carriacou come down on Friday nights for the Saturday market, while the schooners come in from Trinidad the same afternoon. The harbor is crowded with local vessels, whose crews spend the night making merry. In the morning they all depart. The sailing of a West Indian cargo vessel has to be seen to be believed. A large crew and a heavy cargo, complete with deck load, puts the vessel right down to her marks. Yes, they do have plimsoll marks, but whoever places them has an optimistic view of the weather. They are just below the sheer line. On top of the deck load a few goats and

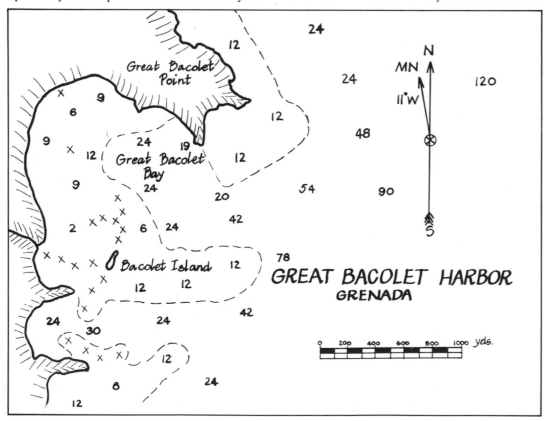

GREAT BACOLET HARBOR
GRENADA

SKETCH CHART 86

chickens will be tethered and you will notice a number of the crew's girl friends going along for the ride, and occasionally passengers as well. Sails go up slowly; first the main, then the fore, amid the squealing of blocks (no West Indian seaman would dream of greasing a block). Then the anchor chain comes in. Usually the windlass won't work, so a tackle is hitched to a chain, which is always old, rusty, and corroded. The anchor comes home accompanied by much shouting, groaning, and singing. Headsails are hoisted, backed, and sheeted home, again amid shouting, confusion, and contrary orders, while the schooner threads its way among the vessels moored in the harbor, seldom, if ever, fouling another boat. As it leaves the harbor, you will notice one person quietly standing at the wheel, saying nothing, observing all, handling the boat beautifully, and completely ignoring the antics of the rest of the crew. He is the skipper. Photographs of a West Indian schooner leaving port miss the best part. Only a tape recorder could catch the true flavor of the show.

Grenville Harbor is sheltered, but its entrance and exit are not easy, and the buoys are unreliable. The last time I was there, there were no range marks, and the outer two buoys were missing. We were informed that "de range mark fall down and de buoy is sunk and we is negotiatin' for a replacement." However, pilotage is cheap. One bottle of Barbados rum seems to be the right price. You will note from the chart that there is either plenty of water or none at all, so you don't have to worry about the pilot running you over shoal spots. The American chart does not have the detailed insert of the harbor which the British one has.

If you are entering on your own, you should stay outside a line drawn from Great Bacolet Point to Telescope Point until the south end of town bears 300 magnetic. Then you may turn inshore, but keep a man aloft to spot the reefs or whatever buoys happen to

be in place. If the sun is in the west, it will be practically impossible to spot buoys or reefs, so do not try to enter after 1400. You should be able to pick up the two small outer buoys marking the reef on the north side of the channel. The range to the outer channel is a forward square white mark atop a piling lined up with a white triangle on shore. The triangle looks just like the eaves of a house and may be very difficult to spot. Look for a large, square, stone building, the old nutmeg factory and now a school. North of this school is a green-painted store under a huge, green shade tree (*ficus benjamina*). Between the store and the tree you will spot the elusive triangle. If you still can't find it, line up the outer range with

the Catholic Church. The church is misplaced on the BA chart; it is actually on a hill in back of town.

Leaving to starboard the two outer buoys which mark the entrance to the channel, run down this range; alter course slightly northward to pass the one-and-a-quarter-fathom spot, marked "Barrel of Beef" on the Sketch Chart, to port. (The local sailors will refer to the eastern group of rocks flanking Luffing Channel as "Barrel of Beef," so be sure not to confuse the two.) As you enter Luffing Channel, you will notice two beacons roughly 30 yards apart along an east-west line. Round up between these two, favoring the eastern one—heading roughly north. This will put you on

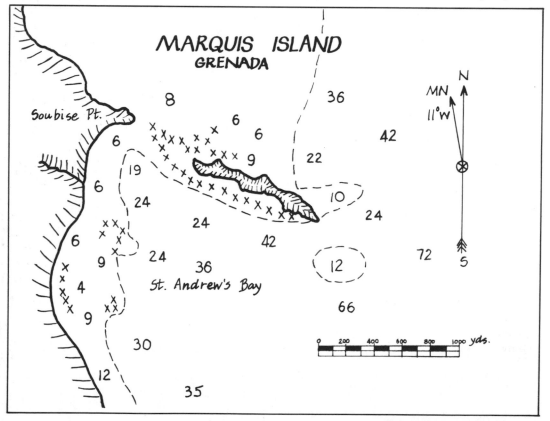

SKETCH CHART 87

GRENADA

the wind for a space of 50 yards. When the western beacon is abeam to port, bear off into the basin and anchor where you see fit. Ten feet of water can be carried through Luffing Channel, and the basin has ample water in its northern half.

Motoring out of Luffing Channel is advisable. Sailing out can be extremely difficult without a very competent crew. Keeping the range in line over the stern while tending sheets and short tacking is a complicated procedure, especially at the outer end of the channel where the gaps in the reefs are no more than 70 to 100 yards wide. Best to motor out

after ten o'clock when the sun is no longer in your eyes. If your engine is out, it is easy to arrange for a tow.

Between Grenville and Bedford Point there are no harbors, and none on the northeast coast of Grenada. When proceeding north, beware of the rock west of Range A, Sketch

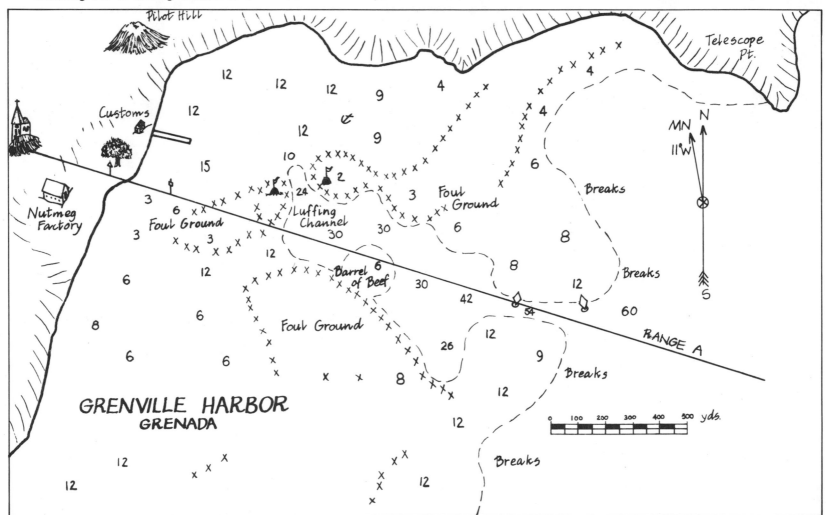

Range A: White triangle ashore in line with white square on the water leads through the outer reefs of Grenville Harbor, 117-297 magnetic.

SKETCH CHART 88

Chart 89, which breaks in heavy weather. If the ground swell is down, a good anchorage can be had in the lee of Sandy Island or Levera Island.

Sandy Island
(BA 2821, NO 25041, Sketch Chart 89)

One may anchor due west of the house on Sandy Island in two fathoms. The tide is very strong here, requiring a Bahamian moor. The wind will be from the east, while the tide will be setting northwest/southeast, which is the axis your boat should lie to. Make sure that both anchors are securely set. The snorkeling is good on the reefs west of Sandy Island, as is the shelling on the reef extending from the south tip. The lovely sand beaches are rarely visited by anyone.

Green Island
(BA 2821, NO 25041, Sketch Chart 89)

The best anchorage due west of the hill is made difficult by 40- to 60-foot depths and a very strong reversing tide. A Bahamian moor will be necessary with about 275 feet on each rode. If you are willing to make this effort, you can enjoy good snorkeling off the south coast and some beautiful beaches.

Levera Island
(BA 2821, NO 25041, Sketch Chart 89)

To the west of Sandy and Green Islands, lies Levera Island, called Sugar Loaf by the locals. The best anchorage is roughly west of Sugar Loaf Peak. Here the water is not particularly deep, but the tide is extremely strong and will reverse itself east and west. Anchor accordingly. This is the best of the small-island anchorages and usually has the least amount of swell. Care must be taken in entering from the west as the one-and-three-quarter-fathom shoal has grown more shallow over the years. Entering or leaving, you should eyeball the deep water. The tide runs anywhere

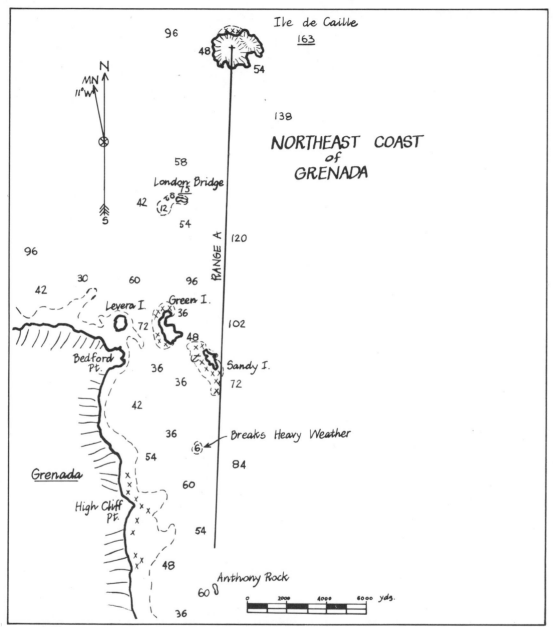

Range A: High land of Caille Island one finger open from eastern end of Sandy Island leads clear of the shoal one-and-a-half miles south of Sandy Island, 010-190 magnetic.

SKETCH CHART 89

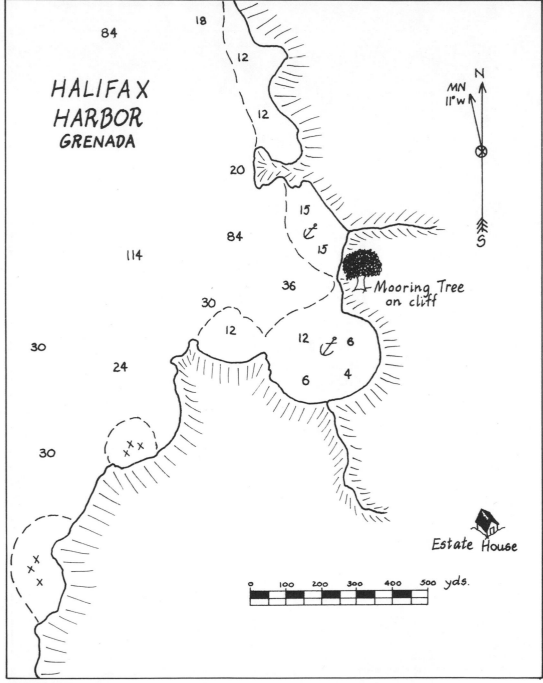

HALIFAX
HARBOR
GRENADA

84

18

12

12

20

15

84

15

114

36

Mooring Tree
on cliff

30

12

30

24

12

6

6

4

30

x x

30

x
x
x

Estate House

0   100   200   300   400   500 yds.

MN
11°W

N

S

SKETCH CHART 90

from one to three knots, and this should be taken into account in planning any swimming expeditions.

Sailing the north and west coasts, the sailor gapes at countless miles of sand beaches off which there are practically no anchorages. It can be an agonizing experience, yet there is really no point in putting in to shore unless you want to turn your insides out. It is, at least, fairly easy sailing along the north and west coasts, with few off-lying hazards. The only danger on the north coast is the seven-foot shoal, six-tenths of a mile west of Levera at 305 magnetic. The shoal is probably more shoal than the charted depth, and it breaks continually in heavy weather. David Point—locally called Tangle Angle—can be rounded close aboard. The west coast of Grenada presents no difficulties. The shore is steep-to, the water very deep, and the winds usually from the east.

Halifax Harbor
(BA 2821, NO 25041, Sketch Chart 90)

This is the only proper harbor north of St. George's on the west coast of the island. Known locally as Black Bay, it can be located by the buildings on Perseverance Estate. These are set well back in the hills and are visible before Halifax Harbor from either the north or south. One fair anchorage is in the southeast corner with Perseverance bearing southeast. This part of the habor is rolly in any sort of swell. Many consider the best anchorage behind the north point, but here again the chart is wrong. The bottom comes up from deep water to two fathoms and quickly shoals to three feet. The three-foot shelf extends about 200 yards offshore. The best method of anchoring here is to drop an anchor on the two-fathom shelf and run a very long stern line ashore to a palm tree or row a stern anchor well onto the three-foot shelf. An alternate method is to anchor off the cliff in deep water and to run a stern line to the large tree on the cliff. It will be a shorter distance from your boat to this tree than to any one of the palm trees. Arrange your bearing to face directly into the swell. The swell will cause you to pitch somewhat, but there will be relatively little rolling about. Halifax is at times a perfect anchorage and at other times completely untenable. Many of the cruising guides tend to overrate its possibilities.

Dragon Bay
(BA 2821, NO 25041, Sketch Chart 91)

Just north of Boismorice Point, Dragon Bay is fact becoming a popular anchorage. It is a place to escape the press of St. George's Harbor without having to go all the way to Halifax. This is a confined anchorage, and the way in must be carefully sounded; once in, you must be prepared to leave on short notice, especially in the winter when the swell can make up in a dangerously short time. However, from June to October in settled weather it is safe and comfortable. At night when the wind dies down, you may swing around unpredictably, so that a Bahamian moor will be required.

Grenada offers anchorages many of whose possibilities have barely been discovered. For this reason, it is an inviting alternative to the popular anchorages on the islands further north. Much of the area between Ile de Ronde and St. Vincent, the area known as the Grenadines, is becoming a virtual thoroughfare, and in years to come, perhaps, boats will be seen rafted ten across in formerly deserted places like the Tobago Cays. This catastrophe is not foreseeable along the coasts of Grenada, where a week or more can be spent in relative seclusion visiting the anchorages I have discussed, or exploring the unexplored.

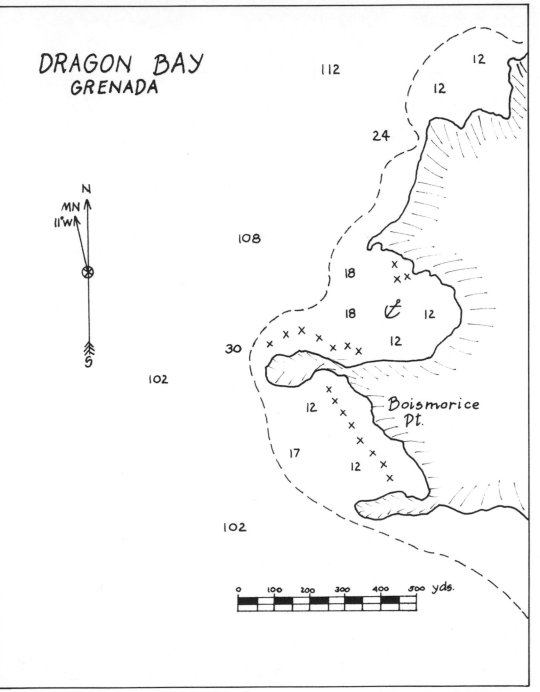

CHAPTER 25

Trinidad & Tobago

NO 24402, 24403, 24405, 24406; BA 479, 482, 483, 505, 508

Trinidad-and-Tobago is one independent state within the British Commonwealth. It was first discovered by the Spanish on Columbus's third voyage. At the head of a small fleet, Columbus entered the Gulf of Paria through the Serpents Mouth and anchored. A minor volcanic eruption shortly caused a tidal wave or bore to sweep through the Gulf, inflicting considerable damage to his fleet. He then moved north across the Gulf and anchored under the south coast of Peninsula de Paria. This was the first stop by a European on the American mainland. The actual anchorage was most likely at Ensenada Cariaquita, as Dr. Camejo of Sargasso has maintained, although this view is disputed by Admiral Morrison's biography of Columbus. Columbus all but ignored the island of Trinidad; the first settlement was not made on the island until much later, in 1552.

Trinidad

Unlike most of the South American colonies, Trinidad did not prosper. By 1780, the population was a scant 300 people. In that year, the colony was opened to settlement by all nations, and by 1797 when the island surrendered to the British without a fight, the population had grown to 18,000. The island remained in British hands for almost two centuries, administered by a governor appointed by the Crown. In 1962, a few years after the British tried unsuccessfully to set up a West Indies Federation, Trinidad and Tobago were granted independence.

In 1970, there was a rebellion by the

Trinidad and Tobago Army Regiment that briefly disturbed the peace. The matter was handled judiciously by the government, the leaders being given jail sentences and subsequently freed on appeal. This was a far more bloodless solution than that which befell the rebellion in 1837 by the black recruits in the West Indian Regiment. The leader, Donald Stewart, was tortured and put to death along with a number of other rebels. Now the only organized civil disturbance occurs during Carnival.

The Trinidadians are a raucous, hard-living people. This is no island for the timid; the number of people that are done in each year by car or motorcycle accidents, stabbings, shootings, or drownings is simple horrendous. Not surprisingly, the police on Trinidad is the only police force among former British colonies that is armed with pistols. A swagger stick is apparently not enough.

Each island has its own accent; Trinidad's is a particularly pleasing one. The language includes some rather picturesque expressions. Trinidad's population is made up of a far-flung blend of English, Chinese, Spanish, East Indian, and African, all worked together to produce some of the most beautiful women of the world. The island's restaurants offer an equal variety of cooking. One of the old standbys is Luciano's on Frederick Street, Port of Spain, where one can gorge himself on almost any combination of food.

The principal reason yachts travel to Trinidad is for mechanical repairs. In the chapter on yacht services I have described the available facilities. Trinidad is the main trans-shipment

port for the Lesser Antilles. The commercial congestion in the harbor is quite beyond belief, second only to the inefficiency that it gives rise to. It may take a month or more to have goods transferred through Port of Spain to points north. If I have important gear being shipped to me through Port of Spain, I usually sail down and pick it up myself.

Trinidad's weather is for the most part governed by the easterly trades. When the island cools off at night, there is usually a calm in the Gulf of Paria. An easterly breeze springs up in the mornings, building to anywhere from ten to 20 knots by the afternoon and dying down at sunset. From time to time, during periods of light winds and very hot days, the island will heat up and a column of warm air rising overland will draw in a wind from the west. The resulting southerly or southwesterly breeze is a cause for great confusion among the weekend racers.

The Trinidad Yachting Association has constructed a clubhouse near the former U.S. Navy Base at Chaguaramas (where BA 482 lists a "fleet landing," just west of the big seaplane hangar north of Point Gourde). The Association conducts races on weekends between January and July. Trinidad Yacht Club is located at Diego Martin, on the outskirts of Port of Spain. A snack bar and showers are available. The club has a slip able to handle boats drawing up to six feet. Another yacht club north of the fueling dock at Pointe-a-Pierre is operated by the Texaco Oil Company. The club is most hospitable. Prior arrangements to use its facilities should be made by contacting Arthur Spence, Texaco, Pointe-a-Pierre. Eight feet can be carried to the old jetty just south of the club. The channel lines up with the jetty, and it should be sounded with the lead line.

Approaching Trinidad from the north, there are no off-lying hazards. The mountainous north coast gives ample warning of approach to land. Both Trinidad and Tobago are well lit and may be approached at night, while the actual entry of harbors should be made in daylight. As you approach Trinidad from seaward, bear in mind that the main light on Chacachacare Island is visible over 37 miles. It is four-and-a-half miles to leeward of the easternmost Boca. Do not head directly for it, as the current will most likely be setting you strongly to the west. If you do not take careful bearings, you will end up well to leeward, leaving you a rough beat east against wind and current. If you happen to be approaching from the southeast, do not enter the Gulf of Paria through Serpents Mouth. This would put you hard on the wind for 35 miles up to Port of Spain, and the first part of this trip would be complicated by the many offshore oil rigs. I would advise rounding the island to windward and entering from the north. The distance may be greater, but the effort will be far less.

The Gulf of Paria may be entered from the north through any of three openings, called Bocas (mouths). Counting from the eastward, these are Boca Grande, Boca de Navios, and Boca de Huevos. The normal flow of current is from the Gulf of Paria into the Caribbean, the current running strongest during an ebbing tide and less fast, though in the same direction, during a flood tide. You should probably plan on using your engine through the Bocas, no matter what the tide. Once you have reached the first or easternmost Boca, power through the rest of the way. If your engine is out of order, use the second Boca which is wider and easier to sail through. Once inside, proceed directly to the big bauxite terminal in Chaguaramas. Customs will clear you there in short order. If you are in need of assistance of any sort, contact the Myers family in the Chaguaramas area. Hugh, Doug, and Harry Myers are skilled yachtsmen and pilots. Their advice will be of considerable value to those not familiar with the area.

Though it is possible to anchor off the bauxite terminal, the bauxite dust blowing off the dock can be most unpleasant. I advise moving on once you have cleared. Go around Pt. Gourde, passing inside of Diego Island, and anchor off the Yachting Association Clubhouse.

Carenage Bay
(BA 483, NO 24405)

This is where the clubhouse is located. A watchman is always on duty. Telephone, showers, a bar, and taxi service to Port of Spain are available.

Cumana Bay
(BA 483, NO 24406)

Further east, this is where the Trinidad Yacht Club will be found. The anchorage is exposed and turbulent, the bottom poor holding.

Port of Spain
(BA 482, NO 24406)

It is possible to go into Port of Spain and lay alongside the Customs dock, but this is not something I would want to do for more than a short while. It is crowded, rough, and filthy. The same holds of the anchorage at Pointe-a-Pierre.

There is, in short, very little to recommend the Gulf of Paria. It is shallow, muddy, and, during summertime, full of jellyfish. No yachtsman wants to linger in this area, unless he has business to conduct or friends ashore. There are, however, a few good anchorages scattered through the area. The cove on the south side of Gaspar Grande in Corsair Bay (NO 24405, BA 479) is attractive and well-sheltered. On Monos Island (BA 479) are two good all-weather anchorages. These are Morris Bay and Grand Fond (or Dehert)

Bay. On the east shore of Boca de Monos is Scotland Bay, which is listed as restricted but is nonetheless used by local yachtsmen without anyone's fussing.

Relatively little cruising is done in the Gulf of Paria, even though there are some excellent anchorages on the Venezuelan Peninsula de Paria. Venezuela requires clearance at Punta Guiria which is time-consuming and out of the way. Besides, the port captain can be downright hostile to yachtsmen. Most Trinidadians prefer the Grenadines and points north for their cruising grounds. The east coast is not amenable to overnight cruising. It is a lee shore with no viable anchorages.

Tobago

Discovered in 1498 and settled in 1639, Tobago was neither zealously colonized nor jealously held, the island changing hands roughly 30 times before the British established ultimate control in 1814. In 1962, along with Trinidad, Tobago was made independent. Lacking good, deep-water harbors, it has never prospered commercially. The island is seldom visited by yachts; lying 90 miles southeast of Grenada, it is hard on the wind on port tack. It is effectively isolated from yachts from Trinidad to the south by the west-running Equatorial current which reaches anywhere from one-and-a-half to three knots. It is a miserable slog, and many a boat that has tried it has wished it hadn't. The Lazzari Brothers aboard *Draconius* are among those who have completed the passage, though they were so worn out on arrival that they never went ashore. It is another matter for the Trinidadian sportfishermen who shuttle back and forth regularly between the two islands. One of the most grueling power boat races of the year is the Trinidad/Tobago over a rough-water stretch of 60 miles. The least rigorous passage is by ferry or by air. Arawak and

255

TRINIDAD & TOBAGO

LIAT operate the air service, although their reputation for reliability is open to question. Tobago is the vacation area for Trinidad. Hotels and restaurants are sprouting up all over the island. Between the end of July and Labor Day, Tobago is inundated by Trinidadians on their summer holiday.

Whatever the reputation of the passage, it is possible to sail from Trinidad to Tobago without killing yourself. The key is to put yourself well to the east before striking out from shore. I recommend a departure from the Bocas timed to the first hour of the ebb tide. Stay close inshore along the north coast of Trinidad; a back eddy runs strongly off to the eastward for quite a few hours. Whether tacking or motoring, you should not allow yourself to get more than three miles offshore. When you reach Galera Point at the northeast corner of Trinidad, stand across to Tobago. On the way across allow for the current that will be sucking you to leeward at a tremendous rate. As you approach the western end of Tobago, watch out for Drecos Bank and Wasp Shoal, both of which break in heavy weather.

An anchorage can be had off Columbus Point below the airport. You can clear through the airport, a procedure that may not be completely legal but it has become something of a habit with those few visiting yachts. The official port of entry is Scarborough. (If you are coming from Trinidad, coastwise clearance for Tobago can be obtained in Trinidad.) There is another anchorage, unnamed, between Columbine and Crown Points (NO 24402, BA 505). It is satisfactory for the most part, though the strong tides may kick things up a bit. If the winds are in the south, Milford Bay is adequate. The bottom falls off steeply so that you must anchor fairly close with a Bahamian moor to keep the tide from swinging you onshore. From here, a dinghy expedition can be made up to Bucco Reef which the Tourist Board vaunts as the most interesting

in the world. Unfortunately, it is so accessible to hotels that literally thousands of people come to tromp across the reef every year. A reef, unlike a Fifth Avenue sidewalk, will not hold up against this sort of wear and tear. I have been told that with the aid of a local pilot seven feet can be carried inside the reef, but I would check out the pilot's credentials carefully.

Bucco Bay
(BA 505, 508; NO 24402)

East of Bucco Reef, this offers good shelter as long as the ground swell is not running in. The entrance favors the Bucco Reef side of the bay. The northeastern portion of the bay is shoal and reef-infested. It is possible, however, to sail in behind the reefs, passing to the west and turning east once south of them. Work your way east as far as your draft permits and anchor. There is a dinghy landing at the village of Bucco where, with any luck, you should be able to locate a taxi.

Plymouth
(BA 505; NO 24402, 24403)

This is Tobago's second city (Scarborough is the largest). As long as the swell is not up—an occasional problem in the winter months—a satisfactory anchorage can be gained tucked up in the northeast corner of the harbor. Sneak in as close as your draft will permit and anchor. Put yourself in the axis of the swell, which tends to sweep around Courland Point. Shoal-draft boats can work their way inshore under the old fort, anchoring in a fathom and a half with Pelican Rock bearing northwest. Care should be taken not to run up on Barrel of Beef, the submerged rock south-southeast of Pelican Rock.

As I have indicated, relatively little is known of Tobago's cruising possibilities, being so seldom visited by yachts. However, I have

it on good authority that the bays on the north coast are exceptionally fine and offer adequate overnight shelter in the summer when the wind is in the south.

Portaluvier Bay
(BA 505, NO 24402)

A fresh-water stream runs in to the head of this bay. The water is deep and best negotiated by running a line ashore and an anchor off the stern to hold you off. Probably best for daytime only.

Bloody Bay
(BA 505, NO 24402)

Here, too, a river runs into the bay. On shore is a beach and behind it some high hills. A pleasant spot, virtually uninhabited.

Man of War Bay
(BA 505, 508; NO 24402, 24403)

The town here is Charlotteville. The best anchorage is not off town, but one-quarter mile north in Pirate's Bay. Work your way into the northeast corner of Pirate's as close inshore as possible, staying south of the detached rock at the north end of the bay. This should be thoroughly sheltered in all normal weather, though it is somewhat susceptible to the swell. It is good swimming and only a dinghy ride to town.

If you aim to beat around the east end of Tobago, wait for a weather-going tide. Against the tide the beat between Melville Island and the northeast corner of Tobago would be difficult. It is probably best to stand north of Melville Island and to cross north and eastward of Melville Island and then run south to the Anse Bateau/Tyrell Bay area. Little Tobago and Goat Island (NO 24402, 24403; BA 505, 508) will afford some shelter from the easterly winds. Because of the strong tide rips near shore, you should keep well out into Tyrell Bay. Goat Island is privately owned, and though I have been told the owners are quite friendly and hospitable, they certainly don't want to be inundated with visiting yachtsmen.

Kings Bay
(BA 505, 508; NO 24402, 24403)

This would be poor with the wind in the southeast. During the winter it is excellent. The shore is steep-to. Run a bow line ashore and an anchor astern to hold you off. Anchor up in the northeast corner off the ruined jetty.

Scarborough
(BA 508, 505; NO 24402)

Between Kings Bay and Scarborough there are a variety of small coves and anchorages for shoal-draft boats. This is an area of exploration for the experienced yachtsman who knows what he is about and it should not be attempted except when the wind is northeast. Scarborough is the main port of entry and the terminal point of the Port of Spain ferry. When the ferry makes a landing, she drops her anchor some distance off and runs alongside, paying out a goodly length of heavy chain which is very likely to land on top of your own rode. Nothing can be done but to pay heed to the ferry schedule in planning your departure. The only thing to watch out for in approaching Scarborough is an area of two- or three-fathom shoals. These will break in heavy weather. Best to stand eastward and come in on the normal steamer range. In the town of Scarborough you will find the usual complement of hotels, restaurants, and supermarkets. A taxi may be hired for a tour of the island. Such a trip is well worthwhile. The wildlife is truly extraordinary.

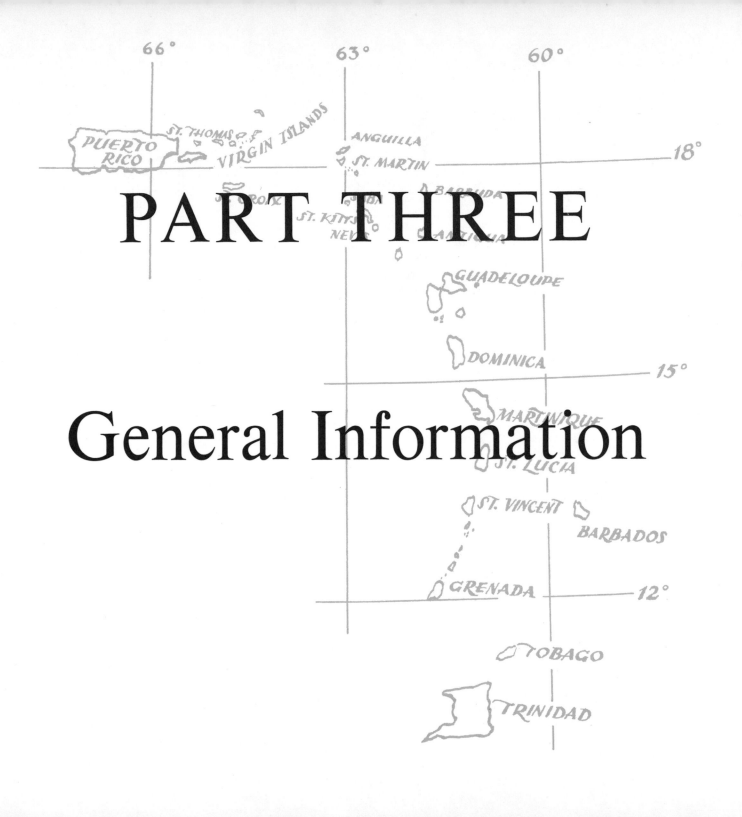

PART THREE

General Information

CHAPTER 26

Leaving

After spending a season cruising the Lesser Antilles, the majority of visiting yachts will be off to some other part of the world. While a few decide to stay for the rest of their days, most now head for North America or Europe.

For boats heading north, the usual departure point is St. Thomas. It has facilities for hauling and other repair work, readily available provisions, and, last but by no means least, duty-free liquor. As to timing, one can leave from St. Thomas heading north at any time of year other than the hurricane season (July through October). During the winter and early spring one has to watch for a norther, but this is the only real danger presented by the weather. Northers never make their way down to the Islands, so it is too easy to set off with the false assurance that the weather seems good. If you listen to the Florida weather reports, however, they will give you more than adequate warning of an approaching storm. If the wind is swinging to the northwest and the temperature is dropping fast, then the norther will be arriving in the Bahamas in another 12 hours. One usually will last anywhere from 24 hours to three days. Regardless of the time of year, any yacht going to North America should carry on board a yachting guide to the Bahamas. Frequently a breakdown will necessitate a stop in these islands, but any competent seaman with a large-scale chart of the entire Bahamas, a yachting guide, and the common sense to wait until the sun is high, can find his way into any of the Bahamian ports in an emergency.

If you are making a passage direct from St. Thomas to Florida, there are two routes that can be used. The more popular, and to my mind the safest, is to leave St. Thomas steering northwest; pick up the light at the north end of San Salvador as a check point, and continue sailing northwest through the NE-NW Providence Channel to Ft. Lauderdale or Miami. While appearing simple, this route nevertheless demands careful navigation. More than one boat has ended up on the rocks of Cacos, San Salvador, or Eleuthra.

Celestial navigation can be quite valuable on this route. The traditional noon sight, however, is useless because the sun in April is almost directly overhead at this latitude. But if you take a morning shot when the sun is directly astern, you can determine your day's progress along your course; and if you take a second sight in the afternoon, when the sun is perpendicular to your course, you can determine your position north or south of the rhumb line. This second sight· is particularly useful on account of the unpredictable nature of the current through the Bahamas. Sometimes it runs northwest, sometimes due west, and occasionally it will run southwest. Its fickleness has led to the demise of several boats.

The other route to Florida, used more in the old days, follows along the coast of Puerto Rico, Hispaniola, and Cuba. The first two of these islands have steep, dangerous coastlines, and the third, Cuba, while well lit along the shore, is politically dangerous. Hugging any of these coasts is not a good idea. The second part of this route is also risky as the Great Bahama Bank is poorly lit—an easy target for the unsuspecting.

Another popular route taken by yachts leaving the Islands is to head directly for the northern part of the U.S. The customary landfalls are either Charleston or Morehead City. From either port it is possible to enter the Inland Waterway and proceed in relative safety to Norfolk, from where, providing the weather forecast is good, you can then set sail for your own particular haven. If the weather forecast is not good, I would strongly recommend against setting out. The usual northwest front comes in hard from the northwest and then swings to the northeast, blowing sometimes as much as 25 knots, dead on the nose, and bringing cold weather with it. These are just the kinds of conditions that exhaust a delivery crew and usually make for trouble of one sort or another.

I personally prefer Charleston to Morehead City as a landfall. Charleston is a large port with no off-lying shoals, and it has a strong radio beacon. Morehead City, on the other hand, has a weak radio beacon, and Cape Lookout shoals extend far enough offshore that one can run aground before ever spotting the lighthouse. And too, if you arrive in Charleston and the weather is good, you can always scoot along the shore up to Morehead City without having to put up with the annoyances of the Waterway.

The route to Charleston and Morehead City can vary. The straight-line distance from St. Thomas to Charleston is 1200 miles, and from St. Thomas to Morehead City is 1160 miles. But the straight-line distance is not necessarily the fastest route. By this route you will be sailing out of the trade-wind belt quickly and diagonally crossing the doldrums, which bodes for many long hours under power. The route I much prefer is to leave St. Thomas heading west of the rhumb line, make a landfall at San Salvador, pass just to windward of Great Abaco and Little Bahama Bank, continue northwest until the Gulf Stream is reached, and then turn due north. Though this is 200 miles farther than the direct route to Charleston, there is a greater chance of holding the wind, and the current is favorable throughout the entire trip. On a 41-foot yawl, we once did this run in seven days and three hours without using the engine.

Some yachtsmen prefer their departure via Bermuda. If you leave St. Thomas and follow the North Star, 800 miles later you will bump into Bermuda. Usually you will boom off on a beautiful beam reach for three-and-a-half days, spend a day in the doldrums, and then run on into Bermuda on a southwesterly. Easy sailing, to say the least. From Bermuda to the States is straightforward sailing, again coasting along on the predominant southwesterly, except that special watch must be maintained for a northwesterly front.

Correct timing is as important as selecting the correct route. Obviously, the hurricane season is to be avoided. This is particularly true when you consider that most hurricanes follow approximately the same course as a boat's course to the States via the Bahamas. Progressing towards the States at 150 miles a day with a hurricane chasing you at a rate of 300 miles a day is not an enviable situation for any boat. If you must sail after June, I would advise taking the Bermuda route. Given a good weather report, with no possible hurricanes building up, you can be out of the hurricane area within 48 hours and be safe for the rest of your trip to Bermuda. Needless to say, in Bermuda you must again check the weather reports thoroughly before setting out for the States. Most hurricanes that begin in the Caribbean follow a course up the coast and pass between Bermuda and the States. If the picture looks good as you set out, only to have a hurricane develop down south after your first day at sea, you should still be able to reach the mainland well before any Caribbean storm could make itself north.

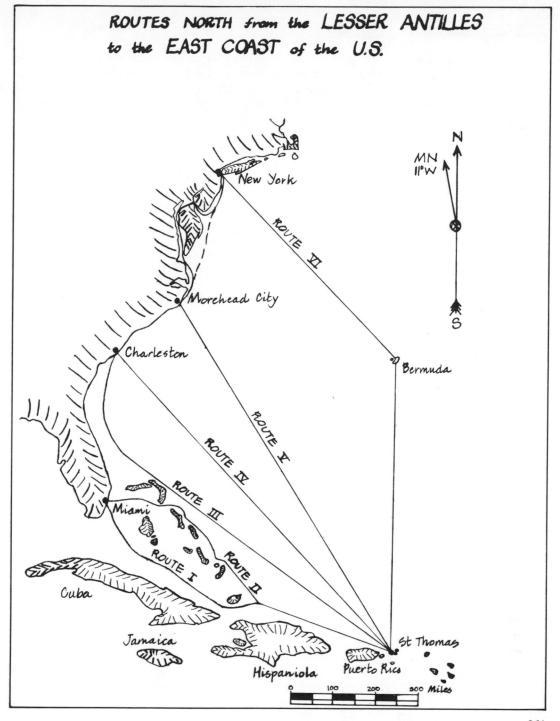

ROUTES NORTH from the LESSER ANTILLES to the EAST COAST of the U.S.

LEAVING

It is worth noting that the pilot charts show a large predominance of gales around Bermuda in the spring and fall. Thus, don't leave before the end of April and no later than early September.

Every spring there is an exodus of yachts north to the States and east to England and the Mediterranean. This exodus becomes a downright flood right after Antigua week. Yachts use Antigua as a departure point because it has all the necessary facilities for marine repair and for provisioning. And Antigua Week offers an opportunity for one last fling before setting out to sea.

To Europe there are essentially two routes one can take—the easy way and the hard. The easy way follows the aforementioned route to Bermuda, continues north until the prevailing westerlies are found, and then swings east to whatever your destination might be. A lesson can be learned from the becalmed 1972 Transatlantic Race. Before leaving Bermuda, establish the exact location of the Azores high and plan your course to avoid it. For safety's sake it is wise to check with the Coast Guard to find the southern limit of the year's crop of icebergs. And, too, a thermometer is a valuable piece of equipment, as a careful running check of the water temperature can tell you whether you are in or out of the Gulf Stream. In it, you are receiving a kick in the right direction and should enjoy a warm crossing; north of it, the temperature drops, fog increases, and the weather on the whole is miserable.

Some boats follow what I call the "hard route" to Europe, usually because they are in a hurry. Leaving Antigua and sailing hard on the wind on the starboard tack, they slog their way against the trades, hoping that by May the wind will have swung south of east. Sometimes this is wishful thinking, sometimes not. Passing out of the trades, they must then power northeastward through the doldrums until they progress far enough north to pick up the prevailing westerlies, with which they can romp on home. In all, this is a rough passage, but, with luck, it can be accomplished quickly. More than one charter boat has deadheaded hard on this route to make good a Mediterranean charter in excellent times.

Still other boats leave the Islands bound west through the Panama Canal. While this might appear to be an easy trip down the trades in balmy Caribbean weather, it can often get quite rough. Along the Venezuelan coast as far as the islands of Curacao, Bonaire, and Aruba, there is usually no difficulty. But west of Aruba you can often encounter heavy weather and large, confused seas. Several boats have been pooped in this region and others have ended up as total losses on the north coast of Colombia. I'm not sure exactly why this nasty weather builds up here, but be forewarned.

Sailing west from Grenada to Panama can often be as dangerous as sailing the same course in an easterly direction (for which see my discussion in the earlier chapter). While the toll of boats lost sailing eastward is legion, there have been boats lost sailing westward as well. In 1973, the 50-foot ketch *Renegade* and the 40-foot cutter *Cygnis* left Grenada for San Diego after complete overhauls. Both were wrecked on the Colombian coast. Similarly, in the summer of 1972, *Eleuthra*, a well-equipped, well-sailed, 57-foot ketch ran into heavy weather and was badly pooped. She came through in the end but not without damage and serious injury to her crew.

This may not be the most cheerful note on which to close, but I have noticed that too often are departures undertaken in a false sense of security. Island cruising confers many joys with little open-ocean weather to contend against. But do not be lulled off guard. Offshore passages can get ugly in any season.

Chartering

One of the amenities of modern times is that there is scarcely a luxury in the world that is not within reach of the average man. It may cost a year's savings for a brief fling, but still, the fact that it can be done at all is a mark of Western World progress—for what that may be worth.

In the Antilles, it's worth a lot; here incomparable sailing is now offered for rent in all types of boats, catering to every taste and budget from fairly spartan to no-comfort-spared opulent. Smaller boats from 28 to 32 feet suitable for a couple can be bare-chartered for as little as $400 a week, while crewed, palatial, 100-foot ketches or schooners go as high as $4,000. In between, of course, is any number of other craft: excellent sailers lacking some of the luxuries; well-appointed motorsailers, with air-conditioning, freezers, stereo—and hopeless windward-going ability; big, comfortable cruising boats; and bare boats of all shapes and sizes.

It is impossible here to give a list of charter brokers in the States or the Islands, as they come and go too rapidly. Consult the boating periodicals' back-of-the-book sections, and start writing for information. Don't be afraid to write to individual boats, as some of the oldest and most experienced skippers do not have brokers but deal directly with the charterer. Others book both direct and through brokers. Still others are exclusive with one broker and book only through him.

The cost of chartering varies drastically. The cheapest head boats (where one person signs up for an individual bunk) charge about $200 per week for bunk and food; drinks are extra. If you pick a relatively small bare boat and cram six aboard, you could get away with as little as $100 a week per person. Six aboard a more commodious bare boat will run to $200 each.

If four people charter a boat with crew in the 45-foot (of which there are only a few) to 60-foot category, prices range from a low of about $250 to a high of $500 per person per week. Six people on the same boat will reduce the per-person charge, of course, but will make for uncomfortably close quarters. Once the boats go over 60 feet, the sky's the limit. Some happen to be moderate, but others are fabulously expensive. Naturally the more you pay, the better the crews and the more elegant the boats. For a price, you get superb cooking, wine with meals, some entertainment, and red-carpet service all the way. Even in this category, however, very few boats take more than six passengers.

A good comparison is to be made with the costs of hotel accommodations. In most cases, on crewed boats liquor is included in the price, so there is no huge room service and bar bill staring you in the face at the end of your vacation. In sum, I would estimate that chartering a crewed yacht works out on a per-day per-person basis to about the same as you would spend ashore. But hotels are as varied as the charter fleet. If you are of the sort to pick a simple, inexpensive hotel, you would probably do likewise in a charter boat. But if you're willing to spend $75 a day each on a hotel with drinks, tips, trips, etc., extra, you'll do very well on a luxury charter boat at the same fee—usually with all extras except tips included in the base price.

Speaking of tipping raises an imponderable. Even though a charter skipper myself, I have observed no hard and fast rules. All I've seen is that an owner-skipper often comes off on the short end of the stick. On *Iolaire* I have practically never received a tip, though my crews almost always have. Whenever I have skippered someone else's boat as a substitute skipper, I have been tipped. I guess it's part of the barbershop tradition, in which the owner of the establishment is not considered in need of a tip.

As for tipping the crew, there are no rigid standards here either, but it should be kept in mind that on many of the yachts the crews are young, eager, out for adventure, do their best to please—and are paid beans. They rely on tips to make a financial go of it. Similarly, by American yachting standards the skippers in the Islands are paid nowhere near what they would receive for a similar job in the States, but are willing to work for less as they enjoy the life and, quite frankly, whatever tips might come their way. Generally, for a good crew who has really tried (and the vast majority do), ten percent of the charter price to be split among them is in order. But like all else, some charter parties have been extremely generous and others very tight-fisted.

Some people who find it awkward to tip the owner-skipper have another much-appreciated way. They send useful items for the boat which they know the owner wouldn't ordinarily buy himself, such as clocks, crockery, lamps, and what have you. Others have been known to invite the skipper to the States for a week or two, and have donated round-trip tickets. Still others offer to chase down spare parts for him, should he cable in an emergency.

All the above are received gratefully, but the best tip you can possibly give an owner-skipper is to charter him again, and the next best thing is to send your friends down to charter his boat. To the skipper, sailing with guests who have been on board before makes the job a lot easier, and friends of previous guests usually turn out to be better prepared at the outset.

Some crewed boats, especially the smaller ones, charge a flat fee for everything and have done with it. But many of the larger boats add a per-person charge to the basic price for consumption of fuel, food and liquor (though this is sometimes itemized separately at the end of the charter), and for laundry, dockage, and port clearance charges. A small fraction of crewed boats charge a flat fee and then deliver an extensive itemized list of extras at the end. This is a system I would urge you to avoid. The last day of a vacation is a poor time for the skipper to work up a swindle sheet and for the charter party to try to check it over.

The most important thing in chartering a crewed boat is that in any case you know fully what kind of deal you are getting into and what the final costs are or are apt to be before you make your final commitment.

On bare boats, arrangements tend to be a lot simpler. Essentially, you pay for the use of the boat, and either the agency or you, the charter party, stocks it for the cruise. If the former, then there is, or should be, a standard set price. But even though it leads to somewhat more complicated fee structures, I think it is better if the agency does the provisioning. In this way you can depart immediately upon your arrival, and don't have to waste a day chasing around a strange city trying to store an empty boat when you would much rather be out sailing.

One thing to remember in bare-boat chartering, however, is that some come with a more or less complete inventory of equipment, and others with only the bare essentials. Make sure you are sent a complete list of what the boat comes with before you sign anything. Some boats, for example, can be supplied with spinnaker and several headsails, while others carry only a rudimentary jib.

The greatest disadvantage of bare-boat chartering is that the lessee is completely responsible for the boat. This is immediately impressed on you by the fact that all bare-boat charterers demand a so-called damage deposit, usually to the amount of the deductible ("excess" to the British) of their insurance policy. If you lose the dinghy (or it is stolen), repayment comes out of your pocket. If you run aground and knock paint off the bottom, the owner has the right to haul the boat and have it sanded and repainted—and there goes your deposit. Thus always run through the equipment list when you are being checked out on the boat; if anything is missing have it noted and co-signed on the list or you will be charged for items you didn't lose as well as for those you did.

Presently this damage deposit is about $500, but now that larger boats are coming through with bigger insurance deductibles, I would guess the deposit would rise to $750 or $1,000 in the not too distant future. Also, you should be prepared to demonstrate your sailing as well as your paying ability. Before the keys are handed over, you will have to demonstrate skills on board the boat you are chartering, showing that you know how to pilot, anchor, and sail.

There is a third type of charter, for the individual who doesn't have too much to spend or hasn't put together a group. Charterers who fill their boats with such individual bookings refer to them as "head boats." I suggest being very careful before booking into one of these. Obtain names of people who have gone on the cruise within the last few months. And if the charterer won't provide you with such references, forget the whole thing. They are used to being asked for names, and should cooperate in supplying you with a proper list.

Some head boats are fastidious operations, even though they may not look as well-maintained or come with as many luxuries as the plusher fleet. Ten days or two weeks of fun and adventure, with sailing lessons thrown in, can be had for a most reasonable price. Most of them have been in business for years, enjoying tons of repeat business, but there are a few that are so bad no one can understand why their owners haven't been thrown in jail for fraud. But don't let this minor risk scare you away from head boats. Just check carefully and only go on one that comes well recommended.

Charter agreements can be written in various ways, but basically the broker agrees to place such-and-such a boat at your disposal (with or without crew as the case may be) for a set period at a set price. The agreement states that the vessel is fully found and ready for sea (in the area where she is to be used—lack of a fog horn or bell doesn't render a boat unseaworthy in the Islands). Frequently if the charter is to begin or end some distance from the boat's home port, a "dead-head" fee of one-half the per-diem rate is charged for delivery or return of the boat. In the case of a crewed boat, the broker (or owner) is responsible for providing a competent crew, who are to be in charge of the safe operation of the boat at all times. The charterer can tell the captain where he wants to go, but the decision to go there or not rests with the skipper.

In the case of bare-boat chartering, the charterer must be able and willing to convince the broker that he is competent enough to handle the boat. If he cannot, all the good bare-boat organizations have stand-by skippers available, and the charterer will have to pay his wages. Further, most all bare-boat agreements stipulate that the boat must be at a safe anchorage before sunset. If you are out after dark and get yourself in trouble, you'll be paying the damages, rather than the insurance company.

If the boat is not ready to leave exactly as promised, or is forced to lay over during the cruise, most agreements provide for one day of "breakdown" per week of charter without penalty. This applies to bare or crewed boat. For example, if you are chartering for three weeks, the boat may not be sailable due to unforeseen breakdown for three days of those three weeks, and no money will be refunded. For every day over that, a per-diem refund is given, or in extreme situations the remaining charter may be cancelled with refund per diem.

Be sure to plan ahead, as the best boats invariably are booked early on. However, if suddenly you decide to charter at the last minute, start phoning reliable brokers. There's an outside chance that some one of them might have a cancellation.

The normal routine in payment calls for a 50 percent deposit, balance due prior to departure. The deposit is stated as non-returnable, for the reason that once the boat is booked, all brokers are notified and its availability crossed off the books. If the charter is cancelled subsequently, it is difficult and often impossible to fill the slot in time. The charter season is relatively short—mainly December to mid-April—and a two-week blank in the middle of it is costly to the charter operation. However, if you notify the broker or charterer of your intent to cancel in such time that they are able to book another charter in your place, your deposit will be returned. There is no legal pressure you can bring to bear in this instance, but most operations are honest about it. A bad reputation on their part can prove to be harmful.

In the early days of the charter business, a boat was usually paid for at the completion of the charter, and personal checks were freely accepted. Unfortunately, all this has gone by the boards now, due to a flood of last-minute cancellations with no deposits securing them, and a bundle of bum checks. Charter operations were getting stung with increasing frequency. Now, practically all charter boats require that payments be made in cash or some sort of certified check prior to the commencement of the charter.

Another recent trend is for the charter operation to deal direct with its clients, rather than through a broker. A look at the economics of the business will show why. Insurance costs alone have doubled and in some cases tripled since 1967, labor costs have tripled, the cost of replacement gear is up at least 50 percent, dockage fees have doubled, and hauling charges, port dues, licensing, and other incidentals have similarly increased. Some brokers are now charging the boats 20 percent of the *gross*—including food—which works out to close to 30 percent of the basic boat price. This is a far cry from the old formula in which the broker received 10 percent of the first $1,000 of the basic price only, and 15 percent of anything over that. Further, many of the brokers insist that the boats they are handling help out with advertising expenses, printing of brochures, and so forth.

And the brokers, too, are getting squeezed, in that more and more charterers are coming to them through travel agencies, with the result that they have to split the commission. Thus a broker may be forced to jack up his commissions even higher. In the face of all this, the mathematics roughly works out that 15 weeks of charter business made direct with the client is equivalent to some 20 weeks of business booked through a broker.

Despite the pinch of the economics, people are continuing to buy new boats and placing them in charter. In a very few cases, with a properly organized and efficiently run boat, purchased for a bargain price, this can be a money-making enterprise. However, I've yet to find someone who knows the business well who will maintain that chartering a boat is a financial success. Most boat owners look on chartering merely as a tolerable way of minimizing the expense of owning a good cruising boat.

In a way it's still a buyer's market, because of the vast variety of different boats to choose from. This will give you the opportunity to match your personality with that of the skipper of a crewed boat, or your sailing preferences with the performance of a bare boat. You should try to do just that, as most brokers can't be bothered with making this important effort. Someone who would prefer a comfortable motorsailer with a crew that waits on him hand and foot is bound to be mighty unhappy on a converted Twelve with a crew forever grinding in sheets. If you really would like to help sail a crewed boat, be sure to specify this to the broker and skipper. Some skippers are happy to let an experienced charter party sail the boat; others don't like to have them do anything but sit and watch. Make sure your desire to do some sailing will be relayed to the skipper.

Likewise with bare boats. Some hot racing designs are available for bare-boat charter, but in the main bare-boat offerings are fat and comfortable, going to windward like a rubber duck. I feel it is essential when bare-boat chartering to be very careful about the kind of boat involved, as well as the organization behind it. Talk to two or three different people who have chartered the boat in question, or at least one of the same type. Further, check the equipment list carefully. Some bare boats are just as bare as Mother Hubbard's cupboard. Others are moderately well equipped or even fully equipped. In most cases, however, there will be a lack of tools on board. Supposedly, the boat is in such fine shape that nothing can possibly go wrong.

CHARTERING

But anyone who's spent more than a day at sea knows it just ain't so with sailboats.

To be sure, bare-boat operators have had nothing but trouble from ham-fisted charter parties who thought they were mechanics and turned generators into spaghetti. They have become a mite chary of leaving even a pair of pliers on board. Many operators will undoubtedly let out a howl of protest at my next suggestion, but I offer it seriously: if the list of tools and spares is not to your mind sufficient and you are an experienced repairer, bring your own. It is amazing how many tools, odds and ends, and components of a sail kit can be crammed into one briefcase. But before you take this drastic step, examine your conscience fairly as to whether you're competent enough to tinker with other people's gear.

Think twice, too, about whether you truly want to undertake a bare-boat voyage. What may be great adventure to the skipper sailing his own boat is apt not to be so thrilling to his wife who has spent the last 50 weeks in a kitchen in Jersey City, only to find herself back at it again in Road Town. Also, it can get mighty nerve-wracking being responsible for the safety of the vessel. Being his own boss, the skipper has to fuss over piloting and navigation, and get up at three in the morning to make sure his anchor is holding. And without an experienced skipper to guide him, a bare-boat charterer is likely to miss many of the best anchorages and places of interest. Finally, accurately predicting tomorrow's wind, weather, and tide conditions is tricky enough in the Antilles even for experienced local skippers, but for the stranger it is virtually impossible.

Not to beat a dead horse, but the following, I think, makes the point pretty well. For many years two highly experienced sailors frequently chartered *Iolaire,* both of them fully capable of sailing a bare boat themselves. When asked why they didn't do so instead of hiring on old *Iolaire*, each had the same answer. "We cruise in our own boats in the summer, and we work like hell in our business in the winter. When we come down here we want to relax. Don lets us sail the boat as much as we care to, but he and the crew do the cooking and navigating and take care of the details. We get in all the sailing we want, while Don does all the worrying."

The arrival of the bare boat has almost completely obliterated the small, crewed charter boats of 40 to 45 feet (there are still a handful around, including my own *Iolaire*), and made it difficult for 55-footers such as *Shango* and *Lincoln* to survive. Thus now most of the crewed charter boats are 65 feet or more. Bare boats, of course, come around 40 feet and range down to under 30. But in either case, before making a final commitment, request letters of reference from people who have chartered the boat recently and from people who have done business with the broker. A reliable skipper and broker will consult their lists of previous charterers and send you some of the names of people in your area. If they are not willing to do this, I would call that sign enough to try someone else.

Now, if I may, a few words in behalf of the skipper. Most people view the life of a charter skipper as an absolute dream. After all, he is given a beautiful yacht with maintenance paid for, cruises the Islands at the owner's expense in addition to getting a salary, entertains charming and often distressingly voluptuous charter parties, visits exotic places, and so on, and so on.

In actuality, though, he has probably brought the boat from the States in the midst of a gale or two, and half his equipment has broken down. So he must spend the next few weeks tinkering with stereo systems, refrigerators, freezers, air-conditioning systems, and all the rest of the fancy gear that owners use to lure their customers but which have an in-variable tendency to stop working at sea. Then on to the "leisurely" cruise, in which he must entertain four or six people seven days a week, 24 hours a day. Many of them are personable, but just one difficult person who expects the skipper to do everything down to handstands on the masthead can make life miserable. And this goes on week in and week out for the entire winter season, with only a one-day break between charters. But on that day our weary skipper does not haul himself off to the nearest saloon. Instead, he must take on stores and fuel and hunt down parts that have been lost by the so-called air-freight service. At other times our brokers are apt to end the charter in Grenada and have one booked for two days later in Martinique. Then they get upset when the skippers become short-tempered.

All this—plus the bother of clearing and entering, supervising each meal, taking guests on diving explorations, etc.—is one relentless strain. But recently the skippers have been clawing for some break in the ceaseless routine, and a number of boats have placed a clause in the agreement calling for the charter party to take at least one dinner ashore each week. I happen to think it's a good idea, and would predict that all will eventually have this stipulation.

As a result of these pressures, when the boys get together at the end of the season or during a rare break, the gatherings tend to go on boisterously to the wee hours of the morning. One well-known marina in the area is run by a man who doesn't drink, swear, or chase women. He tends to get very upset at these carryings on, to the point where he has kicked numerous yachts away from the dock and at one point obtained a court order forever barring certain individuals from the marina. (Which is rather foolish, since the big expensive boats who would be funneling a lot of money to the marina now anchor out, rather than alongside.)

A Brief History of Island Chartering

Like Topsy, the chartering business in the Lesser Antilles seems to have "just done growed." Actually, the whole thing was conceived sort of by accident back in the late '40s when Commander Nicholson, with his wife and two sons, stopped off at English Harbour, en route around the world, to refit their boat. While there they discovered, much to their delight, that tourists were quite anxious to go out sailing for a fee. It struck the Commander as a great way to replenish finances before taking off across the Pacific. One thing led to another, and before long more boats came out from England in quest of the Golden Fleece. Nicholson stayed on to become a charter broker and a leading light in the restoration of the old dockyard at English Harbour.

Eventually V. E. Nicholson & Sons developed into a travel agency, supply store, yacht brokerage office, and managers of hotels—all operated by the Commander and his two sons and daughters-in-law. He is also largely responsible for the creation of Antigua Sailing Week.

The American end of things more or less began in earnest in the middle '50s in St. Thomas. In those days St. Thomas was largely a divorce mill teeming with wronged young women who were establishing residency there for incontestable divorces. The wait was long and there wasn't much to do in the meantime—a ripe situation if ever I've heard one. Boat owners began clustering around Charlotte Amalie like bees to honey.

At that time there were no yacht yards in the Islands that truly could be called yacht yards. All of the owners had to make do with their own wits and skills. My own experiences are a case in point. I reacquired *Iolaire* in 1957 after she had ended up high and dry on the beach in front of the Caribbean Beach Hotel in Lindbergh Bay when her anchor

shackle let go in the swell. (Moral: don't lie in Lindbergh Bay with the swell running in; but if you must, use two anchors.) The underwriters declared her a total loss.

I bought her from the insurance company for $100, as is, where is. As there was no hope of getting her hauled anywhere, I decided to piece her back together right there on the beach. We knocked out the interior, installed framing to hold her together, and proceeded to jack her up, using greenheart wedges and odd bits of timber that were lying around. Two weeks later we had her upright and temporarily patched. We then hired a crane from the West Indian Company to float in and lift her off. After a good deal of maneuvering we got her under tow, brought her to the West Indian Company dock, hoisted her up, and began rebuilding. With the aid of three local shipwrights and a number of prep-school kids on their Christmas vacation, 14 weeks and two days from the date I bought her she was out on charter. She had 13 new planks, new frames, a new rudder, a new bilge stringer, a new interior, and a new engine.

Four years later she was converted from a seven-eighths sloop to a masthead cutter—but not by ordinary processes. While we were beating to windward under reefed main and No. 2 genoa, the jaws sheered off from the poured socket on the headstay, and the whole rig came back on our ears. (I now go to windward under double-headsail rig.) We managed to get the sails off, lashed the rest of the mess to the sides, and hung on to it all night. We arrived in St. Thomas late the next afternoon to discover that there were four days of holidays coming up. We hurried ashore to purchase wood and glue before the stores closed, and with the help of Ruben Petersen, one of St. Thomas's famous old shipwrights, the mast was trimmed and scarfed, and shortened by five feet for a cutter rig.

When everything was ready to go, we

found that there were no cranes available. The mast was stepped with "Norwegian steam." About 20 men picked the mast up bodily and set it on *Iolaire*'s deck. We powered over to *Seaward*, a 77-foot schooner owned by the late Kris Lundal. He rigged his fore gaff as a cargo boom and we started lifting the mast. At this point it was discovered that the anchor windlass didn't work, so we took a couple of turns around the bollard, and all 20 of us, heaving like a tug-of-war on the fall of the tackle, hoisted the spar.

Those were the good old days. The boats certainly were not as fancy or as professionally run as they are today, but in general I think the charter parties had more fun. What the boats lacked in luxuries (running out of ice was normal routine, not the complete tragedy it is now) they made up for in the colorfulness of their crews. Practically everyone had gone through World War II in the service of some country or other, and some had been in prison camps or the underground. They were a roistering, bold, and capable lot, and they did not expect life to be handed to them on a silver platter—quite a different kettle of fish from what is found in the Islands today.

Also, of course, there were no such handy instruments as "cruising guides." The charts were none too good (and for the most part have remained that way), and the mistakes were discovered when someone ran aground or received a bad scare when an uncharted reef slid by close aboard. Obtaining food in the mid '50s was none too easy, either. Outside of St. Thomas shopping became a major project. One always went with some trepidation out into the marketplaces, armed with a large canvas bag or a straw basket. You had to stop at a half-dozen stores at the least. And if you managed to purchase a large load of groceries at one store, the storekeeper always insisted on having a small boy carry it for

CHARTERING

you. For some reason, either out of a sense of quaintness or entrepreneurism, the larger the load the smaller the boy. To go back to one's boat like that often was downright embarrassing.

The crewed charter business developed slowly from the late '50s to the mid '60s, mostly through secondhand boats that had been bought in Europe and brought over to the Islands. Suddenly some people collectively had the brilliant (though I think erroneous) notion that lots of money could be made overnight. Boats were specifically designed for chartering, and even the smallest of them, maybe 55 feet, were running $70,000 delivered. That's a sum that takes an awful lot of chartering to pay off. Since that time the price of such boats has gone even higher, so that the owner-skipper has just about disappeared from the business. As more and more wealthy yachtsmen send their yachts down under hired skippers to latch on to some income while they're not using their boats, the old owner-skipper pulls his belt in a few more notches and keeps on working. For their part (and my own), I must say that what the older boats may lack in creature-comfort is more than made up by the fact that their skippers have been in the Islands for years, and can take a charter party to all sorts of out-of-the-way places that the hired skipper has never heard of.

The new specially built charter boats are, in most cases, floating hotels, complete with air-conditioning, freezers, hi-fi, huge after cabins, and every other wonder of the age. Most of them, unfortunately, have the windward-going quality of a sand barge, and keeping all their equipment running is what gives charter skippers grey hair and ulcers. There are, happily, a few exceptions. John Clegg's *Flica* was converted from a Twelve Metre racer to a Caribbean charter boat, and the famous *Ticonderoga* was rebuilt and converted. For those who want comfort and fabulous sailing ability, a converted Twelve goes into the wind like a train.

I often wonder, with some small degree of modesty, whether the writing of the original *Cruising Guide to the Lesser Antilles* was not what opened the Pandora's Box of the bare-boat fleet. Before this edition appeared in 1966, there was no such guide, and without one, trying to operate bare boats in the Islands would have been next to hopeless. W. R. Van Ost and Tom Kelly were the first to come out with the proper idea: a fleet of boats exactly the same to cut down on the maintenance problem, direct contact with New York, a small yard to maintain the boats, and their own guidebook to keep the fleet out of trouble.

Now, of course, there are fleets of bare boats from one end of the Islands to the other. The competition seems to get fiercer each year, so that owning such a fleet is no longer a guarantee of financial success. That's the way it should be. Investigate carefully before you charter, but come on down—the sailing's glorious.

CHAPTER 28

Provisions and Services

Currency

Money has become more confusing the world over, and the Islands are no exception. Puerto Rico and the U. S. Virgins use the trusty American Greenback, of course; so do the British Virgins. St. Martin's Dutch half, Statia, and Saba use the Dutch guilder. St. Barts, Guadeloupe, Martinique, and the French side of St. Martin use the French franc. With the exception of Trinidad-Tobago and Barbados, each of which has its own currency, the remaining islands deal in EC (Eastern Caribbean) currency, formerly called "Bee Wee." Trinidad-Tobago and Barbados currencies are freely exchangeable in banks with each other and with EC, but unfortunately this is not the case on the street. But perhaps the most irritating thing is that their coins are now all different sizes, so that if you travel from one sector to the other you end up with a jangling pocketful of useless change.

Where EC money exists one runs into a few anomalies, especially in the market. The older people will refer to the cost of something as "a penny." They do not mean the one-cent piece but rather the two-cent piece. This is due to the fact that the present EC cent is the same size as the old British half-penny, and the two-cent piece is the same size as the old British penny.

Apropos of this, until about 1968 there were practically no pay phones on Grenada. The phone company in that year installed nearly a hundred pay phones all over the island. The charge in the phone was three pennies (viz., three of the two-cent pieces). This drained the island's supply of pennies almost completely in a matter of months. Trying to obtain pennies to use in the phone became a major feat; frequently not even the bank had them.

Not only did the lack of pennies cause trouble with the phone system but at that time there were two issues of dimes on the island, one thin and one thick, each with the same diameter. Only the thin dimes would fit in the phone. You could find yourself trying desperately to make a phone call with no pennies or with ten-cent pieces too thick to fit in the phone. This circumstance finally drove the Grenada Yacht Club Bar, for one, to install a free phone rather than to suffer a continual fight chasing pennies.

One thing to remember is that the British pound or the U.S. dollar is freely exchangeable throughout the islands except on the French islands. As the French islands had until recently little trade with the British islands, EC money is discounted on the French islands at a horrible rate. Similarly, French money, although freely exchangeable elsewhere in the world, is practically worthless on a British island. You will have a very difficult job even getting banks to accept French francs. The good old U.S. dollar is still the best method of exchange in the entire Lesser Antilles—the dollar may be floating but it is a long way from sinking. Rates of exchange, of course, vary; rates would also vary depending whether you are changing U.S. dollars, traveler's cheques, personal checks, or coins.

Food

Certainly a key ingredient of an enjoyable cruise is keeping the crew on a varied, wholesome, and plentiful diet. With some planning, it can be done conveniently and economically. The price and availability of certain foods range widely among different islands. Imported produce is particularly expensive, as you pay the American or European retail price plus shipping and duty. (In the Islands, as everywhere else, added costs are passed on to the consumer.) The "supermarkets" of any island stock just about what you would expect to find in a *small* market in America. Only the coffee changes radically from island to island.

The cheapest food in the Lesser Antilles is to be found in Puerto Rico. The supermarkets and shopping centers of the larger towns in Puerto Rico are as vast as in the States. Puerto Rico, being a high island, has the water supply to grow great quantities of produce and to market it at relatively low prices. The U.S. Virgins, on the other hand, import their goods; there's no point tilling crops if you can lay your land off to the developers at $20,000 an acre. What little produce that is home-grown is snapped up before it ever gets to market. At one time, the markets of St. Croix and St. Thomas had some of the finest fruit to be found anywhere. On Saturday mornings you could buy wonderful, small bananas (locally called "figs") and the most delicious pineapples I have ever tasted—so tender you could eat the core. Now all that you will see cultivated is a batch of tasteless tourists!

In the British Virgins the food supply is generally adequate, though not so plentiful as Puerto Rico or St. Thomas. What they lack in variety, however, they make up for in accessibility. One can stop by the small shop next to the Tortola Shipyard and give a couple of bucks to a cab driver to fetch the ice while you do the shopping and enjoy a beer at the pub. Then everything can be loaded directly into the dinghy and off you go.

Proceeding on through the islands, you will find only the basic necessities—at high prices—in Anguilla and St. Barts. St. Martin has a fairly good supermarket of recent vintage. St. Eustatius, a small island, has little food for sale outside of the basics. St. Kitts now has an adequate stock since its long-overdue decision to diversify its agriculture. Their strong suit is fresh produce; they are somewhat understocked in canned goods and meat. The case with Antigua is like that of St. Thomas: everything shipped in at high prices. Best to do your shopping in EC currency in Antigua, as the storekeepers tend to redeem U.S. dollars a notch or two below what the banks will give you.

From Guadeloupe south to Grenada there is no difficulty shopping on the major islands. Every island has at least one market, the ones on Guadeloupe and Martinique being the best. The latter two, both French islands, are the best places to stock up on wines and cheeses, which on the British islands are extremely hard to come by.

Among the charter skippers who keep close tabs on such things, a consensus of opinion ranks St. Lucia as the most inexpensive place to stock a boat. I will cite but one particularly personal example to drive this point home: a case of Heineken in St. Lucia is 35 percent less than in Grenada.

On all the wet islands, such as Martinique, Guadeloupe, or St. Lucia, fresh fruit can be had in abundance, more than you could possibly eat. But always taste the oranges beforehand; some of them are as sour as lemons—great in rum punches but not for much else. Salad ingredients and fresh vegetables also abound. They may be different from the ones you are used to in the States. Christophine, a yellow vegetable with small prickers, is excellent when peeled, pitted, and boiled. Green papaya is prepared the same way. A green vegetable called pumpkin (which it resembles, but isn't) has a delicious taste, something like squash. Various types of squash are available, as are turnips, carrots, beans, eggplant, and plantain. The plantain looks like a large banana. It may be baked or boiled—very good with fish—or fried in "chips" to go with drinks. Breadfruit is good baked, boiled, or fried. There is a wide assortment of potatoes sold under different names from island to island. Here is a list of native produce available in local markets:

Fruits

Banana—Eat fresh or bake with rum or pancakes. Available all year.

Grapefruit—Available most of the year.

Orange—Available most of the year.

Pineapple—July to January.

Custard apple—Pulpy, yellowish, and sweet; July to September.

Golden apple—Yellow when ripe; eat fresh or make into jams or jellies.

Granadilla or Passion Fruit—Can be eaten straight the year 'round. Also, makes a lovely punch: juice of the fruit, water, and condensed milk.

Guava—Varies from round to pear-shaped. Flesh is white, pink, or slightly yellow. Many small seeds in the pulp. Eat fresh, or make into jams, jellies, nectar, or guava cheese. May to September.

Mammee apple—Large (a good eight inches in diameter), with rough brown skin. One to four large seeds, and apricot-flavored pulp. Makes lovely jams, or can be eaten raw. June to September.

Mango—There are various kinds, of which "Julie" and "Cylon" are the best. Makes chutney, jams, or good dessert. April to September.

Seville orange—Year 'round; juice or marmalade.

Soursop—Pulpy, white inside, with numerous seeds. A delightful drink when squeezed, mixed with condensed milk, and served cold. Also, good flavor for ice cream. December to April.

Sugar apple—Pulp is sweet with numerous seeds; eat fresh. July to December.

Papaya or paw paw—Dual purpose: when green, cook as vegetable; when ripened to orange color, eat fresh like melon with lime juice.

Sapodilla—Round or pear-shaped, brownish skin, brown-pink flesh, with flat, shiny seeds. Delicate flavor. January to May.

Mandarin or tangerine—The familiar citrus fruit.

Watermelon—Two kinds: the U.S. type shaped like an American football, or the Venezuelan type, round like a soccer ball.

Vegetables

Avocado—June to November.

Pumpkin or squash—Different from North American pumpkin; yellow flesh; cook and eat as vegetable, or makes delicious soup.

Christophine—Light green, about five inches long, pear-shaped and wrinkled.

Eggplant or aubergine—Beautiful dark purple; slice, dip in egg and bread crumbs, salt lightly, and fry.

Lettuce—Leaf type. To store Island lettuce for any amount of time is difficult, but it can be done. One method is to keep it in a bowl with very little water (too much will rot it). Some people put it in a paper bag and sprinkle in a little water. Others store it in a plastic bag in the ice box, a method which has not shown me great success. I have even known it to be placed in damp earth and kept growing.

Okra—Long, horn-shaped, fibrous on the outside; can be eaten boiled, or as an ingredient in soups such as calaloo.

Pigeon pea—Makes a delicious soup; or serve

as side dish, or use in beef stew. December to March.

Plantain—Similar to banana, but not as sweet and longer with pointed ends. Available year 'round.

Tomato—Year 'round.

Potato—Sweet, similar to American yam. Year 'round.

Corn—September to December.

Calaloo—The large green leaves of the dasheen plant. Cook and serve like spinach; or use as soup base.

Bluggoe—Thick, short, green, looks similar to plantain. Slice thin, fry in deep fat.

Breadfruit—Round and green, about ten inches in diameter. Boil and mash, add seasoning, one egg, some butter, black pepper, and salt; shape into balls, dip in bread crumbs, and fry. Real tasty.

Spices

A vast assortment of spices is found in the Islands. Included are nutmeg, sapote (the tonka bean; can be used in place of vanilla), saffron, ginger, clove, cinnamon, black pepper, bay leaves, and arrowroot (found only on St. Vincent).

Bread presents something of a problem. Readily available and good though it is, it won't keep more than a few days no matter what you do. Best to load up with the various cornbreads, coffee cakes, and bran muffin mixes. This will cut down on trips ashore. Cassava bread is available in the various markets. As for milk, it is advisable to use the powdered or evaporated type. Fresh milk is difficult to find and expensive.

The best buys in liquor are on the American Virgins, St. Martin, St. Barts, and Antigua. Antigua is a late-comer to this list. For years, liquor was expensive here as on all the British islands, due to a heavy excise tax. Antigua, with its many beaches, coves, harbors, and inlets, was an ideal place for smuggling, and it was just a matter of time before the government was soon spending more money paying agents to chase the smugglers than it was collecting in excise tax. Finally some sharp accountant suggested that the tax be reduced to an extent that it would no longer be profitable to smuggle. Sure enough, the smuggling died out, the extra taxmen were put out of work, the government saved money, and Antigua is now an excellent place to stock up on hard liquors. Just the same there is a substantial difference between stores, so shop around a bit. (Watch out for the soft drinks. That's where they really make their money. These are all imported from the States and outrageously expensive. A boatload of thirsty children will put you in the poorhouse.)

Liquor may be readily purchased in bond on Grenada and St. Lucia. In bond, the price is duty free but you are forbidden to open the bottles until you have reached international waters. You may buy as much as you like, although there are restrictions on the quantity you can bring into another country without paying a duty on the excess. On the other islands, I have found the paperwork so laborious that it is not worth the effort.

The best buys in wine are in the French islands. St. Barts is good, Guadeloupe better, and Martinique excellent. In Martinique contact Philippe Lacheren at Socara, 48 Rue Lamartine. He is a young man with excellent taste in wine, generous in his discounts, and a good sailor to boot.

Ice

Obtaining ice in the Antilles is relatively simple. It comes in all shapes and sizes. Block ice is, of course, the best. The worst is shaved ice, which has usually melted by the time you return to your boat. In St. Thomas, block ice can be had within carrying distance of Avery's Boat Yard from ICD Island Cube. Both Burn's Ice Factory, across the street from the Catholic Church near the waterfront, and ICD will deliver. In Road Town, Tortola, ice may be fetched by taxi, so long as the drivers are willing to let you carry it in their cabs. In Anguilla the block ice is so cold that there is no problem with its melting in the back seat. In St. Martin, it has become difficult to obtain and may cost as much as ten cents a pound. It is also available in St. Barts, but also at horrendous prices.

The saga of block ice on Antigua could be a book in itself, but here I will try to be brief. When I first arrived in Antigua in 1960, there was a block ice plant left over from World War II, but it was located by the airport and there was no direct road to it. You had to get at it via St. Johns—roughly a three-hour round trip—hence you did without ice. The English made a virtue of necessity; they drank their rum neat and extolled the pleasures of warm beer. (However, whenever an American yacht arrived, they were more than happy to come aboard for a gam and a nice cold drink.) Within a few more years the plant died, so Carib Marine bought an ice *cube* machine; it produced inadequate quantities of fast-melting little squares at exorbitant prices. More recently, Antigua Slipway also installed an ice-cube maker, but that only compounded the error. The situation was relieved somewhat about 1970, when someone rebuilt the airport ice plant and a new road to the south coast was cut through, reducing the round trip to a little over an hour. That was all well and good, except that the English Harbour crowd had become so used to limping along on a minimal supply of ice that no one bothered to trek out to the airport, and the block ice plant went bust. So cubes it was again, and cubes it remains.

It's possible to buy shaved ice from the government fishery establishment in St. Johns.

PROVISIONS AND SERVICES

The price is right, but the problem is that shaved ice melts so fast that 200 pounds bought in St. Johns ends up as 100 pounds in English Harbour. Somehow the 1973 Race Committee for Antigua Sailing Week managed to have plenty of ice on hand each day in English Harbour. They seem to have achieved the impossible, but how I don't know.

From Guadeloupe south to Grenada ice is relatively abundant. In the main towns particularly, there is no shortage. In the smaller islands of the Grenadines, it is occasionally available. The Bequian schooner captains will bring blocks over from St. Vincent on request. This is a more satisfactory arrangement than buying cubes at the Bequia Slip. There is an ice plant on Petit St. Vincent, but during the winter it is a good idea to call ahead by radio to reserve some. Carriacou has an ice plant in the final stages of collapse; the prognosis is uncertain, but Tom Vickery at the Mermaid Tavern will know whether the freeze is on.

Grenada once had three ice plants, though frequently all three would be broken down at the same time. Now with a new plant installed at Spice Island Boatyard, Prickly Bay, under the eagle eye of Dodd Gorman, ice should always be available.

Fuel and Water

Diesel fuel and gasoline are now generally available throughout the Islands. It is dispensed alongside in most of the major islands. In St. Barts fuel is available alongside in cans only. And water in St. Barts is probably more expensive than wine. In St. Vincent, contact Hazel Store for the fuel tanker truck to come down to the steamer dock. Following are the islands where fuel and water *cannot* be had from alongside: Anguilla, Saba, Stacia, Nevis, Montserrat, Dominica, and Carriacou. Otherwise water is widely available and of good quality.

Electricity

Dockside electricity is at best a sometimes thing throughout the area. On the French and British islands the current is either 440 volt two phase or 220 one phase. For American boats a transformer is needed to step it down to 110 volts single phase. In the U.S. islands it is usually 220 single phase to 110 single phase. These estimations may be too optimistic. Island power plants being erratic to an extreme, voltage may be well below the stated standard. Moored to a dock, you may find the voltage as much as 40 percent below what it is cracked up to be. If you are saddled with a great deal of electrical equipment, my advice is to install a second generator.

Laundry

Laundry is the bugbear of cruising in the Lesser Antilles, inasmuch as washing machines are almost nonexistent. It's a clear case of a seller's market. It is not unusual for a crew of four to be stuck with a $40 laundry bill. Only St. Thomas, St. Croix, and Martinique have laundromats.

The laundromat in Martinique is not too easy to find. It is on the east side of the canal that is west of Fort de France, 200 yards north of the bridge. In Antigua laundry is all done by hand. Mrs. Malone is the person to contact; it is not cheap, but she does a good job. Don't ask for ironing unless you are willing to absorb an astronomical price.

In St. Lucia there is a laundry at the Privateer Marine Services under the scrupulous supervision of Mrs. Gracie Ganter, a woman who has played fairy godmother to visiting yachtsmen for more years than she would care for me to recall. In St. Vincent Miss Phills of Calliaqua (tel. 84249) will pick up the laundry at Mariners Inn and deliver it back the same day. You might as well forget about laundry in the Grenadines. Water is so hard to come by that it is probably cheaper to give the clothes away and buy new ones. In Grenada, there are women along the Mang—West Indian for the Lagoon—who will do the laundry for you. But be sure to make a count of the articles and set an agreed price ahead of time. Occasionally you can have the wash done at the Grenada Steam Laundry.

Marine Supplies

Securing these supplies is something of a problem in the Lesser Antilles. Some suppliers are better than others, but no one is equipped to answer all your needs. Oarlocks, for example, are particularly hard to find—anywhere. Best to carry a spare pair down with you. A good bottom paint is likewise hard to find. At the risk of ruffling a few feathers, I must advise against French and British paints. They have come a long way over the years, but they are still not as good as the American brands. I strongly suggest bringing a few cans of high-quality *tropical* bottom paint down with you. Your non-tropical paint will not hold up very long once you put in to Caribbean waters. There are a number of good bottom paints on the market that are supposed to stand up for a year. (I have had good luck with International "Bottom Cote" for quite a few years.) Before you select one, check with the local yachtsmen of the island for the best brand (never mind the salesman, he is trying to sell his product). Putting old bottom paint on your bottom—paint that has been standing around in the can for over a year—is about as useful as putting fertilizer on the bottom and giving worms vitamin pills. The paint manufacturers and their scientists insist that it is not so but in 20 years down here I have seen it proven so many times that I can no longer believe either the paint manufacturers or the paint salesmen.

What follows is a list of the major marine suppliers in the Lesser Antilles:

Puerto Rico

Nauticenter—50 Covadonga St., San Juan.

Miramar Marine—619 Fernandez Juncos Ave., San Juan.

Hector Sanchez—106 Diego Ave., Santurce.

Florida Wire and Rigging—202 San Augustin, San Juan.

St. Thomas

Island Marine Supply—New Sub Base Rd., Charlotte Amalie; telephone 774-0753.

Ship and Shore—Formerly Sea Saga. Havensight Mall at the entrance to the West Indian dock. Undoubtedly the largest stock of marine supplies east of Nassau.

Power Products—Box 2454, Charlotte Amalie. Onan agent, refrigeration specialist; also sells and tests inflatable life rafts. Located across the street from Yacht Haven.

Harm's Marina—Red Hook; telephone 775-0468.

St. Croix

St. Croix Marine and Development.

Tortola

Tortola Shipyard—This and various other organizations are located in the same complex adjacent to the Fort Burt Hotel.

St. Martin

Island Water World—Located at Simson Lagoon. A rapidly expanding stock, and with direct air links to the U.S. and Europe, it's possible to have things freighted in with little difficulty.

St. Barts

Alma—The Magras family can supply anything from perfume to nuts and bolts; a varied stock of marine goods.

Antigua

Carib Marine or Antigua Slipway—Between them, most yachting needs can be filled.

Guadeloupe

Au Martin Pecheur—9 Rue Sadi Carnot, Pointe-a-Pitre. An unbelievable stock of outboards, dinghies, dories, small sailboats, and various bits and pieces; but no heavy yachting gear as of this writing.

Martinique

Not too much available. Check with Martinique Yacht Charter (dock at the Savan) or Grant's Yard for what's around in Fort de France.

St. Lucia

Privateer Marine Services—Located in Vigie Cove. Constantly improving its stock.

St. Vincent

Practically nothing obtainable, but contact Dave Corrigan, Mariner's Inn, who may be able to help out in an emergency.

Bequia

Lulley's—A shop on the hill above Admiralty Bay. Now one of the major dealers in marine supplies in the lower islands. Also stocks diving gear.

Ken Walker—A machine shop under Lincoln Simmond's sail loft, he has a relatively good supply of engine, generator, and outboard parts. What he doesn't have, he will know where to look for.

Grenada

Grenada Yacht Services—Formerly a major supplier, for the last few years has done little to replenish stock.

Spice Island Boat Yard—Here again, the stock has been depleted, but a major inventory expansion recently took place; thus should have a reliable selection of supplies and paint.

Claude Patterson—For many years one of the few popular and efficient members of the GYS staff, he has opened a small marine supply store next to Lincoln Ross's Combined Workshop on the Mang. Also will help you order parts from the States and guide them through customs.

Trinidad

Very little available. Ask Trinidad Yachting Association for advice.

Sailmakers

Throughout the Islands today, the situation is a lot better than it used to be, but sail repairs are still a problem. There are a few bona fide sailmakers; others are capable of doing an excellent job of repairs; and numerous others claim to be knowledgeable, but in my estimation should not be allowed within ten feet of a valued sail. Here is a list of the better lofts:

St. Thomas

Manfred Dittrick—Hassel Island. King of the sailmakers in the Lesser Antilles. (809) 884-4335.

Aaron Jasper—Water Island. (809) 774-2919.

Martinique

Fidol—Fort de France. No one seems willing to send me his address. Go to the Savan taxi stand, find Joe Ratin, and he will take you there. Or ask at the yacht clubs.

Grenada

Iolaire Enterprises—Box 249, St. George's; telephone 2510. Donald M. Street, Jr. is agent for Cheong Lee Sails. Yours truly measures and draws the specs, and orders them (made from Howe & Bainbridge

U.S. Dacron). If I do say so myself, the cut is good, as are the handwork, fittings, and hardware.

And these are some of the better sail repairers:

Bequia

Lincoln Simmonds—Best of the Bequia sailmakers and repairers. Learned his trade making sails for Island schooners. His handwork is superb.

Grenada

Spice Island Boat Yard—Excellent stock of sailmaking materials, fittings, etc. Resident sailmaker Johnny Philip spends his summers working at Howard Boston's in the States, and does excellent repair work.

Leven Stowe—Contact through Oliver at the yacht club for awnings, hatch covers, sail repairs, and good handwork in general.

Trinidad

Griffith—Contact through Trinidad Yacht Club. Located on Simeon Rd., Petite Valley.

Puerto Rico

Walter Pluss—255 San Jorge St., Santurce.
Dave Seltzer—San Juan; telephone 723-7743.
Windward Sails—Old San Juan. Telephone 725-4585 or 722-8603.

Repairs

As a general rule of thumb, whenever you have the repair parts, almost anything can be put back into working order. It would be impossible to list all the mechanics and carpenters within an area as large as the Lesser Antilles. The numbers and the turnover are too great. I have limited myself to referring previously to some of the better-known servicemen, and in most cases I have given the name of at least one contact on each island who will be able to steer you in the right direction if he can't do the job himself.

The keynote is improvisation. A repairman of Caterpillar Tractors won't know too much about your gearbox, but he wouldn't have too much trouble sizing up your engine or generator. The hotels and stores all have refrigeration systems; the managers and storekeepers will be able to refer you to someone who can repair your mechanical or electrical refrigerator, provided you are carrying all the manuals, descriptive literature, and spare parts with you on board.

The general electrician is not hard to come by; check with the stores or inquire of local yachtsmen. More difficult to find are the electronic specialists who can repair your radio and instruments. What is more disconcerting is that many of the yacht yards are hard pressed even to find competent carpenters and shipwrights. Frequently, carpentry jobs are delayed on account of labor shortage. As an alternative, you may often find good carpenters in the local yachtsmen; some of their work is really superb. As far as shipwrights go, one must distinguish between a shipwright and a joiner, just as one does in European or North American yards. The shipwright who is used to fitting two-inch planks with a seam wide enough to put your thumb through is not the man to repair your snug teak sliding hatch. This is a job for someone from one of the local furniture shops.

If you look for help outside the yards, you can find painting and varnishing labor that is probably the cheapest in the world. You must be sure of whom you are hiring, however, and here again the best way to proceed is by recommendation of local yachtsmen. Don't hire the first kid who walks up the dock claiming to be an excellent painter, varnisher, or whatever else. Some of the kids won't know which end of a brush to use or which side of the sandpaper. But many of them will put in an honest day's work without supervision. A number of these West Indians are also able seamen. The best of them are strong, capable, and cheerful; they never get seasick and almost all of them are better cooks than they will let on. A number have taught themselves celestial navigation and served as skipper, mate, or crew on passages all over the world. However, some others become hopeless if taken more than ten miles from their homes. The backgrounds must be checked.

Hauling Facilities

These have come a long way over the years. When I first came to the Virgin Islands, there were only two major slipways, Creque Slipway, St. Thomas, which was driven by a steam-powered winch, and Vladick Wagner's Slipway on Beef Island, Tortola. The latter was an unpredictable affair; its tracks were misaligned so that practically every heavy boat in the Virgin Islands had jammed on its way up or down at some time or other. Road Town, Tortola, used to have a small slipway that was more trouble than it was worth. It was said to be such a rough track that by the time your boat was back in the water and afloat, all the new caulking had been knocked out of the seams.

But again, the recent growth in yachting has added to one's options. The main dry dock in Martinique, though cheap, has problems of its own. The shipyard which ran the dock used to be reluctant to haul yachts, but a few managed to slip in just the same. When a large ship was standing by to be put into dry dock, the local yachts would begin to gather around. The yard crew would not pay too much attention, and by the time the gates were floated in place to close the dock for draining, the yachts would all have lashed themselves up around the dock sides, their skippers readying themselves for bottom repairs. On at least one occasion this tactic backfired. A number of yachts had followed a freighter into the lock, expecting the freighter to be berthed there for no more than a week, only to discover that the freighter had been hauled for a massive job of replating. By the time the job was complete, some weeks later, the yachts had so dried out that they all but sank when the dock was reflooded.

East of the main steamer dock in Martinique is Grant's Yacht Yard. For a long time his was the only yard with facilities for side-tracking yachts. The yard was a fairly primitive operation. No electricity whatsoever. The drill and drill presses were all hand powered, including a big two-inch drill press which could put a one-inch hole through half-inch plate. This was powered by a fly wheel propelled by two small boys overhead. It was a wondrous contraption, and should have been preserved in a museum somewhere as a last relic of the Industrial Revolution.

Grant's yard is located in the eastern corner of Fort de France east of the main steamer dock. It is a superb small yard capable of hauling boats up to seven feet in draft and of side-tracking a yacht. If the mast is taken out, your boat can be stored in a covered shed, which is a real advantage in rain-drenched Martinique. Grant has excellent carpenters, though little in the way of materials (bring your own). Mechanics and electricians must be sought in the city as none are available at the yard. There are slips alongside, though these are most often crowded.

In the early 1960s Grenada Yacht Services was built by Ken Gooding and Bob Peterson. The yard included a large screw-lift dock which could haul boats of up to ten-foot draft and considerable tonnage. With this asset Grenada became practically overnight the center for yachting in the Lesser Antilles south of St. Thomas. It also became a center of a large-scale chartering business. The labor market and tourism in Grenada benefited immeasurably from the publicity which yachting brought to the island. Originally the dock was to be set up so that yachts could be side-tracked and transferred off the dock. But like many businesses in the islands, this one was undercapitalized, and the side-tracking facilities were never installed. The yard changed hands, and a large synchro-lift dock was built, but still no side-tracking. As a result there is usually a long waiting list for hauling. I might add that due to a number of changes in management, the formerly good rapport between yachtsmen and yard under Gooding and Peterson has disappeared. While GYS has expanded its dockage and hauling facilities in recent years, the yard has not maintained support facilities adequate to the expansion. If you are moored at the end of the dock, you will be expected to carry your own garbage a quarter mile to the open garbage pit at the entrance to the yard. The pit is inhabited by some of the largest rats known to man—some of whom have acquired a taste for sail cloth. Do not leave spare sails in GYS lockers. If you do, don't be surprised to find them with what appears to be a three-inch shell hole through the sail bag. The toilets and showers at GYS are generally considered the foulest outside of Yacht Haven, St. Thomas. Bringing provisions from a taxi to the boat can also be a problem. It makes for a lot of work when you can't lay a hand on a wheelbarrow or push-cart, as is most often the case. For this reason, whenever you are stocking a boat in GYS, load all your food, booze, and laundry into a water-taxi in the Careenage and have him take you.

As an illustration of the feuding that has taken place recently, in 1971 one of our more hot-blooded charter skippers was winding up a charter at GYS. His party was due to fly out of Grenada on an early morning flight, and he was planning to return to St. Vincent to pick up a second party right away. To expedite matters, he had called ahead to GYS to arrange for Customs to be at the dock at 6:00 AM and for the fuel dock to have the hose readied to take on 1600 gallons of diesel at 8:00. At 0100 he docked his 90-foot motor-sailer at the GYS dock. At 0600 there was no sign of Customs, and no one at the fuel pump. In fact, it wasn't until 1500 that he finally got his party cleared and himself fueled for the trip to St. Vincent. The dock crew arrived with the bill, which the skipper examined, noting with some surprise that he had been charged for one day's dockage. He sent back the bill and asked them to strike off the dockage. There was a long argument between the skipper and the dock boss. The skipper simply wrote out a check for the bill minus the dockage. The yard manager began jumping up and down like a jack-in-the-box, yelling to the skipper that he couldn't leave the dockside until every cent of the bill had been paid, to which the skipper replied, "Like hell I can't!" and shoved both engines full ahead. There was the rendering crunch of cleats and planks tearing loose from the dock as the motor-sailer bulled its way into the lagoon. Clear of the dock, the skipper ordered his crew to disconnect the remains of GYS fuel dock from his lines, bid farewell to the yard manager, and steamed off into the blue.

The ill will between GYS and visiting yachtsmen has led many to look elsewhere for yacht facilities in the southern end of the Lesser Antilles. Many of the smaller yachts have turned to Grant's on Martinique. There is a new drydock in the works in St. Vincent and a slipway in Union. In Grenada we have at L'Anse aux Epines (Prickly Bay) one of the cleanest and neatest boatyards and marinas you could find anywhere. It has a cradle which is adaptable to multi-hulls and which can also haul yachts up to 20 tons. You can do your own labor or hire it locally, which certainly reduces the cost of hauling. Dodd Gorman runs the yard with fairness and efficiency.

In Trinidad, the Swan Hunter commercial shipyard may be able to help you out in a pinch, but remember, this is a commercial operation that prefers not to deal with private yachts. Tugs & Lighters of Trinidad can haul most any power boat, but in hauling sail boats there is a draft limit of seven feet, except during spring tides. This again is a commercial yard. Smaller yachts can be variously hauled in Trinidad. Some use the government crane; others weighing less than 15 tons with under seven-foot draft can be hauled at the slipway next to the Harbormaster's office. This is for emergencies only; contact Dougie Meyers for details.

Antigua Slipway, English Harbour, is run by David Simmonds, who happens to be one of the best Lloyd's surveyors in the area. His facility has two slipways, the smaller one for boats of up to 45 feet, the other for yachts of any size up to 160 tons. The latter is particularly useful, as the cradle can be split so that two boats can be hauled at the same time. The yard requires that it do all bottom painting.

A number of small boatyards have sprung up inside Simson's Lagoon, St. Martin. Island Water World is building a marina and it is reported that a 40-ton-capacity Travel Lift will be in operation shortly. The great advantage of hauling in St. Martin is that there is no rain to interrupt your work. The disadvantage is that skilled labor is expensive and hard to come by.

Hauling facilities in the British Virgin Islands are limited. The established organization is the Tortola Shipyard, run by Albie Stewart. Draft is limited to about seven feet. The yard insists on performing all bottom work. A fair amount of supplies are available. The only other hauling is the new slipway at West End, which doesn't have a yard.

St. Croix Marine and Development, run by Bill Chandler, has facilities for hauling and for side-tracking all but the largest yachts. Dick Avery's Boathouse in Charlotte Amalie has a unique mono-railway. To look at it, one may well wonder how it works, but it has been in operation for several years without serious mishap. The only disadvantage is that, as a mono-rail, the main beam is directly under the keel, which makes work on the keel itself impossible. The West India Company Dock at Charlotte Amalie has a crane which can lift up to 20 tons. Antilles Yachting Services, located on the Lagoon, has a large Travel Lift that is capable of hauling at any time or tide. The only trick is threading your way up the channel to the yard. Since water depth and variations in the channel are subject to much debate, I would suggest contacting Tom Kelly of AYS by mail at P.O. Box 721, St. Thomas, or telephone (809) 775-1210 or -1930. AYS is one of the few places in the islands where boats can be stored out of the water.

There are four major shipyards in Puerto Rico. Puerto Rico Dry Dock has cranes for smaller yachts and dry dock facilities for steamships. This is primarily a commercial enterprise, and while larger yachts can be hauled for painting, there is a lack of highly skilled yacht craftsmen. Stateside Shipyard is located on Isla Grande in San Juan. The yard can haul tugs, barges, and larger yachts. Since the yard is under new management, it is probably too early to comment on its reputation. Vaello's Yard is in Catano in San Juan and caters to commercial craft. They will also haul small or large yachts, and they keep a staff of welders, mechanics, and a few woodworkers. Although delays can be expected, this is probably the best bet for the average-sized yacht in San Juan. In the eastern part of Puerto Rico at Fajardo is Isleta Marina, where they haul yachts almost exclusively and can handle drafts to ten feet and length to 65 feet. Their paint work is very competent, as is the shaft and propeller repair. There is limited carpentry service but practically no mechanical or electrical work. Slips are available and owners are permitted to do their own work.

CHAPTER 29

Entry and Communications

You can fly to most of the major islands of the Lesser Antilles, usually transferring from San Juan, Antigua, Barbados, or Trinidad. The inter-island airlines vary from poor to completely unreliable. LIAT (Leeward Islands Air Transport) is the largest inter-island carrier and is convenient in that it services almost every island between St. Thomas and Trinidad. With LIAT, a confirmed reservation means nothing —I have been physically on board a plane, seated, with a confirmed reservation, only to end up spending the night in that same airport while the plane flew on. A second problem is the flight schedules. They are subject to change without notice. A third problem is baggage. Experienced travelers to the Islands always carry a handbag with enough clothes to get them through several days, because it may be that long before they see their baggage again. If you are changing planes in the Islands, under no circumstances should your baggage be checked through to your final destination. This is asking for trouble and your baggage will almost certainly be lost. Take it with you between planes.

One supposedly can ship almost anything from one corner of the earth to the other overnight via air freight. Witness the fact that *Ondine* had a new mast air-freighted to Australia and *Pen Duick* had one sent to Rio this way. Unfortunately, the concept of efficiency has not filtered down to air-freight warehouses in the Lesser Antilles. In the view of most seasoned yachtsmen here, paying for air freight is like contributing to a favorite charity—the money disappears to little noticeable effect.

Lest you think this is mere hearsay, let me provide my own example. In August, 1973, a shipment for *Iolaire* was handed in to Air Canada in Halifax, Nova Scotia. After spending about a week in Halifax, nine weeks in Antigua, and three more weeks in Barbados, it finally arrived in Grenada—in December!

And as far as I can determine it *never* would have arrived if I hadn't spent $100 of my own money on phone calls and cables and about 25 hours' worth of detective work. But even this wasn't a record. An earlier shipment took 11 months and two weeks to reach me, and I was obliged to pay the air-freight fees in full.

All I can suggest is that if you do air-freight anything, make sure you obtain the way-bill number, the routing, and alleged flight number. Better still, send air freight only to major transfer points. Freight shipped to San Juan, St. Thomas, Antigua, Barbados, and Trinidad has a chance of arriving on a direct flight without complication. Air freight to the other islands is undertaken at your own risk— and good luck.

Communications within the Lesser Antilles can be hampered by the large variety of languages and localized patois that seem to spring up everywhere. With a little luck and a phrase book you can probably get by on most of the islands, but my recommendation is to proceed upon stepping ashore directly to the Tourist Information Center. There you will be fitted out with all the useful paraphernalia—a map of the island, street plans, tours, taxis, public transport, or what have you.

Telegraph service out of the British and American islands is excellent. The French service is not. With the British and American services I have sent cables all over the globe, with minor problems arising only in dealing with the U.S. Western Union. One advantage to the British and American systems is that the cable offices have public Telex machines. If you are communicating with anyone who has a Telex, you can wire him direct, rather than having to wait while your cable is passed through various offices or lies ignored on a clerk's desk. When cabling to and from the islands, a night letter will save money. There is frequently a backlog at the retransmission points, and rarely can a cable get through intraday anyway.

It is best not to send mail marked "General Delivery," but rather direct to one of the marinas, yacht clubs, or charter brokers marked "Hold For Arrival." Do not count on your mail being successfully forwarded from one island to another. Inter-island mail is notoriously slow. Here follows a list of reliable groups who will hold mail so marked:

St. Thomas—Yacht Haven Marina
St. Croix—St. Croix Marine and Development (or possibly the ever-friendly Comanche Club)
St. Martin—Island Water World
Antigua—Nicholson, English Harbour
Guadeloupe—I advise against having mail sent to any of the French Islands. The French postal, telegraph and telephone systems leave much to be desired.
Dominica—Anchorage Hotel, Roseau
Martinique—Ditto Guadeloupe
St. Lucia—Carib Cruises
St. Vincent—Mariner's Inn
Grenada—Grenada Yacht Club, or Grenada Yacht Services, or Stevens & Co.

Puerto Rico and the U.S. Virgin Islands have excellent telephone communications to the United States—they are on the direct dialing

ENTRY AND COMMUNICATIONS

system. But as one progresses south, telephone communications of any distance become more and more difficult, and it can sometimes take as long as five hours to get through. You can shorten the delay by calling after 7:00 at night and before 7:00 in the morning. For some reason, it is cheaper to call from the Islands to the States than the other way around.

Most of the yachts in the Lesser Antilles that use radiotelephones have old, low-powered AM sets. Though some of these have been tuned up to give good performance, their efficiency is hampered by the location of many of the shoreside transmitters. Aside from being located far apart, these transmitting stations are manned only from 0800 to 1600 or at "announced times," which change so frequently that I can only recommend that you check with local yachtsmen when you arrive. Furthermore, don't rely on 2182. Though it is supposed to be monitored 24 hours a day for emergency transmission, many people have not been able to raise anybody when calling on this frequency. For this reason I do not think that a radiotelephone is an essential piece of safety equipment in the Islands. But if you have one, make sure you have the working crystals *before* you come down; elsewise, they may not be available.

There are only two reliable, completely equipped radio shore stations in the Lesser Antilles that are capable of transmitting on many different frequencies—North Post Radio, Trinidad, which handles mostly big-ship traffic in the southern Caribbean, and WAH Homeport, St. Thomas, run by Bob Smith (phone 774-8282). Whiskey Alpha Hotel stands by on 2182, transmits on working frequency of 2509, and receives on 2009. It is closely monitored by the FCC; Smith cannot transmit messages to ships or yachts on any of the other marine frequencies without getting himself in trouble, so don't ask him to. WAH broadcasts weather

278

and identifies boats it is holding traffic for at 0900, 1200, 1600, and 2000 hours. It then goes off the air, resuming at 0800. WAH also has VHF equipment (channels 6 and 16, crossover channel 9, harbor channel 12, private yachts 70, fishing vessels 67, commercial 8, and coast 28). They can patch your call into the local or international phone system, and can send cables; charges are most reasonable and the service is good.

British Virgin Island shore stations stand by on 2182, working frequency 2030. Even though it's British, the FCC monitors very strictly.

North Post Radio, Trinidad, stands by on 2182, normally operates on frequencies 2738, 2522, 3165, but they have tuneable sending and receiving sets so they can transmit and receive on any frequency you desire. They stand by on VHF channel 16, transmit traffic on channels 25, 26, 27. If contacted on the radio they can place a call through to anywhere in the world—but the call will have to be made collect.

From Antigua south, all stations stand by and transmit on 2527—working hours approximately 0800-1600 except Sunday, 0800-1000 or 1100.

Most people assume that navigation between the islands is easy, with crystal-clear visibility always enabling one to see the next island before the last island fades away from sight. Not so. Haze can sometimes reduce visibility to two to three miles, particularly in the winter. For this reason, I have included a table of radio stations in the appendix. With the aid of a radio direction finder and aero beacons, one should be able to fix one's position in any weather. (There are several marine beacons, but they are low-powered and not too useful.) In a pinch, even a portable transistor radio can be used to get a rough fix on the commercial stations.

The best weather report on the southern

area is available on 2527 in English Harbour, Antigua, at 0900 every morning. In the northern islands contact WAH 2009.

The exact time is difficult to obtain on WWV in the Islands. However, all the former British islands broadcast the BBC news, complete with a Big Ben time tick, at 0700, 1200, 1600 and 1900. The last beep is accurate enough for the average navigator.

Going south it is very difficult to receive WWV. But sometimes CSU, the Canadian Time Signal Station, can be picked up on 3330, 7335, and 14670 kHz. If you can get it, WWV broadcasts on .5, 2.5, 5, 10, 15 and 20 mHz. It is also receivable on 5870, 8090, 12135, 16180 kHz.

Sailing along the south coast of South America, it is also almost impossible to receive WWV. Spanish stations give their times in Spanish and no really good time tick. The only reliable thing available in the western Caribbean is the time signal (WWV) rebroadcast from the Canal Zone. This is transmitted on 147.85, 5448.5, 110.80, 17697.5 kHz, for five minute intervals at 0455-0500, 1055-1100, 1655-1700, and 2255-2300 Canal Zone time.

Customs and Immigration in the Lesser Antilles varies from island to island and from day to day. I can only say that one must check with local yachtsmen to find out what regulations are currently in effect. Almost every island is a separate entity and though it may be bothersome, you must officially clear out of one and enter the next, even though they may only be a few miles apart. British yachtsmen shouldn't complain, as England governed the majority of these islands for over 200 years. They administered each and every one of them as a separate entity and finally convinced the West Indians that they were not West Indians but rather Anguillans, Antiguans, Dominicans, Vincentians, Grenadians, etc. Once divided, they were conquered; and divided still, they are wreaking revenge in the form of tedious Customs procedures.

You would do well to check Customs regulations before deciding where to send ships stores in bond. At the present time the duty regulations are as follows:

Puerto Rico—Everything subject to duty.

St. Thomas—Goods shipped directly to the boat can be imported duty-free if the goods go on board with a commercial bill of lading, but the duty on marine supplies is so nominal that it is hardly worth the effort of paperwork.

Tortola—Everything is dutiable no matter how it is shipped, unless the yacht is not normally based in the Caribbean and the skipper can convince the collector of Customs that he is merely passing through.

Anguilla, St. Kitts, Nevis—Everything shipped to these destinations goes through St. Martin. Hence, St. Martin's Customs laws apply and it is really best to work through St. Martin from the start.

St. Martin—Both the French and Dutch sides have free ports; no duty.

St. Barts—A free port, but so small that shipping doesn't stop here. Again, use St. Martin.

Statia—Ditto

Antigua—As long as supplies are consigned directly to the yacht and will be used on board, they are duty-free.

Guadeloupe—Same.

Dominica—Immaterial; that is, it's just too damn difficult to ship stores here. It's best to deal with other islands.

Montserrat—Same as Dominica.

Martinique—As long as supplies are consigned directly to the yacht and will be used on board, they are duty-free.

St. Lucia—With a good deal of paperwork, you can have marine supplies shipped duty-free.

St. Vincent—Formerly duty-free for ship's gear. In the winter of 1972-1973 Customs began charging a duty.

Barbados—All marine supplies are duty-free.

Grenada—By law there is a duty on marine supplies but the Commissioner of Customs has been given discretion, which is usually granted, to import goods duty-free. (This has encouraged yachtsmen and benefitted the Grenada economy in the long run.)

Trinidad—Duty-free but lots of paperwork.

In general, there is so much paperwork involved with shipping goods duty-free that it is often easier to pay the nominal Customs brokerage fee and to get on with enjoying the island pleasures. However, in Grenada there are two sources who seem to know the ropes better than most. Claude Paterson or St. Louis Services can get you through all the red tape in no time, and if you're having supplies sent through Grenada, I recommend contacting either one. Paterson: call 3269 or 2063; St. Louis Services: 2921 or 2927.

You will have no problem with Immigration throughout the Islands as long as you are on a boat. However, if you are flying in to join a yacht with only a one-way ticket, you must have a letter from the owner or skipper of your boat explaining that you will be sailing off the island with him. This letter, presented to the Immigration officer at the airport, will be the only way you can get outside the gate. Similarly, if you discharge a crew, he must be able to show his airline ticket home to get off the boat. Semi-permanent visitors are not welcome in the Islands.

U.S. citizens should carry a passport. The French are especially particular about it. A driver's license and a good bluff used to pass, but recently the U.S. Government has begun to fine airlines that have landed passengers without proper documents. Consequently, the airlines have begun to demand passports or, at the very least, proof of citizenship—either a voter regis-

ENTRY AND COMMUNICATIONS

tration card or a birth certificate. Incidentally, when traveling on a boat it is a good idea to keep all your important documents in a waterproof container and to keep them with your other valuables in a safe place.

The penalty in any country for blatantly violating the entering and clearance procedures is the seizure of the yacht. Recently, Island officials have adopted a harder line and you can no longer enjoy playing games with the authorities. While there have been no seizures to date, fines have become stiffer. If you are chartering, remember that your boat passes back and forth through the Islands frequently and that to ask your captain to ignore Customs and Immigration regulations is to invite trouble for his next charter party.

Standard procedure for entering a new country for the first time calls for you to hoist a "Q" flag upon anchoring. If you happen to arrive on a Sunday and do not want to have to pay overtime fees for clearing Customs during non-working hours, you can legally wait 24 hours before checking in, provided no one goes ashore during that time. If you wish to enter immediately, and after an hour of sitting at anchor with your "Q" flag up no one shows up, then the *skipper only* should go ashore with passports, identification papers, and several duplicate copies of the crew list, and either go to the Customs and Immigration office, or call them and have them come down to the harbor. One word of warning—have fenders ready. Customs officials will often come out to your boat in a local dinghy. Local dinghy owners always use tenpenny nails and leave the heads exposed when installing rub strakes on their boats, a quaint habit that will do in your topsides in a matter of seconds.

Customs Procedures

Puerto Rico

Entry ports are San Juan, Fajardo, Ponce,

ENTRY AND COMMUNICATIONS

Mayaguez, Aguadilla. In all cases, haul up "Q" flag, go ashore and phone the nearest U.S. Government Immigration office. They will send a man down who will take care of Customs, Immigration, health, and what not.

St. Thomas

If you are coming from the British Virgins or Puerto Rico, you need only clear Immigration; coming from anywhere else, you must also go through Customs and Health and Agriculture. It is best to go to the Immigration Office at the ferry dock at the western end of St. Thomas harbor, east of the Antilles airboat landing ramp. If no one is on duty at the waterfront, try the airport.

St. John

Cruz Bay; from the head of the dock cross the street, bear left: second story over the travel agency. Good place to enter, simpler than St. Thomas but only a legal point of entry if coming from the British Virgins, not if you have come from the down islands.

Coral Harbor; the same regulations apply as for Cruz Bay, but the Immigration Officer is harder to find. Find the nearest phone and call a taxi. The driver will know where to go and it will save you a long, hot, dry walk.

St. Croix

Christiansted; again, coming from British Virgins or Puerto Rico you only have to clear with Immigration; otherwise you must run the gamut of Customs, health, and agriculture. The offices are on the second floor of the post office in Christiansted. Working hours are 9:00 to 5:00, Monday through Saturday.

Frederiksted; the skipper should go ashore and call Customs and Immigration in Christiansted.

British Virgin Islands

Jost van Dyke, West End, Little Dix Bay,

and Road Town are all ports of entry for the British Virgin Islands. Regulations require that you fill out separate entrance and clearance papers, through if you are only staying a few days, they may let you do both at the same time. You must bring your clearance papers from your last port.

St. Martin

Philipsburg; usually officials will come out in a launch if you have hoisted your "Q" flag. Have your crew list ready.

Statia

No one seems to care about yachts coming or going.

Saba

Formerly, a surf boat came out and took you ashore. The police officer would be on board to receive your crew list, after which you were free to go ashore. Now, with the building of the dock, the surf boats may not be operating and you'll have to get ashore on your own. But don't worry; everything is lazy and relaxed in Saba.

Martinique

Fort de France; anchor off the Savanne and hoist your "Q" flag. A launch should be out shortly; remember to have your fenders ready. The officials will want five copies of the crew list compete with name, date of birth, citizenship, and everything else you can think of that they might want to know. Further, have your ship's registration papers ready. If you are going to be in the area for any length of time, they will issue you a passport for the ship. If you are cruising around the south and east coast of Martinique, you must still notify Customs and Immigration back in Fort de France in order to properly clear the island. If Customs does not come out, land at Martinique Yacht charter pier; Customs and Im-

migration is located at the head of the dock. M. Breton, the Immigration officer, will handle everything.

You can also enter or clear at La Trinite, but this port is inconveniently located and the harbor is poor—there is no good place to land a dinghy. Should you end up there, however, the Customs and Immigration house is located in its own new building at the south end of the harbor.

You may try your luck at entering or clearing at Ste. Anne. I have heard that yachtsmen have met with some success.

Guadeloupe

Pointe-a-Pitre; tie up to the marina dock south of town while your skipper takes the ship's papers to the Customs and Immigration office located at the main steamer dock. The manager of the marina has proven most helpful in these matters.

Deshayes; at the north end of town at the foot of the hill there is a pleasant bar where a more pleasant proprietor has a stack of crew list forms which can be filled out while enjoying an even more pleasant punch. Leave your completed list with the proprietor and go on your way. This is the civilized method.

Les Saintes; ask around for the present location of the Gendarmerie. It seems to change quite frequently. Once found, carry out business as usual. A note of caution: don't tie up your dinghy at the dock. This is where the ferry lands and the ferry captain holds little respect for pleasure craft.

St. Barts

Gustavia; anchor, hoist "Q" flag, skipper should go ashore with all papers, passports, ship's papers, clearance papers from last port. If the friendly gendarme is on duty, these papers will be unnecessary; if the unfriendly gendarme is on duty, you will need them all.

(I have been in hot water with the Customs and Immigration officials of the French West Indies ever since I recommended in my first cruising guide that entering yachts had merely to hand their crew lists to a passing gendarme, who would accept them and promptly lose them. Whatever was the case in the past, those days are gone. I now formally go on record as advising that you adhere to regulations strictly.)

Anguilla

Road Harbor, Boat Harbor, Forest Bay; follow the "Q" flag routine. Anguillan officials are usually very relaxed, so you probably will end up beseeching a police officer onshore to accept your crew list.

Barbuda

To land at Barbuda you must first clear Customs and Immigration in Antigua, so when you're in Antigua, make sure you remember to get permission for landing at Barbuda.

Antigua

St. Johns; tie up to the main steamer dock and hoist "Q" flag. If no one comes, ask at ferry office for present location of Customs and Immigration office.

English Harbour; you will attract more attention and therefore have to wait less if you tie up to the pier with your "Q" flag raised than if you anchor out in the harbor. If you can't seem to raise anybody official, seek out the police station at the entrance to the dockyard and they will help you with everything.

St. Kitts

Basseterre is the only point of entry. Hoist your "Q" flag, and usually the Immigration Officer will come out. If he does not, bring your crew list ashore to the Immigration Office, which is in the new building to the right of the dock.

Nevis

Charlestown; take your crew list ashore to the police station.

Montserrat

Plymouth; here is a place that is strict and where regulations must be exactly adhered to. Anchor directly off the dock and hoist your "Q" flag. Most likely Customs and Immigration will come out to you, but if not, go ashore and find them. Under no circumstances should you move to another anchorage without first clearing Customs.

Dominica

Portsmouth; go ashore with your crew list to the Customs Office. If you plan to stop at Woodbridge on your way south, have Customs apprise Roseau Customs of this fact so that they will not treat you like a rum smuggler.

Roseau; go ashore to the main Customs shed and enter. Do not go on to Woodbridge until you are cleared.

St. Lucia

Castries; you can tie up alongside the main steamer dock. "Q" flag will probably elicit little response, so your skipper will have to search out the Customs and Immigration office. Special note: when coming from Martinique do not anchor in Pigeon Island Cove prior to clearing at Castries. It is illegal and the Police Commissioner's house is on a high hill overlooking the anchorage. He has an eagle eye and will not hesitate to report you.

Vieux Fort; nothing out of the ordinary here. Hoist "Q" flag upon anchoring and send skipper ashore if no one comes out. The police station is the place to go.

St. Vincent

Kingstown; hoist your "Q" flag before you enter the harbor and the lighthouse keeper will alert Customs.

Bequia

Sail up to the end of the bay, anchor, hoist your "Q" flag, send your skipper ashore in the dinghy, and he can clear at the police station.

Union

Anchor at Clifton, hoist "Q" flag, send skipper ashore to Customs, and clear.

Cannouan

Anchor at Charlestown, hoist "Q" flag, send skipper ashore to police station, and clear.

Carriacou

Hillsboro; work your way in as close as possible to the Seaview Inn (conspicuous hotel northeast of town) to avoid the swell, and hope that someone notices your "Q" flag. Customs and Immigration office is at the head of the dock, should your skipper have to row ashore. Obtain coastwise clearance here, but you will have to re-enter St. George's or L'Anse aux Epines when you arrive in Grenada—"The Mainland," as it is known in Carriacou.

Grenada

St. George's; the guard at Grenada Yacht Services can arrange everything for you. Tie up at the fuel dock or moor to the steel mooring buoy north of the dock, hoist your "Q" flag, and let him do the legwork. If your boat is too deep to go up the channel, anchor in the Carenage and hoist your "Q" flag. If officials don't show, your skipper will have to go to the fire station, where the Immigration Office is located at the north end of the building, and to the baggage shack at the main dock, where the Customs office is located.

L'Anse aux Epines; this is Grenada's newest point of entry, with a guard on duty at all times. Follow normal "Q" flag skipper-only-ashore routine, and remember that if you leave St. George's for the south coast of Grenada,

ENTRY AND COMMUNICATIONS

you are required to obtain clearance from the Customs officer at St. George's prior to departure.

Grenville; once you have negotiated the long, tricky channel, don't be so cruel as to send off your skipper right away. Hoist your "Q" flag, set your awning, have a drink, and wait awhile. Then send your skipper ashore.

Barbados

The world's most pleasant place to enter. Anchor off the Carenage. The Harbor police, dressed in natty uniforms, will appear before your "Q" flag reaches the spreaders.

Trinidad

Chaguaramas; proceed to the bauxite terminal (you can't miss it) and anchor off or tie up to the dock. Customs and Immigration office is located within the terminal and is open 24 hours a day.

Port of Spain; go to the head of the main steamer dock where there is a low section to which yachts may be tied. From there it is only a short walk to the head of the dock where Customs and Immigration is located.

All in all, the Customs officials are polite and efficient. If you have a case out of the ordinary—have patience, don't lose your temper, and don't give them a hard time. Otherwise their motto becomes "Why be difficult when, with a little effort, I can be downright ornery?"

CHAPTER 30

Yacht Clubs and Racing

Many visiting yachtsmen do not realize that practically every island in the Lesser Antilles has its own yacht club. In fact, the histories of many of these date back as far as the '20s and '30s. Some clubs, of course, are more recent, having been knocked together in the last several years or so. But whether they are one-room sailing associations or gabled bastions, they are generally hospitable and together they have done a great deal to encourage the lofty pursuit of sailing in the Islands.

It is frequently assumed that the yacht clubs of this area are for members only. At least this is how the signs read. Because sign painting is expensive down here, one must learn to read between the lines. What they mean to say is "members, guests, *and visiting yachtsmen from other clubs* only." For the most part, if you simply come in by boat, you are welcome without question. The only place I was required to show my home yacht club membership card was the club of Fort de France. The Barbados Yacht Club used to be notoriously stuffy, but this attitude has happily changed over recent years. Though they may not do handstands for every visiting yachtsmen, they are certainly courteous.

One quick note: there is no launch service anywhere in the Lesser Antilles.

Yacht Clubs

Club Nautico, San Juan, is located on the eastern end of the northernmost arm of San Juan Harbor (it is shown on the chart). It is a large club with a marina. A bar, restaurant, fuel, water, ice, and showers are all right at hand. Power boats tend to outnumber sailing craft.

Ponce Yacht Club, Ponce, has a small, crowded marina and limited facilities; make arrangements beforehand if at all possible.

The club is popular with visiting yachtsmen, and everyone I have known who has passed through Ponce has sung praises to the hospitality of its members (sometimes in the thick tones of a godawful hangover). There is fuel, water, ice, a restaurant, showers, and hauling facilities for boats up to 40 feet. The club is the home of the Chalang class in which many of the present generation of Puerto Rico's racing yachtsmen have learned their racing sailing. Chalang sloops vary in length from 23 to 28 feet, and are heavily constructed with a fin keel and the rudder on a skeg. They are often raced with more enthusiasm than skill, but they are an excellent training class nonetheless.

Roosevelt Roads Sailing Association has a clubhouse and mooring areas located on the northeast corner of Ensenada Honda (Roosevelt Roads). The Sailing Association sponsors small-boat racing and once a year co-sponsors a Thanksgiving Day Race with Club Nautico de San Juan.

Club Nautico de Puerto Rico has no clubhouse, most of the members of this club also being members of other clubs. Club Nautico de Puerto Rico organizes large-boat racing and it is usually under this flag that Puerto Rican yachtsmen race elsewhere in the Caribbean. With no clubhouse and no permanent address, I recommend contacting this club through Dick Doran, Box 185, Puerto Real, Fajardo, PR 00740.

Federation of Puerto Rico is primarily interested in racing small boats, particularly the Olympic classes and Sunfish. They have a launching facility at Isla Verde, San Juan. Contact Juan R. Torruella, P.O. Box 507, San Juan, PR 00919, if you have any questions.

Club Nautico de Cangrejos is located at Boca de Cangrejos, San Juan. It is for power boats only, as there is a low fixed bridge at the entrance to the club and dock area. The club has its own Travel Lift for power boats.

Club Nautico de Catano specializes in small-boat racing, both power and sail. The clubhouse, with bar, showers, and snack bar, is located at Catano in San Juan Bay.

Club Nautico de Arecibo is, again, a sport-fishing club, with docks, fuel, water, showers, and light meals all available. It is located behind the breakwater at Arecibo. Being on the north coast of Puerto Rico, which is exposed to the winter ground swell, it is not a comfortable long-term stop.

St. Thomas Yacht Club, St. Thomas Harbor, is located due south of the West Indian Company dock. It offers showers, a bar, and a small restaurant. There is a small dinghy dock for those people anchored off.

Virgin Islands Yacht Club, Cowpet Bay (also called Secret Harbor), east end of St. Thomas. This is a very active yacht club with fleets of Sunfish, Flying Dutchmen, and many small cruiser-racers. Its members take part in most of the major cruising-type regattas. They even managed to convince the Olympic Committee

YACHT CLUBS AND RACING

that the Virgins were not part of the U.S. and fielded their own Olympic team. This rare finesse was executed by Rudy Thompson, an ex-charter skipper, who is one of the fastest talkers in the Lesser Antilles. The atmosphere is "country clubbish," with families sailing, swimming, and picnicking en masse over the weekends.

St. Croix Yacht Club, Tague Bay, is an active small-boat club with a hearty fleet of Sunfish and Snipes. They also sponsor a few cruiser races. There is not a great deal of activity here during the week as the club is located well out of town.

St. John Yacht Club, St. John, has followed a new trend in yacht racing. They start out from their home basin on Saturday, race to a good anchorage, spend the night, and race back the next day, a vast improvement over the usual start and finish at the same harbor twice in one weekend.

British Virgin Islands Yacht Group, Road Town, Tortola. This is less an established yacht club than a standing committee that is striving hard to foster sailing in the area by conducting races and by urging people to invest in a boat. I'm certain they will have a proper club house before long. Their current project is the organization of a Tortola Weekend Regatta, the week after Easter. The second running of this regatta produced 55 entrants. For an update on the racing events of this area, write Peter Haycraft or Albie Stewart of Tortola Shipyard.

Antigua Yacht Club, Falmouth Harbor, Antigua. The lifeblood of this energetic club is a fleet of Sunfish which races within the harbor right in front of the club. I can't think of a body of water better suited to this sort of round-the-buoy racing. There is also a good deal of handicap racing among the many charter boats based in English Harbour. The Antigua Yacht Club is the host yacht club for Antigua Week, the extravagant swan song of the winter season.

The week started out as a publicity stunt on the part of the charterers and the Antigua Hotel Association, but it is fast becoming a first-rate regatta that is drawing international attention. The Race Committee has been trying to build up a series of feeder races to and from Antigua before and after Antigua Week, which is commendable. If one crew cannot spare the time, a series of crews could take turns, giving the boat a season's worth of racing in a very short time.

Guadeloupe Yacht Club, Pointe-a-Pitre. Strictly a power-boat club with a very convenient location on the north side of the Carenage. They are most hospitable here. There are showers, a snack bar, and a few cold beers. It is a nice spot to leave your dinghy while shopping in town.

(There is no yacht club in Dominica as yet.)

The Yacht Club of Fort de France, Martinique, is located in the Carenage south of the main shipyard, where unfortunately the waterfront has become a receptacle of all sorts of harbor jetsam. The sailing fleet is made up of Sharks, 420's, Flying Dutchmen, and sundry cruisers and power boats. You will most likely be required to present your club membership here.

Club de Voile, Baie de Fort de France, Martinique. Located on the dock on the western end of the Savanne (a park), this club is likewise heir to quantities of jetsam. It is unsafe to leave a dinghy at the pier here unless you rig a stern anchor to hold it off. From the pier it is a short walk to the ice plant, Customs, and the Martinique Yacht Charter outfit. There are showers and a bar, and an active racing fleet. A four-star restaurant is upstairs.

Francois Yacht Club, Baie de Francois, Martinique, is located about two miles from the town of Francois; there is a small dredged basin south of the club which will carry about six feet and there is a good anchorage directly west of the club. A bar, showers, water, and gasoline are available. A fine French restaurant is attached to the club and on Sundays this is one of the most popular places on the island.

St. Lucia Yacht Club, Gros Islet, St. Lucia, is located on the south side of the channel into the basin. There is an active weekend program of Mirror dinghies. It has a bar and snack bar open during weekends and occasional weekdays.

St. Vincent Yacht Club, Kingstown, is thus far a club without a clubhouse. The principals have been trying to get themselves organized for many years with unpredictable results. The main event of the season is the Bequia Regatta on Whitsunday Weekend, now an outstanding regatta, though in years past the organization has been appalling. The first day is a race from Kingstown around Bequia to Admiralty Bay; a lay day Sunday during which the Bequia working sloops go out to race (and the guests bask on the beach watching the goings-on); and on Whit Monday a race from Admiralty Bay around Bequia to Youngs Island.

Grenada Yacht Club, The Spout, St. George's, is located on a spit of land on the north side of the harbor. Harold la Borde remarked after his circumnavigation in *Honey Bird* that the Grenada Yacht Club had the most spectacular location of any he had seen in the world. Many a late afternoon we have sat on the veranda watching for the green flash of the sun as it dropped beneath the horizon. I might add that the location is not only beautiful, it is practical as well. Where else can you moor quietly in a secure harbor within short rowing distance of shipyard, food, fuel, and shelter?

There are showers available, a snack bar, and a couple of bedrooms. The club conducts an active sailing program. The major offshore races sponsored by the club are the South Coast Race on Easter Sunday, the August Monday Race to Carriacou, and the round-the-island race on the first Sunday in January. A good feature is that the races start from a range mark in front of the club. The start can be watched sitting at the club bar. The Thursday afternoon series, strictly an informal but hard-fought series based on arbitrary handicaps, usually runs from September through Easter. Races begin at 4:30 and finish around 6:00 PM.

Barbados Yacht Club, Bridgetown, is just north of the Holiday Inn. It is a rock-ribbed establishment that boasts a vigorous and varied small-boat fleet. The racing is truly first class, as keen as any to be found in the Islands. The only drawback is the exposed location, which makes mooring a problem. Most of the classes are beach boats that are taken up after every race. Also, there is no dinghy jetty. Dinghies must be dragged up the beach, sometimes through considerable surf. The clubhouse itself is well appointed; also tennis courts, changing rooms, a large reading room, and a gaming room.

Barbados Cruising Club lies immediately south of the Holiday Inn, and suffers from the same exposure problems as the Barbados Yacht Club. There is a bar, showers, and light snacks.

Trinidad Yacht Club, Port-of-Spain, is a ramshackle wooden building, built out over the waters of what has to be the worst anchorage

in the New World. Before the 1973 Trinidad Race my navigator and I sat at the bar watching *Iolaire* pitching uncontrollably in the swell. Just watching her, we both felt slightly seasick. We concluded that the real cause of our queasiness was the club itself swaying on its pilings. Just the same, what the club lacks as an anchorage it more than makes up for in hospitality. It even has its own yacht yard with hauling facilities for boats drawing up to seven feet and room enough to side-track a large fleet of day-sailers and small power boats. Showers and a snack bar are available.

Trinidad Yachting Association, Chaguaramas, is located on what was formerly the U.S. Naval Base in the cove just west of the old seaplane hangar. The club recently received a handsome grant of land from the national government, which is being put to good use in the construction of a new clubhouse, complete with snack bar, bar, showers, and dinghy launching-ramp. Being well away from Port of Spain, the pilferage problem is considerably less than at the Trinidad Yacht Club, and the anchorage far superior. The Trinidad Yachting Association supervises all the major cruiser-type races in the area and most of the small-boat racing.

Texaco Yacht Club, Pointe-a-Pierre, Trinidad, is, as the name sounds, a small company-operated club which is located north of the long Texaco fueling pier. If you are planning to be in the area and would like to use the club, I suggest that you write Arthur Spence, c/o Texaco, Pointe-a-Pierre, Trinidad, and make arrangements beforehand.

San Fernando Yacht Club, San Fernando, Trinidad, is an active, hospitable club open seven days a week. The only problem is getting there, as it is surrounded by shoal water of three to four feet. Not surprisingly, most of the sailing here is done in catamarans. If you are suffi-

ciently shallow-drafted to get anywhere near the club, a warm welcome will be accorded to you. Bar, snacks, and showers are available.

The West Indies Yachting Association was founded in the early '60s to promote dinghy racing and class championships in the southern islands. The founding members were Trinidad, Grenada, and Barbados; later, St. Lucia, St. Vincent, Martinique, and Antigua joined. Venezuela, Tortola, and Guyana are associate members, while St. Thomas and Puerto Rico attend meetings as observers, hopefully soon to become full-fledged members. A great leap forward was made in 1973 when the spring meeting was held in Antigua at the close of Antigua Week, a time when sailors from all corners of the Caribbean are in one place. Hopefully this will have continued and the WIYA will come to truly represent all the West Indies instead of just a few southern islands. Originally formed to promote small-boat racing, cruiser racing is now its most important function, though it still runs the various dinghy championships. Its major achievement has been the adoption of a single handicap rule for all its member clubs, for which Alfred Rapier, Ray and Ron Smith, and John Clegg should receive high marks and a pat on the back. To contact WIYA, write Mr. Kenneth Monplaisier, Box 256, Castries, St. Lucia.

Racing

Yachtsmen have enthusiastically endorsed the Lesser Antilles as the best cruising grounds in the world. I'll not argue. But recognition is due as well to the robust racing in this area. Granted, there is not the depth or quality of competition that you will find on the Solent during Cowes Week, but the consistently fine sailing offered by trade-wind weather is difficult to equal anywhere in the world. Perhaps short on tradition, yacht racing in the Lesser Antilles is always long on strong, steady winds.

In the past, cruising-class races were conducted in the spring and summer at the end of the charter season, since almost all the charter yachts doubled as racing boats. These races were usually spectacular, with five or six 70-footers, glittering with all the finery common to a luxury cruising craft, hitting the starting line at one time. More recently, racing has become a year-round sport, but still the charter boat captains and their elegant yachts seem to find time to lock horns with some of the hotter racing boats that have drifted down to the Islands.

The racing was rather chaotic in the old days; each club had its own special rule, and in most cases the skipper measured his own boat. The result was mass confusion, fighting, and bitterness, and some rules had loopholes big enough to sail a clipper ship through. The new handicap rule, formulated by the West Indies Yachting Association, has proved accommodating to the needs of visiting yachtsmen. The average boat can be fully measured in the water in under two hours and, using a small calculator, its rating can be assigned in another hour. This WIYA rule has been universally accepted in all the racing centers except Puerto Rico. Puerto Rico had been racing under the Pacific Handicap Rule, but later leaned toward the IOR.

The WIYA Rule is supposed to be only a modification of the IOR, but it has been bent so much out of shape that it might as well be considered on its own merits. Fundamentally it's pretty good, but there are a few bad features, as of this writing. For one, basic L is measured by a method that penalizes boats with long overhangs. Older boats with long overhangs take a real licking. Nor is stability measured. Modern boats stand up like churches going to windward, while older boats tend to lay over a good deal further. A major disadvantage of the rule, in my estimation, is that the allowance given to yawls and ketches is not sufficient. I know this is true in the case of a yawl, as by removing my mizzen my rating is reduced. Yet without the weight and windage of the mizzen mast we have a boat that is much faster going to windward and reaching, just as fast dead downwind, and only slightly slower with the wind in the quarter (and there are practically no courses given with the wind in the quarter). Thus we race as a sloop, and I definitely know that despite the smaller sail area she is faster this way.

Actually, this doesn't bother me too much, since my mizzen mast is stepped on deck and I've got a willing crew. (It costs me half a case of beer to take the mizzen out and another half to put it back in; once this book is published, they'll probably charge me a case each way!) However, I feel sorry for larger yawls or boats that have more difficult mizzens and cannot yank them out so easily whenever they race.

At times, I have been accused of trying to get the rule rewritten to benefit myself and *Iolaire*. This is not so. I am trying to get the rule rewritten to encourage *all* boats to race, and not just the streamlined Clorox bottles. If the WIYA would make a substantial change to benefit yawls and ketches, I promise to continue racing as a sloop for two years after the revised rule goes into effect. This, I think, will prove my point that I am not trying to get special advantage for *Iolaire*.

One revision that has recently taken place was granted by the Antigua Week Sailing Committee. In order to give the older boats a chance of overall points placement in a race that had a lot of windward work, they granted a graduated over-age bonus to the older boats. This made the good, well-sailed old boats competitive. Sixty-eight-year-old *Iolaire* managed to place fourth in Division I in 1973, and David Simmonds' *Bocco*, 25 years old, would have won the cruising division had she not missed one race.

As this book is being written, the WIYA is revamping the rule to plug up some of the loopholes. I don't have the details, but I understand that length will be so measured that it will no longer be advantageous to chop the stern off, freeboard will now be subtracted from quarter-beam depth (giving the older boats a better break), and the graduated old-age bonus will be adopted. But, with some justification, stability will not be measured: finding a day of flat calm is an impossibility. They have also indicated a change with regards to mizzens, but it still appears that the bonus given yawls will be insufficient. But they hope that they will have straightened everything out enough to let the rule stand for five years. Let's hope they succeed.

Credit is due to the WIYA for formulating the rule and managing to get all the clubs in the Association to use it. It is a great step forward, as once you have your certificate you can race in any regatta from Caracas to St. Thomas.

In almost every case there is racing for all types, in that most of the clubs—those that don't, should—have the fleet split up into a racing and a cruising division (the latter with no spinnakers). In some big regattas there is also a traditional division—the old gaff-rigged boats, etc.—racing under arbitrary handicap. This means that the really hot hot-shots can have their racing, the more conservative people can get in some low-pressure racing, and the old-timer boats can go out and drink beer and watch everyone else killing themselves, and still have a good time.

Following is a list of the major races and regattas in the Lesser Antilles. While in the past prizes included gifts of hard cash, airplane trips to exotic lands, and the like (offered to spur interest in the then fledgling racing program), now the participants compete for the usual silverware—although the racing is no less fierce or hard fought because of this.

Round Grenada

First Sunday in January; around Grenada clockwise; 40 miles. This is a challenging race for the simple reason that you encounter many different conditions.

Trinidad to Grenada

Easter Weekend; 90 miles. An overnight race, it starts Thursday of Easter Weekend at 1600. Also, there is an around-the-buoys race in Grenada on Sunday (15 miles).

Antigua Week

Early May; several around-the-buoys races varying from approximately 32 to 9 miles. Antigua is the ideal place in the Lesser Antilles to hold a race week. The island itself is low and doesn't obstruct the trades. It is large enough so that numerous different courses can be arranged, ending in a different anchorage almost every night. And it is halfway between Trinidad and St. Thomas, so that boats from all corners of the Caribbean can come together without too long a sail. Originally conceived by clever publicity agents as a kind of Cecil B. De Mille extravaganza, Antigua Week has been attracting a large fleet, many of whom are serious-minded competitors in fast, new boats.

Whitsun Weekend Regatta

Seventh weekend after Easter; the course is St. Vincent to Admiralty Bay, Bequia, about 20 miles. Layover Sunday to watch work boats race and on Monday a race back to St. Vincent counterclockwise around Bequia. This is always an enjoyable weekend with good racing and good partying betweentimes.

Carriacou Regatta

August Monday Weekend (first weekend in August). On Saturday, yachts race from St. George's, Grenada, to Hillsboro on Carriacou; distance about 36 miles. Next morning, the Mermaid Inn race, round the buoys. On Sunday afternoon and Monday, three work-boat races, and everyone disperses on Tuesday. This date is when most of the people who live in the Lesser Antilles are on vacation, so attendance is good and everybody is out for—and finds—a good time.

Petit St. Vincent Regatta

Thanksgiving (American) Weekend; two races, one starting at St. George's, Grenada, the other simultaneously at Kingstown, St. Vincent; both about 42 miles, and both finishing at Petit St. Vincent. Friday and Saturday are two day-races, about 20 miles. Sunday, the St. Vincent boats race back to that port, and the Grenada boats usually cruise more leisurely back home. Some excellent sailing and scenery, but the weekend has suffered from lack of organization. The situation recently has improved; let's hope the trend continues.

Club Nautico Season

The racing in the northern end of the Lesser Antilles has for the most part remained localized, as no intersectional organization was developed to unite the various yacht clubs until 1973, when all became associated with the WIYA.

Club Nautico de Puerto Rico sponsors 14 races a year for cruising-type boats. The races vary from around-the-buoys to the 240-mile annual race around Puerto Rico.

The most important races that Club Nautico de Puerto Rico holds are: The Governors Cup Race, around Puerto Rico, usually in April; El Conquistador Regatta, in June; Constitution Day Race, in July, to Vieques and back; Labor Day Race, a weekend of racing in Fajardo; The Overnight Race, in October, around Culebra and Vieques; The Thanksgiving Day Race, a weekend race to Roosevelt Roads and return to Fajardo. There are also about 10 Series Races held throughout the year. Write Club Nautico de Puerto Rico for details.

Memorial Day Weekend Regatta

St. Thomas to St. Croix, back the next day; 36 miles each way.

Around St. Thomas

July 4th; starting at the V.I. Yacht Club, counterclockwise around the island; about 30 miles. A good, fun race, and always plenty of wind.

Basketweaver Race

Mid-July; V.I. Yacht Club; a complicated course around various islands near St. Thomas, exact course and distance varies from year to year but usually about 30 miles.

August Monday Race

First Monday in August; St. Thomas Yacht Club; St. Thomas to Road Town, Tortola, about 20 miles; Tortola Carnival and then back to St. Thomas.

Pillsbury Sound Race

Mid-August; St. Thomas Yacht Club; about 15 miles.

Race of The Saints

Early September; St. Thomas Yacht Club; 120 miles; the course varies yearly.

Seamanship Race

Late September; Virgin Island Yacht Club; course varies from year to year; about 25 miles.

Around St. John Race

Late October; St. Thomas Yacht Club; about 25 miles.

Sir Francis Drake Cup Race

Second week in November; St. Thomas Yacht Club; course varies from year to year; about 20 miles.

YACHT CLUBS AND RACING

St. Thomas to St. Martin Race

Race one weekend from St. Thomas to St. Martin, 105 miles, then back to St. Thomas the next weekend. The first race is dead to windward against the current; it separates the men from the boys. Coming back downwind is an enjoyable sleigh ride. A recently organized race with as yet no fixed date.

The Tortola Yacht Club is attempting to establish a regatta the weekend after the Governor's Cup Race in Puerto Rico in April. It will provide a good warm-up for Antigua Week and will serve to get the Puerto Rican boats racing further east. It may be tied into some kind of feeder race to Antigua Week. It sounds like a good idea to me.

CHAPTER 31

Native Boats

Sailors cruising the Lesser Antilles will be intrigued by the various types of small boats to be seen there. Each area has its own type of craft that has evolved over a period of years to suit particular conditions and needs. Interestingly, areas separated by only a few miles of open water will have evolved radically different designs.

In Grenada, the southernmost of the Lesser Antilles, there are many good harbors where small boats can safely be left in the water. The fishermen have developed the only inboard-powered fishing launch in the West Indies. These fine-lined, canoe-sterned, round-bottomed launches carry no auxiliary sail or oars, yet they can be seen out in the roughest weather breasting the Atlantic swell. At a distance, with two long bamboo trolling poles, they look like great waterbugs as they rise and fall in the seas. With infinite faith in their little hand-starting two-cylinder Stuart-Turner engines, the Grenada fishermen face the winter trades miles out on the open sea day in and day out.

At the northern end of the chain, the excellent harbors of Antigua, Anguilla, the British Virgin Islands, Puerto Rico, and the Passage Islands have given rise to a boat that also can be moored year round. It has a mast and heavy sailing hull to which an outboard motor has been added in recent years as an auxiliary to the sail.

The remaining islands lack large, natural harbors, and have thus spawned various types of haulable boats, falling into four rough categories: the Bequia whaleboats, the Carib canoes, the Saints boats, and the sailing lighters of St. Kitts and Nevis.

The Grenada launches draw 18 inches on a hull 22 feet long and five feet wide. They have a short deck on both the bow and stern, a short bridgedeck amidships housing the engine, and cockpits fore and aft. The construction is good, but rough. Keel, stem, horn timber, floors, and frames are cedar, but not the cedar as we know it in northern climates; it is rather a hard, close-grained wood, more like oak than anything else, but without oak's tendency to split. All the curved structural members are natural crooks cut out "in da bush." The dry, wind-swept windward shores of the southern islands produce the twisted, close-grained cedar trees that are ideal for frames and floors; the dryer the area, the tougher the wood. The keel and upper two strakes on each side of the boats are heavy pitch pine, and the bottom planking is of light Canadian spruce fastened to the frames by iron boat nails.

The planking is a story in itself. When a boat is built, the backbone is set up, followed by the frames. The lines are faired up with rib-bands, temporary deck beams are fitted, and the sheer strake and the plank below it follow. All planks are fitted straight and untapered. Once the first two upper planks are put on, the garboard is fitted—again, untapered—and as the additional planks are added from the bottom up, they sweep up toward the sheer strake at an acute angle, the final strake being merely a small segment of a circle. This makes a difficult seam to caulk and places the end grain against the side grain. And, since the lower planks often end between frames, it makes it necessary to insert small butt blocks to hold the planks in place. For many years I was unable to find out why all the double-enders in the southern islands were built in this fashion. Finally, I discovered the reason: labor is cheap, lumber expensive, and this method of planking uses less material than the conventional method of lining off and tapering planks.

Most of the Grenada launches have Stuart-Turner engines, which work for the most part, though I don't know why. The design has been basically unchanged for over 40 years—a hand crank, magneto ignition, splash lubrication, and a carburetor that must be flooded manually for starting. There are no flame arresters and there are numerous explosions. The engines never run quite right, but then again, they never quite *don't* run. They will always sputter, spurt, and chug along after a fashion.

One story has it that a group of brilliant engineers "designed" this remarkable instrument over brandy and cigars after a good dinner, jokingly sketching out an engine that would appear to be perfect, but actually wouldn't run at all. After much laughter, they broke up and went home. But two sharp-eyed waiters found the tablecloth, and realizing that here was an engine designed by some of the finest engineers in the country, they decided to build it. The waiters' names?—why, Stuart and Turner!

On *Iolaire* we used to have a Stuart-Turner generator. Like the Grenada launch engines, it had a carburetor that you had to flood, no flame arrester, and a gas tank that vented through the cap, further adding to the fumes in the engine room. Given all the sparks that flew around while the generator was running, I decided that operating the thing was like playing Russian roulette with six shells in the chambers. We dumped it in the middle of the harbor at St. Croix. If anyone wants it, it's probably still there—and probably still works.

As you leave Grenada and sail north, the horizon will be dotted with splotches of white, the sails of the small fishing boats directly descended from the double-ended whaleboats of New Bedford, and undoubtedly the ancestor of the Grenada inboard launch. Though all are of roughly the same lines, these boats vary in size and finish from the roughest of the rough in Mayero, with not a metal fitting on board and flour-sack sails, to the yacht-like boats of Admiralty Bay, some of which actually have stainless steel rigging and Dacron sails, though their owners are still commercial fishermen.

In the old days, the Grenadines (the islands north of Grenada) were the last refuge of the sailing whalers. They would leave New Bedford in the fall with a skeleton crew and sail to Admiralty Bay at Bequia, where they would fill out their crew with local natives, whale until May, then pay off the local crew and return home. This routine was maintained until World War I, and in fact I am told that a few of the schooner whalers from New Bedford came down as late as the winter of 1921. However, that same year the Norwegians established a whaling station on Glover Island, just south of Grenada. They arrived with modern methods and equipment and all but cleaned the area out. The British Government did not permit them to return the following year, but the damage was done and the whaling industry has never recovered. Before the arrival of the Norwegians, about 20 whaleboats operated from Grenada, Ile de Caille, Cannouan, and Bequia. Now the number has been reduced to four, as of this writing.

Many of the crews of the Yankee whalers decided to forego their own fog-bound coast and to remain in the sunny south, thereby giving Bequia such family names as Wallace, King, and Simmons. They taught the islanders to build whaleboats similar to the New England boat. They have changed little if at all through the years; they still use the hand-thrown harpoon, hunt the whale under oars or sail, and tow the carcass in by brute strength. It is really the last refuge of old-time whaling, as even in the Azores crash boats follow the whalers and tugs tow the whale in once it is killed.

The Bequia boats are primarily sailing vessels. A centerboard allows them to work to windward. Rock stone ballast and the weight of six men (some of the crew sit on the windward rail; others hang from trapezes from the mast) keep them stable in the worst of the trade-wind weather. The West Indian fisherman has been using trapezes since time immemorial and it is probably here that our high performance racing sailors learned to dangle from the end of a wire.

The rig is simple: a sloop with a short mast and overlapping genoa. A long bamboo sprit gives the mainsail more height, but when it blows up, this can be quickly reduced by dropping the sprit and tying the peak of the main to the midpoint of the luff. But simplicity doesn't always make for ease of handling, as the West Indian method of stepping the mast proves. On the New England whaleboats, there was a hinge in the aft side of the mast partners that could be opened or shut. The mast was inserted in the step while still horizontal, swung vertical, and secured by closing the hinge. To strike the rig, one had only to open the hinge, ease the jib halyard, and the whole thing lay back nicely in the boat. Simple and easy. Not so with the West Indian rig. They have only a hole in the mast partners; the whole rig must be lifted high, aimed at the step, and dropped. To miss is to crack the garboard; to strike the rig while under tow from an enraged whale is practically impossible.

Like all boats carrying rock stone ballast, the whaleboats are completely open, with no side decks. If capsized or swamped, the boat can be rolled on its side and the rocks tumbled out. Then the boat is righted, and the lightest crew climbs aboard, to bail until she is floating high enough for the rest of the crew to clamber aboard and finish the job. They then carry on with the day's work.

The St. Lucian and St. Vincent pilot-fish boats are lineal descendants of the Bequia whaleboats. They range from 22 to 25 feet, and are similar to the whaleboat with two exceptions: a daggerboard has replaced the centerboard, and the crew is four or five instead of six. Their quarry is the pilot fish, a species of whale about 15 feet long closely resembling a bottle-nosed dolphin, that can be found in the channels to the north and south of St. Vincent. Pilot-fishing is a year-round occupation and even though the techniques of hunting whale and pilot fish are strategically the same, the pilot fishermen seem to use relatively more advanced equipment. They employ small shoulder-held harpoon-guns that are so old looking they seem to contradict the word "advanced." Pilot fishermen had such great success with this gun that the whale men gave it a try. After one season with the gun they had no kills. The next season they reverted to the hand-thrown harpoon and made three kills. Where else in the world do people become more primitive with time?

Slightly smaller than the pilot-fish boats, but still related to the Bequia whaleboat, are the double-enders seen throughout the Grenadines and on the south coast of St. Vincent. These boats are from 16 to 20 feet long and are used for trolling, bottom fishing, and lobster diving. Open and undecked, they are nevertheless seaworthy and can be seen as far away as Carriacou, 40 miles south of Bequia. They are especially interesting to study as they are still in a state of development. The older ones did not have a daggerboard, but relied on their long straight keel to give them the necessary grip on the water. About 20 years ago,

St. Lucian Pilot Fishing Boat

someone installed a daggerboard to increase windward performance. This it succeeded in doing to such a degree that everyone soon copied it. Then someone figured that if you made the daggerboard narrower fore and aft at the top than where it passes through the keel, it would be possible to pivot the board fore and aft, adjusting the center of lateral resistance wherever desired.

Leaks and spray in heavy weather combine to necessitate constant bailing in these boats. The bailer, however, is made of a calabash gourd, which is harder than the planking. Hence, a copper plate is tacked to the inside of the planks in the deepest part of the bilge to take the chafe. Yet another device is the short length of bamboo that is always carried on board: the top section is cut off to make a cup. You can't stand up in heavy weather in these small boats, so if one needs to relieve oneself, the bamboo cup is used and the waste dumped over the side. Practical, these West Indians!

Among West Indians, the Bequians show the most initiative and are the best fishermen and boat builders. They are doing better each year, and the rise in their standard of living is reflected in their boats. Their money is spent refurbishing old boats. and building new ones. Fifteen to 20 years ago, their double-enders were all painted white or gray to the waterline, with a mixture of creosote and Stockholm tar covering the bottom. Fastenings were iron, fittings were all wood, the standing rigging was hemp, and the sails were made from old flour sacks. While this may still be seen, more and more boats are using stainless steel wire to replace the hemp rigging, and sails are being cut from a higher grade of canvas. In some cases, as already noted, Dacron has replaced canvas altogether. Centerboard trunks are being reset in waterproof glue, bronze cleats and fittings are beginning to sprout up, and first-class yacht finishes in bright colors are now sported by many of the boats. Many new boats are copper-fastened, while the copper chafing plate in the bilge has been eliminated with the replacement of calabash gourds by plastic Clorox bottles.

Despite the tendency to modernization, the double-enders are the last remnants of commercial sailing craft in the Islands. As double-enders they have not readily lent themselves to the installation of outboards. They continue to rely solely on their sailing capabilities, which must be especially great to windward on account of the strong westbound current which will carry a boat off to leeward very quickly. The Islanders are proud of their talents, and when they are not racing one another home with the day's catch, they frequently arrange around-the-buoy races among themselves. Entrance fee is $1 per man; the winner gets his money back, and the remaining money is spent on liquid refreshments for a beach party immediately following the race.

These races can be quite exciting, even to the spectator. Usually they are sailed on the exposed coast of Bequia, where a strong current and steep chop prevails. The salt spray and saltier language fly about as the fleet thrashes its way out to windward, "four men up," as the British would say. With full sails set in a breeze that would force the normal cruising boat to reef, the boats present a real sight, especially on a squally day. They disappear one by one into the rain and one by one reappear as the rain passes, still under full sail and bailing like mad.

Several times a year there are organized regattas aimed at bringing out all the local boats for a race. The biggest one is over the August Monday Weekend in Carriacou. The Carriacou regatta was originally started by Linto Rigg, who also started the better known Bahamian Out Island Regatta. Large and small cargo sloops and double-enders of all sizes race in various classes. The competition is tough, which probably explains why some of the boats are maintained like yachts although they are primarily commercial fishing vessels for the rest of the year. Excitement is intense and I can't think of a better way to spend a weekend than anchored in the Carriacou harbor drinking beer and watching the local sailors put on a show of skill, seamanship, and shenanigans, sailing their boats full-tilt around the race course.

Another regatta worth seeing is the Whit Weekend Regatta at Bequia. Lately there have been upwards of 50 Bequia double-enders racing, and an added attraction is provided by younger boys who race model sailboats.

North of Bequia in St. Vincent the role of the Bequia double-ender is fulfilled by the Carib canoe, a distinctive craft that has changed little since Columbus seized one in St. Croix. The Caribs came from South America and worked their way up the chain of islands on raiding expeditions, arriving in their open dugout canoes at San Salvador, The Bahamas, at about the same time as Columbus. These warlike seamen were eventually forced to seek refuge on the islands of Dominica and St. Vincent, and from here their descendants still go to sea in dugouts of the same type used centuries ago.

The Carib dugout is only found on the mountainous islands of the Lesser Antilles, as the lower, flatter islands do not catch enough rainfall to encourage the trees to grow tall and straight. Originally the canoes were made of one single log hollowed out with fire and axe. Now the freeboard is increased by adding two planks on each side. They are quite narrow and seldom longer than 25 feet. The beam is a mere three feet at most, and the depth of the hull is 18 to 24 inches. The midships section is rounded, the ends are long and thin, and the bow and stern are ram-shaped, making the hull longest on the keel. They are rowed with a pair of short oars never more than five feet

Anguilla Schooner

Carib Canoes, Martinique

Carib Canoes, Martinique

long, or in the larger ones with two pair. The steersman alternately steers and paddles with a short canoe paddle. The normal sailing rig consists of a mast about ten feet high stepped in the eyes way up near the bow of the boat. Sails are frequently made of flour sacks, the sail area being measured by the number of 100-pound flour sacks used to make the sail. "She got a small four-sack sail, but she got a great six-sack, too." With the boisterous trade winds, a 10-foot-square scrap of a sail is ample, and the canoes can beat to windward with no semblance of a keel. The natives steer by trimming the sail and shifting their weight, using a paddle only in rough water.

The amazing performance put on by these boats can be seen on the weather coast of Dominica, where the fishermen launch from the small coves on the exposed eastern shore. They beat out against the full force of the winter trades to an offshore shelf about 20 miles to windward. There they douse their sail, heave to, and fish with hand lines. It is a sight to see them on their way home with a bulging flour-sack sail and a monster bow wave as they surf down an Atlantic swell. This makes racing a dinghy tame by comparison.

These canoes are much safer than they appear. Although they have little initial stability, they are held upright by a man on a hiking board, similar to, but shorter than, the springboards used by Chesapeake log canoes. At the approach of a squall, the whole rig can be unstepped in a matter of seconds and, if the squall is especially vicious, lashed together and used as a sea anchor. If the canoe capsizes, the bottom is so thick that the reserve buoyancy floats the canoe high enough to bail out the water easily as soon as the squall passes over.

The physical condition of a canoe will vary according to age, the financial position of its owner, and the use that it is to be put to. The Dominican and St. Lucian canoes are the poorest. The Martinique varieties are the best

built and best maintained. On the east coast they have reached the highest stage of development and regattas are held every summer at Robert, François, and La Trinite. A dozen or so canoes will show up rigged for racing. This consists of the small regular foresail supplemented by a large mainmast, stepped amidships, carrying a large boomless mainsail and rigged in the same fashion as the foresail mast —without stays. The captains ship a large crew, each with his own hiking pole. The canoes have been polished to within an inch of their lives, and betting runs high. In fact, there is so much interest that several enterprising local merchants have supported a boat in return for a handsome advertisement on the sail.

Exactly when the races are held has been kept a secret for many years—it seems that military clearance is needed to find out the information. If you should be lucky enough to stumble upon a race, the scene is most enjoyable.

Many of the spectator boats are a development of the dugout, almost 35 feet long, with only four feet of beam. They are too large to be made out of one log. Instead, the bottom is formed and hollowed out from a single tree, while the frames are cut from a second tree and bolted to the sides, one or two planks to a side. A small transom is installed, just large enough to take a 10- or 15-horsepower outboard. With a rounded bottom unconducive to planing, these heavy boats still do better than 15 knots at full steam—certainly a good speed-to-length ratio.

The large powered canoe has evolved from the nature of the east coast of Martinique. A detailed chart will show numerous coves, harbors, islands, and peninsulas. Much of the land is too steep and rugged for roads, and the islands can be reached only by boat. Nevertheless, the coast is populated. Many of the wealthier Martinicans are attracted during the

summer months by the cool sea breeze on this side of the island. Their sole means of transportation is by boat and the large powered canoe serves admirably as a water taxi. Their boatmen think nothing of making the trip from Fort de France to Castries, a distance of 35 miles across open ocean.

In Guadeloupe and its surrounding islands, one encounters another type of small boat, generally referred to as the Saints boat. The name derives from the large concentration of this type of boat in Iles de Saintes, a group of small, dry islands eight miles south of Guadeloupe. The Saints boats are without a doubt the best-built boats in the entire Lesser Antilles. They come in all sizes, and until recent times they were always the same shape. They had a straight keel with slight drag, hollow garboards, a steeply rising floor, ample beam, hollow waterlines fore and aft, a great flare to the bow, a heart-shaped stern, and a pleasing sheer. The bow was quite high, its height and flare allowing the boat to rise to the sea without taking water in even the roughest weather. The low freeboard aft allowed hand lines or nets to be handled with ease, while the flare increased the beam as the boat became loaded, increasing stability at the same time.

The addition of an outboard motor has changed the design slightly. While the heart-shaped stern produced beautiful, sleek lines for rowing and sailing, it also produced a severe squatting problem when an outboard was placed on the stern and revved up to high speed. To prevent this squatting, the Saints boats have evolved a flatter, rounded stern that offers more buoyancy.

But they are still beautifully built. The frames are natural crooks, and each frame is a single piece from gunwale to keel. In fact, the frames are so small and well finished that they appear almost steam bent. Floors are also natural crooks, one to each frame, and are securely fastened to both the keel and frame.

Saints Boats, Iles des Saintes

NATIVE BOATS

The mast step always crosses at least three frames, safely supporting the thrust of the mast. The planking is mahogany and the seams are so tightly fitted that the boats are caulked with a single strand of cotton wicking worked in by a very sharp iron.

The rig is typically West Indian—a genoa jib and a low-aspect leg-of-mutton mainsail. (I have a feeling the West Indian fishermen are more fond of the genoa than the modern ocean-racing skipper.) Mast hoops are twisted out of vines, or sections of large-diameter bamboo. Spars are either bamboo or a local wood called silver bally. Stability is achieved by perching a large crew on the weather rail or by hiking out on a trapeze.

But, alas, outboards have taken some of the sport out of fishing in a Saints boat. It used to be that once the fishing was completed for the day, the men would set sail and enjoy a wild sleigh ride home from the fishing grounds. Although they would power out against the wind, there was still good reason to sail home in light of the cost of gasoline. But today convenience has won out over expense and the sailing world has suffered yet another loss. Still, even the motorized vessels provide a different kind of spectacle to the visiting yachtsmen. You may someday find yourself crossing the Dominican channel in squally weather with huge steep seas that make your crew feel exceptionally brave to be out there, when suddenly you happen upon a 16-foot dinghy hove to under oars with the crew calmly fishing as if they were in the middle of the lake in Central Park. It's enough to put your nose slightly out of joint.

The one other distinctive type of boat that has developed in the Lesser Antilles is the sailing lighter of St. Kitts and Nevis. Neither of these islands has a dock, and when a freighter arrives, everything must be taken ashore by launch. The islands offer only partial protection from the wind and the sea, and

the anchorages tend to be rough. The type of vessels that has evolved is the clumsiest looking imaginable. The boats are heavily constructed to withstand a pounding against the sides of docks and freighters. Ranging in size from 35 to 45 feet, they are open like a barge, have a transom stern, and an outboard rudder. Perhaps it is the rig that seems most clumsy. One unstayed mast, extremely short, is stepped quite far forward, and raked further forward so that the masthead is directly over the stem. The boom is just about the same length as the mast and points skyward at about a 45-degree angle, making room for the cargo that may be heaped as high as ten feet above the gunwale. The aerodynamics of the rig leaves much to be desired. The larger barges add sail area by means of a genoa, and by using a long boom stretching 15 feet beyond the transom and a gaff about five feet long from the masthead. Watching them handle these heavily laden, cranky sailing barges without the aid of an engine is worth the trip to these two islands. But you will have to go soon. Motor tugs have already started to arrive. In the near future commercial sail craft will have become a thing of the past.

Antigua, Anguilla, the British Virgins, Puerto Rico, and the Passage Islands have developed another type of boat, smaller than the Nevis/St. Kitts variety. These boats from the northern islands have a remarkable similarity, as they evolve from very similar circumstances. In these northern islands there are numerous good harbors and coves where the boats can be left in the water rather than hauled up on the beach. Local economics also necessitates that these boats be able to do a variety of jobs from fishing to carrying freight of all types, including occasional passengers.

There has evolved a sloop about 24 feet long. It has a straight keel with much drag to it, raked stem and sternpost, hollow garboards, hard bilges, plenty of beam (beam-

length ratio: one to three), a high bow, and pleasing sheer. The draft will vary greatly according to its home port and its trading route. Most of them draw three to four feet, but the Anegada boats are likely to be built with deeper drafts, as they have a beat of 50 miles from St. Thomas to Anegada. Fifty miles to windward against a fresh trade is hard going in any boat. Some of the Puerto Rican boats carry fruit from Puerto Rico to St. Thomas—another long beat—and here again draft has been increased to give better windward ability. Occasionally a boat is seen with a wet fish well, very common in the Bahamas but relatively uncommon in the Lesser Antilles.

The rigs of the boats are interesting. The West Indians love to do things the hard way; frequently there is only one sheet to the genoa, which must be passed around the mast every time the boat tacks; it is belayed directly to a wooden pin rail, with no lead block at all. The main is a low-aspect leg-of-mutton sail, and a sharp rake to the mast brings the halyard over the cargo hatch. The sail is usually longer on the foot than on the luff, and is cut very full. Going to windward the genoa is sheeted flat, and the main eased, so that the boat is sailing on the genoa and the leech of the main with the whole luff of the main aback. Standing rigging consists of a headstay and two side shrouds (usually of manila), ironwork, a stem band, and two chain plates. It is worthy to note that the Anegada boats have developed slightly differently, probably because of their long downwind sail in open water to the market in St. Thomas. While other of these boats are decked, the Anegada variety is mostly undecked, except for a turtleback deck aft to prevent being pooped by a following sea. They are thus lighter, and can carry more cargo. The Anegada boat's mainsail is also shaped differently. It is loose-footed and set to a sprit in the manner of a New Haven Sharpie. Since the tack of the sail is well below the gooseneck,

St. Kitts Lighter

Dominican Cargo Sloop

the sail itself acts as a boom vang and prevents the boom from rising when running dead before the wind. All these boats use whisker poles to wing out their genoas when sailing downwind. They are a sight to see with all their canvas hung out to a fair breeze over a hull so laden that each sea sloshes aboard.

Once in a while you will notice an Anegada sloop with fancy stainless steel rigging, stem band, and chain plates. Among the many boats that have been lost to the reefs off Anegada, there have been several classy ocean racers and cruisers. *Ondine* is probably the most famous. Once abandoned, these boats are stripped by the Anegada natives, who have been salvaging wrecks as a livelihood for hundreds of years. Stainless steel rigging is one of the benefits of living near a yachting graveyard.

Principal Visual Navigation Aids

Key to Abbreviations

Alt	Alternating	M	Sea Miles
B	Black	m	Meters
Bl	Blue	Mo(A)	Morse Code Light or Fog Signal
By	Buoy	min	Minutes
C	Cape	Occ	Occulting
Dia	Diaphone	Or	Orange
Dir	Directional	Pt	Point
F	Fixed	Qk Fl	Quick Flashing
Fl	Flashing	R	Red
ft	Feet	Ra Bn	Radio Beacon
G	Green	rk	Rock
Gp Fl	Group Flashing	S	South
Gp Fl(1 + 2)	Composite Group Flashing	sec	Seconds
Gp Occ	Group Occulting	Sq	Square
hor	Horizontal	vert	Vertical
Int Qk Fl	Interrupted Quick Flashing	Vis	Visible
Iso	Isophase (Equal Interval)	W	White
Lat	Latitude	Whis	Whistle
Long	Longitude	yds	Yards
Lt V	Light Vessel	Ω	Radar Reflector

Puerto Rico

North Coast

Punta Borinquen. 18°30′N, 67°09′W Gp. Fl.W. (2) 15 sec. 24M gray twr. NW. side of island.

Arecibo. 18°29′N, 66°42′W Fl.W. 20 sec. 20M W. twr. on dwelling E. side of entrance to Puerto Arecibo on Pta. Morrillos.

Puerto San Juan. 18°28′N, 66°07′W Fl.W. 10 sec. 20M sq. brick twr. on Moro Castle E. side of entrance to San Juan Harbor Obscured from 281°-061°.

Cabras. Iso. W. 6 sec. 9M NW. point of Isla de Cabras W. side of entrance to San Juan Harbor.

Leading Lights Vis. 2° each side of rangeline.
Front Qk. Fl.W. R. [] W. stripe on B. house on piles.
Rear Occ. W. 4 sec. R. [] W. stripe on W. twr. above house.

The channels into San Juan Harbor are well lit. Vessels desiring yacht harbor should make the turn at No. 11 Lt. Qk.Fl.G. and continue along San Antonio Channel, between Isla San Juan and Isla Grande.

Boca de Cangrejos 'BC' Mo.(A) W. Ω By. B. and W. vert. stripes 6½ M E. of Puerto San Juan Lt.

Punta Picua No. 2. Fl.W. 4 sec. Ω By. R. 9M WNW. of Cabo San Juan Lt. 2M N. of Punta Picua.

Cabo San Juan. 18°23′N, 65°37′W Fl.W. 15 sec. 23M twr. on W. dwelling on highest point of cape.

Las Cucarachas. Fl.W. 6 sec. 7M W. twr. R. lantern 1½ M NNE. Cabo San Juan Lt.

East Coast

Bajo Laja No. 1. Fl.W. 6 sec. Ω By. B. 1½ M S. of Cabo San Juan Lt. at entrance to channel to Fajardo.

Isla Palominos No. 2. Fl.R. 4 sec. By. R. marks W. coast of island 3½ M E. of Fajardo.

Cayo Largo No. 1A. Fl.G. 4 sec. marks westerly shoal 2½ M SE. of Fajardo.

Cabeza de Perro. Fl.W. 6 sec. R. sector 8M R. structure on E. point of island. W. from 161°-021°, R. West of 021° and 161°.

Bajos Chinchoro Del Sur. Fl.W. 4 sec. R. and W. checkered sq. on W. twr. 3¼ M ESE. of Cabeza de Perro Lt.

Cabeza de Perro No. 7. Fl.W. 6 sec. By. B. 1½ M SE. of Cabeza de Perro Lt.

Isla Cabras. Occ. W. 4 sec. 9M R. and W. striped [] on twr. on E. side of island NW. side of Pasaje de Vieques.

Ensenada Honda No. 1. Fl.W. 6 sec. Ω By. B. marks S. side of entrance to Roosevelt Roads Naval Base.

Ensenada Honda No. 2. Fl.R. 4 sec. Ω By. R. marks N. side of entrance to Roosevelt Roads Naval Base.

Culebra Island Restricted Area North '2RA'. 18°26′N, 65°17′W Fl.W.

APPENDIX A

4 sec. Ω By. R. marks N. limit of Danger Area off Culebra Island. This area is used by the U.S. Navy for bombing and gunnery practice.

Culebra Island Restricted Area Northeast '4RA'. Fl.W. 4 sec. Ω By. R. 4½ M ESE. of '2RA' Lt. By. marks NE. limit of Danger Area.

Piedra Stevens No. 1. Fl.W. 4 sec. By. B. ¾ M NNW. of Pta. Noroeste NW. point of Culebra Island.

Cayo Lobito. Fl.W. 6 sec. 8M B. sq. W. twr. 3M SE. of Piedra Stevens No. 1 Lt.

Isla Culebrita. Gp. Fl.W. (2) 20 sec. 13M gray and R. twr. on dwelling (obscured 125°-142°) E. of Culebra Island W. side of Virgin Passage.

Grampus Shoal No. 2. Fl.R. 4 sec. By. R. 5M SSE. of Isla Culebrita Lt.

Point Soldado. Fl.W. 2½ sec. W. twr. near S. point of Culebra Island No. 2 Lt. Fl.R. 4 sec. By. R. ¾ M E. of Pt. Soldado Lt.

Melones Point. Fl.W. 6 sec. W. twr. extremity of point W. side of Culebra Island.

Hodgkins Shoal No. 6. Fl.R. 4 sec. Ω By. R. 6M N. of Pta. Mulas Lt. on Vieques Island.

'6RA'. Lt. Ω By. R. 1M SE. of Hodgkins Shoal No. 6 Lt. marks S. limit of Restricted Area Danger Zone.

Punta Mulas. Occ. W. 4 sec. 2 R. sectors 9M R. from 068°-107° covers Bajo Comandante and Arrecifes Corona and Mosquito, 122°-141° covers Caballo Blanco; W. twr. on dwelling on point E. side of Bahia de Mulas N. shore of Vieques Island.

Punta Este. Fl.W. 6 sec. R. twr. on point E. end of Vieques Island.

Punta Conejo. Fl.W. 6 sec. W. daymark on twr. on E. side of point 3M E. of Puerto Ferro Lt. S. shore of Vieques Island.

Puerto Ferro. Fl.W. 4 sec. 7M W. twr. on dwelling on outer point on W. side of entrance to Puerto Ferro S. shore of Vieques Island.

South Coast

Punta Tuna. 17°59′N, 65°53′W Gp. Fl.W. (2) 30 sec. 16M W. twr. on dwelling on point E. side of Puerto Maunabo.

Punta Figuras. Fl.W. 6 sec. R. sector 8M R. N. of 079° W. twr. on point E. side of Puerto Arroyo 9½ M W. of Punta Tuna Lt.

No. 2. Lt. Fl.W. 4 sec. By. R. 3½ M SSE. of Pta. Figuras Lt.

Las Mareas 'LM'. 17°54′N, 66°11′W Mo. (A) W. Ω B. and W. vert. stripes.

Bahia de Jobos. Fl.W. 2½ sec. 6M W. [] twr. on E. point easternmost of Cayos de Ratones at entrance to Bahia de Jobos.

Isla Caja de Muertos. 17°54′N, 66°31′W Fl.W. 30 sec. 13M gray twr. on center of flat roofed dwelling.

Rio Bucana. Qk. Fl.W. 6M pole on outer end of jetty 1½ M E. of entrance to Playa de Ponce.

Bahia de Ponce.

(Port)	(Starboard)
No. 1. Lt. Fl.G. 4 sec. Ω By. B.	**No. 2 Lt.** Fl.R. 4 sec. Ω By. B.

Cayo Cardona. Fl.W. 4 sec. 12M W. twr. on dwelling.

No. 5 Lt. Fl.G. 4 sec. Ω By. B.	**No. 6 Lt.** Fl.R. 4 sec. By. R.

Bahia De Ponce

Leading Lights
Front Qk. Fl.W. W. daymark B. bullseye on twr.
Rear Iso. R. 6 sec. W. daymark B. vert. stripe on twr.

Bahia De Tallaboa

Leading Lights 353°.
Front Qk. Fl.G. Or. □ B. center on twr.
Rear F.G. Or. □ B. center on twr.

(Port)	(Starboard)
No. 1 Lt. Fl.W. 4 sec. By. B.	**No. 4 Lt.** Fl.R. 4 sec. Ω By. R.
No. 5 Lt. Fl.G. 2½ sec. Ω By. B.	
No. 7A Lt. Fl.G. 2½ sec. Ω B. daymark.	
	No. 10 Lt. Fl.R. 2½ sec. By. R.

Bahia De Guanica

No. 2 Lt. Fl.W. 4 sec. By. R. 2M S. of Guanica Lt.

No. 5 Lt. Fl.G. 4 sec. By. B.

No. 6 Lt. Fl.R. 4 sec. By. R.

Guanica. Fl.W. 6 sec. 8M W. twr. on Punta Meseta E. side of entrance to harbor, obscured by Punta Brea to seacoast traffic W. of 044°.

Cabo Rojo. 17°56′N, 67°11′W F. Fl.W. 10 sec. 15M gray twr. on dwelling on SE. point of cape.

Mona Passage East Shoal No. 2. Fl.W. 6 sec. Ω By. R. 4½ M SW. of Cabo Rojo Lt.

West Coast

Mona Island. 18°05′N, 67°51′W Gp. Fl.W. (3) 30 sec. 18M B. twr. on W. dwelling R. roof on Cabo Este, Mona Island, W. side of Mona Canal (obscured 045°-181°).

Mona Passage East Shoal No. 4. Fl.W. 6 sec. By. R. 10M NW. of Mona Passage East Shoal No. 2 Lt.

Mona Passage East Shoal No. 6. Fl.W. 6 sec. By. R. 5½ M NNW. of Mona Passage East Shoal No. 4 Lt.

Arrecife Tourmaline No. 8. Fl.W. 6 sec. By. R. 6½ M NE. of Mona Passage East Shoal No. 6 Lt. W. side of reef.
Mayaguez Harbor. Fl.W. 6 sec. 7M W. house on pile structure.
No. 3 Lt. Fl.G. 4 sec. By. B. 2½ M WNW. of Mayaguez marks N. side of harbor entrance.
No. 4 Lt. Fl.W. 4 sec. By. R. marks S. side of harbor entrance.
Punta Higuero. Occ. W. 4 sec. 9M gray twr. on point between Bahia Mayaguez and Aguadilla.

Virgin Islands (U.S.)

St. Thomas

South Coast

Savana Island. 18°20′N, 65°05′W Fl.W. 4 sec. 6M W. twr. SW. part of island 2½ M W. of westernmost point of St. Thomas.
Sail Rock No. 1. 18°17′N, 65°06′W Fl.W. 10 sec. By. B.
Buck Island. 18°17′N, 64°54′W Fl.W. 4 sec. 8M W. twr. on highest point of island.
St. Thomas Aero Lt. 18°20′N, 64°58′W Alt. Fl.W. and G. 10 sec.
West Gregerie Channel No. 2. Fl.R. 4 sec. Ω By. R. 1¾ M S. of St. Thomas Aero Lt. W. side of Porpoise Rks. Shoal marks entrance to West Gregerie Channel.
West Gregerie Channel No. 4. Fl.R. 2½ sec. By. R. off Providence Point on Water Island E. side of channel.
West Gregerie Channel No. 5. Fl.G. 4 sec. By. B. off Regis Point marks W. side of channel.
West Gregerie Channel No. 6. Fl.W. 4 sec. R. daymark on dolphin off Sandy Point Rk. on Water Island at end of channel.
East Gregerie Channel No. 2. Fl.R. 2½ sec. By. R. off Cowell Point S. end of Hassel Island marks E. side of channel entrance.
East Gregerie Channel No. 3. Fl.G. 4 sec. By. B. off Banana Point S. end of Water Island marks end of channel.
St. Thomas Harbor Entrance No. 2. 18°19′N, 64°55′W Fl.W. 6 sec. By. R. marks E. side of entrance to Charlotte Amalie Harbor.
St. Thomas Harbor Entrance No. 3. Fl.W. 4 sec. By. B. ¼ M E. of East Gregerie Channel Lt. No. 2 at Cowell Point marks mid-channel of harbor entrance.
Berg Hill. 18°21′N, 64°56′W
> **Leading Lights 344°.**
> Front Qk. Fl.G. R. and W. daymark Vis. 2° each side.
> Rear Occ. G. 4 sec. R. and W. daymark Vis. 2° each side.

St. Thomas Harbor Entrance No. 6. Fl.R. 4 sec. By. R. off Rupert Rock E. side of entrance to harbor.
Current Rock. 18°19′N, 64°50′W Fl.R. 6 sec. W. twr. on S. side at St. James Bay entrance to Pillsbury Sound.

St. John

Two Brothers. 18°21′N, 64°49′W Fl.W. 6 sec. W. twr. with B. and W. daymark NE. end of Pillsbury Sound ¾ M NW of Stevens Cay Lt.
Stevens Cay. Fl.W. 4 sec. W. twr. with B. and W. daymark ½ M W. of Cruz Bay Lt.
Cruz Bay. Fl.R. 4 sec. W. twr. with B. and W. daymark S. side of entrance to Cruz Bay W. end of St. John.
Johnson Reef '1 JR'. 18°22′N, 64°46′W Fl.G. 4 sec. Ω By. B.

St. Croix

North Coast

Hamms Bluff. 17°46′N, 64°52′W Gp. Fl.W. (2) 30 sec. 27M W. twr. on bluff NW. point of St. Croix Island Vis. 053°-265° partly obscured 053°-062°.
Christiansted Harbor Entrance No. 1. 17°46′N, 64°42′W Fl.W. 2½ sec. By. B. ¼ M NW. of Long Reef.
> **Leading Lights 164°.**
> Front Qk. Fl.W. twr. near Old Fort E. of harbor entrance.
> Rear Iso. W. 6 sec. W. pole.

Christiansted Harbor Entrance No. 4. Qk. Fl.R. Ω By. R. W. side of entrance channel off Long Reef.
Buck Island. 17°47′N, 64°37′W Fl.W. 4 sec. 6M R. twr. on highest point of island.

South Coast

Lime Tree Bay No. 1. 17°41′N, 64°44′W Fl.W. 10 sec. Ω By. B., channel marked by lit and unlit buoys.
Lime Tree Bay
> **Leading Lights 334°.**
> Front F.G. R. [] on pole.
> Rear F.R. R. [] on pole.

Port Harvey No. 3. 17°41′N, 64°45′W Fl.W. 4 sec. 7M B. sq. daymark on pile, channel marked by lit and unlit buoys.

Port Harvey.
    Leading Lights
        Front F.G. R. and W. daymark on twr. Vis. 1° each side.
        Rear F.G. R. and W. daymark on twr. Vis. 1° each side.
Southwest Cape. 17°41′N, 64°54′W Fl.W. 6 sec. 7M R. twr. on cape SW. end of St. Croix Island.

West Coast

Frederiksted Harbor. 17°43′N, 64°53′W Fl.W. 2 R. sectors 4 sec. 8M W. twr. S. side of inner end of wharf R. Vis. 000°-044°30′, 137°-180°, W. Vis. 044°30′-137°.
Frederiksted Pier. Two F.R. on corners of pier.

Virgin Islands (U.K.)

Tortola

Road Town. 18°25′N, 64°37′W.
    Leading Lights 290°.
        Front F.R. 3M on mast at head of pier.
        Rear F.R. 3M corner of customhouse.

Virgin Gorda

St. Thomas Bay. 18°27′N, 64°26′W.
    Leading Lights 109°02′.
        Front Two F.R. 5M head of Little Dix Bay.
        Rear F.G. 5M at foot of jetty.

Leeward Islands

Sombrero Island. 18°36′N, 63°26′W Fl.W. 5 sec. 18M R. twr. SE. side of island near Point Ray.
Anguilla Islet. 18°09′N, 63°11′W Fl.W. 10 sec. 8M alum. twr. with R. top just off SW. point of Anguilla Island.

St. Martin (N., F.)

Grande Bay. 18°01′N, 63°04′W Fl.W. 4 sec. 6M wooden post on site of old Fort Amsterdam, S. end of St. Martin Island Vis. 300°-096°.
Simson Bay. Alt. Fl.W. G. 6 sec. 13M aviation light on station building 3½ M WNW. of Grande Bay Lt.
Marigot Bay. 18°04′N, 63°06′W F.W. 3M W. mast SW. corner of old fort obscured when bearing S. of 155° difficult to distinguish from lights of town W. coast of St. Martin Island.

St. Barthelemy (F.)

Fort Gustave. 17°54′N, 62°51′W Gp. Occ. W. R. G. (2) 6 sec. W. 14M, R. 10M, G. 9M, W. twr. W. Vis. 054°-071°, G. Vis. 071°-095°, W. Vis. 095°-111°, R. Vis. 111°-160°, obscured 160°-340°, R. Vis. 340°-054° on W. coast of St. Barthelemy Island.

St. Eustatius (N.)

Orange Town. 17°29′N, 62°59′W F.W. 2M on roof of Customs Office near landing place on St. Eustatius Island.

St. Christopher (U.K.)

Basse Terre Bay. 17°18′N, 62°43′W.

    Leading Lights
        Front F.R. 10M metal mast at Treasury Pier.
        Rear F.R. 10M lantern on wall.

Fort Thomas. Occ. W. 5 sec. 14M metal mast W. end of harbor ¾ M SW. of Basse Terre Bay Leading Lts.
Fort Smith. F.G. 2M concrete block E. side of harbor 1M SE. of Basse Terre Bay Leading Lts.

Nevis (U.K.)

Charlestown. 17°08′N, 62°37′W F.R. post at foot of pier W. coast of Nevis.
Long Point. 17°05′N, 62°35′W Fl.W. 7½ sec. 10M W. twr. at SW. point of island.

Montserrat (U.K.)

Plymouth. 16°42′N, 62°13′W F.R. mast at end of wharf SW. coast of Montserrat.

Antigua (U.K.)

Sandy Island. 17°08′N, 61°55′W Fl.W. 15 sec. 13M W. twr. 2M W. of entrance to St. Johns Harbor on W. coast of Antigua.
Pillar Rock. Fl.G. 5M W. house 'Pillar Rock' in B., on S. side of entrance to St. Johns Harbor, Vis. 067°-093° obscured 093°-108° visible then to shore SE. of Lt.
St. Johns Harbor

    Leading Lights 113°.
    Front Qk. Fl.R.
    Rear Iso. R. 6 sec.

Fort James. Fl.R. 5M W. pillar N. side of entrance to harbor 1M E. of

Pillar Rock Lt.
Parham Sound. 17°07′N, 61°48′W Fl.W. 10 sec. twr. aviation light NE. part of Antigua.

Guadeloupe (F.)

Port Louis. 16°25′N, 61°32′W F.G. 8M G. platform on W. twr. on beach just N. of landing.
Anse Bertrand. F.R. 9M W. twr. 4M N. along W. coast of Grande-Terre.
Port du Moule. 16°20′N, 61°21′W F.G. 8M W. twr. W. side of port entrance.
LeGozier. 16°12′N, 61°30′W Gp. Fl.R. (2) 10 sec. 14M W. twr. Vis. 259°-115° obscured on certain bearings toward Pointe Caraibe.
Pointe a Pitre. 16°13′N, 61°32′W.

> **Leading Lights** 348°.
> Front Qk. Fl.W. 12M W. twr.
> Rear Qk. Fl.W. 14M R. mast.

Saint Marie. 16°06′N, 61°34′W F.G. 7M W. sq. twr. at the foot of E. pier.
Trois Rivieres. 15°58′N, 61°39′W Iso. W. R. G. 4 sec. W. 13M, R. 9M, G. 8M, W. twr. R. top on SE. point of Guadeloupe G. Vis. 275°-349° W. Vis. 349°-054°, R. Vis. 054°-068°.
Pointe du Vieux Fort. 15°57′N, 61°43′W Gp. Fl.W. (2 + 1) 20 sec. 15M conical twr. SW. point of Guadeloupe.
Basse Terre. F.R. 5M W. pylon on quay near Custom House 3½ M N. of Pointe du Vieux Fort Lt.
Anse a la Barque. Gp. Fl.W. (2) 6 sec. 12M W. sq. twr. R. top on N. side of entrance 6M N. of Basse Terre Lt.
Anse a la Barque. F.G. 7M W. twr. G. top ½ M E. of entrance light.
Bourg des Saintes. 15°52′N, 61°35′W F.W. 3M concrete column at foot of wharf on Terre d'en Haut, Isles des Saintes S. of Guadeloupe.

Marie Galante (F.)

Grand Bourg. 15°53′N, 61°19′W Fl.W. 4 sec. 8M W. post R. top on wharf SW. part of Marie Galante.
Saint Louis. F.R. 8M W. sq. twr. W. of church 4½ M N. of Grand Bourg Lt.
Capesterre. 15°54′N, 61°31′W.

> **Leading Lights** 315°.
> Front F.R. 8M W. and R. twr.
> Rear F.R. 8M W. and R. twr.

Windward Islands

Dominica (U.K.)

Roseau. 15°17′N, 61°24′W Fl.R. 2 sec. 8M on shore.
Fort Young. Occ. R. 8M W. concrete structure 1M N. of Roseau Lt.
Portsmouth. 15°34′N, 61°28′W F.R. 1M on mast at foot of pier in Prince Rupert Bay NW. coast of Dominica.

Martinique (F.)

Precheur Point. 14°48′N, 61°14′W Fl.R. 10 sec. 14M iron twr. stone base on NW. corner of Martinique.
La Carvelle. 14°46′N, 60°53′W Gp. Fl.W. (3) 15 sec. 29M R. and W. twr. on NE. point of Martinique, Vis. 113°-345°.
Cabrit Islet. 14°23′N, 60°52′W Fl.R. 5 sec. 18M R. pylon Vis. 228°-106° and 107°-108° off SE. point of Martinique.
Negro Point. 14°36′N, 61°06′W Fl.W. 5 sec. 17M W. twr. Vis. 300°-126° N. side of entrance to Baie de Fort de France.
Banc Mitan. Qk. Fl.W. Ω By. R. and B. bands 9M W. side of shoal 1M SE. of Negro Point Lt.
Fort de France.

> **Leading Lights** 004°.
> Front Iso. G. 4 sec. 17M B. and W. pylon.
> Rear Iso. G. 4 sec. 18M B. and W. pylon.

St. Lucia (U.K.)

Vigie. 14°02′N, 61°01′W Gp. Fl.W. (2) 10 sec. 24M W. twr. R. roof on summit N. side of entrance to Port Castries Vis. 039°-212° partially obscured by Pigeon Island 206°-209°.
Tapion Rock. Fl.W. 3 sec. 8M old battery ½ M S. of Vigie Lt. on S. side of entrance to Port Castries.
Port Castries.

> **Leading Lights** 121°.
> Front F.R. 5M W. wharf of Market Place.
> Rear F.R. 5M 1M E. of Tapion Rock Lt.

Morne Belle Vue. 13°45′N, 60°57′W Fl.W. 10 sec. 20M aviation light 1¾ M N. of Brandon Point Lt.
Brandon Point. 13°43′N, 60°57′W Fl.W. 5 sec. 19M twr. Vis. 197°-123° at SE. point of St. Lucia.

St. Vincent (U.K.)

Fort Charlotte. 13°09′N, 61°15′W Gp. Fl.W. (3) 20 sec. 16M octag-

onal structure SW. coast of St. Vincent ¾ M N. of Kingstown Harbor.
Kingstown Harbor.

>**Leading Lights** 041°.
>Front F.R. at head of jetty.
>Rear F.R. 7M on cupola of building.

Barbados

Ragged Point. 13°10′N, 59°26′W Fl.W. 15 sec. 21M W. twr. on W. coast of Barbados.
South Point. 13°03′N, 59°32′W Gp. Fl.W. (3) 30 sec. 17M R. and W. twr. southernmost point of Barbados.
Bridgetown Carenage. Fl.G. 2M wooden post S. side of entrance 1¾ M S. of Bridgetown Breakwater Lt.
Bridgetown Breakwater. 13°06′N, 59°38′W Gp. Fl.W. (3) 5 sec. 12M.
Bridgetown Quay. Occ. R. 5 sec. 6M on quay ½ M W. of breakwater light.
Harrison Point. 13°18′N, 59°39′W Gp. Fl.W. (2) 15 sec. 20M W. twr. NW. side of island.

Grenadine Islands (U.K.)

Carriacou Island, Jack a Dan. 12°30′N, 61°28′W Qk. Fl.R. 3M Vis. 243°-182°.
Bequia, Admiralty Bay. 13°00′N, 61°15′W F.R. at head of pier.

Grenada

Saline Point. 12°00′N, 61°48′W Gp. Fl.W. (3) 15 sec. 17M twr. SW. point of Grenada.
St. George's Harbor. 12°03′N, 61°46′W F.R. 15M on brick building extremity of N. bastion of Fort George Vis. 056°30′-151°.
Two pair of F.R. range lights 132° and 068° respectively lead into the harbor.

Tobago

Tobago. 11°30′N, 60°32′W Fl.W. 15 sec. 16M steel twr. Visible 85°-325°, −331° partially obscured, −9° obscured. To NE. point of island.
Scarborough. 11°10′N, 60°44′W Gp. Fl.W. (2) 20 sec. 29M W. rectangular bldg. with twr. To Fort George visible 258°-90°.
Crown (Browns) Pt. 11°09′N, 60°51′W Gp. Fl.W. (4) 20 sec. 11M steel twr. on SW. extremity of island.

Trinidad (U.K.)

Galera Pt. 10°50′N, 60°55′W Gp. Fl.W. (5) 20 sec. 12M W. concrete twr. NE. extremity of island. Obscured to W. between land and 107°.
Brigand Hill. 10°30′N, 61°04′W Gp. Fl.W. (2 + 1) 30 sec. 20M W. steel twr.
Chacachacare I. 10°42′N, 61°45′W Fl.W. 10 sec. 26M W. concrete twr.
Chacachacare Beacon. Fl.W. 2 sec. 11M W. steel structure W. ☐ rectangle in line 36° with above clears Diamond Rock.
North Post. 10°44′N, 61°34′W Fl.W. 5 sec. 15M beacon. To Pt. a Diable, visible only 87°-252°.

(Puerto Rico to Grenada reprinted by kind permission of Reed's Nautical Almanac, *American East Coast Edition 1974.)*

Radio Navigation Aids

Island	Morse	Description/Location	kHz	Call Sign	Range or Power
Bermuda	KB	Kindley Aero	375	-.- -...	50 miles
Bermuda	BDA	Gibbs Hill L. S.	295	-... -.. .-	120 miles
Puerto Rico	O	Isla Mona L. S.	296	---	75 miles
Puerto Rico	DDP	San Juan Aero (Vega Baja)	391	-.. -.. .--.	75 miles
Puerto Rico	SJ	north coast	330	... .---	
Puerto Rico	L	San Juan	318	.-..	55 miles
Puerto Rico	NRR	Roosevelt Roads Aero	264	-. .-. .-.	150 watts
Puerto Rico	X	Punta Tuna L. S.	288	-..-	55 miles
St. Croix	STX	Hamilton	224	... - -..-	100 watts
St. Thomas	STT	Truman	239	... - -	
St. Martin	PJM	St. Martin Aero (Juliana)	308	.--. .--- --	1,200 watts
St. Barts	BY		338	-... -.--	50 miles
Antigua	ZDX	Antigua Aero (Coolidge)	369	--.. -.. -..-	1,200 watts
Antigua	ANU		351	.- -. ..-	
Guadeloupe	FXG	Guadeloupe Aero (Pointe-a-Pitre)	300	..-. -..- --.	1,000 watts
Guadeloupe	AR	middle of island	402	.- .-.	
Dominica	DOM	Melville Hall (northeast)	273	-.. --- --	100 miles
Martinique	FXF	Martinique Aero (Fort de France)	314	..-. -..- ..-.	3,000 watts
Martinique	FF	middle of island	281	..-. ..-.	
St. Lucia	SLU	St. Lucia Aero (Vigie)	415	... .-.. ..-	
St. Lucia	BNE	southeast coast	375	-... -. .	
Barbados	8PV	Barbados Aero (Seawell)	345	---.. .--. ...-	1,200 watts
St. Vincent	SV	Arnos Vale (south)	403	... ...-	
Grenada	ZGT	Pearls (northeast)	362	--.. --. -	150 watts
Tobago	TAB	Crown Point Aero (southwest)	323	- .- -...	100 watts
Trinidad	POS	Piarco (center of island)	382	.--. --- ...	1,200 watts

Radio Stations

Island	Station	Location of Transmitter	Power (Watts)	Frequency (kHz)	Language
Puerto Rico	WPAB	Ponce	5,000 S(1)	550	Spa.
	WKAQ	San Juan	5,000 N(1)	580	Spa.
	WAPA	San Juan	10,000 N(1)	680	Spa.
	WIAC	San Juan	10,000 N(1)	740	Spa.
	WKVM	San Juan	25,000 N(1)	810	Spa.
	WHOA	Hato Rey	5,000 N(1)	870	Spa.
	WIPR	Hato Rey	10,000 N(1)	940	Spa.
	WIVV	Vieques	5,000 (1)	1370	Eng.
St. Croix	WSTX	Ft. Augusta	5,000	970	Eng.
St. Thomas	WSTA	St. Thomas	250 (1)	1340	Eng.
	WVWI	St. Thomas	1,000 (1)	1000	Eng.
Tortola	ZBVI	Road Town	10,000 (2)	780	Eng.
St. Martin	PJD2	Philipsburg	10,000	1295	Eng.
Anguilla	R. Anguilla	The Valley	500 (2)	1505	Eng.
Antigua	ABBS	St. John's	5,000 (2)	620	Eng.
	ZDK		10,000 (2)	1100	Eng. Eng.
St. Kitts	ZIZ	Basseterre	5,000 S(1)	555	Eng.
	R. Paradise	Basseterre	50,000 S(1)	1265	Eng.
Montserrat	R. Antilles	O'Garro's	125,000 S	930	Eng. Fr. Spa.
	R. Montserrat	Plymouth	1,000 S(1)	885	Eng.
Guadeloupe	ORTF	Arnouville	20,000 (2)	640	Fr.
		Citerne	4,000 S	1420	Fr.
Dominica	R. Dominica	St. Joseph	10,000 (1)	595	Eng.
	ZGBC	Gr. Savanne	10,000	1060	Eng.
Martinique	ORTF	Ft. de France	50,000 S(1)	1310	Fr.
St. Lucia	R. St. Lucia	Babonneau	10,000 N	660	Fr. Eng.
	R. Caribbean	Castries	10,000 N(1)	840	Fr. Eng.
Barbados	R. Barbados	Black Rock	10,000 (2)	900	Eng.
St. Vincent	R. St. Vincent	Brighton	500/10,000 (2)	705	Eng.
Grenada	R. Grenada	St. George's	500 S(2)	535	Eng.
		Carriacou	10	1045	Eng.
		Sauteurs	100 N(1)	1040	Eng.
Trinidad	NBS-610 Radio	Chaguaramas	10,000 (2)	610	Eng.
	R. Trinidad	Caroni	20,000 (2)	730	Eng.

Key:

N—Reception better in northerly direction

S—Reception better in southerly direction

(1)—Reception better west of island chain

(2)—Reception better east of island chain

—Compiled by Ray Smith, Grenada

Holidays

What with the variety of local customs, manners of setting dates, sporadic observation by private enterprise, and the vast assortment of royalty and heroes that abounds in the Islands, it is impossible to provide a list of holidays that will hold together year after year. However, it is important to know at least the approximate dates of holidays, because without this knowledge, customs procedures and shopping for parts or provisions after a passage can be totally frustrating. Here then is a list as complete as I could make it, with exact dates where they could be provided, and with approximate ones otherwise.

Puerto Rico

New Year's Day
Three Kings' Day Eve: January 5, whole day
Three Kings' Day: January 6
De Hostos' Birthday: January 11, half day
George Washington's Birthday: Monday of the week of the 22nd, half day
Abolition Day: March 22, half day
Jose de Diego's Birthday: April 16, half day
Good Friday
Memorial Day: as in U.S.
Independence Day: as in U.S.
Luis Munoz Rivera's Birthday: July 17, half day
P. R. Constitution Day: July 25
Jose Barbosa's Birthday: July 27, half day
Labor Day: as in U.S.
Columbus Day: as in U.S., half day
Veterans Day: as in U.S.
Discovery of P.R.: November 19
Thanksgiving: as in U.S.
Christmas Eve: whole day
Christmas
New Year's Eve: whole day

U.S. Virgins

New Year's Day
Three Kings' Day: January 6; end of St. Croix Festival
Roosevelt's Birthday: January 30
Washington's Birthday: as in U.S.; donkey races in St. Croix
Transfer Day: March 31; in observance of the physical transfer of the Danish West Indies to the U.S. in 1917
Holy Thursday: Thursday before Easter
Good Friday
Easter Monday: Monday after Easter
Carnival Week: Usually the last week in April; Friday and Saturday of this week are legal holidays; parades and fairs all week
Whit Monday: about seven weeks after Easter; Monday following Feast of Pentacost
Memorial Day: as in U.S.; boat races from St. Thomas to St. Croix
Organic Act Day: June 22; celebrating the 1936 act granting civil government and universal sufferage to the Virgins
Independence Day: as in U.S.; celebrated big on St. John
Supplication Day: July 25; Islanders attend churches to pray for deliverance from hurricanes; it must work, as there has been no severe damage since 1924
August Monday: First Monday in August; yacht races from St. Thomas to Tortola
Labor Day: as in U.S.
Primary Election: Second Tuesday in September
Columbus Day: as in U.S.
Local Thanksgiving: October 25; thanks given for relief from hurricanes
Liberty Day: November 1; commemorates the bloodless revolution on St. Croix in 1915
Veterans Day: as in U.S.
General Election: First Tuesday after first Monday in November
St. Croix Christmas Festival: about December 18-January 6
Christmas Day
Second Christmas Day: December 26

APPENDIX D

British Virgins

New Year's Day
Good Friday
Easter Monday: Monday after Easter
Whit Monday: seventh Monday after Easter
Sovereign's Birthday: June 2; lots of uniformed parades
Territory Day: July 1
August Monday: First Monday in August
St. Ursula's Day: October 21
Prince of Wales' Birthday: November 14
Christmas
Boxing Day: December 26

Anguilla

New Year's Day
Statehood Day: February 27
Good Friday
Easter Monday: Monday after Easter
Labour Day: first Monday in May
Whit Monday: seventh Monday after Easter
Queen's Birthday: as directed by H. M. The Queen
August Monday: first Monday in August
Prince of Wales' Birthday: November 14
Boxing Day: December 26
National Carnival: usually December 26 through January 2

St. Kitts

New Year's Day
Good Friday
Easter Monday
Labour Day: May 1
Whit Monday: seventh Monday after Easter
Queen's birthday: usually second Saturday in June
August Bank Holiday: first Monday in August
Statehood Day: February 27
Prince Charles' Birthday: November 14
Boxing Day: December 26

(Note: shopping hours usually are 8.00 a.m.-12.00 noon, 1.00 p.m.-4.00 p.m. Half-day closing Thursday at 1.00 p.m. Banks open 8.00 a.m. to 12.00 noon, Mondays to Fridays; 8.00 a.m. to 11.00 a.m., Saturdays.)

Antigua and Barbuda

New Year's Day
Good Friday
Easter Monday
Labour Day: May 1
Queen's Official Birthday: as decreed
August Monday: first Monday in August
State Day: November 1
Boxing Day: December 26

(Note: shopping hours usually are 8.00 a.m. to 12.00 noon, 1.00 p.m. to 4.00 p.m. Half-day closing Thursday at 1.00 p.m. Banks open 8.00 a.m. to 12.00 noon, Mondays through Fridays; 8.00 a.m. to 11.00 a.m., Saturdays.)

Martinique, St. Barts, Guadeloupe

New Year's Day
Carnival: Monday and Tuesday before Ash Wednesday
Holy Thursday
Good Friday
Holy Saturday
Easter Monday
Labour Day: May 1
Ascension Day
Whit Monday
Bastille Day: July 14
Assumption Day: August 15
All Saints Day: November 1
All Souls Day: November 2
Armistice Day: November 11
Christmas Day

(Note: normal business hours are Monday through Friday 8.00 a.m. to 12.00 noon, 2.30 p.m. to 5.30 p.m.; Saturday, half day. Saturday is the best day for visiting the market, 8.00 a.m. to 12.00 noon, 3.00 p.m. to 7.00 p.m.)

Dominica

New Year's Day
Carnival: Monday and Tuesday before Ash Wednesday
Good Friday

Easter Monday
May Day: May 1
Whit Monday
Commonwealth Day: As decreed
August Monday: first Monday in August
Dominica Day: November 3
Christmas Day
Boxing Day: December 26
Merchants Holiday: December 27

(Note: shop hours are 8.00 a.m. to 1.00 p.m., 2.00 p.m. to 4.00 p.m., weekdays; Saturday, half day.)

St. Lucia

New Year's Days: January 1 and 2
Carnival: 2 days before Ash Wednesday
Good Friday
Easter Monday
Labour Day: May 1
Whit Monday
Corpus Christi
Emancipation Day: first Monday in August
Thanksgiving Day: October 2
Queen's Birthday: As decreed
Saint Lucia's Day: December 13
Christmas Day
Boxing Day: December 26

(Note: most stores close half day on Wednesday; banks close Saturdays at 11.00 a.m.)

St. Vincent

New Year's Days: January 1 and 2
Discovery Day: January 22
Carnival: Monday and Tuesday before Ash Wednesday
Good Friday
Easter Monday
Labour Day: May 1
Whit Monday
Queen's Birthday: As decreed
Corpus Christi
Emancipation Day: first Monday in August

Thanksgiving Day: November, provisionally a Monday after the hurricane season
Christmas Day
Boxing Day: December 26

(Note: most stores and government offices close half day on Saturday. Some operate a five-day week, closed all day Saturday.)

Grenada

New Year's Days: January 1 and 2
Good Friday
Easter Monday
Easter Tuesday
Labour Day: May 1
Whit Monday
Corpus Christi
Queen's Birthday: June, usually second Saturday
August Monday: first Monday in August
August Tuesday: Tuesday after first Monday
National Day: August 15
Christmas
Boxing Day: December 26

(Note: usually an additional 20 are declared during the course of the year! Most stores close half day on Thursday, open Saturday. Government, banks, law offices Monday through Friday.)

Trinidad & Tobago

New Year's Day
Carnival: Monday and Tuesday before Ash Wednesday
Good Friday
Easter Monday
May Day: May 1
Whit Monday
Corpus Christi
Discovery Day: first Monday in August
Independence Day: August 31
Divali: November, depends on phase of moon
Eid-ul-Fitr: November, depends on phase of moon
Christmas Day
Boxing Day: December 26
D.M.S. Day: subject of petition

Index

Donald M. Street, Jr., author of *The Ocean Sailing Yacht,* is known to thousands of yachtsmen as a contributor to major sailing periodicals. He now writes regularly for Sail Magazine. Mr. Street has been living in Grenada, where he also acts as a marine insurance broker, a sailmaker's representative, and the charter-skipper of his 45-foot yawl, *Iolaire*. A member of the Royal Ocean Racing Club, after some two decades of sailing and chronicling these waters, he rightly deserves his reputation as the Dean of Caribbean Yachting.

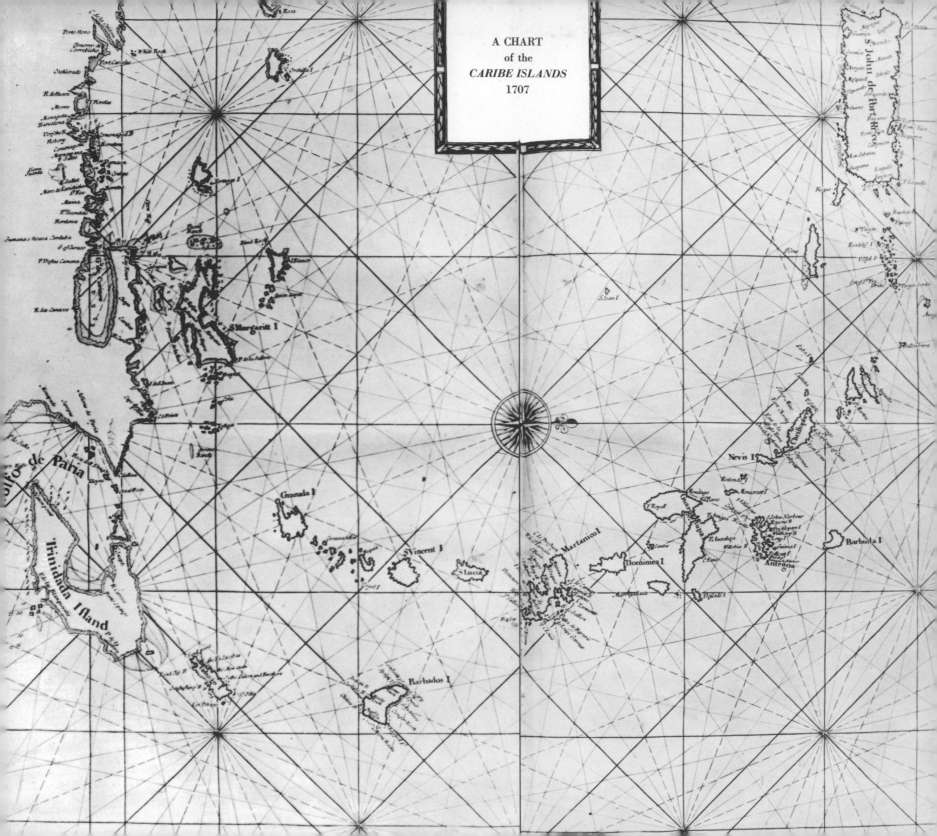

A CHART
of the
CARIBE ISLANDS
1707